MANAGERIAL ECONOMICS

Sixth Edition

W. Bruce Allen
The Wharton School
University of Pennsylvania

Neil A. Doherty
The Wharton School
University of Pennsylvania

Keith Weigelt
The Wharton School
University of Pennsylvania

Edwin Mansfield
late of University of Pennsylvania

MANAGERIAL ECONOMICS

Theory, Applications, and Cases

Sixth Edition

W. W. NORTON & COMPANY
NEW YORK • LONDON

Dedication:

To Edwin Mansfield, a pioneer of managerial economics

MANAGERIAL ECONOMICS
Theory, Applications, and Cases, Sixth Edition
Edwin Mansfield, W. Bruce Allen, Neil A. Doherty, and Keith Weigelt

The text of this book is composed in Rotis Serif
Composition by Matrix Composition
Manufacturing by Quebecor
Book design by Rubina Yeh
Manufacturing director: Roy Tedoff

Library of Congress Cataloging-in-Publication Data
Managerial economics : theory, applications, and cases / W. Bruce Allen . . . [et al.].—6th ed.
   p. cm.
  Includes bibliographical references and index.
  ISBN 0-393-92496-3
  1. Managerial economics. I. Allen, W. Bruce.

  HD30.22.M354 2004
  338.5'024'658—dc22

                                                        2004058323

W. W. Norton & Company, Inc., 500 Fifth Avenue, New York, N.Y. 10110
    www.wwnorton.com
W. W. Norton & Company Ltd., Castle House, 75/76 Wells Street, London W1T 3QT

1 2 3 4 5 6 7 8 9 0

CONTENTS

Chapter 2   ## Optimization Techniques 39

Chapter 5   Estimating Demand Functions   153

Chapter 8

Technological Change and Industrial Innovation 293

Chapter 9   The Analysis of Costs   325

Part Four   Market Structure, Strategic Behavior, and Pricing   375

Chapter 10   Perfect Competition   377

Chapter 11   Monopoly and Monopolistic Competition   405

Chapter 12 Sophisticated Monopoly Pricing 451

Chapter 13 Oligopoly 523

Chapter 16　Auctions　643

Chapter 17　Moral Hazard and Principal-Agent Problems 671

Chapter 20   Managerial Economics: Taking a Global View   789

A character made famous by Lewis Carroll is used by biologists to show why progress is a relative measure. Alice encountered the Red Queen in *Through the Looking Glass*. Though the Queen is a model of perpetual motion, she travels hardly any distance because her world travels with her. This idea of relative change is hardly confined to the fantasies of Carroll or the world of biology. In 1903, traffic traveled through central London at an average of 12 mph. The leisurely pace was largely determined by the physical limits of horses. Over the succeeding 100 years, man developed the internal combustion engine to overcome the physical limits of horses. However, traffic in central London in 2003 only averaged 9 mph. The increased speed of transportation was offset by the increase in traffic congestion. Progress is indeed relative.

The relativity of progress also exists between textbooks and the subjects they cover. For, unless a textbook stays ahead of the changes in a complex world, a revision doesn't necessarily equal progress. We believe that this sixth edition of *Managerial Economics* represents progress. By taking into account the latest changes in the business world, this edition will better prepare our readers for their future managerial tasks. As stated in the fifth edition, our goal in making changes is to better integrate the Mansfield tradition within the changing business world. We see five mainstays of this tradition:

1. To tightly couple practice to theory.
2. To use formal analysis.
3. To use mathematics as a tool, not an end.
4. To update materials to remain current with the changing business landscape.
5. To listen and learn from the experiences of readers and instructors.

The three of us teach the Managerial Economics course at The Wharton School. It is required for most MBA students, taken in their first-semester. Our charge is to develop a class to help students transfer economic principles to the business world. We find to do so requires us to accomplish several goals. It is these goals that have guided our revisions for this sixth edition. The first goal is to establish economics as a decision-making framework. We need to get students to see past the equations and graphs and understand why, as managers, they want to follow its general precepts. For example, the precepts of marginal analysis or backward induction. Secondly, we want to establish the integrative nature of economics. Economic models permeate all business disciplines. Thirdly, we want to accomplish the above without sacrificing the formal analysis that underlies rational choice. For without it, knowledge is speculative. The objectivity of mathematics brings focus to a business discussion. After all, most managers realize that demand should increase if prices drop, but fewer are able to quantify the sales increase. We want to produce managers who could do the latter. Our final goal is to acknowledge that at times managers can be boundedly rational. We wanted to show students how boundedly rational managers might act, and help them to understand how behavior is affected.

As they did in the fifth edition, these four goals guided our revisions in this edition. It is not so much that economic principles change, rather change is manifested in how managers apply the principles. As the business world becomes more global, complex, and competitive, managers need to use more sophisticated decision-making models. Providing managers with these models, and the ability to apply them to the real world, was a primary goal in our revision efforts.

As we explain below, most of the changes in the sixth edition reflect our desire to give readers the ability to make better decisions in today's complex business world. The book reflects this desire in both content and organization. New content has been added to better reflect developments in the business world. For instance, the game theory chapter is entirely new and illustrates important strategic principles managers need to follow. Also, our treatment of pricing has been expanded and re-organized. The following are the major additions and changes made to the sixth edition:

1. **New Content**–In the fifth edition we added two new chapters to reflect our shift to treating economics as a model of managerial decision-making. The

two chapters were on auctions and moral hazard, especially as applied to principal-agent issues. We continue that path in this sixth edition with six chapters of essentially new material.

Chapter 14–Game Theory   This chapter has been re-written and updated. Game theory is explained more in terms of behavioral principles. For example, dominant strategy and backward induction. We show how issues like reputation-building, credible signals, and repeated games can change managerial behavior. As we explain the various concepts, all our game examples follow the interaction between two rivals—Allied and Barkley. We show how game models can reflect the added complexity of the real world.

Chapter 18–Adverse selection   This chapter is entirely new material and should be thought of as a companion to our chapter on moral hazard. Adverse selection and moral hazard are two sides of the same coin. Adverse selection is more focused on "hidden" information, while moral hazard is focused on "hidden" actions. But, they share behavioral principles that lead to similar actions. For example, they both recommend that incentive schemes can alter managerial behavior.

The remaining four chapters examine managerial pricing under different market structures. All chapters give a more comprehensive treatment of the optimal pricing options, conditional on market structure. We also changed the logical flow of introducing options to better reflect our understanding of economic models and behavior. We feel these changes will make it easier for students to understand how market structure changes impact managerial decisions.

Chapter 10–Pure Competition   This chapter looks at managerial actions in a perfectly competitive market. It covers such topics as pricing where marginal cost is equal to price, average and marginal cost curves, producer surplus, the market's social welfare and long run market equilibrium.

Chapter 11–Monopoly and Monopolistic Competition   This chapter examines managerial decisions in markets characterized by either a monopoly or monopolistic competition. It covers such topics as pricing and output decisions in a monopoly, the use of cost plus pricing, the output of multiproduct firms, the pricing of joint products, the use of advertising, and pricing and output decisions in a monopolistic competitive market.

Chapter 12–Sophisticated Pricing   This chapter examines the managerial use of sophisticated pricing schemes. It covers three pricing schemes— bundling, two-part tariffs, and price discrimination. Each of these schemes is being seen with greater frequency in many different markets. We show how and why these pricing schemes work. We also look at pricing within the firm by examining transfer pricing options.

Chapter 13–Oligopoly Pricing   This chapter looks at managerial decisions in oligopolistic markets. It covers such topics as Cournot and Stackelberg pricing, and dominant price leaders.

2. **New Cases and Applications**   This textbook has long been viewed as the best expression of Edwin Mansfield's special talents as an economist and business consultant. As one who spent a great deal of time applying microeconomics in the business world, Professor Mansfield believed deeply in the power of example. For the Fifth Edition we introduced ten new cases. In the Sixth Edition we introduce over two dozen additional cases. The cases are consistently interwoven into the main body of the text, and they also appear in a variety of boxed inserts. Every step of the way, students are presented with economic ideas and their applications, and real instances when the ideas at hand have been critical to solving managerial problems. More than one hundred cases and applications appear in the book (see the endpapers). New or significantly revised cases in this edition include:

    - The Yankees Buy A-Rod's Contract
    - Paying for Early SAT Scores
    - Textbook Prices: At home and Overseas
    - Variable Pricing for Baseball Tickets
    - Therma-Stent and Cost-Plus Pricing
    - Printers and Product Tying
    - Personal Seat Licenses and Sports Teams
    - New Yorker Magazine and Bundling
    - AT&T and Bundling
    - Wal-Mart and Home Depot
    - Seagoing Chemical Haulers
    - Drug Sales
    - Disposable Syringes
    - Genetic Testing
    - Shell Oil
    - Information Technology and Productivity
    - Airbus

3. The **E-Media Package**   which addresses the desire of the business student and the need of the business instructor to integrate electronic media into the curriculum. The Sixth Edition comes complete with a powerful group of electronic ancillaries, including the student website and PowerPoint slides, all of which are detailed below.

    - **Spreadsheet Exercises**   Over 40 spreadsheet exercises, several new to this edition, have been written by Stephen Erfle of Dickinson College. Some of the exercises are tutorial in nature, designed to help the student work through various principles and models. Others are designed as labs, suitable for use as homework problems.
    - **Economics News Service**   Every week an article from a major newspaper is posted on the site, along with annotation and questions connect-

ing the article back to specific chapters in the book. This helps the student see that the principles they learn in *Managerial Economics, 6th Edition* are manifested in the news stories they encounter every day.

- **Review Quizzes** Multiple-choice questions for every chapter offer the student a chance to check their understanding of the chapter they just read. The results of these quizzes can be emailed to the instructor, enabling the instructor to assign them as a homework assignment.
- **PowerPoint Slides** All figures in the textbook will be reproduced for PowerPoint and available for download from the book's Internet site.

ANCILLARIES

Study Guide and Casebook This popular supplement includes eight full-length case studies in which students become the managers, tackling practical problems with real data and economic analysis.

Instructor's Manual and Test-Item File This IM-TIF includes suggestions for lectures and discussion topics as well as exam questions. It is available in print and digital form, and the test bank is also available as a CTIF. Revised by Kathryn Nantz of Fairfield University.

PART

1

Introduction

Introduction to
Managerial Economics

What do Boeing, the Walt Disney Company, and the Toyota Motor Company have in common? All three, like countless other firms, have used the well-established principles of managerial economics to improve their profitability. Managerial economics draws on economic analysis for such concepts as cost, demand, profit, competition, pricing, entry strategy, and market protection strategy. It attempts to bridge the gap between the purely analytical problems that intrigue many economic theorists and the day-to-day decisions managers face. It now offers powerful tools and approaches for managerial policymaking, like game theory and sophisticated pricing policies such as bundling and two-part tariffs.

In this opening chapter, we begin our study by presenting several case studies illustrating just some of the problems managerial economics can help solve. Although they cover only a small sample of the situations in which managerial economics is useful, these illustrations provide a reasonable first impression of the nature of managerial economics and its relevance to real business decisions. To aid in elucidating the application to business decisions, strategically placed sections, called Concepts in Context, Consultant's Corner, and Analyzing Managerial Decisions, directly point the reader to applications of the adjacent concept in the text. Also, we examine the relationship between managerial economics and such related disciplines as microeconomics and the decision sciences, including statistics.

Next, we take up basic models of decision making, as well as the theory of the firm. Since managerial economics is concerned with the ways in which business executives and other policymakers should make decisions, it is important at the outset that the nature of this decision-making process be analyzed and that the motivation of firms be discussed. Since profits play so major a role in business decision making, we define profit and recognize how the economist's definition of profit differs from that of the accountant. Finally, we present an overview of the basic principles of demand and supply, a central topic examined much more completely in subsequent chapters.

Boeing's Struggle to Retain Market Leadership

To illustrate how managerial economics can help managers, consider the issues facing managers at the Boeing Company. Boeing was once the world's largest producer of commercial aircraft. Beginning in the 1970s, Boeing managers mapped out a two-prong approach to retaining market leadership. The company would be the low-cost producer and the technological leader in the industry. By 1980, the company had achieved a market share of 81 percent, a sevenfold lead over its nearest competitor. And, Boeing was able to accomplish this feat while maintaining high profit margins. One industry expert estimated that, in 1991, Boeing realized a profit of $45 million on every 747 aircraft it sold for $150 million.

Boeing's principal rival since the 1980s has been Airbus, a joint venture of British, French, German, and Spanish aerospace firms. Starting with the delivery of their first plane in 1974, Airbus quickly moved into the number-two spot behind Boeing. By 1997, Airbus achieved a market share of over 33 percent, while Boeing's share was reduced to under 65 percent.[1] Not only did Airbus reduce Boeing's market share, the company also assumed the lead in technological advances and challenged Boeing for low-cost leadership. This aggressive move by Airbus also forced Boeing managers to drop prices and rely more heavily on discounts to sell their planes. By 1994, the net earnings of Boeing had fallen 31 percent relative to 1991 levels, primarily due to the increased competition offered by Airbus. In 2003, Airbus reported that it will build more commercial planes than Boeing.[2]

Managerial economics can help us better understand how Airbus was so quickly able to erode Boeing's market domination. Chapter 9 provides some

[1] *Wall Street Journal*, April 30, 1997.

[2] www.ainonline.com/Publications/farn/farn_02.

rationale to explain how Airbus was able to reduce its costs to approach those of Boeing. For example, this chapter illustrates how the costs of aircraft production are affected by the number of planes built. Chapter 8 helps us understand how further cost savings can be realized by reducing the development time of new aircraft models. Finally, Chapter 20 helps us understand how national trade policy may have helped Airbus in its quest to challenge Boeing.

The Disney Corporation: Expansion of the Magic Kingdom

The Disney Corporation has always been known as a mecca for creative talent and energy. However, after its founder, Walt Disney, died in 1966, the company was adrift for decades. Although the company retained high brand recognition, its managers seemed unable to turn this recognition into increased sales and profits. Because of this lack of performance, in the early 1980s, the company was attacked by a series of corporate raiders, including Saul Steinberg and Irwin Jacobs. In desperation, the directors hired Michael Eisner as the new CEO.

Eisner and his management team have unlocked the value of the Disney name and positioned the Magic Kingdom for the twenty-first century. In 20 years, Eisner's team has increased revenues tenfold to over $25 billion in 2002.[3] Disney now ranks among the 100 biggest global firms and the second largest global media company (behind Time-Warner). Disney holdings include the following: ABC television and radio networks; 10 U.S. television and 59 U.S. radio stations; ownership in over 10 cable channels, including ESPN International, the global leader in sports networking (with 24-hour broadcasting in 21 languages to over 165 countries); several major film, video, and television studios, including Disney, Miramax, and Buena Vista; several major record labels; theme parks in the United States, Japan, and France; the Disney Cruise Line; and 600 Disney retail stores worldwide.

In expanding the Magic Kingdom, Eisner's team has used analyses based on managerial economics principles. For example, after studies indicated that increases in advertising would raise theme park attendance and profits, the team launched a series of successful advertising campaigns.

Eisner's team has also shown its ability to use both simple and sophisticated pricing techniques to improve firm performance. When the Disney animated classic film *Pinocchio* was released on videocassette, it was initially priced at $79.95 (as were most videocassettes). At this price only 100,000 copies were sold in the first two months. Eisner's team decided to drop the price to $29.95,

---

[3]*2002 Disney Fact Book* at //disney.go.com/investors/financial/factbook/2002.

and promptly sold over 300,000 copies. Disney has also been a leader in using sophisticated pricing strategies, such as bundling. They have bundled together a Disney cruise with a stay at their Disneyworld theme park in Florida, a McDonald kid's meal and action figures from their movies, and several of their cable channels to cable customers. They also practice price discrimination. Consumers who buy a Disney videocassette find coupons for merchandise at Disney retail stores. These and other pricing strategies are examined in Chapter 12. With the help of these techniques, Disney has given its shareholders 20 percent annual earnings growth for 14 consecutive years and an annualized return on equity of 18.5 percent.

In What Size Production Runs Should Toyota Produce Its Cars?

Firms must decide how to produce their products. Firms that produce multiple products on an assembly line must decide how much of a given product they should produce in a production run—in essence, the length of the production run. Long production runs lower the costs associated with changing over the production line to produce a different product (setup costs), while shorter runs lower the costs associated with raw material and final product inventory (inventory carrying charges). More frequent, smaller production runs mean high setup costs and low inventory costs. Less frequent, larger production runs have the reverse effect.

Toyota Motor Company (and many other producers) face exactly this problem. What production run is optimal to minimize the combined costs of setup and inventory? In Chapter 7, we discuss how Toyota's significant decrease in setup costs enabled it to significantly decrease its optimal production runs and hence to decrease its total costs.

The model used in the Toyota case is called the *economic order quantity* (EOQ) model. It is the mainstay of supply chain management. Using it (in sophisticated versions), companies determine the optimal amount of a product needed each time they place an order. In the simple model, the firm trades off ordering cost and inventory costs. As the model is expanded, reliability in delivery time plays a major role in determining the optimal EOQ. We discuss this model in Chapter 7.

Relationships of Managerial Economics to Other Disciplines

Having considered three case studies illustrating the sorts of problems managerial economics can help solve, we can begin to describe how managerial

FIGURE
1.1

Relationship between Managerial Economics and Related Disciplines

Managerial economics provides a link between economic theory and the decision sciences in the analysis of managerial decision making.

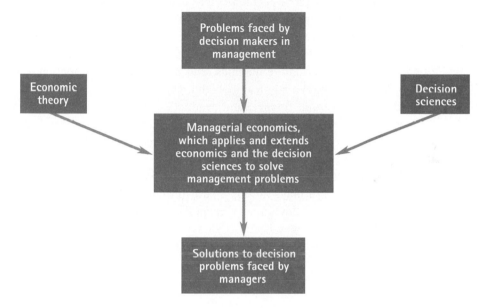

economics is related to other disciplines. As shown in Figure 1.1, managerial economics provides a link between economic theory and the decision sciences in the analysis of managerial decision making. Traditional economic theory, which consists of microeconomics (focusing on individual consumers, firms, and industries) and macroeconomics (focusing on aggregate output, income, and employment), contains a considerable amount of material that bears on managerial decision making; the role of microeconomics is particularly important in this regard. Managerial economics draws heavily from microeconomics, as well as from other areas of economic theory.

But managerial economics is quite different from microeconomics. Whereas microeconomics is largely descriptive (that is, it attempts to describe how the economy works without indicating how it should operate), managerial economics is largely prescriptive (that is, it attempts to establish rules and techniques to fulfill specified goals). For example, microeconomics is concerned with the way in which computer manufacturers like IBM price their products, while managerial economics is concerned with how they *should* price their products. Of course, this is a difference of emphasis and degree not of kind, but it nonetheless is important.

As shown in Figure 1.1, managerial economics draws heavily on the decision sciences as well as traditional economics. The decision sciences provide ways to analyze the impact of alternative courses of action. Managerial economics uses optimization techniques, such as differential calculus and mathematical programming, to determine optimal courses of action for decision makers. To implement these techniques, statistical methods must be employed to estimate the relationships between relevant variables and forecast their values. Thus, managerial economics has arisen from a complex mixture of various parts of economics and the decision sciences, including statistics.

Managerial economics plays two important roles in the study of business administration. First, the course in managerial economics, like courses in accounting, quantitative methods, and management information systems, provides fundamental analytical tools that can and should be used in other courses, such as marketing, finance, and production. Second, the course in managerial economics, like courses in business policy, can serve an integrating role, showing how other areas, such as marketing, finance, and production, must be viewed as a whole to fulfill the goals of the firm.

Although managerial economics is at the heart of the study of business administration, it plays no less a part in the management of nonbusiness organizations such as government agencies, hospitals, and schools. Regardless of whether one manages Eastman Kodak, the Mayo Clinic, or the University of Hawaii, one must pay attention to the efficient allocation of resources. Waste is waste, wherever it occurs. The principles of managerial economics are as important in reducing waste in nonbusiness organizations as in firms.

The Basic Process of Decision Making

Both for firms and for nonbusiness organizations, the process of decision making can be divided into five basic steps, as indicated in Figure 1.2. These steps are as follows.[4]

Step 1. Establish or Identify the Objectives

In making any decision, you, as the decision maker, should determine what are the organization's (or individual's) objectives. Unless you know what it is you are trying to achieve, there is no sensible way to make the decision. For example, consider the managers of Black and Decker, the power tool manufacturer, who had to decide in the 1970s whether the firm's consumer power tools should be redesigned. Their objectives were to bolster the company's profits, attain a

---

[4]For further discussion, see H. Simon, "The Decision-Making Process," in E. Mansfield, ed., *Managerial Economics and Operations Research* (5th ed.; New York: Norton, 1987).

FIGURE 1.2

Basic Process of Decision Making

This process can be divided into these five basic steps.

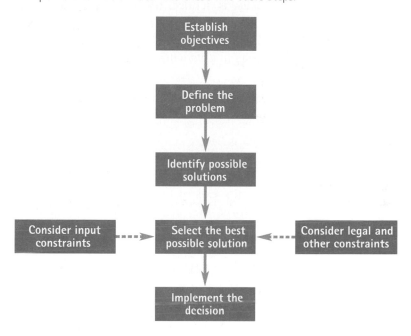

15 percent annual growth rate, remain independent, and service world markets.[5]

Step 2. Define the Problem

One of the most difficult parts of decision making is to determine exactly what the problem is. Frequently, executives confront a situation that is judged to be unsatisfactory. For example, Black and Decker's management felt it had to change the operations drastically if it were to continue to be a domestic manufacturer doing business internationally. To meet this challenge, it had to determine exactly what the problem was, since otherwise it had little chance of solving that problem. After considerable study, it concluded that the problem was the likelihood of increased foreign competition and the possibility that double insulation of power tools would be legally required. (*Double insulation* means

[5]A. Lehnerd, "Revitalizing the Manufacture and Design of Mature Global Products," in B. Guile and H. Brooks, eds., *Technology and Global Industry* (Washington, DC: National Academy Press, 1987).

that an additional insulation barrier is placed in an electric device to protect the user from electric shock if the main insulation system fails.)

Step 3. Identify Possible Solutions

Once the problem is defined, try to construct and identify possible solutions. For example, Black and Decker considered a variety of options, including more effective production and marketing of its products based on existing designs, as well as redesigning its entire product line.

Step 4. Select the Best Possible Solution

Having identified the set of alternative possible solutions, evaluate each one and determine which is best, given the objectives of the organization. In the case of Black and Decker, studies indicated that the best solution was to redesign the firm's consumer power tools. Black and Decker's managers "decided that a window of opportunity existed to improve their product lines and manufacturing capability. Moreover, they decided that if they did not take time to do it right the first time, they would never have the time or resources to do it over."[6]

Step 5. Implement the Decision

Once a particular solution has been chosen, it must be implemented in order to be effective. Even organizations as disciplined as armies find it difficult to carry out orders effectively. Since even the best decisions come to naught if they are not carried out, this phase of the decision-making process is of crucial importance. In the case of Black and Decker, the organization of the firm was changed, and a new job—vice president of operations—was created so that manufacturing, product development, and advanced manufacturing engineering were all under one manager. The firm's top management made sure the decision was implemented properly.

The Theory of the Firm

Although managerial economics is not concerned solely with the management of business firms, this is its principal field of application. To apply managerial economics to business management, we need a **theory of the firm**, a theory indicating how firms behave and what their goals are. Firms are complex organizations that vary enormously. Any theory or model (which means the same as theory) must be a simplification. The trick is to construct a model in such a way that irrelevant and unimportant considerations and variables are neglected,

[6]Ibid., p. 50.

but the essential factors—those that have an important effect on the phenomena the model is designed to illuminate—are included.

The basic model of the business enterprise stems from what economists designate as the theory of the firm. In its most stripped-down version, this theory assumes that the firm tries to maximize its profits. But this version is too stark to be useful in many circumstances, particularly where a problem facing the firm has important dynamic elements and risk is involved. A richer version of this theory assumes that the firm tries to maximize its wealth or value. At present, this version is the dominant theory used by managerial economists.

To understand this theory, we must spell out what managerial economists mean by the **value** of the firm. Since a firm's value can be defined in a variety of ways,[7] it will prevent confusion if we provide a detailed definition at this point. Put briefly, *a firm's value will be defined here as the present value of its expected future cash flows.* In later chapters, we will learn more about what is meant by "cash flow." For present purposes, we can regard a firm's cash flow as the same as its profit. (For those who are unfamiliar with the concept of a "present value" or who want to review this concept, a detailed discussion is provided in Appendix A.)

Therefore, expressed as an equation, the value of the firm equals

$$\text{Present value of expected future profits} = \frac{\pi_1}{1+i} + \frac{\pi_2}{(1+i)^2} + \cdots + \frac{\pi_n}{(1+i)^n}$$

$$\text{Present value of expected future profits} = \sum_{t=1}^{n} \frac{\pi_t}{(1+i)^t} \tag{1.1}$$

where π_t is the expected profit in year t, i is the interest rate, and t goes from 1 (next year) to n (the last year in the planning horizon). Because profit equals total revenue (TR) minus total cost (TC), this equation can also be expressed as

$$\text{Present value of expected future profits} = \sum_{t=1}^{n} \frac{\text{TR}_t - \text{TC}_t}{(1+i)^t} \tag{1.2}$$

where TR_t is the firm's total revenue in year t, and TC_t is its total cost in year t.

A careful inspection of equation (1.2) suggests how a firm's managers and workers can influence its value. Consider, for example, the Ford Motor Company. Its marketing managers and sales representatives work hard to increase its total revenues, while its production managers and manufacturing engineers strive to reduce its total costs. At the same time, its financial managers play a major role in obtaining capital and, hence, influence equation (1.2); while its research and development personnel invent new products and processes that

---

[7]For example, one could define a firm's *value* as its book value or liquidating value, among others.

both increase the firm's total revenues and reduce its total costs. All these diverse groups affect Ford Motor's value, defined here as the present value of its expected profits.

The Role of Constraints

To repeat, managerial economists generally assume that managers want to maximize firm value, as defined in equations (1.1) and (1.2). However, this does not mean that managers have complete control over firm value and can set it at any level they choose. On the contrary, managers must cope with the fact that there are many constraints on what they can achieve in this regard.

The constraints that limit the extent to which a firm's value can be increased are of various kinds. For one thing, the amount of certain types of inputs may be limited. In the relevant period of time, managers may be unable to obtain more than a particular amount of specialized equipment, skilled labor, essential materials, or other inputs. Particularly if the period of time is relatively short, these input constraints may be quite severe. For example, because it takes many months to expand the capacity of a steel plant, many short-run problems facing a steel firm must be solved on the basis of the recognition that plant capacity is essentially fixed. However, in dealing with longer-run problems, the firm has more flexibility and can alter (within limits) its capacity.

Another important type of constraint that limits managerial actions is legal or contractual in nature. For example, a firm may be bound to pay wages exceeding a certain level because the minimum wage laws stipulate that it must do so. Also, it must pay taxes in accord with federal, state, and local laws. Further, it must act in accord with its contracts with customers and suppliers—or take the legal consequences. A wide variety of laws (ranging from environmental laws to antitrust laws to tax laws) limit what managers can do, and the contracts and other legal agreements made by them further constrain their actions. As indicated in Figure 1.3, these constraints limit how much profit a firm can make as well as the value of the firm itself.

Because there are constraints on a firm's actions and behavior, the relevant techniques used to analyze many of a firm's problems are **constrained optimization techniques,** such as Lagrangian multipliers (described in Chapter 2).

What Are Profits?

Throughout previous sections, we have repeatedly encountered the term *profits*. Practically all published profit figures are based on the accountants' definition of profits. It is important at the outset to recognize that managerial economists define *profits* somewhat differently. In particular, when economists

FIGURE
1.3

Determinants of the Value of a Firm

A firm's value depends on factors influencing TR_t, TC_t, and i, as well as the constraints it faces.

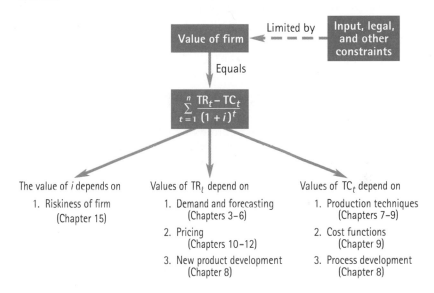

| | Limited by | Input, legal, and other constraints |
| Value of firm | | |

Equals

$$\sum_{t=1}^{n} \frac{TR_t - TC_t}{(1 + i)^t}$$

The value of i depends on	Values of TR_t depend on	Values of TC_t depend on
1. Riskiness of firm (Chapter 15)	1. Demand and forecasting (Chapters 3–6)	1. Production techniques (Chapters 7–9)
	2. Pricing (Chapters 10–12)	2. Cost functions (Chapter 9)
	3. New product development (Chapter 8)	3. Process development (Chapter 8)

speak of profit, they mean profit after taking account of the capital and labor provided by the owners. Therefore, suppose that the owners of the San Jose Shoe Store, who receive profits but no salary or wages, put in long hours for which they could receive $40,000 in 2004 if they worked for someone else. Also suppose that, if they invested their capital somewhere other than in this firm, they could obtain a return of $24,000 on it in 2004. Under these circumstances, if the store's 2004 accounting profit is $60,000, economists would say that the firm's economic profits in 2004 were $60,000 − $40,000 − $24,000, or −$4,000, rather than the $60,000 shown in the store's accounting statements. In other words, the economists' concept of profit includes only what the owners make above and beyond what their labor and capital employed in the business could earn elsewhere. In this case, that amount is negative.

The differences between the concepts used by the accountant and the economist reflect the difference in their functions. The accountant is concerned with controlling the firm's day-to-day operations, detecting fraud or embezzlement, satisfying tax and other laws, and producing records for various interested groups. The economist is concerned primarily with decision making and rational choice among prospective alternatives. While the figures published on profits almost always conform to the accountant's, not the economist's, concept, the economist's is the more relevant one for many kinds of decisions. (And this, of course, is recognized by sophisticated accountants.) For example, suppose the owners of the San Jose Shoe Store are trying to decide whether they should continue in business. If they are interested in making as much money as possible, the answer depends on the firm's profits as measured by the economist not the accountant. If the firm's economic profits are greater than (or equal to) zero, the firm should continue in existence; otherwise, it should not. Hence, if 2004 is a good indicator of its prospective profitability, the San Jose Shoe Store should not stay in existence.

Reasons for the Existence of Profit

Why do economic profits exist? Three important reasons are innovation, risk, and monopoly power. Suppose that an economy is composed of competitive industries, entry into these industries is completely free, and no changes in technology—no new processes, no new products, and no other innovations—are permitted. Moreover, suppose that everyone can predict the future with perfect accuracy. Under these conditions, there will be no profits, because people will enter industries where profits exist, eventually reducing these profits to zero, and leave industries where losses exist, eventually reducing these negative profits to zero.

But in reality, innovations of various kinds are made. For example, Boeing, (recall page 4) introduces its 777 (a new twin-engined wide-bodied jet) or Intel, the California electronics firm, introduces the microprocessor (a computer on a chip). The people who carry out these bold schemes are the **innovators,** those with vision and the daring to back it up. The innovators are not necessarily the inventors of new techniques or products, although in some cases the innovator and the inventor are the same. Often the innovator takes another's invention, adapts it, and introduces it to the market. Profits are a reward earned by successful innovators.

Risk also exists in the real world. Indeed one hazard in attempting to be an innovator is the risk involved. Profit is a reward for bearing risk. Assuming that people like to avoid risk, they prefer relatively stable, sure earnings to relatively unstable, uncertain earnings—*if the average level of earnings is the same.* Consequently, to induce people to take the risks involved in owning businesses in various industries, a profit—a premium for risk—must be paid them.

Another reason for the existence of profits is that markets are not perfectly competitive. Under perfect competition, there is a tendency in the long run for economic profits to disappear. But this is not the case if an industry is a monopoly or oligopoly. Instead, profits may well exist in the long run in such imperfectly competitive industries. Monopoly profits are fundamentally the result of "contrived scarcities." The monopolist takes account of the fact that the more it produces, the smaller the price it will receive. In other words, the monopolist realizes that it will spoil the market if it produces too much. Consequently, it pays the monopolist to limit its output, and this contrived scarcity is responsible for the existence of its profits.

Organizational Factors and "Satisficing"

Although managerial economists generally assume that managers want to maximize profit (and hence their value, as defined in equation (1.1)), other assumptions can be made. To see why it sometimes is sensible to make other assumptions, you must recognize that in many firms, particularly big ones, it is hard to know exactly where, how, and by whom decisions are made. Some firms, rather than being run by a single owner-manager, have large numbers of people in middle management, as well as the top brass occupying key management positions, all of whom participate in varying degrees in the formulation of company policy. Various groups within the firm develop their own party lines, and intrafirm politics is an important part of the process determining company policy. For example, if a firm is composed of two divisions (each making a different product), each division may fight to maintain and expand its share of the firm's budget, and each may try to put the other in a subordinate position. Political struggles within the firm may play an important role in determining its objectives.

Under such circumstances, a firm may "satisfice" rather than attempt to maximize profit. In other words, it may aim at a satisfactory rate of profit rather than the maximum figure. A firm's aspiration level is the boundary between unsatisfactory and satisfactory outcomes. For example, the aspiration level might be a particular goal, such as "Our profit for this year should be $5 million." The firm may abandon the attempt to maximize profits because intrafirm politics rule out such a goal—and because the calculations required are too complicated and the available data too poor. Instead, the firm may attempt to attain certain minimal levels of performance.[8]

If the environment facing the firm is relatively constant, the aspiration level may tend to be slightly higher than the firm's performance. If performance is improving, the aspiration level may tend to lag behind actual performance. And if performance is decreasing, the aspiration level may tend to be above actual performance. Of course, if the aspiration level is close to the maximum profit, the findings obtained by assuming satisficing are likely to be similar to those obtained by assuming profit maximization.

---

[8]For example, see H. Simon, "Theories of Decision-Making in Economic and Behavioral Science," reprinted in *Microeconomics: Selected Readings*, ed. E. Mansfield (5th ed.; New York: Norton, 1985).

ANALYZING MANAGERIAL DECISIONS

Shell Gains by Giving Safe-Driving Advice

McDonald's sponsors Ronald McDonald houses so that parents of a sick child can be near the child's hospital and receive support from similarly situated parents. Texaco sponsored the opera. Many corporations sponsor public television. Shell Oil created television ads to notify viewers that it will send them a booklet on safe driving and how to cope with problems on the road. All of this occurs without Shell mentioning its products.

While a cost stream for such behavior is evident (TV ads are expensive—the total campaign cost Shell $50 million), the revenue stream isn't quite so explicit. So why do these companies do it? Is such behavior consistent with profit maximizing? Is it satisficing?

According to a survey by Cone Inc., a strategic marketing consultant, and Roper Starch Worldwide Inc., a poll of 2,000 Americans showed that 80 percent of Americans have a more positive image of companies aligned with social issues, and *two-thirds would probably switch brands to one associated with a good cause.*

While Shell hasn't released the revenue stream impact of its campaign, the above survey results suggest that revenues increase as a result of what is known as "cause branding" and such behavior may be very compatible with the goal of profit maximizing.

Source: Sullivan Allannia, "Advertising: Shell Gains by Giving Safe-Driving Advice," *Wall Street Journal*, February 18, 1999, Sec. B, p. 9.

Managerial Interests and the Principal-Agent Problem

Satisficing is not the only alternative to the assumption of profit maximization. When differences arise between profit maximization and the interests of the management group, executives are likely to follow policies favoring their own interests.[9] Important in this regard is the separation of ownership from control in the large corporation in the United States. The owners of the firm—the stockholders—usually have little detailed knowledge of the firm's operations. Even if the board of directors is made up largely of people other than top management, top management usually has a great deal of freedom as long as it seems to be performing adequately. Consequently, the behavior of the firm may be dictated in part by the interests of the management group, the result being

[9]See R. Marris, *The Economic Theory of "Managerial" Capitalism* (New York: Free Press, 1964). For a study of intrafirm organization, see O. Williamson, *Markets and Hierarchies: Analysis and Antitrust Implications* (New York: Free Press, 1975).

ANALYZING MANAGERIAL DECISIONS

How Disney Dealt with the Principal-Agent Problem

As you have already seen (on page 5), the Walt Disney Company brought in Michael Eisner, a Paramount executive, as CEO in 1984. The firm's board of directors agreed to pay Eisner a salary of $750,000, plus a $750,000 bonus for signing on, plus an annual bonus equal to 2 percent of the dollar amount by which the firm's net income exceeded a 9 percent return on shareholders' equity. In addition, he received options on 2 million shares of Disney stock, which meant that he could purchase them from the firm at any time during the five-year life of the contract for only $14 per share.*

(a) At the end of 1984, shareholders' equity was about $1.15 billion. How much would Eisner's 1985 bonus have been if Disney's net income that year were $100 million? If it were $200 million? (b) In 1987, the price of Disney stock rose to about $20 per share. How much were Eisner's options worth? (c) Eisner's bonus was $2.6 million in 1986 and $6 million in 1987. Including the stock options he exercised, his compensation in 1988 was about $41 million, a record at that time for any U.S. executive. In 1993, his total compensation was about $202 million, again a record. Had Disney's owners provided a substantial incentive for Eisner to work hard to increase the firm's profits? (d) A shareholder who invested $100 in Disney stock at the beginning of Eisner's tenure would have seen its value rise to $1,460 in 1994. Was this why there was no substantial outcry from the firm's owners about Eisner's compensation? (e) Eisner is reported to have said: "You've got to . . . pretend you're playing with your own money."

SOLUTION (a) Since 9 percent of $1.15 billion equals $103.5 million, Eisner's bonus would have been zero if Disney's net income were $100 million, and his bonus would have been 0.02 ($200 million − $103.5 million) = $1.93 million if Disney's net income were $200 million. (b) 2 million × ($20 − $14) = $12 million. (c) Yes. (d) Yes. (e) No.[†]

*J. Flower, *Prince of the Magic Kingdom* (New York: Wiley, 1991), p. 261.
[†]For further discussion, see Flower, *Prince of the Magic Kingdom*; P. Milgrom and J. Roberts, *Economics, Organization, and Management* (Englewood Cliffs, N.J.: Prentice-Hall, 1992); and *Business Week*, April 25, 1994.

higher pay and more perquisites (and a larger staff) for managers than otherwise would be true.

Economists designate this as the *principal-agent problem*. A firm's managers are *agents* who work for the firm's owners, who are the *principals*. The principal-agent problem is that the managers may pursue their own objectives, even though this decreases the profits of the owners. Consider Joseph Wagner, a manager of a local textile firm. Because the cost of the benefits (large staff, company-paid travel, and so on) that he receives from the firm is borne entirely by the owners, he has an incentive to increase these benefits substantially. Since the owners of the firm find it difficult to distinguish between those benefits that bolster profits and those that do not do so, the manager has some leeway.

To deal with this problem, firms often establish contracts with their managers that give the latter an incentive to pursue objectives that are reasonably close to profit maximization. Thus, the firm's owners might give the managers a financial stake in the success of the firm. Many corporations have adopted stock option plans, whereby managers can purchase shares of common stock at less than market price. These plans give managers an incentive to promote the firm's profits and act in accord with the owners' interests. There is some evidence that these plans do have an effect. For example, according to one recent study, if managers own between 5 and 20 percent of a firm, the firm is likely to perform better (in terms of profitability) than if they own less than 5 percent. In some firms, managers are forced to purchase stock, and boards of directors are being compensated in stock. This, and other moral hazard issues, are discussed extensively in Chapter 17.

Demand and Supply: A First Look

Having described the nature of managerial economics, we turn now to an overview of the basic principles of demand and supply. Any manager, whether in Tokyo, Singapore, New York, or Toronto, must understand these basic principles, which are taken up in more detail in subsequent chapters. Our purpose here is to take a preliminary look at this topic, our first task being to define what we mean by a *market*.

For present purposes, a *market* can be defined as a group of firms and individuals that are in touch with each other in order to buy or sell some good. Of course, not every person in a market has to be in contact with every other person in the market. A person or firm is part of a market even if it is in contact with only a subset of the other persons or firms in the market.

On first inspection, concepts like "market" and "good" seem completely clear, but precise definitions of specific markets and goods can be complicated, for interesting reasons. Consider the case of Staples Inc., which in 1997 attempted to merge with Office Depot. As is the case in many large-scale mergers, the United States Federal Trade Commission (FTC) evaluated the proposed merger to be sure the new firm would not command excessive power in the market for office supplies. Staples argued that the combined entity would have less than a 6 percent share of that $185 billion market. Staples' argument was that you could buy paper clips at any stationary store, a drug store, Wal-Mart, Kmart, wherever. You could buy computers from a number of bricks and mortar computer stores as well as online. And so on for any other element of office supplies.

Thus, argued Staples, what's the problem with a resulting new entity that controls only 6 percent of the market? The FTC on the other hand viewed the market as one of the "category killers"—a market in which by one-stop shopping, one could satisfy all one's office supply needs. With the exception of some local and regional players, the FTC viewed this as a market with three major players: Staples, Office Depot, and Office Max. A merger between Staples and Office Depot would leave only two category killers left. An FTC study showed that when the market had three category killers in it, "prices are significantly lower than in two chain markets."[10]

Therefore, one can see that in addition to beauty being in the eye of the beholder, it is also the case that what constitutes a market (or a good) is also in the eye of the beholder. The FTC's view prevailed and Staples gave up its attempt to merge with Office Depot.

Effective business management often requires careful thinking about markets. Consider now the case of the Coca-Cola Company. In addition to all the variants of Coke (diet, caffeine free, diet caffeine free), it also makes Sprite and Minute Maid Orange Juice. Its major competitor in the soft drink business is Pepsi. If one considers the market as brown carbonated cola soft drinks, Coke and Pepsi combined have about an 80 percent share of the market. The same figure holds if the market is all soft drinks.

But how does Coke view its market? According to Douglas Ivester, recently retired CEO of Coke, its "stomach share," that is, Coke's share of potable liquids that a human can put in his or her stomach, is how Coke views its market. Coke estimates that each person needs to consume an average of 64 ounces of fluids each day to survive. Coke currently accounts for less than 2 ounces of that total. So rather than a 40 percent or so market share, Coke views itself as having about a 3 percent market share—competing with coffee, tea, water (Coke now has a bottled water)—whatever's potable.[11]

A firm that is too myopic may neglect to understand that what consumers want is for a need to be satisfied and not necessarily by the firm's product. If Coke felt that the market was soft drinks, it could find that profits could dissipate rapidly because other potable liquids could fulfill customers' needs.

FedEx determined that customers cared only about their package, good, document, and so on getting to its destination within a certain time period. The customer did not care how it got there, so FedEx went from an airline to a transportation company to a logistics provider—a company that uses whatever mode of transportation or means is available to deliver the item on time. UPS has done the same but from the starting base of trucking.

---

[10]"The FTC, Proudly Ensuring Its Survival at Your Expense," *Wall Street Journal*, April 8, 1997.

[11]"Pop Culture: A Coke and a Perm? Soda Giant Is Pushing Into Unusual Locales," *Wall Street Journal*, May 8, 1997.

Managers must know their current market as they and others perceive it and plan for the future market. In doing so, they must view product competition (other products that substitute for their product in fulfilling consumer needs), geographical competition (spatial separation may insulate you from competitors), and temporal competition (hours of operation and seasonality may influence the market).

Now, we turn to the model of supply and demand, the economist's most basic tool for analyzing markets.

The Demand Side of a Market

Every market has a demand side and a supply side. The *demand* side can be represented by a *market demand curve*, which shows the amount of the commodity buyers would like to purchase at various prices. Consider Figure 1.4, which shows the demand curve for copper in the world market in the 1990s.[12] The figure shows that about 11.7 million metric tons of copper will be demanded annually if the price is $1.00 per pound, about 11 million metric tons will be demanded annually if the price is $1.10 per pound, and about 10.3 million metric tons will be demanded annually if the price is $1.20 per pound. An important reason why copper is demanded in such substantial amounts is that it is very useful in constructing equipment to generate and transmit electricity.

The demand curve in Figure 1.4 shows the total demand—worldwide—at each price. Any demand curve pertains to a particular period of time, and the shape and position of the demand curve depend on the length of the period. The demand curve for copper slopes downward to the right. In other words, the quantity of copper demanded increases as the price falls. This is true of the demand curves of most commodities: They almost always slope downward to the right. This makes sense; one would expect increases in a good's price to result in a smaller quantity demanded.

Any demand curve is based on the assumption that the tastes, incomes, and number of consumers, as well as the prices of other commodities, are held constant. Changes in any of these factors are likely to shift the position of a commodity's demand curve. Therefore, if consumers' tastes shift toward goods that use considerable copper or if consumers' incomes increase (and they hence buy more goods using copper), the demand curve for copper would shift to the right. In other words, holding the price of copper constant, more copper would be demanded than before. Much more will be said on this score in later sections (and in Chapter 3).

---

[12]We are indebted to officials of the U.S. Bureau of Mines for providing relevant information. Of course, these estimates, based on a variety of studies of the copper industry, are only rough approximations, but they are good enough for present purposes.

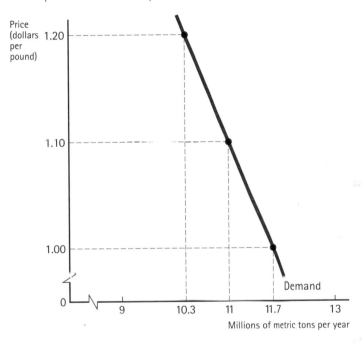

FIGURE 1.4

The Market Demand Curve for Copper, World Market

The market demand curve for copper shows the amount of copper that buyers would like to purchase at various prices.

CONCEPTS IN CONTEXT

The Market for Quick Turnaround Results of SAT Tests

For years, the College Board (the owners of the SAT test) charged a single posted price for taking the exam. It still does. But it added an additional feature. You can pay more (specifically $13 more) and get the result in two weeks' time. It first started giving the results by phone for the additional $13. But now, if you use the Internet to register for the SAT, you can go online (two weeks after having taken the exam) and get the results for an extra $13. Or, you can wait another eight days and receive the results for free by mail or online. What is the value of getting the score eight days early? If the SAT people calculated correctly, it is $13 (and the College Board has customers at that price).

Source: "Can't Wait for SAT Scores? That'll Be $13," *Philadelphia Daily News*, March 11, 2002.

FIGURE

1.5

The Market Supply Curve for Copper, World Market

The market supply curve for copper shows the amount of copper that sellers would offer at various prices.

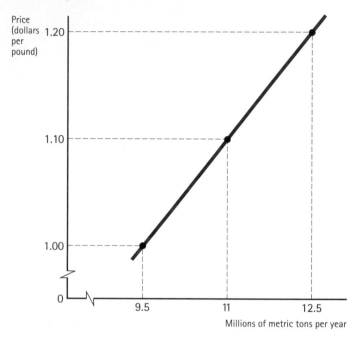

The Supply Side of a Market

The *supply* side of a market can be represented by a *market supply curve* that shows the amount of the commodity sellers would offer at various prices. Let us continue with the case of copper. Figure 1.5 shows the supply curve for copper in the world market in the 1990s, based on estimates made informally by industry experts.[13] According to the figure, about 9.5 million metric tons of copper would be supplied per year if the price of copper were $1.00 per pound, about 11 million tons if the price were $1.10 per pound, and about 12.5 million tons if the price were $1.20 per pound.

Note that the supply curve for copper slopes upward to the right. In other words, the quantity of copper supplied increases as the price increases. This

[13]Officials of the U.S. Bureau of Mines provided relevant information. This supply curve is based on a variety of studies and assumptions. While it is only a rough approximation, it is good enough for present purposes.

seems plausible, since increases in price give a greater incentive for firms to produce copper and offer it for sale. Also, there is more incentive to extract the copper from scrap metal. Empirical studies indicate that the supply curves for a great many commodities share this characteristic of sloping upward to the right.

Any supply curve is based on the assumption that technology, which we define as society's pool of knowledge regarding the industrial arts, is held constant. As technology progresses, it becomes possible to produce commodities more cheaply, so that firms often are willing to supply a given amount at a lower price than formerly. Therefore, technological change often causes the supply curve to shift to the right. This certainly has occurred in the case of copper. There have been many important technological innovations in copper production, ranging from very large flotation cells to in-pit crushers of ore and conveyor belts to transport ore to the mill.

The supply curve for a product is also affected by the prices of the resources (labor, capital, and land) used to produce it. Decreases in the prices of these inputs make it possible to produce commodities more cheaply, so that firms may be willing to supply a given amount at a lower price than they formerly would. Therefore, decreases in the prices of inputs may cause the supply curve to shift to the right. On the other hand, increases in the prices of inputs may cause it to shift to the left. For example, if the wage rates of workers in the copper industry increase, the supply curve for copper may shift to the left.

Equilibrium Price

The two sides of a market, demand and supply, interact to determine the price of a commodity. To illustrate, consider the copper market. Let us put both the demand curve for copper (in Figure 1.4) and the supply curve for copper (in Figure 1.5) together in the same diagram. The result, shown in Figure 1.6, helps us determine the **equilibrium price** of copper. An *equilibrium price is a price that can be maintained. Any price that is not an equilibrium price cannot be maintained for long, since fundamental factors are at work to cause a change in price.*

Let us see what would happen if various prices were established in the market. For example, if the price were $1.20 per pound, the demand curve indicates that 10.3 million metric tons of copper would be demanded, while the supply curve indicates that 12.5 million metric tons would be supplied. Therefore, if the price were $1.20 per pound, there would be a mismatch between the quantity supplied and the quantity demanded per year, since the rate at which copper is supplied would be greater than the rate at which it is demanded. Specifically, as shown in Figure 1.6, there would be an *excess supply* of 2.2 million metric tons. Under these circumstances, some of the copper supplied by

FIGURE

1.6

Equilibrium Price of Copper, World Market

The equilibrium price is $1.10 per pound, since the quantity demanded equals the quantity supplied at this price.

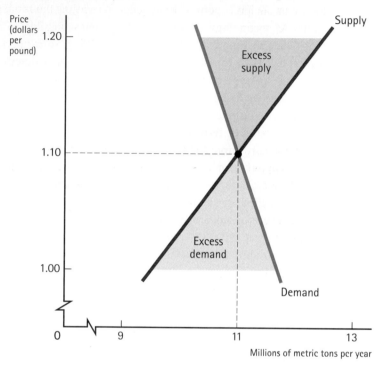

producers could not be sold, and as inventories of copper built up, suppliers would tend to cut their prices to get rid of unwanted inventories. Thus, a price of $1.20 per pound would not be maintained for long—and for this reason, $1.20 per pound is not an equilibrium price.

If the price were $1.00 per pound, on the other hand, the demand curve indicates that 11.7 million metric tons would be demanded, while the supply curve indicates that 9.5 million metric tons would be supplied. Again, we find a mismatch between the quantity supplied and the quantity demanded per year, since the rate at which copper is supplied would be less than the rate at which it is demanded. Specifically, as shown in Figure 1.6, there would be an *excess demand* of 2.2 million metric tons. Under these circumstances, some consumers who want copper at this price would be turned away empty-handed. There would be a shortage. And, given this shortage, suppliers would find it profitable to increase the price, and competition among buyers would bid the price up. Therefore, a price of $1.00 per pound could not be maintained for long—so $1.00 per pound is not an equilibrium price.

The equilibrium price must be the price where the quantity demanded equals the quantity supplied. Obviously, this is the only price at which there is no mismatch between the quantity demanded and the quantity supplied and consequently the only price that can be maintained for long. In Figure 1.6, the price at which the quantity supplied equals the quantity demanded is $1.10 per pound, the price where the demand curve intersects the supply curve. Therefore, $1.10 is the equilibrium price of copper under the circumstances visualized in Figure 1.6, and 11 million metric tons is the equilibrium quantity.

Actual Price

Of course, the price we really are interested in is the *actual price*—the price that really prevails—not the equilibrium price. In general, economists simply assume that the actual price approximates the equilibrium price, which seems reasonable enough, since the basic forces at work tend to push the actual price toward the equilibrium price. Therefore, if conditions remain fairly stable for a time, the actual price should move toward the equilibrium price.

To see that this is true, consider the market for copper, as described in Figure 1.6. What if the price somehow is set at $1.20 per pound? As we saw in the previous section, there is downward pressure on the price of copper under these conditions. Suppose the price, responding to this pressure, falls to $1.15 per pound. Comparing the quantity demanded with the quantity supplied at $1.15 per pound, we find that there is still downward pressure on price, since the quantity supplied exceeds the quantity demanded at $1.15 per pound. The price, responding to this pressure, may fall to $1.12 per pound, but comparing the quantity demanded with the quantity supplied at this price, we find that there is still a downward pressure on price, since the quantity supplied exceeds the quantity demanded at $1.12 per pound.

So long as the actual price is greater than the equilibrium price, there will be a downward pressure on price. Similarly, so long as the actual price is less than the equilibrium price, there will be an upward pressure on price. Hence, there is always a tendency for the actual price to move toward the equilibrium price. But this movement may not be fast. Sometimes it takes a long time for the actual price to get close to the equilibrium price because, by the time it gets close, the equilibrium price changes (due to shifts in either the demand curve, the supply curve, or both). All that safely can be said is that the actual price moves toward the equilibrium price. But, of course, this information is of great value, since frequently all that a manager needs to know is the direction in which a price will change.

CONCEPTS IN CONTEXT

Different Prices for the Same Product

If there is no collusion, a free market allows produc-ers to charge what the market will bear. Evidence sug-gests that European consumers seem to be willing to pay much more than consumers in the United States for consumer electronics products. For instance, a Sony DVD player in France was priced at 349 Euros while the same Sony DVD in the United States was priced at $160; an iMacG4 with a 17-inch screen was selling for 2,630 Euros in France but $1,995 in the United States (about $650 less). Even allowing for the French 19.6 percent value added tax, the products were much cheaper in the United States. Not only does this hold for the France–United States compar-ison on consumer electronics, the pattern seems to hold for consumer electronics throughout Europe.

As a result, savvy people who live in Europe and travel to the "New World" make sure to stock up on electronic equipment here because they know that almost everything is much cheaper here than in Europe.

Here is another example. While you probably paid something over $100 for this text in the United States, you might find it interesting that a student in India paid $30 for the exact same book (printed, by the way, in the United States). Any-body booking a flight to Calcutta?

Source: "You Paid What?! Europe's High Prices Break No Laws, but Collusion Does," *International Herald Tribune,* November 11, 2002.

What If the Demand Curve Shifts?

Any supply-and-demand diagram like Figure 1.6 is essentially a snapshot of the situation during a particular period of time. The results in Figure 1.6 are limited to a particular period because the demand and supply curves in the fig-ure, like any demand and supply curves, pertain only to a certain period. What happens to the equilibrium price of a product when its demand curve changes? This is an important question because managers must try to anticipate and fore-cast the changes that will occur in the prices of their products (as well as the prices of their inputs).

To illustrate the effects of a shift to the left of the demand curve, consider the situation in the copper industry during the 1980s. Because of the recession during the early 1980s and reductions in the growth rate of electric power out-put, there was a decrease in the demand for copper. Also, due in part to the substitution of fiber optics and other materials for copper, there was a further decrease in copper demand. This meant, of course, that the demand curve for copper shifted *to the left*, as shown in the left-hand panel of Figure 1.7. Accord-ing to this panel, one would expect that this leftward shift of the demand curve would have resulted in a decrease in the price of copper, from P to P_1.

FIGURE
1.7

Effects of Leftward and Rightward Shifts of the Demand Curve on the Equilibrium Price of Copper

A leftward shift of the demand curve results in a decrease in the equilibrium price; a rightward shift results in an increase in the equilibrium price.

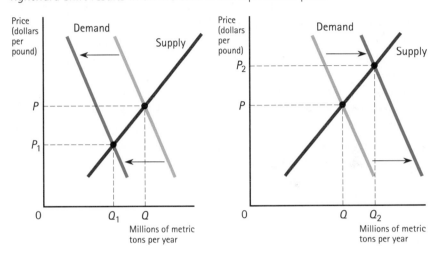

In fact, the price of copper dropped severely during this period. In 1980, the price was about $1 per pound; in 1986, it was about $0.60 per pound. Therefore, our theory predicts exactly what occurred. It is important to recognize how momentous this price drop was—and how important it was for managers to understand why it occurred. Kennecott Copper, the nation's largest copper producer, cut operations at its Utah Copper Division by two-thirds and experienced heavy losses in the mid-1980s. Kennecott's president, G. Frank Joklik, was all too aware that this drastic price cut was due in part to a leftward shift in the demand curve for copper.[14]

On the other hand, suppose that the market demand curve for copper shifts *to the right*, as in the late 1980s. During this period, the United States saw considerable economic growth and the demand for copper increased. As indicated in the right-hand panel of Figure 1.7, we would expect that such a rightward shift of the demand curve would result in an increase in the price of copper, from P to P_2. In fact, the price of copper did increase during the late 1980s, from about $0.60 per pound in 1986 to about $1.30 per pound in 1989. Therefore, in both the early and late 1980s, the price of copper behaved in accord with our simple demand-and-supply analysis.

[14]T.L. Wheelen and J.D. Hunger, *Cases in Strategic Management and Business Policy* (Boston: Addison-Wesley-Longman, 1983).

CONCEPTS IN CONTEXT

Baseball Discovers the Law of Supply and Demand

It started, several years ago, with the Colorado Rockies looking for a way to obtain more revenue but, at the same time, not wishing to heap additional expense on their loyal season ticket holders (who buy tickets for every game or an aggregation of games as a bundle). As of the 2003 season, the Rockies have been joined by 11 other teams, making the number slightly less than half of the 30 major league baseball teams. Doing what? Practicing what they call *variable pricing*. In lay terms, they are charging more for games with desirable teams as opponents, such as teams that are traditional rivals, teams with "superstars", and the like.

While the concept is nothing new for many other goods or services (e.g., Miami Beach hotel rooms cost more in February than in July, phone calls are more expensive in daytime hours than in nighttime hours), it is new for baseball.

Historically, the price for seat X in the stadium was price Y for each of the team's 81 home games. Now seat X is priced higher on opening day, on fireworks night, or when the New York Yankees or San Francisco Giants (because of Barry Bonds) or another traditional rival comes to town. The basic premise is the law of supply and demand. While the number of seats in the ballpark remain fixed, the attractiveness of a seat to a potential buyer is not constant.

Bill Iannicello, vice president of ticket sales for the New York Mets, states, "The demand for games with particular opponents is certainly greater than for others. The same is true for summer versus spring or fall dates, and weekends versus weekdays. We tried to look at it on a game by game level."

Frank Maloney, the director of ticket sales for the Chicago Cubs stated, "I think people under-stand the theory. [Authors' note: As students of managerial economics, we hope you do!] If I'm a realistic fan, I know prices are going to go up one way or another. So when we raise prices on only 19 dates of 81, which is what we did, I think that they see that as a pretty good deal." Maloney adds that variable pricing is "an idea that makes too much sense." [Authors' note: And cents, too.]

All 12 teams have their own version of variable pricing. The Mets' scheme is most sophisticated. There are four tiers: gold (17 dates), silver (21 dates), bronze (27 dates), and value (16 dates). In the 2002 season, before the Mets adopted variable pricing, all seats were priced at the bronze level. For the exact same seat, the gold price is $53, the silver price is $48, the bronze price is $43, and the value price is $38. Tampa Bay has 13 prime games, 55 regular games, and 13 value games. Weekday afternoon games in April are the cheapest way to see the Cubs play. But 18 summer weekend games and the season opener are the most expensive. The remainder of the games are at the regular price. St. Louis charges a $2 premium on seats between May 16 and August 28. Atlanta charges $3 extra for seats on Friday nights and Saturdays in the summer. San Francisco adds on an extra $1 to $4 depending on the seat location for every weekend game and the season opener.

What is next? Teams play 162 games to determine who wins the division pennant (there are six divisions). Those winners plus two wild cards (teams with the best won-lost record who did not win their division) have won the right to enter postseason play (which ultimately leads to two of the eight teams playing in the World Series, the winner being crowned World Champions). The divisions have "pennant races," which become evident in September and October. Some division winners are not determined until the last several games of the season. Right now, variable pricing is based on ex ante (as much as nine months before the games are actually played) feelings about what games the fans will really want to see. True variable pricing will see price changing very close to game time. Teams that have a chance to win the division (i.e., that are still in the pennant race in September and October) will be expected to raise prices on unsold tickets for those games. This will occur under other circumstances, too. If Barry Bonds is coming to town and already has 70 home runs, expect to see ticket prices rise. Coming to a ball park near you—*real time* variable pricing.

Source: "All Games Are Not Created Equal as Teams Turn to Variable Pricing," *Philadelphia Inquirer*, April 2, 2003, pp. E-1 and E-4.

What If the Supply Curve Shifts?

What happens to the equilibrium price of a product when its supply curve changes? For example, suppose that, because of technological advances in copper production, firms like Kennecott Copper are willing and able to supply more copper at a given price than they used to, with the result that the supply curve shifts *to the right*, as shown in the right-hand panel of Figure 1.8. What will

FIGURE
1.8

Effects of Leftward and Rightward Shifts of the Supply Curve on the Equilibrium Price of Copper

A leftward shift in the supply curve results in an increase in the equilibrium price; a rightward shift results in a decrease in the equilibrium price.

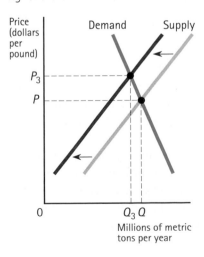

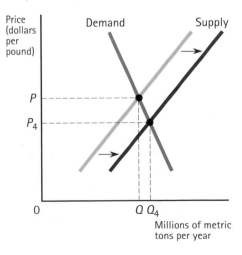

be the effect on the equilibrium price? Clearly, it will fall from P (where the original supply curve intersects the demand curve) to P_4 (where the new supply curve intersects the demand curve).

On the other hand, suppose that there is a marked increase in the wage rates of copper workers, with the result that the supply curve shifts *to the left*, as shown in the left-hand panel of Figure 1.8. What will be the effect? The equilibrium price will increase from P (where the original supply curve intersects the demand curve) to P_3 (where the new supply curve intersects the demand curve).

How Russia Glutted the Aluminum Market: A Case Study

The basic principles of supply and demand are useful in understanding many markets, not just the copper market. Consider, for example, the fascinating and interesting case of aluminum (Figure 1.9). Before the breakup of the Soviet Union in 1991, its aluminum industry primarily served military needs. When those needs decreased because of the decline in cold war tensions, Russia and the other newly independent states in the former Soviet Union began selling aluminum on the world market. In four years, Russian exports rose over 600 percent, pushing the supply curve for aluminum to the right. The result, as shown in Figure 1.9, was a severe drop in the price of aluminum, from about 80 cents per pound in 1990 to about 47 cents in November 1993.

Because of the lower price of aluminum, about 20 percent of U.S. aluminum capacity was idled by the end of 1993, and about 5,000 aluminum workers lost their jobs. Aluminum producers in the United States complained strongly to the federal government, which took up the issue with the Russian government. In January 1994, the world's leading aluminum-producing countries met in Brussels to formulate a plan to cope with the enormous glut of aluminum. One outcome was that Russia agreed to cut its annual output by about 15 percent during the next two years. Western producers were also expected to reduce output. The effect was expected to be a shift of the supply curve to the left, which would raise price. In fact, the price rose to 56 cents per pound in February 1994 and soared to about 90 cents per pound in December 1994.

While this was a very unpleasant episode for aluminum producers (and workers), it was a boon to users of aluminum, who paid low prices. Clearly, managers of both aluminum-producing firms and aluminum-using firms have an intense interest in the ups and downs of the aluminum market—and to understand these ups and downs, they need to know the basic principles of demand

FIGURE
1.9

Effect of a Shift in the Supply Curve in the Early 1990s on the Equilibrium Price of Aluminum

Because of the rightward shift in the supply curve due to large sales on the world market by Russia and other newly independent states in the former Soviet Union, the equilibrium price fell from about 80 cents to about 47 cents.

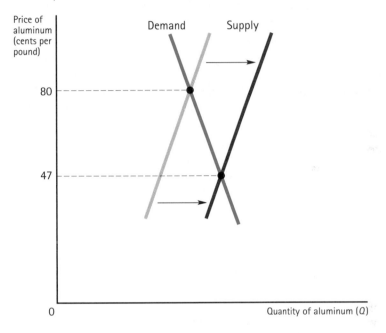

and supply we discussed. Managers in other industries must know these principles too. Much more is said on this score in subsequent chapters.[15] Virtually every issue of the *Wall Street Journal* and the *Financial Times* (in the commodities section) contains a story on a commodity price change due to shifts or anticipated shifts in demand and supply curves. Test your knowledge of the concepts of demand and supply curves by examining the stories and explaining what happened in the market by drawing demand and supply curves and then shifts.

[15]For further discussion of this case, see *New York Times*, February 13, 1994, and December 6, 1994; *Philadelphia Inquirer*, March 18, 1994; *Business Week*, March 28, 1994; WEFA Group, *Industrial Analysis Service Monthly Update*, February 1994; and *Wall Street Journal*, June 9, 1994.

CONCEPTS IN CONTEXT

Problems in the Potato Market

The United States is one of the world's leading producers of potatoes. Idaho is a particularly famous source of this product, but other states like Maine, Oregon, and Washington are important, too. In 1995, farmers in Idaho and elsewhere planted more potatoes than usual, and growing conditions were unusually favorable. Frost, pests, and diseases were of limited importance. The result was a marked shift to the right of the supply curve for potatoes. The 1996 crop was the largest in U.S. history, almost 49 billion pounds. Consequently, the price of potatoes per 100-pound sack nosedived from about $8 in 1995 to about $1.75 in 1996. According to leading potato producers, farmers lost about $1,000 per acre on the 1996 crop.

Unfortunately, this is not the only problem facing U.S. potato producers. The potato market today is dominated by french fries, which are becoming popular throughout the world. But as demand for french fries grows in various countries, producers of french fries are trying to establish local sources of potatoes. For example, according to the chairman of McCain Foods, the world's leading producer of frozen french fries, "If we're in England, we're buying all of the potatoes we can buy in England."* Obviously, this reduces the export of potatoes by U.S. producers. While U.S. exports of french fries have increased considerably in recent years, there is the feeling that this growth may slow considerably.†

*New York Times, April 12, 1997, p. 35.
†For further discussion, see ibid.

Summary

1. Managerial economics draws heavily on economics (particularly microeconomics) and the decision sciences. In contrast to microeconomics, which is largely descriptive, managerial economics is prescriptive. Courses in managerial economics provide fundamental analytical tools as well as play a major integrating role. Managerial economics is at the core of the management of nonbusiness organizations like government agencies as well as the management of firms.

2. Both for nonbusiness organizations and firms, the process of decision making can be divided into the following five steps: (1) Establish or identify the organization's objectives. (2) Define the problem. (3) Identify possible solutions. (4) Select the best possible solution. (5) Implement the decision.

3. To apply managerial economics to business management, we need a theory of the firm. According to the theory accepted by most managerial economists, the firm tries to maximize its value, defined as the present value of its expected future cash flows (which for now are equated with profits). However, this maximization occurs subject to constraints, since the firm

has limited inputs, particularly in the very short run, and must act in accord with a variety of laws and contracts.

4. Managerial economists define profits somewhat differently from the way accountants do. When economists speak of profit, they mean profit over and above what the owners' labor and capital employed in the business could earn elsewhere. To a considerable extent, the differences between the concepts of profit used by the accountant and the economist reflect the difference in their functions.

5. Three important reasons for the existence of profits are innovation, risk, and monopoly power. Profits and losses are the mainsprings of a free enterprise economy. They are signals that indicate where resources are needed and where they are too abundant. They are important incentives for innovation and risk taking. They are society's reward for efficiency.

6. Although managerial economists generally assume that firms want to maximize profit (and hence their value), it is recognized that a principal-agent problem arises if managers pursue their own interests, even though this decreases the profits of the owners. To deal with this problem, the owners often give the managers a financial stake in the success of the firm.

7. Every market has a demand side and a supply side. The market demand curve shows the amount of a product that buyers would like to purchase at various prices. The market supply curve shows the amount of a product that sellers would offer at various prices. The equilibrium price is the price where the quantity demanded equals the quantity supplied.

8. Both demand curves and supply curves shift over time; this results in changes in a product's price. Rightward shifts in the demand curve (and leftward shifts in the supply curve) tend to increase price. Leftward shifts in the demand curve (and rightward shifts in the supply curve) tend to decrease price.

Problems

1. In 1991, Bantam Books agreed to pay General Norman Schwarzkopf, who led U.S. forces in the Persian Gulf war against Iraq, $6 million for the rights to his not-yet-written memoirs. According to one leading publisher, Bantam would earn profits of about $1.2 million from the book if it sold 625,000 copies in hardcover. On the other hand, if it sold 375,000 copies in hardcover it would lose about $1.3 million.

   a. Publishing executives stated that it was very hard to sell more than 500,000 copies of a nonfiction hardcover, and very exceptional to sell 1 million copies. Was Bantam taking a substantial risk in publishing this book?

   b. In early 1993, Bantam announced that Schwarzkopf's book, *It Doesn't Take a Hero*, had already sold over 1 million copies and was the second most successful Bantam hardcover ever, behind only *Iacocca*, which sold 2.6 million copies in its hardcover edition. Did Bantam make a profit on this book? If so, was this profit, at least in part, a reward for risk bearing?

2. According to Paul Kagan Associates, a market research firm in Carmel, California, the average price of a combined AM/FM radio station fell from about $6.2 million in 1987 to about $1.8 million in 1990. From the mid-1980s to the early 1990s, the Federal Communications Commission, which regulates the airwaves, approved over a thousand new radio stations. Did this action by the commission help to cause the price decrease? Why or why not?

3. "No self-respecting [top] executive joining a company from the outside these days does so without a front-end, or signing, bonus. And in many cases, the bonus is in the seven figures. At the same time, the entering executive may be given a bonus guarantee; hence, he does not have to worry that, if the company's fortunes sag right after he joins, he will lose some or all of his normal bonus. Typically, the bonus guarantee lasts for two or three years, although [sometimes] . . . the guarantee turns out to be for life."[16] Do long-term bonus guarantees help to solve the principal-agent problem or do they tend to exacerbate it? Why?

4. What are the five basic steps in decision making? After the stock market crash on October 19, 1987, when the Dow-Jones average plummeted about 500 points, Louis Eckhardt, a New York broker, had to decide whether to buy Dow Chemical's stock. In his particular decision-making process, describe each of these five steps.

5. If the interest rate is 10 percent, what is the present value of the Monroe Corporation's profits in the next 10 years?

Number of years in the future	Profit (millions of dollars)
1	8
2	10
3	12
4	14
5	15
6	16
7	17
8	15
9	13
10	10

6. The profits of Du Pont de Nemours and Company in 1997 were about $2.4 billion. Does this mean that Du Pont's economic profit equaled $2.4 billion? Why or why not?

[16]G. Crystal, *In Search of Excess* (New York: Norton, 1991).

7. William Howe must decide whether to start a business renting beach umbrellas at an ocean resort during June, July, and August of next summer. He believes that he can rent each umbrella to vacationers at $5 a day, and he intends to lease 50 umbrellas for the three-month period for $3,000. To operate this business, he does not have to hire anyone (but himself), and he has no expenses other than the leasing costs and a fee of $3,000 per month to rent the location of the business. Howe is a college student, and if he did not operate this business, he could earn $4,000 for the three-month period doing construction work.

   a. If there are 80 days during the summer when beach umbrellas are demanded and Howe rents all 50 of his umbrellas on each of these days, what will be his accounting profit for the summer?

   b. What will be his economic profit for the summer?

8. If the demand curve for wheat in the United States is

$$P = 12.4 - 4Q_D$$

where P is the farm price of wheat (in dollars per bushel) and Q_D is the quantity of wheat demanded (in billions of bushels), and the supply curve for wheat in the United States is

$$P = -2.6 + 2Q_S$$

where Q_S is the quantity of wheat supplied (in billions of bushels), what is the equilibrium price of wheat? What is the equilibrium quantity of wheat sold? Must the actual price equal the equilibrium price? Why or why not?

9. During the 1980s, lumber prices averaged between $195 and $250 per thousand square feet. In 1993, the price hit $491. According to some observers, this price increase was due to a boom in housing construction; according to others, it was because the federal government was reducing the amount of federal forest open to logging. Did both groups feel that it was due to a shift in the demand curve for lumber? Did both feel that it was due to a shift in the supply curve for lumber? If not, which group emphasized the demand side of the market and which emphasized the supply side?

10. From October 1994 to March 1995, the price of cotton increased from $0.65 to over $1 per pound, the highest level since the Civil War. According to *Business Week*, "Supplies have dwindled because of poor crops in China, India, and Pakistan. At the same time, consumers, undeterred by rising costs, have pumped up demand for cotton-rich casual clothing, as well as home furnishings made from cotton."[17]

    a. Was this price increase due to a shift in the demand curve for cotton, a shift in the supply curve for cotton, or both?

    b. Did this price increase affect the supply curve for clothing? If so, how?

[17]*Business Week*, March 13, 1995, p. 83

11. On October 2, 1994, a revival of *Show Boat*, the great Broadway musical by Jerome Kern and Oscar Hammerstein, opened at the Gershwin Theater in New York. While the hit songs (like "Ole Man River" and "Make Believe") were old favorites, the top ticket price of $75 was new. Never before had a regularly priced ticket for an open-ended Broadway run been this high. The show's weekly gross revenues, operating costs, and profits were estimated to be as follows, depending on whether the top ticket price was $75 or $65 (the normal top price prior to this show):

	Top price of $75	Top price of $65
Gross revenues	$765,000	$680,000
Operating costs	600,000	600,000
Profit	165,000	80,000

a. With a cast of 71 people, a 30-piece orchestra, and more than 500 costumes, *Show Boat* cost about $8 million to stage. This investment was in addition to the operating costs (such as salaries and theater rent). How many weeks would it take before the investors got their money back, according to these estimates, if the top price were $65? If it were $75?

b. George Wachtel, director of research for the League of American Theaters and Producers, has said that about one in three shows that opened on Broadway in recent years has at least broken even. Were the investors in *Show Boat* taking a substantial risk?

c. According to one Broadway producer, "Broadway isn't where you make the money any more. It's where you establish the project so you can make the money. When you mount a show now, you really have to think about where it's going to play later." If so, should the above profit figures be interpreted with caution?

d. If the investors in this revival of *Show Boat* make a profit, will this profit be, at least in part, a reward for risk bearing?

12. In July 1993, the price of a pound of green, or unroasted, coffee was about $0.52. In early 1994, there was concern among coffee traders that Brazil's crop, the world's largest, would be smaller than expected. According to the U.S. Department of Agriculture, Brazil's 1994 crop was expected to be 18 percent below that in 1993 because of severe freezes. Brazil exported about 77 million pounds of coffee in April 1994, the smallest monthly shipment since April 1989. In Colombia, another very important coffee producer, the coffee crop was reduced by worm infestation; and in Java, Indonesia's largest coffee-producing region, heavy rains hampered the harvest. Whereas the price of coffee was $0.52 in July 1993, it rose to about $1.38 in June 1994. Why?

Optimization Techniques

CHAPTER 2

Carly Fiorina, chairperson of Hewlett-Packard, purchased the Compaq Computer Company in 2002. Why? Because she and her colleagues felt the acquisition would enhance the performance of Hewlett-Packard. As we learned in Chapter 1, managerial economics is concerned with the ways in which managers make decisions in order to maximize the effectiveness or performance of the organization they manage. To understand how this can be done, you must understand the basic optimization techniques taken up in this chapter.

To begin, we describe the nature of marginal analysis. While simple in concept, marginal analysis is a powerful tool that illuminates many central aspects of decision making regarding resource allocation. Economists think at the margins. It is intuitive that one would undertake a project if the additional (marginal) benefit one received from undertaking the project exceeded the additional (marginal) cost incurred by undertaking the project. Virtually all the rules of optimal behavior of firms and individuals that we study are driven by this concept.

Next, we examine the basic elements of differential calculus, including the rules of differentiation and the use of a derivative to maximize a function (such as profit) or minimize a function (such as cost). Differentiation tells us what changes will occur in one variable (the dependent variable) when a small (marginal) change is made in another variable (the independent variable). Therefore, the marginal analysis first discussed can be implemented by the use of differentiation.

Finally, we take up constrained optimization and include an optional section on Lagrangian multipliers. While we want to maximize the profits of our firm (or minimize the costs of production), such maximization or minimization is often subject to constraints (such as producing a certain amount to adhere to a contract or utilizing a certain amount of labor in a union agreement).

Since Lagrangian multipliers require more mathematical sophistication than the rest of this chapter, the section in which they are discussed can be skipped without loss of continuity.

Functional Relationships

To understand the optimization techniques described in this chapter, you must know how economic relationships are expressed. Frequently, the relationship between two or more economic variables can be represented by a table or graph. For example, Table 2.1 shows the relationship between the price charged by the Cherry Corporation and the number of units of output the company sells per day. Figure 2.1 represents the same relationship using a graph.

While tables and graphs are extremely helpful and are used often in this book, another way of expressing economic relationships is through equations. How can the relationship between the number of units sold and the price in Table 2.1 (and Figure 2.1) be expressed in the form of an equation? One way is to use the following functional notation:

$$Q = f(P) \tag{2.1}$$

where Q is the number of units sold and P is price. This equation should be read as: "The number of units sold is a function of price," which means that

TABLE 2.1

Relationship between Price and Quantity Sold, Cherry Corporation

Price per unit	Number of units sold per day
$10	150
$20	100
$30	50
$40	0

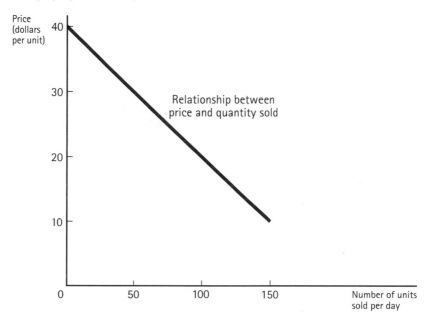

FIGURE
2.1

Relationship between Price and Quantity Sold, Cherry Corporation

This graph presents the data in Table 2.1.

the number of units sold *depends* on price. In other words, the number of units sold is the *dependent* variable, and price is the *independent* variable.

While equation (2.1) is useful, it does not tell us how the number of units sold depends on price. A more specific representation of this relationship is

$$Q = 200 - 5P \qquad (2.2)$$

Comparing this equation with the data in Table 2.1 (and Figure 2.1), you can verify that these data conform to this equation. For example, if the price equals $10, the number of units sold should be $200 - 5(10) = 150$, according to the equation. This is exactly what Table 2.1 (and Figure 2.1) shows. Regardless of what price you choose, the number of units sold is the same, no matter whether you consult Table 2.1, Figure 2.1, or equation (2.2).

Marginal Analysis

Whether economic relationships are expressed as tables, graphs, or equations, marginal analysis has enabled managers to use these relationships more

TABLE 2.2

Relationship between Output and Profit, Roland Corporation

(1) Number of units of output per day	(2) Total profit	(3) Marginal profit	(4) Average profit
0	0		—
		100	
1	100		100
		150	
2	250		125
		350	
3	600		200
		400	
4	1,000		250
		350	
5	1,350		270
		150	
6	1,500		250
		50	
7	1,550		221.4
		−50	
8	1,500		187.5
		−100	
9	1,400		155.5
		−200	
10	1,200		120

effectively. The **marginal value** of a dependent variable is defined as the change in this dependent variable associated with a one-unit *change* in a particular independent variable. As an illustration, consider Table 2.2, which indicates in columns 1 and 2 the total profit of the Roland Corporation if the number of units produced equals various amounts. In this case, total profit is the dependent variable and output is the independent variable. Therefore, the marginal value of profit, called **marginal profit,** is the *change* in total profit associated with a one-unit *change* in output.

Column 3 of Table 2.2 shows the value of marginal profit. If output increases from zero to one unit, column 2 shows that total profit increases by $100 (from $0 to $100). Therefore, marginal profit in column 3 equals $100 if output is between zero and one unit. If output increases from one to two units, total profit increases by $150 (from $100 to $250). Therefore, marginal profit in column 3 equals $150 if output is between one and two units.

The central point to bear in mind about a marginal relationship of this sort is that the dependent variable—in this case, total profit—is maximized when its marginal value shifts from positive to negative. To see this, consider Table 2.2. So long as marginal profit is positive, the Roland Corporation can raise its total profit by increasing output. For example, if output is between five and six units, marginal profit is positive ($150); therefore, the firm's total profit goes up (by $150) if output is increased from five to six units. But, when marginal profit shifts from positive to negative, total profit falls, not goes up, with any further increase in output. In Table 2.2, this point is reached when the firm produces seven units of output. If output is increased beyond this point (to eight units), marginal profit shifts from positive to negative—and total profit goes down (by $50). So, as stated previously, the dependent variable—in this case, total profit—is maximized when its marginal value shifts from positive to negative.

Since managers are interested in determining how to maximize profit (or other performance measures), this is a very useful result. It emphasizes the importance of looking at marginal values, and the hazards that may arise if average values are used instead. In Table 2.2, **average profit**—that is, total profit divided by output—is shown in column 4. It may seem eminently reasonable to choose the output whose average profit is highest. Countless managers have done so. But this is not the correct decision if one wants to maximize profit. Instead, as stressed in the previous paragraph, one should choose the output where marginal profit shifts from positive to negative.

To prove this, one need only find the output in Table 2.2 at which average profit is highest. Based on a comparison of the figures in column 4, this output is five units; and according to column 2, total profit at this output equals $1,350. In the paragraph before last, we found that the output where marginal profit shifts from positive to negative is seven units; and according to column 2, total profit at this point equals $1,550. Clearly, total profit is $200 higher if output is seven rather than five units. Hence, if the managers of this firm were to choose the output at which average profit is highest, they would sacrifice $200 per day in profits.

It is important to understand the relationship between average and marginal values: Because the marginal value represents the change in the total, the average value must increase if the marginal value is greater than the average value; by the same token, the average value must decrease if the marginal value is less than the average value. Table 2.2 illustrates these propositions. For the first to fifth units of output, marginal profit is greater than average profit. Since the extra profit from each additional unit is greater than the average, the average is pulled up as more is produced. For the sixth to tenth units of output, marginal profit is less than average profit. Since the extra profit from each additional unit is less than the average, the average is pulled down as more is produced.

Relationships between Total, Marginal, and Average Values

To explore further the relationships between total, marginal, and average values, consider Figure 2.2, which shows the relationships between total, average, and marginal profit, on the one hand, and output, on the other hand, for the

FIGURE
2.2

Total Profit, Average Profit, and Marginal Profit, Roland Corporation

The average and marginal profit curves in panel B can be derived geometrically from the total profit curve in panel A.

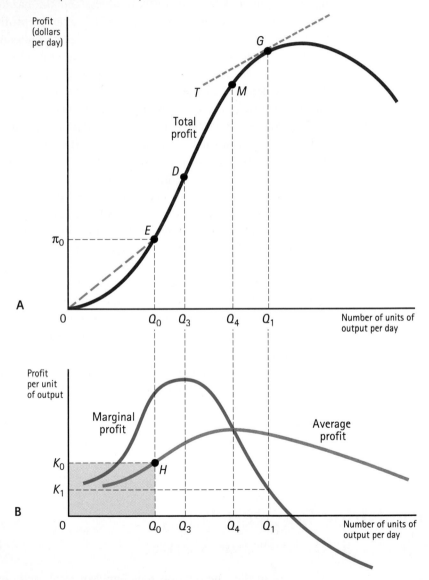

Roland Corporation. The relationship between output and profit is exactly the same as in Table 2.2, but rather than using particular numbers to designate output or profit, we use symbols such as Q_0 and Q_1 for output levels and π_0 for a profit level. The results are of general validity, not true for only a particular set of numerical values.

At the outset, note that Figure 2.2 contains two panels. The upper panel (panel A) shows the relationship between total profit and output, while the lower panel (panel B) shows the relationship between average profit and marginal profit, on the one hand, and output, on the other. The horizontal scale of panel A is the same as that of panel B, the result being that a given output, like Q_0, is the same distance from the origin (along the horizontal axis) in panel A as in panel B.

In practice, one seldom is presented with data concerning both (1) the relationship between total profit and output and (2) the relationship between average profit and output, because it is relatively simple to derive the latter relationship from the former. How can this be done? Take any output, say Q_0. *At this output, average profit equals the slope of the straight line from the origin to point E, the point on the total profit curve corresponding to output Q_0.* To see that this is the case, note that average profit at this output level equals π_0/Q_0, where π_0 is the level of total profit if output is Q_0. Because the slope of any straight line equals the vertical distance between two points on the line divided by the horizontal distance between them, the slope of the line from the origin to point E equals π_0/Q_0.[1] Thus, the slope of line OE equals average profit at this output. (In other words, K_0 in panel B of Figure 2.2 is equal to the slope of line OE.) To determine the relationship between average profit and output from the relationship between total profit and output, we repeat this procedure for each level of output, not Q_0 alone. The resulting average profit curve is shown in panel B.

Turning to the relationship between marginal profit and output (in panel B), it is relatively simple to derive this relationship too from the relationship between total profit and output (in panel A). Take any output, say Q_1. *At this output, marginal profit equals the slope of the tangent to the total profit curve (in panel A) at the point where output is Q_1.* In other words, marginal profit equals the slope of line T in Figure 2.2, which is tangent to the total profit curve at point G. As a first step toward seeing why this is true, consider Figure 2.3, which provides a magnified picture of the total profit curve in the neighborhood of point G.

Recall that marginal profit is defined as the extra profit resulting from a very small increase (specifically, a one-unit increase) in output. If output

[1]The vertical distance between the origin and point E equals π_0, and the horizontal distance between these two points equals Q_0. Therefore, the vertical distance divided by the horizontal distance equals π_0/Q_0.

FIGURE

2.3

Marginal Profit Equals the Slope of the Tangent to the Total Profit Curve

As the distance between Q_1 and Q_2 becomes extremely small, the slope of line T becomes a very good estimate of $(\pi_2 - \pi_1)/(Q_2 - Q_1)$.

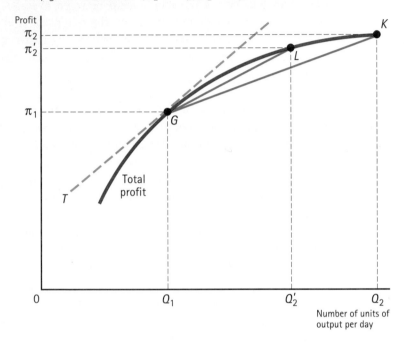

increases from Q_1 to Q_2, total profit increases from π_1 to π_2, as shown in Figure 2.3. Therefore, the extra profit per unit of output is $(\pi_2 - \pi_1)/(Q_2 - Q_1)$, which is the slope of the GK line. But this increase in output is rather large. Suppose that we decrease Q_2 so that it is closer to Q_1. In particular, let the new value of Q_2 be Q_2'. If output increases from Q_1 to Q_2', the extra profit per unit of output equals $(\pi_2' - \pi_1)/(Q_2' - Q_1)$, which is the slope of the GL line. If we further decrease Q_2 until the distance between Q_1 and Q_2 is extremely small, the slope of the tangent (line T) at point G becomes a very good estimate of $(\pi_2 - \pi_1)/(Q_2 - Q_1)$. In the limit, for changes in output in a very small neighborhood around Q_1, the slope of the tangent is marginal profit. (This slope equals K_1 in panel B of Figure 2.2.) To determine the relationship between marginal profit and output from the relationship between total profit and output, we repeat this procedure for each level of output, not Q_1 alone. The resulting marginal profit curve is shown in panel B of Figure 2.2.

Sometimes one is given an average profit curve like that in panel B but not the total profit curve. To derive the latter curve from the former, note that total profit equals average profit times output. Hence, if output equals Q_0, total profit equals K_0 times Q_0. In other words, π_0 in panel A equals the area of rectangle $0K_0HQ_0$ in panel B. To derive the relationship between total profit and output from the relationship between average profit and output, we repeat this procedure for each level of output. That is, we find the area of the appropriate rectangle of this sort corresponding to each output, not Q_0 alone. The resulting total profit curve is shown in panel A.

Finally, two further points should be made concerning the total, average, and marginal profit curves in Figure 2.2. First, you should be able to tell by a glance at panel A that marginal profit increases as output rises from zero to Q_3 and that it decreases as output rises further. Why is this so obvious from panel A? Because the slope of the total profit curve increases as one moves from the origin to point D. In other words, lines drawn tangent to the total profit curve become steeper as one moves from the origin to point D. Since marginal profit equals the slope of this tangent, it must increase as output rises from zero to Q_3. To the right of point D, the slope of the total profit curve decreases as output increases. That is, lines drawn tangent to the total profit curve become less steep as one moves to the right of point D. Consequently, since marginal profit equals the slope of this tangent, it too must decrease when output rises beyond Q_3.

Second, panel B of Figure 2.2 confirms the following proposition: *The average profit curve must be rising if it is below the marginal profit curve, and it must be falling if it is above the marginal profit curve.* At output levels below Q_4, the average profit curve is below the marginal profit curve; therefore, the average profit curve is rising because the higher marginal profits are pulling up the average profits. At output levels above Q_4, the average profit curve is above the marginal profit curve; therefore, the average profit curve is falling because the lower marginal profits are pulling down the average profits. At Q_4, the straight line drawn from the origin to point M is just tangent to the total cost curve. Therefore, the average profit and marginal profit are equal at output Q_4.

The Concept of a Derivative

In the case of the Roland Corporation, we used Table 2.2 (which shows the relationship between the firm's output and profit) to find the profit-maximizing output level. Frequently, a table of this sort is too cumbersome or inaccurate to be useful for this purpose. Instead, an equation is used to represent the relationship between the variable we are trying to maximize (in this case, profit) and the variable or variables under the control of the decision maker (in this case, output). Given an equation of this sort, the powerful concepts and techniques of differential calculus can be employed to find optimal solutions to the decision maker's problem.

In previous sections, we defined the *marginal value* as the change in the dependent variable resulting from a one-unit change in an independent variable. If Y is the dependent variable and X is the independent variable,

$$Y = f(X) \tag{2.3}$$

according to the notation in equation (2.1). Using Δ (called *delta*) to denote change, a change in the independent variable can be expressed as ΔX, and a change in the dependent variable can be expressed as ΔY. Thus, the marginal value of Y can be estimated by

$$\frac{\text{Change in } Y}{\text{Change in } X} = \frac{\Delta Y}{\Delta X} \tag{2.4}$$

For example, if a two-unit increase in X results in a one-unit increase in Y, $\Delta X = 2$ and $\Delta Y = 1$; this means that the marginal value of Y is about $^1/_2$. That is, the dependent variable Y increases by about $^1/_2$ if the independent variable X increases by 1.[2]

Unless the relationship between Y and X can be represented as a straight line (as in Figure 2.4), the value of $\Delta Y/\Delta X$ is not constant. For example, consider the relationship between Y and X in Figure 2.5. If a movement occurs from point G to point H, a relatively small change in X (from X_1 to X_2) is associated with a big change in Y (from Y_1 to Y_2). Therefore, between points G and H, the value of $\Delta Y/\Delta X$, which equals $(Y_2 - Y_1)/(X_2 - X_1)$, is relatively large. On the other hand, if a movement occurs from point K to point L, a relatively large change in X (from X_3 to X_4) is associated with a small change in Y (from Y_3 to Y_4). Consequently, between points K and L, the value of $\Delta Y/\Delta X$, which equals $(Y_4 - Y_3)/(X_4 - X_3)$, is relatively small.

The value of $\Delta Y/\Delta X$ is related to the steepness or flatness of the curve in Figure 2.5. Between points G and H, the curve is relatively *steep*; this means that a *small* change in X results in a *large* change in Y. Consequently, $\Delta Y/\Delta X$ is relatively large. Between points K and L, the curve is relatively *flat*; this means that a *large* change in X results in a *small* change in Y. Consequently, $\Delta Y/\Delta X$ is relatively small.

---

[2]Why do we say that Y increases by about 1/2, rather than by exactly 1/2? Because Y may not be linearly related to X. More is said on this subject in the next paragraph of the text.

FIGURE
2.4

Linear Relationship between *Y* and *X*

The relationship between *Y* and *X* can be represented as a straight line.

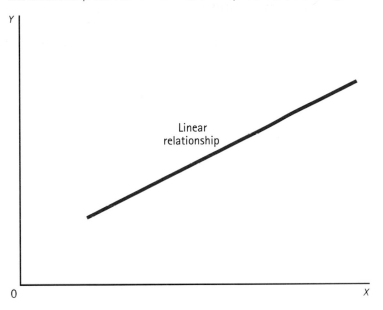

The derivative of Y with respect to X is defined as the limit of ΔY/ΔX as ΔX approaches zero. Since the derivative of *Y* with respect to *X* is denoted by *dY/dX*, this definition can be restated as

$$\frac{dY}{dX} = \underset{\Delta X \to 0}{limit} \frac{\Delta Y}{\Delta X} \tag{2.5}$$

which is read "The derivative of *Y* with respect to *X* equals the limit of the ratio ΔY/ΔX as ΔX approaches zero." To understand what is meant by a limit, consider the function $(X - 2)$. What is the limit of this function as *X* approaches 2? Clearly, as *X* gets closer and closer to 2, $(X - 2)$ gets closer and closer to zero. What is the limit of this function as *X* approaches zero? Clearly, as *X* gets closer and closer to zero, $(X - 2)$ gets closer and closer to −2.

Graphically, the derivative of *Y* with respect to *X* equals the *slope* of the curve showing *Y* (on the vertical axis) as a function of *X* (on the horizontal axis). To see this, suppose we want to find the value of the derivative of *Y* with respect to *X* when *X* equals X_5 in Figure 2.6. A rough measure is the

FIGURE
2.5

How the Value of $\Delta Y/\Delta X$ Varies Depending on the Steepness or Flatness of the Relationship between Y and X

Between points G and H, since the curve is steep, $\Delta Y/\Delta X$ is large. Between points K and L, since the curve is flat, $\Delta Y/\Delta X$ is small.

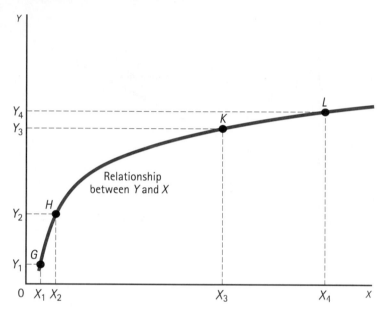

value of $\Delta Y/\Delta X$ when a movement is made from point A to point C; this measure equals

$$(Y_7 - Y_5)/(X_7 - X_5)$$

which is the slope of the AC line. A better measure is the value of $\Delta Y/\Delta X$ when a movement is made from point A to point B; this measure equals

$$(Y_6 - Y_5)/(X_6 - X_5)$$

which is the slope of the AB line. Why is the latter measure better than the former? Because the distance between points A and B is less than the distance between points A and C, what we want is the value of $\Delta Y/\Delta X$ when ΔX is as small as possible. Clearly, *in the limit, as ΔX approaches zero, the ratio $\Delta Y/\Delta X$ is equal to the slope of the line M, which is drawn tangent to the curve at point A.*

FIGURE
2.6

Derivative as the Slope of the Curve

When X equals X_5, the derivative of Y with respect to X equals the slope of line M, the tangent to the curve at point A.

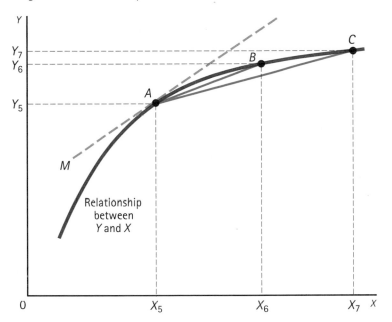

How to Find a Derivative

Managers want to know how to optimize the performance of their organizations. If Y is some measure of organizational performance and X is a variable under a particular manager's control, he or she would like to know the value of X that maximizes Y. To find out, it is very useful, as we shall see in the next section, to know the derivative of Y with respect to X. In this section, we learn how to find this derivative.

Derivatives of Constants

If the dependent variable Y is a constant, its derivative with respect to X is always zero. That is, if $Y = a$ (where a is a constant),

$$\frac{dY}{dX} = 0 \tag{2.6}$$

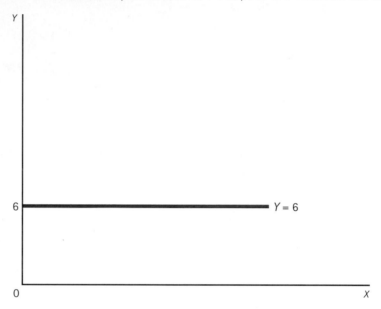

FIGURE

2.7

Case in Which $Y = 6$

In this case, dY/dX equals zero, since the slope of this horizontal line equals zero.

EXAMPLE Suppose that $Y = 6$, as shown in Figure 2.7. Since the value of Y does not change as X varies, dY/dX must be equal to zero. To see how this can also be shown geometrically, recall from the previous section that dY/dX equals the slope of the curve showing Y as a function of X. As is evident from Figure 2.7, this slope equals zero, which means that dY/dX must equal zero.

Derivatives of Power Functions

A power function can be expressed as

$$Y = aX^b$$

where a and b are constants. If the relationship between X and Y is of this kind, the derivative of Y with respect to X equals b times a multiplied by X raised to the $(b - 1)$ power:

$$\frac{dY}{dX} = baX^{b-1} \tag{2.7}$$

EXAMPLE Suppose that

$$Y = 3X$$

which is graphed in panel A of Figure 2.8. Applying equation (2.7), we find that

$$\frac{dY}{dX} = 1 \cdot 3 \cdot X^0 = 3$$

FIGURE
2.8

Case in Which $Y = 3X$

In this case, dY/dX equals 3, since the slope of the line in panel A equals 3.

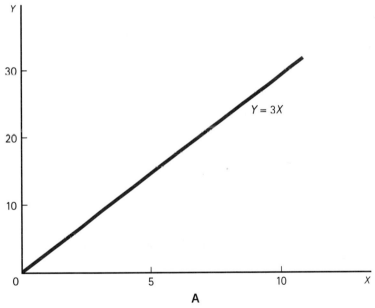

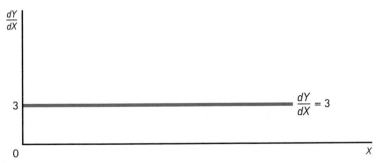

since $a = 3$ and $b = 1$. Therefore, the value of dY/dX graphed in panel B of Figure 2.8 is 3, regardless of the value of X. This makes sense, since the slope of the line in panel A is 3, regardless of the value of X. Recall once again from the previous section that dY/dX equals the slope of the curve showing Y as a function of X. In this case (as in Figure 2.7), this "curve" is a straight line.

EXAMPLE Suppose that

$$Y = 2X^2$$

which is graphed in panel A of Figure 2.9. Applying equation (2.7), we find that

$$\frac{dY}{dX} = 2 \cdot 2 \cdot X^1 = 4X$$

since $a = 2$ and $b = 2$. Therefore, the value of dY/dX, which is graphed in panel B of Figure 2.9, is proportional to X. As would be expected, dY/dX is negative when the slope of the curve in panel A is negative and positive when this slope is positive. Why? Because, as we stressed repeatedly, dY/dX equals this slope.

Derivatives of Sums and Differences

Suppose that U and W are two variables, each of which depends on X. That is,

$$U = g(X) \text{ and } W = h(X)$$

The functional relationship between U and X is denoted by g and that between W and X is denoted by h. Suppose further that

$$Y = U + W$$

In other words, Y is the sum of U and W. If so, the derivative of Y with respect to X is equal to the sum of the derivatives of the individual terms:

$$\frac{dY}{dX} = \frac{dU}{dX} + \frac{dW}{dX} \qquad (2.8)$$

On the other hand, if

$$Y = U - W$$

FIGURE
2.9

Case in Which $Y = 2X^2$

In this case, $dY/dX = 4X$, since the slope of the curve in panel A equals $4X$.

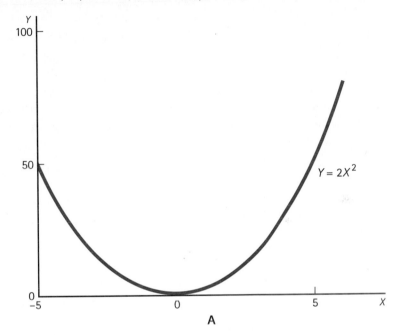

$Y = 2X^2$

A

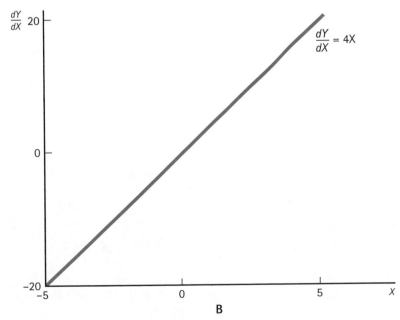

$\dfrac{dY}{dX} = 4X$

B

CONCEPTS IN CONTEXT

The Allocation of the TANG Brand Advertising Budget

In the 1960's, US astronauts drank TANG on their trips in space. Forty years later, Kraft Foods sells TANG in more than 80 countries. Eighty five percent of TANG's sales come from developing markets, where Kraft customizes the beverage to the specific taste preferences and nutritional needs of each market.

Managers and analysts use differential calculus to help solve all sorts of problems. Consider the work that Young and Rubicam, the prominent advertising agency, did for one of its Kraft foods (General Foods at the time) accounts, TANG beverages. TANG is the trademark for an instant breakfast drink with an orange flavor. Young and Rubicam did a study to estimate the effects of advertising expenditures on the sales of TANG and found that the relationships between advertising expenditures and sales in two districts were*

$$S_1 = 10 + 5A_1 - 1.5A_1^2$$

and $$S_2 = 12 + 4A_2 - 0.5A_2^2$$

where S_1 is the sales of TANG (in millions of dollars per year) in the first district, S_2 is its sales in the second district, A_1 is the advertising expenditure on TANG in the first district, and A_2 is the advertising expenditure in the second district.

Young and Rubicam wanted to determine the amount of additional sales that an extra dollar of advertising would generate in each district. To answer this question, the derivative of sales with respect to advertising expenditure was calculated for each district:

$$\frac{dS_1}{dA_1} = 5 - 3A_1$$

and $$\frac{dS_2}{dA_2} = 4 - A_2$$

Thus in each district, the effect on sales of an extra dollar of advertising expense, depended on the amount spent on advertising. Supposing that $0.5 million was being spent on advertising in the first district and that $1 million was being spent on advertising in the second district:

$$\frac{dS_1}{dA_1} = 5 - 3(0.5) = 3.5$$

and $$\frac{dS_2}{dA_2} = 4 - 1 = 3$$

Consequently, an extra dollar of advertising generated an extra $3.50 of sales in the first district and an extra $3.00 of sales in the second district.

On the basis of these findings, Young and Rubicam made a number of recommendations to General Foods (recall that TANG is now part of Kraft Foods) concerning the regional allocation of the TANG advertising budget. In particular, it recommended that, if General Foods wanted to boost the total sales of TANG, more should be spent on advertising in the first district and less should be spent on it in the second district. This would not mean an increase in General Foods's total advertising budget, since the extra advertising expenditure in the first district would be offset by the reduced advertising expenditure in the second district.

How did Young and Rubicam come to this conclusion? The fact that an extra dollar of advertising would result in a greater addition to sales in the first district than in the second indicated that a reallocation of the advertising budget was called for. To see this, consider what would happen if a dollar extra were spent on advertising in the first district and a dollar less spent in the second. The result, as indicated previously, would be an extra $3.50 of sales in the first district and a $3.00 reduction in sales in the second. The overall effect would be a $3.50 − $3.00 = $0.50 increase in total sales. Thus, if General Foods wanted to increase the sales of TANG beverages, a reallocation of the advertising budget in favor of the first district was to be recommended.[†]

*Although these equations are of the form derived by Young and Rubicam, the numerical coefficients are hypothetical. For present purposes, this is of no consequence. Our purpose here is to describe the general features of this case and how differential calculus played a role, not the specific numbers. The methods that can be used to estimate such coefficients are described in Chapter 5. Also, note that sales in each district are assumed to depend on the level of advertising in this district only.

[†]F. DeBruicker, J. Quelch, and S. Ward, *Cases in Consumer Behavior* (2d ed; Englewood Cliffs, NJ: Prentice-Hall, 1986). This case has been simplified in various respects for pedagogical reasons.

the derivative of Y with respect to X is equal to the difference between the derivatives of the individual terms:

$$\frac{dY}{dX} = \frac{dU}{dX} - \frac{dW}{dX} \tag{2.9}$$

EXAMPLE Consider the case in which $U = g(X) = 3X^3$ and $W = h(X) = 4X^2$. If $Y = U + W = 3X^3 + 4X^2$,

$$\frac{dY}{dX} = 9X^2 + 8X \tag{2.10}$$

To see why, recall from equation (2.8) that

$$\frac{dY}{dX} = \frac{dU}{dX} + \frac{dW}{dX} \tag{2.11}$$

Applying equation (2.7),

$$\frac{dU}{dX} = 9X^2 \text{ and } \frac{dW}{dX} = 8X$$

Substituting these values of the derivatives into equation (2.11), equation (2.10) follows.

EXAMPLE Suppose that $Y = U - W$, where $U = 8X^2$ and $W = 9X$. Then

$$\frac{dY}{dX} = 16X - 9$$

since, according to equation (2.9),

$$\frac{dY}{dX} = \frac{dU}{dX} - \frac{dW}{dX}$$

and, applying equation (2.7),

$$\frac{dU}{dX} = 16X \text{ and } \frac{dW}{dX} = 9$$

Derivatives of Products

The derivative of the product of two terms is equal to the sum of the first term multiplied by the derivative of the second plus the second term times the derivative of the first. Consequently, if $Y = UW$,

$$\frac{dY}{dX} = U\frac{dW}{dX} + W\frac{dU}{dX} \qquad (2.12)$$

EXAMPLE If $Y = 6X(3 - X^2)$, we can let $U = 6X$ and $W = 3 - X^2$; then

$$\begin{aligned}
\frac{dY}{dX} &= 6X\frac{dW}{dX} + (3 - X^2)\frac{dU}{dX} \\
&= 6X(-2X) + (3 - X^2)(6) \\
&= -12X^2 + 18 - 6X^2 \\
&= 18 - 18X^2
\end{aligned}$$

The first term, $6X$, is multiplied by the derivative of the second term, $-2X$, and the result is added to the second term, $3 - X^2$, times the derivative of the first, 6. As indicated, the result is $18 - 18X^2$.

Derivatives of Quotients

If $Y = U/W$, the derivative of Y with respect to X equals

$$\frac{dY}{dX} = \frac{W(dU/dX) - U(dW/dX)}{W^2}. \qquad (2.13)$$

In other words, the derivative of the quotient of two terms equals the denominator times the derivative of the numerator minus the numerator times the derivative of the denominator—all divided by the square of the denominator.

EXAMPLE Consider the problem of finding the derivative of the expression

$$Y = \frac{5X^3}{3 - 4X}$$

If we let $U = 5X^3$ and $W = 3 - 4X$,

$$\frac{dU}{dX} = 15X^2 \text{ and } \frac{dW}{dX} = -4$$

Consequently, applying equation (2.13),

$$\frac{dY}{dX} = \frac{(3 - 4X)(15X^2) - 5X^3(-4)}{(3 - 4X)^2}$$

$$= \frac{45X^2 - 60X^3 + 20X^3}{(3 - 4X)^2}$$

$$= \frac{45X^2 - 40X^3}{(3 - 4X)^2}$$

Derivatives of a Function of a Function (Chain Rule)[3]

Sometimes a variable depends on another variable, which in turn depends on a third variable. For example, suppose that $Y = f(W)$ and $W = g(X)$. Under these circumstances, the derivative of Y with respect to X equals

$$\frac{dY}{dX} = \left(\frac{dY}{dW} \right)\left(\frac{dW}{dX} \right) \tag{2.14}$$

In other words, to find this derivative, we find the derivative of Y with respect to W and multiply it by the derivative of W with respect to X.

EXAMPLE Suppose that $Y = 4W + W^3$ and $W = 3X^2$. To find dY/dX we begin by finding dY/dW and dW/dX:

$$\frac{dY}{dW} = 4 + 3W^2$$

$$= 4 + 3(3X^2)^2$$
$$= 4 + 27X^4$$

$$\frac{dW}{dX} = 6X$$

---

[3]This section can be skipped without loss of continuity.

Then, to find dY/dX, we multiply dY/dW and dW/dX:

$$\frac{dY}{dX} = (4 + 27X^4)(6X)$$

$$= 24X + 162X^5$$

Using Derivatives to Solve Maximization and Minimization Problems

Having determined how to find the derivative of Y with respect to X, we now take up the way to determine the value of X that maximizes or minimizes Y. *The central point to recognize is that a maximum or minimum point can occur only if the slope of the curve showing Y on the vertical axis and X on the horizontal axis equals zero.* To see this, suppose that Y equals the profit of the Monroe Company and X is its output level. If the relationship between Y and X is as shown by the curve in panel A of Figure 2.10, the maximum value of Y occurs when $X = 10$, and at this value of X the slope of the curve equals zero.

Since the derivative of Y with respect to X equals the slope of this curve, it follows that Y can be a maximum or minimum only if this derivative equals zero. To see that Y really is maximized when this derivative equals zero, note that the relationship between Y and X in Figure 2.10 is

$$Y = -50 + 100X - 5X^2 \tag{2.15}$$

which means that

$$\frac{dY}{dX} = 100 - 10X \tag{2.16}$$

Therefore, if this derivative equals zero,

$$100 - 10X = 0$$
$$X = 10$$

This is the value of X where Y is maximized, as we saw in the previous paragraph. The key point here is that, *to find the value of X that maximizes or minimizes Y, we must find the value of X where this derivative equals zero.* Panel B of Figure 2.10 shows graphically that this derivative equals zero when Y is maximized.

FIGURE
2.10

Value of the Derivative When *Y* Is a Maximum

When *Y* is a maximum (at *X* = 10), *dY*/*dX* equals zero.

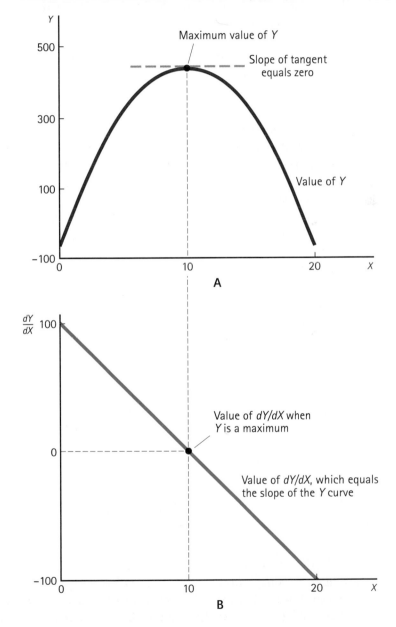

However, on the basis of only the fact that this derivative is zero, one cannot distinguish between a point on the curve where Y is maximized and a point where Y is minimized. For example, in Figure 2.11, this derivative is zero both when $X = 5$ and when $X = 15$. In the one case (when $X = 15$), Y is a maximum; in the other case (when $X = 5$), Y is a minimum. To distinguish between a maximum and a minimum, one must find the *second derivative of Y with respect to X, which is denoted d^2Y/dX^2 and is the derivative of dY/dX.* For example, in Figure 2.10, the second derivative of Y with respect to X is the derivative of the function in equation (2.16); therefore, it equals -10.

The second derivative measures the slope of the curve showing the relationship between dY/dX (the first derivative) and X. Just as the first derivative (that is, dY/dX) measures the slope of the Y curve in panel A of Figure 2.11, so the second derivative (that is, d^2Y/dX^2) measures the slope of the dY/dX curve in panel B of Figure 2.11. In other words, just as the first derivative measures the slope of the total profit curve, the second derivative measures the slope of the marginal profit curve. The reason why the second derivative is so important is that it is always *negative* at a point of *maximization* and always *positive* at a point of *minimization.* Therefore, *to distinguish between maximization and minimization points, all we have to do is determine whether the second derivative at each point is positive or negative.*

To understand why the second derivative is always negative at a maximization point and always positive at a minimization point, consider Figure 2.11. When the second derivative is negative, this means that the slope of the dY/dX curve in panel B is negative. Because dY/dX equals the slope of the Y curve in panel A, this in turn means that the slope of the Y curve decreases as X increases. At a maximum point, such as when $X = 15$, this must be the case. On the other hand, when the second derivative is positive, this means that the slope of the dY/dX curve in panel B is positive, which is another way of saying that the slope of the Y curve in panel A increases as X increases. At a minimum point, such as when $X = 5$, this must be the case.

EXAMPLE   To illustrate how one can use derivatives to solve maximization and minimization problems, suppose that the relationship between profit and output at the Kantor Corporation is

$$Y = -1 + 9X - 6X^2 + X^3$$

where Y equals annual profit (in millions of dollars) and X equals annual output (in millions of units). This equation is valid only for values of X that equal 3 or less; capacity limitations prevent the firm from producing more than 3 million units per year. To find the values of output that maximize or

FIGURE
2.11

Using the Second Derivative to Distinguish Maxima from Minima

At maxima (such as $X = 15$), d^2Y/dX^2 is negative; at minima (such as $X = 5$), d^2Y/dX^2 is positive.

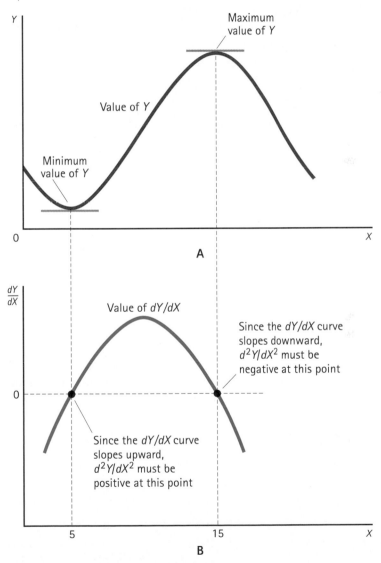

minimize profit, we find the derivative of Y with respect to X and set it equal to zero:

$$\frac{dY}{dX} = 9 - 12X + 3X^2 = 0 \qquad (2.17)$$

Solving this equation for X, we find that two values of X—1 and 3—result in this derivative being zero.[4]

To determine whether each of these two output levels maximizes or minimizes profit, we find the value of the second derivative at these two values of X. Taking the derivative of dY/dX, which is shown in equation (2.17) to equal $9 + 12X + 3X^2$, we find that

$$\frac{d^2Y}{dX^2} = -12 + 6X$$

If $X = 1$

$$\frac{d^2Y}{dX^2} = -12 + 6(1) = -6$$

Since the second derivative is negative, profit is a maximum (at 3) when output equals 1 million units. If $X = 3$,

$$\frac{d^2Y}{dX^2} = -12 + 6(3) = 6$$

Since the second derivative is positive, profit is a minimum (at -1) when output equals 3 million units.

---

[4]If an equation is of the general quadratic form, $Y = aX^2 + bX + c$, the values of X where Y is 0 are

$$X = \frac{-b \pm (b^2 - 4ac)^{0.5}}{2a}$$

In the equation in the text, $a = 3$, $b = -12$, and $c = 9$. Hence,

$$X = \frac{12 \pm (144 - 108)^{0.5}}{6} = 2 \pm 1$$

Therefore, $Y = 0$ when X equals 1 or 3.

Marginal Cost Equals Marginal Revenue and the Calculus of Optimization

Once you know how elementary calculus can be used to solve optimization problems, it is easy to see that the fundamental rule for profit maximization—set marginal cost equal to marginal revenue—has its basis in the calculus of optimization. Figure 2.12 shows a firm's total cost and total revenue functions. Since total profit equals total revenue minus total cost, it is equal to the vertical distance between the total revenue and total cost curves at any level of output. This distance is maximized at output Q_1, where the slopes of the total revenue and total cost curves are equal. Since the slope of the total revenue curve is marginal revenue and the slope of the total cost curve is marginal cost, this means that profit is maximized when marginal cost equals marginal revenue.

FIGURE 2.12

Marginal–Revenue–Equals–Marginal–Cost Rule for Profit

At the profit-maximizing output of Q_1, marginal revenue (equal to the slope of line R) equals marginal cost (the slope of line S).

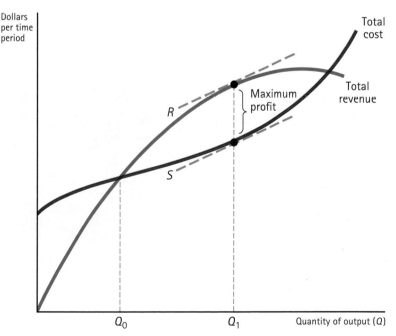

ANALYZING MANAGERIAL DECISIONS

The Optimal Size of a Nursing Home

The nursing home industry takes in about $70 billion a year and is growing rapidly because of the aging of the U.S. population. According to Peter Sidoti of Nat West Securities Corporation, "Nursing homes are the only area in health care where there is a shortage."[*] A study by Niccie McKay of Trinity University has estimated that the average cost per patient-day of a nursing home (owned by a chain of for-profit homes) is

$$Y = A - 0.16X + 0.00137X^2$$

where X is the nursing home's number of patient-days per year (in thousands) and A is a number that depends on the region in which the nursing home is located (and other such factors) but not on X.

(a) On the basis of the results of this study, how big must a nursing home be (in terms of patient-days) to minimize the cost per patient-day? (b) Show that your result minimizes, rather than maximizes, the cost per patient-day. (c) Is the number of patient-days a good measure of a nursing home's output? Why or why not?

SOLUTION (a) To find the value of X that minimizes Y, we set the derivative of Y with respect to X equal to zero:

$$= -0.16 + 0.00274X = 0$$

Therefore, $X = 0.16/0.00274 = 58.4$ thousands of days.

(b) Since

$$\frac{d^2Y}{dX^2} = 0.00274$$

d^2Y/dX^2 is positive. So, Y must be a minimum, not a maximum, at the point where $dY/dX = 0$.

(c) It is a crude measure, since some patients require far more complex and intensive care than others.[†]

[*]New York Times, February 27, 1994, p. F5.
[†]For further discussion, see N. McKay, "The Effect of Chain Ownership on Nursing Home Costs," Health Services Research, April 1991.

Inspection of Figure 2.12 shows that Q_1 must be the profit-maximizing output. Outputs below Q_0 result in losses (since total cost exceeds total revenue) and obviously do not maximize profit. As output increases beyond Q_0, total revenue rises more rapidly than total cost, so profit must be going up. So long as the slope of the total revenue curve (which equals marginal revenue) exceeds the slope of the total cost curve (which equals marginal cost), profit will continue to rise as output increases. But, when these slopes become equal (which means that marginal revenue equals marginal cost), profit no longer will rise but will be at a maximum. Since these slopes become equal at an output of Q_1, this must be the profit-maximizing output. After output Q_1, profit decreases (because marginal cost exceeds marginal revenue).

Using calculus, one can readily understand why firms maximize profit by setting marginal cost equal to marginal revenue. The first thing to note is that

$$\pi = TR - TC,$$

where π equals total profit, TR equals total revenue, and TC equals total cost. Taking the derivative of π with respect to Q (output), we find that

$$\frac{d\pi}{dQ} = \frac{dTR}{dQ} - \frac{dTC}{dQ}$$

For π to be a maximum, this derivative must be zero, so it must be true that

$$\frac{dTR}{dQ} = \frac{dTC}{dQ} \tag{2.18}$$

And since marginal revenue is defined as $d\,TR/dQ$ and marginal cost is defined as $d\,TC/dQ$, marginal revenue must equal marginal cost.[5]

Partial Differentiation and the Maximizations of Multivariable Functions

Up to this point, we have been concerned solely with situations in which a variable depends on only one other variable. Although such situations exist, in many cases, a variable depends on a number (often a large number) of other

---

[5]Two points should be noted. (1) For profit to be maximized, $d^2\pi/dQ^2$ must be negative. (2) The analysis in this section (as well as in earlier sections) results in the determination of a *local* maximum. Sometimes a local maximum is not a global maximum. For example, under some circumstances, the profit-maximizing (or loss-minimizing) output is zero, as we shall see in Chapter 10.

CONCEPTS IN CONTEXT

An Alleged Blunder in the Stealth Bomber's Design

Managerial economics is of great use in the aerospace industry, but this does not mean that errors will not occur sometimes. The B-2 "Stealth" bomber cost billions of dollars to develop. According to Joseph Foa, an emeritus professor of engineering at George Washington University, its design is fundamentally flawed because two aerodynamicists made a mistake: They mistook a minimum point for a maximum point.

The B-2 is basically a jet-powered "flying wing" aircraft. In a secret study for the Air Force, the two aerodynamicists, William Sears and Irving Ashkenas (then at the Northrop Corporation), used mathematical formulas to determine how an aircraft's volume should be proportioned between wing and fuselage to maximize its range. Taking the derivative of range with respect to volume, they found that this derivative equaled zero when the total volume was almost all in the wing. Hence,

they concluded that a "flying wing" design would maximize range.

But in a subsequent analysis, Foa showed that the second derivative was positive, not negative, under these circumstances. Hence, the "flying wing" design *minimized* the range; it did not maximize it. In Foa's words, "The flying wing was the aerodynamically worst possible choice of configuration."

This is a very interesting example of how important it is to look at the second derivative to make sure that you do not confuse a maximization point with a minimization point. While the backers of the B-2 bomber claim that it is a good plane despite this error, no one denies that the error is an embarrassment.*

*This discussion is based on W. Biddle, "Skeleton Alleged in the Stealth Bomber's Closet," *Science*, May 12, 1989.

variables, not just one. For example, the Merrimack Company produces two goods, and its profit depends on the amount that it produces of each good. That is,

$$\pi = f(Q_1, Q_2) \tag{2.19}$$

where π is the firm's profit, Q_1 is its output of the first good, and Q_2 is its output of the second good.

To find the value of each of the independent variables (Q_1 and Q_2 in this case) that maximizes the dependent variable (π in this case), we need to know the marginal effect of each independent variable on the dependent variable, *holding constant the effect of all other independent variables*. For example, in this case, we need to know the marginal effect of Q_1 on π when Q_2 is held constant, and we need to know the marginal effect of Q_2 on π when Q_1 is held constant. To get this information, we obtain the partial derivative of π with respect to Q_1 and the partial derivative of π with respect to Q_2.

To obtain the partial derivative of π with respect to Q_1, denoted $\partial\pi/\partial Q_1$, one applies the rules for finding a derivative (on pages 47–60) to equation (2.19), but treats Q_2 as a constant. Similarly, to obtain the partial derivative of π with respect to Q_2, denoted $\partial\pi/\partial Q_2$, one applies these rules to equation (2.19), but treats Q_1 as a constant.

EXAMPLE   Suppose that the relationship between the Merrimack Company's profit (in thousands of dollars) and its output of each good is

$$\pi = -20 + 113.75Q_1 + 80Q_2 - 10Q_1^2 - 10Q_2^2 - 5Q_1Q_2 \qquad (2.20)$$

To find the partial derivative of π with respect to Q_1, we treat Q_2 as a constant and find that

$$\frac{\partial\pi}{\partial Q_1} = 113.75 - 20Q_1 - 5Q_2$$

To find the partial derivative of π with respect to Q_2, we treat Q_1 as a constant and find that

$$\frac{\partial\pi}{\partial Q_2} = 80 - 20Q_2 - 5Q_1$$

Once we have derived the partial derivatives, it is relatively simple to determine the values of the independent variables that maximize the dependent variable. All we have to do is set *all the partial derivatives equal to zero*. In the case of the Merrimack Company,

$$\frac{\partial\pi}{\partial Q_1} = 113.75 - 20Q_1 - 5Q_2 = 0 \qquad (2.21)$$

$$\frac{\partial\pi}{\partial Q_2} = 80 - 20Q_2 - 5Q_1 = 0 \qquad (2.22)$$

Equations (2.21) and (2.22) are two equations in two unknowns. Solving them simultaneously, we find that profit is maximized when $Q_1 = 5.0$ and $Q_2 = 2.75$. In other words, to maximize profit, the firm should produce 5.0 units of the

FIGURE
2.13

Relationship between π, Q_1, and Q_2

At M, the point where π is a maximum, the surface representing this relationship is flat; its slope with regard to either Q_1 or Q_2 is zero.

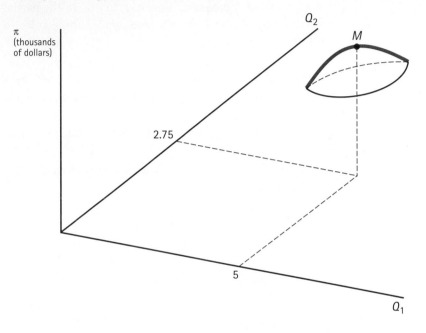

first good and 2.75 units of the second good per period of time. If it does this, its profit will equal \$374.375 thousand per period of time.[6]

To see why all the partial derivatives should be set equal to zero, consider Figure 2.13, which shows the relationship in equation (2.20) between π, Q_1, and Q_2, in the range where π is close to its maximum value. As you can see, this relationship is represented by a three-dimensional surface. The maximum value of π is at point M, where this surface is level. A plane tangent to this surface at point M is parallel to the Q_1Q_2 plane; in other words, its slopes with respect to either Q_1 or Q_2 must be zero. Since the partial derivatives in equations (2.21) and (2.22) equal these slopes, they too must equal zero at the maximum point, M.[7]

[6]Inserting 5.0 for Q_1 and 2.75 for Q_2 in equation (2.20), we find that

$$\pi = -20 + 113.75(5) + 80(2.75) - 10(5)^2 - 10(2.75)^2 - 5(5)(2.75) = 374.375$$

[7]The second-order conditions for distinguishing maxima from minima can be found in any calculus book. For present purposes, a discussion of these conditions is not essential. Also note that the techniques presented in this section result in a local maximum, not necessarily a global maximum (recall footnote 5).

ANALYZING MANAGERIAL DECISIONS

The Effects of Advertising on the Sales of TANG

On page 56, we encountered Young and Rubicam's study to estimate the effects of advertising expenditures on the sales of TANG, an instant breakfast drink marketed by General Foods (currently marketed by Kraft Foods). Specifically, the agency found that the relationship between advertising expenditures and sales in two districts were

$$S_1 = 10 + 5A_1 - 1.5A_1^2$$

and

$$S_2 = 12 + 4A_2 - 0.5A_2^2$$

where S_1 is TANG's sales (in millions of dollars per year) in the first district, S_2 is its sales in the second district, A_1 is the advertising expenditure (in millions of dollars per year) on TANG in the first district, and A_2 is the advertising expenditure in the second district.

(a) If General Foods wants to maximize TANG's sales in the first district, how much should it spend on advertising? (b) If General Foods wants to maximize TANG's sales in the second district, how much should it spend on advertising? (c) Show that your answers to parts a and b maximize, rather than minimize, sales. (d) Would you recommend that General Foods attempt to maximize TANG's sales? Why or why not?

SOLUTION (a) To find the value of A_1 that maximizes S_1, we set the derivative of S_1 with respect to A_1 equal to zero:

$$\frac{dS_1}{dA_1} = 5 - 3A_1 = 0$$

Here, $A_1 = 5/3$ million dollars. (b) To find the value of A_2 that maximizes S_2, we set the derivative of S_2 with respect to A_2 equal to zero:

$$\frac{dS_2}{dA_2} = 4 - A_2 = 0$$

Here, $A_2 = 4$ million dollars. (c) Since $d^2S_1/dA_1^2 = -3$, S_1 must be a maximum at the point where $dS_1/dA_1 = 0$. Since $d^2S_2/dA_2^2 = -1$, S_2 must be a maximum at the point where $dS_2/dA_2 = 0$. If S_1 and S_2 were minimized, not maximized, the second derivatives would be positive, not negative. (d) No. As stressed in Chapter 1, firms generally are assumed to be interested in maximizing profit, not sales. In general, a firm is unlikely to increase its sales if it means a decrease in its profits. But, in some cases, a firm may do this because, although profits may fall in the short run, they may increase in the long run. For example, a firm may make some sales at a loss to gain customers who eventually will enhance the firm's profits.[*]

[*]See F.S. DeBruicker, J.A. Quelch, and S. Ward, *Cases in Consumer Behavior* (2nd ed.; Englewood Cliffs, NJ: Prentice-Hall, 1986).

Constrained Optimization

As we learned in Chapter 1, managers of firms and other organizations generally face constraints that limit the options available to them. A production manager may want to minimize his or her firm's costs but may not be permitted to produce less than is required to meet the firm's contracts with its customers. The top managers of a firm may want to maximize profits, but in the short run, they may be unable to change its product or augment its plant and equipment.

Constrained optimization problems of this sort can be solved in a number of ways. In relatively simple cases in which there is only one constraint, one can use this constraint to express one of the decision variables—that is, one of the variables the decision maker can choose—as a function of the other decision variables. Then, one can apply the techniques for unconstrained optimization described in the previous sections. In effect, what one does is convert the problem to one of unconstrained maximization or minimization.

To illustrate, suppose that the Kloster Company produces two products and that its total cost equals

$$TC = 4Q_1^2 + 5Q_2^2 - Q_1Q_2 \tag{2.23}$$

where Q_1 equals its output per hour of the first product and Q_2 equals its output per hour of the second product. Because of commitments to customers, the number produced of both products combined cannot be less than 30 per hour. Kloster's president wants to know what output levels of the two products minimize the firm's costs, given that the output of the first product plus the output of the second product equals 30 per hour.

This constrained optimization problem can be expressed as follows:

Minimize $TC = 4Q_1^2 + 5Q_2^2 - Q_1Q_2$
subject to $Q_1 + Q_2 = 30$

Of course, the constraint is that $(Q_1 + Q_2)$ must equal 30. Solving this constraint for Q_1, we have

$$Q_1 = 30 - Q_2$$

Substituting $(30 - Q_2)$ for Q_1 in equation (2.23), it follows that

$$
\begin{aligned}
TC &= 4(30 - Q_2)^2 + 5Q_2^2 - (30 - Q_2)Q_2 \\
&= 4(900 - 60Q_2 + Q_2^2) + 5Q_2^2 - 30Q_2 + Q_2^2 \\
TC &= 3600 - 270Q_2 + 10Q_2^2
\end{aligned}
\tag{2.24}
$$

The methods of unconstrained optimization just described can be used to find the value of Q_2 that minimizes TC. As indicated in earlier sections, we must obtain the derivative of TC with respect to Q_2 and set it equal to zero:

$$\frac{dTC}{dQ_2} = -270 + 20Q_2 = 0$$
$$20Q_2 = 270$$
$$Q_2 = 13.5$$

To make sure that this is a minimum, not a maximum, we obtain the second derivative, which is

$$\frac{d^2TC}{dQ_2^2} = 20$$

Since this is positive, we have found a minimum.

To find the value of Q_1 that minimizes total cost, recall that the constraint requires that

$$Q_1 + Q_2 = 30$$

which means that

$$Q_1 = 30 - Q_2$$

Since we know that the optimal value of Q_2 is 13.5, it follows that the optimal value of Q_1 must be

$$Q_1 = 30 - 13.5 = 16.5$$

Summing up, if the Kloster Company wants to minimize total cost subject to the constraint that the sum of the output levels of its two products be 30, it should produce 16.5 units of the first product and 13.5 units of the second product per hour.[8] (In other words, it should produce 33 units of the first product and 27 units of the second product every 2 hours.)

---

[8]Substituting 16.5 for Q_1 and 13.5 for Q_2 in equation (2.23), the firm's total cost will equal

$$TC = 4(16.5)^2 + 5(13.5)^2 - (16.5)(13.5)$$
$$= 4(272.25) + 5(182.25) - 222.75$$
$$= 1089 + 911.25 - 222.75$$
$$= 1777.5, \quad \text{or} \quad \$1,777.50$$

Lagrangian Multipliers[9]

If the technique described in the previous section is not feasible because the constraints are too numerous or complex, the method of Lagrangian multipliers can be used. This method of solving constrained optimization problems involves the construction of an equation—the so-called Lagrangian function—that combines the function to be minimized or maximized and the constraints. This equation is constructed so that two things are true: (1) When this equation is maximized (or minimized), the original function we want to maximize (or minimize) is in fact maximized (or minimized). (2) All the constraints are satisfied.

To illustrate how one creates a Lagrangian function, consider once again the problem faced by the Kloster Company. As indicated in the previous section, this firm wants to minimize $TC = 4Q_1^2 + 5Q_2^2 - Q_1 Q_2$, subject to the constraint that $Q_1 + Q_2 = 30$. The first step in constructing the Lagrangian function for this firm's problem is to restate the constraint so that an expression is formed that is equal to zero:

$$30 - Q_1 - Q_2 = 0 \qquad (2.25)$$

Then, if we multiply this form of the constraint by an unknown factor, designated λ (*lambda*), and add the result to the function we want to minimize (in equation (2.23)), we get the Lagrangian function, which is

$$L_{TC} = 4Q_1^2 + 5Q_2^2 - Q_1 Q_2 + \lambda(30 - Q_1 - Q_2) \qquad (2.26)$$

For reasons specified in the next paragraph, we can be sure that, if we find the unconstrained maximum (or minimum) of the Lagrangian function, the solution will be exactly the same as the solution of the original constrained maximization (or minimization) problem. In other words, to solve the constrained optimization problem, all we have to do is optimize the Lagrangian function. For example, in the case of the Kloster Company, we must find the values of Q_1, Q_2, and λ that minimize L_{TC} in equation (2.26). To do this, we must find the partial derivative of L_{TC} with respect to each of these three variables—Q_1, Q_2, and λ:

$$\frac{\partial L_{TC}}{\partial Q_1} = 8Q_1 - Q_2 - \lambda$$

$$\frac{\partial L_{TC}}{\partial Q_2} = -Q_1 + 10Q_2 - \lambda$$

$$\frac{\partial L_{TC}}{\partial \lambda} = -Q_1 - Q_2 + 30$$

[9]This section can be skipped without loss of continuity.

As indicated in the section before last, we must set all three of these partial derivatives equal to zero in order to minimize L_{TC}:

$$8Q_1 - Q_2 - \lambda = 0 \qquad (2.27)$$
$$-Q_1 + 10Q_2 - \lambda = 0 \qquad (2.28)$$
$$-Q_1 - Q_2 + 30 = 0 \qquad (2.29)$$

It is important to note that the partial derivative of the Lagrangian function with regard to λ (that is, $\partial L_{TC}/\partial \lambda$), when it is set equal to zero (in equation (2.29)), is the constraint in our original optimization problem (recall equation (2.25)). This, of course, is always true because of the way the Lagrangian function is constructed. So, if this derivative is zero, we can be sure that this original constraint is satisfied. And, if this constraint is satisfied, the last term on the right of the Lagrangian function is zero, so the Lagrangian function boils down to the original function that we wanted to maximize (or minimize). Consequently, by maximizing (or minimizing) the Lagrangian function, we solve the original constrained optimization problem.

Returning to the Kloster Company, equations (2.27), (2.28), and (2.29) are three simultaneous equations with three unknowns—Q_1, Q_2, and λ. If we solve this system of equations for Q_1 and Q_2, we get the optimal values of Q_1 and Q_2. Subtracting equation (2.28) from equation (2.27), we find that

$$9Q_1 - 11Q_2 = 0 \qquad (2.30)$$

Multiplying equation (2.29) by 9 and adding the result to equation (2.30), we can solve for Q_2:

$$-9Q_1 - 9Q_2 + 270 = 0$$
$$\underline{9Q_1 - 11Q_2 = 0}$$
$$-20Q_2 + 270 = 0$$
$$Q_2 = 270/20 = 13.5$$

Therefore, the optimal value of Q_2 is 13.5. Substituting 13.5 for Q_2 in equation (2.29), we find that the optimal value of Q_1 is 16.5.

The answer we get is precisely the same as in the previous section: The optimal value of Q_1 is 16.5, and the optimal value of Q_2 is 13.5. In other words, the Kloster Company should produce 16.5 units of the first product and 13.5 units of the second product per hour. But, the method of Lagrangian multipliers described in this section is more powerful than that described in the previous section for at least two reasons: (1) It can handle more than a single constraint, and (2) the value of λ provides interesting and useful information to the decision maker.

Specifically λ, called the Lagrangian multiplier, measures the change in the variable to be maximized or minimized (TC in this case) if the constraint is relaxed by one unit. For example, if the Kloster Company wants to minimize total cost subject to the constraint that the total output of both products is 31 rather than 30, the value of λ indicates by how much the minimum value of TC will increase. What is the value of λ? According to equation (2.27),

$$8Q_1 - Q_2 - \lambda = 0$$

Since $Q_1 = 16.5$ and $Q_2 = 13.5$,

$$\lambda = 8(16.5) - 13.5 = 118.5$$

Consequently, if the constraint is relaxed so that total output is 31 rather than 30, the total cost will go up by $118.50.

For many managerial decisions, information of this sort is of great value. Suppose that a customer offers the Kloster Company $115 for one of its products, but to make this product, Kloster would have to stretch its total output to 31 per hour. On the basis of the findings of the previous paragraph, Kloster would be foolish to accept this offer, since this extra product would raise its costs by $118.50, which is $3.50 more than the amount the customer offers to pay for it.

Comparing Incremental Costs with Incremental Revenues

Before concluding this chapter, we must point out that many business decisions can and should be made by comparing incremental costs with incremental revenues. Typically, a manager must choose between two (or more) courses of action, and what is relevant is the difference in costs between the two courses of action, as well as the difference in revenues between them. For example, if the managers of a machinery company are considering whether to add a new product line, they should compare the incremental cost of adding the new product line (that is, the extra cost resulting from its addition) with the incremental revenue (that is, the extra revenue resulting from its addition). If the incremental revenue exceeds the incremental cost, the new product line will add to the firm's profits.

Note that *incremental* cost is not the same as *marginal* cost. Whereas marginal cost is the extra cost from a very small (one-unit) increase in output, **incremental cost** is the extra cost from an output increase that may be very substantial. Similarly, **incremental revenue**, unlike marginal revenue, is the

Planning to Meet Peak Engineering Requirements*

A leading computer manufacturer, after analyzing the history of its product development projects, found regular patterns of laborpower buildup and phaseout in its projects. Specifically, the number of engineers required to carry out such a project t months after the start of the project could be approximated reasonably well by

$$Y = at - bt^2, \qquad \text{for } 0 \leq t \leq a/b$$

where Y is the number of engineers required t months after the start of the project, and a and b are numbers that vary from project to project (and that depend on the kind of product being developed).

The computer manufacturer wanted to use these results to estimate when the number of engineers required to carry out a particular product development project would hit its peak and how great this peak requirement would be. Estimates of this sort would help the firm's managers plan the allocation and utilization of the firm's engineering staff and alert them to situations in which its staff might have to be expanded or supplemented. The project for which the firm's managers wanted these estimates was to begin immediately. On the basis of previous experience with projects of this type, the firm's managers estimated that a would be about 18 and b would be about 1 for this project.

If you were a consultant to this firm, how would you make the estimates wanted by the firm's managers?

Source: This section is based on an actual case, although the equations and the situation have been simplified somewhat for pedagogical purposes.

extra revenue from an output increase that may be very substantial. For example, suppose that you want to see whether a firm's profits will increase if it doubles its output. If the incremental cost of such an output increase is $5 million and the incremental revenue is $6 million, the firm will increase its profits by $1 million if it doubles its output. Marginal cost and marginal revenue cannot tell you this, because they refer to only a very small increase in output, not to a doubling of it.

While it may seem very easy to compare incremental costs with incremental revenues, there in fact are many pitfalls. One of the most common errors is the failure to recognize the irrelevance of sunk costs. Costs incurred in the past often are irrelevant in making today's decisions. Suppose you are going to make a trip and you want to determine whether it will be cheaper to drive your car or to go by plane. What costs should be included if you drive your car? Since the only incremental costs incurred will be the gas and oil (and a certain amount of wear and tear on tires, engine, and so on), they are the only costs that should be included. Costs incurred in the past, such as the original price of the car, and costs that will be the same regardless of whether you make the trip by car or plane, such as your auto insurance, should not be included. On the other hand, if you are thinking about buying a car to make this and many other trips, these costs should be included.[10]

To illustrate the proper reasoning, consider the actual case of an airline that has deliberately run extra flights that do no more than return a little more than their out-of-pocket costs. Assume that this airline is faced with the decision of whether to run an extra flight between city A and city B. Assume that the fully allocated costs—the out-of-pocket costs plus a certain percent of overhead, depreciation, insurance, and other such costs—are $5,500 for the flight. Assume that the out-of-pocket costs—the actual sum that this airline has to disburse to run the flight—are $3,000 and the expected revenue from the flight is $4,100. In such a case, this airline will run the flight, which is the correct decision, since the flight will add $1,100 to profit. The incremental revenue from the flight is $4,100, and the incremental cost is $3,000. Overhead, depreciation, and insurance would be the same whether the flight is run or not. Therefore, fully allocated costs are misleading here; the relevant concept of costs is out-of-pocket, not fully allocated, costs.

Errors of other kinds can also mar firms' estimates of incremental costs. For example, a firm may refuse to produce and sell some items because it is already working near capacity and the incremental cost of producing them is judged to be very high. In fact, however, the incremental cost may not be so high because the firm may be able to produce these items during the slack season (when there is plenty of excess capacity), since the potential customers may be willing to accept delivery then.

Also, incremental revenue frequently is misjudged. Take the case of a firm that is considering the introduction of a new product. The firm's managers may estimate the incremental revenue from the new product without taking proper account of the effects of the new product's sales on the sales of the firm's existing products. Whereas they may think that the new product will not cut into the sales of existing products, it may in fact do so, with the result that their estimate of incremental revenue may be too high.

Summary

1. Functional relationships can be represented by tables, graphs, or equations. The marginal value of a dependent variable is defined as the change in this

---

[10]This example is worked out in more detail in the paper by E. Grant and W. Ireson in E. Mansfield, ed., *Managerial Economics and Operations Research: Techniques, Applications, and Cases,* 5th ed.: New York: W. W. Norton, 1983).

variable associated with a one-unit change in a particular independent variable. The dependent variable achieves a maximum when its marginal value shifts from positive to negative.

2. The derivative of Y with respect to X, denoted dY/dX, is the limit of the ratio $\Delta Y/\Delta X$ as ΔX approaches zero. Geometrically, it is the slope of the curve showing Y (on the vertical axis) as a function of X (on the horizontal axis). We have provided rules that enable us to find the value of this derivative.

3. To find the value of X that maximizes or minimizes Y, we determine the value of X where dY/dX equals zero. To tell whether this is a maximum or a minimum, we find the second derivative of Y with respect to X, denoted d^2Y/dX^2, which is the derivative of dY/dX. If this second derivative is negative, we have found a maximum; if it is positive, we have found a minimum.

4. A dependent variable often depends on a number of independent variables, not just one. To find the value of each of the independent variables that maximizes the dependent variable, we determine the partial derivative of Y with respect to each of the independent variables, denoted $\partial Y/\partial X$ and set it equal to zero. To obtain the partial derivative of Y with respect to X, we apply the ordinary rules for finding a derivative; however, all independent variables other than X are treated as constants.

5. Managers of firms and other organizations generally face constraints that limit the options available to them. In relatively simple cases in which there is only one constraint, we can use this constraint to express one of the decision variables as a function of the other decision variables, and we can apply the techniques for unconstrained optimization.

6. In more complex cases, constrained optimization problems can be solved by the method of Lagrangian multipliers. The Lagrangian function combines the function to be maximized or minimized and the constraints. To solve the constrained optimization problem, we optimize the Lagrangian function.

7. Many business decisions can and should be made by comparing incremental costs with incremental revenues. Typically, a manager must choose between two (or more) courses of action, and what is relevant is the difference between the costs of the two courses of action, as well as the difference between their revenues.

Problems

1. One very important question facing hospitals is this: How big must a hospital be (in terms of patient-days of care) to minimize the cost per patient-

day? According to one well-known study, the total cost (in dollars) of operating a hospital (of a particular type) can be approximated by

$$C = 4,700,000 + 0.00013X^2$$

where X is the number of patient-days.
   a. Derive a formula for the relationship between cost per patient-day and the number of patient-days.
   b. On the basis of the results of this study, how big must a hospital be (in terms of patient-days) to minimize the cost per patient-day?
   c. Show that your result minimizes, rather than maximizes, the cost per patient-day.
2. The Trumbull Company has developed a new product. Trumbull's chairperson estimates that the new product will increase the firm's revenues by $5 million per year and result in extra out-of-pocket costs of $4 million per year, the fully allocated costs (including a percentage of overhead, depreciation, and insurance) being $5.5 million.
   a. Trumbull's chairperson feels that it would not be profitable to introduce this new product. Is the chairperson right? Why or why not?
   b. Trumbull's vice president for research argues that since the development of this product has already cost about $10 million, the firm has little choice but to introduce it. Is the vice president right? Why or why not?
3. For the Martin Corporation, the relationship between profit and output is the following:

Output (number of units per day)	Profit (thousands of dollars per day)
0	−10
1	−8
2	−5
3	0
4	2
5	7
6	12
7	21
8	22
9	23
10	20

   a. What is the marginal profit when output is between 5 and 6 units per day? When output is between 9 and 10 units per day?
   b. At what output is average profit a maximum?
   c. Should the Martin Corporation produce the output where average profit is a maximum? Why or why not?

4. Determine the first derivative of each of the following functions:
   a. $Y = 3 + 10X + 5X^2$
   b. $Y = 2X(4 + X^3)$
   c. $Y = 3X/(4 + X^3)$
   d. $Y = 4X/(X - 3)$

5. The total cost function at the Duemer Company is $TC = 100 + 4Q + 8Q^2$, where TC is total costs and Q is the output.
   a. What is marginal cost when output is 10?
   b. What is marginal cost when output is 12?
   c. What is marginal cost when output is 20?

6. The Bartholomew Company's profit is related in the following way to its output: $\pi = -40 + 20Q - 3Q^2$, where π is total profit and Q is output.
   a. If the firm's output equals 8, what is its marginal profit?
   b. Derive an equation relating the firm's marginal profit to its output.
   c. What output maximizes the firm's profit?

7. Determine the second derivative of the following functions:
   a. $Y = 4 + 9X + 3X^2$
   b. $Y = 4X(3 + X^2)$
   c. $Y = 4X(2 + X^3)$
   d. $Y = (4/X) + 3$

8. The Mineola Corporation hires a consultant to estimate the relationship between its profit and its output. The consultant reports that the relationship is

$$\pi = 10 - 6Q + 5.5Q^2 - 2Q^3 + 0.25Q^4$$

   a. The consultant says that the firm should set Q equal to 1 to maximize profit. Is it true that $d\pi/dQ = 0$ when $Q = 1$? Is π at a maximum when $Q = 1$?
   b. Mineola's executive vice president says that the firm's profit is a maximum when $Q = 2$. Is this true?
   c. If you were the chief executive officer of the Mineola Corporation, would you accept the consultant's estimate of the relationship between profit and output as correct?

9. Find the partial derivative of Y with respect to X in each of the following cases:
   a. $Y = 10 + 3Z + 2X$
   b. $Y = 18Z^2 + 4X^3$
   c. $Y = Z^{0.2}X^{0.8}$
   d. $Y = 3Z/(4 + X)$

10. The Stock Corporation makes two products, paper and cardboard. The relationship between π, the firm's annual profit (in thousands of dollars), and its output of each good is

$$\pi = -50 + 40Q_1 + 30Q_2 - 5Q_1^2 - 4Q_2^2 - 3Q_1Q_2$$

where Q_1 is the firm's annual output of paper (in tons) and Q_2 is the firm's annual output of cardboard (in tons).

   a. Find the output of each good that the Stock Corporation should produce if it wants to maximize profit.

   b. If the community in which the firm is located imposes a tax of $5,000 per year on the firm, will this alter the answer to part a? If so, how will the answer change?

11. The Miller Company uses skilled and unskilled labor to do a particular construction project. The cost of doing the project depends on the number of hours of skilled labor and the number of hours of unskilled labor used, the relationship being

$$C = 4 - 3X_1 - 4X_2 + 2X_1^2 + 3X_2^2 + X_1X_2$$

where C is cost (in thousands of dollars), X_1 is the number of hours (in thousands) of skilled labor, and X_2 is the number of hours (in thousands) of unskilled labor.

   a. Find the number of hours of skilled labor and the number of hours of unskilled labor that minimizes the cost of doing the project.

   b. If the Miller Company has to purchase a license costing $2,000 to do this project (and if the cost of this license is not included in C), will this alter the answer to part a? If so, how will the answer change?

12. Ilona Stafford manages a small firm that produces wool rugs and cotton rugs. Her total cost per day (in dollars) equals

$$C = 7X_1^2 + 9X_2^2 - 1.5X_1X_2$$

where X_1 equals the number of cotton rugs produced per day and X_2 equals the number of wool rugs produced per day. Because of commitments to retail stores that sell her rugs to consumers, she must produce 10 rugs per day, but any mix of wool and cotton rugs is acceptable.

   a. If she wants to minimize her costs (without violating her commitment to the retail stores), how many cotton rugs and wool rugs should she produce per day? (Do not use the method of Lagrangian multipliers.)

   b. Does it seem reasonable that she would want to minimize cost in a situation of this sort? Why or why not?

   c. Can she produce fractional numbers of rugs per day?

13. a. Use the method of Lagrangian multipliers to solve problem 12.

   b. Do you get the same answer as you do without using this method?

   c. What does λ equal? What does this mean?

Demand and Forecasting

Demand Theory

CHAPTER 3

Demand is half of the equation to determine a firm's profits.

Managers, therefore, spend enormous amounts of time, energy, and money analyzing the demand for their products. This analysis of demand can be difficult. Intuitively, we know that price influences the quantity demanded for our product. But many other variables do too: the price of substitute products, the price of complementary products, the state of the economy, disposable personal income, advertising expenditures, the quality of the product, people's tastes, government regulations, and so on.

Some of the variables (endogenous) that influence our demand are under the manager's control, such as price, advertising, and quality, while other variables are exogenous to the manager, such as the prices of substitute and complementary goods, the state of the economy, disposable personal income, and government regulation. The manager wants to understand the impact of these (and other) variables on the product, so that he or she can make decisions on endogenous variables and plan a reactive strategy to changes in exogenous variables.

Suppose a firm wishes to change its price. What will be the impact on quantity demanded of its product? What will be the impact on the firm's total

TABLE 3.1	Market Demand Schedule for Laptops, 2004	
Price per computer (dollars)		**Quantity demanded per year (thousands)**
3,000		800
2,750		975
2,500		1,150
2,250		1,325
2,000		1,500

revenues? The same questions can be asked for a change in any variable listed previously. Without knowledge of the firm's demand, the manager cannot answer these important questions.

This chapter introduces market demand functions and discusses how changes in the listed variables cause the demand function to shift or cause movements along the function.

A critical application of our marginal analysis, called *elasticity*, is introduced. Elasticity tells us how the percentages of quantity change given a small (marginal) percentage change in one of the listed variables. When the changed variable is the firm's price, the elasticity also tells us how total revenue changes. Having estimates of elasticities can help managers make decisions about how to price their products and how to anticipate quantity and revenue changes when uncontrollable variables change.

The Market Demand Curve

The **market demand schedule** for a good is a table that shows the total quantity of the good that would be purchased at each price. For example, suppose that the market demand schedule for laptop computers in 2004 is as shown in Table 3.1.[1] According to this table, 1.5 million laptop computers are demanded per year if the price is $2,000 per computer, 800,000 are demanded if the price is $3,000, and so on. Another way of presenting the data in Table 3.1 is by a **market demand curve**, which is a plot of the market demand schedule on a graph. The vertical axis of the graph measures the price per unit of the good,

---

[1]These numbers are hypothetical but adequate for present purposes. In subsequent chapters, we provide data describing the actual relationship between the price and quantity demanded of various goods. At this point, the emphasis is on the concept of a market demand schedule, not on the detailed accuracy of these numbers.

FIGURE
3.1

Demand Curve for Laptops

This demand curve is a graphical representation of the figures in Table 3.1.

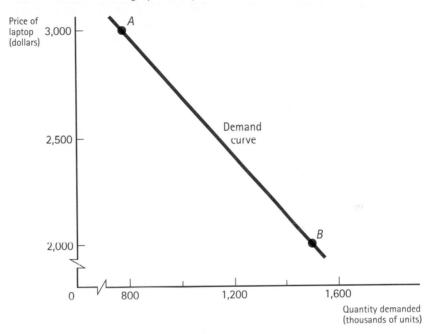

and the horizontal axis measures the quantity of the good demanded per unit of time. Figure 3.1 shows the market demand curve for laptop computers in 2004, based on the figures in Table 3.1.

In Chapter 1, we had an introductory look at the market demand curve. Now we study this topic in more detail. Three things should be noted concerning Figure 3.1. First, the market demand curve shows the *total* quantity of laptop computers demanded at each price, not the quantity demanded from a *particular* firm. We discuss the demand for a particular firm's product in the next section of this chapter. Second, the market demand curve for laptop computers slopes downward to the right. In other words, the quantity of laptop computers demanded increases as the price falls. As we pointed out in Chapter 1, this is true of the demand curve for most goods: They almost always slope downward to the right. Third, the market demand curve in Figure 3.1 pertains to a particular period of time: 2004. As you recall from Chapter 1, any demand curve pertains to some period of time, and its shape and position depend on the length and other characteristics of this period. For example, if we were to estimate the market demand curve for laptop computers for the first week in 2004, it would be a different curve from the one in Figure 3.1, which pertains to the whole year. The difference arises partly because consumers can adapt their purchases more fully to changes in the price of laptop computers in a year than in a week.

In addition to the length of time period, what factors determine the position and shape of the market demand curve for a good? As indicated in Chapter 1, one important factor is the **tastes of consumers**. If consumers show an increasing preference for a product, the demand curve shifts to the right; that is, at each price, consumers want to buy more than they did previously. Alternatively, for each quantity, consumers are willing to pay a higher price. On the other hand, if consumers show a decreasing preference for a product, the demand curve shifts to the left, since, at each price, consumers want to buy less than previously. Alternatively, for each quantity, consumers are willing to pay only a lower price. For example, as shown in Figure 3.2, if people find that laptop computers are more helpful than they thought and they begin to use them more and give them in larger numbers to their children and others, the demand curve

FIGURE
3.2

Effect of an Increased Preference for Laptops on the Market Demand Curve

The demand curve for laptops shifts to the right.

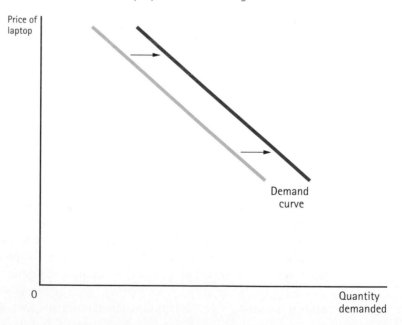

for laptop computers may shift to the right. The greater is the shift in preferences, the farther the demand curve shifts.

Another factor that influences the position and shape of a good's market demand curve is the **level of consumer incomes.** For some types of products, the demand curve shifts to the right if per capita income increases, whereas for other types of commodities, the demand curve shifts to the left if per capita income rises. In the case of laptop computers, one would expect that an increase in per capita income would shift the demand curve to the right, as shown in Figure 3.3. Still another factor that influences the position and shape of a good's market demand curve is the **level of other prices.** For example, one would expect that the quantity of laptop computers demanded would increase if the price of software for such computers fell drastically.

Finally, the position and shape of a good's market demand curve is also affected by the size of the population in the relevant market. If the population increases, one would expect that, if all other factors were held equal, the quantity of laptop computers demanded would increase. Of course, the population generally changes slowly, so this factor often has little effect in the very short run.

FIGURE 3.3

Effect of an Increase in Per Capita Income on the Market Demand Curve for Laptops

The demand curve shifts to the right.

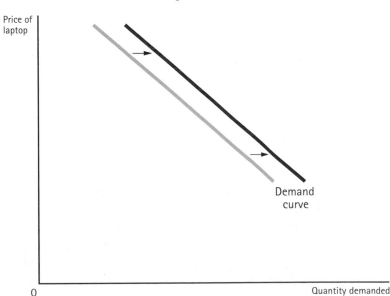

Industry and Firm Demand Functions

Building on the results of the previous section, we can define the **market demand function** for a product, which is the relationship between the quantity demanded of the product and the various factors that influence this quantity. Put generally, this market demand function can be written as

$$\text{Quantity demanded of good } X = Q = f(\text{price of } X, \text{ incomes of consumers, tastes of consumers, prices of other goods, population, advertising expenditures, and so forth}).$$

To be useful for analytical and forecasting purposes, this equation must be made more specific. For example, if good X is laptop computers, the market demand function might be

$$Q = b_1 P + b_2 I + b_3 S + b_4 A \tag{3.1}$$

where Q equals the number of laptop computers demanded in a particular year, P is the average price of laptop computers in that year, I is per capita disposable income during that year, S is the average price of software during that year, and A is the amount spent on advertising by producers of laptop computers in that year. The assumption in equation (3.1) is, of course, that the relationship is linear. (Also, we assume for simplicity that the population in the relevant market is essentially constant.)

Going a step further, it generally is necessary for managers and analysts to obtain numerical estimates of the values of b in equation (3.1). Employing the statistical techniques described in Chapter 5, one usually can estimate these so-called parameters of the demand function. To illustrate the sorts of results that might be obtained, we might find that

$$Q = -700P + 200I - 500S + 0.01A \tag{3.2}$$

According to equation (3.2), a \$1 increase in the price of a laptop computer results in a decrease in the quantity demanded of 700 units per year, a \$1 increase in per capita disposable income results in a 200-unit increase in the quantity demanded, a \$1 increase in the price of software reduces the quantity demanded by 500 units per year, and a \$1 increase in advertising raises the quantity demanded by 0.01 unit per year.

It is important to understand the relationship between the market demand function and the demand curve. The market demand curve shows the relationship between Q and P when all other relevant variables are held constant. For example, suppose that we want to know the relationship between quantity demanded and price if per capita disposable income is $13,000, if the average price of software is $400, and if advertising expenditure is $50 million. Since $I = 13,000$, $S = 400$, and $A = 50,000,000$, equation (3.2) becomes

$$Q = -700P + 200(13,000)$$
$$-500(400) + 0.01(50,000,000) \tag{3.3}$$

or

$$Q = 2,900,000 - 700P \tag{3.4}$$

Solving this equation for P, we obtain

$$P = 4,143 - 0.0014290Q$$

which is graphed in Figure 3.1. This is the demand curve for laptop computers, given that I, S, and A are held constant at the stipulated levels.

Given the market demand function, managers and analysts can readily quantify the shifts in the demand curve that result from changes in the variables other than the product's price. For example, how much of a shift will occur in the demand curve if the price of software falls from $400 to $200? Inserting 200 (rather than 400) for S in equation (3.3), we find that

$$Q - 3,000,000 - 700P \tag{3.5}$$

Solving this equation for P, we obtain

$$P = 4,286 - 0.0014290Q \tag{3.6}$$

which is graphed (together with the demand curve based on $S = 400$) in Figure 3.4. Clearly, the demand curve has shifted to the right, the quantity demanded being 100,000 more than when $S = 400$ (if P is held constant).

Market demand functions can be formulated for individual firms as well as for entire industries. That is, one can formulate an equation like equation (3.2) to predict the sales of an individual producer of laptop computers. In such an equation, the quantity demanded of the firm's good would be inversely related to its price but directly related to the prices charged by its competitors, and it would be directly related to its advertising expenditures but inversely related to the advertising expenditures of its competitors. It is important to distinguish between industry and firm demand functions, since they are quite different. Both are important to managers, because firms often are interested in the effects of variables like disposable income and advertising on industry sales, as well as on the sales of their own firms—which obviously are of primary significance.

Demand Curve for Laptops

If the price of software falls from $400 to $200, the demand curve shifts to the right by 100,000 units.

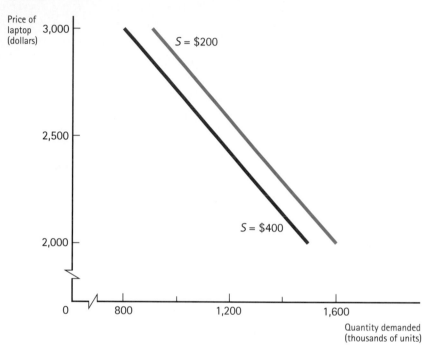

The Price Elasticity of Demand

Market demand curves vary with regard to the sensitivity of quantity demanded to price. For some goods, a small change in price results in a big change in quantity demanded; for other goods, a big change in price results in a small change in quantity demanded. To indicate how sensitive quantity demanded is to changes in price, economists use a measure called the **price elasticity of demand**. The price elasticity of demand is defined to be *the percentage change in quantity demanded resulting from a 1 percent change in price.* More precisely, it equals

$$\eta = \left(\frac{P}{Q}\right)\frac{dQ}{dP} \tag{3.7}$$

Suppose that a 1 percent reduction in the price of cotton shirts results in a 1.3 percent increase in the quantity demanded in the United States. If so, the price elasticity of demand for cotton shirts is −1.3. The price elasticity of demand generally varies from one point to another on a demand curve. For instance, the price elasticity of demand may be higher in absolute value when the price of cotton shirts is high than when it is low. Similarly, the price elasticity of demand varies from market to market. For example, India may have a different price elasticity of demand for cotton shirts from that of the United States.

The price elasticity of demand for a product must lie between zero and negative infinity. If the price elasticity is zero, the demand curve is a vertical line; that is, the quantity demanded is unaffected by price. If the price elasticity is negative infinity, the demand curve is a horizontal line; that is, an unlimited amount can be sold at a particular price ($15 in Figure 3.5), but nothing can be sold if the price is raised even slightly. Figure 3.5 shows these two limiting cases.

FIGURE
3.5

Demand Curves with Zero and Infinite Price Elasticities of Demand

The demand curve is a vertical line if the price elasticity is zero and a horizontal line if it is negative infinity.

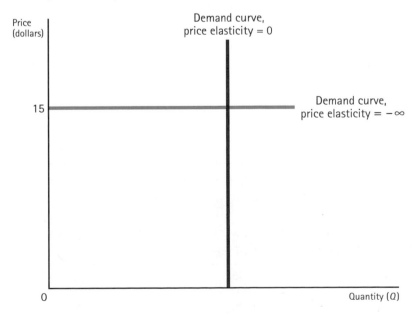

Point and Arc Elasticities

If we have a market demand schedule showing the quantity of a commodity demanded in the market at various prices, how can we estimate the price elasticity of market demand? Let ΔP be a change in the price of the good and ΔQ be the resulting change in its quantity demanded. If ΔP is very small, we can compute the point elasticity of demand:

$$\eta = \frac{\Delta Q}{Q} \div \frac{\Delta P}{P} \tag{3.8}$$

For instance, consider Table 3.2, where data are given for very small increments in the price of a commodity. If we want to estimate the price elasticity of demand when the price is between $0.9995 and $1, we obtain

$$\eta = \frac{20{,}002 - 20{,}000}{20{,}000} \div \frac{99.95 - 100}{100} = -0.2$$

Note that we used $1 as P and 20,000 as Q. We could have used $0.9995 as P and 20,002 as Q, but it would have made no real difference to the answer.

But, if we have data concerning only large changes in price (that is, if ΔP and ΔQ are large), the answer may vary considerably depending on which value of P and Q is used in equation (3.8). Consider the example in Table 3.3. Suppose that we want to estimate the price elasticity of demand in the price range between $4 and $5. Then, depending on which value of P and Q is used, the answer is

$$\eta = \frac{40 - 3}{3} \div \frac{4 - 5}{5} = -61.67$$

TABLE
3.2

Quantity Demanded at Various Prices (Small Increments in Price)

Price (cents per unit of commodity)	Quantity demanded per unit of time (units of commodity)
99.95	20,002
100.00	20,000
100.05	19,998

TABLE
3.3

Quantity Demanded at Various Prices (Large Increments in Price)

Price (dollars per unit of commodity)	Quantity demanded per unit of time (units of commodity)
3	50
4	40
5	3

or

$$\eta = \frac{3 - 40}{40} \div \frac{5 - 4}{4} = -3.70$$

The difference between these two results is very large. To avoid this difficulty, it is advisable to compute the arc elasticity of demand, which uses the average value of P and Q:

$$\eta = \frac{\Delta Q}{(Q_1 + Q_2)/2} \div \frac{\Delta P}{(P_1 + P_2)/2}$$

$$\eta = \frac{\Delta Q(P_1 + P_2)}{\Delta P(Q_1 + Q_2)} \tag{3.9}$$

where P_1 and Q_1 are the first values of price and quantity demanded, and P_2 and Q_2 are the second set. Therefore, in Table 3.3,

$$\eta = \frac{40 - 3}{(40 + 3)/2} \div \frac{4 - 5}{(4 + 5)/2} = -7.74$$

Using the Demand Function to Calculate the Price Elasticity of Demand

As we saw in a previous section, estimates frequently are made of the demand function for particular products. In equation (3.2), we provided the following hypothetical demand function for laptop computers:

$$Q = -700P + 200I - 500S + 0.01A$$

Given such a demand function, how can you calculate the price elasticity of demand?

The first step is to specify the point on the demand curve at which this price elasticity is to be measured. Assuming that per capita disposable income (I) is $13,000, the average price of software (S) is $400, and advertising expenditure (A) is $50 million, we know from equation (3.4) that the relationship between quantity demanded and price is

$$Q = 2,900,000 - 700P \tag{3.10}$$

Suppose we want to measure the price elasticity of demand when price equals $3,000. At this point on the demand curve (point A in Figure 3.1),

$$Q = 2,900,000 - 700(3,000)$$
$$= 800,000.$$

Next, we must evaluate the partial derivative of Q with respect to P. Applying Chapter 2's rules for finding a derivative to equation (3.10), we find that the desired derivative equals

$$\frac{dQ}{dP} = -700$$

According to equation (3.7), to obtain the price elasticity of demand, we must multiply dQ/dP by P/Q. Performing this multiplication, we get

$$-700\frac{3,000}{800,000} = -2.62$$

which means that the price elasticity of demand equals -2.62.

As a further illustration, let us calculate the price elasticity of demand when price equals $2,000 rather than $3,000. At this point on the demand curve (point B in Figure 3.1),

$$Q = 2,900,000 - 700(2,000)$$
$$= 1,500,000$$

Since $dQ/dP = -700$,

$$\eta = \left(\frac{dQ}{dP}\right)\left(\frac{P}{Q}\right) = (-700)\frac{2,000}{1,500,000} = -0.93$$

FIGURE
3.6

Values of the Price Elasticity of Demand at Various Points along a Linear Demand Curve

The price elasticity increases in absolute value as price rises, approaching negative infinity as quantity approaches zero.

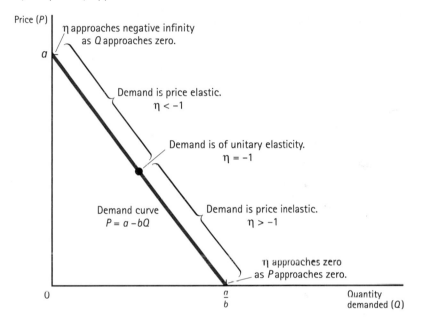

Therefore, the price elasticity of demand equals −0.93.

An important thing to note is that the price elasticity of demand can vary greatly from point to point on a particular demand curve. As we have just seen, on the demand curve in Figure 3.1, the price elasticity of demand is −2.625 at point *A* but only −0.93 at point *B*. For any linear demand curve, the price elasticity of demand varies from zero to negative infinity, as shown in Figure 3.6. If

$$P = a - bQ$$

where *a* is the intercept of the demand curve on the price axis and *b* is the slope (in absolute terms) of the demand curve, it follows that

$$Q = \frac{a}{b} - \frac{1}{b}P$$

CONCEPTS IN CONTEXT

Fur Demand in Russia

Historically, Russia has been an important exporter of furs like mink, fox, and sable; for example, in 1993, over $60 million worth of pelts was sent abroad. But in 1994, Russia exported only $30 million worth of pelts. "We were taken by surprise at first," said Andrei Nyukhalov, deputy director of Russia's largest fur farm. "We thought nobody was going to buy the fur. Then we realized they were buying it all in Russia."*

In 1995, the fur stores in Moscow were very busy. The high-priced furs sold well, and the cheaper coats were difficult to keep in stock. Why? Because newly rich Russians, flaunting their new wealth and anxious to keep warm during the tough Russian winter (six months long), purchased fur in unprecedented amounts. The market in Russia was simply exploding, said Jay Mechutan, a New York fur importer.[†]

Given the Russian climate, the substantial demand for fur was understandable. Two-thirds of the Russian land mass stays frozen from October to April. Also, the demand for fur was promoted by a shift from expensive to more moderate priced furs. Russian fur producers seemed to be turning their attention from mink and sable to cheaper furs like lambskin, nutria, and some varieties of fox, all of which sold for less than $1,000 per coat.

*"Russia Answers Capitalism: Let the People Have Fur," *New York Times,* October 12, 1995, p. A6.
[†]Ibid., p. A1.

Therefore, the price elasticity of demand is

$$\left(\frac{dQ}{dP}\right)\left(\frac{P}{Q}\right) = \frac{-1}{b}\ \frac{a - bQ}{Q}$$

Clearly, if the demand curve is linear, the price elasticity approaches zero as P ($= a - bQ$) gets very small and approaches negative infinity as Q gets very small.

Price Elasticity and Total Money Expenditure

Managers are interested in questions like these: Will an increase in price result in an increase in the total amount spent by consumers on their product? Or, will an increase in price result in a decrease in the total amount spent by consumers on their product? The answers depend on the price elasticity of demand, as we show in this section.

Suppose that the demand for the product is price elastic; that is, the price elasticity of demand is less than -1. The total amount of money spent by consumers on the product equals the quantity demanded times the price per unit. In this situation, if the price is reduced, the percentage increase in quantity demanded is greater than the percentage reduction in price (since this follows from the definition of the price elasticity of demand). It then follows that a price reduction must lead to an increase in the total amount spent by consumers on the commodity. Similarly, if the demand is price elastic, a price increase leads to a reduction in the amount of money spent on the commodity.

If the demand for the product is price inelastic (which means that the price elasticity of demand is greater than -1), a price decrease leads to a reduction in the total amount spent on the commodity and a price increase leads to an increase in the amount spent on the commodity. If the demand is of unitary elasticity (which means that the price elasticity of demand equals -1), an increase or decrease in price has no effect on the amount spent on the commodity.

As an illustration, consider the case shown in Figure 3.7. The demand curve shown there is a rectangular hyperbola, which means that

$$Q = \frac{m}{P} \tag{3.11}$$

FIGURE
3.7

Demand Curve with Unitary Elasticity at All Points

The demand curve is a rectangular hyperbola if the price elasticity of demand is always -1.

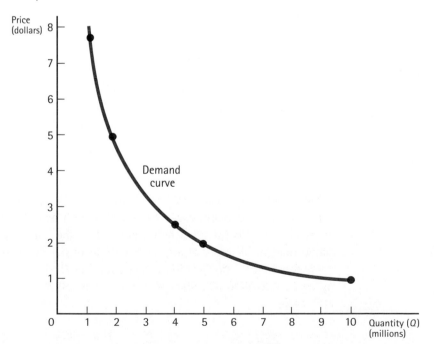

where Q is the quantity demanded of the good, P is its price, and m is some constant. This kind of demand curve is of unitary elasticity at all points. Hence, changes in price have no effect on the total amount spent on the product. It is evident from equation (3.11) that, regardless of the price, the total amount spent on the product will be m ($10 million in Figure 3.7).

Total Revenue, Marginal Revenue, and Price Elasticity

To its producers, the total amount of money spent on a product equals their total revenue. Therefore, to the Ford Motor Company, the total amount spent on its cars (and other products) is its total revenue. Suppose that the demand curve for a firm's product is linear; that is,

$$P = a - bQ \tag{3.12}$$

where a is the intercept on the price axis and b is the slope (in absolute terms), as shown in panel A of Figure 3.8. Thus, the firm's total revenue equals

$$\begin{aligned} TR &= PQ \\ &= (a - bQ)Q \\ &= aQ - bQ^2 \end{aligned} \tag{3.13}$$

An important concept is marginal revenue, which, as we know from Chapter 2, is defined as dTR/dQ. We use this concept repeatedly in subsequent chapters. In the present case,

$$\begin{aligned} MR &= \frac{dTR}{dQ} \\ &= \frac{d(aQ - bQ^2)}{dQ} \\ &= a - 2bQ \end{aligned} \tag{3.14}$$

which is also shown in panel A of Figure 3.8. Comparing the marginal revenue curve with the demand curve, we see that both have the same intercept on the vertical axis (this intercept being a) but that the marginal revenue curve has a slope that (in absolute terms) is twice that of the demand curve.

According to the definition in equation (3.7), the price elasticity of demand, η, equals $(dQ/dP)(P/Q)$. Since $dQ/dP = -1/b$ and $P = a - bQ$, it follows that, in this case,

$$\eta = \frac{-1}{b} \frac{a - bQ}{Q} \tag{3.15}$$

FIGURE
3.8

Relationship between Price Elasticity, Marginal Revenue, and Total Revenue

If demand is price elastic, marginal revenue is positive and increases in quantity result in higher total revenue. If demand is price inelastic, marginal revenue is negative and increases in quantity result in lower total revenue.

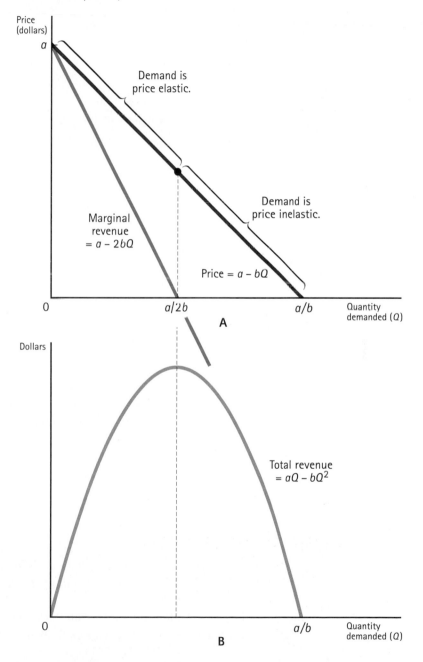

ANALYZING MANAGERIAL DECISIONS

The Demand for Newsprint

In early 1995, there was a sharp increase in the price of newsprint, the paper used by newspapers. Since newsprint is the second-largest expense for U.S. newspapers (after salaries), publishers were concerned about the price hike. Suppose that the demand for newsprint can be represented as

$$Q_1 = 17.3 - 0.0092P + 0.0067I$$

where Q_1 equals the quantity demanded (in kilograms per capita), P is the price of newsprint (in dollars per metric ton), and I is income per capita (in dollars).

(a) If 1 million people are in the market, and per capita income equals $10,000, what is the demand curve for newsprint? (b) Under these circumstances, what is the price elasticity of demand if the price of newsprint equals $400 per metric ton? (c) According to a 1984 study,* the demand curve for newsprint in the northeastern United States is

$$Q_2 = 2,672 - 0.51P$$

where Q_2 is the number of metric tons of newsprint demanded (in thousands). What is the price elasticity of demand for newsprint in the northeastern United States if price equals $500 per metric ton? (d) On the basis of this study, will the 1995 price increase result in an increase or decrease in the amount spent on newsprint in the northeastern United States? Why?

SOLUTION (a) Since 1 million people are in the market and Q_1 equals per capita quantity demanded, the quantity demanded equals 1 million times Q_1. Letting Q_1' be the quantity demanded (in millions of kilograms),

$$Q_1' = 17.3 - 0.0092P$$
$$+ 0.0067(10,000)$$
$$= 84.3 - 0.0092P$$

(b) Since $dQ_1'/dP = -0.0092$, the price elasticity of demand equals $-0.0092\ P/Q_1'$. Because $P = 400$ and $I = 10,000$, Q_1' must equal $17.3 - 0.0092(400) + 0.0067(10,000) = 80.62$ million kilograms. Therefore, the price elasticity of demand equals $-0.0092(400/80.62) = -0.0456$. (c) Since $dQ_2/dP = -0.51$ and $P = 500$, the price elasticity of demand equals $-0.51(500)/[2,672 - 0.51(500)] = -0.1055$. (d) It will result in an increase in the amount spent on newsprint because the demand for newsprint is price inelastic.

* F. Guder and J. Buongiorno, "An Interregional Analysis of the North American Newsprint Industry," *Interfaces*, September–October 1984, pp. 85–95.

Therefore, whether η is greater than, equal to, or less than -1 depends on whether Q is greater than, equal to, or less than $a/2b$. As shown in Figure 3.8, demand is price elastic if $Q < a/2b$; it is of unitary elasticity if $Q = a/2b$; and it is price inelastic if $Q > a/2b$.

Panel B in Figure 3.8 plots the firm's total revenue against the quantity demanded of its product. As would be expected, at quantities where marginal revenue is positive, increases in quantity result in higher total revenue; at quantities where marginal revenue is negative, increases in quantity result in lower total revenue. Why would this be expected? Because, as pointed out, marginal revenue is the derivative of total revenue with respect to quantity. So, if marginal revenue is positive (negative), increases in quantity must increase (decrease) total revenue.

Another thing to note about Figure 3.8 is that, at quantities where demand is price elastic, marginal revenue is positive; at quantities where it is of unitary elasticity, marginal revenue is zero; and at quantities where it is price inelastic, marginal revenue is negative. This is no accident. In general, whether or not the demand curve is linear, this is the case. To see why, recall that by definition,

$$MR = \frac{dTR}{dQ}$$

Since total revenue equals price times quantity, it follows that

$$MR = \frac{d(PQ)}{dQ}$$

Using the rule for differentiating a product (given in Chapter 2),

$$MR = P\frac{dQ}{dQ} + Q\frac{dP}{dQ}$$

Because $dQ/dQ = 1$,

$$MR = P + Q\frac{dP}{dQ}$$

$$= P\left[1 + \left(\frac{Q}{P}\right)\left(\frac{dP}{dQ}\right)\right]$$

And since the definition of the price elasticity of demand implies that $(Q/P)(dP/dQ) = 1/\eta$,

$$MR = P\left(1 + \frac{1}{\eta}\right) \tag{3.16}$$

Equation (3.16) is a famous result, which shows that if $\eta < -1$, marginal revenue must be positive; if $\eta > -1$, marginal revenue must be negative; and if $\eta = -1$, marginal revenue must be zero. (This is what we set out to prove.)

Concepts in Context

Elasticity in Use

Aside from the Wal-Mart Zorro price slasher cutting prices from levels like $12.79 to $10.56, most of us are accustomed to seeing prices that end in 0s, 5s, or 9s. But prices that end in any integer are becoming more common. In addition, prices for the exact same item may differ substantially in stores of the same chain, even if the stores are located close (or far) from one another. Why? Because elasticity is being used to generate optimal (or closer to optimal) prices in a price optimization model. The model is designed to generate the ideal price for every item, in each store, at any given time. Longs Drug Stores, a drug store chain with 390 stores in the lower 48 U.S. states is a user of such a model. D'Agostino's, a 23-store grocery chain in New York, claims that such a model has increased unit revenues by 10 percent, unit volume by 6 percent, and net profits by 2 percent. ShopKo used the model in 141 stores and reports gross profit margins increased by 24 percent. Payback periods for the purchase and use of such pricing systems is estimated to be a year (despite their expensive price tag).

Rather than marking up costs, benchmarking on competitors' prices, or guessing, the price optimization models use data mining techniques. Scanned transactions from cash registers, responses to sales promotions, and the like, are used to estimate an individual demand curve *for each product in each store*. Much of the modeling is based on the airline yield management systems (see Chapter 12). The driving goal behind the modeling is to find the "crossover point between driving sales and giving away margin unnecessarily." That is consultant-speak. Let us put it in economist-speak.

Airline yield management models attempt to equate marginal expected revenues on each fare class. For instance, suppose that two fare classes, 1 and 2, exist. As just shown, marginal revenue (MR) is equal to $MR = P[1 + (1/\eta)]$, and so equating marginal revenues for classes 1 and 2 yields

$$MR_1 = P_1[1 + (1/\eta_1)] = P_2[1 + (1/\eta_2)] = MR_2$$

Think about why a business with two different demand curves for the same product (e.g., business and leisure travelers for an airline seat, spring and summer demands for a bathing suit, location 1 and location 2 demands for Pampers) would want to equate marginal revenues of those demand curves. If the marginal revenue on fare type 2 exceeds the marginal revenue on fare type 1, then it would pay the airline to switch seats out of fare type 1 and into fare type 2. Since the cost of moving a person in fare type 1 is likely to be the same as the cost of moving a person in fare type 2, the airline can increase revenues while leaving costs the same by such a switch. Such a move must increase the airline's bottom line. (If the equated marginal revenues equal the marginal cost of moving a passenger, profits are not only improved, they are maximized).

How would an elasticity model do this in retailing? Consider the optimal discounting of a product over time. The subscript 1 stands for the first time period and the subscript 2 stands for the second time period. If the marginal revenue is higher in period 2 than in period 1, you would want to shift some of the merchandise from period 1 to period 2 (or if 1 and 2 referred to stores, shift some product from store 1 to store 2).

Suppose that $\eta_1 = -2$ and $\eta_2 = -3$, then

$MR_1 = P_1[1 + (1/-2)] = P_1[1 - (1/2)] = P_1/2 = P_2[1 + (1/-3)] = P_2[1 - (1/3)] = 2P_2/3 = MR_2$

Or $P_2 = 0.75P_1$; that is, the optimal discount on the product would be to sell the good in time period 2 for 25 percent off of the price from time period 1. Lowering price increases the quantity demanded (because demand curves have an inverse relationship between price and quantity); hence the term driving sales. But lowering price too much or too little will not yield the seller the optimal profit margin, that is, the profit margin that yields maximum profits. This can be done only where $MR_1 = MR_2 (= MC)$.

ShopKo, by analyzing several years' worth of sales data, estimates a seasonal demand curve for each product (approximately 300 of them). The analysis predicts how many units would sell each week at various prices. The software uses sales history "to predict how sensitive customer demand would be to price changes, what economists call 'price elasticity'." The software then uses the price elasticity information, the number of weeks until the product is outdated, and such factors into a system of mathematical models to determine the most profitable price cuts on each item.

A recent article in the *Economist* ("The Price Is Wrong") notes that supermarket chains "can quickly and easily track customers' 'elasticity'—how their buying habits change in response to a price rise or discount." Supermarkets such as D'Agostino's in New York and Dominicks in Chicago use elasticity-based models to help them in making pricing decisions.

Source: "The Power of Optimal Pricing," *Business 2.0*, September, 2002, pp. 68–70. "Priced to Move: Retailers Try to Get Leg up on Markdowns with New Software." *Wall Street Journal*, August 7, 2001.

In later chapters, we use equation (3.16) repeatedly. Study it carefully and understand it. To illustrate its meaning, what is the value of the marginal revenue if the price is \$10 and the price elasticity of demand is -2? On the basis of equation (3.16), it equals $10(1 - 1/2) = \$5$.

Using Price Elasticity of Demand: Application to Philip Morris

In 1993, Philip Morris cut cigarette prices by 18 percent. Its major competitor (RJ Reynolds) matched the price cut. Not surprisingly, the quantity sold of Philip Morris's cigarettes increased (by 12.5 percent). In a June 13, 1994, article referring to the perils of a price cut, *Fortune* reported that Philip Morris's profits fell by 25 percent, the result of a bad pricing strategy.

While all the information is not available, do not be surprised by the qualitative fall in profits. A rough estimate of the price elasticity of demand for Philip Morris's cigarettes ($\%\Delta Q/\%\Delta P$) is $12.5\%/-18\% = -0.694$; it is inelastic. As just demonstrated, cutting the price when demand is inelastic decreases total revenues. Since output increased (by 12.5 percent), total cost increased. Since profits are total revenue less total cost, and total revenue decreased and total cost increased, profits had to fall.

Using Price Elasticity of Demand: Public Transit

Consider another example where your knowledge of elasticity and its properties give you a qualitative answer (and with more information, you would have the quantitative answer). The fare (price) elasticity for public transportation service in the United States is about −0.3 (that is, fairly inelastic). All transit systems in the United States lose money. Keeping the deficit under control is a constant battle because typical subsidizers (federal, state, and local governments) are reluctant to fund transit (because of their own deficit problems) in many jurisdictions. Can you guess which transit systems they are?

They tend to be the ones with the high transit fares. Here is where your knowledge of elasticity comes in. How is the general manager of the transit system going to raise the needed revenues? With an inelastic demand, raising fares increases revenues. Raising fares decreased ridership, hence, decreasing total cost. Therefore, the bottom line of the transit agency improves as total revenue increases and total cost decreases.

Determinants of the Price Elasticity of Demand

Table 3.4 shows the price elasticity of demand for selected products in the United States. What determines whether the demand for a product is price clastic or price inelastic? Why does the price elasticity of demand for fresh apple products in the United States equal −1.159 while the short-run price elasticity of demand for gasoline in Canada lies between −0.01 and −0.2?

1. The price elasticity of demand for a product depends heavily on the number and closeness of the substitutes available. If a product has lots of close substitutes, its demand is likely to be price elastic. If the product's price is increased, a large proportion of its buyers will turn to the close substitutes available; if its price is reduced, a great many buyers of substitutes will switch to this product. The extent to which a product has close substitutes depends on how narrowly it is defined. As the definition of the product becomes narrower and more specific, the product would be expected to have more close substitutes, and its demand would be expected to become more price elastic. Hence, the demand for a particular brand of gasoline is likely to be more price elastic than the overall demand for gasoline, and the demand for gasoline is likely to be more price elastic than the demand for all fuels taken as a whole.

TABLE
3.4

Own Price Elasticities of Demand, Selected Goods, and Services from Global Locations

Good/Service	Elasticity
Agricultural products	
Apples (US)[1]	−1.159
Potatoes (UK)[3]	−0.13
Oranges (US)[2]	−0.62
Lettuce (US)[2]	−2.58
Products from animals/fish	
1-percent milk (US)[5]	−0.54 to −0.74
Cheese (UK)[3]	−1.36
Cheese (US)[6]	−0.595
Meat (China)[4]	−0.06 to −0.18
Beef/veal (UK)[3]	−1.45
Manufactured agricultural products	
Beer and malt beverages (US)[6]	−2.83
Wine (UK/Ireland)[7]	1.12
Wine and brandy (US)[6]	−0.198
Cigarettes (US)[7]	−0.107
Bread (UK)[3]	−0.26
Energy	
Gasoline—short run (Canada)[8]	−0.01 to −0.2
Gasoline—long run (Canada)[8]	−0.4 to −0.8
Transportation	
Domestic cars (US)[12]	−0.78
European cars (US)[12]	−1.09

(Continues on next page)

2. The price elasticity of demand for a product may depend on the importance of the product in consumers' budgets. It is sometimes claimed that the demand for products like thimbles, rubber bands, and salt may be quite inelastic, since the typical consumer spends only a very small fraction of his or her income on such goods. In contrast, for products that bulk larger in the typical consumer's budget, like major appliances, the elasticity of demand may tend to be higher, since consumers may be more conscious of and influenced by price changes in the case of goods that require larger outlays. However, although a tendency of this sort is sometimes hypothesized, there is no guarantee that you can count on it being true.

3. The price elasticity of demand for a product is likely to depend on the length of the period to which the demand curve pertains. (As pointed out, every

TABLE 3.4

Own Price Elasticities of Demand, Selected Goods, and Services from Global Locations (Continued)

Good/Service	Elasticity
Other manufactured goods	
Clothing and footwear (UK/Ireland)[8]	−0.94
Other goods (UK/Ireland)[8]	−0.85
Services	
Child care (North America)[11]	−0.570
Government health care (Kenya)[12]	−0.100

[1]C. Elmore, Chapter 10, "Use of 2.4-D in Orchard, Vineyard, and Soft Fruit Production in the United States," Phenoxy Herbicides, December 20, 1998, found at *piked.agn.uiuc.edu/piap/assess2/ch10.htm.*

[2]D. Suits, "Agriculture," in Walter Adams and James Brock, eds., *The Structure of American Industry,* (10th ed.; Englewood Cliffs, NJ: Prentice-Hall, 2000).

[3]AEF116: 1.6: Major market response concepts and measures 1: The demand side and its elasticities found at *www.staff.ncl.ac.uk/davidharvey/AEF116/1.6/1.6/html.*

[4]Millennium Institute, China Agricultural Project found at *www.threshold21.com/chinaag/report/appendix.html.*

[5]A Regional Economic Analysis of Dairy Compacts: Implications for Missouri Dairy Producers, Section IV—Economic Analysis of Dairy Compact, circa 1999, found at *agebb.missouri.edu/commag/dairy/bailey/compact/sect4.htm.*

[6]Emilo Pagoulatos and Robert Sorensen, "What Determines the Elasticity of Industry Demand," *International Journal of Industrial Organization,* Vol. 4, 1986.

[7]C. O'Donoghue, "Carbon Dioxide, Energy Taxes, and Household Income," Department of Statistics and Social Policy, London School of Economics, October 13, 1998.

[8]"Potential for Fuel Taxes to Reduce Greenhouse Gas Emissions in Transportation," Hagler Bailly Canada for Department of Public Works and Government Services, Hull, Quebec, June 11, 1990 found at *www.tc.gc.ca/envattairs/sub . . . udy1/Final_report/Final_Report. html.*

[9]P. McCarthy, "Market Price and Income Elasticities of New Vehicle Demands," *Review of Economics and Statistics,* Vol. 78(3), August 1990, 543–547.

[10]E. Brynjolfsson, "Some Estimates of the Contribution of Information Technology to Consumer Welfare," MIT Sloan School, Working Paper 3647-094, January 1994.

[11]D. Chaplin et al., "The Price Elasticity of Child Care Demand: A Sensitivity Analysis," found at *www.cpc.unc.edu/pubs/ppp_papers/1997/chaplin.html.*

[12]Section 4: The Basics of Markets and Health Care Markets: Box 4.4: Demand for Health Care in Kenya found at *www.worldbank.org/wbi/healthflagship/learning/module1/box4_4.htm.*

market demand curve pertains to a certain time interval.) Demand is likely to be more elastic, or less inelastic, over a long period of time than over a short period of time, because the longer the period of time, the easier it is for consumers and firms to substitute one good for another. If, for instance, the price of oil should decline relative to other fuels, the consumption of oil in the day after the price decline would probably increase very little.

| TABLE 3.5 | Elasticities of Demand for Air Tickets between the United States and Europe |

Elasticities of Demand for Air Tickets between the United States and Europe

Type of ticket	Price elasticity	Income elasticity
First class	−0.45	1.50
Regular economy	−1.30	1.38
Excursion	−1.83	2.37

Source: J. Cigliano, "Price and Income Elasticities for Airline Travel: The North Atlantic Market," *Business Economics*, September 1980.

But over a period of several years, people would have an opportunity to take account of the price decline in choosing the type of fuel to be used in new houses and renovated old houses. In the longer period of several years, the price decline would have a greater effect on the consumption of oil than in the shorter period of one day.[2]

Uses of the Price Elasticity of Demand

Managers display an avid interest, and for good reason, in the price elasticity of demand for their products. Consider Table 3.5, which provides estimates of the price elasticity of demand for first-class, regular economy, and excursion air tickets between the United States and Europe. The price elasticity of demand for first-class air tickets is much lower in absolute value than for regular economy or excursion tickets, owing in part to the fact that the people who fly first class—often business travelers and relatively wealthy people—are unlikely to change their travel plans if moderate increases or decreases occur in the price of an air ticket. Airline executives have studied these data carefully, with an eye toward the pricing of various kinds of tickets. Because the price elasticity of demand for first-class air tickets is relatively low in absolute value, they have nudged up the prices for such tickets.

It is important to recognize that no manager interested in maximizing profit will set the price at a point where the demand for his or her product is price

[2]However, for durable goods like automobiles, the price elasticity of demand may be greater in absolute value in the short run than in the long run. If the price of automobiles goes up, the quantity demanded is likely to fall sharply, because many consumers put off buying a new car. But, as time goes on and old cars wear out, the quantity of automobiles demanded tends to increase.

inelastic. To see why this is a mistake, recall from equation (3.16) that marginal revenue must be negative if demand is price inelastic (that is, if $\eta > -1$). If marginal revenue is negative, a firm can increase its profit by raising its price and lowering its output. Why? Because its total revenue will increase if it sells less. (This, after all, is what it means to say that marginal revenue is negative.) Since the firm's total cost does not rise if less is sold, its profits go up if it sells less.

Market researchers are continually engaged in studies to estimate the price elasticity of demand for particular products. The results enable firms to answer questions like these: How much of an increase in sales can we expect if we reduce our price by 5 percent? To increase the amount we sell by 10 percent, how much must we reduce price? These are fundamental questions of the sort that firms confront repeatedly.

For example, take the soft drink industry. The price elasticity of demand for RC Cola has been estimated to be about -2.4, which means that the amount sold is very sensitive to price. A 1 percent reduction in the price of RC Cola (holding the prices of its competitors constant) results in a 2.4 percent increase in the quantity sold. Coke is even more price elastic, the price elasticity being about -5.5. Therefore, a 1 percent reduction in the price of Coke (holding the prices of its competitors constant) results in a 5.5 percent increase in the quantity sold.[3] Clearly, the managers of RC and Coke need this information to function effectively, and they and their opposite numbers in firms across the country spend plenty to obtain such information.

Price Elasticity and Pricing Policy

To see more specifically how managers use information concerning the price elasticity of demand for their products, consider in more detail the important topic of pricing. According to equation (3.16),

$$MR = P\left(1 + \frac{1}{\eta}\right)$$

From Chapter 2, we know that marginal revenue equals marginal cost if a firm is maximizing profit, which means that

$$MC = P\left(1 + \frac{1}{\eta}\right) \tag{3.17}$$

[3] J. Nevin, "Laboratory Experiments for Estimating Consumer Demand," *Journal of Marketing Research,* August 1974.

where MC equals marginal cost. (To obtain equation (3.17), we substitute MC for MR on the left-hand side of equation (3.16).) Solving equation (3.17) for P, we obtain

$$P = MC\left(\frac{1}{1 + 1/\eta}\right) \tag{3.18}$$

While equation (3.18) looks rather innocuous, it is in fact a very powerful, useful result. What it says is that the optimal price of a product depends on its marginal cost and its price elasticity of demand. Suppose that the marginal cost of a particular type of shirt is $10 and its price elasticity of demand equals -2. According to equation (3.18), its optimal price is

$$P = 10\left(\frac{1}{1 - 1/2}\right)$$
$$= \$20$$

For present purposes, the central point to note is that the optimal price depends heavily on the price elasticity of demand. Holding constant the value of marginal cost, a product's optimal price is inversely related to its price elasticity of demand. Therefore, if the shirt's price elasticity of demand were -5 rather than -2, its optimal price would be

$$P = 10\left(\frac{1}{1 - 1/5}\right)$$
$$= \$12.50$$

Given the importance of the price elasticity of demand in determining the optimal price of a product, it is not hard to see why managers are so intent on obtaining at least rough estimates of its value. (In Chapters 10–13, we say much more about optimal pricing policies.)

The Income Elasticity of Demand

As was stressed in previous sections, price is not the only factor that influences the quantity demanded of a product. Another important factor is the level of money income among the consumers in the market. If shoppers have plenty of money to spend, the quantity demanded of men's suits is likely to be greater than it would be if they were poverty-stricken. Or if incomes in a particular city are high, the quantity demanded of cognac is likely to be greater than it would be if incomes were low.

The **income elasticity of demand** for a particular good is defined to be *the percentage change in quantity demanded resulting from a 1 percent change in consumers' income.* More precisely, it equals

$$\eta_I = \left(\frac{dQ}{dI}\right)\left(\frac{I}{Q}\right) \tag{3.19}$$

where Q is quantity demanded and I is consumers' income. For some products, the income elasticity of demand is positive, indicating that increases in consumers' money income result in increases in the amount of the good consumed. For example, one would generally expect luxury items like gourmet foods to have positive income elasticities. Other goods have negative income elasticities, indicating that increases in money income result in decreases in the amount of the good consumed. For example, inferior grades of vegetables and clothing might have negative income elasticities. In calculating the income elasticity of demand, it is assumed that the prices of all commodities are held constant.

Whether the income elasticity of demand for a firm's product is high or low can have a great impact on the firm's opportunities and problems. Firms making products with high income elasticities are likely to grow relatively rapidly as incomes rise in an expanding economy, whereas firms making products with low income elasticities are likely to experience more modest expansion. On the other hand, if the economy is jolted by a serious depression and incomes fall sharply, firms making products with low income elasticities are likely to experience less of a decrease in output than those making products with high income elasticities.

In forecasting the long-term growth of the quantity demanded for many major products, the income elasticity of demand is of key importance. According to studies done by the U.S. Department of Agriculture, the income elasticity of demand for milk has been about 0.5, which means that a 1 percent increase in disposable income is associated with about a 0.5 percent increase in the quantity demanded of milk. But, in a study done in Britain, the income elasticity of bread has been about −0.17, which means that a 1 percent increase in disposable income is associated with about a −0.17 percent decrease in the quantity demanded of bread. Table 3.5 indicates that the income elasticity of demand for first-class air tickets between the United States and Europe is 1.50, which means that a 1 percent increase in disposable income is associated with a 1.50 percent increase in the quantity demanded of such tickets. Table 3.6 shows the income elasticity of demand for other commodities from across the world. In measuring income elasticities, income can be defined as the aggregate income of consumers (as in Table 3.6) or as per capita income (as in the next section), depending on the circumstances.

TABLE
3.6

Income Elasticity of Demand, Selected Commodities, Global

Good	Elasticity
Agricultural products	
Grain (China)[1]	−0.12 to +0.15
Potatoes (UK)[2]	−0.32
Potatoes (US)[3]	+0.15
Oranges (US)[3]	+0.83
Apples (US)[3]	+1.32
Lettuce (US)[3]	+0.88
Animal products	
Meat (China)[1]	+0.1 to +1.2
Milk (UK)[2]	+0.05
Milk (US)[3]	+0.50
Cream (US)[3]	+1.72
Eggs (UK)[2]	−0.21
Eggs (US)[3]	+0.57
Processed food products	
Bread (UK)[2]	−0.17
Other cereal products (UK)[2]	+0.18
Automobiles	
Domestic cars (US)[4]	+1.62
European cars (US)[4]	+1.93
Asian cars (US)[4]	+1.65

[1]Millennium Institute, China Agricultural Project found at *www.threshold21.com/chinaag/report/appendix.html*.

[2]AEF116: 1.6: Major market response concepts and measures 1: The Demand side and its elasticities found at *www.staff.ncl.ac.uk/david.harvey/AEF116/1.6/1.6.html*.

[3]D. Suits, "Agriculture" in Adams and Brock, eds. *The Structure of American Industry*.

[4]P. McCarthy, "Market Price and Income Elasticities of New Vehicle Demands."

Using the Demand Function to Calculate the Income Elasticity of Demand

In a previous section, we learned how to calculate the price elasticity of demand based on a product's demand function. Here, we see how the income elasticity of demand can be calculated. Suppose that the demand function for good X is

$$Q = 1{,}000 - 0.2P_X + 0.5P_Y + 0.04I$$

where Q is the quantity demanded of good X, P_X is the price of good X, P_Y is the price of good Y, and I is per capita disposable income. The income elasticity of demand is

$$\eta_I = \left(\frac{dQ}{dI}\right)\left(\frac{I}{Q}\right)$$

$$= 0.04\,\frac{I}{Q}$$

If $I = 10,000$ and $Q = 1,600$,

$$\eta_I = 0.04\left(\frac{10,000}{1,600}\right) = 0.25$$

Therefore, the income elasticity of demand equals 0.25, which means that a 1 percent increase in per capita disposable income is associated with a 0.25 percent increase in the quantity demanded of good X.

Cross Elasticities of Demand

In addition to price and income, still another factor influencing the quantity demanded of a product is the price of other commodities. Holding constant the product's own price (as well as the level of money incomes) and allowing the price of another product to vary may result in important effects on the quantity demanded of the product in question. By observing these effects, we can classify pairs of commodities as **substitutes** or **complements,** and we can measure how close the relationship (either substitute or complementary) is. Consider two commodities, good X and good Y. If good Y's price goes up, what is the effect on Q_X, the quantity of good X demanded? The **cross elasticity of demand** is defined as *the percentage change in the quantity demanded of good X resulting from a 1 percent change in the price of good Y.* Expressed in terms of derivatives,

$$\eta_{XY} = \left(\frac{dQ_X}{dP_Y}\right)\left(\frac{P_Y}{Q_X}\right) \tag{3.20}$$

Goods X and Y are classified as substitutes if the cross elasticity of demand is positive. For instance, an increase in the price of wheat, when the price of corn remains constant, tends to increase the quantity of corn demanded; therefore, η_{XY} is positive, and wheat and corn are classified as substitutes. On the other hand, if the cross elasticity of demand is negative, goods X and Y are classified as complements. For example, an increase in the price of software may tend to decrease the purchase of personal computers when the price of personal computers remains constant; therefore, η_{XY} is negative and software and personal computers are classified as complements.

CONSULTANT'S CORNER

Estimating the Demand for Rail Passenger Business by Amtrak

Amtrak (the national passenger railroad in the United States) has used its aggregate demand model to obtain its forecasts of systemwide passenger revenues. The first part of its model was a multivariate, linear regression that forecasts its systemwide passenger miles—the dependent variable (a passenger mile is one passenger moved one mile). Explanatory variables are disposable personal income; Amtrak's average fare; the ratio of Amtrak's average fare to the airlines' average fare; retail gasoline price; dummy variables to reflect such events as weather, holidays, strikes, and derailments; and dummy variables to reflect seasonal variation.

The most important determinant of rail passenger miles was disposable personal income (a proxy variable for the strength of the U.S. economy). From the regression, a 1 percent increase in disposable personal income was expected to yield a 1.8 percent increase in systemwide passenger miles.

(a) Explain the rationale for each of the explanatory variables appearing in the model and what signs (positive or negative) you expect for their regression coefficients. (b) How did Amtrak use this forecast of systemwide passenger miles to obtain their estimate of systemwide passenger revenues? (c) What is Amtrak's estimate of income elasticity of demand for passenger service (based on income level of the economy as a whole)? If U.S. disposable personal income per capita increases from $27,000 to $28,000, what's your prediction for the increase in train passenger miles in the new situation (all other independent variables remaining constant)? Will this prediction be 100 percent accurate? Why or why not? (d) Even though disposable personal income rose throughout the 2000s, Amtrak's market share of intercity passenger miles decreased. Can you explain this?

To illustrate the calculation of cross elasticities, suppose once again that the demand function for good X is

$$Q_X = 1,000 - 0.2P_X + 0.5P_Y + 0.04I$$

where Q_X is the quantity demanded of good X, P_X is the price of good X, P_Y is the price of good Y, and I is per capita disposable income. The cross elasticity of demand between goods X and Y is

$$\eta_{XY} = \left(\frac{dQ_X}{dP_Y}\right)\left(\frac{P_Y}{Q_X}\right)$$
$$= 0.5\frac{P_Y}{Q_X}$$

Although the value of the cross elasticity depends on the values of P_Y and Q_X, the goods always are substitutes, since η_{XY} must be positive, regardless of the values of P_Y and Q_X. If $P_Y = 500$ and $Q_X = 2,000$,

$$\eta_{XY} = 0.5\left(\frac{500}{2,000}\right) = 0.125$$

The cross elasticity of demand is of fundamental importance to firms because they continually must do their best to anticipate what will happen to their own sales if their rivals change their prices. To do so, they need information concerning the cross elasticities of demand. Table 3.7 shows the cross elasticities of demand for selected pairs of commodities. In Chapter 5, we take up some of the statistical techniques used to estimate them.

TABLE
3.7

Cross Elasticity of Demand, Selected Pairs of Commodities, Global

Change of price of good	Change of quantity of good	Cross price elasticity
European/Asian cars	US domestic cars	+0.28[1]
European/US domestic cars	Asian cars	+0.61[1]
US domestic/Asian cars	European cars	+0.76[1]
Australian public transit	Australian auto ownership	+0.1 to +0.3[2]
Irish coal	Irish natural gas	+0.4[3]
Irish coal	Irish oil	+0.7[3]
Kenyan government Provided health care	Mission or private sector Provided health care in Kenya	+0.023[4]
US durum wheat	US hard red spring wheat	+0.04[5]
US hard red winter wheat	US white wheat	+1.80[5]
UK beef/veal	UK pork	0.00[6]
UK mutton/lamb	UK beef/veal	+0.25[6]

[1]P. McCarthy, "Market Price and Income Elasticities of New Vehicle Demand."

[2]J. Luk and S. Hepburn, "A Review of Australian Travel Demand Elasticities," Working Document No.: TE 93/004, 1993, Australian Road Research Board.

[3]Competition Authority Decision of 30 January 1998, relating to a proceeding under Section 4 of the Competition Act 1991: Notification No. CA/15/97—Statoil Ireland Ltd./Clare Oil Company Ltd.—Share Purchase Agreement and Service Employment Agreement. Decision No. 490 found at www.irlgov.ie/compauth/dec490. htm.

[4]Section 4: The Basics of Markets and Health Care Markets: Box 4.4: Demand for Health Care in Kenya found at www.worldbank.org/wbi/heathflagship/learning/module1/box4_4.htm.

[5]Wheat Yearbook, March 30, 1998, Economic Research Services, United States Department of Agriculture, Washington, DC 20036-5831.

[6]AEF116: 1.6: Major market response concepts and measures 1: The demand side and its elasticities found at www.staff.ncl.ac.uk/david.harvey/AEF116/1.6/1.6.html.

The Advertising Elasticity of Demand

Although the price elasticity, income elasticity, and cross elasticities of demand are the most frequently used elasticity measures, they are not the only ones. For example, firms sometimes find it useful to calculate the **advertising elasticity of demand**. Suppose that the demand function for a particular firm's product is

$$Q = 500 - 0.5P + 0.01I + 0.82A$$

where Q is the quantity demanded of the product, P is its price, I is per capita disposable income, and A is the firm's advertising expenditure. The advertising elasticity is defined as *the percentage change in the quantity demanded of the product resulting from a 1 percent change in advertising expenditure*. More precisely, it equals

$$\eta_A - \left(\frac{dQ}{dA}\right)\left(\frac{A}{Q}\right) \tag{3.21}$$

In this case, since $dQ/dA = 0.82$,

$$\eta_A = 0.82 \frac{A}{Q}$$

If A/Q, the amount of advertising per unit of the product demanded, is $2,

$$\eta_A = 0.82(2) = 1.64$$

This elasticity is useful because it tells the firm's managers that a 1 percent increase in advertising expenditure results in a 1.64 percent increase in the quantity demanded. In later chapters, we see how information of this sort can be used to help guide major managerial decisions.

The Constant-Elasticity Demand Function

In previous sections of this chapter, we generally assumed that the demand function is linear. That is, the quantity demanded of a product has been assumed to be a linear function of its price, the prices of other goods, consumer income, and other variables. Another mathematical form frequently used is the **constant-elasticity demand function**. If the quantity demanded (Q) depends only on the product's price (P) and consumer income (I), this mathematical form is

$$Q = aP^{-b_1}I^{b_2} \tag{3.22}$$

Therefore, if $a = 200$, $b_1 = 0.3$, and $b_2 = 2$,

$$Q = 200P^{-0.3}I^2$$

An important property of this demand function is that the price elasticity of demand equals $-b_1$, regardless of the value of P or I. (This accounts for it being called the *constant-elasticity demand function*.) To see this, let us differentiate Q with respect to price:

$$\frac{\partial Q}{\partial P} = -b_1 a P^{-b_1-1} I^{b_2}$$

$$= \frac{-b_1}{P} a P^{-b_1} I^{b_2}$$

$$= \frac{-b_1}{P} Q$$

Therefore,

$$\left(\frac{P}{Q}\right)\left(\frac{\partial Q}{\partial P}\right) = -b_1 \tag{3.23}$$

Since the left-hand side of equation (3.23) is defined to be the price elasticity of demand, it follows that the price elasticity of demand equals $-b_1$, a constant whose value does not depend on P or I.

Similarly, the income elasticity of demand equals b_2, regardless of the value of P or I. To prove this, differentiate Q with respect to income:

$$\frac{\partial Q}{\partial I} = b_2 a P^{-b_1} I^{b_2-1}$$

$$= \frac{b_2}{I} a P^{-b_1} I^{b_2}$$

$$= \frac{b_2}{I} Q.$$

Therefore,

$$\left(\frac{\partial Q}{\partial I}\right)\left(\frac{I}{Q}\right) = b_2 \tag{3.24}$$

Since the left-hand side of equation (3.24) is defined to be the income elasticity of demand, it follows that the income elasticity of demand equals b_2, another constant whose value does not depend on P or I.

ANALYZING MANAGERIAL DECISIONS

Price Cutting at the *London Times*

The *London Times*, owned by Rupert Murdoch, is one of the leading newspapers in the world. In September 1993, the *London Times* lowered its price from 45 pence to 30 pence, while the prices of its rivals remained unchanged. The numbers of newspapers sold by the *London Times* and its rivals in August 1993 and May 1994 were as follows:

	August 1993	May 1994
London Times	355,000	518,000
Daily Telegraph	1,024,000	993,000
Independent	325,000	277,000
Guardian	392,000	402,000

(a) Based on these figures, what was the price elasticity of demand for the *London Times*? (b) Was the cross electricity of demand between the *Daily Telegraph* and the *London Times* positive or negative? Would you expect it to be positive or negative? Why? (c) Did this price reduction increase or decrease the *London Times* total revenue from newspaper sales? (d) On the basis of newspaper sales alone, was this price reduction profitable? (e) Peter Stothard, editor of the *London Times*, pointed out that "the increase in circulation . . . made the paper a more attractive vehicle for advertisers."[*] If so, could this price reduction be profitable?

SOLUTION (a) Based on these figures, the arc elasticity was

$$\eta = \frac{518,000 - 355,000}{(355,000 + 518,000)/2} \div \frac{30 - 45}{(45 + 30)/2} = -0.9336$$

This assumes that the demand curve did not shift between August 1993 and May 1994. (b) Positive, since a cut in the price of the *London Times* reduced the quantity sold of the *Daily Telegraph*. It would be expected to be positive since the *London Times* and the *Daily Telegraph* are substitutes. (c) Total revenue from newspaper sales fell from 355,000 × 45 pence = 15,975,000 pence to 518,000 × 30 pence = 15,540,000 pence. This is to be expected since price was cut when demand was inelastic. (d) No. Since total revenue fell and total cost did not fall (because the output of papers increased), profits went down. (e) If the increase in advertising revenue due to the newspaper's higher circulation were large enough, it could offset the decline in profit from newspaper sales.[†]

[*]*New York Times*, June 13, 1994, p. D7.
[†]For further discussion, see ibid.

The constant-elasticity demand function is often used by managers and managerial economists, for several reasons. First, in contrast to the linear demand function, this mathematical form recognizes that the effect of price on quantity depends on the level of income and that the effect of income on quantity depends on the level of price. The multiplicative relationship in equation (3.22) is often more realistic than the additive relationship in equation (3.1). Second, like the linear demand function, the constant-elasticity demand function is relatively easy to estimate. If we take logarithms of both sides of equation (3.22),[4]

$$\log Q = \log a - b_1 \log P + b_2 \log I \tag{3.25}$$

Since this equation is linear in the logarithms, the parameters (a, b_1, and b_2) can readily be estimated by regression analysis. In Chapter 5, we learn how such estimates can be made.

Summary

1. The market demand curve for a product shows how much of the product will be demanded at each price. The market demand curve shifts in response to changes in tastes, incomes, the prices of other products, and the size of the population.

2. The market demand function for a product is an equation showing how the quantity demanded depends on the product's price, the incomes of consumers, the prices of other products, advertising expenditure, and additional factors. Holding all factors other than the product's price constant, one can derive the market demand curve for the product from the market demand function. Market demand functions can be formulated for individual firms as well as for entire industries.

3. The price elasticity of demand is the percentage change in quantity demanded resulting from a 1 percent change in price; more precisely, it equals $(dQ/dP)(P/Q)$. Whether a price increase (or decrease) results in an increase in the total amount spent by consumers on a product depends on the price elasticity of demand.

4. Marginal revenue is the change in total revenue resulting from a one-unit increase in quantity; that is, it equals the derivative of total revenue with respect to quantity. Marginal revenue equals $P(1 + 1/\eta)$, where P is price and η is the price elasticity of demand.

5. The price elasticity of demand for a product tends to be elastic if the product has a large number of close substitutes. Also, it often tends to be more elastic in the long run than in the short run. It is sometimes asserted that the demand for a product is relatively price inelastic if the product accounts for a very small percentage of the typical consumer's budget, but this need not be the case.

---

[4]A review of some basic points regarding logarithms may be of use. To begin with, X equals the logarithm of Y (that is, $\log Y$) if $10^X = Y$. Therefore, the logarithm of the product of two variables (say, Y_1 and Y_2) equals the sum of the logarithms of these variables; that is, $\log (Y_1 Y_2) = \log Y_1 + \log Y_2$. Also, the logarithm of Y^C equals $C \log Y$.

6. The optimal price for a product depends on its price elasticity of demand as well as on its marginal cost. To maximize profit, a firm should set its price equal to MC[1/(1 + 1/η)], where MC is marginal cost and η is the price elasticity of demand.

7. The income elasticity of demand is the percentage change in quantity demanded resulting from a 1 percent increase in consumer income; that is, it equals $(dQ/dI)(I/Q)$, where I is the income of consumers. The income elasticity of demand may be positive or negative. Like the price elasticity of demand, it is of major importance in forecasting the long-term growth in the quantity demanded for many major products.

8. The cross elasticity of demand is the percentage change in the quantity demanded of product X resulting from a 1 percent increase in the price of product Y; in other words, it equals $(dQ_X/dP_Y)(P_Y/Q_X)$. If X and Y are substitutes, it is positive; if they are complements, it is negative. This elasticity is important for managers, because they must try to understand and forecast the effects of changes in other firms' prices on their own firm's sales.

9. If a demand curve is linear, the price elasticity of demand varies from point to point on the demand curve. As price approaches zero, the price elasticity of demand also approaches zero. As quantity demanded approaches zero, the price elasticity approaches negative infinity. In contrast, for a constant-elasticity demand function, the price elasticity of demand is the same regardless of the product's price. Both linear demand functions and constant-elasticity demand functions are used frequently by managers and managerial economists.

Problems

1. The Dolan Corporation, a maker of small engines, determines that in 2004 the demand curve for its product is

$$P = 2,000 - 50Q$$

where P is the price (in dollars) of an engine and Q is the number of engines sold per month.

a. To sell 20 engines per month, what price would Dolan have to charge?

b. If it sets a price of $500, how many engines will Dolan sell per month?

c. What is the price elasticity of demand if price equals $500?

d. At what price, if any, will the demand for Dolan's engines be of unitary elasticity?

2. The Johnson Robot Company's marketing officials report to the company's chief executive officer that the demand curve for the company's robots in 2004 is

$$P = 3,000 - 40Q$$

where P is the price of a robot and Q is the number sold per month.

a. Derive the marginal revenue curve for the firm.

b. At what prices is the demand for the firm's product price elastic?

c. If the firm wants to maximize its dollar sales volume, what price should it charge?

3. After a careful statistical analysis, the Chidester Company concludes that the demand function for its product is

$$Q = 500 - 3P + 2P_r + 0.1I$$

where Q is the quantity demanded of its product, P is the price of its product, P_r is the price of its rival's product, and I is per capita disposable income (in dollars). At present, $P = \$10$, $P_r = \$20$, and $I = \$6,000$.

a. What is the price elasticity of demand for the firm's product?

b. What is the income elasticity of demand for the firm's product?

c. What is the cross elasticity of demand between its product and its rival's product?

d. What is the implicit assumption regarding the population in the market?

4. The Haas Corporation's executive vice president circulates a memo to the firm's top management in which he argues for a reduction in the price of the firm's product. He says that such a price cut will increase the firm's sales and profits.

a. The firm's marketing manager responds with a memo pointing out that the price elasticity of demand for the firm's product is about -0.5. Why is this fact relevant?

b. The firm's president concurs with the opinion of the executive vice president. Is she correct?

5. According to J. Fred Bucy, former president of Texas Instruments, his firm continually made detailed studies of the price elasticity of demand for each of its major products to determine how much its sales would increase if it changed its price by a particular amount.[5] For example, Texas Instruments had to estimate the effect of a 10 percent reduction in the price of the TI-55, a hand calculator the company produced, and whether such a price reduction would increase sales by a large enough amount to be profitable.

---

[5]See his paper in J. Backman and J. Czepiel, eds., *Changing Marketing Strategies in a New Economy* (Indianapolis: Bobbs-Merrill, 1977).

In 1982, Texas Instruments reduced the price of its 99/4A home computer from $299 to $199, and its rivals followed suit. If the price elasticity of demand was less than -1, did the price cut increase the amount spent on such computers?

6. The Hanover Manufacturing Company believes that the demand curve for its product is

$$P = 5 - Q$$

where P is the price of its product (in dollars) and Q is the number of millions of units of its product sold per day. It is currently charging a price of $1 per unit for its product.

   a. Evaluate the wisdom of the firm's pricing policy.

   b. A marketing specialist says that the price elasticity of demand for the firm's product is -1.0. Is this correct?

7. On the basis of historical data, Richard Tennant has concluded: "The consumption of cigarettes is . . . [relatively] insensitive to changes in price. . . . In contrast, the demand for individual brands is highly elastic in its response to price. . . . In 1918, for example, Lucky Strike was sold for a short time at a higher retail price than Camel or Chesterfield and rapidly lost half its business."

   a. Explain why the demand for a particular brand is more elastic than the demand for all cigarettes. If Lucky Strike raised its price by 1 percent in 1918, was the price elasticity of demand for its product greater than -2?

   b. Do you think that the demand curve for cigarettes is the same now as it was in 1918? If not, describe in detail the factors that have shifted the demand curve, and whether each has shifted it to the left or right.

8. According to S. Sackrin of the U.S. Department of Agriculture, the price elasticity of demand for cigarettes is between -0.3 and -0.4, and the income elasticity of demand is about 0.5.

   a. Suppose the federal government, influenced by findings that link cigarettes and cancer, were to impose a tax on cigarettes that increased their price by 15 percent. What effect would this have on cigarette consumption?

   b. Suppose a brokerage house advised you to buy cigarette stocks because, if incomes rise by 50 percent in the next decade, cigarette sales would be bound to spurt enormously. What would be your reaction to this advice?

9. Using the PIMS (Profit Impact of Market Strategies) survey of major U.S. firms, Michael Hagerty, James Carman, and Gary Russell estimated that, on the average, the advertising elasticity of demand was only about 0.003. Doesn't this indicate that firms spend too much on advertising?

10. Market researchers at the Lawrence Corporation estimate that the demand function for the firm's product is

$$Q = 50P^{-1.5}I^{0.5}$$

where Q is the quantity demanded, P is the product's price, and I is per capita disposable income. The marginal cost of the firm's product is estimated to be \$10. Population is assumed to be constant.

a. Lawrence's price for its product is \$20. Is this the optimal price? Why or why not?

b. If it is not the optimal price, write a brief memorandum indicating what price might be better and why.

11. The McCauley Company hires a marketing consultant to estimate the demand function for its product. The consultant concludes that this demand function is

$$Q = 100P^{-3.1}I^{2.3}A^{0.1}$$

where Q is the quantity demanded per capita per month, P is the product's price (in dollars), I is per capita disposable income (in dollars), and A is the firm's advertising expenditures (in thousands of dollars).

a. What is the price elasticity of demand?

b. Will increases in price result in increases or decreases in the amount spent on McCauley's product?

c. What is the income elasticity of demand?

d. What is the advertising elasticity of demand?

e. If the population in the market increases by 10 percent, what is the effect on the quantity demanded if P, I, and A are held constant?

12. The Schmidt Corporation estimates that its demand function is

$$Q = 400 - 3P + 4I + 0.6A$$

where Q is the quantity demanded per month, P is the product's price (in dollars), I is per capita disposable income (in thousands of dollars), and A is the firm's advertising expenditures (in thousands of dollars per month). Population is assumed to be constant.

a. During the next decade, per capita disposable income is expected to increase by \$5,000. What effect will this have on the firm's sales?

b. If Schmidt wants to raise its price enough to offset the effect of the increase in per capita disposable income, by how much must it raise its price?

    c. If Schmidt raises its price by this amount, will it increase or decrease the price elasticity of demand? Explain. Make sure your answers reflect the fact that elasticity is a negative number.

13. The marketing manager of the Summers Company must formulate a recommendation concerning the price to be charged for a new product. According to the best available estimates, the marginal cost of the new product will be $18 and the price elasticity of demand for this product will be -3.0.

    a. What recommendation should she make if Summers wants to maximize profit?

    b. If her recommendation is accepted, what will be the new product's marginal revenue?

Consumer Behavior and Rational Choice

Market demand was discussed in Chapter 3. But market demand for a product is just the aggregate of individual demands. How do individual consumers form their demands for products? How do the variables discussed in Chapter 3 (prices, income, advertising, tastes) influence an individual consumer's demand for a product? Firms need to understand what consumers' tastes and preferences are and how consumers are influenced by changes in those and other variables that managers can or cannot control.

We assume that our consumer is rational and wishes to maximize his or her well-being. Well-being is a function of the goods one consumes. However, the amount of goods he or she can consume is constrained by income. Therefore, using the techniques of constrained maximization from Chapter 2, we show how a consumer's demand curve is derived from the rational behavior of an individual who maximizes his or her well-being given the prices of goods, personal tastes and preferences for goods, and income. We develop the concepts of utility functions, indifference curves, and budget lines. Using them, we derive the consumer's demand curve for a good (food). We show how the consumer's demand curve shifts when income changes.

Many firms use focus groups of consumers to help them understand what variables influence consumer demands and how consumers trade off one variable versus another. For instance, Dell Computer has run focus groups in which customers estimate how much they would pay for a given function.

Firms often use market research firms to survey consumers in person, over the telephone, or using questionnaires—all designed to assess consumer demand characteristics.

Indifference Curves

To make things as simple as possible, we assume that there are only two goods—food and clothing. This assumption can easily be relaxed. To understand the theory of consumer behavior, you must know what an indifference curve is. *An indifference curve contains points representing market baskets among which the consumer is indifferent.* To illustrate, consider Jennifer Popovich, a consumer in South Pasadena, California. Certain market baskets—that is, certain combinations of food and clothing (the only commodities)—are equally desirable for her. For example, she may be indifferent between a market basket containing 50 pounds of food and five pieces of clothing and a market basket containing 100 pounds of food and two pieces of clothing. These two market baskets can be represented by two points, K and L in Figure 4.1. In addition, other market baskets, each of which can be represented by a point in Figure 4.1, are just as desirable to Ms. Popovich as those represented by points K and L. If we connect all these points, we get a curve that represents market baskets that are equally desirable to the consumer. In our case, Ms. Popovich is indifferent among all the market baskets represented by points on curve I_1 in Figure 4.1. Curve I_1 is therefore called an **indifference curve**.

Three important things should be noted about any consumer's indifference curves:

1. *A consumer has many indifference curves not just one.* If Ms. Popovich is indifferent among all the market baskets represented by points on I_2 in Figure 4.1, I_2 is another of her indifference curves. Moreover, one thing is certain. She prefers any market basket on I_2 to any market basket on I_1, since I_2 includes market baskets with as much clothing as and more food than (or as much food as and more clothing than) the market baskets on I_1. (Of course, consumers sometimes become so satiated with a commodity that they prefer less of it to more, but we assume for simplicity that this is not the case here.) Consequently, it must be true that market baskets on higher indifference curves like I_2 must be preferred to market baskets on lower indifference curves like I_1.

2. *Every indifference curve must slope downward and to the right, so long as the consumer prefers more of each commodity to less.* If one market basket

FIGURE
4.1

Two of Ms. Popovich's Indifference Curves

The curves I_1 and I_2 are two of Ms. Popovich's indifference curves. Each shows market baskets that are equally desirable to Ms. Popovich.

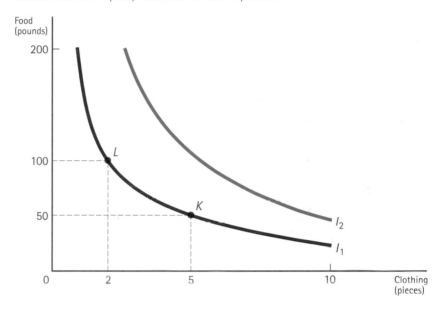

has more of one commodity than a second market basket, it must have less of the other commodity than the second market basket, assuming that the two market baskets are to yield equal satisfaction to the consumer. This must be true so long as more of each commodity is preferred over less by the consumer.

3. *Indifference curves cannot intersect.* If they did, this would contradict the assumption that more of a commodity is preferred to less. For example, suppose that I_1 and I_2 in Figure 4.2 are two indifference curves and that they intersect. If this is the case, the market basket represented by point D is equivalent in the eyes of the consumer to the one represented by point C, since both are on indifference curve I_1. Moreover, the market basket represented by point E is equivalent in the eyes of the consumer to the one represented by point C, since both are on indifference curve I_2. And this means that the market basket represented by point E must be equivalent in the eyes of the consumer to the one represented by point D. But this is impossible because market basket E contains the same amount of food and two more pieces of clothing than market basket D. Since we are assuming more of a commodity is preferred to less, market basket E must be preferred to market basket D.

FIGURE
4.2

Intersecting Indifference Curves: A Contradiction

Indifference curves cannot intersect. If they did, the consumer would be indifferent between *D* and *C*, since both are on indifference curve I_1, and between *E* and *C*, since both are on indifference curve I_2. But this implies that he or she must be indifferent between *D* and *E*, which is impossible since *E* contains the same amount of food and two more pieces of clothing than *D*, and we are assuming more of a commodity is preferred to less.

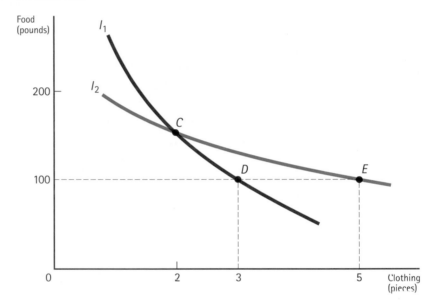

The Marginal Rate of Substitution

Some consumers value an extra unit of a particular good highly; they would be willing to give their eyeteeth to get an extra unit of it. Other consumers do not value an extra unit of this good at all highly; they would give up little of anything to get an extra unit of it. Obviously, in studying consumer behavior, it is useful to have a measure of the relative importance attached by the consumer to the acquisition of another unit of a particular good. The measure that economists use is called the **marginal rate of substitution.**

The marginal rate of substitution of good X for good Y is defined as the number of units of good Y that must be given up if the consumer, after receiving an extra unit of good X, is to maintain a constant level of satisfaction. Obviously, the larger the number of units of good Y that the consumer is willing to give up to get an extra unit of good X, the more important good X is (relative to good *Y*) to the consumer. To measure the marginal rate of substitution, we can obtain the slope of the consumer's indifference curve and multiply this slope by −1. This gives us the number of units of good *Y* that the consumer is willing to give up for an extra unit of good *X*.

To illustrate, consider consumer preferences with regard to the characteristics of automobiles. Two of the key characteristics of an automobile are stylishness and performance (for example, speed, gasoline mileage, and handling). Some consumers are willing to trade off a lot of stylishness for a little extra performance. For these consumers, the indifference curves in Figure 4.3 are relatively steep, as in the left-hand panel of Figure 4.3. The marginal rate of substitution of performance for stylishness is relatively high, since the slope of the indifference curves (times −1) is relatively large. On the other hand, other consumers are willing to trade off a lot of performance for a little extra stylishness. For these consumers, the indifference curves in Figure 4.3 are relatively flat, as in the right-hand panel of Figure 4.3. The marginal rate of substitution of performance for stylishness is relatively low, since the slope of the indifference curves (times −1) is relatively small.

FIGURE 4.3

Indifference Curves of Consumers with High and Low Marginal Rates of Substitution of Performance for Stylishness

The left-hand panel shows the indifference curves of consumers who are willing to trade off a lot of stylishness for a little extra performance. The right-hand panel shows the indifference curves of consumers who are willing to trade off a lot of performance for a little extra stylishness.

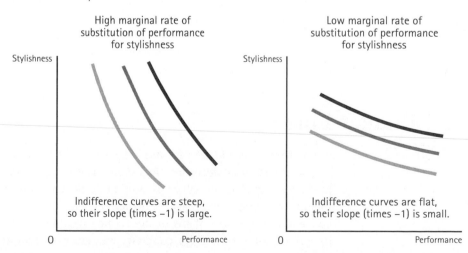

The Concept of Utility

As we have seen, the consumer's indifference curves are a representation of his or her tastes. Given all the indifference curves of a particular consumer, we attach a number, a **utility**, to each of the market baskets that might confront him or her. *This utility indicates the level of enjoyment or preference attached by this consumer to this market basket.* More specifically, it summarizes the preference ranking of market baskets. Since all market baskets on a given indifference curve yield the same amount of satisfaction, they would have the same utility. Market baskets on higher indifference curves would have higher utilities than market baskets on lower indifference curves.

The reason why we attach these utilities to market baskets is that, once this is done, we can tell at a glance which market baskets the consumer would prefer over other market baskets. If the utility attached to one market basket is higher than that attached to another market basket, the consumer prefers the first over the second. If the utility attached to the first market basket is lower than the second, he or she prefers the second over the first. If the utility attached to the first market basket equals the second, he or she is indifferent between the two market baskets.

How should we pick these utilities? Any way will do, as long as market baskets on the same indifference curve receive the same utility and market baskets on higher indifference curves receive higher utilities than market baskets on lower indifference curves. For example, if the consumer prefers market basket R to market basket S, and market basket S to market basket T, the utility of market basket R must be higher than the utility of market basket S, and the utility of market basket S must be higher than the utility of market basket T. But any set of numbers conforming to these requirements is an adequate measure of utility. Therefore, the utility of market baskets R, S, and T may be 30, 20, and 10 or 6, 5, 4, respectively. Both are adequate utility measures, since all that counts is that the utility of market basket R be higher than that of market basket S, which in turn should be higher than that of market basket T. Put differently, both provide a correct ordering or ranking of market baskets in terms of levels of consumer satisfaction.

The Budget Line

The consumer would like to maximize his or her utility, which means that he or she wants to achieve the highest possible indifference curve. But whether a particular indifference curve is attainable depends on the consumer's money income and commodity prices. Exactly what constraints are imposed on the consumer by the size of his or her money income and the nature of commodity prices? To make things concrete, we return to Jennifer Popovich. Suppose that her total income is $600 per week and that she can spend this amount on only two commodities, food and clothing. Needless to say, it is unrealistic to assume that there are only two commodities in existence, but to repeat what was said earlier, this simplification makes it easier to present the model, and the results can easily be generalized to cases where more than two commodities exist.

Under these circumstances, the answer to how much of each commodity Ms. Popovich can buy depends on the price of a pound of food and the price of a piece of clothing. Suppose the price of a pound of food is $3 and the price of a piece of clothing is $60. Then, if she spent all her income on food, she could buy 200 pounds of food per week. On the other hand, if she spent all her income on clothing, she could buy 10 pieces of clothing per week. Or she could, if she wished, buy some food and some clothing. There are a large number of combinations of amounts of food and clothing that she could buy, and each such combination can be represented by a point on the line in Figure 4.4. This line is called her **budget line**. *A consumer's budget line shows the market baskets*

FIGURE
4.4

Ms. Popovich's Budget Line

The consumer's budget line shows the market baskets that can be purchased, given the consumer's income and prevailing commodity prices. This budget line assumes that Ms. Popovich's income is $600 per week, that the price of a pound of food is $3, and that the price of a piece of clothing is $60.

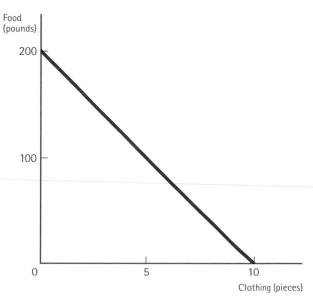

that he or she can purchase, given the consumer's income and prevailing market prices.

To obtain the equation for Jennifer Popovich's budget line, note that

$$YP_f + XP_c = I \tag{4.1}$$

where Y is the amount she buys of food, X is the amount she buys of clothing, P_f is the price of food, P_c is the price of clothing, and I is her income. The left-hand side of equation (4.1) equals the total amount she spends on food and clothing; what equation (4.1) says is that this amount must equal her income. For simplicity, we assume that she saves nothing. (This assumption can be relaxed.) Solving equation (4.1) for Y, we obtain

$$Y = \frac{I}{P_f} - \frac{P_c}{P_f}X \tag{4.2}$$

which is the equation for her budget line.

A shift occurs in the consumer's budget line if changes occur in the consumer's money income or commodity prices. In particular, an increase in money income means that the budget line rises, and a decrease in money income means that the budget line falls (parallel to the original line since a change in I does not affect the slope). This is illustrated in Figure 4.5, which shows Ms. Popovich's

---

FIGURE 4.5

Ms. Popovich's Budget Line at Money Incomes of $300, $600, and $900 per Week

The higher the consumer's money income, the higher is the budget line. Holding commodity prices constant, the budget line's slope remains constant.

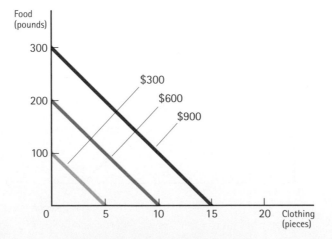

FIGURE
4.6

Ms. Popovich's Budget Line at Food Prices of $3 and $6 per Pound

Holding constant Ms. Popovich's money income at $600 per week and the price of a piece of clothing at $60, the budget line cuts the vertical axis farther from the origin when the price of food is $3 than when it is $6.

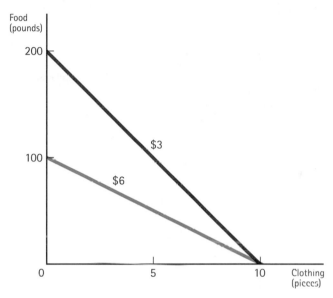

budget line at money incomes of $300, $600, and $900 per week. Her budget line moves upward as her income rises.

Also, commodity prices affect the budget line. A decrease in a commodity's price causes the budget line to cut this commodity's axis at a point farther from the origin. Figure 4.6 shows Ms. Popovich's budget line when the price of a pound of food is $3 and when it is $6. You can see that the budget line cuts the vertical, or food, axis farther from the origin when the price of food is $3 per pound. This is because the change in the price of food alters the slope of the budget line, which equals $-P_c/P_f$ (as shown in equation (4.2)).

The Equilibrium Market Basket

Given the consumer's indifference curves and budget line, we are in a position to determine the consumer's equilibrium market basket—the market basket that, among all those items the consumer can purchase, yields the maximum utility. The first step is to combine the indifference curves with the budget line on the

FIGURE
4.7

Equilibrium Market Basket

Ms. Popovich's equilibrium market basket is at point H, containing 100 pounds of food and five pieces of clothing. This is the point on her budget line that is on the highest indifference curve she can attain, I_2.

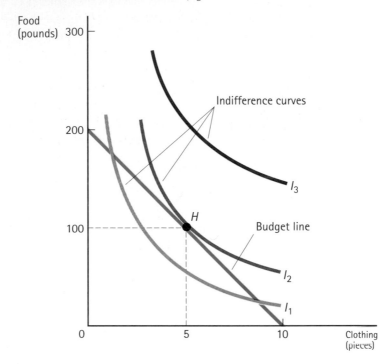

same graph. Figure 4.7 brings together Ms. Popovich's indifference curves (from Figure 4.1) and her budget line (from Figure 4.4). On the basis of the information assembled in Figure 4.7, it is a simple matter to determine her equilibrium market basket. *Her indifference curves show what she wants*: Specifically, she wants to attain the highest possible indifference curve. Therefore, she would rather be on indifference curve I_2 than on indifference curve I_1 and on indifference curve I_3 than on indifference curve I_2. But, as we emphasize, she cannot choose any market basket she likes. *The budget line shows which market baskets her income and commodity prices permit her to buy.* Consequently, she must choose some market basket on her budget line.

Clearly, *the consumer's choice boils down to choosing that market basket on the budget line that is on the highest indifference curve. This is the equilibrium market basket.* For example, Ms. Popovich's equilibrium market basket is at point H in Figure 4.7; it consists of 100 pounds of food and five pieces of clothing

CONCEPTS IN CONTEXT

Effect of a Time Constraint on Consumer Behavior

For consumers, time can be as important as money. For example, suppose that Mildred Evans, an avid sports fan who goes regularly to baseball and football games, decides that she can devote no more than 24 hours per month to attending such games and that she can spend no more than $120 per month on baseball and football tickets. Since she lives much closer to the local baseball stadium than to the nearest football stadium, it takes 4 hours to see a baseball game but 6 hours to see a football game. The price of each baseball ticket is $10, and the price of each football ticket is $40.

Let B be the number of baseball games and F be the number of football games she attends per month. If she spends a total of $120 per month on tickets,

$$40F + 10B = 120 \qquad (4.3)$$

Why? Because $40F$ is the amount spent on football tickets, and $10B$ is the amount spent on baseball tickets, so $40F + 10B$ is the total amount spent per month on baseball and football tickets, which must equal $120. From equation (4.3), it follows that

$$F = 3 - B/4 \qquad (4.4)$$

This is the equation for the *budget line*, plotted in the following graph.

But this ignores the time constraint. If she spends a total of 24 hours per month at baseball and football games,

$$6F + 4B = 24. \qquad (4.5)$$

Why? Because $6F$ equals the number of hours spent at football games and $4B$ equals the num-

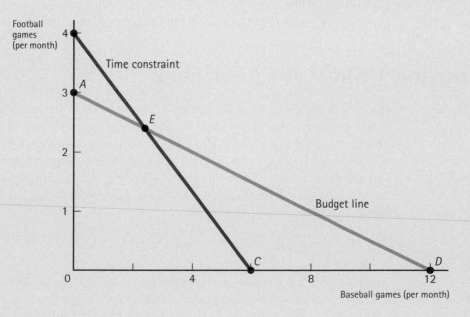

ber of hours spent at baseball games, so $6F + 4B$ equals the total number of hours spent at baseball and football games, which must equal 24. From equation (4.5), it follows that

$$F = 4 - 2B/3 \qquad (4.6)$$

This is the equation for the time constraint, plotted in the graph.

To keep within both the time and expenditure constraints, she must pick a market basket on line segment AE or line segment EC in the graph. Note that the time constraint cuts down on the number of feasible market baskets. Given that she wants to devote only 24 hours per month to

attending baseball and football games, she must be content with market baskets along line segment EC rather than line segment ED, which would be available if there were no time constraint.

per week. This is her equilibrium market basket because any other market basket on the budget line is on a lower indifference curve than point H. But, will a consumer like Ms. Popovich choose this market basket? Admittedly, it may take some time for the consumer to find out that this is the best market basket for him or her under the circumstances, but eventually one would expect a consumer to come very close to acting in the predicted manner.

Maximizing Utility: A Closer Look

Let us look more closely at the market basket at point H, the one Ms. Popovich chooses. Clearly, this market basket is at the point where the budget line is tangent to an indifference curve. Since the slope of the indifference curve equals -1 times the marginal rate of substitution of clothing for food (see page 130) and the slope of the budget line is $-P_c/P_f$ (see page 133), it follows that Ms. Popovich, if she maximizes utility, chooses in equilibrium to allocate her income between food and clothing so that

$$MRS = P_c/P_f \qquad (4.7)$$

where MRS is the marginal rate of substitution of clothing for food.

To understand what this means, recall that the marginal rate of substitution is the rate at which the consumer is *willing* to substitute clothing for food, holding his or her total level of satisfaction constant. Hence, if the marginal rate of substitution is 4, the consumer is willing to give up 4 pounds of food to obtain one more piece of clothing. On the other hand, the price ratio, P_c/P_f, is the rate at which the consumer is able to substitute clothing for food. So, if P_c/P_f is 3, he or she *must* give up 3 pounds of food to obtain one more piece of clothing.

What equation (4.7) is saying is this: The rate at which the consumer is willing to substitute clothing for food (holding satisfaction constant) must equal the rate at which he or she is able to substitute clothing for food. Otherwise, it is always possible to find another market basket that increases the consumer's satisfaction. And this means, of course, that the present market basket is not the one that maximizes consumer satisfaction.

To illustrate, suppose that Ms. Popovich chooses a market basket for which the marginal rate of substitution of clothing for food is 4. Suppose that the price ratio, P_c/P_f, is 3. If this is the case, Ms. Popovich can obtain an extra piece of clothing if she buys 3 less pounds of food, since the price ratio is 3. But an extra piece of clothing is worth 4 pounds of food to Ms. Popovich, since the marginal rate of substitution is four. Therefore, she can increase satisfaction by substituting clothing for food—and this will continue to be the case so long as the marginal rate of substitution exceeds the price ratio. Conversely, if the marginal rate of substitution is less than the price ratio, Ms. Popovich can increase satisfaction by substituting food for clothing. Only when the marginal rate of substitution equals the price ratio does her market basket maximize her utility.

Corner Solutions

While in this case Ms. Popovich chooses the market basket where the budget line is tangent to an indifference curve (the market basket at point H in Figure 4.7), this is not always true. In particular, the consumer may consume *none* of some goods because even tiny amounts of them (or the minimum amount of them that can be bought) are worth less to the consumer than they cost. For example, although your money income may be big enough to afford some Beluga caviar (which you would enjoy), you may not purchase any because even a bit would be worth less to you than it would cost.

Figure 4.8 shows the situation graphically. For simplicity, we assume that there are only two goods, Beluga caviar and pizza. Given the position of your indifference curves, you would maximize utility by choosing market basket W, which contains all pizza and no Beluga caviar at all. This market basket maximizes your utility because it is on a higher indifference curve than any other market basket on the budget line. It is a *corner solution*, in which the budget line touches the highest achievable indifference curve along an axis (in this case, the vertical axis).

FIGURE
4.8

Corner Solution

The market basket that maximizes your utility is *W*, which lies on the vertical axis.

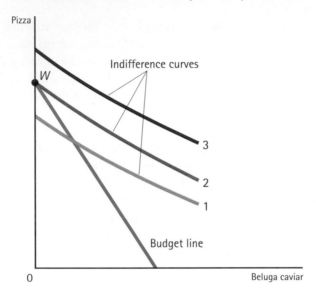

If the consumer purchases some of both commodities, the marginal rate of substitution must equal the price ratio if utility is maximized. This was shown in the previous section. But if the consumer does not purchase both commodities, this is not the case.

Representing the Process of Rational Choice

Of what practical use is the theory of consumer behavior? Later in this chapter, we describe how this theory helps us interpret and analyze demand curves, but for now, we want to emphasize that, apart from its usefulness as a theoretical tool, it can be applied to practical decision making. Many problems people and organizations face are of the following type: *The person or organization has a certain amount of money to spend and must decide how much to allocate to a number of different uses.* For example, a person may have a certain money income, and the problem is how much to spend on various goods and services. Or a philanthropic foundation like the Ford Foundation must determine how much of its money to allocate each year to various kinds of research and educational purposes.

Faced with a problem of this sort, the economist's model of consumer behavior can be of some help. All these problems are basically the same as that facing the consumer, and the economist's model of consumer behavior shows the rational approach to their solution. Thus, the model does not apply only to consumers. It can be useful in any situation where a person or organization must allocate a fixed amount of money among alternative uses. *This model is much more than a theory of consumer behavior; it is a theory of rational choice.* That is, it is a theory that indicates how one should go about making choices.

A model like this is useful because it shows what factors are important to the decision maker and how these factors should be combined to come to a decision. At first glance, this statement may not mean much, but put yourself in the position of the people making a decision. They have lots of factors that they might weigh and try to measure in coming to a decision. Chances are good that they will look at the wrong factors or give some factors improper weight. The economist's model of consumer behavior can be useful in indicating which factors are relevant and how they should be used.

In subsequent chapters, we explain in detail how this model can be applied to help improve managerial decision making. For now, you may want to try problem 11 at the end of this chapter. See if you can figure out how this model sheds light on a state's choice between mass transit and highways. (The answer is provided at the end of the book.)

Deriving the Individual Demand Curve

A consumer's individual demand curve shows how much he or she would purchase of the good in question at various prices of this good (when other prices and the consumer's income are held constant). In this section, we show how our theory can be used to derive the consumer's demand curve. In particular, we return to the case of Ms. Popovich and show how her demand curve for food can be derived.

Assuming that food and clothing are the only goods, Ms. Popovich's weekly income is $600, and the price of clothing is $60 per piece of clothing, Ms. Popovich's budget line is budget line 1 in Figure 4.9 when the price of food is $3 per pound. As we saw in Figure 4.7, Ms. Popovich will buy 100 pounds of food per week under these circumstances.

But, if the price of food increases to $6 per pound and her income and the price of clothing remain constant, her budget line would be budget line 2 in Figure 4.9 and she would attain her highest indifference curve, I_1, by choosing the market basket corresponding to point K, a market basket containing 50 pounds of food per week. Therefore, if the price of food is $6 per pound, she will buy 50 pounds of food per week.

FIGURE
4.9

Effect of a Change in Price on Ms. Popovich's Equilibrium Market Basket

If the price of a pound of food is $3, Mrs. Popovich's budget line is such that her equilibrium market basket is at point *H*, where she buys 100 pounds of food per week. If the price of a pound of food is $6, Mrs. Popovich's budget line is such that her equilibrium market basket is at point *K*, where she buys 50 pounds of food per week.

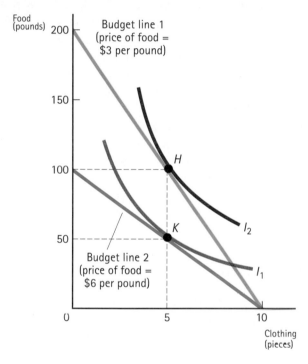

We derived two points on Ms. Popovich's individual demand curve for food, those corresponding to food prices of $3 and $6 per pound. Figure 4.10 shows these two points, *U* and *V*. To obtain more points on her individual demand curve for food, all we have to do is assume a particular price of food, construct the budget line corresponding to this price (holding her income and the price of clothing constant), and find the market basket on this budget line that is on her highest indifference curve. Plotting the amount of food in this market basket against the assumed price of food, we obtain a new point on her individual demand curve for food. Connecting all these points, we get her complete individual demand curve for food, shown in Figure 4.10. (In this situation, the amount of clothing consumed was the same under both pricing scenarios for food. This does not have to be the case.)

Ms. Popovich's Individual Demand Curve for Food

Ms. Popovich's individual demand curve for food shows the amount of food she would buy at various prices.

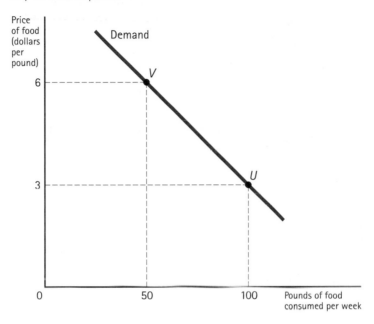

Deriving the Market Demand Curve

We just described how each consumer's individual demand curve for a commodity can be derived, given the consumer's tastes and income as well as the prices of other commodities. Suppose that we obtain the individual demand curve for each of the consumers in the market. How can these individual demand curves be used to derive the market demand curve?

The answer is easy. *To derive the market demand curves, we obtain the horizontal sum of all the individual demand curves.* In other words, to find the total quantity demanded in the market at a certain price, we add up the quantities demanded by all the individual consumers at that price.

Table 4.1 shows the individual demand curves for food of four families: the Millers, Sarafians, Chases, and Grubers. For simplicity, suppose these four families constitute the entire market for food. (This assumption can easily be relaxed; it just makes things simple.) Then, the market demand curve for food is shown in the last column of Table 4.1. Figure 4.11 shows the families' individual demand curves for food as well as the resulting market demand curve.

TABLE
4.1

Individual Demand Curves and Market Demand Curve for Food

Price of food (dollars per pound)	Individual demand (hundreds of pounds per month)				Market demand
	Miller	Sarafian	Chase	Gruber	
3.00	51.0	45.0	5.0	2.0	103
3.20	43.0	44.0	4.2	1.8	93
3.40	36.0	43.0	3.4	1.6	84
3.60	30.0	42.0	2.6	1.4	76
3.80	26.0	41.4	2.4	1.2	71
4.00	21.0	41.0	2.0	1.0	65

FIGURE
4.11

Individual Demand Curves and Market Demand Curve for Food

The market demand curve is the horizontal sum of all the individual demand curves.

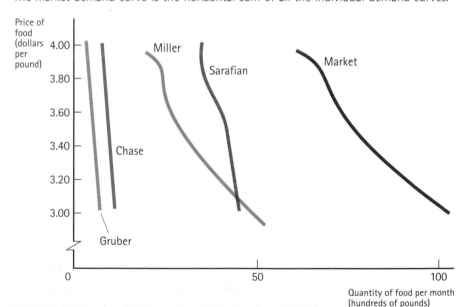

To illustrate how the market demand curve is derived from the individual demand curves, suppose that the price of food is $3 per pound. Then, the total quantity demanded in the market is 103 hundreds of pounds per month, since this is the sum of the quantities demanded at this price by the four families. (As shown in Table 4.1, this sum equals 51.0 + 45.0 + 5.0 + 2.0, or 103 hundreds of pounds.)

Consumer Surplus

One of the most important lessons of our analysis of demand is that individual consumers may value a good above its market price. This is a simple but powerful idea. An individual's demand curve tells us the unit price (P_x) that the individual is willing to pay to purchase a given number of units of a product (say, X). Because the demand curve (usually) is downward sloping, the curve indicates that the consumer values goods $X - 1, X - 2$, and so forth, at a greater amount than the value of the Xth good purchased (say, at values P_{X-1}, P_{X-2}). The price value for each number of units demanded is called the **consumer's reservation price** for that particular unit of good.

The difference between what an individual is *willing* to pay and what that individual *has* to pay for a good is called **consumer surplus.** Alternatively, consumer surplus is the actual price paid subtracted from the reservation price.

When a market price is determined, in a market context, the last individual (or set of individuals) to purchase the good is the individual whose reservation price just equals the market price. All other purchasers of the good have reservation prices exceeding the market price. Hence, all these individuals "gained" a consumer surplus, since they paid less for the good than they were willing to pay. If we aggregate all the individuals' consumer surpluses, we have the consumer surplus for the good at that price. Simply put, the consumer surplus for a good is the area below the demand curve but above the price charged, area A in Figure 4.12.

We have more to say about consumer surplus in later chapters, when we introduce the analogous idea pertaining to the production side of the market, called the *producer surplus*, and the summation of consumer and producer surplus, called the *total surplus*. Economists use these concepts to describe the efficiency of markets and the social benefits of market transactions. For now, we draw a simpler observation. As a business manager, so long as the demand curve for your good or service is downward sloping, you would generate more revenue for your firm if you could charge each consumer his or her reservation price or if you could simply charge higher prices to groups of consumers who value the good more highly than others. Relative to charging a single market price, such a policy would amount to capturing some of the consumer

FIGURE
4.12

The Consumer Surplus for a Price of P_x

The consumer surplus for an individual is the area under the demand curve but above the price (P_x) paid (area A). The same definition holds for a market demand curve.

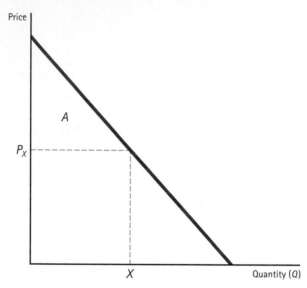

surplus for the benefit of your firm. Even though various legal, practical, and economic constraints limit the extent to which firms can charge different prices for the same good, beyond these constraints, the practice is widespread. Examples include airline tickets, automobiles sold at dealerships where haggling is the norm, and goods and services offered at discounts through coupon systems and other special offers.

Summary

1. An indifference curve contains points representing market baskets among which the consumer is indifferent. If the consumer prefers more to less of both commodities, an indifference curve must have a negative slope.
2. Market baskets on higher indifference curves provide more satisfaction than those on lower indifference curves. Utility is a number that indexes the level of satisfaction derived from a particular market basket. Market baskets with higher utilities are preferred over market baskets with lower utilities.

CONSULTANT'S CORNER

The Trade-off Between Risk and Return

Ms. Jackson has $1 million, which she must allocate between U.S. government securities and common stocks. If she invests it all in U.S. government securities, she will receive a return of 5 percent, and there is no risk. If she invests it all in common stock, she expects to receive a return of 10 percent and there is considerable risk. If she invests half in U.S. government securities and half in common stocks, she expects to receive a return of 7.5 percent and there is some risk. Line *RT* in the graph that follows shows the expected return and extent of risk from all possible allocations of the $1 million between these two types of securities.

Investors differ in how much risk they will accept to obtain a higher expected return. This investor's indifference curves are shown in the graph.

Why do these indifference curves slope *upward* to the right, whereas the other indifference curves in this chapter slope *downward* to the right? How should this investor allocate the $1 million between U.S. government securities and common stocks? (Much more will be said about problems of this sort in Chapter 15.)

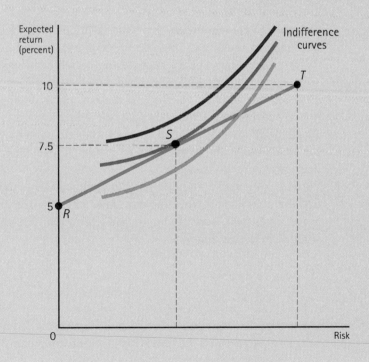

3. The marginal rate of substitution shows how many units of one good must be given up if the consumer, after getting an extra unit of another good, is to maintain a constant level of satisfaction. To obtain the marginal rate of substitution, multiply the slope of the indifference curve by −1.

4. The budget line contains all the market baskets the consumer can buy, given his or her money income and the level of each price. Increases in income push the budget line upward and parallel to the old budget line; changes in the price ratio alter the budget line's slope.

5. To attain the highest level of satisfaction compatible with the budget line, the consumer must choose the market basket on the budget line that is on the highest indifference curve. This market basket is at a point where the budget line is tangent to an indifference curve (unless there is a corner solution).

6. The consumer who maximizes utility will choose in equilibrium to allocate his or her income so that the marginal rate of substitution of one good for another good equals the ratio of the prices of the two goods (unless there is a corner solution).

7. The theory of consumer behavior is often used to represent the process of rational choice. Frequently, a person or organization has a certain amount of money to spend and must decide how much to allocate to a number of different uses. This theory indicates how such decisions should be made.

8. A consumer's demand curve shows how much the consumer would purchase of the good in question at various prices of the good when other prices and the consumer's income are held constant. The theory of consumer behavior can be used to derive the consumer's demand curve, and the market demand curve can be obtained by summing the individual demand curves horizontally.

9. Consumer surplus is the difference between what a consumer is willing to pay for a good and what the consumer pays for the good in the market. Clever managers want to figure out pricing policies to extract consumer surplus from consumers.

Problems

1. The market for athletic shoes experienced a big shift in the early 1990s, as sales of hiking shoes increased by over 27 percent, while those of other types of athletic shoes grew much more slowly (or declined). According to Jim Reid of the Coleman Company, "The baby boomers are getting to an age where they are more interested in doing things with families rather than individual sports."[1]

[1] *New York Times*, February 13, 1994, p. 6F.

   a. If the typical baby boomer regards each pair of hiking shoes as equally desirable as two pairs of jogging shoes, what do his or her indifference curves (between hiking shoes and jogging shoes) look like? Assume that this is true regardless of how many pairs of each type of athletic shoes he or she has.

   b. Do they have the typical shape of indifference curves? Why or why not?

2. In recent years, fresh bagel sales have been growing at about 30 percent per year. Once considered an ethnic food to be eaten only with cream cheese and lox, bagels now "have become the new doughnut to bring to the office," according to Michael Goldstein of Goldstein's Bagel Bakery in Pasadena, California.[2] But one problem with bagels is that they get stale fast. In the words of Ray Lahvic, editor emeritus of *Bakery Production and Marketing,* "the worst thing in the world is a day-old bagel."[3] If a market researcher asserts that the slope of the typical consumer's indifference curves between fresh bagels and day-old bagels is −1, would you agree with this assertion? Why or why not?

3. On a piece of graph paper, plot the quantity of lamb consumed by Ms. Turner along the vertical axis and the quantity of rice she consumes along the horizontal axis. Draw the indifference curve that includes the following market baskets. Each of these market baskets gives equal satisfaction.

Market basket	Lamb (pounds)	Rice (pounds)
1	2	8
2	3	7
3	4	6
4	5	5
5	6	4
6	7	3
7	8	2
8	9	1

4. In the previous question, what is the marginal rate of substitution of rice for lamb? How does the marginal rate of substitution vary as Ms. Turner consumes more lamb and less rice? Is this realistic?

5. Suppose that Richard has an after-tax income of $500 per week and must spend it all on food or clothing. If food is $5 per pound and clothing is $10 per piece, draw his budget line on a piece of graph paper, where the amount of food is measured along the vertical axis and the amount of clothing is measured along the horizontal axis.

[2]*Philadelphia Inquirer,* December 28, 1993.

[3]Ibid.

6. In the previous problem, what is the budget line if Richard's weekly income increases to $600? What is the budget line if his income is $500 but the price of food increases to $10 per pound? What is his budget line if his income is $500 but the price of clothing increases to $20 per piece? Draw each of these budget lines on the piece of graph paper used in the previous problem.

7. Maria has budgeted a total of $9 to spend on two goods, chips and salsa. She likes to consume a unit of chips in combination with a unit of salsa. Any unit of chips that she cannot consume in combination with a unit of salsa is useless. Similarly, any unit of salsa that she cannot consume in combination with chips is useless. If the price of a unit of chips is 50 cents and the price of a unit of salsa is 10 cents, how many units of each good does she purchase?

8. In the following diagram, we show one of Jane's indifference curves and her budget line.

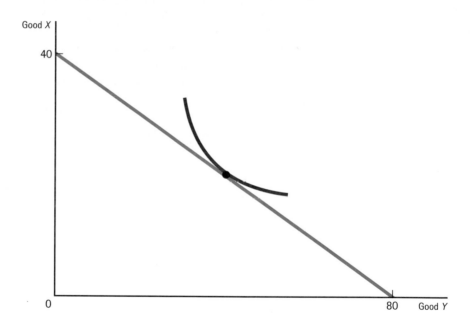

a. If the price of good X is $100, what is her income?
b. What is the equation for her budget line?
c. What is the slope of the budget line?
d. What is the price of good Y?
e. What is her marginal rate of substitution in equilibrium?

9. Sarah has $300 to allocate between opera tickets and movie tickets. The price of each opera ticket is $60, and the price of each movie ticket is $6. Her marginal rate of substitution of opera tickets for movie tickets equals

five, regardless of what market basket she chooses. How many opera tickets does she purchase?

10. Suppose that Milton has $50 to be divided between corn and beans and that the price of beans is $0.50 per pound. What will be the relationship between the price of corn and the amount of corn he will buy if $U = \log Q_c + 4 \log Q_b$, where U is his utility, Q_c is the quantity of corn he consumes (in pounds), and Q_b is the quantity of beans he consumes (in pounds)?

11. In 1993, the state of New York received $3 billion (from federal sources and a state petroleum tax) to be spent during the mid-1990s on highways and/or mass transit (subways, buses, and urban rail lines), both of which could be used to meet the transportation needs of the state's population.

   a. If each mile of mass transit costs $20 million, what is the maximum number of miles of mass transit that these funds would have enabled the state to construct?

   b. If each mile of highway costs $10 million, what is the maximum number of miles of highways that these funds would have enabled the state to construct?

   c. If the number of miles of mass transit constructed is put on the vertical axis of a graph and the number of miles of highways constucted is put on the horizontal axis, can a budget line (showing the maximum number of miles of mass transit that could be constructed, given each number of miles of highways constructed) be drawn for the state? If so, what is the slope of this budget line? (Assume that the $3 billion is the only source of funds for mass transit or highway construction.)

   d. If the public and the state government agree that every extra mile of mass transit adds three times as much to the state's transportation capability as an extra mile of highways, how much of the $3 billion should be spent on mass transit (if the objective is to maximize transportation capability)?

Estimating Demand
Functions

W hen Sergio Zyman was the marketing chief of Coca-Cola, he once indicated that his company, one of the world's biggest advertisers, would put less emphasis on traditional newspaper, magazine, and TV ads and more emphasis on new marketing techniques like special programs on cable TV and product tie-ins with movies. All firms, not just Coke, must constantly reevaluate and adjust their marketing strategies. As stressed repeatedly in previous chapters, an effective manager must have a good working knowledge of the demand function for his or her firm's products.

The previous two chapters were concerned with the theory of demand; now we learn how to estimate a product's demand function. Consumer surveys and market experiments can be useful in providing such information, but the technique most frequently used to estimate demand functions is regression analysis.

While managers use some or all of these techniques (we mentioned the use of focus groups by Dell Computer in Chapter 4), the technique most frequently used to estimate demand functions is regression analysis (even much of the data gathered by questionnaire and focus group is analyzed by regression). In Chapter 3, we showed how Amtrak estimated its demand function with regression analysis. Since regression analysis is used repeatedly in subsequent chapters to estimate production functions and cost functions and for forecasting, we devote considerable attention to this basic technique in this chapter.

The Identification Problem

While it is very important that managers have reasonably accurate estimates of the demand functions for their own (and other) products, this does not mean that it is always easy to obtain such estimates. One problem that may arise in estimating demand curves should be recognized at the outset. Given the task of estimating the demand curve for a particular product, you might be inclined to plot the quantity demanded of the product in 2003 versus its 2003 price, the quantity demanded in 2002 versus its 2002 price, and so forth. If the resulting plot of points for 2001 to 2003 were as shown in Figure 5.1, you might be tempted to conclude that the demand curve is DD'.

Unfortunately, things are not so simple. Price, as we saw in Chapter 1, is determined by both the demand and supply curves for this product if the

FIGURE
5.1

Price Plotted against Quantity, 2001–2003

The curve DD' is unlikely to be a good estimate of the demand curve.

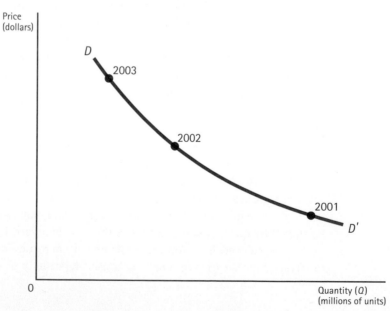

market is competitive. Specifically, the equilibrium value of price is at the level where the demand and supply curves intersect. The important point to note is that the demand and supply curves for this product may have been different each year. So, as shown in Figure 5.2, the supply curve may have shifted (from S_{01} in 2001 to S_{02} in 2002 to S_{03} in 2003), and the demand curve may have shifted (from D_{01} in 2001 to D_{02} in 2002 to D_{03} in 2003). As indicated in Figure 5.2, DD' is not even close to being a good approximation to the demand curve for this product in any of these three years.

In the situation in Figure 5.2, if you were to conclude that DD' was the demand curve, you would underestimate (in absolute value) the price elasticity of demand for this product in 2003 and 2002 and overestimate it (in absolute value) in 2001. In 2003, you would think that, if price were lowered from \$30 to \$28, the quantity demanded would increase from 10 to 12 million units per year. In fact, as shown in Figure 5.2, such a price reduction would result in an increase of the quantity demanded to 18, not 12, million units per year. This is a mammoth error in anyone's book.

FIGURE
5.2

Estimated Demand Curve Contrasted with Actual Demand Curves

The estimated demand curve DD' is not at all similar to the actual demand curves.

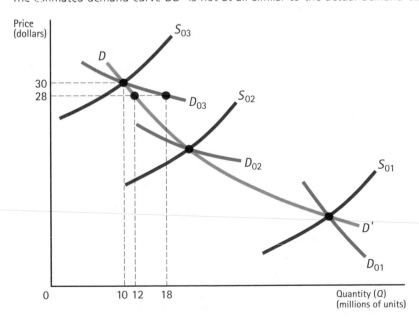

FIGURE
5.3

Fixed Demand Curve and Shifting Supply Curve

In this special case, *DD'* does represent the actual demand curve.

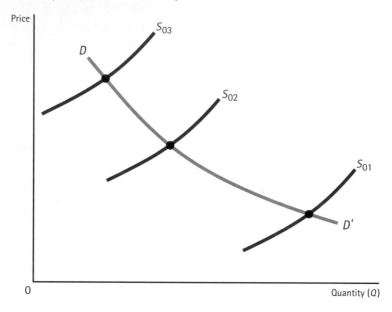

The point is that, because we are not holding constant a variety of non-price variables like consumer tastes, incomes, the prices of other goods, and advertising, we cannot be sure that the demand curve was fixed during the period when the measurements were made. If the demand curve was fixed and only the supply curve changed during the period, we could be confident that the plot of points in Figure 5.1 represents the demand curve. As shown in Figure 5.3, the shifts in the supply curve trace out various points on the demand curve we want to measure.

How can we estimate a demand curve if it has not remained fixed in the past? There are many ways, some simple, some very complex. Econometric techniques recognize that price and quantity are related by both the supply curve and the demand curve and both these curves shift in response to nonprice variables. Some basic econometric techniques, such as regression analysis, are presented later in this chapter; others are too complex to be taken up here.[1]

---

[1]See J. Johnston, *Econometric Methods* (3d ed.; New York: McGraw-Hill, 1984); J. Kmenta, *Elements of Econometrics* (2d ed.; New York: Macmillan Co., 1986); or E. Berndt, *The Practice of Econometrics* (Reading, MA: Addison-Wesley, 1991).

Consumer interviews and market experiments are also widely used, as indicated in the next three sections.

Consumer Interviews

To obtain information concerning the demand function for a particular product, firms frequently interview consumers and administer questionnaires concerning their buying habits, motives, and intentions. Firms may also run focus groups in an attempt to discern consumers' tastes. For example, a firm might ask a random sample of consumers how much more gasoline they would purchase if its price were reduced by 5 percent. Or, a market researcher might ask a sample of consumers whether they liked a new type of perfume better than a leading existing brand, and if so, how much more they would be willing to pay for it (than for the existing brand).

Unfortunately, consumer surveys of this sort have many well-known limitations. The direct approach of simply asking people how much they would buy of a particular commodity at particular prices often does not seem to work very well. Frequently, the answers provided by consumers to such a hypothetical question are not very accurate. However, more subtle approaches can be useful. Interviews indicated that most buyers of a particular baby food selected it on their doctor's recommendation and that most of them knew very little about prices of substitutes. This information, together with other data, suggested that the price elasticity of demand was quite low in absolute value.[2]

Despite the limitations of consumer interviews and questionnaires, many managers believe that such surveys can reveal a great deal about how their firms can serve the market better. For example, the Campbell Soup Company's researchers contacted close to 110,000 people to talk about the taste, preparation, and nutritional value of food. On the basis of these interviews, Campbell changed the seasonings in five Le Menu dinners and introduced a line of low-salt soups (called Special Request). Some of the factors influencing the quality of survey results can be quite subtle. For example, according to research findings, there are sometimes advantages in respondents' keypunching answers, rather than verbalizing them, because the respondents tend to answer emotional questions more honestly this way.[3]

---

[2]J. Dean, "Estimating the Price Elasticity of Demand," in E. Mansfield, ed., *Managerial Economics and Operations Research* (4th ed.; New York: Norton, 1980).

[3]*New York Times*, November 8, 1987, p. 4F. Also, see W. Baumol, "The Empirical Determination of Demand Relationships," in *Managerial Economics and Operations Research*, ed. Mansfield.

Market Experiments

Another method of estimating the demand curve for a particular commodity is to carry out direct market experiments. The idea is to vary the price of the product while attempting to keep other market conditions fairly stable (or to take changes in other market conditions into account). For example, a manufacturer of ink conducted an experiment some years ago to determine the price elasticity of demand for its product. It raised the price from 15 cents to 25 cents in four cities and found that demand was quite inelastic. Attempts were made to estimate the cross elasticity of demand with other brands as well.

Controlled laboratory experiments can sometimes be carried out. Consumers are given money and told to shop in a simulated store. The experimenter can vary the prices, packaging, and location of particular products, and see the effects on the consumers' purchasing decisions. While this technique is useful, it suffers from the fact that consumers participating in such an experiment know that their actions are being monitored. For that reason, their behavior may depart from what it normally would be.

Before carrying out a market experiment, weigh the costs against the benefits. Direct experimentation can be expensive or risky because customers may be lost and profits cut by the experiment. For example, if the price of a product is raised as part of an experiment, potential buyers may be driven away. Also, since they are seldom really controlled experiments and since they are often of relatively brief duration and the number of observations is small, experiments often cannot produce all the information that is needed. Nonetheless, market experiments can be of considerable value, as illustrated by the following actual case.

L'eggs: A Market Experiment

L'eggs Products, a subsidiary of the Hanes Corporation, markets L'eggs Pantyhose, the first major nationally branded and advertised hosiery product distributed through food and drug outlets. According to some estimates, it has been the largest-selling single brand in the hosiery industry. Jack Ward, group product manager of the firm, was interested in determining the effect on sales of four temporary promotion alternatives: a 40-cent price reduction for a package containing two pairs, a 25-cent price reduction for a package containing two pairs, a 20-cent price reduction per pair, and a coupon mailed to homes worth 25 cents off if a pair was purchased.[4]

---

[4]The material in this section is based on F. DeBruicker, J. Quelch, and S. Ward, *Cases in Consumer Behavior* (2d ed.; Englewood Cliffs, NJ: Prentice-Hall, 1986).

To test these four promotion alternatives, Jerry Clawson, director of marketing research, decided that each would be implemented in a carefully chosen test market, and the results would be compared with another market where no unusual promotion was carried out. Specifically, there was a 40-cent reduction (for two pairs) in Syracuse, New York; a 25-cent reduction (for two pairs) in Columbus, Ohio; a 20-cent reduction (for one pair) in Denver, Colorado; and a 25-cent coupon in Cincinnati, Ohio. The results in these markets were compared with those in Boise, Idaho, where no special promotion occurred.

According to the firm's sales research group, the results were as follows: "The two for 40¢-off promotion (Syracuse) was the most effective with a net short-term cumulative increase in sales of 53 percent felt over six weeks. The 20¢ price-off promotion (Denver) was the second most effective, with a net cumulative short-term increase of 20 percent felt over eight weeks. . . . The 25¢ coupon promotion (Cincinnati) was the least effective with a 3 percent short-term increase in sales felt over eight weeks."[5]

This is an example of how firms go about obtaining information concerning their market demand functions. In this case, the firm's managers were interested in the effects of both the form and size of the price cut, and they were concerned only with a temporary price cut. In other cases, firms are interested in the effects of more long-term price changes or of changes in product characteristics or advertising. But, regardless of these differences, marketing research of this sort can play an important role in providing data for the estimation of demand functions.

Regression Analysis

Although consumer interviews and direct market experiments are important sources of information concerning demand functions, they are not used as often as regression analysis. Suppose that a firm's demand function is

$$Y = A + B_1 X + B_2 P + B_3 I + B_4 P_r \tag{5.1}$$

where Y is the quantity demanded of the firm's product, X is the selling expense (such as advertising) of the firm, P is the price of its product, I is the disposable income of consumers, and P_r is the price of the competing product sold by its rival. What we want are estimates of the values of A, B_1, B_2, B_3, and B_4. Regression analysis enables us to obtain them from historical data concerning Y, X, P, I, and P_r.

---

[5]Ibid., p. 335. The validity of these results is discussed there also.

CONSULTANT'S CORNER

Marketing Plans at the Stafford Company

The Stafford Company developed a new type of electric drive. When the design engineering for this machine was finished, Stafford's managers began to make long-range plans concerning marketing this product. By means of field surveys and the analysis of published information, the firm's market research personnel estimated that about 10,000 electric drives of this general sort would be sold per year. The share of the total market that Stafford's new product would capture depended on its price. According to the firm's market research department, the relationship between price and market share was as follows:

Price	Market share
$ 800	11.0
900	10.2
1,000	9.2
1,100	8.4
1,200	7.5
1,300	6.6
1,400	5.6

Stafford's managers wanted advice in setting the price for their new drive, and to help determine the optimal price, they wanted a simple equation expressing the annual quantity demanded of the new product as a function of its price. They also wanted whatever information could readily be provided concerning the reliability of this equation. In particular, they were interested in whether they could safely use this equation to estimate the quantity demanded if price were set at $1,500 or $1,600.

Prepare a brief report supplying the information requested. (Note that the figures on market share in the table are expressed in percentage points. Thus, if the price of Stafford's new product is set at $800, it will capture 11.0 percent of the market for electric drives of this general sort, according to the market research department.)

Source: This section is based on an actual case, although the numbers and situation are disguised somewhat.

In the rest of this chapter, we describe the nature and application of regression analysis, a statistical technique that can be used to estimate many types of economic relationships, not just demand functions. We begin with the simple case in which the only factor influencing the quantity demanded is the firm's selling expense, then turn to the more complicated (and realistic) case in which the quantity demanded is affected by more than one factor, as it is in equation (5.1).

Regression analysis describes the way in which one variable is related to another. (As we see later in this chapter, regression techniques can handle more than two variables, but only two are considered at present.) Regression analysis derives an equation that can be used to estimate the unknown value of one variable on the basis of the known value of the other variable. For example, suppose that the Miller Pharmaceutical Company is scheduled to spend

TABLE
5.1

Selling Expense and Sales, Miller Pharmaceutical Company, Sample of Nine Years

Selling expense (millions of dollars)	Sales (millions of units)
1	4
2	6
4	8
8	14
6	12
5	10
8	16
9	16
7	12

$4 million next year on selling expense (for promotion, advertising, and related marketing activities) and it wants to estimate its next-year's sales, on the basis of the data in Table 5.1 regarding its sales and selling expense in the previous nine years. In this case, although the firm's selling expense next year is known, its next year's sales are unknown. Regression analysis describes the way in which the firm's sales are historically related to its selling expense.

Simple Regression Model

As you recall from Chapter 1, a **model** is a simplified or idealized representation of the real world. In this section, we describe the model—that is, the set of simplifying assumptions—on which regression analysis is based. We begin by visualizing a population of all relevant pairs of observations of the independent and dependent variables. For instance, in the case of the Miller Pharmaceutical Company, we visualize a population of pairs of observations concerning sales and selling expense. This population includes all the levels of sales corresponding to all the levels of selling expense in the history of the firm.

The mean of a variable equals the sum of its values divided by their number. Therefore, the mean of a variable that assumes four values, 3, 2, 1, and 0, is $(3 + 2 + 1 + 0)/4$, or 1.5. Regression analysis assumes that *the mean value of Y, given the value of X, is a linear function of X.* In other words, the mean value of the dependent variable is assumed to be a linear function of the independent variable, the equation of this being $A + BX$, as shown in Figure 5.4.

FIGURE

5.4

Regression Model

The mean value of Y, given the value of X, falls on the population regression line.

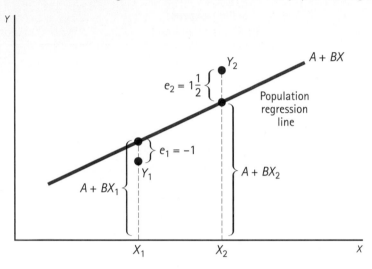

This straight line is called the **population regression line** or the **true regression line.**

Put differently, regression analysis assumes that

$$Y_i = A + BX_i + e_i \tag{5.2}$$

where Y_i is the ith observed value of the dependent variable and X_i is the ith observed value of the independent variable. Essentially, e_i is an **error term,** that is, a random amount that is added to $A + BX_i$ (or subtracted from it if e_i is negative). Because of the presence of this error term, the observed values of Y_i fall around the population regression line, not on it. Hence, as shown in Figure 5.4, if e_1 (the value of the error term for the first observation) is -1, Y_1 lies 1 below the population regression line. And if e_2 (the value of the error term for the second observation) is $+1.50$, Y_2 lies 1.50 above the population regression line. Regression analysis assumes that the values of e_i are independent and their mean value equals zero.[6]

[6]The values of e_1 and e_2 are independent if the probability distribution of e_1 does not depend on the value of e_2 and the probability distribution of e_2 does not depend on the value of e_1. Regression analysis also assumes that the variability of the values of e_i is the same, regardless of the value of X. Many of the tests described subsequently assume too that the values of e_i are normally distributed. For a description of the normal distribution, see Appendix B.

Although the assumptions underlying regression analysis are unlikely to be met completely, they are close enough to the truth in a sufficiently large number of cases that regression analysis is a powerful technique. Nonetheless, it is important to recognize at the start that, if these assumptions are not at least approximately valid, the results of a regression analysis can be misleading.

Sample Regression Line

The purpose of a regression analysis is to obtain the mathematical equation for a line that describes the average relationship between the dependent and independent variables. This line is calculated from the sample observations and is called the **sample** or **estimated regression line**. It should not be confused with the population regression line discussed in the previous section. Whereas the population regression line is based on the entire population, the sample regression line is based on only the sample.

The general expression for the sample regression line is

$$\hat{Y} = a + bX$$

where $\hat{Y}$ is the value of the dependent variable predicted by the regression line, and a and b are estimators of A and B, respectively. (An estimator is a function of the sample observations used to estimate an unknown parameter. For example, the sample mean is an estimator often used to estimate the population mean.) Since this equation implies that $\hat{Y} = a$ when $X = 0$, it follows that a is the value of $\hat{Y}$ at which the line intersects the Y axis. Therefore, a is often called the Y **intercept** of the regression line. And b, which clearly is the slope of the line, measures the change in the predicted value of Y associated with a one-unit increase in X.

Figure 5.5 shows the estimated regression line for the data concerning sales and selling expense of the Miller Pharmaceutical Company. The equation for this regression line is

$$\hat{Y} = 2.536 + 1.504X$$

where $\hat{Y}$ is sales in millions of units and X is selling expense in millions of dollars. What is 2.536? It is the value of a, the estimator of A. What is 1.504? It is the value of b, the estimator of B. For the moment, we are not interested in how this equation was determined; what we want to consider is how it should be interpreted.

At the outset, note the difference between Y and $\hat{Y}$. Whereas Y denotes an *observed* value of sales, $\hat{Y}$ denotes the *computed* or *estimated* value of sales,

FIGURE

5.5

Sample Regression Line

This line is an estimate of the population regression line.

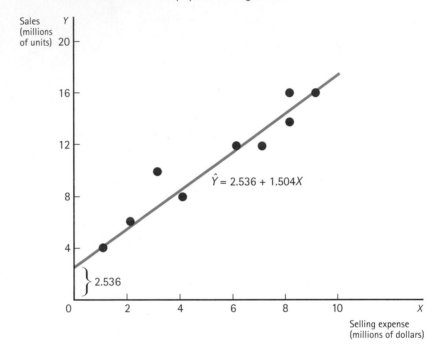

based on the regression line. For example, the first row of Table 5.1 shows that, in the first year, the actual value of sales was 4 million units when selling expense was $1 million. Therefore, Y = 4.0 millions of units when $X = 1$. In contrast, the regression line indicates that $\hat{Y} = 2.536 + 1.504(1)$, or 4.039 millions of units when $X = 1$. In other words, while the regression line predicts that sales will equal 4.039 millions of units when selling expense is $1 million, the actual sales figure under these circumstances (in the first year) was 4 million units.

It is essential to be able to identify and interpret the Y intercept and slope of a regression line. What is the Y intercept of the regression line in the case of the Miller Pharmaceutical Company? It is 2.536 millions of units. This means that, if the firm's selling expense is zero, the estimated sales would be 2.536 millions of units. (As shown in Figure 5.5, 2.536 millions of units is the value of the dependent variable at which the regression line intersects the vertical axis.) What is the slope of the regression line in this case? It is 1.504. This means that the estimated sales go up by 1.504 millions of units when selling expense increases by $1 million.

Method of Least Squares

The method used to determine the values of a and b is the so-called method of least squares. Since the deviation of the ith observed value of Y from the regression line equals $\hat{Y}_i - Y_i$, the sum of these squared deviations equals

$$\sum_{i=1}^{n} (Y_i - \hat{Y}_i)^2 = \sum_{i=1}^{n} (Y_i - a - bX_i)^2 \tag{5.3}$$

where n is the sample size.[7] Using the minimization technique presented in Chapter 2, we can find the values of a and b that minimize the expression in equation (5.3) by differentiating this expression with respect to a and b and setting these partial derivatives equal to zero:

$$\frac{\partial \sum_{i=1}^{n} (Y_i - \hat{Y}_i)^2}{\partial a} = -2 \sum_{i=1}^{n} (Y_i - a - bX_i) = 0 \tag{5.4}$$

$$\frac{\partial \sum_{i=1}^{n} (Y_i - \hat{Y}_i)^2}{\partial b} = -2 \sum_{i=1}^{n} X_i (Y_i - a - bX_i) = 0 \tag{5.5}$$

Solving equations (5.4) and (5.5) simultaneously and letting $\overline{X}$ equal the mean value of X in the sample and $\overline{Y}$ equal the mean value of Y, we find that

$$b = \frac{\sum_{i=1}^{n} (X_i - \overline{X})(Y_i - \overline{Y})}{\sum_{i=1}^{n} (X_i - \overline{X})^2} \tag{5.6}$$

$$a = \overline{Y} - b\overline{X} \tag{5.7}$$

The value of b in equation (5.6) is often called the **estimated regression coefficient**.

---

[7]As pointed out in Chapter 1, Σ is the mathematical summation sign. What does ΣX_i mean? It means that the numbers to the right of the summation sign (that is, the values of X_i) should be summed from the lower limit on i (which is given below the Σ sign) to the upper limit on i (which is given above the Σ sign):

$$\sum_{i=1}^{n} X_i$$

means the same thing as $X_1 + X_2 + \cdots + X_n$.

TABLE
5.2

Computation of ΣX_i, ΣY_i, ΣX_i^2, ΣY_i^2, and $\Sigma X_i Y_i$

	X_i	Y_i	X_i^2	Y_i^2	$X_i Y_i$
	1	4	1	16	4
	2	6	4	36	12
	4	8	16	64	32
	8	14	64	196	112
	6	12	36	144	72
	5	10	25	100	50
	8	16	64	256	128
	9	16	81	256	144
	7	12	49	144	84
Total	50	98	340	1,212	638

$\overline{X} = 50/9 = 5.556$
$\overline{Y} = 98/9 = 10.889$

From a computational point of view, it frequently is easier to use a somewhat different formula for b than the one given in equation (5.6). This alternative formula, which yields the same answer as equation (5.6), is

$$b = \frac{n \sum_{i=1}^{n} X_i Y_i - \left(\sum_{i=1}^{n} X_i\right)\left(\sum_{i=1}^{n} Y_i\right)}{n \sum_{i=1}^{n} X_i^2 - \left(\sum_{i=1}^{n} X_i\right)^2}$$

In the case of the Miller Pharmaceutical Company, Table 5.2 shows the calculation of $\Sigma X_i Y_i$, ΣX_i^2, ΣX_i, and ΣY_i. Based on these calculations,

$$b = \frac{9(638) - (50)(98)}{9(340) - 50^2} = 1.504$$

Therefore, the value of b, the least-squares estimator of B, is 1.504, which is the result given in the previous section. In other words, an increase in selling expense of $1 million results in an increase in estimated sales of about 1.504 millions of units.

Having calculated b, we can readily determine the value of a, the least-squares estimator of A. According to equation (5.7),

$$a = \overline{Y} - b\overline{X}$$

where $\overline{Y}$ is the mean of the values of Y, and $\overline{X}$ is the mean of the values of X. Since, as shown in Table 5.2, $\overline{Y} = 10.889$ and $\overline{X} = 5.556$, it follows that

$$a = 10.889 - 1.504(5.556)$$
$$= 2.536$$

Therefore, the least-squares estimate of A is 2.536 millions of units, which is the result given in the previous section.

Having obtained a and b, it is a simple matter to specify the average relationship in the sample between sales and selling expense for the Miller Pharmaceutical Company. This relationship is

$$\hat{Y} = 2.536 + 1.504X \tag{5.8}$$

where $\hat{Y}$ is measured in millions of units and X is measured in millions of dollars. As we know, this line is often called the *sample regression line*, or the *regression of Y on X*. It is the line presented in the previous section and plotted in Figure 5.5. Now, we see how this line is derived. (However, a computer usually does the calculations.)

To illustrate how a regression line of this sort can be used, suppose that the managers of the firm want to predict the firm's sales if they decide to devote \$4 million to selling expense. Using equation (5.8), they would predict that its sales would be

$$2.536 + 1.504(4) = 8.55. \tag{5.9}$$

Since sales are measured in millions of units, this means that sales would be expected to be 8.55 million units.

Coefficient of Determination

Once the regression line has been calculated, we want to know how well this line fits the data. There can be huge differences in how well a regression line fits a set of data, as shown in Figure 5.6. Clearly, the regression line in panel F of Figure 5.6 provides a much better fit than the regression line in panel B of the same figure. How can we measure how well a regression line fits the data?

The most commonly used measure of the goodness of fit of a regression line is the coefficient of determination. For present purposes, it is not necessary to know the formula for the coefficient of determination, because it is seldom calculated by hand. It is a particular item, often designated by R^2, or R-sq on a computer printout, as we shall see in the section after next.

FIGURE
5.6

Six Regression Lines: Coefficient of Determination
Equals 0, 0.2, 0.4, 0.6, 0.8, and 1.0

When there is only one independent variable, the coefficient of determination is often designated by r^2, rather than R^2, but computer printouts generally use R^2, regardless of the number of independent variables. We use R^2 here, even though there is only one independent variable. See footnote 8.

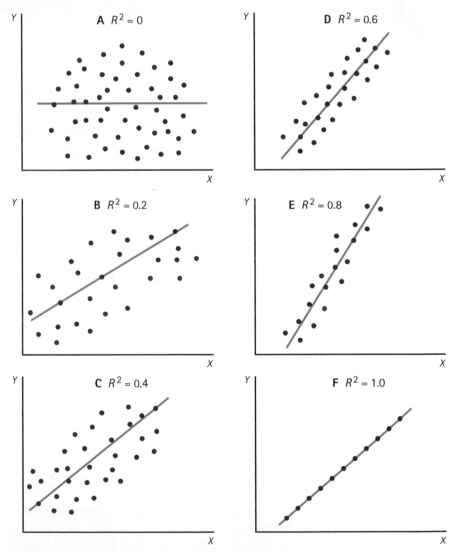

How the Japanese Motorcycle Makers Used the Coefficient of Determination

In late 1982, Harley-Davidson asked the International Trade Commission (ITC), a federal agency that investigates possible injuries to U.S. firms and workers from imports, for relief from Japanese imports of heavyweight motorcycles. According to Harley-Davidson, the Japanese were selling their motorcycles at prices too low for it to meet. On the basis of Section 201 of the 1974 Trade Act, the ITC can impose tariffs or quotas on imported goods to provide "additional time to permit a seriously injured domestic industry to become competitive." But to receive such tariff or quota relief, the industry must demonstrate that the injuries it suffers are due to increased imports, not some other cause such as bad management or a recession.

Harley-Davidson's petition to the ITC was contested by the major Japanese motorcycle makers: Honda, Kawasaki, Suzuki, and Yamaha. One of their arguments was that general economic conditions, not Japanese imports, were the principal cause of Harley-Davidson's declining share of the market. In other words, they attributed Harley-Davidson's problems to the recession of the early 1980s. They pointed out that heavyweight motorcycles, which cost about $7,000, were a "big-ticket luxury consumer product" and that their sales would be expected to fall in a recession.

To back up this argument, John Reilly of ICF, Inc., the Japanese firms' chief economic consultant, calculated a regression, where Harley-Davidson's sales were the dependent variable and the level of blue-collar employment (a measure of general economic conditions) was the independent variable. He showed that the coefficient of determination was about 0.73. Then, he calculated a regression where Harley-Davidson's sales were the dependent variable, and the level of sales of Japanese motorcycles was the independent variable. He showed that the coefficient of determination was only about 0.22. From this comparison of the two coefficients of determination, he concluded that Harley-Davidson's sales were much more closely related to general economic conditions than to the level of sales of Japanese motorcycles.

Of course, this analysis tells us nothing about the effects of the price of Japanese motorcycles on Harley-Davidson's sales and profits. From many points of view, what was needed was an estimate of the market demand function for Harley-Davidson's motorcycles. Such an analysis would have related Harley-Davidson's sales to the price of Harley-Davidson's motorcycles, the price of Japanese motorcycles, the level of disposable income, and other variables discussed in Chapter 3. In any event, despite the evidence cited, the Japanese motorcycle manufacturers did not prevail. On the contrary, the ITC supported Harley-Davidson's petition, and on April 1, 1983, President Ronald Reagan imposed a substantial tariff (almost 50 percent) on imported (large) motorcycles.*

*See "Revving up for Relief: Harley-Davidson at the ITC," a case in the Study Guide accompanying this textbook. For further discussion, see J. Gomez-Ibanez and J. Kalt, *Cases in Microeconomics* (Englewood Cliffs, NJ: Prentice-Hall, 1990); P.C. Reid, *Well Made in America;* Lessons from Harley-Davidson on Being the Best (New York: McGraw-Hill, 1989); and *New York Times,* July 20, 1997.

The value of the coefficient of determination varies between 0 and 1. *The closer it is to 1, the better the fit; the closer it is to 0, the poorer the fit.* In the case of the Miller Pharmaceutical Company, the coefficient of determination between sales and selling expense is 0.97, which indicates a very good fit. To get a feel for what a particular value of the coefficient of determination means, look at the six panels of Figure 5.6. Panel A shows that, if the coefficient of determination is 0, there is no relationship at all between the independent and dependent variables. Panel B shows that, if the coefficient of determination is 0.2, the regression line fits the data rather poorly. Panel C shows that, if it is 0.4, the regression line fits better but not very well. Panel D shows that, if it is 0.6, the fit is reasonably good. Panel E shows that, if it is 0.8, the fit is good. Finally, panel F shows that, if it is 1.0, the fit is perfect.[8] (A fuller discussion of the coefficient of determination is provided in the appendix to this chapter.

Multiple Regression

In previous sections of this chapter, we discussed regression techniques in the case in which there is only one independent variable. In practical applications of regression techniques, it frequently is necessary and desirable to include two or more independent variables. Now, we extend the treatment of regression to the case in which there is more than one independent variable.

Whereas a **simple regression** includes only one independent variable, a **multiple regression** includes two or more independent variables. Multiple regressions ordinarily are carried out on computers with the aid of statistical software packages like Minitab, SAS, or SPSS. So, there is no reason for you to learn how to do them by hand. The first step in multiple regression analysis is to identify the independent variables and specify the mathematical form of the equation relating the mean value of the dependent variable to these independent variables.

---

[8]If one is doing the calculations by hand, a convenient formula for the coefficient of determination is

$$r^2 = \frac{\left[n \sum_{i=1}^{n} X_i Y_i - \left(\sum_{i=1}^{n} X_i \right)\left(\sum_{i=1}^{n} Y_i \right) \right]^2}{\left[n \sum_{i=1}^{n} X_1^2 - \left(\sum_{i=1}^{n} X_i \right)^2 \right]\left[n \sum_{i=1}^{n} Y_1^2 - \left(\sum_{i=1}^{n} Y_i \right)^2 \right]}$$

Table 5.2 contains the quantities to be inserted in this formula.

Note too that the square root of r^2, called the **correlation coefficient**, is also used to measure how well a simple regression equation fits the data. (The sign of the square root is the same as that of b.)

As pointed out in the note to Figure 5.6, computer printouts generally refer to the coefficient of determination as R^2, although statisticians often call it r^2 when there is only one independent variable.

In the case of the Miller Pharmaceutical Company, suppose that the firm's executives feel that its sales depend on its price, as well on its selling expense. More specifically, they assume that

$$Y_i = A + B_1X_i + B_2P_i + e_i \qquad (5.10)$$

where X_i is the selling expense (in millions of dollars) of the firm during the ith year and P_i is the price (in dollars) of the firm's product during the ith year (measured as a deviation from \$10, the current price). Of course, B_2 is assumed to be negative. This is a different model from that in equation (5.2). Here, we assume that Y_i (the firm's sales in the ith year) depends on two independent variables, not one. Of course, there is no reason why more independent variables cannot be added, so long as data are available concerning their values and there is good reason to expect them to affect Y_i. But, to keep matters simple, we assume that the firm's executives believe that only selling expense and price should be included as independent variables.[9]

The object of multiple regression analysis is to estimate the unknown constants A, B_1, and B_2 in equation (5.10). Just as in the case of simple regression, these constants are estimated by finding the value of each that minimizes the sum of the squared deviations of the observed values of the dependent variable from the values of the dependent variable predicted by the regression equation. Suppose that a is an estimator of A, b_1 is an estimator of B_1, and b_2 is an estimator of B_2. Then, the value of the dependent variable Y_i predicted by the estimated regression equation is

$$\hat{Y}_i = a + b_1X_i + b_2P_i$$

and the deviation of this predicted value from the actual value of the dependent variable is

$$Y_i - \hat{Y}_i = Y_i - a - b_1X_i - b_2P_i$$

If these deviations are squared and summed, the result is

$$\sum_{i=1}^{n} (Y_i - \hat{Y}_i)^2 = \sum_{i=1}^{n} (Y_i - a - b_1X_i - b_2P_i)^2 \qquad (5.11)$$

where n is the number of observations in the sample. As pointed out earlier, we choose the values of a, b_1, and b_2 that minimize the expression in equation (5.11). These estimates are called *least-squares estimates*, as in the case of simple regression.

[9]As in the case of simple regression, it is assumed that the mean value of e_i is zero and that the values of e_i are statistically independent (recall footnote 6).

Sales, Selling Expense, and Price, Miller Pharmaceutical Company, Sample of Nine Years

Selling expense (millions of dollars)	Sales (millions of units)	Price (less $10)
2	6	0
1	4	1
8	16	2
5	10	3
6	12	4
4	8	5
7	12	6
9	16	7
8	14	8

Computer programs, described in the following section, are available to calculate these least-squares estimates. Based on the data in Table 5.3, the computer output shows that $b_1 = 1.758$, $b_2 = -0.352$, and $a = 2.529$. Consequently, the estimated regression equation is

$$Y_i = 2.529 + 1.758X_i - 0.352P_i \qquad (5.12)$$

The estimated value of B_1 is 1.758, as contrasted with our earlier estimate of B, which was 1.504. In other words, a $1 million increase in selling expense results in an increase in estimated sales of 1.758 million units, as contrasted with 1.504 million units in the simple regression in equation (5.8). The reason these estimates differ is that the present estimate of the effect of selling expense on sales holds constant the price, whereas the earlier estimate did not hold this factor constant. Since this factor affects sales, the earlier estimate is likely to be a biased estimate of the effect of selling expense on sales.[10]

[10]Of course, this regression is supposed to be appropriate only when X_i and P_i vary in a certain limited range. If P_i is large and X_i is small, the regression would predict a negative value of sales, which obviously is inadmissible. But, as long as the regression is not used to make predictions for values of X_i and P_i outside the range of the data given in Table 5.3, this is no problem. For simplicity, we assume in equation (5.10) that the effect of price on the mean value of sales (holding selling expense constant) can be regarded as linear in the relevant range. Alternatively, we could have assumed that it was quadratic or the constant-elasticity demand function discussed in Chapter 3 might have been used.

Color Balance and Shelf-Life Performance of Polaroid Film

In 1947, the prototype of the instant camera was demonstrated to the Optical Society of America. A year later, the Polaroid made the first instant camera and film available to the public. The single-step photographic process enabled pictures to be developed in 60 seconds. Unfortunately, Polaroid did not see the potential for the digital camera fast enough, and although they subsequently developed digital cameras, they were no longer the leader in the photography market. In addition, "one-hour" photo developing at the local drugstore, supermarket, or photo shop took away some of the advantage of Polaroid's "instant" pictures. In 2001, they voluntarily declared bankruptcy.

Sixty five percent of the assets (and trademark name) of the company were purchased by One Equity Partners (part of J.P. Morgan Chase) in 2002. Primary PDC (the interests of the old Polaroid Corporation

own the other 35% of the new Polaroid Corporation. According to the new corporate description by Yahoo Finance, "the company makes instant film and camera, digital cameras, professional imaging equipment, and security ID-card systems." Its I-Zone instant camera is the nation's top-selling camera. So, while digital cameras are prevalent, many people take pictures using film cameras.

Regression analysis is important in many aspects of managerial economics, not just in estimating demand functions. For example, this technique helped the Polaroid Corporation, a leading manufacturer of cameras and film, to supply film at the peak of its usefulness. An extremely important consideration to Polaroid was how well films maintain their sensitivity, and whether they provided satisfactory photographic results and for how long. Information of this sort, together with

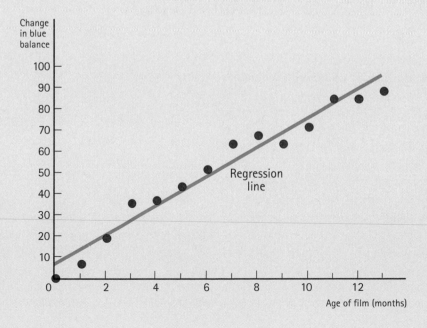

data concerning average elapsed time between the purchase and utilization of film, enabled Polaroid to make manufacturing adjustments to help consumers get good performance from Polaroid film.

One important characteristic of film is color balance—its ability to produce color. To see the effects of film age on color balance, Polaroid took 14 samples at monthly intervals, up to 13 months after manufacture. For each sample, the change in blue balance was measured. As shown in the graph, the color balance becomes bluer (that is, "cooler," not as "warm") as the film ages.

Using the techniques described in this chapter, Polaroid estimated the regression line:

$$\hat{Y} = 8.194 + 6.756X,$$

where Y is the change in blue balance and X is the age (in months) of the film. The coefficient of determination was 0.966, which indicates a close fit to the data.

According to Polaroid officials, this application of regression analysis was important. Together with data regarding consumer purchase and use patterns, it enabled "Polaroid to manufacture film that shifted those characteristics which determine picture quality to their optimum setting by the time the film was being used. In essence, Polaroid had the information to compensate in its manufacturing process for crucial alterations in film performance that happened as a result of the aging process."*

*D. Anderson, D. Sweeney, and T. Williams, *Statistics for Business and Economics* (3d ed.; St. Paul, MN: West, 1987), p. 523.

ANALYZING MANAGERIAL DECISIONS

How Good are *Ward's* Projections of Auto Output?

The automobile industry and its suppliers, as well as other industries and government agencies, try in a variety of ways to forecast auto output in the United States. Each month, *Ward's Automotive Reports* asks eight U.S. automakers to state their domestic production plans for the next three to eight months. The following figure shows actual domestic auto production and *Ward's* projections made at the beginning of each quarter. The average error is about a half-million cars per year, or about 6 percent.

To obtain a more precise estimate of the relationship between *Ward's* projections and actual output, Ethan Harris regressed actual output *(Y)* on *Ward's* projection *(X)* and the error in *Ward's* projection during the previous quarter *(E)*, the result being

$$Y = 0.275 + 0.909X + 0.277E$$

The multiple coefficient of determination equals 0.838.

(a) If *Ward's* projection is 1 million cars higher in one quarter than in another, would you expect actual output to be 1 million cars higher? Why or why not? (b) If *Ward's* projection was 100,000 cars too high in the previous quarter, is it likely that actual output would be higher than if the projection had been 100,000 cars too low in the previous

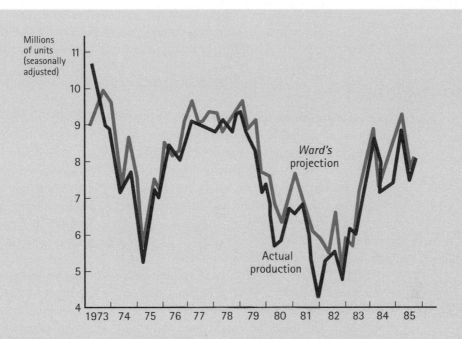

quarter? (c) Does the regression provide a good or poor fit to the data?

SOLUTION (a) No. According to the equation, if X increases by 1 million, Y would be expected to increase by 0.909 times 1 million, or 909,000 (if E remains the same). (b) Under these circumstances, it is likely that actual output would be higher than it would if the projection had been 100,000 cars too low in the previous quarter. To see this, note that the regression coefficient of E in the regression equation is positive. Therefore, increases in E tend to be associated with increases in Y. (c) The fact that the multiple coefficient of determination is about 0.8 indicates that the fit is good (about like that in panel E of Figure 5.6).*

---

*For further discussion, see E. Harris, "Forecasting Automobile Output," *Federal Reserve Bank of New York Quarterly Review*, Winter 1985–86, reprinted in *Managerial Economics and Operations Research*, ed. Mansfield.

Software Packages and Computer Printouts

With few exceptions, regression analyses are carried out on computers, not by hand. Therefore, it is important that you know how to interpret computer printouts showing the results of regression calculations. Because there is a wide variety of "canned" programs for calculating regressions, no single format or list of items is printed out. However, the various kinds of printouts are sufficiently similar that it is worthwhile looking at two illustrations—Minitab and SAS—in some detail.

Figure 5.7 shows the Minitab printout from the multiple regression of the Miller Pharmaceutical Company's sales (designated as C1) on its selling expense (C2) and price (C3). According to this printout, the regression equation is

$$C1 = 2.529 + 1.758C2 - 0.352C3$$

The column headed "Coef" shows the estimated regression coefficient of each independent variable (called a "Predictor" on the printout). The intercept of the regression is the top figure in this vertical column (the figure in the horizontal row where the "Predictor" is "Constant"). The coefficient of determination (called R-sq) is shown in the middle of the printout. For a multiple regression, the coefficient of determination is often called the *multiple coefficient of determination.*[11]

Figure 5.8 shows the SAS printout for the same regression. To find the intercept of the equation, obtain the figure (2.529431) in the horizontal row labeled "INTERCEP" that is in the vertical column called "Parameter Estimate." To find the regression coefficient of selling expense, obtain the figure (1.758049) in the horizontal row labeled "C2" that is in the vertical column called "Parameter Estimate." To find the regression coefficient of price, obtain the figure (−0.351870) in the horizontal row labeled "C3" that is in the vertical column called "Parameter Estimate." The multiple coefficient of determination is the figure (0.9943) to the right of "R-square."

Interpreting the Computer Printout

The following additional statistics are also of considerable importance: the standard error of estimate, the F statistic, and the t statistic. Each is discussed briefly next. For more detailed discussions of each, see any business statistics textbook.[12]

The Standard Error of Estimate

A measure often used to indicate the accuracy of a regression model is the standard error of estimate, which is *a measure of the amount of scatter of individ-*

---

[11]The positive square root of the multiple coefficient of determination is called the *multiple correlation coefficient,* denoted R. It too is sometimes used to measure how well a multiple regression equation fits the data.

The *unadjusted* multiple coefficient of determination—R-sq in Figure 5.7—can never decrease as another independent variable is added; a related measure without this property is the *adjusted* multiple coefficient of determination—R-sq (adj.) in Figure 5.7. The latter is often denoted $\bar{R}^2$.

[12]For example, E. Mansfield, *Statistics for Business and Economics* (5th ed.; New York: Norton, 1994).

FIGURE 5.7   Minitab Printout of Results of Multiple Regression

```
MTB > regress c1 on 2 predictors in c2 and c3

The regression equation is
C1 = 2.53 + 1.76 C2 - 0.352 C3

Predictor           Coef         Stdev      t-ratio         p
Constant          2.5294        0.2884         8.77     0.000
C2               1.75805       0.06937        25.34     0.000
C3              -0.35187       0.07064        -4.98     0.002

s = 0.3702        R-sq = 99.4%     R-sq(adj) = 99.2%

Analysis of Variance

SOURCE        DF            SS           MS          F         p
Regression     2       144.067       72.033     525.72     0.000
Error          6         0.822        0.137
Total          8       144.889

SOURCE        DF        SEQ SS
C2             1       140.667
C3             1         3.399
```

FIGURE 5.8   SAS Printout of Results of Multiple Regression

```
Dependent Variable: C1

Analysis of Variance

                          Sum of        Mean
Source          DF       Squares       Square      F Value     Prob>F

Model            2     144.06678     72.03339      525.718     0.0001
Error            6       0.82211      0.13702
C Total          8     144.88889

     Root MSE      0.37016     R-square       0.9943
     Dep Mean     10.88889     Adj R-sq       0.9924
     C.V.          3.39944

Parameter Estimates

                  Parameter      Standard      T for H0:
Variable    DF     Estimate         Error    Parameter=0    Prob > |T|

INTERCEP     1     2.529431    0.28842968          8.770        0.0001
C2           1     1.758049    0.06937127         25.343        0.0001
C3           1    -0.351870    0.07064425         -4.981        0.0025
```

FIGURE
5.9

Four Regression Lines: Standard Error of Estimate Equals 1.5, 1.0, 0.5, and 0.25

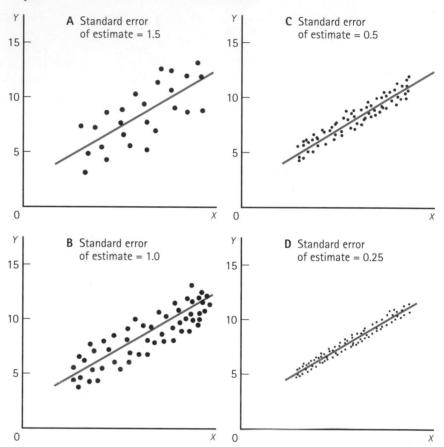

ual observations about the regression line. The standard error of estimate is denoted by "s" in the Minitab printout in Figure 5.7 and by "ROOT MSE" in the SAS printout in Figure 5.8. A comparison of these printouts shows that, in the Miller Pharmaceutical multiple regression, the standard error is about 0.37 million units of sales. Of course, the answer is always the same, no matter which package we use.

To illustrate what the standard error of estimate measures, consider Figure 5.9. In panel A, the standard error of estimate is 1.5, which is much higher than in panel D, where it is 0.25. This is reflected in the much greater scatter in the points around the regression line in panel A than in panel D. As pointed out already, what the standard error of estimate measures is the amount of such scatter. Clearly, the amount of scatter decreases as we move from panel A to panel B to panel C to panel D. Similarly, the standard error of estimate decreases as we move from panel A to panel B to panel C to panel D.

The standard error of estimate is useful in constructing prediction intervals, that is, intervals within which there is a specified probability that the dependent variable will lie. If this probability is set at 0.95, a very approximate prediction interval is

$$\hat{Y} \pm 2s_e \tag{5.13}$$

where $\hat{Y}$ is the predicted value of the dependent variable based on the sample regression and s_e is the standard error of estimate. For example, if the predicted value of the Miller Pharmaceutical Company's sales is 11 million units, the probability is about 0.95 that the firm's sales will be between 10.26 ($=11 - 2 \times 0.37$) million units and 11.74 ($=11 + 2 \times 0.37$) million units. However, it is important to note that equation (5.13) is a good approximation only if the independent variable is close to its mean; if this is not true, more complicated formulas must be used instead.[13]

The F Statistic

Frequently, the analyst wants to know whether any of the independent variables really influences the dependent variable. In the case of the Miller Pharmaceutical Company, the marketing director may ask whether the data indicate that either selling expense or price really influences the firm's sales. To answer such a question, one utilizes the F statistic, which is also included in the computer printout. The value of F is provided in the fifth horizontal row from the bottom of figures in the Minitab printout (Figure 5.7) and in the top horizon-

---

[13]The formula for the standard error of estimate is

$$\left[\sum_{i=1}^{n} (Y_i - \hat{Y}_i)^2/(n - k - 1)\right]^{0.5}$$

where k is the number of independent variables.

If the error term is normally distributed (see Appendix B for a description of the normal distribution), the exact prediction interval (with 0.95 probability) is

$$\hat{Y} \pm t_{0.025}s_e \left[\frac{n + 1}{n} + \frac{(X^* - \bar{X})^2}{\sum_{i=1}^{n} X_i^2 - \left(\sum_{i=1}^{n} X_i\right)^2/n}\right]^{0.5}$$

where $t_{0.025}$ is the value of a variable with the t distribution with $(n - 2)$ degrees of freedom that is exceeded with probability of 0.025, X^* is the value of the independent variable, and n is the sample size. (The t distribution is taken up in Appendix B.) This assumes that there is only one independent variable. For further discussion, see Mansfield, *Statistics for Business and Economics*.

tal row of figures in the SAS printout (Figure 5.8). Both printouts indicate that the value of F in the Miller Pharmaceutical case equals about 525.72.

Large values of F tend to imply that at least one of the independent variables has an effect on the dependent variable. Tables of the F distribution, a probability distribution named (or initialed) after the famous British statistician R. A. Fisher, are used to determine *the probability that an observed value of the F statistic could have arisen by chance, given that none of the independent variables has any effect on the dependent variable* (see Appendix B). This probability too is shown in the computer printout. It is denoted by "p" (immediately to the right of F) in the Minitab printout, and by "Prob.F" (immediately to the right of F VALUE) in the SAS printout. The value of this probability is 0.0001 (SAS) or 0.000 (Minitab); the difference is due to rounding.

Having this probability in hand, it is easy to answer the marketing director's question. Clearly, the probability is extremely small—only about 1 in 10,000—that one could have obtained such a strong relationship between the dependent and independent variables sheerly by chance. Therefore, the evidence certainly suggests that selling expense or price (or both) really influences the firm's sales.

The t Statistic

Managers and analysts often are interested in whether a particular independent variable influences the dependent variable. For example, the president of the Miller Pharmaceutical Company may want to determine whether the amount allocated to selling expense really affects the firm's sales. As we know from equation (5.12), the least-squares estimate of B_1 is 1.758, which suggests that selling expense has an effect on sales. But this least-squares estimate varies from one sample to another, and by chance it may be positive even if the true value of B_1 is zero.

To test whether the true value of B_1 is zero, we must look at the t statistic of B_1, which is presented in the printout. For Minitab, recall that B_1 is the regression coefficient of C2, since selling expense is denoted by C2. Therefore, to find the t statistic for B_1, we must locate the horizontal row of figures in the printout where the "Predictor" is C2 and obtain the figure in the vertical column called "t-ratio." If SAS is used, find the horizontal row of figures where the "Variable" is C2 and obtain the figure in the vertical column called "T for H0: Parameter = 0." If the error terms in the regression (that is, e_i) are normally distributed, the t statistic has a well-known probability distribution—the t distribution (see Appendix B).

All other things equal, the bigger is the value of the t statistic (in absolute terms), the smaller the probability that the true value of the regression coefficient in question really is zero. Based on the t distribution, it is possible to calculate *the probability, if the true value of the regression coefficient is zero, that the t statistic is as large (in absolute terms) as we observe.* This probability too is presented in the computer printout. For both Minitab and SAS, this probability is immediately to the right of the t statistic. For Minitab, it is in the vertical column labeled "p"; for SAS, it is in the vertical column labeled "Prob > T." Regardless of whether Minitab or SAS is used, this probability is shown to be about 0.0001 (see Figures 5.7 and 5.8).

Given this probability, we can readily answer the question put forth by the president of the Miller Pharmaceutical Company. Recall that the president wanted to know whether the amount allocated to selling expense really affects the firm's sales. Given the results obtained in the previous paragraph, it seems extremely likely that the amount allocated to selling expense really does affect sales. After all, according to the previous paragraph, the probability is only about 1 in 10,000 that chance alone would have resulted in as large a t statistic (in absolute terms) as we found, based on the firm's previous experience.[14]

Multicollinearity

One important problem that can arise in multiple regression studies is **multicollinearity**, a situation in which two or more independent variables are very highly correlated. In the case of the Miller Pharmaceutical Company, suppose that there had been a perfect linear relationship in the past between the firm's selling expense and its price. In a case of this sort, it is impossible to estimate the regression coefficients of both independent variables (X and P) because the data provide no information concerning the effect of one independent variable, holding the other independent variable constant. All that can be observed is the

---

[14]Note that this is a *two-tailed test* of the hypothesis that selling expense has no effect on sales. That is, it is a test of this hypothesis against the alternative hypothesis that the true regression coefficient of selling expense is either positive or negative. In many cases, a *one-tailed test*—for example, in which the alternative hypothesis states that the true regression coefficient is positive only—may be more appropriate.

Frequently, a manager would like to obtain an interval estimate for the true value of a regression coefficient. In other words, he or she wants an interval that has a particular probability of including the true value of this regression coefficient. To find an interval that has a probability equal to $(1 - \alpha)$ of including this true value, you can calculate

$$b_1 \pm t_{\alpha/2}s_{b1} \qquad (5.14)$$

where s_{b1} is the standard error of b_1 (in the horizontal row labeled "C2" and the vertical column labeled "Stdev" in the Minitab printout, or in the horizontal row labeled "C2" and the vertical column labeled "Standard Error" in the SAS printout) and where $t_{\alpha/2}$ is the $\alpha/2$ point on the t distribution with $(n - k - 1)$ degrees of freedom (see Appendix B). If α is set equal to 0.05, you obtain an interval that has a 95 percent probability of including B_1. In the case of the Miller Pharmaceutical Company, since, $B_1 = 1.758$, $s_{b1} = 0.069$, and $t_{0.025} = 2.447$ it follows that a 95 percent confidence interval for B_1 is

$$1.758 \pm 2.447 \, (0.069)$$

or 1.589 to 1.927. For further discussion, see any business statistics textbook.

effect of both independent variables together, given that they both move together in the way they have in previous years.

Regression analysis estimates the effect of each independent variable by seeing how much effect this one independent variable has on the dependent variable when other independent variables are held constant. If two independent variables move together in a rigid, lockstep fashion, there is no way to tell how much effect each has separately; all we can observe is the effect of both combined. If there is good reason to believe that the independent variables will continue to move in lockstep in the future as they have in the past, multicollinearity does not prevent us from using regression analysis to predict the dependent variable. Since the two independent variables are perfectly correlated, one of them in effect stands for both and we therefore need use only one in the regression analysis. However, if the independent variables cannot be counted on to continue to move in lockstep, this procedure is dangerous, since it ignores the effect of the excluded independent variable.

In reality, you seldom encounter cases in which independent variables are perfectly correlated, but you often encounter cases in which independent variables are so highly correlated that, although it is possible to estimate the regression coefficient of each variable, these regression coefficients cannot be estimated at all accurately. To cope with such situations, it sometimes is possible to alter the independent variables in such a way as to reduce multicollinearity. Suppose that a managerial economist wants to estimate a regression equation where the quantity demanded per year of a certain good is the dependent variable and the average price of this good and disposable income of U.S. consumers are the independent variables. If disposable income is measured in money terms (that is, without adjustment for changes in the price level), there may be a high correlation between the independent variables. But if disposable income is measured in real terms (that is, with adjustment for changes in the price level), this correlation may be reduced considerably. Therefore, the managerial economist may decide to measure disposable income in real rather than money terms to reduce multicollinearity.

If techniques of this sort cannot reduce multicollinearity, there may be no alternative but to acquire new data that do not contain the high correlation among the independent variables. Whether you (or your board of directors) like it or not, there may be no way to estimate accurately the regression coefficient of a particular independent variable that is very highly correlated with some other independent variable.

Serial Correlation

In addition to multicollinearity, another important problem that can occur in regression analysis is that the error terms (the values of e_i) are not indepen-

FIGURE
5.10

Serial Correlation of Error Terms

If the error term in one year is positive, the error term in the next year is almost always positive. If the error term in one year is negative, the error term in the next year is almost always negative.

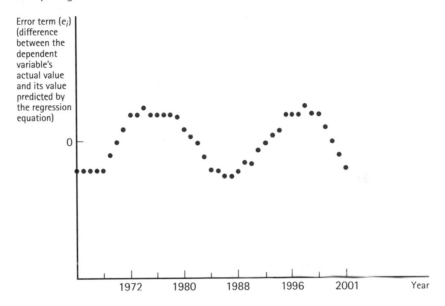

dent; instead, they are serially correlated. For example, Figure 5.10 shows a case in which, if the error term in one period is positive, the error term in the next period is almost always positive. Similarly, if the error term in one period is negative, the error term in the next period almost always is negative. In such a situation, we say that the errors are *serially correlated* (or *autocorrelated*, which is another term for the same thing).[15] Because this violates the assumptions underlying regression analysis, it is important that we be able to detect its occurrence. (Recall that regression analysis assumes that the values of e_i are independent.)

To see whether serial correlation is present in the error terms in a regression, we can use the Durbin-Watson test. Let $\hat{e}_i$ be the difference between Y_i

---

[15]This is a case of positive serial correlation. (It is the sort of situation frequently encountered in managerial economics.) If the error term in one period tends to be positive (negative) and if the error term in the previous period is negative (positive), this is a case of negative serial correlation. More is said about this subsequently.

and $\hat{Y}_i$, the value of Y_i predicted by the sample regression. To apply the Durbin-Watson test, we (or in most cases, the computer) must calculate

$$d = \frac{\displaystyle\sum_{i=2}^{n} (\hat{e}_i - \hat{e}_{i-1})^2}{\displaystyle\sum_{i=1}^{n} \hat{e}_i^2} \tag{5.15}$$

Durbin and Watson provided tables that show whether d is so high or so low that the hypothesis that there is no serial correlation should be rejected. (Note that d is often called the Durbin-Watson statistic.)

Suppose we want to test this hypothesis against the alternative hypothesis that there is **positive** serial correlation. (Positive serial correlation would mean that e_i is directly related to e_{i-1}, as in Figure 5.10.) If so, we should reject the hypothesis of no serial correlation if $d < d_L$ and accept this hypothesis if $d > d_U$. If $d_L \leq d \leq d_U$, the test is inconclusive. The values of d_L and d_U are shown in Appendix Table 7. (Note that these values depend on the sample size n and on k, the number of independent variables in the regression.) On the other hand, suppose the alternative hypothesis is that there is **negative** serial correlation. (Negative serial correlation means that e_i is inversely related to e_{i-1}.) If so, we should reject the hypothesis of no serial correlation if $d > 4 - d_L$ and accept this hypothesis if $d < 4 - d_U$. If $4 - d_U \leq d \leq 4 - d_L$, the test is inconclusive.[16]

One way to deal with the problem of serial correlation, if it exists, is to take first differences of all the independent and dependent variables in the regression. For example, in the case of the Miller Pharmaceutical Company, we might use the change in sales relative to the previous year (rather than the level of sales) as the dependent variable. And the change in selling expense relative to the previous year (rather than the level of selling expense) and the change in price relative to the previous year (rather than the level of price) might be used as the independent variables in the regression.[17]

---

[16]For a two-tailed test of both positive and negative serial correlation, reject the hypothesis of no serial correlation if $d < d_L$ or if $d > 4 - d_L$, and accept this hypothesis if $d_U < d < 4 - d_U$. Otherwise, the test is inconclusive. For a two-tailed test, the significance level is double the significance level shown in Appendix Table 7.

[17]The use of first differences, while useful in some cases, is not always appropriate. For further discussion, see Johnston, *Econometric Methods.*

It is also important to avoid specification errors, which result when one or more significant explanatory variables is not included in the regression. If specification errors arise, the estimated regression coefficients may be biased and the regression equation may not predict very well. Also, problems can arise if the independent variables in a regression contain substantial measurement errors, since the regression coefficients of these variables often tend to be biased toward zero.

FIGURE

5.11

Residuals Indicating That the Variation in the Error Terms Is Not Constant

As you can see, the residuals vary less when X is small than when it is large.

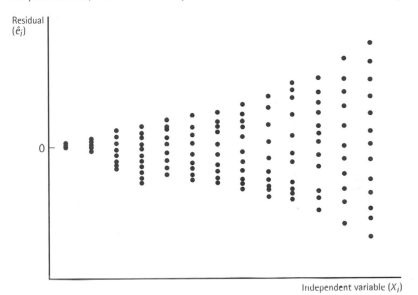

Further Analysis of the Residuals

In the previous section, we used $\hat{e}_i$ (the difference between the actual value of Y_i and its value predicted by the sample regression) to test for serial correlation. Since it is a measure of the extent to which Y_i *cannot* be explained by the regression, $\hat{e}_i$ is often called the **residual** for the *i*th observation. Now we describe additional ways in which the residuals—that is, the values of $\hat{e}_i$—can be used to test whether the assumptions underlying regression analysis are met. We begin by plotting the value of each residual against the value of the independent variable. (For simplicity, we suppose only one independent variable.) That is, we plot $\hat{e}_i$ against X_i, which is the independent variable.

Suppose that the plot is as shown in Figure 5.11. As you can see, the values of the residuals are much more variable when X_i is large than when it is small. In other words, the variation in $\hat{e}_i$ increases as X_i increases. Since regression analysis assumes that *the variation in the error terms is the same, regardless of the value of the independent variable*, the plot in Figure 5.11 indicates that this assumption is violated. Two ways to remedy this situation are to use a

FIGURE

5.12

Residuals Indicating That the Relationship between the Dependent and Independent Variables Is Nonlinear, Not Linear

The residuals are negative when X is very small or very large and positive when X is of medium size.

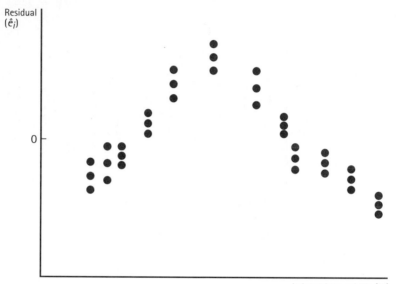

weighted least-squares regression or to change the form of the dependent variable. For example, we might use log Y rather than Y as the dependent variable.[18]

If the plot of $\hat{e}_i$ against X_i looks like Figure 5.12, this is an indication that the relationship between the dependent and independent variables is not linear. When X is very low and very high, the linear regression *overestimates* the dependent variable, as shown by the fact that the residuals tend to be negative. When X is of medium size, the linear regression underestimates the dependent variable, as shown by the fact that the residuals tend to be positive. It appears that a quadratic relationship fits the data better than a linear one. So, rather than assume that equation (5.2) holds, we should assume that

$$Y_i = A + B_1X_i - B_2X_i^2 + e_i$$

Using the multiple regression techniques described previously, the values of A, B_1, and B_2 can be estimated.

[18]For further details, see Johnston, *Econometric Methods*.

Summary

1. An identification problem may occur if price in various periods is plotted against quantity demanded and the resulting relationship is used to estimate the demand curve. Because nonprice variables are not held constant, the demand curve may have shifted over time. Nonetheless, sophisticated econometric methods may be used to estimate the demand function. Also, market experiments and consumer interviews may be of value. For example, firms sometimes vary price from one city or region to another, to see what the effects are on quantity demanded. An actual illustration of this sort was the evaluation of the four promotion alternatives by L'eggs Products.

2. Regression analysis is useful in estimating demand functions and other economic relationships. The regression line shows the average relationship between the dependent variable and the independent variable. The method of least squares is the standard technique used to fit a regression line to a set of data. If the regression line is $\hat{Y} = a + bX$ and if a and b are calculated by least squares,

$$b = \frac{\sum_{i=1}^{n} (X_i - \bar{X})(Y_i - \bar{Y})}{\sum_{i=1}^{n} (X_i - \bar{X})^2}$$

and

$$a = \bar{Y} - b\bar{X}$$

This value of b is often called the *estimated regression coefficient*.

3. Whereas a simple regression includes only one independent variable, a multiple regression includes more than one independent variable. An advantage of multiple regression over a simple regression is that you frequently can predict the dependent variable more accurately if more than one independent variable is used. Also, if the dependent variable is influenced by more than one independent variable, a simple regression of the dependent variable on a single independent variable may result in a biased estimate of the effect of this independent variable on the dependent variable.

4. The first step in multiple regression analysis is to identify the independent variables and specify the mathematical form of the equation relating the mean value of the dependent variable to the independent variables. For example, if Y is the dependent variable and X and P are identified as the independent variables, one might specify that

$$Y_i = A + B_1 X_i + B_2 P_i + e_i$$

ANALYZING MANAGERIAL DECISIONS
How Fed Economists Forecast Auto Output

Since purchases by the auto industry account for more than half of the rubber and lead consumed in this country as well as a major portion of the steel, aluminum, and a variety of other materials, it is obvious that many firms and government agencies, as well as the auto firms themselves, are interested in forecasting auto output. The Federal Reserve Bank of New York has published an article describing how the regression techniques described in this chapter have been used for this purpose. According to the author, Ethan Harris, the quantity of autos produced quarterly depends on five variables: (1) real disposable income, (2) the ratio of retail auto inventories to sales, (3) the average price of new cars (relative to the overall consumer price index), (4) the price level for nonauto durable goods, and (5) the prime rate (the interest rate banks charge their best customers).

The regression results follow. The probability that the t statistic for each of the regression coefficients is as large (in absolute terms) as it is here, if the true value of the regression coefficient is zero, is less than 0.01, except for the case of the nonauto price.

The value of the adjusted multiple coefficient of determination is 0.862, the standard error of estimate is 532, and the Durbin-Watson statistic (d) is 2.26. According to Ethan Harris, this regression equation has predicted auto output with a mean (absolute) error of about 6.9 percent.

(a) Would you expect the regression coefficient of the inventory-sales ratio to be negative? If so, why? (b) Can we be reasonably sure that the true value of the regression coefficient of the inventory-sales ratio is not zero? Why or why not? (c) Is there evidence of positive serial correlation

of the error terms? (d) Can we use this regression as an estimate of the demand curve for autos? Why or why not?

SOLUTION (a) Yes. If inventories are large relative to sales, one would expect auto firms to produce less than they would if inventories were small. (b) Yes. According to the preceding discussion, the probability that the t statistic for the regression coefficient of the inventory-sales ratio would be as great as 6.1 (in absolute terms) would be less than 0.01 if the true regression coefficient were zero. Hence, if this true regression coefficient were zero, it is exceedingly unlikely that the t statistic (in absolute terms) would equal its observed value or more. (c) No. Since the value of n is approximately 50 and $k = 5$, Appendix Table 7 shows that $d_L = 1.26$ and $d_U = 1.69$ if the significance level equals 0.025. The observed value of the Durbin-Watson statistic (2.26) is greater than d_U (1.69); this means that we should accept the hypothesis that there is no positive serial correlation. (d) No. One important indication that this is true is that the regression coefficient of the auto price is positive. Clearly, this regression equation cannot be used as an estimate of the demand curve for autos.

Variable	Regression coefficient	t statistic
Constant	−22,302	−4.5
Disposable income	12.9	6.6
Prime rate	−97.8	−3.2
Inventory-sales ratio	−19.9	−6.1
Auto price	230	5.0
Nonauto price	6.0	2.1

where e_i is an error term. To estimate B_1 and B_2 (called the *true regression coefficients* of X and P) as well as A (the intercept of this true regression equation), we use the values that minimize the sum of squared deviations of Y_i from $\hat{Y}_i$, the value of the dependent variable predicted by the estimated regression equation.

5. In a simple regression, the coefficient of determination is used to measure the closeness of fit of the regression line. In a multiple regression, the multiple coefficient of determination, R^2, plays the same role. The closer R^2 is to 0, the poorer the fit; the closer it is to 1, the better the fit.

6. The F statistic can be used to test whether any of the independent variables has an effect on the dependent variable. The standard error of estimate can help to indicate how well a regression model can predict the dependent variable. The t statistic for the regression coefficient of each independent variable can be used to test whether this independent variable has any effect on the dependent variable. Computer printouts show the probability that the t statistic is as big (in absolute terms) as we observed, given that this independent variable has no effect on the dependent variable.

7. A difficult problem that can occur in multiple regression is multicollinearity, a situation in which two or more of the independent variables are highly correlated. If multicollinearity exists, it may be impossible to estimate accurately the effect of particular independent variables on the dependent variable. Another frequently encountered problem arises when the error terms in a regression are serially correlated. The Durbin-Watson test can be carried out to determine whether this problem exists. Plots of the residuals can help to detect cases in which the variation of the error terms is not constant or where the relationship is nonlinear not linear.

Problems

1. The Klein Corporation's marketing department, using regression analysis, estimates the firm's demand function, the result being

$$Q = -104 - 2.1P + 3.2I + 1.5A + 1.6Z$$
$$R^2 = 0.89$$
$$\text{Standard error of estimate} = 108$$

where Q is the quantity demanded of the firm's product (in tons), P is the price of the firm's product (in dollars per ton), I is per capita income (in dollars), A is the firm's advertising expenditure (in thousands of dollars), and Z is the price (in dollars) of a competing product. The regression is based on 200 observations.

a. According to the computer printout, the probability is 0.005 that the t statistic for the regression coefficient of A would be as large (in absolute terms) as it is in this case if in fact A has no effect on Q. Interpret this result.

b. If $I = 5,000$, $A = 20$, and $Z = 1,000$, what is the Klein Corporation's demand curve?

c. If $P = 500$ (and the conditions in part b hold), estimate the quantity demanded of the Klein Corporation's product.

d. How well does this regression equation fit the data?

2. Since all the Hawkins Company's costs (other than advertising) are essentially fixed costs, it wants to maximize its total revenue (net of advertising expenses). According to a regression analysis (based on 124 observations) carried out by a consultant hired by the Hawkins Company,

$$Q = -23 - 4.1P + 4.2I + 3.1A$$

where Q is the quantity demanded of the firm's product (in dozens), P is the price of the firm's product (in dollars per dozen), I is per capita income (in dollars), and A is advertising expenditure (in dollars).

a. If the price of the product is $10 per dozen, should the firm increase its advertising?

b. If the advertising budget is fixed at $10,000, and per capita income equals $8,000, what is the firm's marginal revenue curve?

c. If the advertising budget is fixed at $10,000, and per capita income equals $8,000, what price should the Hawkins Company charge?

3. The 1980 sales and profits of seven steel companies were as follows:

Firm	Sales ($ billions)	Profit ($ billions)
Armco	5.7	0.27
Bethlehem	6.7	0.12
Bundy	0.2	0.00
Carpenter	0.6	0.04
Republic	3.8	0.05
U.S. Steel (now USX)	12.5	0.46
Westran	0.5	0.00

a. Calculate the sample regression line, where profit is the dependent variable and sales is the independent variable.

b. Estimate the 1980 average profit of a steel firm with 1980 sales of $2 billion.

c. Can this regression line be used to predict a steel firm's profit in 2006? Explain.

4. The Cherry Manufacturing Company's chief engineer examines a random sample of 10 spot welds of steel. In each case, the shear strength of the weld and the diameter of the weld are determined, the results being as follows:

Shear strength (pounds)	Weld diameter (thousandths of an inch)
680	190
800	200
780	209
885	215
975	215
1,025	215
1,100	230
1,030	250
1,175	265
1,300	250

a. Does the relationship between these two variables seem to be direct or inverse? Does this accord with common sense? Why or why not? Does the relationship seem to be linear?

b. Calculate the least-squares regression of shear strength on weld diameter.

c. Plot the regression line. Use this regression line to predict the average shear strength of a weld $1/5$ inch in diameter. Use the regression line to predict the average shear strength of a weld $1/4$ inch in diameter.

5. The Kramer Corporation's marketing manager calculates a regression, where the quantity demanded of the firm's product (designated as "C1") is the dependent variable and the price of the product (designated as "C2") and consumers' disposable income (designated as "C3") are independent variables. The Minitab printout for this regression follows:

```
MTB > regress c1 on 2 predictors in c2 and c3
The regression equation is
C1 = 40.8 - 1.02 C2 + 0.00667 C3

Predictor       Coef        Stdev      t-ratio          p
Constant      40.833        1.112        36.74      0.000
C2           -1.02500      0.06807      -15.06      0.000
C3           0.006667      0.005558       1.20      0.244

s=1.361                   R-sq=91.6%           R-sq(adj)=90.8%
Analysis of variance

SOURCE          DF          SS          MS         F          p
Regression       2       422.92      211.46    114.11     0.000
Error           21        38.92        1.85
Total           23       461.83

SOURCE          DF       SEQ SS
C2               1       420.25
C3               1         2.67
```

a. What is the intercept of the regression?

b. What is the estimated regression coefficient of the product's price?

c. What is the estimated regression coefficient of disposable income?

d. What is the multiple coefficient of determination?

e. What is the standard error of estimate?

f. What is the probability that the observed value of the F statistic could arise by chance, given that neither of the independent variables has any effect on the dependent variable?

g. What is the probability, if the true value of the regression coefficient of price is zero, that the t statistic is as large (in absolute terms) as we observe?

h. What is the probability, if the true value of the regression coefficient of disposable income is zero, that the t statistic is as large (in absolute terms) as we observe?

i. Describe briefly what this regression means.

6. Railroad executives must understand how the costs incurred in a freight yard are related to the output of the yard. The two most important services performed by a yard are switching and delivery, and it seems reasonable to use the number of cuts switched and the number of cars delivered during a particular period as a measure of output. (A cut is a group of cars that rolls as a unit onto the same classification track; it is often used as a unit of switching output.) A study of one of the nation's largest railroads assumed that

$$C_i = A + B_1 S_i + B_2 D_i + e_i$$

where C_i is the cost incurred in this freight yard on the ith day, S_i is the number of cuts switched in this yard on the ith day, D_i is the number of cars delivered in this yard on the ith day, and e_i is an error term. Data were obtained regarding C_i, S_i, and D_i for 61 days. On the basis of the procedures described in this chapter, these data were used to obtain estimates of A, B_1, and B_2. The resulting regression equation was

$$\hat{C}_i = 4{,}914 + 0.42 S_i + 2.44 D_i$$

where $\hat{C}_i$ is the cost (in dollars) predicted by the regression equation for the ith day.[19]

a. If you were asked to evaluate this study, what steps would you take to determine whether the principal assumptions underlying regression analysis were met?

[19]For a much more detailed account of this study, see E. Mansfield and H. Wein, "A Managerial Application of a Cost Function by a Railroad," a case in the Study Guide accompanying this textbook.

b. If you were satisfied that the underlying assumptions were met, of what use might this regression equation be to the railroad? Be specific.

c. Before using the study's regression equation, what additional statistics would you like to have? Why?

d. If the Durbin-Watson statistic equals 2.11, is there evidence of serial correlation in the residuals?

7. Mary Palmquist, a Wall Street securities analyst, wants to determine the relationship between the nation's gross domestic product (GDP) and the profits (after taxes) of the General Electric Company. She obtains the following data concerning each variable:

Year	Gross domestic product (billions of dollars)	General Electric's profits (millions of dollars)
1965	688	355
1966	753	339
1967	796	361
1968	868	357
1969	936	278
1970	982	363
1971	1,063	510
1972	1,171	573
1973	1,306	661
1974	1,407	705
1975	1,529	688
1976	1,706	931

a. What are the least-squares estimates of the intercept and slope of the true regression line, where GE's profits are the dependent variable and GDP is the independent variable?

b. On the average, what effect does a $1 increase in gross domestic product seem to have on the profits of GE?

c. If Ms. Palmquist feels that next year's GDP will be $2 trillion, what forecast of GE's profits will she make on the basis of the regression?

d. What is the coefficient of determination between the nation's gross domestic product and GE's profits?

e. Do the results obtained in previous parts of this problem prove that changes in GE's profits are caused by changes in the gross domestic product? Can we be sure that GE's profit is a linear function of the GDP? What other kinds of functions might be as good or better?

f. If you were the financial analyst, would you feel that this regression line was an adequate model to forecast GE's profits? Why or why not?

8. In the manufacture of cloth, the weft packages should not disintegrate unduly during weaving. A direct measure of the tendency to disintegrate exists, but it is laborious and uneconomical to carry out. In addition, there are indirect measures based on laboratory tests. The Brockway Textile Company would like to determine the extent to which one of these indirect measures is correlated with the direct measure. If the correlation is high enough, the firm believes that it may be able to use the indirect measure instead of the direct measure.

An experiment was carried out in which both the direct and indirect measures of the tendency to disintegrate were calculated for 18 lots of packages. The results follow:

Lot	Measure	
	Direct	Indirect
1	31	6.2
2	31	6.2
3	21	10.1
4	21	8.4
5	57	2.9
6	80	2.9
7	35	7.4
8	10	7.3
9	0	11.1
10	0	10.7
11	35	4.1
12	63	3.5
13	10	5.0
14	51	4.5
15	24	9.5
16	15	8.5
17	80	2.6
18	90	2.9

a. What is the coefficient of determination between the two measures?
b. What linear regression line would you use to predict the value of the direct measure on the basis of knowledge of the indirect measure?
c. On the basis of your findings, write a brief report indicating the factors to be weighed in deciding whether to substitute the indirect measure for the direct measure.

9. The Kingston Company hires a consultant to estimate the demand function for its product. Using regression analysis, the consultant estimates the demand function to be

$$\log Q = 2.01 - 0.148 \log P + 0.258 \log Z$$

where Q is the quantity demanded (in tons) of Kingston's product, P is the price (in dollars per ton) of Kingston's product, and Z is the price (in dollars per ton) of a rival product.

a. Calculate the price elasticity of demand for Kingston's product.

b. Calculate the cross elasticity of demand between Kingston's product and the rival product.

c. According to the consultant, $\bar{R}^2 = 0.98$ and the standard error of estimate is 0.001. If the number of observations is 94, comment on the goodness of fit of the regression.

10. During the 1960s, the Boston and Maine Railroad conducted an experiment in which it reduced fares by about 28 percent for approximately a year to estimate the price elasticity of demand. This large fare reduction resulted in essentially no change in the railroad's revenues.

a. What problems exist in carrying out an experiment of this sort?

b. Taken at face value, what seemed to be the price elasticity of demand?

11. Because of a shift in consumer tastes, the market demand curve for high-quality red wine has shifted steadily to the right. If the market supply curve has remained fixed (and is upward sloping to the right), there has been an increase over time in both the price of such wine and in the quantity sold.

a. If one were to plot price against quantity sold, would the resulting relationship approximate the market demand curve?

b. If not, what would this relationship approximate?

12. The Brennan Company uses regression analysis to obtain the following estimate of the demand function for its product:

$$\log Q = 2 - 1.2 \log P + 1.5 \log I$$

where Q is quantity demanded, P is price, and I is consumers' disposable income.

a. Brennan's president is considering a 5 percent price reduction. He argues that these results indicate that such action will result in a 6 percent increase in the number of units sold by the firm. Do you agree? Why or why not?

b. The firm's treasurer points out that, according to the computer printout, the probability that the t statistic of $\log P$ is as large (in absolute value) as it is, given that $\log P$ has no real effect on $\log Q$, is about 0.5. He says that the estimate of the price elasticity is unreliable. Do you agree? Why or why not?

c. How can the firm obtain a more accurate estimate of the price elasticity of demand?

Appendix: The Coefficient of Determination and the Concept of Explained Variation

In this appendix, we provide a fuller explanation of what the coefficient of determination is and how it can be interpreted. To begin with, we must discuss the concept of variation, which refers to a sum of squared deviations. The total variation in the dependent variable Y equals

$$\sum_{i=1}^{n} (Y_i - \bar{Y})^2 \qquad (5.16)$$

In other words, the total variation equals the sum of the squared deviations of Y from its mean.

To measure how well a regression line fits the data, we divide the total variation in the dependent variable into two parts: the variation that *can* be explained by the regression line and the variation that *cannot* be explained by the regression line. To divide the total variation in this way, we must note that, for the ith observation,

$$(Y_i - \bar{Y}) = (Y_i - \hat{Y}_i) + (\hat{Y}_i - \bar{Y}) \qquad (5.17)$$

where $\hat{Y}_i$ is the value of Y_i that would be predicted on the basis of the regression line. In other words, as shown in Figure 5.13, the discrepancy between Y_i and the mean value of Y can be split into two parts: the discrepancy between Y_i and the point on the regression line directly below (or above) Y_i and the discrepancy between the point on the regression line directly below (or above) Y_i and $\bar{Y}$.

It can be shown that[20]

$$\sum_{i=1}^{n} (Y_i - \bar{Y})^2 = \sum_{i=1}^{n} (Y_i - \hat{Y}_i)^2 + \sum_{i=1}^{n} (\hat{Y}_i - \bar{Y})^2 \qquad (5.18)$$

---

[20]To derive this result, we square both sides of equation (5.17) and sum the result over all values of i. We find that

$$\sum_{i=1}^{n} (Y_i - \bar{Y})^2 = \sum_{i=1}^{n} [(Y_i - \hat{Y}_i) + (\hat{Y}_i - \bar{Y})]^2$$

$$= \sum_{i=1}^{n} (Y_i - \hat{Y}_i)^2 + \sum_{i=1}^{n} (\hat{Y}_i - \bar{Y})^2 + 2 \sum_{i=1}^{n} (Y_i - \hat{Y}_i)(\hat{Y}_i - \bar{Y})$$

The last term on the right hand side equals zero, so equation (5.18) follows.

FIGURE
5.13

Division of $(Y_i - \bar{Y})$ into Two Parts: $(Y_i - \hat{Y}_i)$ and $(\hat{Y}_i - Y)$

This division is carried out to measure how well the regression line fits the data.

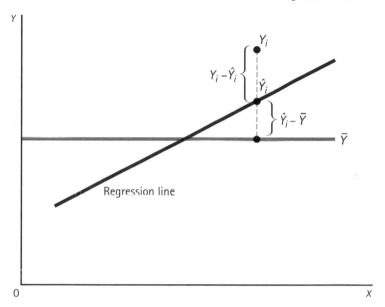

The term on the left-hand side of this equation shows the total variation in the dependent variable. The first term on the right-hand side measures the *variation in the dependent variable not explained by the regression*. This is a reasonable interpretation of this term, since it is the sum of squared deviations of the actual observations from the regression line. Clearly, the larger is the value of this term, the poorer the regression equation fits the data. The second term on the right-hand side of the equation measures the *variation in the dependent variable explained by the regression*. This is a reasonable interpretation of this term, since it shows how much the dependent variable would be expected to vary on the basis of the regression alone.

To measure the closeness of fit of a simple regression line, we use the **coefficient of determination**, which equals

$$1 - \frac{\sum_{i=1}^{n} (Y_i - \hat{Y}_i)^2}{\sum_{i=1}^{n} (Y_i - \bar{Y})^2} \tag{5.19}$$

In other words, the coefficient of determination equals

$$1 - \frac{\text{variation not explained by regression}}{\text{total variation}}$$

$$= \frac{\text{variation explained by regression}}{\text{total variation}} \tag{5.20}$$

Clearly, the coefficient of determination is a reasonable measure of the closeness of fit of the regression line, since it equals the proportion of the total variation in the dependent variable explained by the regression line. The closer it is to 1, the better the fit; the closer it is to 0, the poorer the fit.

When a multiple regression is calculated, the multiple coefficient of determination is used to measure the goodness of fit of the regression. The multiple coefficient of determination is defined as

$$R^2 = 1 - \frac{\sum_{i=1}^{n} (Y_i - \hat{Y}_i)^2}{\sum_{i=1}^{n} (Y_i - \overline{Y})^2} \tag{5.21}$$

where $\hat{Y}_i$ is the value of the dependent variable that is predicted from the regression equation. So, as in the case of the simple coefficient of determination covered earlier,

$$R^2 = \frac{\text{variation explained by regression}}{\text{total variation}} \tag{5.22}$$

This means that *R² measures the proportion of the total variation in the dependent variable explained by the regression equation.*

Business and
Economic Forecasting

CHAPTER 6

Many corporations have corporate economists or hire consulting firms to forecast sales or profits. These forecasts can be done on a short-term basis, for example, next quarter, or on a longer-term basis, for the next year, five years, or ten years. Security analysts forecast quarterly and yearly earnings, and one can hear their consensus via First Call before earnings are about to be released. Popular business press publications, like *Business Week* and the *Wall Street Journal*, offer similar results. The Federal Reserve and the Department of Commerce also conduct business forecasts as do trade associations for their industries.

Managers of all sorts are routinely involved in decision making that is informed by forecasts. Sales forecasts, for instance, may dictate raw material orders, production run schedules, and hiring decisions. An organization's mid-level managers are likely to make these decisions. On the other hand, long-term growth forecasts for an industry may entail capital expansion or disinvestment of assets, decisions likely to be made by higher-level managers within the organization, most likely with the board of directors' approval.

In this chapter, we take up the techniques used by many business and economic forecasters. As you work through these subjects, keep in mind that economic forecasting is not an exact science. Too many variables exist to precisely model the economic system or even a small part of it. Even so, most corporations prefer rigorous data to intuition or hunch (and, in fact, managers have a fiduciary responsibility to the owners of the firm to practice due diligence in following rational procedures for decision making). Recently, dot.coms and other new economy businesses were started with virtually no business plans and no concept of the market. While some success stories exist, most ventures failed, and after an initial "love affair" with Internet startups, the financial community has now declared that "red is dead"; that is, they do not throw funding at firms that cannot project a profit within a reasonable period of time.

As we shall see, regression (which we studied in Chapter 5) plays a major role in many of these forecasting techniques, including the econometric models that are the staple of the leading private and public economic forecasters.

Survey Techniques

One of the simplest forecasting devices is to survey firms or individuals to determine what they believe will occur. Consider the surveys carried out to forecast firms' expenditures. For example, the U.S. Department of Commerce and the Securities and Exchange Commission conduct surveys of business intentions to buy plant and equipment. Still other surveys are aimed at measuring consumer intentions. The Survey Research Center at the University of Michigan and other such groups provide information on planned purchases of automobiles, appliances, and housing. Also, they indicate the extent of consumer confidence in the economy, which is an important factor influencing consumers' spending decisions. Surveys of this type are of value in forecasting the sales of many products. They provide a wealth of information to the forecaster.

At least two types of information can be obtained from surveys. First, they can provide us the respondent's forecast of some variable over which he or she has no control. For example, the University of Michigan obtains data from consumers concerning their forecasts of the rate of inflation. Second, surveys can provide us information concerning what people or firms believe they will do. For example, the National Federation of Independent Business surveys firms to determine whether, and to what extent, they plan to increase their prices.[1]

Suppose a survey is used to forecast some variable, such as the sales of a particular firm. How can we determine how reliable this forecasting technique seems to be? One commonly used measure of the size of the forecast error is the root-mean-squared forecast error, which is defined as

$$E = \left(\sum_{i=1}^{n} (Y_i - F_i)^2 / n \right)^{0.5}$$

[1] See W. Dunkelberg, "The Use of Survey Data in Forecasting," in E. Mansfield, ed., *Managerial Economics and Operations Research* (4th ed.; New York: Norton, 1980).

where F_i is the ith forecast, Y_i is the corresponding actual value, and n is the number of forecasts for which we have data concerning the size of the forecast errors. Therefore, if the forecasts for 2001, 2002, and 2003 are $110 million, $120 million, and $130 million, and if the actual values are $105 million, $122 million, and $127 million, respectively, the root-mean-squared forecast error equals

$$\sqrt{\frac{(105 - 110)^2 + (122 - 120)^2 + (127 - 130)^2}{3}} = 3.56$$

or $3.56 million dollars. This measure of forecast error is used to evaluate forecasts, no matter whether they are based on surveys or other techniques. Clearly, the lower is the root-mean-squared forecast error, the better the forecasting technique.

Taking Apart a Time Series

Although surveys are of considerable use, most major firms seem to base their forecasts in large part on the quantitative analysis of economic time series. The classic approach to economic forecasting, devised primarily by economic statisticians, was essentially descriptive. It assumed that an economic time series could be decomposed into four components: trend, seasonal variation, cyclical variation, and irregular movements. More specifically, it assumed that the value of an economic variable at a certain time could be represented as the product of each of these four components. For example, the value of a company's sales in January 2003 was viewed as equal to

$$Y = T \times S \times C \times I \tag{6.1}$$

where T is the trend value of the firm's sales during that month, S is the seasonal variation attributable to January, C is the cyclical variation occurring that month, and I is the irregular variation that occurred then.[2] Each of these components is defined next.

Trend

A trend is a relatively smooth long-term movement of a time series. For instance, the civilian labor force of the United States increased rather steadily between 1947 and 2002, as shown in Figure 6.1. Hence, there has been an upward trend in the U.S. civilian labor force. Of course, not all trends are upward. The trend

---

[2]In some versions of this model, the components are added rather than multiplied. That is, it is assumed that

$$Y = T + S + C + I$$

where Y is the value of the time series.

FIGURE
6.1

Civilian Labor Force of the United States, 1947–2002

This series exhibits a strong upward trend.
Source: Bureau of Labor Statistics.

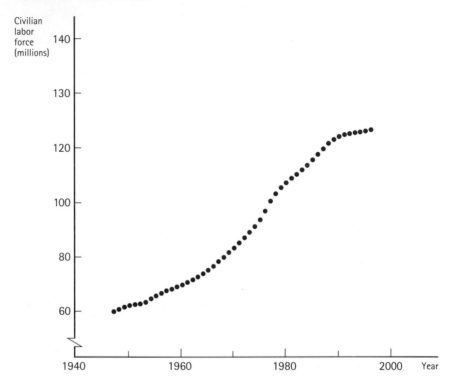

in farm employment in the United States has generally been downward, as shown in Figure 6.2.[3] Whether upward or downward, the trend of a time series is represented by a smooth curve. In equation (6.1), *T* is the value of the firm's sales predicted for January 2003, on the basis of such a curve.

Seasonal Variation

In a particular month, the value of an economic variable is likely to differ from what would be expected on the basis of its trend because of seasonal factors. For example, consider the sales of a firm that produces Christmas trees. Since the demand for Christmas trees is much higher in the winter than in the summer, one would expect that the monthly time series of the firm's sales would show a pronounced and predictable seasonal pattern. Specifically, sales each

[3]In still other cases, the trend is horizontal; that is, there is no upward or downward tendency in the time series. In these cases, it is often said that there is no trend.

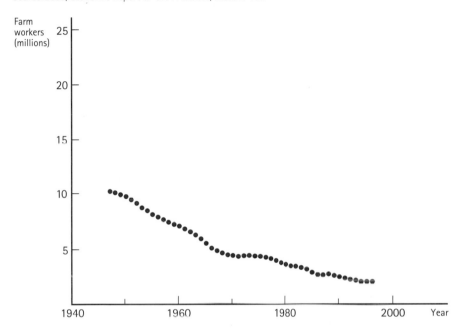

FIGURE 6.2

Farm Employment in the United States, 1947–2001

This series exhibits a strong downward trend.

Source: 2003, Economic Report of the President, Table B-100

year would tend to be higher in December than during the rest of the year. As we shall see, it is possible to calculate *seasonal indexes* that estimate how much each month departs from what would be expected on the basis of its trend. In equation (6.1), we must multiply the trend value T by the seasonal index S to allow for the effect of this seasonal variation.

Cyclical Variation

Another reason why an economic variable may differ from its trend value is that it may be influenced by the so-called business cycle. The general tempo of economic activity in our society has exhibited a cyclical nature, with booms being followed by recessions and recessions being followed by expansions. These cycles have not been regular or consistent (which is one reason why many economists prefer the term *business fluctuations* to *business cycles*); but unquestionably there has been a certain cyclical ebb and flow of economic activity, which has been reflected in a great many time series. For this reason, $T \times S$ is multiplied by C, which is supposed to indicate the effect of cyclical variation on the firm's sales in equation (6.1).

Irregular Variation

Once it has been multiplied by both S and C, the trend value T has been altered to reflect seasonal and cyclical forces. But in addition to these forces, *a variety of short-term, erratic forces is also at work*. Their effects are represented by I. Essentially, I reflects the effects of all factors other than the trend, seasonal variation, and cyclical variation. According to the classic model, these irregular forces are too unpredictable to be useful for forecasting purposes.

How to Estimate a Linear Trend

Managerial economists have carried out many studies to estimate the trend, seasonal variation, and cyclical variation in particular economic time series. In this and the following sections of this chapter, we encounter the methods used to estimate a trend; in subsequent sections, we take up seasonal and cyclical variation. First, we consider the case in which the long-term overall movement of the time series seems to be fairly close to linear. For example, this seems true for the sales of the ABC Corporation during the period 1988 to 2002. (These sales are plotted in Figure 6.3.) In a case in which the trend seems to be linear,

---

FIGURE
6.3

Linear Trend in Sales, ABC Corporation, 1988–2002

The ABC Corporation's sales have risen rather steadily throughout the period.

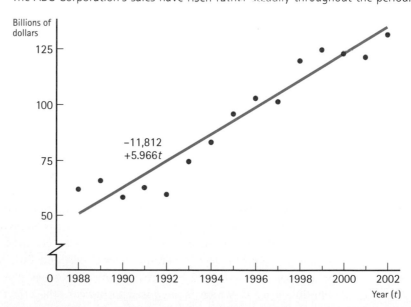

analysts frequently use the method of least squares to calculate the trend. In other words, they assume that, if the long-term forces underlying the trend were the only ones at work, the time series would be approximately linear. Specifically, they assume that

$$Y_t = A + Bt \tag{6.2}$$

where Y_t is the trend value of the variable at time t. (Note that t assumes values like 2000 or 2001 if time is measured in years.) The **trend value** is the value of the variable that would result if only the trend were at work. The deviation of Y, the actual value of the variable, from the trend value is the **deviation from trend**.

To illustrate the calculation of a linear trend, we examine the ABC Corporation's annual sales from 1988 to 2002. Since sales in year t is the dependent variable and t is the independent variable, it follows from our discussion in Chapter 5 that

$$b = \frac{\displaystyle\sum_{t=t_0}^{t_0+n-1} (S_t - \bar{S})(t - \bar{t})}{\displaystyle\sum_{t=t_0}^{t_0+n-1} (t - \bar{t})^2} \tag{6.3}$$

and

$$a = \bar{S} - b\bar{t} \tag{6.4}$$

where S_t is sales (in billions of dollars) in year t, t_0 is the earliest year in the time series (that is, 1988), $t_0 + n - 1$ is the latest year in the time series (that is, 2002), b is an estimate of B, and a is an estimate of A.

Inserting the data underlying Figure 6.3 into equations (6.3) and (6.4), we find that the trend line is

$$S_t = -11,812 + 5.966t \tag{6.5}$$

This trend line is plotted in Figure 6.3.

How to Estimate a Nonlinear Trend

Many time series do not exhibit linear trends. In some such cases, a quadratic function of time provides an adequate trend. Such a trend can be represented as

$$Y_t = A + B_1 t + B_2 t^2$$

FIGURE
6.4

Exponential Trend, Assuming β = 1.5, α = 1

Many time series have exponential trends.

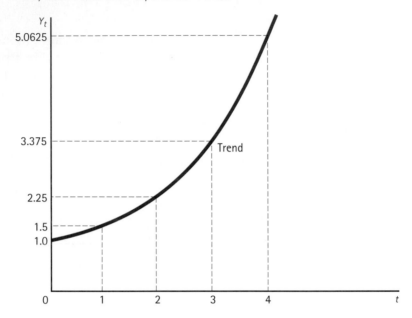

To estimate A, B_1, and B_2, we can use the multiple regression techniques described in Chapter 5. As indicated there, standard computer programs are available to make these computations. The regression contains two independent variables: t and t^2. Whether a quadratic trend is more appropriate than a linear trend can be determined by seeing whether it fits the data significantly better than a linear trend.

For many variables, an exponential curve provides a better-fitting trend than a quadratic curve. The equation for such a trend (shown in Figure 6.4) is

$$Y_t = \alpha\beta^t \tag{6.6}$$

where Y_t is the trend value of the time series at time t. A trend of this sort seems to fit many business and economic time series. It represents a situation in which the variable grows at a constant percentage rate per year. Therefore, if a firm's sales grow at about 5 percent per year, they are likely to exhibit an exponential trend.

If there is an exponential trend, we can take logarithms of both sides of equation (6.6):

$$\log Y_t = A + Bt \tag{6.7}$$

where $A = \log \alpha$, and $B = \log \beta$. Since equation (6.7) is linear, we can estimate A and B by the method of least squares. Then, we can take antilogs of A and B to estimate α and β, the unknown coefficients in equation (6.6). (The average rate of increase of Y_t equals $\beta - 1$.)[4] In this way, we can estimate the nonlinear trend shown in equation (6.6).

Seasonal Variation

Many time series consist of monthly or quarterly rather than annual data. For such time series, managerial economists and decision makers must recognize that seasonal variation is likely to be present in the series. Seasonal variation in many economic time series is due to the weather. For example, sales of soft drinks are higher in the summer than in the winter. In other cases, such as sales of Christmas trees, seasonal variation is due to the location of a specific holiday (Christmas) on the calendar. Still other reasons for seasonal variation are the fact that some industries tend to grant vacations at a particular time of year, taxes have to be paid at certain times of the year, or schools tend to open at particular times of the year.

Managerial economists have devised methods for estimating the pattern of seasonal variation in a particular time series. In other words, they can determine the extent to which a particular month or quarter is likely to differ from what would be expected on the basis of the trend and cyclical variation in the same series. (In terms of the traditional model in equation (6.1), they can determine the value of S for each month or quarter.) For example, the marketing vice president for a manufacturer of soft drinks may tell the company's board of directors that U.S. production of soft drinks tends in June to be 5.9 percent higher than what the trend and cyclical variation in soft drink production would

---

[4]If Y grows at a constant rate of $100r$ percent per year,

$$Y_t = Y_0(1 + r)^t$$

where Y_0 is the value of Y in some base year (say 1990) and Y_t is its value t years after the base year. Taking logarithms of both sides of this equation,

$$\log Y_t = \log Y_0 + [\log (1 + r)]t$$

Therefore, $\log (1 + r)$ equals B, and the antilog of B (which is β) equals $(1 + r)$. Consequently, $r = \beta - 1$. In other words, as stated in the text, the average rate of increase of Y_t (which is r) equals $\beta - 1$. (Mathematical review: If X is the logarithm of Y, Y is called the antilog of X.)

Seasonal Variation in Production of Soft Drinks in the United States

Month	Seasonal index	Month	Seasonal index
January	93.4	July	112.4
February	89.3	August	113.4
March	90.7	September	108.3
April	94.9	October	103.9
May	99.0	November	95.8
June	105.9	December	93.0

indicate. Or she may tell them that U.S. production of soft drinks in December tends to be 7.0 percent lower than the trend and cyclical variation would indicate.

The seasonal variation in a particular time series is described by a figure for each month, the **seasonal index,** *which shows the way in which that month tends to depart from what would be expected on the basis of the trend and cyclical variation in the time series.* For example, Table 6.1 shows the seasonal variation in U.S. production of soft drinks. January's production tends to be about 93.4 percent of the amount expected on the basis of trend and cyclical variation, February's production tends to be about 89.3 percent of this amount, March's production tends to be about 90.7 percent of this amount, and so on. Figures of this sort can be used in a number of ways. *One important application is to forecast what the time series will be in the future.* For example, suppose that on the basis of the trend and cyclical variation, it appears likely that about 30 million gallons of soft drinks will be produced next January. If this is the case, a reasonable forecast of actual January production is 0.934(30 million) = 28.02 million gallons, since January's production tends to be 93.4 percent of the amount expected based on trend and cyclical variation.

Calculation of Seasonal Variation

One way of calculating the seasonal variation in a time series is to use the regression techniques described in Chapter 5. Suppose, for example, that a business analyst has a time series composed of quarterly values; that is, each observation pertains to the first, second, third, or fourth quarter of a year. If the analyst believes that the time series has a linear trend, he or she may assume that the value of the observation at time t equals

$$Y = A + B_1 t + B_2 Q_1 + B_3 Q_2 + B_4 Q_3 + e_t \qquad (6.8)$$

where Q_1 equals 1 if time t is the first quarter and 0 otherwise, Q_2 equals 1 if time t is the second quarter and 0 otherwise, Q_3 equals 1 if time t is the third quarter and 0 otherwise, and e_t is an error term.

It is important to understand the meaning of B_1, B_2, B_3, and B_4 in equation (6.8). Clearly, B_1 is the slope of the linear trend, but what are B_2, B_3, and B_4? The answer is that B_2 *is the difference between the expected value of an observation in the first quarter and the expected value of an observation in the fourth quarter when the effects of the trend are removed.* (The **expected value** of an observation is its long-term mean value. To find its expected value, one multiplies each possible value of the observation by the probability of this value, and sums up the results.) To see that this is true, note that, if an observation pertains to time t, the first quarter of a particular year, its expected value equals

$$A + B_1 t + B_2$$

according to equation (6.8). Similarly, if an observation pertains to time $t + 3$, the fourth quarter of the same year, its expected value equals

$$A + B_1(t + 3)$$

according to equation (6.8). Therefore, the difference between the expected value of an observation in the first quarter and the expected value of an observation in the fourth quarter equals

$$(A + B_1 t + B_2) - [A + B_1(t + 3)] = B_2 - 3B_1$$

And, if we remove the effects of the trend (which is responsible for the last term on the right, $3B_1$), this difference equals B_2; this is what we set out to prove. When the effects of the trend are removed, one can show in the same way that B_3 is the difference between the expected value of an observation in the second quarter and the expected value of an observation in the fourth quarter, and B_4 is the difference between the expected value of an observation in the third quarter and the expected value of an observation in the fourth quarter.

Consequently, if equation (6.8) is valid, the analyst can represent the seasonal variation in the time series by the three numbers B_2, B_3, and B_4. To estimate each of these numbers, ordinary multiple regression techniques can be used. The dependent variable is Y, and the independent variables are t, Q_1, Q_2, and Q_3. The last three independent variables (Q_1, Q_2, and Q_3) are dummy variables. (A dummy variable is a variable that can assume only two values: 0 or 1.) Using the regression methods described in Chapter 5, the constants in equation (6.8) (A, B_1, B_2, B_3, and B_4) can be estimated by the ordinary least-squares technique.

ANALYZING MANAGERIAL DECISIONS

Forecasting the Demand for Blood Tests

North Carolina Memorial Hospital (now part of University of North Carolina Hospitals) has been interested in forecasting the number of blood tests it will perform. A simple model has been constructed that assumes that the number of tests per month increases according to a linear trend, and that the seasonal variation can be represented in the way described in equation (6.9). In other words, it is assumed that

$$Q = A + B_1 t + B_2 M_1$$
$$+ B_3 M_2 + \cdots + B_{12} M_{11} + e_t,$$

where Q is the number of blood tests performed at the hospital in month t, M_1 equals 1 if month t is January and 0 otherwise, ..., M_{11} equals 1 if month t is November and 0 otherwise, and e_t equals an error term. Therefore, B_2 is the difference between January and December in the expected number of tests, B_3 is the difference between February and December in the expected number of tests, and so on (when the effects of the trend are removed).

(a) Indicate how one can estimate the values of A, B_1, B_2, ..., B_{12}. (b) Potential patients are reluctant to seek medical care during the Christmas holidays. Would you expect B_2 to be positive or negative? Why? (c) According to the hospital, the model forecasts "are being used to plan vacation schedules for . . . employees and to order supplies for the tests."* Why would forecasts of this sort be useful for these purposes? (d) Forecasts based on this simple model have been reported to be "excellent." Forecasting errors have averaged only about 4.4 percent. On the other hand, forecasts based on exponential smoothing (a technique described in the chapter appendix) did not perform so well. Do you think that a model of this sort will always outperform exponential smoothing?

SOLUTION (a) The values of these parameters can be estimated by calculating a multiple regression, where Q is the dependent variable and t, M_1, M_2, ..., M_{11} are the independent variables. (b) Positive, because B_2 is the difference between January and December in the expected number of tests when the effects of the trend are removed. Because patients tend not to want such tests during the holidays, December would be expected to be below January in this regard. (c) If one can forecast the demand for blood tests, it is possible to estimate the number of employees and the quantity of supplies needed at various times. Clearly, this information is useful in scheduling vacations and purchases, among other things. (d) No. In some cases, one forecasting technique works well; in others, it works less well. No technique is universally better than the others discussed in this chapter.

*E. Gardner, "Box-Jenkins vs. Multiple Regression: Some Adventures in Forecasting the Demand for Blood Tests," *Interfaces*, August 1979, pp. 49–54.

When using this procedure, the analyst assumes that seasonal effects are added to the trend value, as shown in equation (6.8). This differs from the traditional model in equation (6.1), where it is assumed that seasonal effects multiply the trend value (see footnote 2). The former assumption is appropriate in some cases, whereas the latter assumption is appropriate in others. Techniques based on both assumptions are useful.[5]

To illustrate how this regression procedure can be used to estimate the seasonal variation in monthly data, suppose you have monthly data concerning the sales of a particular firm. If there is a linear trend, you can assume that

$$Y = A + B_1 t + B_2 M_1 + B_3 M_2 + \ldots + B_{12} M_{11} + e_t \qquad (6.9)$$

where Y is the firm's sales in month t, M_1 equals 1 if month t is January and 0 otherwise, M_2 equals 1 if month t is February and 0 otherwise, $\ldots$, M_{11} equals 1 if month t is November and 0 otherwise, and e_t equals an error term. Using ordinary multiple regression techniques, you can estimate A, B_1, B_2, $\ldots$, B_{12}. The estimates of B_2, B_3, $\ldots$, B_{11}, and B_{12} indicate the seasonal variation in the firm's sales. In particular, B_2 is the difference between January and December in the expected value of sales, B_3 is the difference between February and December in the expected value of sales, and so on, until B_{12} is the difference between November and December in the expected value of sales (when the effects of the trend are removed).

Cyclical Variation

Time series in business and economics frequently exhibit cyclical variation, such variation often being termed the **business cycle**. To illustrate what we mean by the business cycle or **business fluctuations**, we look at how national output has grown in the United States since 1929. Figure 6.5 shows the behavior of gross domestic product (GDP) in constant dollars in the United States since 1929. Clearly, output has grown considerably during this period; indeed, GDP is more than five times what it was 70 years ago. But this growth has not been steady. While the long-term trend has been upward, there have been periods, such as 1929–1933, 1937–1938, 1944–1946, 1948–1949, 1953–1954, 1957–1958, 1969–1970, 1973–1975, 1980, 1981–1982, and 1990–1991, when national output declined.

The **full-employment level** of GDP is the total amount of goods and services that could have been produced if there had been full employment. Figure

---

[5]To calculate the seasonal variation based on the latter assumption, a four-quarter—or 12-month if the data are monthly—moving average can be used. For the details, see any business statistics book.

FIGURE
6.5

Gross Domestic Product (GDP) (1987 Dollars), United States, 1929–2002 (Excluding World War II)

National output has fluctuated considerably.

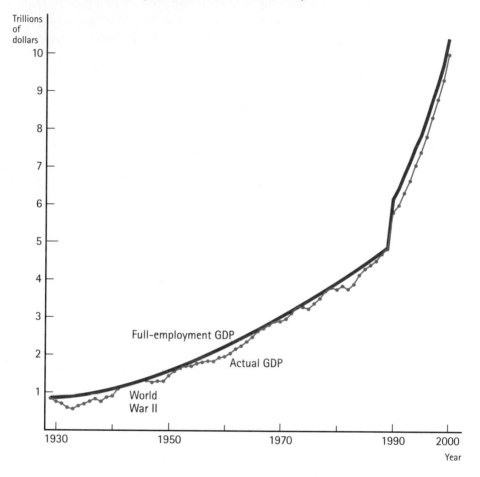

6.5 shows that national output tends to rise and approach (and perhaps exceed)[6] its full-employment level for a while, then falters and falls below this level, then rises to approach it once more, then falls below it again, and so on. For example, output fell far below the full-employment level in the depressed 1930s but rose again to this level once we entered World War II. This movement of national output is sometimes called the *business cycle*, but it must be recognized that these "cycles" are far from regular or consistent.

[6]During a period of inflationary pressure, national output may exceed its full-employment level.

FIGURE
6.6

Four Phases of Business Fluctuations

The peak occurs when national output is highest relative to its full-employment value; the trough occurs when national output is lowest relative to its full-employment value.

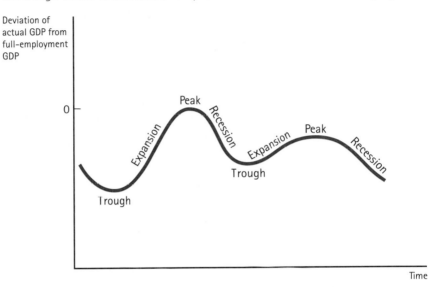

Each cycle can be divided by definition into four phases, as shown in Figure 6.6. *The* **trough** *is the point where national output is lowest relative to its full-employment level.* **Expansion** *is the subsequent phase during which national output rises. The* **peak** *occurs when national output is highest relative to its full-employment level. Finally,* **recession** *is the subsequent phase during which national output falls.*[7]

Many business and economic time series go up and down with the business cycle. For example, industrial output tends to be above its trend line at the peak of the business cycle and tends to fall below its trend line at the trough. Similarly, such diverse series as the money supply, industrial employment, and stock prices reflect the business cycle. However, not all series go up and down at exactly the same time. Some turn upward before others at a trough, and some turn downward before others at a peak. As we shall see, the fact that some time series tend to precede others in cyclical variation sometimes is used to forecast the pace of economic activity.

[7]The peak and trough may also be defined in terms of deviations from the long-term trend of GDP rather than in terms of deviations from the full-employment level of GDP.

Elementary Forecasting Techniques

In general, all forecasting techniques are extremely fallible, and all forecasts should be treated with caution. Nonetheless, businesses and government agencies have no choice but to make forecasts, however crude. Since firms, governments, and private individuals must continually make decisions that hinge on what they expect will happen, they must make implicit forecasts even if they do not make explicit ones. Therefore, the central question is how best to forecast, not whether to forecast. In this section, we present some elementary forecasting techniques that are commonly applied. Even among small firms, evidence indicates that about three-quarters of the firms use techniques of this sort.[8] However, these techniques should be viewed as crude first approximations rather than highly sophisticated methods. More sophisticated techniques are taken up subsequently.

The simplest type of forecasting method is a straightforward extrapolation of a trend. For example, let us return to the ABC Corporation. At the end of 2002, suppose that ABC Corporation managers wanted to forecast its 2003 sales. During the period 1988–2002, we know from our earlier discussion that the firm's sales could be represented (approximately) by the trend line

$$S_t = -11,812 + 5.966t$$

where t equals the year in question. To forecast its 2003 sales, the ABC Corporation could simply insert 2003 for t in this equation. Thus, the forecast for 2003 is

$$-11,812 + 5.966(2003) = 138.4$$

or 138.4 billion dollars. As shown in Figure 6.7, this forecast is a simple extension, or extrapolation, of the trend line into the future.

Decision makers often need forecasts of monthly rather than annual amounts. In such cases, it is necessary to recognize that seasonal variation, as well as trend, is likely to affect the value for a particular month. To see how a forecast can be made under such circumstances, consider a clothing manufacturer that wants to forecast its sales during each month of 2004. On the basis of data for each month during the period 1973 to 2003, the firm determines that its sales seem to conform to the trend

$$S_t = 12,030 + 41t$$

---

[8]R. Coccari, "How Quantitative Business Techniques Are Being Used," *Business Horizons*, July 1989.

FIGURE

6.7

Simple Trend Extrapolation to Forecast 2003 Sales of the ABC Corporation

The forecast is $138.4 billion.

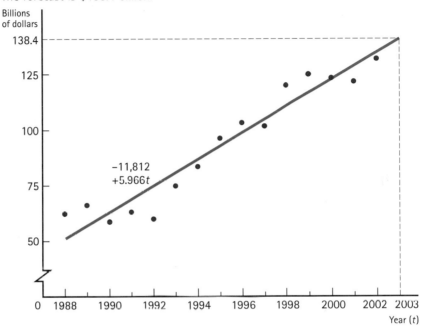

where S_t is the trend value of the firm's monthly sales (in thousands of dollars) and t is time measured in months from January 2003. If this trend continues, the expected sales for each month in 2004 would be as shown in the second column of Table 6.2. But this ignores whatever seasonal variation exists in the firm's sales. To include seasonal variation, suppose that the clothing manufacturer's marketing manager analyzes past sales data and finds that the monthly seasonal index for sales is as shown in the third column of Table 6.2. (Seasonal effects here are multiplicative, not additive.) If this seasonal pattern continues in 2004 as in the past, we would expect that actual sales each month would equal the trend value (in the second column) times the seasonal index (in the third column) divided by 100. The result, which is shown in the fourth column of Table 6.2, is a forecast that includes both the trend and the seasonal variation.

Needless to say, this entire procedure is simply a mechanical extrapolation of the firm's sales data into the future. The assumption is made that the past trend and the past seasonal variation will continue. Moreover, it is assumed

TABLE
6.2

Forecast of Sales of Clothing Manufacturer, 2004

Month	Forecast trend value of sales[a]	Seasonal index	Forecast sales (reflecting both trend and seasonal variables)[a]
January	12,522	90	11,270
February	12,563	80	10,050
March	12,604	80	10,083
April	12,645	90	11,380
May	12,686	110	13,955
June	12,727	120	15,272
July	12,768	80	10,214
August	12,809	110	14,090
September	12,850	120	15,420
October	12,891	100	12,891
November	12,932	100	12,932
December	12,973	120	15,568

[a]Expressed in units of $1,000.

that the trend and seasonal variation are the predominant factors that will determine sales in the coming months. The validity of this assumption depends on many considerations, including the extent to which the time series in question (in this case, sales) is affected by cyclical factors and the extent to which the economy is likely to change its cyclical position. In the next section, we turn our attention to a particular method of forecasting business fluctuations.

How Leading Indicators Are Used

Managers and analysts want to modify their forecasts to reflect prospective overall changes in economic activity. For example, if the president of the clothing firm in Table 6.2 is convinced that a serious depression will occur in 2004, he is likely to modify the forecasts in Table 6.2 accordingly. But how does the president of the clothing firm—or anyone else—predict whether there is going to be a depression? There are a variety of ways of doing this, all of which are very imperfect. In this section, we discuss an essentially empirical approach, reserving a discussion of more sophisticated techniques for a later section.

One of the simplest ways to forecast business fluctuations is to use **leading indicators,** which are certain economic series that typically go down or up before gross domestic product does. The National Bureau of Economic Research carries out detailed and painstaking examinations of the behavior of various economic variables over a long period of time and attempts to find out whether each variable turns downward before, at, or after the peak of the business cycle and whether it turns upward before, at, or after the trough. Variables that go down before the peak and up before the trough are called **leading series**. Variables that go down at the peak and up at the trough are called **coincident series**. Variables that go down after the peak and up after the trough are called **lagging series**.

According to the bureau, some important leading series are new orders for durable goods, the average workweek, building contracts, stock prices, certain wholesale prices, and claims for unemployment insurance. These are the variables that tend to turn downward before the peak and upward before the trough.[9] Coincident series include employment, industrial production, corporate profits, and gross domestic product, among many others. Some typical lagging series are retail sales, manufacturers' inventories, and personal income.

These leading series—or leading indicators, as they often are called—are used frequently as forecasting devices. There are sound economic reasons why these series turn downward before a peak or upward before a trough: In some cases, leading series indicate changes in spending in strategic areas of the economy, while in others, they indicate changes in managers' and investors' expectations. To guide business executives in their planning, it is important to try to spot turning points—peaks and troughs—in advance. This, of course, is the toughest part of economic forecasting. Economists sometimes use leading indicators as evidence that a turning point is about to occur. If a large number of leading indicators turn down, this is viewed as a sign of a coming peak. The upturn of a large number of leading indicators is thought to signal an impending trough.

Experience with leading indicators has been only partially successful. The economy has seldom turned downward in recent years without a warning from these indicators, but unfortunately these indicators have turned down on a number of occasions—in 1952 and 1962, for example—when the economy did not turn down subsequently. Therefore, leading indicators sometimes provide false signals. Also, in periods of expansion, they sometimes turn downward too far ahead of the real peak. And in periods of recession, they sometimes turn upward only a very short while before the trough, so that we turn the corners before anything can be done. Nonetheless, leading indicators are not worthless; they are watched closely and used to supplement other, more sophisticated forecasting techniques.[10]

---

[9]Of course, claims for unemployment insurance turn upward before the peak and downward before the trough.

[10]See R. Ratti, "A Descriptive Analysis of Economic Indicators," in *Managerial Economics and Operations Research*, ed. Mansfield.

CONSULTANT'S CORNER

Deciding Whether to Finance the Purchase of an Oil Field

In 1985, a leading bank was deciding whether to approve a loan application from an oil and gas company. This loan was to finance the purchase of an oil and gas field. The bank projected the oil and gas company's most likely production levels and profits and estimated how much money the company would have available to meet its debt. To make these estimates, it was necessary to forecast the price of crude oil. In the bank's view, the oil industry had very good prospects for returning to the prosperity of the 1970s.

The 15-year forecast of the oil price that was provided by the bank's head office for the purpose of evaluating this loan was as follows:

You now have the benefit of hindsight, but even in 1985 you should have been suspicious of the bank's forecast. If the bank hired you to evaluate its forecasting procedure in this case, what comments would you make?

Source: This section is based on an actual case, although the numbers and situation are simplified somewhat.

Year	Price (par barrel)	Year	Price (per barrel)
1986	$25	1994	$41
1987	27	1995	43
1988	29	1996	45
1989	31	1997	47
1990	33	1998	49
1991	35	1999	51
1992	37	2000	53
1993	39		

Students interested in learning more about these leading indicators should visit the website of The Conference Board (www.conference-board.org). The Conference Board is a nonprofit organization that provides economic reports and data about business issues and sponsors the business cycle indicators website. The website not only shows a time series for the leading indicators but also discusses their implications for the U.S. economy. In addition, the site reports the leading indicators for other countries.

How Econometric Models Are Used

Managers and analysts have tended in recent years to base their forecasts more and more on multiple regression techniques and multiequation models. Increased emphasis has been put on the construction and estimation of an equation or system of equations to show the effects of various independent variables on the variable or variables one wants to forecast. For example, one may want to estimate the quantity of automobiles produced by U.S. auto firms next quarter. According to a study published by the Federal Reserve Bank of New York (described on page 188), the following regression equation is useful for this purpose:[11]

$$A = -22,302 + 12.9D - 97.8I - 19.9R + 230P + 6.0N$$

where A is the quantity of autos produced quarterly, D is real disposable income, I is the prime interest rate, R is the inventory-sales ratio, P is the auto price, and N is the nonauto price level. To forecast the quantity of autos produced quarterly, one estimates the values of the independent variables and inserts them into this equation.

Multiequation models have been used to forecast many variables, such as gross domestic product. The Wharton model, a pioneer in this field, contained hundreds of equations variously intended to explain the level of expenditures by households, the level of business investment, aggregate output and employment, and wages, prices, and interest rates. The forecasts produced by the Wharton model (and other large models like it) have been followed closely by major business firms and government agencies. Indeed, some firms (like General Electric) have constructed their own multiequation models. Of course, this does not mean that these large models have an unblemished forecasting record; on the contrary, they, like all other forecasting techniques, are quite fallible. However, these models continue to be used in business and government.

Both the single-equation model used to forecast the quantity of autos produced and the Wharton model, with its hundreds of equations, are examples of econometric models. An **econometric model** is a system of equations (or a single equation) estimated from past data used to forecast economic and business variables. The essence of any econometric model is that it blends economic theory with modern statistical methods.

John Hancock and Timberland: A Case Study

The John Hancock Mutual Life Insurance Company manages timberland for investors, who reap gains when either the timber or the land is sold at a profit.

---

[11]E. Harris, "Forecasting Automobile Output," *Federal Reserve Bank of New York Quarterly Review*, Winter 1985–86, reprinted in *Managerial Economics and Operations Research*, ed. Mansfield.

ANALYZING MANAGERIAL DECISIONS

Forecasting Shipments of Cement by CEMCO

CEMCO, a small cement producer, has used an econometric model to forecast its sales and profits. According to this model, national cement shipments depend on the amount of residential construction and business fixed investment. Assuming its price is unchanged, CEMCO's shipments of cement are assumed to depend on national cement shipments. Holding national cement shipments constant, CEMCO can increase its shipments by reducing its price. However, its rivals are likely to meet such a price cut, whereas they are less likely to match a price increase.

This year, CEMCO shipped 453,000 tons of cement. Based on this model and alternative assumptions concerning the firm's future price, the forecasted shipments for next year and the year after next were as follows (in thousands of tons):

Assumed future change in CEMCO's price	Next year	Year after next
No price change	468	457
10 percent price increase	306	296
10 percent price decrease	473	459

(a) As stated, the firm's model assumes that (1) national cement shipments depend on the amount of residential construction and business fixed investment, and (2) its shipments depend on national cement shipments (if its price does not change). Does it appear that the company expected both residential construction and business fixed investment to be higher in the year after next than in next year? Why or why not? (b) With regard to increases in price, does the demand for the firm's cement seem to be price elastic or price inelastic? Explain. (c) Does the price elasticity of demand seem to be lower for price decreases than for price increases? Is this reasonable? Why or why not?

SOLUTION (a) No. If the company had expected both residential construction and business fixed investment to be higher in the year after next than in next year, it would have forecasted an increase in national cement shipments, which in turn would have implied an increase in CEMCO's cement shipments (assuming no price change). In fact, as shown in the table, it forecasted that its cement shipments would be lower in the year after next than in next year. (b) Price elastic. A 10 percent increase in price seems to reduce shipments by about one-third. (c) Yes. It seems reasonable if, as stated, the firm's rivals are likely to meet a price reduction but unlikely to meet a price increase.*

*F. G. Adams, *The Business Forecasting Revolution* (New York: Oxford University Press, 1986), pp. 219–236. A couple of numbers have been changed for pedagogical reasons.

Hancock's holdings include 1.8 million acres of forests, mostly in the Southeast and the Pacific Northwest. The firm uses econometric models to estimate future demand for timber, as well as changes in wood and paper prices. On the basis of these estimates, Hancock executives decide what kinds of trees to plant, how to manage their growth, and when to harvest them.

In early 1994, Hancock's economists were predicting rising prices in the next three or four years as the national economy grew and the supply of commercial timber declined. Investors in timberland were getting returns of 20 to 30 percent per year from their investment, but Hancock recognized that the profit rate was likely to decline over time to a 9 to 15 percent rate. Econometric models were used to try to maintain the profit rate at a high level.[12]

The Purvere Corporation: A Numerical Example

To illustrate the nature of multiequation econometric models, consider the Purvere Corporation, a seller of aircraft. Purvere's total revenues come from three sources: the sale of the equipment, servicing the equipment, and the sale of accessories to customers who buy equipment or have it serviced. On the basis of regression analysis, Purvere's managers have found that its revenues from each of these sources can be represented by the following three equations:

$$E_t = 100 - 4P_t + 0.02G_t \tag{6.10}$$
$$S_t = 10 + 0.05E_{t-1} \tag{6.11}$$
$$A_t = 25 + 0.1Y_t \tag{6.12}$$

where E_t is the company's revenue from equipment sales in year t, P_t is the price of its equipment, G_t is gross domestic product (in billions of dollars), S_t is its revenue from servicing its equipment, A_t is its revenue from accessory sales, and Y_t is its total sales (which equal $E_t + S_t + A_t$). The values of E_t, S_t, A_t, and P_t are expressed in millions of dollars.

According to equation (6.10), Purvere's equipment sales are inversely related to its price and directly related to gross domestic product. According to equation (6.11), its service revenues are directly related to its equipment sales during the previous year (because the equipment is serviced about a year after it is bought). According to equation (6.12), its revenue from accessory sales is directly related to its total sales.

Purvere's president wants to use this model to forecast next year's total sales, which equal (in year t)

$$Y_t = E_t + S_t + A_t = (100 + 10 + 25) - 4P_t + 0.02G_t + 0.05E_{t-1} + 0.1 \ Y_t$$

Therefore,

$$(1 - 0.1)Y_t = 135 - 4P_t + 0.02G_t + 0.05E_{t-1}$$

or

$$Y_t = \frac{1}{0.9}(135 - 4P_t + 0.02G_t + 0.05 \ E_{t-1}) \tag{6.13}$$

---

[12]*New York Times*, February 20, 1994.

This equation can be used to forecast next year's value of Y if we know the price of Purvere's equipment next year, the value of GDP next year, and the firm's revenues from equipment sales this year. Suppose that price will be 10 and that this year's equipment sales will be 100. Then,

$$Y_t = \frac{1}{0.9} (135 - 4(10) + 0.05(100) + 0.02G_t)$$

$$= \frac{1}{0.9} (100 + 0.02G_t)$$

To forecast Y_t, we must know G_t, the value of gross domestic product next year. Obviously, the best we can do is to utilize the best available forecast of next year's GDP. Suppose that Purvere's president decides to rely on the forecast of a large econometric model (like Wharton's), which is that GDP next year will be about \$6,250 billion. If so, his sales forecast for next year would be

$$Y_t = \frac{1}{0.9} [100 + 0.02(6,250)] = \frac{1}{0.9} (225) = 250$$

or \$250 million.

Note that Purvere's president links his company model in equations (6.10) to (6.12) to the large econometric model, which is providing the forecasted value of G_t. This is frequently the way managers have used the forecasts of macroeconomic models like the Wharton model.

Before leaving this example, it is important to recognize that it is highly simplified. Firms frequently use multiequation models containing many variables, not just the handful contained in equations (6.10) to (6.12). Some of these additional variables utilized to forecast company sales were identified and discussed in Chapter 3. General Electric, for example, has used an iterative process "in which the initial values are obtained from individual economic relationships but the final results are strongly influenced by the experience, 'feel,' and intuition of business economists. This procedure has the advantage of 'taking everything into account' along with the disadvantage of being time consuming. The GE group, like the large model forecasters, forecasts more than a hundred economic variables, including items of special interest to the company such as total appliance sales and electric power generation."[13]

"Study Your Residuals"

Before concluding this chapter, it is important to consider Nobel laureate Paul A. Samuelson's well-known statement: "To the scientific forecaster I say, 'Always

---

[13]S. McNees, "The Recent Record of Thirteen Forecasters," *New England Economic Review*, September 1981, p. 291.

study your residuals.'" What Samuelson meant was that, in evaluating any forecasting technique, it is useful to calculate the difference between each observation and what the technique predicts this observation will be. These differences—or residuals (defined in Chapter 5)—are very useful in indicating whether your forecasting technique excludes some important explanatory variables and whether its assumptions are valid.

To illustrate, suppose you are using an econometric model to forecast your firm's sales and the difference between each year's sales and what this model predicts these sales to be is as shown in Figure 6.8. To improve this technique, you should think hard about why the model made the errors that it did. Based on Figure 6.8, it might occur to you, for example, that many of the years when the residuals were large and positive were years when your firm had an unusually large sales force and that many of the years when the residuals were large and negative were years when your firm had an unusually small sales force. If the size of your firm's sales force is not included as an independent variable in your model, there may be good reason to include it.

By continually studying your forecasting errors and improving your forecasting techniques, significant progress can be made. Although it generally is

FIGURE 6.8

Residuals from Sales Forecasting Model

The years (1989 and 1997) when the residuals are large and negative are ones when the sales force was small; the years (1993 and 2000) when they are large and positive are ones when the sales force was large.

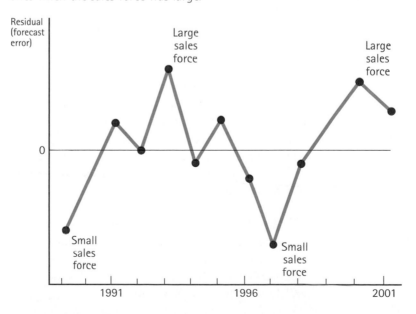

unrealistic to expect business and economic forecasts to be very precise, they are likely to be considerably more trustworthy than forecasts that are not based on the principles of managerial economics.

Summary

1. Although surveys are of considerable use, most major firms seem to base their forecasts in large part on the quantitative analysis of economic time series. The classical approach to business forecasting assumes that an economic time series can be decomposed into four components: trend, seasonal variation, cyclical variation, and irregular movements.

2. If the trend in a time series is linear, simple regression may be used to estimate an equation representing the trend. If it seems to be nonlinear, a quadratic equation may be estimated by multiple regression or an exponential trend may be fitted. An exponential trend is appropriate when the variable increases at a relatively constant percentage rate per year. To fit such a trend, we use the logarithm of the variable, not the variable itself, as the dependent variable in the regression.

3. The seasonal variation in a particular time series is described by a figure for each month (the seasonal index) that shows the extent to which that month's value typically departs from what would be expected on the basis of trend and cyclical variation. Such seasonal indexes, together with the trend, can be useful for forecasting. Regression analysis, including dummy variables, can be employed to estimate seasonal indexes.

4. Cyclical variation, as well as trend and seasonal variation, is reflected in many time series. Variables that go down before the peak and up before the trough are called *leading indicators*. If a large number of leading indicators turn downward, this is viewed as a sign of a coming peak. If a large number turn upward, this is thought to signal an impending trough. Although these indicators are not very reliable, they are watched closely and are used to supplement other, more-sophisticated forecasting techniques.

5. The simplest kind of forecasting method is a straightforward extrapolation of a trend. To allow for seasonal variation, either multiplicative or additive seasonal effects can be included. This entire procedure is simply a mechanical extrapolation of the time series into the future.

6. In recent years, managerial economists have tended to base their forecasts less on simple extrapolations and more on equations (or systems of equations) showing the effects of various independent variables on the variable (or variables) one wants to forecast. These equations (or systems of equations), which are estimated using the techniques described in Chapter 5, are called *econometric models*. Examples are the models used by CEMCO and General Electric, as well as the model of auto output published by the Federal Reserve Bank of New York.

Problems

1. The following seasonal index was calculated for the room occupancy of a motel located on a major interstate highway in the Southeast. The motel's customers are largely tourists and commercial truckers who regularly travel this highway. This index is based on actual data.[14]

January	74.8	July	116.8
February	79.8	August	117.4
March	92.9	September	105.4
April	108.8	October	103.7
May	107.5	November	100.3
June	112.0	December	80.6

 a. Is there pronounced seasonal variation in this motel's business? All other things equal, by what percentage, on the average, does room occupancy in the peak month exceed that in the lowest month?

 b. What factors would you expect to be responsible for the observed seasonal variation? In calculating the seasonal index, it was assumed that the index for a particular month like January was the same from year to year. Some observers have questioned whether this assumption is correct, given that a recession occurred in 1990 and 1991. Why might the recession have changed the pattern of seasonal variation?

 c. If you were the motel's manager, how might a seasonal index of this sort be of use? Be specific.

2. The Union Carbide Corporation's sales during the period 1960 to 1975 follow:

Year	Sales (billions of dollars)	Year	Sales (billions of dollars)
1960	1.5	1968	2.7
1961	1.6	1969	2.9
1962	1.6	1970	3.0
1963	1.7	1971	3.0
1964	1.9	1972	3.3
1965	2.1	1973	3.9
1966	2.2	1974	5.3
1967	2.5	1975	5.7

 a. Fit a linear trend line to these data.

 b. Fit an exponential trend line to these data.

---

[14]B. Bettegowda, "Calculation of Seasonal Index for Motel Room Occupancy," National Technological University.

c. In 1980, Union Carbide's sales were $9.994 billion. Suppose that in 1976, both the linear trend line and the exponential trend line had been used to forecast the firm's 1980 sales. Which forecast would have been more accurate?

d. In 1984, Union Carbide's sales were $9.508 billion. Suppose that in 1976, both the linear trend line and the exponential trend line had been used to forecast the firm's 1984 sales. Which forecast would have been more accurate?

3. The Milton Company's statistician calculates a seasonal index for the firm's sales; the results are shown in the second column. The firm's monthly 2001 sales are shown in the third column.

Month	Seasonal index	2001 sales (millions of dollars)
January	97	2.5
February	96	2.4
March	97	2.7
April	98	2.9
May	99	3.0
June	100	3.1
July	101	3.2
August	103	3.1
September	103	3.2
October	103	3.1
November	102	3.0
December	101	2.9

a. If one divides each month's sales figure by its seasonal index (divided by 100), it is said to be "deseasonalized." That is, the seasonal element is removed from the data. Why is this true?

b. Calculate deseasonalized sales figures for 2001.

c. Why would the managers of the Milton Company want deseasonalized sales figures?

4. The equation describing the sales trend of the Secane Chemical Company is

$$S_t = 21.3 + 1.3t$$

where S_t is the sales (in millions of dollars per month) of the firm and t is time measured in months from January 1995. The firm's seasonal index of sales is

January	103	May	101	September	121
February	80	June	104	October	101
March	75	July	120	November	75
April	103	August	139	December	78

a. Construct a monthly sales forecast for the firm for 2001.

b. Why would the managers of the Secane Chemical Company want monthly sales forecasts of this kind?

5. On October 4, 2002, the U.S. Department of Commerce announced that the index of leading indicators rose 0.6 percent in August 2002.

a. During August, the average workweek rose. Is the average workweek among the leading indicators? If so, did its increase help to raise the index?

b. During August, stock prices rose. Is the level of stock prices among the leading indicators? If so, did its increase help to raise the index?

6. The Allen Company's monthly sales have the following trend:

$$C_t = 4.12 + 0.32t$$

where C_t is the sales (in millions of dollars per month) of the firm and t is time measured in months from July 1994. The firm's seasonal index of sales is

January	81	May	137	September	79
February	98	June	122	October	101
March	102	July	104	November	74
April	76	August	101	December	125

a. Construct a monthly sales forecast for the firm in 2002.

b. The firm's president feels strongly that a recession will occur in late 2002. Would this influence your answer to part a? If so, how?

7. The sales of Sears, Roebuck were as follows during 1978 to 1990:

Year	Sales (billions of dollars)	Year	Sales (billions of dollars)
1978	22.9	1985	40.7
1979	24.5	1986	42.3
1980	25.2	1987	45.9
1981	27.4	1988	50.3
1982	30.0	1989	53.8
1983	35.9	1990	56.0
1984	38.8		

a. Calculate a linear trend based on these data.

b. Sears, Roebuck's sales in 1991 were about $57.2 billion. If you had used a least-squares trend line based on 1978 to 1990 data to forecast its 1991 sales, how big a forecasting error would have resulted?

c. In 1992, Sears, Roebuck's sales were $52.3 billion. If you had used a least-squares trend line based on 1978 to 1990 data to forecast its 1992 sales, how big a forecasting error would have resulted?

8. In the Wharton econometric model, housing starts (divided by the number of households) were specified to be a function of (1) the mortgage rate, (2) a consumer sentiment index, (3) capacity utilization, (4) the occupancy rate, and (5) deposit inflows into savings intermediaries.

a. Indicate why each of these five variables might be expected to influence the number of housing starts.

b. What factors influence these five variables? What sort of multiequation system might be constructed for forecasting purposes?

9. The General Electric Corporation's sales from 1950 to 1976 were as follows:

Year	Sales (billions of dollars)	Year	Sales (billions of dollars)
1950	2.2	1964	4.9
1951	2.6	1965	6.2
1952	3.0	1966	7.2
1953	3.5	1967	7.7
1954	3.3	1968	8.4
1955	3.5	1969	8.4
1956	4.1	1970	8.8
1957	4.3	1971	9.6
1958	4.2	1972	10.5
1959	4.5	1973	11.9
1960	4.2	1974	13.9
1961	4.5	1975	14.1
1962	4.8	1976	15.7
1963	4.9		

a. Using the method of least squares, derive a linear trend.

b. Plot General Electric's sales against time. Also, plot the trend line derived in part a against time. (Time here is the year to which the sales figure pertains.)

c. Does a visual inspection of how well the linear trend fits suggest that an exponential trend would do better? That a quadratic trend would do better?

      d. Using this linear trend, what would have been the sales forecast for General Electric in 1994? How accurate would it have been?

10. The SAS printout of the regression of the IBM Corporation's annual sales (designated "Y") on the year to which the sales figure pertains (designated "YEAR") follows. This regression is based on data for 1974 to 1986.

```
DEP VARIABLE: Y
ANALYSIS OF VARIANCE
```

SOURCE	DF	SUM OF SQUARES	MEAN SQUARE	F VALUE	PROB>F
MODEL	1	2164.18549	2164.18549	288.750	0.0001
ERROR	11	82.44527481	7.49502498		
C TOTAL	12	2246.63077			

	ROOT MSE	2.737704	R-SQUARE	0.9633	
	DEP MEAN	29.43846	ADJ R-SQ	0.9600	
	C.V.	9.299753			

PARAMETER ESTIMATES

VARIABLE	DF	PARAMETER ESTIMATE	STANDARD ERROR	T FOR HO: PARAMETER=0	PROB>|T|
INTERCEP	1	-6798.29780	401.80637	-16.919	0.0001
YEAR	1	3.44835165	0.20293215	16.993	0.0001

      a. If you had used this regression as a linear trend in 1986, what would have been your forecast of IBM's 1987 sales, based on this trend?

      b. IBM's actual sales in 1987 were $54.2 billion. How accurate would your forecast have been?

Appendix: Exponential Smoothing and Forecasting

A frequently used method of calculating a trend is by **exponential smoothing**. According to this method, *the trend value at time t is a weighted average of all available previous values, where the weights decline geometrically as one goes backward in time.* As an illustration, suppose that a firm has been in existence for five years and its sales have been $2 million, $6 million, $6 million, $4 million, and $8 million (see Figure 6.9). Then, the trend value in the fifth year would be a weighted average of $2 million, $6 million, $6 million, $4 million, and $8 million, where the weights decline geometrically as we go backward in time. Specifically, the weight attached to the observation at time t equals θ, the weight attached to the observation at time $t - 1$ equals $(1 - \theta)\theta$, the weight attached to the observation at time $t - 2$ equals $(1 - \theta)^2\theta$, the weight attached to the observation at time $t - 3$ equals $(1 - \theta)^3\theta$, . . . , and the weight attached to the observation at the earliest relevant time (time 0) equals $(1 - \theta)^t$. Clearly, the weights decline geometrically as one goes backward in time; that is, the weight attached to the observation at time $t - 1$ is $(1 - \theta)$ times the weight attached to the observation at time t; the weight attached to the observation at

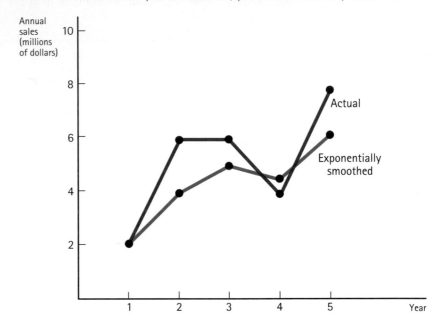

FIGURE
6.9

Sales of Firm, Actual and Exponentially Smoothed

Year 1 is the firm's first year in existence, year 2 is its second year, and so on.

time $t - 2$ is $(1 - \theta)$ times the weight attached to the observation at time $t - 1$; and so on.

To calculate an exponentially smoothed time series, choose a value of θ, which is designated the **smoothing constant**. If we choose a value of 0.5 for θ, the exponentially smoothed value of the firm's sales in each of the five years is

$$S_0 = 2$$
$$S_1 = (0.5)(6) + (1 - 0.5)(2) = 4$$
$$S_2 = (0.5)(6) + (1 - 0.5)(0.5)(6) + (1 - 0.5)^2(2) = 5$$
$$S_3 = (0.5)(4) + (1 - 0.5)(0.5)(6)$$
$$+ (1 - 0.5)^2(0.5)(6) + (1 - 0.5)^3(2) = 4.5$$
$$S_4 = (0.5)(8) + (1 - 0.5)(0.5)(4) + (1 - 0.5)^2(0.5)(6)$$
$$+ (1 - 0.5)^3(0.5)(6) + (1 - 0.5)^4(2) = 6.25$$

where S_0 is the exponentially smoothed value of the firm's sales in the first year of its existence, S_1 is this value in the second year, S_2 the value in the third year, and so on. Figure 6.9 shows both the original time series and the exponentially smoothed time series.

To compute the value of such a smoothed time series at time t, all you really need is the value of the smoothed time series at time $t - 1$ and the actual value of the time series at time t. This is because the smoothed value of the time series at time t is a simple weighted average of the smoothed value at time $t - 1$ and the actual value at time t. If S_t is the smoothed value at time t,

$$S_t = \theta Y(t) + (1 - \theta)S_{t-1} \tag{6.14}$$

where $Y(t)$ is the value of the time series at time t.[15] So, to calculate an exponentially smoothed time series, you do not need to keep all the previous values of the actual time series; *all you need to keep is the value of the exponentially smoothed series in the previous period.* From this information alone (together with the current value of the series and the smoothing constant), you can calculate the smoothed value of the series in the current period. For instance, consider the firm in the previous paragraph. If the firm's sales in its sixth year of existence are $10 million, the smoothed value of sales for the sixth year is

$$(0.5)(10) + (1 - 0.5)(6.25) = 8.125$$

or $8.125 million.

In choosing the value of the smoothing constant θ, you must pick a number between 0 and 1. (In other words, $0 \leq \theta \leq 1$.) If θ is close to 1, past values of the time series are given relatively little weight (compared with recent values) in calculating smoothed values. If θ is close to 0, past values of the time series are given considerable weight (as compared with recent values) in calculating smoothed values. If the time series contains a great deal of random variation, it is often advisable to choose a relatively small value of θ, since this results in relatively little weight put on $Y(t)$, which is influenced more than S_{t-1} by this variation. On the other hand, if one wants the smoothed time series to reflect relatively quickly whatever changes occur in the average level of the time series, the value of θ should be set at a high level.

---

[15]Let us prove that equation (6.14) is true. If $Y(t)$ is the actual value of the time series at time t, then equation (6.14) implies that

$$\begin{aligned} S_t &= \theta Y(t) + (1 - \theta)S_{t-1} \\ &= \theta Y(t) + (1 - \theta)[\theta Y(t - 1) + (1 - \theta)S_{t-2}] \\ &= \theta Y(t) + (1 - \theta)\theta Y(t - 1) + (1 - \theta)^2[\theta Y(t - 2) + (1 - \theta)S_{t-3}] \\ &\;\;\vdots \\ &= \theta Y(t) + (1 - \theta)\theta Y(t - 1) + (1 - \theta)^2\theta Y(t - 2) + \cdots + (1 - \theta)^t Y(0) \end{aligned}$$

Since the right-hand side of the last line is equivalent to the definition of an exponentially smoothed time series in the first paragraph of this appendix, it follows that equation (6.14) is true.

How to Forecast the Sales of Paper, According to McKinsey

Bill Barnett of McKinsey and Company, a leading management consulting firm, described how a management team constructed a forecast of the sales of uncoated white paper in the United States. The first step was to divide the total demand into more homogeneous components. Then, in each of these end-use categories, the analysts tried to identify, understand, and forecast the factors influencing demand.

To illustrate, take the case of reprographics paper. The management team, using existing data, divided reprographics paper into two types: plain-paper copy paper and nonimpact page printer paper. With regard to plain-paper copy paper, there was evidence that sales tended to be directly related to the level of business activity (as measured by macroeconomic variables like the gross domestic product). Holding the level of business activity constant, it appeared that the quantity of plain-paper copy paper demanded was related to the average cost (including labor time, equipment,

and paper) of making a copy. As indicated in the graph, the analysts found an inverse relationship between the average cost per copy and the quantity demanded.

Because further declines in cost per copy seemed unlikely, the management team forecasted a slowing in the growth of sales of plain-paper copy paper. Since 1983, there seemed to be a decrease in the rate of growth of sales of this product; the team forecasted that this decrease would continue. (In addition, the analysts looked carefully at how sensitive their conclusions were to alternative assumptions regarding the rate of growth of the gross domestic product and the rate of reduction of cost per copy.) According to Barnett, this sort of approach to sales forecasting is frequently very effective.

Source: The material on which this was based comes from F. W. Barnett, "Four Steps to Forecast Total Market Demand," *Harvard Business Review*, HBR 88401, 1988.

Forecasting Based on Exponential Smoothing

Exponential smoothing is also used for forecasting purposes. When used in this way, the basic equation for exponential smoothing is

$$F_t = \theta A(t-1) + (1-\theta)F_{t-1} \qquad (6.15)$$

where $A(t-1)$ is the actual value of the time series at time $(t-1)$ and F_t is the forecast for time t. Because the forecast is being made at time $(t-1)$, the actual value of the time series at this time is known. The forecast for time t is simply a weighted average of the actual value at time $(t-1)$ and the forecasted value for time $(t-1)$, where the actual value is weighted by θ and the

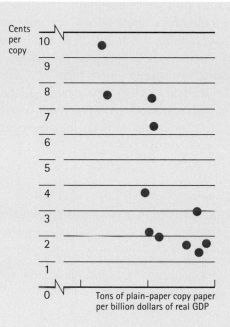

Tons of plain-paper copy paper per billion dollars of real GDP

(a) Can regression techniques be used to estimate the relationship between cost per copy and the quantity demanded of plain-paper copy paper? If so, how?

(b) What statistic would you use to measure the strength of this relationship?

(c) Can one calculate the elasticity of demand for plain-paper copy paper with respect to cost per copy? Of what use might it be?

(d) During the relevant period, the quantity demanded of plain-paper copy paper grew at an average annual rate of 7 percent. Does this mean that an exponential curve provides the best representation of the trend in quantity demanded?

(e) Does the procedure just described to forecast demand result in a seasonal index for sales of plain-paper copy paper? If not, how might such a seasonal index be calculated? Of what use might it be?

(f) How might this forecasting procedure utilize the results of econometric models?

End-use category	Percent of total sales
Business forms	25
Commercial printing	25
Reprographics	20
Envelopes	10
Other converting	5
Stationery and tablet	5
Books	5
Other	5
Total	100

forecasted value is weighted by $(1 - \theta)$. It can readily be demonstrated that the forecast for time t is the weighted sum of the actual values prior to time t, where the weight attached to each value declines geometrically with the age of the observation.

To see how exponential smoothing can be used for forecasting purposes, we return to the firm in Figure 6.9, which had been in existence for five years. Sales during the first year were $2 million, and we assume that the firm's sales forecast for the first year was also $2 million. What will be its sales forecast for the second year? To make such a forecast, the firm begins by choosing a value for the smoothing constant θ. (Values of 0.3 or less are often used.) Suppose that a value of 0.2 is chosen. Then the forecast for the second year is $0.2(2) + 0.8(2) = 2$, or $2 million. Since the firm's actual sales in the second year turn out to be $6 million, its sales forecast for the third year will be 0.2(6) + 0.8(2) = 2.8, or $2.8 million. Since the firm's actual sales in the third year turn out to be $6 million, its sales forecast for the fourth year will be 0.2(6) + 0.8(2.8) = 3.44, or $3.44 million. And so on. Exponential smoothing is often used in this way to make forecasts, particularly where there is a need for a cheap, fast, and rather mechanical method to make forecasts for a large number of items. For example, to implement various kinds of inventory control models, demand forecasts for hundreds or thousands of items may be required.

Problem

The Dickson Corporation wants to calculate an exponentially smoothed time series from the following data:

1989	2	1994	28
1990	4	1995	38
1991	8	1996	50
1992	12	1997	70
1993	20	1998	90

a. Calculate an exponentially smoothed time series, letting the smoothing constant equal $1/4$.

b. Calculate an exponentially smoothed time series, letting the smoothing constant equal $1/2$.

c. Calculate an exponentially weighted time series, letting the smoothing constant equal $3/4$.

Production and Cost

Production Theory

CHAPTER 7

Once managers determine the demand for the firm's product or service, their job is far from over. Now, they must choose the most profitable way to use the firm's resources to produce the good or service. They must ask many questions, including these: What is the optimal level of output? How should we decide between (among) alternative manufacturing processes? How will investment in manufacturing equipment affect labor costs? Will building a new plant increase or decrease costs?

To answer these (and other) questions, managers must understand the production process. Simply stated, production issues are concerned with how scarce resources (inputs) are used to produce the firm's product or service (output). A production function simply specifies the efficient relationship between inputs and outputs.

Good managers realize that *production* refers to more than the physical transformation of inputs into outputs. Production involves all activities associated with providing the goods and services, such as employment practices, acquisition of capital resources, and product distribution. Indeed, as much of the economy becomes more services oriented, the transformation of inputs into outputs (which had more of a "blue collar" tone in the "old economy") now has more of a "white collar" tone. Consulting and investment banking and the disimmediation of the links between manufacturing and the ultimate consumer use the inputs of data, computers, and brainpower to produce output—buy or sell the stock, IPO the stock at 35, or ponder the consultant's recommendation. This is as much of a production process as taking coal, iron ore, massive plants, and blue-collar labor to manufacture steel.

To maximize profits, managers must strive to produce the good or service efficiently and at a minimal cost by constantly keeping abreast of new methods and comparing their production performance with that of their rivals (benchmarking).

The study (and understanding) of the production process is fundamental to gaining insight into cost analysis. While demand analysis gave us the total revenue portion of the profit equation, cost analysis gives us total cost—the other required portion of the profit equation. But costs evolve from the production process. One cannot understand cost unless one understands the production process.

Production analysis also enables managers to understand the integrated nature of the firm, the relationships among the various factors employed by the firm and among the functional units.

The Production Function with One Variable Input

For any product, the production function is a table, a graph, or an equation showing the maximum output rate of the product that can be achieved from any specified set of usage rates of inputs. The production function summarizes the characteristics of existing technology at a given time; it shows the technological constraints that the firm must reckon with. In this chapter, we assume that the firm takes the production function as given; in the next chapter, when we analyze the process of technological change, we study the firm's attempts to change the production function.

Consider the simplest case, in which there is one input whose quantity is fixed and one input whose quantity is variable. Suppose that the fixed input is the service of five machine tools, the variable input is labor, and the product is a metal part. Suppose that John Thomas, owner of the Thomas Machine Company, a very small machine shop, decides to find out what the effect on annual output would be if he were to apply various numbers of units of labor during the year to the five machine tools (and if he maximizes output). He discovers that one full-time laborer can make 49 hundred parts per year on the machines. But Thomas can make more parts per year by hiring more workers, as we see in Table 7.1. The results in Table 7.1 can be regarded as the production function in this situation where the Thomas Machine Company maximizes the output of the labor and machines it uses. Alternatively, the curve in Figure 7.1,

TABLE
7.1

Output of Metal Parts When Various Amounts of Labor Are Applied to Five Machine Tools, Thomas Machine Company

Amount of labor (L)	Amount of capital (# of machines)	Output of parts (Q, hundreds per year)
0	5	0
1	5	49
2	5	132
3	5	243
4	5	376
5	5	525
6	5	684
6.67	5	792.59
7	5	847
8	5	1,008
9	5	1,161
10	5	1,300
11	5	1,419
12	5	1,512
13	5	1,573
14	5	1,596
15	5	1,575

which presents exactly the same results, can be regarded as the production function. In fact, the numbers in Table 7.1 (and Table 7.2) are derived from the relationship $Q = 30L + 20L^2 - L^3$.

The production function provides basic information concerning the nature of a firm's production technology; it shows us the maximum total output that can be realized by using each combination of quantities of inputs. Two other important concepts are the average product and the marginal product of an input. The **average product** of an input is total product (that is, total output) divided by the amount of the input used to produce this amount of output. The **marginal product** of an input is the addition to total output resulting from the addition of the last unit of the input when the amounts of other inputs used are held constant.[1]

---

[1]More precisely, the marginal product of an input is the derivative of output with regard to the quantity of the input. That is, if Q is output and x is the quantity of the input, the marginal product of the input equals dQ/dx if the quantity of all other inputs is fixed.

FIGURE
7.1

Relationship between Total Output
and Amount of Labor Used on Five Machine Tools,
Thomas Machine Company

Total output increases as labor increases at an increasing rate (up to 6.67 units of labor) and increases at a decreasing rate (until slightly more than 14 units of labor). Thereafter, output decreases as more units of labor are deployed. Managers will never willfully deploy labor in the latter circumstance. The production function shows the relationship between output (in this case, number of parts produced) and input (in this case, units of labor).

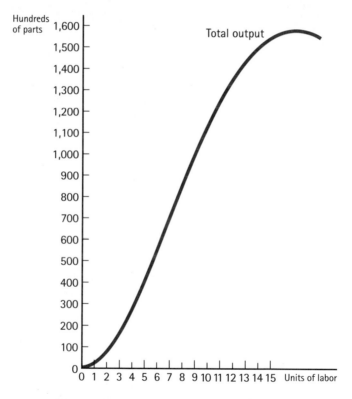

Returning to the Thomas Machine Company, we can calculate the average product and the marginal product of labor, based on the production function in Table 7.1. Both the average product and the marginal product of labor vary, of course, depending on how much labor is used. If $Q(L)$ is the total output rate when L units of labor are used per year, the average product of labor when L units of labor are used per year is $Q(L)/L$. And the marginal product of labor

TABLE
7.2

Average and Marginal Products of Labor, Thomas Machine Company

Amount of labor (units)	Amount of capital (number of machines)	Output of parts (Q, hundreds of parts)	Average product (Q/L)	Marginal product ($\Delta Q/\Delta L$)[a]	Marginal product (dQ/dL)[a]
0	5	0	—	—	—
1	5	49	49	49	67
2	5	132	66	83	98
3	5	243	81	111	123
4	5	376	94	133	142
5	5	525	105	149	155
6	5	684	114	159	162
6.67	5	792.59	118.89	162.89	<u>163.33</u>
7	5	847	121	<u>163</u>	163
8	5	1,008	126	161	158
9	5	1,161	129	153	147
10	5	1,300	<u>130</u>	139	<u>130</u>
11	5	1,419	129	119	107
12	5	1,512	126	93	78
13	5	1,573	121	61	43
14	5	1,596	114	23	2
15	5	1,575	105	−19	−45

[a]The figures in the $\Delta Q/\Delta L$ column pertain to the interval between the indicated amount of labor and one unit less than the indicated amount of labor. The figures in the dQ/dL column are the continuous marginal product, that is, $dQ/dL = MP_L = 30 + 40L − 3L^2$.

MP, when between L and $(L − 1)$ units of labor are used per year is $Q(L) − Q(L − 1)$. Hence, the average product of labor is 49 hundred parts per unit of labor when one unit of labor is used, and the marginal product of labor is 83 hundred parts per unit of labor when between one and two units of labor are used. The results for other amounts of labor are shown in Table 7.2.

The average product curve for labor is shown in Figure 7.2; the numbers are derived from Table 7.1. As is often (but not always) the case for production processes, the average product of labor (which is the only variable input in this case) rises, reaches a maximum (at $L = 10$ and $Q/L = 130$), then falls. Figure 7.2 also shows the marginal product of labor. These numbers are taken from the last column of Table 7.2. The marginal product of labor also rises,

FIGURE
7.2

Average and Marginal Product Curves for Labor

Marginal product exceeds average product when the latter is increasing and is less than average product when the latter is decreasing. (Output per unit of labor is measured in hundreds of parts.)

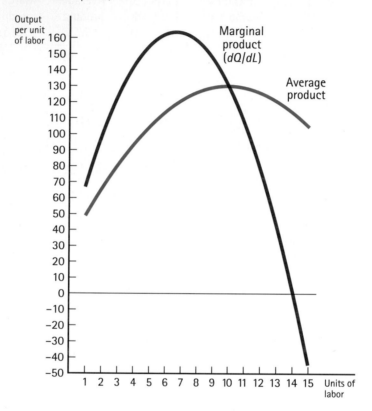

reaches a maximum (at $L = 6.67$ and marginal product $= 163.33$), then falls. This, too, is typical of many production processes. Figure 7.2 shows that marginal product equals average product when the latter reaches a maximum; that is, $MP = AP = 130$, when $L = 10$.

Note that we have two definitions of *marginal product*. The first ($\Delta Q/\Delta L$) assumes that we can employ labor only in discrete units, as in a laborer or a labor-hour. This may be due to employment laws or negotiated contracts with labor. The second (dQ/dL) assumes that we can employ labor continuously, as in 1.25 workers or 1.33 workers. This could occur by using part-time workers or workers who work more or less time than in a standard day's work.

ANALYZING MANAGERIAL DECISIONS

The Yankees' Deal for Alex Rodriguez

In February 2004, the New York Yankees assumed the richest contract in sports by trading players to the Texas Rangers for shortstop Alex Rodriguez. Rodriguez was working under a 10-year, $252 million contract that he signed with the Rangers in 2000. As soon as the deal was announced, commentators speculated about whether the contract was economically sensible. In fact, when one looks at the underlying economics, the Yankees appear to have gotten the best player in baseball, at a relatively bargain basement price.

First, the Yankees receive $67 million in cash from the Rangers, the largest sum to trade hands in the history of baseball. This reduces the Yankees liability to Rodriguez to roughly $112 million. The expected payouts to the players the Yankees got rid of because of the trade were approximately $13.3 million. Rodriguez will receive $15 million in 2004, but he has agreed to defer $1 million. Hence, the added cost of Rodriguez to the Yankees' payroll in 2004 is roughly $750,000.

For future years, the payouts to Rodriguez are the following: $15 million for the next three seasons; $16 million in 2007–08; $17 million in 2009; and $18 million in 2010. Rodriguez will defer $1 million for the first four years at zero percent interest and receive the $4 million in 2011.

Because of their high payroll costs, the Yankees must pay a luxury tax (which is split among the other baseball teams). In 2004, the Yankees estimate their payroll will equal $190 million (this is higher than the 10 lowest payroll teams). A payroll of $190 million would cost the Yankees $21 million in luxury taxes.

The total revenue for the Yankees is estimated to be $330 million in 2004. Approximately $110 million is generated from 3.5 million paying customers (ticket prices were increased an average of 10 percent for the 2004 season). The Yankees also receive $60 million from the YES Network, $10 million from WCBS radio, and over $30 million from national television, licensing, and sponsorship revenues. The team also receives revenue from local sponsorships and game concessions.

The Yankees expect the addition of Alex Rodriguez to increase attendance even in the face of increasing ticket prices (after the trade was announced, the ticket office was swamped with ticket requests). These additional fans also presumably will spend more at the games on snacks, drinks, and merchandise.

After all the factors are considered, most experts believe the marginal benefit to the Yankees is greater than the additional costs for Rodriguez's contract.

Source: "Sports Business: Steinbrenner Has Got It, and He Loves to Flaunt It," *New York Times*, February 17, 2004.

Which one you use depends on your situation: Are you constrained to an integer number of workers or can you employ fractions of a worker (or worker hour)?

To see why MP equals AP when AP is maximized, we apply the calculus techniques presented in Chapter 2. If x is the amount of the variable input used and Q is the output rate, then the average product of the variable input is Q/x

and the marginal product of the variable input is dQ/dx (see footnote 1). From Chapter 2, we know that

$$\frac{d(Q/x)}{dx} = \frac{x(dQ/dx) - Q(dx/dx)}{x^2}$$

$$= \frac{1}{x}\left(\frac{dQ}{dx} - \frac{Q}{x}\right)$$

When the average product is a maximum, $d(Q/x)/dx$ equals zero. Therefore,

$$\frac{d(Q/x)}{dx} = \frac{1}{x}\left(\frac{dQ}{dx} - \frac{Q}{x}\right) = 0$$

which means that dQ/dx must equal Q/x when the average product is a maximum. But, since dQ/dx is the marginal product and Q/x is the average product, this proves the proposition in the previous paragraph: When the average product is a maximum, the average product equals the marginal product.

The Law of Diminishing Marginal Returns

Having defined the production function and the average and marginal products of an input, we are ready to present one of the most famous laws of managerial economics—the law of **diminishing marginal returns**. This law states that, *if equal increments of an input are added and the quantities of other inputs are held constant, the resulting increments of the product decrease beyond some point; that is, the marginal product of the input diminishes.* This law is illustrated by Table 7.2; beyond 7 (6.67 if labor is treated as a continuous input) units of labor, the marginal product of labor decreases.

Three things should be noted concerning the law of diminishing marginal returns. First, this law is an empirical generalization, not a deduction from physical or biological laws. Second, it is assumed that technology remains fixed. The law of diminishing marginal returns cannot predict the effect of an additional unit of input when technology is allowed to change. Third, it is assumed that the quantity of at least one input is being held constant. The law of diminishing marginal returns does not apply to cases where there are increases in all inputs.

It is not hard to see why the law of diminishing marginal returns holds true. Take, for example, the case of the Thomas Machine Company, which has a fixed number of machine tools. If this firm hires more and more workers, the marginal product of a worker eventually begins to decrease, because workers have to wait in line to use the machine tools and the extra workers have to be assigned to less and less important tasks.

The Optimal Level of Utilization of an Input

If a firm has one fixed input and one variable input, how much of the variable input should it utilize? This is a very important question for the managers of business firms, large and small. To answer it, we must define the marginal revenue product of the variable input and the marginal expenditure on the variable input. These two concepts must be understood if we are to answer the question.

The **marginal revenue product** (MRP) is the amount that an additional unit of the variable input adds to the firm's total revenue. That is, letting MRP_Y be the marginal revenue product of input Y,

$$MRP_Y = \frac{\Delta TR}{\Delta Y} \tag{7.1}$$

where ΔTR is the change in total revenue resulting from a change of ΔY in the amount of input Y used by the firm.[2] It can easily be proven that the marginal revenue product of input Y equals input Y's marginal product times the firm's marginal revenue. To see this, note that marginal revenue (MR) equals $\Delta TR/\Delta Q$, where ΔQ is the change in the firm's output, and that

$$MRP_y = \frac{\Delta TR}{\Delta Y} = \left(\frac{\Delta TR}{\Delta Q} \right)\left(\frac{\Delta Q}{\Delta Y} \right)$$

Since $\Delta Q/\Delta Y$ equals input Y's marginal product (MP_Y), it follows that

$$MRP_Y = MR(MP_Y) \tag{7.2}$$

which is what we set out to prove.

The **marginal expenditure** (ME) is the amount that an additional unit of the variable input adds to the firm's total costs. That is, letting ME_Y be the marginal expenditure on input Y,

$$ME_Y = \frac{\Delta TC}{\Delta Y} \tag{7.3}$$

where ΔTC is the change in total cost resulting from a change of ΔY in the amount of input Y used by the firm.[3] If the firm can buy all it wants of input Y at a price of $10 a unit, ME_Y equals $10. In some cases, however, the firm must pay a higher price for input Y to get more of it; in such cases, ME_Y exceeds

[2] More precisely, $MRP_Y = d\text{TR}/dY$.
[3] More precisely, $ME_Y = d\text{TC}/dY$.

the price of input Y. Note that $\Delta TC/\Delta Y$ can be written as $(\Delta TC/\Delta Q)(\Delta Q/\Delta Y)$, where $\Delta TC/\Delta Q$ is the change in the firm's total cost (ΔTC) divided by the firm's change in output (ΔQ). Like $\Delta TR/\Delta Q$ is marginal revenue, $\Delta TC/\Delta Q$ is the firm's marginal cost (MC), or the change in the firm's total cost as its output is changed by a small amount.

To maximize its profits, the firm should utilize the amount of input Y where the marginal revenue product equals the marginal expenditure. In other words, the firm should set

$$MRP_Y = ME_Y \qquad (7.4)$$

This follows from our discussion of marginal analysis in Chapter 2. To maximize profit, a firm should expand any activity as long as the marginal benefits exceed the marginal costs. It should stop expanding it when the marginal benefit (in this case, MRP_Y) equals the marginal cost (in this case, ME_Y). To generalize this further, rewrite (7.4) as

$$(\Delta TR/\Delta Q)(\Delta Q/\Delta Y) = (\Delta TC/\Delta Q)(\Delta Q/\Delta Y)$$

or

$$\Delta TR/\Delta Q = \Delta TC/\Delta Q$$

or

$$MR = MC$$

We have therefore derived one of the most important rules of managerial economics—the firm should stop expanding its output when marginal revenue equals marginal cost (more on this in a later discussion).

The Rondo Corporation: A Numerical Example

To illustrate, consider the case of the Rondo Corporation, a producer of pocket calculators that has a fixed amount of plant and equipment but that can vary the number of workers it hires per day. The relationship between the number of calculators produced per day (Q) and the number of workers hired per day (L) is

$$Q = 98L - 3L^2 \qquad (7.5)$$

The Rondo Corporation can sell all the calculators it can produce (with its current plant and equipment) for $20 per calculator, so its marginal revenue equals

ANALYZING MANAGERIAL DECISIONS

How to Determine the Optimal Horsepower for an Oil Pipeline

Crude oil is carried by pipelines from oil fields and storage areas over hundreds of miles to urban and industrial centers. The output of such a pipeline is the amount of oil carried per day, and the two principal inputs are the diameter of the pipeline and the horsepower applied to the oil carried. Leslie Cookenboo of the Exxon Corporation estimated the production function for a pipeline with a 10-inch diameter to be as follows:

$$Q = 286H^{0.37}$$

where Q is the amount of crude oil carried per day and H is horsepower.

(a) Derive a formula for the marginal product of horsepower. (b) Do increases in horsepower result in diminishing marginal returns? (c) Derive a formula for the average product of horsepower. (d) If the marginal revenue from an extra unit of crude oil carried per day is $2, what is the marginal revenue product of horsepower? (e) If an oil-pipeline firm can add all the horsepower it wants at a price of $30 per unit of horsepower, what is the marginal expenditure on horsepower? (f) Under these circumstances, what amount of horsepower should an oil-pipeline firm use?

SOLUTION (a) The marginal product of horsepower equals $dQ/dH = 0.37(286)H^{-0.63} = 105.82H^{-0.63}$. (b) Yes. The marginal product of horsepower decreases as horsepower increases, as shown by the formula in the answer to part a. Specifically, $dMP_H/dH = -0.2331H^{-1.63} < 0$. (c) The average product of horsepower equals $Q/H = 286H^{-0.63}$. (d) Using equation (7.2), the marginal revenue

product of horsepower equals $2 times $(105.82H^{-0.63}) = $211.64H^{-0.63}$. (e) $30. (f) Using equation (7.4), the firm should set the marginal revenue product of horsepower equal to marginal expenditure:

$$211.64H^{-0.63} = 30$$
$$H^{-0.63} = 0.14175$$
$$H = 22.22.$$

The optimal amount of horsepower is 22.22 units.*

*For further discussion, see L. Cookenboo, "Production Functions and Cost Functions in Oil Pipelines," in the Study Guide accompanying this textbook.

$20. It can also hire as many workers as it likes for $40 per day. How many workers should it hire per day?

To apply the results of the previous section, we must determine the marginal revenue product of labor (MRP_L) and the marginal expenditure on labor (ME_L) in this firm. Using equation (7.2),

$$MRP_L = 20MP_L$$

since the firm's marginal revenue equals $20. Since $MP_L = dQ/dL$,

$$MRP_L = 20 \; \frac{d(98L - 3L^2)}{dL} = 20(98 - 6L)$$

If MRP_L is to equal ME_L, the number of workers hired must be such that

$$20(98 - 6L) = 40$$

since the firm's marginal expenditure on labor equals $40. Solving this equation, we find that L must equal 16. So, if the Rondo Corporation wants to maximize profit, it should hire 16 workers per day.

The Production Function with Two Variable Inputs

Up to this point, we have been concerned with the case where there is only one variable input. Now, we take up the more general case, where there are two variable inputs. These variable inputs can be thought of as working with one or more fixed inputs, or they may be thought of as the only two inputs (in which case the situation is the long run, since all inputs are variable). In either case, it is easy to extend the results to as many inputs as we like.

When we increase the number of variable inputs from one to two, the production function becomes slightly more complicated, but it is still the relationship between various combinations of inputs and the maximum amount of output that can be obtained from them. Really, the only change is that output is a function of two variables rather than one. To illustrate, suppose that the Monroe Machine Company, which produces a metal part (different from that produced by the Thomas Machine Company), can vary the quantities of both machine tools and labor. Its production function is given in Table 7.3. The average product of either machine tools or labor can be computed simply by dividing the total output by the amount of either machine tools or labor used. The marginal product of each input can be obtained by holding the other input

TABLE
7.3

Production Function, Two Variable Inputs, Monroe Machine Company

Amount of labor (units)	Number of machine tools (hundreds of parts produced per year)			
	3	4	5	6
1	5	11	18	24
2	14	30	50	72
3	22	60	80	99
4	30	81	115	125
5	35	84	140	144

constant. For example, the marginal product of a machine tool when four units of labor are used and when between three and four machine tools are used is 51 hundred parts per machine tool; the marginal product of labor when four machine tools are used and when between three and four units of labor are used is 21 hundred parts per unit. If X_1 is the amount of the first input and X_2 is the amount of the second input, the production function is

$$Q = f(X_1, X_2) \tag{7.6}$$

where Q is the firm's output rate. The marginal product of the first input is $\partial Q/\partial X_1$; the marginal product of the second input is $\partial Q/\partial X_2$.

One can also represent the production function by a surface, like that in Figure 7.3. The production surface is $OAQB$.[4] The height of a point on this surface denotes the quantity of output. Dropping a perpendicular down from a point on the production surface to the "floor" and seeing how far the resulting point is from the labor and machine tool axes indicates how much of each input is required to produce this much output. For example, to produce $G'G$ units of output requires OB_1 ($= A_1G'$) units of labor and OA_1 ($= B_1G'$) machine tools. Conversely, one can take any amounts of machine tools and labor, say, OA_2 machine tools and OB_2 units of labor, and find out how much output they produce by measuring the height of the production surface at D', the point where labor input is OB_2 and machine tool input is OA_2. According to Figure 7.3, the answer equals $D'D$.

---

[4]This surface is not meant to represent the numerical values in Table 7.3 but is a general representation of how a production surface of this sort is likely to appear.

FIGURE
7.3

Production Function, Two Variable Inputs

The production surface, $0AQB$, shows the amount of total output that can be obtained from various combinations of quantities of machine tools and labor

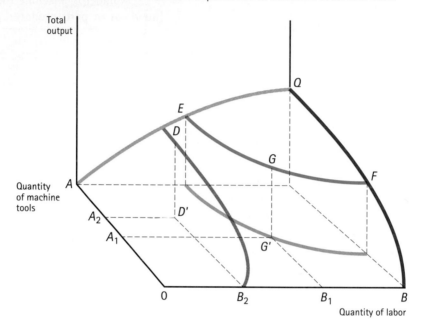

The production function does not include many of the different ways in which a given output can be produced because it includes only efficient combinations of inputs. For example, if two units of labor and three units of capital can produce one unit of output, this combination of inputs and output will not be included in the production function if it is also possible to produce one unit of output with two units of labor and two units of capital. The former input-output combination is clearly inefficient, since it is possible to obtain the result with the same amount of labor and less capital.

Isoquants

An **isoquant** is a curve showing all possible (efficient) combinations of inputs that are capable of producing a certain quantity of output. If we know the production function, we can readily derive the isoquant pertaining to any level of output. In Figure 7.3, suppose we want to find the isoquant corresponding to an output of $G'G$. All we need do is to cut the production surface at the height

ANALYZING MANAGERIAL DECISIONS

How Nucor Stays on the Production Function

Nucor is one of the largest steel firms in the United States, although it did not focus on steel production until the 1960s. By 2003, the company had achieved sales of over $6 billion and had never recorded a loss in over 35 years. More remarkably, its performance has far outstripped that of more traditional steel manufacturers like U.S. Steel. For example, when the average integrated steel company in the United States produced 400 tons of steel per employee, Nucor produced about 980 tons per employee. What actions have Nucor's managers implemented to achieve this superior performance?

One difference is that Nucor is a "minimill" not an integrated steel firm. The minimills have a different production function from that of the integrated mills. They use electric arc furnaces to make steel products from scrap metal. In 1999, Nucor was the nation's largest steel recycler, as it used over 10 million tons of scrap steel in its steel production.

Another reason for Nucor's outstanding performance is the company's focus on the efficient use of resources. Management has executed strategies that keep the company on an efficient production function. As pointed out on page 252, the production function includes only efficient input combinations. For example, if a unit of output can be produced with three units of labor and three units of capital, an input combination containing four units of labor and three units of capital should not be used because it is more costly. Inefficient firms are off the production function. They produce less output than is possible given their input combinations. Hence, they have higher costs.

Efficient production does not occur because of random luck. It is clearly governed by managerial decisions and requires an integrated set of policies. In Nucor's case, the firm employs over 7,000 people. So, how does management keep employees focused on efficient production?

Nucor uses the following multiprong approach:

1. It maintains a simple, streamlined organizational structure that encourages decentralized decision making. Most divisions use only three layers of management. Each division is treated as a profit center and is expected to earn a 25 percent return on total assets.

2. The company acts as the general contractor in building new plants. It locates in rural areas where land is cheap (and unions are weak). Also, each plant is located near water and is served by at least two railroad lines to keep freight rates low. Nucor recruits employees to help build the plant. This allows it to observe the working habits of individuals. Those with good working habits are recruited to work in the plant when it opens. It also brings workers from other plants (who have already built plants) to join the constuction team. Using these methods Nucor is able to build a plant at a lower cost and in about 33 percent less time than competitors.

3. All employees are subject to performance-related compensation plans. For example, production employees are paid weekly bonuses based on the productivity of their work group. Using this team approach, Nucor is able to lower its monitoring costs because employees monitor each other. Bonuses are based on the

capabilities of the equipment and average 80 percent to 150 percent of an employee's base pay. The more output a team produces, the higher are the bonuses.

4. Nucor treats all employees equally. Benefits are the same regardless of organizational position. There are no company cars, executive dining rooms, or corporate jets.

5. The firm's focus on output does not mean that quality suffers. Employees are committed to providing the highest quality steel at a competitive price. To reinforce this commitment to quality, most of Nucor's divisions are ISO 9000 Certified.*

6. Finally, Nucor regards itself as a technological leader. It was the first firm to produce thin-slab casting at a minimill and searches worldwide for new developments in steel production. This emphasis on innovation is reinforced by the firm's flat organizational structure. Decisions can be made and implemented quickly because of it.

[5]ISO 9000 is a set of quality standards. To receive ISO 9000 certification, managers must fulfill various quality assurance requirements and be audited by an external registrar. If a firm's quality assurance system is approved by this registrar, the firm is awarded an ISO 9000 certification and is allowed to advertise it to all customers.

of $G'G$ parallel to the base plane, the result being EGF, and drop perpendiculars from EGF to the base. Clearly, this results in a curve that includes all efficient combinations of machine tools and labor that can produce $G'G$ metal parts. Using the notation in equation (7.6), an isoquant shows all combinations of X_1 and X_2 such that $f(X_1, X_2)$ equals a certain output rate.

Several isoquants, each pertaining to a different output rate, are shown in Figure 7.4. The two axes measure the quantities of inputs that are used. In contrast to the previous diagrams, we assume that labor and capital—not labor and machine tools (a particular form of capital)—are the relevant inputs in this case. The curves show the various combinations of inputs that can produce 100, 200, and 300 units of output. For example, consider the isoquant pertaining to 100 units of output per period of time. According to this isoquant, it is possible to attain this output rate if L_0 units of labor and K_0 units of capital are used per period of time. Alternatively, this output rate can be attained if L_1 units of labor and K_1 units of capital—or L_2 units of labor and K_2 units of capital—are used per period of time.

The Marginal Rate of Technical Substitution

As we have just seen, ordinarily, a particular output can be produced in a number of efficient ways. The **marginal rate of technical substitution** shows the rate at which one input can be substituted for another input if output remains

FIGURE

7.4

Isoquants

These three isoquants show the various combinations of capital and labor that can produce 100, 200, and 300 units of output.

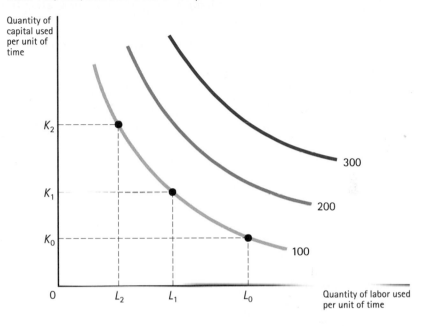

constant. If, as in equation (7.6), the quantity of output produced by a firm is a function of the amounts of two inputs used,

$$Q = f(X_1, X_2)$$

the marginal rate of technical substitution (MRTS) is

$$\text{MRTS} = -\frac{dX_2}{dX_1} \tag{7.7}$$

given that Q is held constant (and X_2 is on the y axis of the isoquant graph and X_1 is on the x axis).

Geometrically, the marginal rate of technical substitution is -1 times the slope of the isoquant. This makes sense, since dX_2/dX_1 is the slope of the isoquant. Note that the marginal rate of technical substitution equals MP_1/MP_2, where MP_1 is the marginal product of input 1 and MP_2 is the marginal product of input 2. To show why, it is useful to point out that

$$dQ = \frac{\partial Q}{\partial X_1}\, dX_1 + \frac{dQ}{\partial X_2}\, dX_2$$

Since output is maintained at a constant level, $dQ = 0$, which means that

$$\frac{\partial Q}{X_1}\, dX_1 + \frac{\partial Q}{\partial X_2}\, dX_2 = 0$$

Therefore,

$$\frac{dX_2}{dX_1} = \frac{-(\partial Q/\partial X_1)}{\partial Q/\partial X_2} = -\frac{MP_1}{MP_2} \tag{7.8}$$

Since $MRTS = -dX_2/dX_1$, it follows that $MRTS = MP_1/MP_2$.

There are vast differences in how readily various inputs can be substituted for one another. For example, in some production processes, one kind of labor can easily be substituted for another; in others, this is not true at all. In extreme cases, no substitution among inputs is possible; to produce a unit of output, a fixed amount of each input is required. In other words, inputs must be used in fixed proportions. Figure 7.5 shows the firm's isoquants in such a case; as you can see, they are right angles. Very few production processes allow no substitution at all among inputs, but in some cases the amount of substitution is very limited. If perfect substitutability of inputs were possible, isoquants would be straight lines connecting the two axes.

While no substitution is a limiting assumption, in the short run, it may approximate many firms' situations. Assuming that no substitution exists, Wassily Leontief collected information from firms in a given industrial sector on how much of each input (measured in dollars) they used to produce their output (in dollars). He then aggregated the output and input data for all firms in a given industrial sector by type. The amount spent on the various inputs was then summed and subtracted from the value of the output (giving a residual or profit for the industry). He did this for many industrial sectors. The dollar value of each input in each industry was then divided by the dollar value of the output of that industry. The result is a production function in terms of the cents of each input required to produce a dollar's worth of output for each industry. This is the fixed input-output production function (i.e., no substitution among inputs).

Consider a highly simplified production function for the steel industry:

Iron ore = 0.5
Coal = 0.4
Labor = 0.1

FIGURE
7.5

Isoquants in the Case of Fixed Proportions

If inputs must be used in fixed proportions, the isoquants are right angles.

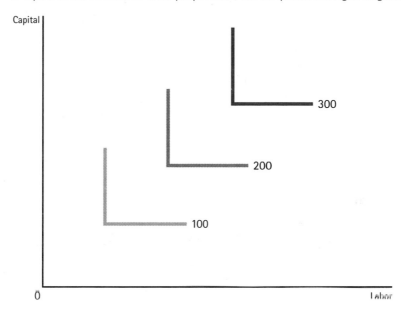

Therefore, it takes 40 cents of coal to make a dollar's worth of steel.

The use of this production function (which, in addition to assuming no substitutability of inputs for each other, also does not assume that inputs are used efficiently, it merely measures what is currently being done in the industry) is called *input-output analysis* and won Leontief the Nobel Prize in Economics in 1973.

To illustrate how it is used, consider a $1 million increase in the demand for steel. The Leontief model would state that $500,000 more iron ore would be required or 0.5 × $1,000,000; $400,000 more coal would be required or 0.4 × $1,000,000; and $100,000 more labor would be required or 0.1 × $1,000,000. All of these dollar figures can be divided by unit prices to get units of iron ore, units of coal, and units of labor required.

Furthermore, since a production function for coal exists, say,

$$\text{Machinery} = 0.6$$
$$\text{Labor} = 0.4$$

then a $1 million increase in steel demand and the subsequent $400,000 increase in coal demand mean a $240,000 increase or 0.6 × $400,000 increase in machinery demand.

But, since machinery also has a production function that undoubtedly involves steel, an increase in steel demand entails yet a further increase in steel demand. Therefore, Leontief's analysis (actually Walras's, 1874) shows the interdependence of the economy through the production functions (since the output of one sector is the input to other sectors).

Many governments, like those of the United States and Japan, and many private sector institutions have developed and use very large and sophisticated input-output models to aid in their policy and managerial decision making.

Isoquants may also have positively sloped segments, or bend back on themselves, as shown in Figure 7.6. Above $0U$ and below $0V$, the slope of the isoquants is positive, which implies that increases in both capital and labor are required to maintain a certain output rate. If this is the case, the marginal product of one or the other input must be negative. Above $0U$, the marginal product of capital is negative; therefore, the output increases if less capital is used while the amount of labor is held constant. Below $0V$, the marginal product of labor is negative; therefore, the output increases if less labor is used while the amount of capital is held constant. The lines $0U$ and $0V$ are called **ridge lines**.

No profit-maximizing firm operates at a point outside the ridge lines, since it can produce the same output with less of both inputs, which must be cheaper. Consider point H in Figure 7.6. Because this is a point where the isoquant is positively sloped (and so outside the ridge lines) it requires a greater amount of both labor and capital than some other point (for example, point E) on the same isoquant. Since both capital and labor have positive prices, it must be cheaper to operate at point E than at point H. The moral is this: Do not operate at a point outside the ridge lines if you want to maximize profit.

The Optimal Combination of Inputs

A firm that wants to maximize profit will try to minimize the cost of producing a given output or maximize the output derived from a given level of cost.[5] Suppose the firm takes input prices as given and there are two inputs, capital and labor, that vary in the relevant time period. What combination of capital and labor should the firm choose if it wants to maximize the quantity of output derived from the given level of cost?

To begin to answer this question, we determine the various combinations of inputs that the firm can obtain for a given expenditure. For example, if capital and labor are the inputs and the price of labor is P_L per unit and the price

---

[5]The conditions for minimizing the cost of producing a given output are the same as those for maximizing the output from a given cost. This is shown in the present section. Therefore, we can view the firm's problem in either way.

FIGURE
7.6

Economic Region of Production

No profit-maximizing firm operates at a point outside the ridge lines, OU and OV.

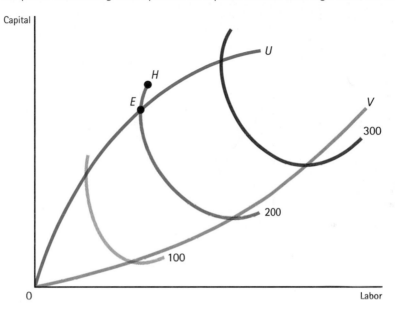

of capital is P_K per unit, the input combinations that can be obtained for a total outlay of M are such that

$$P_L L + P_K K = M \qquad (7.9)$$

where L is the amount of the labor input and K is the amount of the capital input. Given M, P_L, and P_K, it follows that

$$K = \frac{M}{P_K} - \frac{P_L L}{P_K} \qquad (7.10)$$

Hence, the various combinations of capital and labor that can be purchased, given P_L, P_K, and M, can be represented by a straight line like that shown in Figure 7.7. (Capital is plotted on the vertical axis, labor is plotted on the horizontal.) This line, which has an intercept on the vertical axis equal to M/P_K and a slope of $-P_L/P_K$, is called an **isocost curve**.

If we superimpose the relevant isocost curve on the firm's isoquant map, we can determine graphically which combination of inputs maximizes the output

FIGURE

7.7

Isocost Curve

The isocost curve shows the combinations of inputs that can be obtained for a total outlay of M.

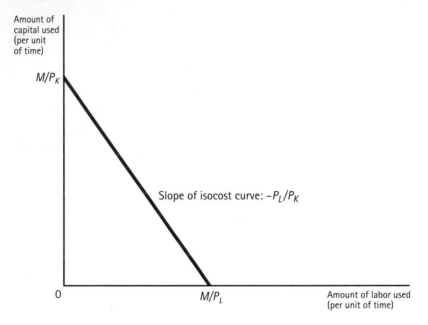

for the given expenditure. The firm should pick the point on the isocost curve that is on the highest isoquant, for example, R in Figure 7.8. This is a point where the isocost curve is tangent to the isoquant. Since the slope of the isocost curve is the negative of P_L/P_K and the slope of the isoquant is the negative of MP_L/MP_K (as pointed out in the previous section), it follows that the optimal combination of inputs is one where $MP_L/MP_K = P_L/P_K$. Or put differently, the firm should choose an input combination where $MP_L/P_L = MP_K/P_K$.

If there are more than two inputs, the firm maximizes output by distributing its expenditures among various inputs in such a way that the marginal product of a dollar's worth of any one input is equal to the marginal product of a dollar's worth of any other input used. That is, the firm will choose an input combination such that

$$\frac{MP_a}{P_a} = \frac{MP_b}{P_b} = \cdots = \frac{MP_n}{P_n} \tag{7.11}$$

FIGURE
7.8

Maximization of Output for a Given Cost

To maximize the output for a given cost, the firm should choose the input combination at point R.

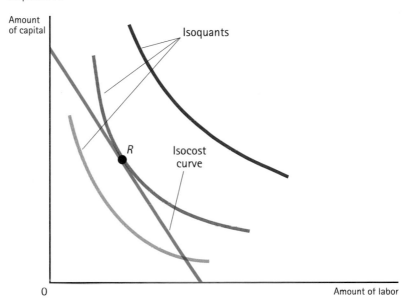

where MP_a, MP_b, ... , MP_n are the marginal products of inputs a, b, ... , n; and P_a, P_b, ... , P_n are the prices of inputs a, b, ... , n. (For further proof of the decision rule in equation (7.11), see the chapter appendix.)

To determine the input combination that minimizes the cost of producing a given output, we use a graph similar to Figure 7.8. Moving along the isoquant corresponding to the stipulated output level, we must find the point on the isoquant that lies on the lowest isocost curve, for example, S in Figure 7.9. Input combinations on isocost curves like C_0 that lie below S are cheaper than S, but they cannot produce the desired output. Input combinations on isocost curves like C_2 that lie above S produce the desired output but at a higher cost than S. It is obvious that the optimal point, S, is a point where the isocost curve is tangent to the isoquant. Therefore, to minimize the cost of producing a given output or to maximize the output from a given cost outlay, the firm must equate MP_L/MP_K and P_L/P_K; this means that $MP_L/P_L = MP_K/P_K$. And if more than two inputs are needed, the firm must satisfy equation (7.11).

FIGURE
7.9

Minimization of Cost for a Given Output

To minimize the cost of producing the amount of output corresponding to this isoquant, the firm should choose the input combination at point S.

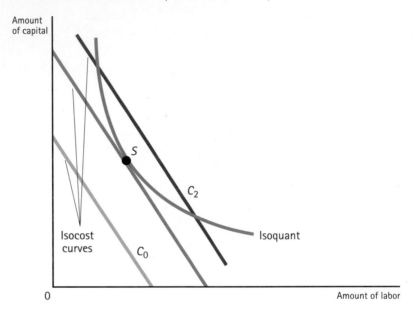

The Beiswanger Company: A Numerical Example

To illustrate how the technique presented in the previous section can be used, consider the Beiswanger Company, a small firm engaged in engineering analysis. Beiswanger's president has determined that the firm's output per month (Q) is related in the following way to the number of engineers (E) and technicians used (T):

$$Q = 20E - E^2 + 12T - 0.5T^2 \qquad (7.12)$$

The monthly wage of an engineer is \$4,000, and the monthly wage of a technician is \$2,000. If Beiswanger allots \$28,000 per month for the total combined wages of engineers and technicians, how many engineers and technicians should it hire?

On the basis of the previous section, if the Beiswanger Company is to maximize output, it must choose a combination of engineers and technicians such that

$$\frac{MP_E}{P_E} = \frac{MP_T}{P_T} \tag{7.13}$$

where MP_E is the marginal product of an engineer, MP_T is the marginal product of a technician, P_E is the wage of an engineer, and P_T is the wage of a technician. Taking partial derivatives of Q in equation (7.12) with respect to E and T, we find that

$$MP_E = \frac{\partial Q}{\partial E} = 20 - 2E \tag{7.14a}$$

$$MP_T = \frac{\partial Q}{\partial T} = 12 - T \tag{7.14b}$$

Inserting these expressions for MP_E and MP_T into equation (7.13) and noting that $P_E = 4,000$ and $P_T = 2,000$, it follows from equation (7.13) that

$$\frac{20 - 2E}{4,000} = \frac{12 - T}{2,000}$$

$$\frac{2,000(20 - 2E)}{4,000} = 12 - T$$

$$10 - E = 12 - T$$

$$T = E + 2$$

Since Beiswanger will spend $28,000 per month on the total combined wages of engineers and technicians,

$$4,000E + 2,000T = 28,000$$

Substituting $(E + 2)$ for T,

$$4,000E + 2,000(E + 2) = 28,000$$

This means that $E = 4$ (and $T = 6$). So, to maximize the output from the $28,000 outlay on wages, Beiswanger should hire four engineers and six technicians.

The Miller Company:
Another Numerical Example

To show how the analysis in the section before last can be used to determine the input combination that minimizes the cost of producing a given output, consider the Miller Company, for which the relationship between output per hour (Q) and the number of workers (L) and machines (K) used per hour is

$$Q = 10(LK)^{0.5}$$

The wage of a worker is $8 per hour, and the price of a machine is $2 per hour. If the Miller Company produces 80 units of output per hour, how many workers and machines should it use?

According to equation (7.11), the Miller Company should choose an input combination such that

$$\frac{MP_L}{P_L} = \frac{MP_K}{P_K}$$

where MP_L is the marginal product of a worker, MP_K is the marginal product of a machine, P_L is the wage of a worker, and P_K is the price of using a machine. Since $Q = 10(LK)^{0.5}$,

$$MP_L = \frac{\partial Q}{\partial L} = 5\left(\frac{K}{L}\right)^{0.5}$$

$$MP_K = \frac{\partial Q}{\partial K} = 5\left(\frac{L}{K}\right)^{0.5}$$

So, if $MP_L/P_L = MP_K/P_K$

$$\frac{5(K/L)^{0.5}}{8} = \frac{5(L/K)^{0.5}}{2}$$

Multiplying both sides of this equation by $(K/L)^{0.5}$, we get

$$\frac{5K}{8L} = \frac{5}{2}$$

which means that $K = 4L$. Since $Q = 80$,

$$10(LK)^{0.5} = 80$$
$$10[L(4L)]^{0.5} = 80$$
$$L = 4$$

Therefore, to minimize cost, the Miller Company should hire four workers and use 16 machines.

The Optimal Lot Size

In previous sections, we describe how a firm's managers can find the input combination that minimizes the cost of producing a particular quantity of output. In this section, we extend our analysis to include more than one time period and recognize that many firms produce goods in lots or batches, which are produced intermittently. A central question for such firms is this: What is the optimal lot size? Managerial economists have devoted considerable attention to this question. By using the optimization techniques described in earlier chapters, this question can readily be answered, extending our analysis in previous sections.

Suppose that the Monarch Company, a manufacturer of trucks, has to produce 100,000 parts of a particular type, since each of its trucks requires such a part. Each time the firm begins to produce this type of part, it incurs a setup cost of $20,000 because it has to devote considerable labor time to setting up the equipment that produces this part. The advantage of producing large lots is that this cuts the total setup cost incurred during the year. If the firm were to produce its annual requirement of 100,000 parts in one huge lot, it would have to set up the equipment only once, the result being that its total setup cost for the year would be $20,000. If it produced its annual requirement of 100,000 parts in two lots (each of 50,000), it would have to set up the equipment twice, the result being that the total setup cost for the year would be $40,000. The relationship between the size of a lot and the annual total setup cost is shown in Figure 7.10.

Firms often do not produce large lots because these result in large inventories that are expensive to maintain and finance. If, for example, the firm produces all 100,000 of the parts in one huge lot at the beginning of the year, its inventory equals 100,000 parts at the beginning of the year and zero parts at the end of the year. Its average inventory is 50,000 parts, as shown in the left-hand panel of Figure 7.11. On the other hand, if the firm produces the annual requirement of 100,000 parts in two lots (each of 50,000 units), its inventory equals 50,000 parts at the beginning of the year and zero parts at the end of six months; then, after the second lot is produced, its inventory jumps back up to 50,000 parts, after which it declines once again to zero parts at the end of the year. Therefore, its average inventory is 25,000 parts, as shown in the right-hand panel of Figure 7.11.

If the annual cost of holding inventory is proportional to the average inventory, the relationship between the size of a lot and the annual cost of holding inventory is as shown in Figure 7.12.[6] Adding the annual setup cost for each lot size (taken from Figure 7.10 and reproduced in Figure 7.12) to the inventory cost, we obtain the total annual cost for each lot size. Under the conditions shown in Figure 7.12, the optimal lot size is 25,000, where the total annual costs are at a minimum.

---

[6]Robert Delaney of Cass Logistics estimates that the cost of carrying a dollar's worth of inventory for a year is 21 cents.

Relationship between the Size of the Lot and Annual Setup Cost

The larger is the lot size, the lower the annual setup cost.

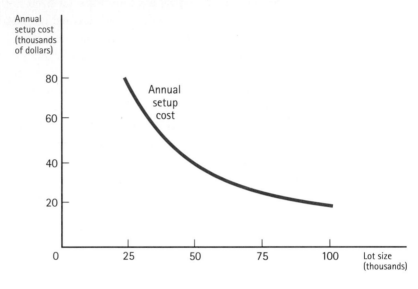

Size of Inventory during the Year

Average inventory is 50,000 parts if the lot size equals 100,000 and 25,000 parts if the lot size equals 50,000.

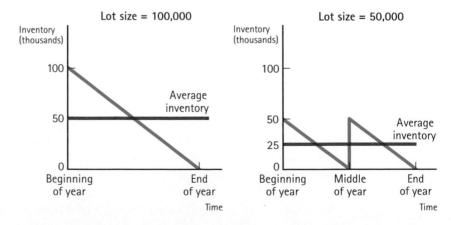

FIGURE
7.12

Relationship between Size of Lot and Total Annual Cost

Setup cost decreases as lot size increases, because fewer setups occur. The cost of carrying inventory increases as lot size increases, because supply exceeds demand more often and goods remain in inventory for a long time period. Total costs are the vertical summation of the two costs. The optimal lot size (which minimizes total cost) is where the two cost curves intersect. Total cost is the sum of the cost of carrying inventory and the setup cost. Therefore, the total cost curve is the vertical sum of the cost-of-carrying-inventory curve and the setup cost curve. For example, if the optimal lot size is 25,000, annual setup cost equals OH, as does annual inventory carrying cost and total annual cost equals $20H = OK$.

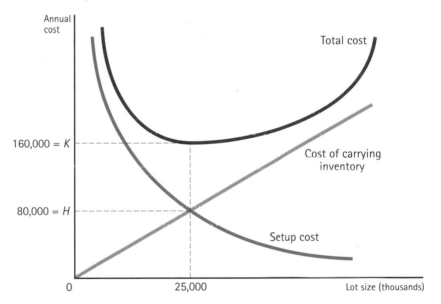

In general, how can we determine the optimal lot size? Total annual setup cost equals $20,000Q/L$ dollars, where Q is the total annual requirement of the relevant part and L is the number of identical parts of this sort produced in a lot. If $6.40 is the annual cost of holding each identical part of this sort in inventory for a year, the annual cost of holding inventory equals $6.40L/2$ dollars. Adding the annual setup cost and the annual cost of holding inventory, we obtain the following expression for the total annual cost:

$$C = 6.4L/2 + 20,000Q/L$$

To minimize total annual cost, we set

$$\frac{dC}{dL} = 3.2 - \frac{20{,}000Q}{L^2} = 0$$

Solving for L, we find that, to minimize total annual cost, we should have

$$L = \left(\frac{20{,}000Q}{3.2} \right)^{0.5} \tag{7.15}$$

More generally, the optimal lot size equals $(2SQ/b)^{0.5}$, where S is the cost per setup and b is the annual cost of carrying each good of this sort in inventory. Note that this optimal lot size occurs when inventory holding costs equal setup costs, or $6.4L/2 = 20{,}000Q/L$, or $3.2L^2 = 20{,}000Q$, which gives the same result as equation (7.15). It can also be shown that the optimal (minimum) total cost is $(2bSQ)^{0.5}$.

In the case of the Monarch Company, Q equals 100,000. Therefore, to minimize total annual cost, L should equal $[20{,}000(100{,}000)/3.2]^{0.5} = (625$ million$)^{0.5} = 25{,}000$. In other words, the optimal lot size is 25,000, which means that 25,000 identical parts of this sort should be produced in each lot. (Of course, there is no reason for the number of setups per year to be an integer number. For example, one could have five setups during each two-year period, or two and a half setups per year.)[7]

What Toyota Taught the World

The Japanese taught the rest of the world a great deal about production. For one thing, they succeeded in lowering the cost per setup, thus reducing the optimal lot size. For example, in the late 1970s, Toyota Motor Company's workers took about 10 minutes to set up the 800-ton presses used in forming auto hoods and fenders, whereas this took about 6 hours in the United States (see Table 7.4 for other cases). To see that such a reduction in the cost per setup reduces the optimal lot size, consider the Monarch Company, discussed in the previous section. If this firm could reduce the cost per setup from \$20,000 to \$5,000, the optimal lot size would be $(5{,}000Q/3.2)^{0.5}$, not $(20{,}000Q/3.2)^{0.5}$, which means that the optimal lot size is cut in half to 12,500 (holding Q constant).

A big advantage of reducing lot sizes is that less inventory has to be held. At least one senior Japanese manager stated that "inventory is the root of all evil." Toyota's famous just-in-time production system calls for every part's

---

[7]See J. Magee, "Guides to Inventory Policy: Functions and Lot Sizes," in E. Mansfield, ed., *Managerial Economics and Operations Research* (5th ed.; New York: Norton, 1987).

TABLE 7.4	Reductions in Time Required to Set up Selected Machines, Japanese Firms

Firm	Machine	Initial setup time	New setup time
Toyota	Bolt maker	8 hours	1 minute
Mazda	Ring gear cutter	6.5 hours	15 minutes
Mazda	Die casting machine	1.5 hours	4 minutes
Mitsubishi	8-arbor boring machine	24 hours	3 minutes

Source: J. Blackburn, Time-Based Competition (Homewood, IL: Business One Irwin, 1991), p. 178.

arrival just when it is needed or just when a machine is available. This can result in a great increase in efficiency. Less work-in-process inventory cuts the cost of holding inventory as well as speeds up the production cycle time and makes it simpler to monitor the progress of work through the factory.[8] Note that as S goes to zero, L goes to zero, and hence $L/2$ (average inventory held) goes to zero. Hence, Toyota's lowering of setup costs enabled it to follow a policy of virtually no inventory.

Many U.S. firms have come to use just-in-time production systems. The results have sometimes been stunning. For example, consider Northern Telecom's plant in Santa Clara, California, which makes printed circuit boards. Managers report that output increased by 25 percent, without additional workers and that inventories were reduced by over 80 percent.

Another technique adopted by the Japanese is focused manufacturing. For example, Toyota, in making forklift trucks, restricted its production to a comparatively narrow line of six families of trucks in its factory in Nagoya. In this way, it reduced the complexity of its production operations, which in turn decreased the number of parts, the level of inventories, the required amount of supervision, and the number of errors and defects. Table 7.5 compares the average cost of producing a forklift truck at Toyota with that at a West European factory that produced 20 families of trucks in its factory. As you can see, Toyota's cost was about 20 percent lower than the West European firm's.[9]

European, U.S., and other firms responded by adopting similar techniques. For example, the West European manufacturer of forklift trucks in Table 7.5

[8]R. Hayes and S. Wheelwright, Restoring Our Competitive Edge (New York: Wiley, 1984). Also, see National Research Council, "The Japanese Cost and Quality Advantages in the Auto Industry," in Managerial Economics and Operations Research, ed. Mansfield.

[9]J. Abegglen and G. Stalk, Kaisha: The Japanese Corporation (New York: Basic Books, 1985). Of course, from a marketing point of view, there can be disadvantages in reducing the variety of products produced. They must be balanced against the cost reductions.

TABLE
7.5

Cost of Producing a Forklift Truck (European Cost = 100)

	Factory	
	West European	Toyota
Number of product families	20	6
Cost per truck		
Materials	75	65
Direct labor	4	2
Overhead	21	14
Total cost	100	81

Source: Abegglen and Stalk, *Kaisha.*

reduced the number of product families made in its plant from 20 to 6. The result was about the same as in Japan: Cost per truck fell by 19 percent.[10] One important point that this illustrates is that Japanese firms have no monopoly on production knowledge and expertise. Indeed, many of the ideas that the Japanese utilized with great success (for example, quality control techniques) originated in the United States.

Returns to Scale

In previous sections, we learned how technology in a particular industry can be represented by a production function and described the characteristics of production functions (and of related concepts like the marginal and average product) that seem to hold in general for production processes. However, one important characteristic of production functions has not been described: how output responds in the long run to changes in the scale of the firm. Suppose we consider a long-run situation in which all inputs are variable, and suppose the firm increases the amount of all inputs by the same proportion. What would happen to output?

Clearly, there are three possibilities: First, output may increase by a larger proportion than each of the inputs. For example, doubling all inputs may lead to more than a doubling of output. This is the case of **increasing returns to scale**. Second, output may increase by a smaller proportion than each of the

[10]Ibid.

inputs. For example, doubling all inputs may lead to less than a doubling of output. This is the case of **decreasing returns to scale.** Third, output may increase by exactly the same proportion as the inputs. For example, doubling all inputs may lead to a doubling of output. This is the case of **constant returns to scale.**

It may seem that production functions must necessarily exhibit constant returns to scale. If two factories are built with the same plant and the same types of workers, it may appear obvious that twice as much output would result than if one such plant is built. But things are not so simple. If a firm doubles its scale, it may be able to use techniques that could not be used at the smaller scale. Some inputs are not available in small units; for example, we cannot install half a robot. Because of indivisibilities of this sort, increasing returns to scale may occur. So, although one could double a firm's size by simply building two small factories, this may be inefficient. One large factory may be more efficient than two smaller factories of the same total capacity because it is large enough to use certain techniques and inputs that the smaller factories cannot employ.

Increasing returns to scale also arise because of certain geometrical relations. Since the volume of a box that is $2 \times 2 \times 2$ feet is 8 times as great as the volume of a box that is $1 \times 1 \times 1$ foot, the former box can carry 8 times as much as the latter box. But, since the area of the six sides of the $2 \times 2 \times 2$-foot box is 24 square feet and the area of the six sides of the $1 \times 1 \times 1$-foot box is 6 square feet, the former box only requires 4 times as much wood as the latter. Greater specialization also can result in increasing returns to scale: As more workers and machines are used, it is possible to subdivide tasks and allow various inputs to specialize. Also, economies of scale may arise because of probabilistic considerations; for example, because the aggregate behavior of a bigger number of customers tends to be more stable, a firm's inventory may not have to increase in proportion to its sales.

Why do decreasing returns to scale occur? The most frequently cited reason is the difficulty of coordinating a large enterprise. It can be difficult even in a small firm to obtain the information required to make important decisions; in a large firm, the difficulties tend to be greater. It can be difficult even in a small firm to be certain that management's wishes are being carried out; in a larger firm, these difficulties tend to be greater. Although the advantages of a large organization are obvious, there are often great disadvantages. For example, in certain kinds of research and development, there is evidence that large engineering teams tend to be less effective than smaller ones and that large firms tend to be less effective than small ones.

Whether there are constant, increasing, or decreasing returns to scale in a particular situation is an empirical question that must be settled case by case. There is no simple, all-encompassing answer. In some industries, the available evidence may indicate that increasing returns are present over a certain range

CONSULTANT'S CORNER

Choosing the Size of an Oil Tanker

Over 60 percent of crude oil output is transported by oil tankers. The product is the largest commodity in transocean trade, accounting for 40 percent of all ocean shipments, by weight. Oil tankers can be regarded as a large cylinder. The surface area of a cylinder is not proportional to its volume; instead, as a cylinder's volume increases, its surface area goes up less than proportionately. Therefore, a tanker that can carry 300,000 deadweight tonnes is only about twice as broad, long, and deep as one that can carry 30,000 tonnes.

Since the 1970s, the size of oil tankers has increased, as indicated next:

Year	Average oil tanker size (thousands of deadweight tonnes)
1973	64.0
1978	103.0
1985	146.0
2000	220.0

The oil tanker business is cyclical in nature. It is characterized by periods of overcapacity (and low prices) and undercapacity (and high prices). For example, in 1999, Standard and Poor's either lowered ratings or downwardly revised outlooks for 23 of the 34 public shipping companies it covers.

In the fall of 2003, some analysts believed that pricing conditions in the oil tanker market would improve because of a strong U.S. economy and strong economies in Asia (especially China). If you were a consultant to a shipping company interested in building a new tanker, would you advise the company to build a tanker of 200,000 tonnes or 20,000 tonnes?

Sources: www.eagibson.co.uk/posidonia; www.standardandpoors.com/ratings/corporates/shipping.htm; www.europa.eu.int/scadplus/leg (Maritime safety communications of 21 March 2000 to Parliament).

of output. In other industries, decreasing or constant returns may be present. Moreover, it is important to note that the answer is likely to depend on the level of output considered. There may be increasing returns to scale at small output levels and constant or decreasing returns to scale at larger output levels.

The Output Elasticity

To measure whether there are increasing, decreasing, or constant returns to scale, the output elasticity can be computed. The **output elasticity** *is defined as the percentage of change in output resulting from a 1 percent increase in all inputs.* If the output elasticity exceeds 1, there are increasing returns to scale; if it equals 1, there are constant returns to scale; and if it is less than 1, there are decreasing returns to scale.

As an illustration, consider the Lone Star Company, a maker of aircraft parts, which has the following production function:

$$Q = 0.8L^{0.3}K^{0.8}$$

where Q is the number of parts produced per year (measured in millions of parts), L is the number of workers hired, and K is the amount of capital used. This is a Cobb-Douglas production function (named after Charles Cobb and Paul Douglas, who pioneered in its application), which is discussed in more detail in the section after next.

To calculate the output elasticity at the Lone Star Company, let us see what happens to Q if we multiply both inputs (L and K) by 1.01. Clearly, the new value of Q, that is, Q', equals

$$\begin{aligned} Q' &= 0.8(1.01L)^{0.3}(1.01K)^{0.8} \\ &= 0.8(1.01)^{1.1}L^{0.3}K^{0.8} \\ &= (1.01)^{1.1}(0.8L^{0.3}K^{0.8}) \\ &= (1.01)^{1.1}Q \\ &= 1.0110054840Q \end{aligned}$$

Therefore, if the quantity of both inputs increases by 1 percent, output increases by slightly more than 1.1 percent; this means that the output elasticity is approximately 1.1. It is exactly 1.1 for an infinitesimal change in input use (of both inputs). Since a 1 percent change is larger than infinitesimal, the increase in output is slightly larger than 1.1.

How Firms Obtain Information About the Production Function: Competitive Benchmarking at Xerox

Having discussed at length the key role of the production function in managerial decision making, we must look carefully at how managers obtain information concerning the production function. How does Hewlett-Packard or Merck or Exxon Mobil find out how to get the most out of a particular combination of inputs and what is the maximum output obtainable from this input combination? One way that firms try to solve this problem is by sending out teams of engineers and technicians to visit other firms to obtain information concerning best-practice methods and procedures. In this way, they try to determine whether they are operating on the industry production function—or whether they are inefficient relative to other firms. This practice, known as **competitive**

TABLE
7.6

Comparison of Warehouse Operations

Measure of output per worker per day	L. L. Bean	Xerox
Orders per worker per day	550	117
Lines per worker per day[a]	1,440	497

[a]A line is a standard measure of travel distance for one trip to a storage bin.

Source: Hayes, Wheelwright, and Clark, *Dynamic Manufacturing.*

benchmarking, produced valuable results for many companies, such as the Xerox Corporation.

In 1979, Xerox, confronted with a falling share of the market and reduced profitability of its basic copier business, began a searching examination of its methods. Starting with an engineering study of rival products, including an examination of Fuji Xerox, its partly owned subsidiary in Japan, Xerox's executives found strong evidence that it was not as efficient as its major Japanese rivals.[11]

Interestingly, Xerox found that it could learn a great deal from firms in seemingly unrelated fields. For example, Xerox executives, intent on improving their warehousing operations, searched for a firm to study in this regard. After looking in trade journals and discussing warehousing systems with consultants, they decided to visit L.L. Bean, the Maine apparel and footwear seller, which acquired a strong reputation for customer service and had distribution problems similar to Xerox's.

Xerox's managers found that, although L.L. Bean's warehouse operations were largely manual, it had achieved a high degree of output per worker. Table 7.6 compares output per worker in L.L. Bean's warehouse operation with that in a proposed operation at Xerox. In large part, Bean's superiority could be attributed to differences in methods; it arranged materials so that big-selling items were closer to stock pickers, and it chose storage locations to minimize forklift travel distance.

In this way, Xerox learned the production function for this type of warehousing operation. On the basis of these findings, it modernized its own warehousing operations. Competitive benchmarking is a very important technique, applicable in a wide variety of areas. Xerox's top managers felt that it was responsible for much of the improvement in the firm's performance during the 1980s. Many other firms swear by the effectiveness and significance of this technique.

---

[11]This section is based largely on R. Hayes, S. Wheelwright, and K. Clark, *Dynamic Manufacturing* (New York: Free Press, 1988).

Measurement of Production Functions

Although techniques like competitive benchmarking are valuable, they generally can provide only part of the information managers need concerning production functions. Therefore, managerial economists have devised other methods, based largely on the regression techniques described in Chapter 5, to measure production functions. As we see in subsequent sections of this chapter, the results often have proven very useful. One of the first steps in estimating a production function is to choose the mathematical form of the production function. If labor and capital are the only inputs used, one possible mathematical form is the following cubic equation:

$$Q = aLK + bL^2K + cLK^2 - dL^3K - eLK^3 \qquad (7.16)$$

where Q is output, L is the quantity of labor input, and K is the quantity of capital input. This mathematical form exhibits first increasing and then decreasing returns to scale. Also, the marginal product of each input first increases and then decreases as more and more of the input is used. To see that this is true, consider the marginal product of labor, which equals

$$\frac{\partial Q}{\partial L} = (aK + cK^2 - eK^3) + 2bKL - 3dKL^2$$

Clearly, the marginal product of labor is a quadratic function of the amount of labor used; it increases at first if $(b/3d > L)$ then decreases (as $L > b/3d$) as more and more labor is employed.

Another mathematical form that is more commonly used is the Cobb-Douglas form, encountered in the section before last. With only two inputs, this form is

$$Q = aL^bK^c \qquad (7.17)$$

One advantage of this form is that the marginal productivity of each input depends on the level of all inputs employed, which is often realistic. Consider the marginal product of labor, which equals

$$\frac{\partial Q}{\partial L} = baL^{b-1}K^c = b\left(\frac{Q}{L}\right) = b(AP_L)$$

Obviously, the marginal product of labor depends on the values of both L and K. Another advantage is that, if logarithms are taken of both sides of equation (7.17),

$$\log Q = \log a + b \log L + c \log K \qquad (7.18)$$

The regression techniques in Chapter 5 can be used to estimate b and c (as well as log a). If we regress log Q on log L and log K, the regression coefficients are these estimates.

Note that, if the Cobb-Douglas production function is used, we can easily estimate the returns to scale. If the sum of the exponents (that is, $b + c$) exceeds 1, increasing returns to scale are indicated; if the sum of the exponents equals 1, constant returns to scale prevail; and if the sum of the exponents is less than 1, decreasing returns to scale are indicated. This is because, if the Cobb-Douglas production function prevails, the output elasticity equals the sum of the exponents. For example, in the section before last, the output elasticity of the Lone Star Company was 1.1, which equaled the sum of the exponents (0.3 and 0.8).

There is no cut-and-dried way to determine which mathematical form is best, since the answer depends on the particular situation. Frequently, a good procedure is to try more than one mathematical form and see which fits the data best. The important thing is that the chosen form provide a faithful representation of the actual situation. To determine whether this is the case, it often is useful to see how well a particular estimated production function can forecast the quantity of output resulting from the combination of inputs actually used.

Three Types of Statistical Analysis

Having chosen a mathematical form for the production function, there remains the question of which of three types of data to use. One possibility is to use time-series data concerning the amount of various inputs used in various periods in the past and the amount of output produced in each period. For example, you might obtain data concerning the amount of labor, the amount of capital, and the amount of various raw materials used in the steel industry during each year from 1958 to 2003. On the basis of such data and information concerning the annual output of steel during 1958 to 2003, you might estimate the relationship between the amounts of the inputs and the resulting output, using regression techniques like those discussed in Chapter 5.

The second possibility is to use cross-section data concerning the amount of various inputs used and output produced in various firms or sectors of the industry at a given time. For example, you might obtain data concerning the amounts of labor, capital, and raw materials used in various firms in the steel industry in 2003. On the basis of such data and information concerning the 2003 output of each firm, you might use regression techniques to estimate the relationship between the amounts of the inputs and the resulting output.

The third possibility is to use technical information supplied by the engineer or the agricultural scientist. This information is collected by experiment or from experience with the day-to-day workings of the technical process.

Advantages are gained from approaching the measurement of the production function from this angle because the range of applicability of the data is known, and unlike time-series and cross-section studies, we are not restricted to the narrow range of actual observations.[12]

Regardless of which approach you use, it is important to recognize that the data may not always represent technically efficient combinations of inputs and output. For example, because of errors or constraints, the amount of inputs used by the steel industry in 2003 may not have been the minimum required to produce the 2003 output of the steel industry. Since the production function theoretically includes only efficient input combinations, a case of this sort should be excluded if our measurements are to be pristine pure. In practice, however, such cases are not always excluded (or recognized), and the resulting estimate of the production function contains errors on this account.

Another important difficulty is the measurement of capital input. The principal problem stems from the fact that the stock of capital is composed of various types and ages of machines, buildings, and inventories. Combining them into a single measure—or a few measures—is not easy. In addition, errors can arise because various data points assumed to be on the same production function are in fact on different ones. Moreover, biases can occur because of identification problems somewhat similar to those discussed on pages 154 to 156.

With regard to the engineering approach, it is difficult to combine the results for the processes for which engineers have data into an overall plant or firm production function. Since engineering data generally pertain to only a part of the firm's activities, this is often a very hard job. For example, engineering data tell us little or nothing about the firm's marketing or financial activities.

The Telephone Industry in Canada: A Case Study

Despite these difficulties, estimates of production functions have proved of considerable interest and value. To illustrate the empirical results that have been obtained, A. Dobell, L. Taylor, L. Waverman, T. Liu, and M. Copeland found that the production function in the telephone industry in Canada was

$$Q = AL^{0.70}K^{0.41} \qquad (7.19)$$

where A is the level of output when both L and K equal 1.[13] On the basis of this equation, it appears that a 1 percent increase in labor (holding the amount

---

[12]For an illustration of this approach, see L. Cookenboo, "Production Functions and Cost Functions in Oil Pipelines," in the Study Guide accompanying this textbook.

[13]A. Dobell, L. Taylor, L. Waverman, T. Liu, and M. Copeland, "Communications in Canada," *Bell Journal of Economics and Management Science*, 1972.

of capital constant) results in approximately a 0.70 percent increase in output. To prove that this is true, note that

$$\frac{\partial Q}{\partial L} = 0.70 \, AL^{-0.30} \, K^{0.41}$$

$$= 0.70 \, \frac{Q}{L}$$

Therefore,

$$\left(\frac{\partial Q}{\partial L} \right)\left(\frac{L}{Q} \right) = 0.70 \tag{7.20}$$

Since $(\partial Q/\partial L)(L/Q)$ is (approximately) equal to the percentage increase in output resulting from a 1 percent increase in labor, a 1 percent increase in labor results in an approximate 0.70 percent increase in output.

On the basis of the estimated production function in equation (7.19), one can also determine the effect on output of a 1 percent increase in capital. Because

$$\frac{\partial Q}{\partial K} = 0.41 \, AL^{0.70}K^{-0.59}$$

$$= 0.41 \, \frac{Q}{K}$$

it follows that a 1 percent increase in capital raises the output of the telephone industry by approximately 0.41 percent. Why? Because $(\partial Q/\partial K)(K/Q) = 0.41$.

In addition, equation (7.19) provides valuable information concerning returns to scale. Because the production function is of the Cobb-Douglas form, the output elasticity equals the sum of the exponents; that is, it equals $0.70 + 0.41 = 1.11$ (recall the discussion on page 276). Since the output elasticity is the percentage of change in output resulting from a 1 percent increase in all inputs, this means that a 1 percent increase in all inputs would result in approximately a 1.11 percent increase in output. Clearly, these results indicate increasing returns to scale.

Estimated production functions of this sort are of enormous value to managers and analysts, since they enable the manager or analyst to estimate the marginal product of each input and determine whether there are increasing, decreasing, or constant returns to scale. As we have stressed, information of this kind is of fundamental importance in deciding how to minimize a firm's costs. In a world where competition is intense and costs matter greatly, it is no wonder that firms find estimated production functions valuable.

Poultry Production in the United States: Another Case Study

As a further illustration, consider the production of broiler chickens, which is a big industry in the United States (2002 production value: $13.4 billion). To estimate the production function, an experiment was carried out in which broilers were fed various amounts of corn and soybean oilmeal and the gain in weight of each broiler was carefully measured.[14] On the basis of regression analysis of the sort described in Chapter 5, it was found that

$$G = 0.03 + 0.48C + 0.64S - 0.02C^2 - 0.05S^2 - 0.02CS \qquad (7.21)$$

where G is the gain in weight (in pounds per broiler), C is pounds of corn per broiler, and S is pounds of soybean oilmeal per broiler. The multiple coefficient of determination (R^2) is very high, about 0.998.

Using equation (7.21), we can obtain isoquants for poultry production. Suppose we want to obtain the isoquant pertaining to a weight gain of 1 pound. In other words, we want to find the various combinations of amounts of corn per broiler and soybean oilmeal per broiler that results in a weight gain per broiler of 1 pound. To find these combinations, we set $G = 1$:

$$1 = 0.03 + 0.48C + 0.64S - 0.02C^2 - 0.05S^2 - 0.02CS \qquad (7.22)$$

Then, we set C equal to various values and determine each resulting value of S. For example, suppose that $C = 1$. Then,

$$1 = 0.03 + 0.48(1) + 0.64S - 0.02(1^2) - 0.05S^2 - 0.02(1)S$$

or

$$1 = 0.03 + 0.48 - 0.02 + (0.64 - 0.02)S - 0.05S^2$$

Solving $0.05S^2 - 0.62S + 0.51 = 0$ by the quadratic formula yields

$$S = [0.62 \pm (0.62^2 - 4(0.05)(0.51))^{0.5}]/2(0.05)$$
$$= [0.62 \pm (0.3844 - 0.0102)^{0.5}]/0.1$$
$$= [0.62 \pm (0.2824)^{0.5}]/0.1$$
$$= (0.62 \pm 0.5314)/0.1$$

[14]Organization for Economic Cooperation and Development, *Interdisciplinary Research in Input/Output Relationships and Production Functions to Improve Decisions and Efficiency for Poultry Production* (Paris: Author, 1966).

FIGURE
7.13

Isoquant for 1–Pound Weight Gain for a Broiler and Isocost Curve If Corn Price Is $^3/_4$ of Soybean Oilmeal Price

The optimal input combination is 1.35 pounds of corn and 0.61 pounds of soybean oilmeal.

Source: Organization for Economic Cooperation and Development, Interdisciplinary Research.

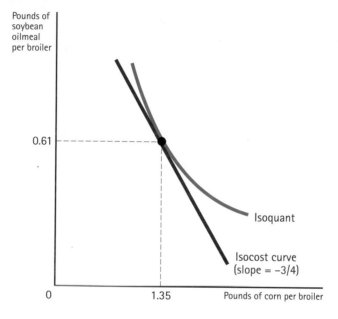

Therefore, $S = 1.1514/0.1 = 11.514$, or $S = 0.08858/0.1 = 0.886$. Consequently, if a broiler is to gain 1 pound of weight, it must be fed 0.886 pounds of soybean oilmeal, as well as 1 pound of corn.[15]

If we let $C = 1.1$, we can find the corresponding value of S by substituting 1.1 for C in equation (7.22) and solving for S. If we let $C = 1.2$, we can find the corresponding value of S by substituting 1.2 for C in equation (7.22) and solving for S. Proceeding in this way, we can find more and more points on the isoquant corresponding to a weight gain of 1 pound. The resulting isoquant is shown in Figure 7.13. Isoquants of this sort are of great importance to managers. Coupled with data regarding input prices, they can be used to determine how much of each input should be used to minimize costs (recall Figure 7.9).

---

[15]To obtain this expression for S, we use the formula in footnote 4, Chapter 2 (see page 64). There is another possible value of S, which corresponds to the use of the plus sign (rather than the minus sign) before $(b^2 - 4ac)^{0.5}$ in this formula, but this other value is not relevant here.

In fact, poultry producers use the isoquant in Figure 7.13 to determine how much corn and soybean oilmeal to feed a broiler if they want a 1-pound weight gain. To see how they do this, suppose that the price of a pound of corn is three-quarters the price of a pound of soybean oilmeal. Then, the slope of each isocost curve in Figure 7.13 equals $-3/4$, since, as pointed out in Figure 7.7, the slope equals -1 times the price of the input on the horizontal axis (corn) divided by the price of the input on the vertical axis (soybean oilmeal). For the cost of the weight gain to be at a minimum, the isocost curve should be tangent to the isoquant; this means that the slope of the isoquant should also equal $-3/4$. As shown in Figure 7.13, this occurs when 1.35 pounds of corn and 0.61 pounds of soybean oilmeal are used. Therefore, this is the optimal input combination if the price of a pound of corn is three-quarters the price of a pound of soybean oilmeal.

Summary

1. The production function is the relationship among the quantities of various inputs used per period of time and the maximum quantity of the good that can be produced per period of time. Given the production function for a particular firm, one can calculate the average product of an input and the marginal product of an input.

2. To determine how much of a particular input to utilize, a firm should compare the marginal revenue product of the input with the marginal expenditure on the input. To maximize profit, the firm should utilize the amount of the input that results in making the marginal revenue product equal to the marginal expenditure.

3. An isoquant is a curve showing all possible (efficient) combinations of inputs that are capable of producing a particular quantity of output. The marginal rate of technical substitution shows the rate at which one input can be substituted for another input if output remains constant. No profit-maximizing firm will operate at a point where the isoquant is positively sloped.

4. To minimize the cost of producing a particular output, a firm should allocate its expenditures among various inputs in such a way that the ratio of the marginal product to the input price is the same for all inputs used. Graphically, this amounts to choosing the input combination where the relevant isoquant is tangent to an isocost curve.

5. Many firms produce goods in lots. The optimal lot size equals $(2SQ/b)^{0.5}$, where S is the cost per setup, Q is the total annual requirement of the relevant good, and b is the annual cost of holding each good of this sort in inventory. It is important that firms produce lots of approximately optimal size; otherwise, their costs will be higher than necessary or desirable.

6. If the firm increases all inputs by the same proportion and output increases by more (less) than this proportion, there are increasing (decreasing) returns to scale. Increasing returns to scale may occur because of indivisibility of inputs, various geometrical relations, or specialization. Decreasing returns to scale can also occur; the most frequently cited reason is the difficulty of managing a huge enterprise. Whether there are constant, increasing, or decreasing returns to scale is an empirical question that must be settled case by case.

7. Competitive benchmarking is frequently used to obtain information concerning the production function. Also, using techniques of the sort described in Chapter 5, business analysts, engineers, and others have estimated production functions in many firms and industries. Statistical analyses of time-series and cross-section data, as well as engineering data, have been carried out. For example, many studies have fit the Cobb-Douglas production function to the data. The results have proven of considerable value to managers, here and abroad.

Problems

1. In the Elwyn Company, the relationship between output (Q) and the number of hours of skilled labor (S) and unskilled labor (U) is

$$Q = 300S + 200U - 0.2S^2 - 0.3U^2$$

The hourly wage of skilled labor is $10 and the hourly wage of unskilled labor is $5. The firm can hire as much labor as it wants at these wage rates.
   a. Elwyn's chief engineer recommends that the firm hire 400 hours of skilled labor and 100 hours of unskilled labor. Evaluate this recommendation.
   b. If the Elwyn Company decides to spend a total of $5,000 on skilled and unskilled labor, how many hours of each type of labor should it hire?
   c. If the price of a unit of output is $10 (and does not vary with output), how many hours of unskilled labor should the company hire?

2. On the basis of a regression analysis like those in Chapter 5, the Washington Company finds that its production function is

$$\log Q = 1.50 + 0.76 \log L + 0.24 \log K$$

where Q is its daily output, L is the number of workers employed per day, and K is the number of machines used per day. The Washington Company's product is sold in a competitive market at a price per unit of $10. The firm cannot influence the wage of workers or the price of machines.

    a. If the wage of a worker is $30 per day, how many workers per unit of output should the firm hire?

    b. What percentage of the firm's revenues are spent on labor? Why?

    c. Will this percentage vary depending on the daily wage of a worker? Why or why not?

3. A consulting firm specializing in agriculture determines that the following combinations of hay and grain consumption per lamb will result in a 25-pound gain on a lamb:

Pounds of hay	Pounds of grain
40	130.9
50	125.1
60	120.1
70	115.7
80	111.8
90	108.3
110	102.3
130	97.4
150	93.8

    a. The firm's president wants to estimate the marginal product of a pound of grain in producing lamb. Can he do so on the basis of these data?

    b. The firm's president is convinced that constant returns to scale prevail in lamb production. If this is true and hay and grain consumption per lamb are the only inputs, how much gain accrues if the hay consumption per lamb is 100 pounds and the grain consumption per lamb is 250.2 pounds?

    c. What is the marginal rate of technical substitution of hay for grain when between 40 and 50 pounds of hay (and between 130.9 and 125.1 pounds of grain) are consumed per lamb?

    d. A major advance in technology occurs that allows farmers to produce a 25-pound gain on a lamb with less hay and grain than the preceding table indicates. If the marginal rate of technical substitution (at each rate of consumption of each input) is the same after the technological advance as before, can you draw the new isoquant corresponding to a 25-pound gain on a lamb?

4. The Ascot Corporation, which produces stationery, hires a consultant to estimate its production function. The consultant concludes that

$$Q = 0.9P + 0.06L$$

where Q is the number of pounds of stationery produced by Ascot per year, L is the number of hours of labor per year, and P is the number of pounds of paper used per year.

a. Does this production function seem to include all the relevant inputs? Explain.

b. Does this production function seem reasonable if it is applied to all possible values of L? Explain.

c. Does this production function exhibit diminishing marginal returns?

5. A Cobb-Douglas production function was estimated for six types of farms. There were five inputs in the production function: (1) land, (2) labor, (3) equipment, (4) livestock and feed, and (5) other resource services. The exponent of each input was as follows:

| | | | | Exponent | |
Farm type	Land	Labor	Equipment	Livestock and feed	Other resource services
Crop farms	0.24	0.07	0.08	0.53	0.02
Hog farms	0.07	0.02	0.10	0.74	0.03
Dairy farms	0.10	0.01	0.06	0.63	0.02
General farms	0.17	0.12	0.16	0.46	0.03
Large farms	0.28	0.01	0.11	0.53	0.03
Small farms	0.21	0.05	0.08	0.43	0.03

a. Do there appear to be increasing returns to scale in any of these six types of farms?

b. In what type of farm does a 1-percent increase in labor have the largest percentage effect on output?

c. On the basis of these results, would you expect that output would increase if many of the farms included in this sample were merged?

6. According to the chief engineer at the Zodiac Company, $Q = AL^\alpha K^\beta$, where Q is the output rate, L is the rate of labor input, and K is the rate of capital input. Statistical analysis indicates that $\alpha = 0.8$ and $\beta = 0.3$. The firm's owner claims the plant has increasing returns to scale.

a. Is the owner correct?

b. If β were 0.2 rather than 0.3, would she be correct?

c. Does output per unit of labor depend only on α and β? Why or why not?

7. On the basis of data obtained by the U.S. Department of Agriculture, the relationship between a cow's total output of milk and the amount of grain it is fed is as follows:

Amount of grain (pounds)	Amount of milk (pounds)
1,200	5,917
1,800	7,250
2,400	8,379
3,000	9,371

(This relationship assumes that forage input is fixed at 6,500 pounds of hay.)

a. Calculate the average product of grain when each amount is used.
b. Estimate the marginal product of grain when between 1,200 and 1,800 pounds are fed, when between 1,800 and 2,400 pounds are fed, and when between 2,400 and 3,000 pounds are fed.
c. Does this production function exhibit diminishing marginal returns?

8. The owner of the Hughes Car Wash believes that the relationship between the number of cars washed and labor input is

$$Q = -0.8 + 4.5L - 0.3L^2$$

where Q is the number of cars washed per hour and L is the number of people employed per hour. The firm receives $5 for each car washed, and the hourly wage rate for each person employed is $4.50. The cost of other inputs like water is trivial; hence, they are ignored.

a. How many people should be employed to maximize profit?
b. What will be the firm's hourly profit?
c. Is this relationship between output and labor input valid for all values of L? Why or why not?

9. An electronics plant's production function is $Q = 5LK$, where Q is its output rate, L is the amount of labor it uses per period of time, and K is the amount of capital it uses per period of time. The price of labor is $1 per unit of labor, and the price of capital is $2 per unit of capital. The firm's vice president for manufacturing hires you to determine which combination of inputs the plant should use to produce 20 units of output per period.

a. What advice would you give him?
b. Suppose that the price of labor increases to $2 per unit. What effect will this have on output per unit of labor?
c. Is this plant subject to decreasing returns to scale? Why or why not?

10. In its Erie, Pennsylvania, plant, General Electric has installed a flexible manufacturing system to produce locomotives. Flexible manufacturing systems, which are very sophisticated forms of factory automation, operate with a minimum of manual intervention. They are integrated systems of machines

under full programmable control. According to General Electric, the new system compares as follows with the old one:

	Old system	New system
Number of machines	29	9
Number of workers	86	16
Annual output	4,100	5,600

a. Does the new system increase the average product of labor?

b. Does it increase the average product of machines?

c. According to a study by Harvard's Ramchandran Jaikumar, U.S. firms generally do not exploit flexible manufacturing systems as well as they might. For one thing, the percentage of time that such systems are actually functioning, rather than awaiting adjustments or repair, seems to be relatively low. He believes that U.S. firms should invest more in skilled engineering personnel. Can steps of this sort result in shifts of the production function?

d. How can a firm determine whether such steps are worthwhile?[16]

11. The Arbor Company produces metal fasteners. The cost per setup is $8,000 and the annual cost of holding each fastener in inventory for a year is $40. What is the optimal lot size if the Arbor Company produces each of the following annual outputs?

a. 1,000

b. 10,000

c. 100,000

12. Volvo A.B., the Swedish auto firm, opened a new car-assembly plant at Uddevalla in 1988. The idea was to have a small team of highly skilled workers build an entire car. According to the proponents, this would reduce the tedium associated with the conventional assembly line and cut absenteeism and turnover among workers. In 1991, there were reports that it took 50 hours of labor to assemble a car at Uddevalla, in contrast to 25 hours at Volvo's conventional assembly plant at Ghent, Belgium. If you were Volvo's chief executive officer, what questions would you ask Uddevalla's managers, and what steps would you take?

13. Porsche, the German producer of sports cars, almost went bankrupt in 1992. It then remade itself, on the basis of Japanese manufacturing techniques. Several measures of the changes in the efficiency of its manufacturing process follow:

---

[16]For further discussion, see S. Miller, *Impacts of Industrial Robotics* (Madison: University of Wisconsin Press, 1988); R. Jaikumar, "Postindustrial Manufacturing," *Harvard Business Review*, November–December 1986; and E. Mansfield, "Flexible Manufacturing Systems: Economic Effects in Japan, United States, and Western Europe," *Japan and the World Economy*, 4, 1992, 1–16.

	Manufacturing area (square yards)	Manufacturing time (hours)	Manufacturing flaws (per car)	Inventory levels (parts)	Managers
Before	765	120	6	8,490	328
After	514	72	3	1,600	226

Source: *New York Times*, January 20, 1996.

    a. Why was it desirable to reduce the manufacturing area?

    b. Why was it desirable to reduce the manufacturing time?

    c. Why was it desirable to reduce inventory levels?

14. During the 1950s and 1960s, the Toyota Motor Company originated and developed the just-in-time system of production, which has had an enormous effect in Japan and elsewhere. According to this system, materials, parts, and components are produced and delivered just before they are needed. One advantage is that inventories of parts and of work in process are reduced considerably, but this is only part of the story. In addition, the time and cost required to change from the production of one part or model to another are reduced; this cuts setup costs and enables the firm to produce small lots economically.

    A careful comparison of an automobile plant using the just-in-time system with an automobile plant not using it resulted in the following data:[17]

	Plant using just-in-time system	Plant not using just-in-time system
Cars produced per day	1,000	860
Total factory workers	1,000	2,150
Workers per car per day		
Direct labor	0.79	1.25
Overhead personnel	0.21	1.25
Total	1.00	2.50

    a. On the basis of this comparison, does it appear that the average product of labor is higher with the just-in-time system than without it?

    b. Does such a system increase the average product of overhead personnel to a greater extent than it does the average product of direct labor?

    c. If changeovers from one part or model to another require a great deal of time, the required planning and management effort is greater than it would be if such changeovers could be accomplished quickly. Does this help to explain why the average product of overhead personnel increases so much?

[17] Abegglen and Stalk, *Kaisha.*

d. According to James Abegglen and George Stalk, "Many Japanese companies by adopting the just-in-time system doubled the productivity of their factory labor forces and almost doubled the productivity of the assets they employed." Did this result in a shift in these firms' isoquants, or a movement along fixed isoquants?

Appendix: Lagrangian Multipliers and Optimal Input Combinations

In this chapter, we stated that equation (7.11) must be satisfied if a firm is to maximize output for a given expenditure level or if it is to minimize the cost of producing a specified amount of output. In this appendix, we show how the decision rule in equation (7.11) can be derived using the method of Lagrangian multipliers (discussed in Chapter 2). To simplify matters, the firm is assumed to employ only two inputs.

Maximizing Output from a Specified Expenditure Level

Suppose that a firm's production function is

$$Q = f(X_1, X_2)$$

where Q is output, X_1 is the amount used of the first input, and X_2 is the amount used of the second input. The firm's total expenditure on both inputs is specified to equal E^*. Therefore,

$$X_1 P_1 + X_2 P_2 = E^*$$

where P_1 is the price of the first input and P_2 is the price of the second input. The firm wants to maximize the quantity of output from this specified level of expenditure. So, the firm wants to maximize Q, where

$$Q = f(X_1, X_2) \tag{7.23}$$

subject to the constraint that

$$E^* - X_1 P_1 - X_2 P_2 = 0 \tag{7.24}$$

Following the procedure described in Chapter 2, we can use Lagrangian multipliers to solve this problem. The first step is to construct the Lagrangian function, which is the right-hand side of equation (7.23) plus λ times the left-hand side of equation (7.24):

$$L_1 = f(X_1, X_2) + \lambda(E^* - X_1P_1 - X_2P_2)$$

where λ is the Lagrangian multiplier. Taking the partial derivatives of L_1 with respect to X_1, X_2, and λ and setting them all equal to zero, we obtain

$$\frac{\partial L_1}{\partial X_1} = \frac{\partial f(X_1, X_2)}{\partial X_1} - \lambda P_1 = 0 \qquad (7.25)$$

$$\frac{\partial L_1}{\partial X_2} = \frac{\partial f(X_1, X_2)}{\partial X_2} - \lambda P_2 = 0 \qquad (7.26)$$

$$\frac{\partial L_1}{\partial \lambda} = E^* - X_1P_1 - X_2P_2 = 0 \qquad (7.27)$$

These are the conditions for output maximization subject to the expenditure constraint.

Letting MP$_1$ be the marginal product of the first input and MP$_2$ be the marginal product of the second input, the following is true (by definition):

$$\frac{\partial f(X_1, X_2)}{\partial X_1} = \frac{\partial Q}{\partial X_1} = MP_1$$

$$\frac{\partial f(X_1, X_2)}{\partial X_2} = \frac{\partial Q}{\partial X_2} - MP_2$$

Equations (7.25) and (7.26) can be restated

$$MP_1 - \lambda P_1 = 0$$
$$MP_2 - \lambda P_2 = 0$$

which implies that

$$MP_1 = \lambda P_1 \qquad (7.28)$$
$$MP_2 = \lambda P_2 \qquad (7.29)$$

Dividing each side of equation (7.28) by the corresponding side of equation (7.29), we find that

$$\frac{MP_1}{MP_2} = \frac{P_1}{P_2}$$

or

$$\frac{MP_1}{P_1} = \frac{MP_2}{P_2} \tag{7.30}$$

which is the decision rule in equation (7.11) when there are only two inputs. Therefore, we have proven what we set out to prove—that this decision rule can be derived using the method of Lagrangian multipliers when the object is to maximize output subject to an expenditure constraint.

Minimizing the Cost of a Specified Amount of Output

Suppose this firm is committed to produce a specified quantity of output, Q^*, which means that

$$f(X_1, X_2) = Q^*$$

The firm's problem is to minimize its costs, which equal

$$C = X_1P_1 + X_2P_2 \tag{7.31}$$

subject to the constraint that

$$Q^* - f(X_1, X_2) = 0 \tag{7.32}$$

Following the procedure described in Chapter 2, we can use the method of Lagrangian multipliers to solve this problem. The first step is to construct the Lagrangian function, which is the right-hand side of equation (7.31) plus λ times the left-hand side of equation (7.32):

$$L_2 = X_1P_1 + X_2P_2 + \lambda[Q^* - f(X_1, X_2)]$$

where λ is the Lagrangian multiplier. Taking the partial derivatives of L_2 with respect to X_1, X_2, and λ and setting them all equal to zero, we obtain

$$\frac{\partial L_2}{\partial X_1} = P_1 - \lambda \frac{\partial f(X_1, X_2)}{\partial X_1} = 0 \tag{7.33}$$

$$\frac{\partial L_2}{\partial X_2} = P_2 - \lambda \frac{\partial f(X_1, X_2)}{\partial X_2} = 0 \tag{7.34}$$

$$\frac{\partial L_2}{\partial \lambda} = Q^* - f(X_1, X_2) = 0 \tag{7.35}$$

These are the conditions for cost minimization subject to the output constraint.

Substituting MP_1 for $\partial f(X_1, X_2)/\partial X_1$ and MP_2 for $\partial f(X_1, X_2)/\partial X_2$ in equations (7.33) and (7.34), we get

$$P_1 - \lambda MP_1 = 0$$
$$P_2 - \lambda MP_2 = 0$$

which implies that

$$P_1 = \lambda MP_1 \qquad (7.36)$$
$$P_2 = \lambda MP_2 \qquad (7.37)$$

Dividing each side of equation (7.36) by the corresponding side of equation (7.37), we find that

$$\frac{P_1}{P_2} = \frac{MP_1}{MP_2}$$

or

$$\frac{MP_1}{P_1} = \frac{MP_2}{P_2}$$

which is the decision rule in equation (7.11) when there are only two inputs. Therefore, we have proven what we set out to prove—that this decision rule can be derived using the method of Lagrangian multipliers when the object is to minimize cost subject to an output constraint.

Technological Change
and Industrial Innovation

The United States is generally viewed as having the highest labor productivity (output per labor hour) in the world. Our high standard of living is strongly correlated with this high labor productivity. However, in recent years, the rate of growth of labor productivity has fallen below that of other nations. For example, between 1947 and 1973, productivity in the United States grew annually at an average of 2.8 percent. This average growth rate dropped to 1.1 percent between 1973 and 1998. Hence, the question facing the United States is whether it can sustain its productivity lead over other developed nations. Since output depends on all inputs, the level of capital inputs (both private and public) and the improvement in the quality of labor (via education) certainly has an impact on productivity growth in the United States.

Companies in the United States have traditionally been at the forefront in using new technologies. Their long-term profitability and market successes are often based on new products or processes. Most of these advances in products or processes are the result of an active commitment to devoting resources to research and development. After all, increases in productivity do not occur haphazardly but are the result of active management of the research and development process. This management not only includes the initial development of a product or process but also the implementation issues involved in getting new products to market.

In this chapter, we discuss various models and techniques for measuring productivity and examine several research and developmental models. These models have proven useful in both helping managers oversee research and development programs and bringing new products to market.

Technological Change

Technological change—the advance of technology—often takes the form of new methods of producing existing products and new techniques of organization, marketing, and management. Technological change results in a change in the production function. If the production function were readily observable, a comparison of the production function at two different times would provide the manager with a simple measure of the effect of technological change during the intervening period. If there were only two inputs, labor and capital, and constant returns to scale, the characteristics of the production function at a given date could be captured fully by a single isoquant.[1] One could simply look at the changing position of this isoquant to see the effects of technological change. If this isoquant shifted from position A to position B in Figure 8.1 during a certain period of time, technological change had less impact during this period than it would have had if the curve had shifted to position C.

Technological change may also result in the availability of new products. Videocassette recorders, for example, did not exist several decades ago; now they are commonplace. Palm pilots and laptop computers did not exist a decade ago; today, many managers rely on them. Nylon was first brought to market in the 1930s; today it is hard to imagine what life would be like without it. In many cases, the availability of new products can be regarded as a change in the production function, since they are merely more efficient ways of meeting old wants if these wants are defined with proper breadth. This is particularly true in the case of new goods used by firms, which may result in little or no change in the final product shipped to consumers. In other cases, however, the availability of new products cannot realistically be viewed as a change in the production function, since the new products represent an important difference in kind.

---

[1]Recall from Chapter 7 that, if there are constant returns to scale, an x percent increase in all inputs results in an x percent increase in output. Hence, if there are constant returns to scale, there is at a given time a unique relationship between capital input per unit of output and labor input per unit of output. This relationship holds for any output and completely summarizes the efficient input combinations.

FIGURE
8.1

Change over a Period of Time in the Position of an Isoquant

If the isoquant shifted from position *A* to position *B*, technological change had less impact than if it had shifted to position *C*.

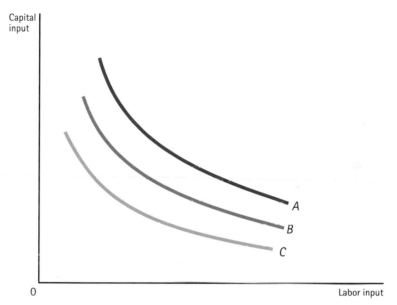

Labor Productivity

Managers have long been interested in productivity—the ratio of output to input. The oldest and most commonly studied productivity measure is labor productivity, output per hour of labor. One determinant of the rate of growth of labor productivity is the rate of technological change: A high rate of technological change is likely to result, all other things being equal, in a high rate of growth of labor productivity. However, the rate of technological change is not the sole determinant of the rate of growth of labor productivity; as a consequence, although labor productivity is often used to measure the rate of technological change, it is in fact an incomplete measure.

Figure 8.2 shows how changes in labor productivity can produce false signals concerning the rate of technological change. Suppose the relevant isoquant is II' and the input prices at the beginning of the period are such that the isocost curves are *A*, *B*, *C*, and so on. The least-cost combination of inputs is L_1

FIGURE
8.2

Productivity Increase without Technological Change

Because labor becomes more expensive relative to capital, labor productivity increases.

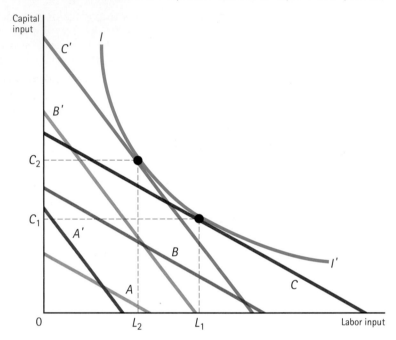

of labor and C_1 of capital. Now suppose that input prices change and labor becomes more expensive relative to capital; as a result, the isocost curves shift to A', B', C', and so on. Under these new circumstances, the least-cost combination of inputs to produce the same output is L_2 of labor and C_2 of capital. Since output remains constant and labor input decreases, labor productivity increases as a result of the change in input prices. But this productivity increase is not an indication of technological change, there being no change at all in the production function.

Total Factor Productivity

A better measure of the rate of technological change is **total factor productivity,** which relates changes in output to changes in both labor and capital inputs, not changes in labor inputs alone. Assume that the production function is of the simple form

$$Q = \alpha(bL + cK) \tag{8.1}$$

where Q is the quantity of output, L is the quantity of labor, K is the quantity of capital, and b and c are constants. Dividing both sides of equation (8.1) by $(bL + cK)$,

$$\frac{Q}{bL + cK} = \alpha \tag{8.2}$$

which is total factor productivity. In this simple case, changes in total factor productivity measure changes in efficiency.

If a firm uses more than two inputs, total factor productivity equals

$$\frac{Q}{a_1 I_1 + a_2 I_2 + \cdots + a_n I_n} \tag{8.3}$$

where I_1 is the amount of the first input used, I_2 is the amount of the second input used, . . . , and I_n is the amount of the nth input used. In calculating total factor productivity, firms often let a_1 equal the price of the first input, a_2 equal the price of the second input, . . . , and a_n equal the price of the nth input in some base period, as we shall see next. The principal advantage of total factor productivity over labor productivity is its inclusion of more types of inputs, not labor alone. It otherwise shares many of the limitations of labor productivity. Note that $\Sigma_i P_i X_i$, where P_i is unit input cost and X_i is amount of input used, is just the firm's total cost (TC). Then Q/TC is just the inverse of the firm's average total cost (ATC). To maximize productivity, minimize ATC. But firms want to maximize profits. That rarely occurs when firms minimize ATC.

Firms calculate total factor productivity to measure changes over time in the efficiency of their operations. It is important for a firm's managers to be aware of the extent to which productivity has increased in response to new techniques and other factors. For example, consider flexible manufacturing systems, a major innovation in industries like machinery (recall problem 10 in Chapter 7). According to Messerschmidt, a leading German firm, the flexible manufacturing system it installed at its Augsburg facility reduced the labor requirements to produce a given output by over 50 percent and reduced the capital investment required by 10 percent.[2]

To calculate the changes in total factor productivity for a firm or plant over a period of time, managers must obtain data concerning the quantities of output and inputs utilized in each period. For example, suppose that the Landau Company uses three inputs—labor, energy, and raw materials. In 2002, it uses 10,000 hours of labor, 100,000 kilowatt-hours of energy, and 5,000 pounds of materials to produce 400,000 pounds of output. In 2003, it uses 12,000 hours

[2]National Research Council, *Toward a New Era in Manufacturing* (Washington, D.C.: National Academy Press, 1986), p. 118.

of labor, 150,000 kilowatt-hours of energy, and 6,000 pounds of materials to produce 700,000 pounds of output. What is total factor productivity in each year?

As a first step toward answering this question, we must get data concerning the price of each input in some base period, say, 2002. Suppose that the price of labor is $8 per hour, the price of a kilowatt-hour of energy is $0.02, and the price of a pound of materials is $3. Then, inserting these figures into the expression in (8.3), we find that total factor productivity in 2002 is

$$\frac{400,000}{8(10,000) + 0.02(100,000) + 3(5,000)} = 4.12$$

and total factor productivity in 2003 is

$$\frac{700,000}{8(12,000) + 0.02(150,000) + 3(6,000)} = 5.98$$

Therefore, from 2002 to 2003, total factor productivity increased by 45 percent—from 4.12 to 5.98.

Note that the base-year input prices are used for all years, not just the base year. For example, the 2002 input prices would be used for all years, not just 2002, in the case of the Landau Company. In this way, we hold constant input prices and do not let changes in them over time affect our results.[3]

Using Total Factor Productivity to Track Factory Performance

To illustrate how changes in total factor productivity can be used to track factory performance, consider a manufacturing plant studied by Harvard's Robert Hayes, Steven Wheelwright, and Kim Clark.[4] Figure 8.3 shows the behavior of total factor productivity in this plant during a 10-year period. As you can see, total factor productivity increased at a healthy pace up to 1976. This was the period during which the plant was started up. Because it takes time for a factory to operate properly, one would expect that total factor productivity would increase substantially in this startup phase.

From 1977 to 1983, there was no evidence of any strong, persistent increase in total factor productivity. Instead, there was an increase in 1977 to 1979, a

---

[3]Of course, this does not mean that the value of total factor productivity is not affected by the base-year prices. For example, if the price of labor in the base period were $10 (rather than $8) per hour, our results would be different. But changes *over time* in input prices are not allowed to influence our results.

[4]R. Hayes, S. Wheelwright, and K. Clark, *Dynamic Manufacturing* (New York: Free Press, 1988).

FIGURE
8.3

Total Factor Productivity, Actual Manufacturing Plant

Total factor productivity increased up to 1976, but in 1982 was only slightly higher than in 1976.

Source: Hayes, Wheelwright, and Clark, *Dynamic Manufacturing.*

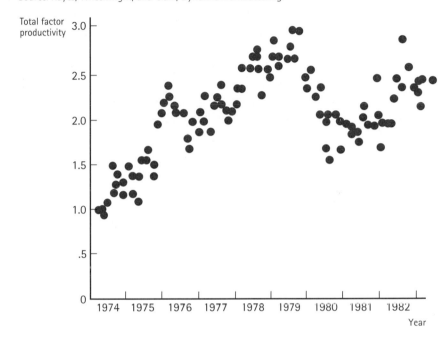

fall in 1979 to 1980, and an increase in 1981 to 1982. In 1982, total factor productivity was only somewhat higher than in 1976. The data in Figure 8.3 indicate that this factory experienced little in the way of technological change from 1977 to 1983. Hayes, Wheelwright, and Clark report that these data triggered an investigation of the causes for this poor performance, which indicated that it was due in considerable part to the way the factory managed equipment introductions.[5] Obviously, this information was of use to the firm's top managers.

In passing, note the fact that total factor productivity fell during 1979 to 1980 does not mean that there was negative technological change then. If the factory's sales decreased during this period, perhaps because of cyclical factors (recall Chapter 6), this could cause such a decline in total factor productivity. Also, it sometimes takes time for new equipment to reach its full efficiency. When equipment is first used, productivity may fall temporarily because of "teething" problems.

[5]Ibid.

Research and Development: A Learning Process

Particularly in science-based industries like electronics and chemicals, a firm's success depends on the extent and nature of the research and development that it carries out. Research and development encompasses work of many kinds. Basic research is aimed purely at the creation of new knowledge, applied research is expected to have a practical payoff, and development is aimed at the reduction of research findings to practice. Inventions can occur in either the research phase or the development phase of organized research and development activity.

Chance plays a crucial role in research and development, and a long string of failures frequently occurs before any kind of success is achieved. A research or development project can be regarded as a process of uncertainty reduction, or learning. Suppose, for example, a firm that is trying to fabricate a part can use one of two alloys and it is impossible to use standard sources to determine their characteristics. Suppose that strength is of paramount importance and the firm's estimates of the strengths of the alloys, alloy X and alloy Y, are represented by the probability distributions in part A of Table 8.1. If the firm were forced to make a choice immediately, it would probably choose alloy Y, since it believes that there is better than a 50–50 chance that alloy Y will turn out to be stronger than alloy X.

However, there is a good chance that this decision might turn out to be wrong, with the consequence that the part would be weaker than if alloy X had been used. Therefore, the firm may decide to perform a test prior to making the

TABLE 8.1

Subjective Probability Distribution of Strength of Alloys X and Y

| | Probabilities | | | |
| | A. Before test | | B. After test | |
Extent of strength	Alloy X	Alloy Y	Alloy X	Alloy Y
Exceptionally high	0.20	0.30	0.10	0.10
Very high	0.40	0.50	0.20	0.80
High	0.20	0.10	0.60	0.10
Medium	0.10	0.05	0.10	0.00
Low	0.10	0.05	0.00	0.00
Total	1.00	1.00	1.00	1.00

selection. On the basis of the test results, the firm formulates new estimates, represented by the probability distributions in part B of Table 8.1. These probability distributions show less dispersion than the distributions in part A; in other words, the firm believes it is able to pinpoint more closely the strength of each alloy in part B than in part A. Because of the tests, the firm feels more certainty concerning which alloy will prove stronger.

Parallel Development Efforts

Research and development is more risky than most other economic activities. Many development projects use parallel efforts to help cope with the uncertainty. For example, in the development of the atomic bomb, there were several methods of making fissionable materials and no consensus among scientists as to which of these alternatives was the most promising. To make sure that the best one was not discarded, all methods were pursued in parallel. The wisdom of this decision was borne out by the fact that the first method to produce appreciable quantities of fissionable material was one considered relatively unpromising early in the development program's history.

How can a firm's managers tell whether it is optimal to run parallel research and development efforts? What factors determine the optimal number of parallel efforts? Suppose that a firm can select x approaches, spend C dollars on each one over a period of n months, choose the one that looks most promising at the end of the period, and carry it to completion, dropping the others. Suppose that the only relevant criterion is the extent of the development costs, the usefulness of the result and the development time, assumed to be the same regardless of which parallel effort is pursued. For further simplification, suppose that all approaches look equally promising. Under these circumstances, the optimal value of x (the number of parallel research and development efforts) is inversely related to C and directly related to the amount learned in the next n months. As the cost of running each effort increases, the optimal number of parallel efforts decreases. As the prospective amount of learning increases, the optimal number of parallel efforts goes up.

To illustrate why it is sometimes cheaper to run parallel development efforts, consider a case in which each approach has a 50–50 chance of costing $5 million and a 50–50 chance of costing $8 million. Since we assume that all approaches are equally promising, these probabilities are the same for all approaches. The expected total cost of development is the sum of the total costs of development if each possible outcome occurs times the probability of the occurrence of this outcome. If a single approach is used, the expected total costs of development are

$$0.5(\$5 \text{ million}) + 0.5(\$8 \text{ million}) = \$6.5 \text{ million} \tag{8.4}$$

since there is a 0.5 probability that total costs with any single approach will be $5 million and a 0.5 probability that they will be $8 million.

If two approaches are run in parallel and if the true cost of development using each approach can be determined after C dollars are spent on each approach, the expected total costs of development are

$$0.25(\$8 \text{ million}) + 0.75(\$5 \text{ million}) + C = \$5.75 \text{ million} + C \qquad (8.5)$$

If each approach is carried to the point at which C dollars have been spent on it and the cheaper approach is chosen at that point (the other approach is dropped). Why? Because there is a 0.25 probability that total costs with the better of the two approaches will be $8 million and a 0.75 probability that they will be $5 million. In addition, there is the certainty that a cost of C will be incurred for the approach that is dropped. (The C dollars spent on the project that is not dropped are included in its total costs, given previously.) The reason why there is a 0.25 chance that total costs with the better of the two approaches is $8 million is that this will occur only when the total cost of both approaches turns out to be $8 million—and the probability that this will occur is 0.5 times 0.5, or 0.25. Comparing equation (8.4) with equation (8.5), it is obvious that the expected total cost of development is lower with two parallel approaches than with a single approach if C is less than $750,000.

More generally, if the probability is P that the development cost will be C_1 and $(1 - P)$ that it will be C_2 (where $C_2 < C_1$), the expected cost if a single approach is used is

$$PC_1 + (1 - P)C_2$$

If two approaches are run in parallel, the expected cost is

$$P^2C_1 + (1 - P^2)C_2 + C$$

which is less than the cost of a single approach if

$$C < (1 - P)(P)(C_1 - C_2) \qquad (8.6)$$

Therefore, if the inequality in (8.6) holds, two parallel approaches result in a lower expected cost than a single approach.[6]

---

[6]See R. Nelson, "Uncertainty, Learning, and the Economics of Parallel Research and Development Efforts," *Review of Economics and Statistics*, 1961, for an early paper on this topic. Also, see B. Dean and J. Goldhar, eds., *Management of Research and Innovation* (Amsterdam: North-Holland, 1980), vol. 15 of Studies in the Management Sciences.

What Makes for Success?

Even companies in the same industry may differ markedly in their ability to make research and development (R and D) pay off commercially. During a four-year period, for instance, three evenly matched chemical companies found the proportion of their R and D expenditures that earned a profit to be 69 percent, 54 percent, and 39 percent, respectively. These differences are too large to be attributed to errors of measurement or definition. What can explain them?[7]

An R and D project's likelihood of economic success is the product of three factors: (1) the probability of technical success, (2) the probability of commercialization (given technical success), and (3) the probability of economic success (given commercialization). One econometric study shows that all three of these probabilities are directly related to how quickly an R and D project is evaluated for its economic, as opposed to technical, potential. Also, in those companies whose R and D staff members do not work closely or responsively with the marketing staff, the integration of R and D activity with market realities is haphazard, belated, or both. Commercially successful innovation depends on just this sort of integration. Numerous case studies of successful and unsuccessful innovation come to the same conclusion: The closer is the link between marketing and R and D, the greater is the probability of commercialization (given technical completion).

Consider, by way of illustration, the experience of three chemical companies of roughly the same size and level of R and D expenditure that underwent reorganization at roughly the same time. In two of them, the reorganization produced a closer integration of R and D with marketing by improving the channels of communication between them as well as by noticeably increasing marketing's input to R and D decision making. In the third, however, integration decreased; R and D paid even less attention to marketing than it had before the reorganization.

Data on the probability of commercialization (given technical completion) of 330 R and D projects in these companies (projects carried out anywhere from three to seven years before reorganization to five to eight years after it) are highly suggestive. They show an increase of about 20 percentage points for the two companies that more closely linked R and D with marketing and a decrease of about 20 percentage points for the third.

---

[7]For references and sources of information for the data presented in this and the next three sections, see E. Mansfield, "How Economists See R and D," *Harvard Business Review*, November–December 1981. Also, see K. Clark and T. Fujimoto, *Product Development Performance* (Boston: Harvard Business School Press, 1991); R. Stobaugh, *Innovation and Competition* (Boston: Harvard Business School Press, 1988); and E. Mansfield, *Innovation, Technology, and the Economy* (Aldershot, UK: Elgar, 1995).

More generally, a substantial portion of a company's R and D efforts may lie fallow because other parts of the company do not make proper use of them. One survey of executive opinion has noted the widely held belief that the economic success rate of R and D projects would increase by half if marketing and production people fully exploited them. If this figure is anywhere close to the truth, the faulty interface between R and D and the other functions has a very serious effect on the productivity of industrial R and D.

Project Selection

However well-founded the fears of excessively detailed control, some managerial oversight of R and D is essential. To make effective use of its R and D capacity, a company must spell out its business objectives and communicate them to its scientists and engineers. Research, after all, makes sense only when undertaken in areas relevant to economic goals.

Simply taking on a team of scientists and allowing them to do research in their favorite fields may produce novel results but results that are unlikely to have much immediate commercial value. Most companies, therefore, have found it worthwhile to make economic evaluations of both project proposals and continuing projects. Without question, these evaluations are useful, since they force managers to make their assumptions explicit. Research suggests that the sooner such evaluations are carried out, the greater a project's chances of ultimate commercial success.

The nature of these evaluations is different for a research than a development project. As a project moves from the laboratory toward the market, it receives more intensive scrutiny from both the technical and economic angles. In the early research phase, the screening of proposals probably is quick and informal, since costs at this stage are still low and predicting outcomes is very difficult. But, as projects enter the development phase, where costs and predictability are higher, they require a far more detailed process of economic evaluation.

Managerial economists have developed a number of more or less sophisticated models to help solve these problems of evaluation. Some employ relatively straightforward adaptations of capital budgeting techniques. For example, the net present value or internal rate of return (concepts developed in a basic course in finance) of each project may be calculated and compared. The more complicated versions of these models have not found extensive use, for the following reasons: (1) Many of the models fail to recognize that R and D is essentially a process of buying information, unsuccessful projects can provide valuable information, and as a result, the real task is to facilitate sequential decision making under conditions of uncertainty. (2) Application of the more-sophisticated models is not cheap. (3) Perhaps most important, the models often rest on overly optimistic estimates that are not very reliable—estimates that

CONCEPTS IN CONTEXT

Parallel Development Efforts at IBM

The IBM Corporation, which spends billions of dollars per year on research and development, is one of the world's leading high-technology companies. Nonetheless, IBM, like other firms, must face the fact that R and D is a risky activity: It is not able to predict with confidence whether a particular R and D project will be successful. Recognizing this fact, parallel development efforts have played a major role in IBM's history, as indicated by the following quotation from one IBM manager:

Parallel projects are crucial—no doubt of it. When I look back over the last dozen products we've introduced, I find in well over half the instances the big development project that we "bet on" via the system came a cropper somewhere along the way. In every instance—and we've gone back and taken a

look and I do mean every—there were two or three (about five once) other small projects, you know, four-to-six person groups, two people in one instance, who had been working on parallel technology or parallel development efforts. It had been with scrounged time and bodies. But that's a time-honored thing. We wink at it. It pays off. Looking at the projects where the initial bets failed, the subsequently developed project came in ahead of the original schedule in three instances. It's just amazing what a handful of dedicated people can do when they are really turned on. Of course they had an advantage. Since they were so resource-constrained, they had to design a simple product in the first place.*

*Bartlett, *Cases in Strategic Management.*

reflect both the uncertainty of the undertaking and the desire by researchers and others to "sell" projects to top management.

Innovation

An invention, when applied for the first time, is called an **innovation**. The distinction between an invention and an innovation becomes somewhat blurred in cases like Du Pont's nylon, in which the inventor and the innovator are the same firm. In these circumstances, the final stages of development may entail at least a partial commitment to a market test. However, in many cases, the firm that is the inventor is not in a position to—and does not want to—apply its invention, because its business is invention, not production; because it is a supplier, not a user, of the equipment embodying the innovation; or for some other reason. In these cases, the distinction remains relatively clear-cut.

Regardless of whether the break between invention and innovation is clean, innovation is a key stage in the process leading to the full evaluation and utilization of an invention. The innovator—the firm that is first to apply the invention—must be willing to take the risks involved in introducing a new and untried process, good, or service. In many cases, these risks are high. Although R and D can provide a great deal of information regarding the technical characteristics and cost of production of the invention—and market research can provide considerable information regarding the demand for it—many areas of uncertainty can be resolved only by actual production and marketing of the invention. By obtaining needed information regarding the actual performance of the invention, the innovator plays a vital social role.

Time-Cost Trade-offs

For a particular innovator, there is likely to be a time-cost trade-off function, like that in Figure 8.4. If the firm cuts the total time taken to develop and

---

FIGURE
8.4

Time-Cost Trade-off Function and Optimal Duration of the Project

The optimal duration of the project is t^* years.

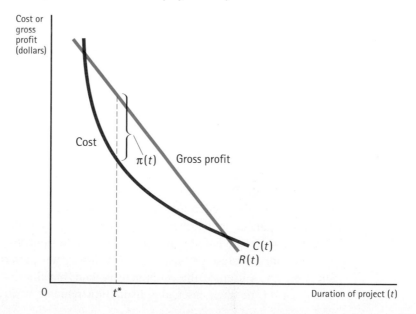

introduce the innovation, it incurs higher costs. As the development schedule is shortened, more tasks must be carried out concurrently rather than sequentially, and since each task provides information useful in carrying out the others, there are more false starts and wasted designs. Also, diminishing returns set in as more and more technical workers are assigned simultaneously to the project.

Faced with this time-cost trade-off function, how quickly should the firm develop and introduce the innovation? Clearly, the answer depends on the relationship between the present value of profit (gross of innovation cost) from the innovation and how quickly the firm develops and introduces it. (For a detailed discussion of the concept of present value, see Appendix A.) If $R(t)$ is the present value of gross profit if the duration of the project is t years and the time-cost trade-off function is $C(t)$, profit equals

$$\pi(t) = R(t) - C(t) \tag{8.7}$$

and the first-order condition for profit maximization is

$$\frac{dC}{dt} = \frac{dR}{dt} \tag{8.8}$$

In Figure 8.4, the optimal duration of the project is t^* years, since $\pi(t)$, which is the vertical difference between $R(t)$ and $C(t)$, is greatest when this is the duration of the project.

To illustrate, consider the Hanover Company, which wants to develop a new plastic. Its vice president for research and development believes that the time-cost trade-off function for this project is

$$C = 520 - 100t + 5t^2$$

where C is cost (in thousands of dollars) and t is the duration of the project (in years). This equation assumes that $t \geq 1$, since it is believed that the project cannot be carried out in less than a year. Hanover's president believes that

$$R = 480 - 20t$$

where R is the present value of profit (gross of innovation cost) from the innovation (in thousands of dollars). Since

$$\frac{dC}{dt} = \frac{d(520 - 100t + 5t^2)}{dt} = -100 + 10t$$

$$\frac{dR}{dt} = \frac{d(480 - 20t)}{dt} = -20$$

it follows from equation (8.8) that the firm should choose t so that

$$-100 + 10t = -20$$
$$t = 8$$

In other words, the Hanover Company should carry out the project in about eight years.

The Learning Curve

In many industries, technological change is due in considerable part to the learning and on-the-job experience that occurs as a firm produces more and more of a given item. Therefore, holding the firm's output rate constant, its average cost declines with increases in its cumulative total output (that is, the total number of items of this sort that it has produced in the past). For example, production of the first 100 machine tools of a particular type may require about 50 percent more hours of labor than production of the second 100 machine tools of this type, even though the number of machine tools produced per month remains about the same. Thus, the average cost of this machine tool falls substantially as cumulative total output grows.

One should distinguish between cost reductions due to learning and those due to greater current output. Holding constant the number of these machine tools produced by this firm in the past, it is quite possible that the average cost of producing such a machine tool during the current period declines as more of them are produced. But, this is different from learning. Holding constant the number of such machine tools produced currently, if the average cost is inversely related to the firm's previous total output of this machine tool, this is due to learning.

Managers, economists, and engineers often use the learning curve to represent the extent to which the average cost of producing an item falls in response to increases in its cumulative total output. Figure 8.5 shows the learning curves for two actual products: a piece of optical equipment (produced by Optical Equipment Company) and a portable turbine (produced by Solar International, Inc.). As you can see, learning results in major reductions in the average cost of both products. Of course, these cost reductions are not automatic: They occur only if workers and managers strive for increased efficiency. But for many products of this sort, a doubling of cumulative output tends to produce about a 20 or 30 percent reduction in average cost.

Applications of the Learning Curve

Many firms adopted pricing strategies based on the learning curve. Consider the case of Texas Instruments, a major producer of semiconductor chips and other

FIGURE
8.5

Learning Curves

Average cost declines with increases in cumulative total output.

Source: R. Hayes and S. Wheelwright, *Restoring Our Competitive Edge* (New York: Wiley, 1984). The cost data are incomplete, but this makes no difference for present purposes.

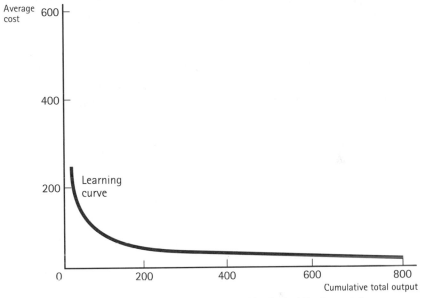

A. Optical equipment produced by Optical Equipment Company

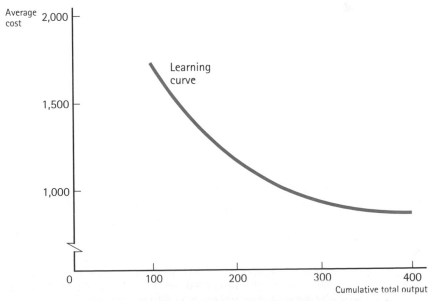

B. Portable turbine produced by Solar International, Inc.

ANALYZING MANAGERIAL DECISIONS

The Time-Cost Trade-off Function for Airliners

Keith Hartley of the University of York and W. Corcoran of the University of Newcastle (both British universities) estimated the time-cost trade-off function for the development of airliners (like the Boeing 707 or McDonnell Douglas DC-10) in the United States and the United Kingdom. Their results are shown in the graph.

(a) If an aircraft manufacturer in the United Kingdom decides to reduce the duration of a development project by 10 percent, by about how much will the cost of the project increase? (b) Holding the duration of a development project constant, does the cost of the project tend to be different in the United States from that in the United Kingdom? (c) What factors may account for this difference between the United States and the United Kingdom in the time-cost trade-off function for airliners?

SOLUTION (a) The cost increases by about 15 percent. To see this, let $t' = 0.9t$. Then, according to the formula in the graph, $C(t') = A(t')^{-1.3} = A(0.9t)^{-1.3} = 0.9^{-1.3}At^{-1.3} = 0.9^{-1.3}C(t) = 1.15C(t)$, since $0.9^{-1.3} = 1.15$. Thus, C increases by

about 15 percent when t is reduced by 10 percent (to $0.9t$). (b) Yes. The cost tends to be less in the United States than in the United Kingdom. (c) Hartley and Corcoran suggest that one factor may be that U.S. aircraft manufacturers benefit from defense contracts to a greater extent than their British counterparts. Therefore, the U.S. manufacturers can develop a commercial airliner more cheaply (holding the duration of the development project constant) than the British firms. (More will be said on this score in Chapter 18.)*

*For further discussion, see K. Hartley and W. Corcoran, "The Time-Cost Tradeoff Function for Airliners, "*Journal of Industrial Economics,* March 1978, 204–222.

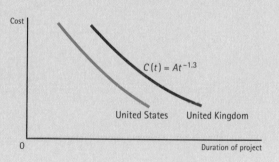

electronic products. When the semiconductor industry was relatively young, Texas Instruments priced its product at less than its then-current average costs to increase its output rate and its cumulative total output. Believing that the learning curve was relatively steep, it hoped that this would reduce its average costs to such an extent that its product would be profitable to produce and sell at this low price. This strategy was extremely successful. As Texas Instruments continued to cut its price, its rivals began to withdraw from the market, its output continued to go up, its costs were reduced further, and its profits rose.[8]

[8]For a classic paper concerning learning curves, see K. Arrow, "The Economic Implications of Learning by Doing," *Review of Economic Studies,* June 1962. The Boston Consulting Group was a leading advocate of its application to corporate planning.

The learning curve is expressed as

$$C = aQ^b \tag{8.9}$$

where C is the input cost of the Qth unit of output produced. If this relationship holds exactly, a is the cost of the first unit produced. The value of b is negative, since increases in cumulative total output reduce cost. If the absolute value of b is large, cost falls more rapidly with increases in cumulative total output than it would if the absolute value of b were small. Taking logarithms of both sides of equation (8.9),

$$\log C = \log a + b \log Q \tag{8.10}$$

In this logarithmic form, b is the slope of the learning curve.

To estimate the learning curve from historical data concerning cost and cumulative output, one can use the regression techniques in Chapter 5. As shown in equation (8.10), log C is a linear function of log Q. Therefore, to estimate a and b, we can regress log C on log Q. (In other words, log C is the equivalent of Y in Chapter 5, and log Q is the equivalent of X.) Of course, the values of a and b vary from product to product and firm to firm.

To illustrate how the learning curve can be used in specific cases, suppose that the controller of the Killian Company, a maker of a particular type of machine tool, finds that, for her firm, the learning curve (in logarithmic form) is

$$\log C = 4.0 - 0.30 \log Q$$

where C is expressed in dollars. (That is, log $a = 4.0$ and $b = -0.30$.) From this equation, she can estimate how much the cost per unit will go down in the future. For example, if she wants to estimate the cost of the 100th machine tool of a particular type, the answer is

$$\log C = 4.0 - 0.30 \log 100 = 4.0 - 0.30(2) = 3.4$$

Since the antilog of 3.4 is 2,512, the answer is that the cost will be $2,512.

Henry Ford's Model T and Douglas Aircraft's DC-9

The learning curve is nothing new. Between 1908 and 1923, the price of Henry Ford's famous Model T automobile fell from over $3,000 to under $1,000, owing in considerable measure to cost reductions due to learning. Ford worked hard to push costs down in this way. Standardization was increased. His product line was less diverse than those of his competitors, and model improvements occurred less frequently. The production throughput time was reduced, and the division of labor was increased.

However, not all firms have been as successful as the Ford Motor Company in reducing costs in this way. In cases in which labor turnover is high or a firm cannot obtain workers with the necessary skills, expected cost reductions due to learning may not materialize. For example, when Douglas Aircraft planned the production of the DC-9 airframe, it anticipated little problem in getting qualified workers. But when the time came, the labor market was so tight in Los Angeles that Douglas soon lost 12,000 of the 35,000 workers it hired. The result was that, contrary to the firm's expectations, costs did not fall as a result of learning, substantial losses were incurred, and the firm was forced into a merger (resulting in McDonnell Douglas, which is now part of Boeing).[9]

Diffusion Models

Another type of technological forecasting technique is based on the use of econometric diffusion models, which analyze the rate at which an innovation spreads. Although these models forecast the diffusion of new processes and products already in existence rather than the occurrence of future inventions, this limitation may be less important than it seems, since the inventions that already occurred are sometimes all that really matter in the short and the intermediate runs. In part, this is because it frequently takes a long time for an invention to be commercially introduced. For example, it took about nine years before catalytic cracking, a major innovation in oil refining, was first used.

The diffusion process, like the earlier stages in the creation and assimilation of new processes and products, is essentially a learning process. However, rather than being confined to a research laboratory or a few firms, the learning takes place among a considerable number of users and producers. When the innovation first appears, potential users are uncertain of its nature and effectiveness, and they tend to view its purchase as an experiment. Sometimes, considerable additional research and development is required before the innovation is successful; sometimes, despite attempts at redesign and improvement, the innovation never is a success. Information regarding the existence, characteristics, and availability of the innovation is circulated by the producers through advertisements and sales representatives; information regarding the reaction of users to the innovation tends to be circulated informally and through the trade press.

Figure 8.6 illustrates an important aspect of the process by which new techniques spread throughout an industry. The figure shows the probability that a

[9]J. Macklin, "Douglas Aircraft's Stormy Flight Path," *Fortune*, December 1966.

FIGURE
8.6

Relation between Probability of a Nonuser's Adopting a Process Innovation and the Proportion of Firms Already Using the Innovation

This relationship tends to be direct.

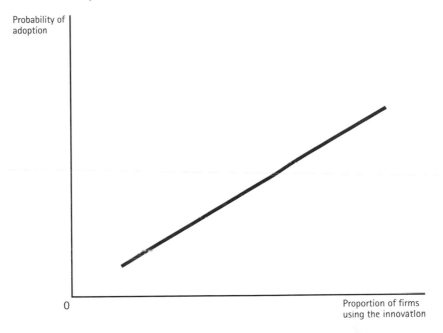

firm not using an innovation will adopt it in the next few months is influenced by the proportion of firms in the industry already using it. Specifically, as the number of firms adopting an innovation increases, the probability of its adoption by a nonuser increases. This is because the risks associated with its introduction grow smaller, competitive pressures mount, and bandwagon effects increase as experience and information regarding an innovation accumulate.

Other important aspects of the diffusion process are brought out by Figure 8.7. Panel A shows that the probability that a nonuser will adopt the innovation is higher for more profitable innovations than for less profitable innovations, holding constant the proportion of firms in the industry already using it. The more profitable the investment in an innovation promises to be, the greater is the probability that a firm's estimate of its potential profitability compensates for the risks involved in its installation.

Panel B of Figure 8.7 shows that the probability a nonuser will adopt the innovation is higher for innovations requiring fairly small investments,

FIGURE
8.7

Effect of Profitability of the Innovation and the Size of Investment Required to Adopt the Innovation on Probability of Adoption

This probability tends to be directly related to profitability and inversely related to the size of the investment.

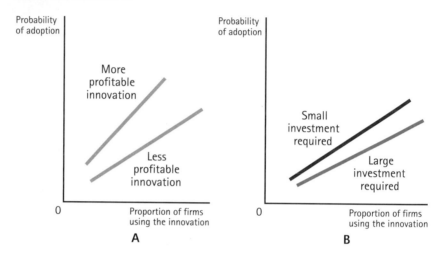

holding constant the proportion of firms in the industry that are already using it (and the profitability of the innovation). This is because firms are more cautious before committing themselves to large, expensive projects; and they have more difficulty in financing them.

If the relationship in Figure 8.6 holds, it can be shown that $P(t)$, the proportion of firms using the innovation, increases in accord with the S-shaped growth curve shown in Figure 8.8. The formula for this growth curve (often called the *logistic curve*) is

$$P(t) = \frac{1}{1 + e^{-(A + B_t)}} \tag{8.11}$$

where A and B are parameters that vary from innovation to innovation. Whether the diffusion process goes on slowly, as in curve L in Figure 8.8, or quickly, as in curve M, depends on the profitability of the innovation and the size of investment it requires. This model has much in common with the models used by epidemiologists to represent the spread of contagious diseases. Firms in a wide

FIGURE
8.8

Growth over a Period of Time in the Proportion of Firms Using the Innovation

Both growth curves L and M are S-shaped.

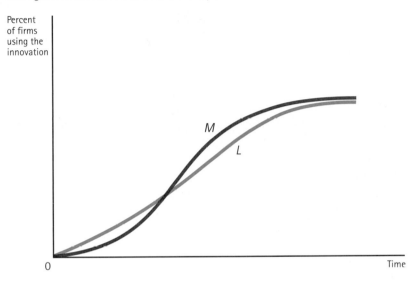

variety of industries have found that it can explain reasonably well the available data concerning the diffusion process.[10]

Forecasting the Rate of Diffusion of Numerically Controlled Machine Tools

To illustrate the use of diffusion models for forecasting, consider a study carried out for the Small Business Administration to forecast the percentage of firms in the tool and die industry that would be using numerically controlled machine tools two years after the time of the study.[11] When the study was

---

[10]See E. Mansfield, *Industrial Research and Technological Innovation* (New York: Norton, 1968); E. Mansfield et al., *The Production and Application of New Industrial Technology* (New York: Norton, 1977); V. Mahajan and Y. Wind, eds., *Innovation Diffusion Models of New Product Acceptance* (Cambridge, MA: Ballinger, 1986); and E. Mansfield, "Contributions of New Technology to the Economy," in *Technology, R and D, and the Economy*, ed. Bruce Smith and Claude Barfield (Washington, DC: Brookings Institution and American Enterprise Institute, 1996).

[11]See Mansfield et al., *The Production and Application of New Industrial Technology.*

Information Technology and Productivity Growth

The U.S. Bureau of Labor Statistics reports the annual output per worker in the United States increased by 4.8% in 2002, and over 5% in 2003. During the 1980's and 1990's the annual growth in output per worker was less than 2.7%. While many articles attribute this productivity increase to the expanded use of information technology (IT), recent research shows that technology alone only accounts for a small percentage of the increase. More important than technology is how managers re-design their work processes around the technology.

Professors Eric Brynjolfsson of MIT and Lorin Hitt of the The Wharton School studied over 1,100 large U.S. corporations. They concluded the critical question facing managers should not be, "Does IT pay off", but "How can we best use computers?" They found that complementary organizational capital assests couples with IT provide most of the increases in productivity. These complementary assests include human capital, training, work processes and routines, knowledge transfer, and corporate culture and value. For every dollar invested in IT hardware, companies spend up to nine dollars on these complementary assests. Their conclusion is that IT does not in itself produce productivity gains, rather it is the management around the use of IT that produces the gains.

For example, they examined the use of IT in both Wal-Mart and K-Mart. They found that while Wal-Mart did have a greater use of IT per employee, the bigger differences were in how the organization is designed around IT. Decision-making in Wal-Mart is more decentralized, there is a greater use of teams, and compensation is more performance based.

Technological advances like electric motors and robotics essentially replaced the brawn of humans. Computers are different since they do not replace the decision-making abilites of humans, rather they complement those abilities. In fact, studies find companies that use IT extensively employ workers who are better trained, educated, and skilled. These companies leverage this combination of computers and cognitive power by empowering employees through the use of intranets and database sharing. They also motivate their employees to make good decisions by structuring performance based incentive systems.

While IT itself holds the potenial for increased productivity within a firm, this potential is only realized when managers take the appropriate actions to re-design organizational assests to complement the technology. Brynjolfsson and Hitt suggest a set of organizational design changes to enhance the productitivy of IT systems. These include:

- automation of routine tasks
- use of highly skilled employees
- decentralized decision-making
- more efficient information flow
- greater use of performance based incentives

References: Lohr, Steven. "Technology and worker efficiency", *The New York Times* (nytimes.com), February 2, 2004. brynjolfsson, Erik. http://ebusiness.mit.edu/erik/Optimize/

carried out, about 20 percent of the firms in the National Tool, Die, and Precision Machining Association were using numerically controlled machine tools. To use the model described in the previous section, data were obtained, both from a mail survey and an interview study, of the past growth over time in the percentage of tool and die firms using such machine tools. Based on these data, and using the regression techniques in Chapter 5, estimates of A and B in equation (8.11) were made. To see how these estimates were calculated, note that equation (8.11) implies that

$$\ln \{P(t)/[1 - P(t)]\} = A + Bt \tag{8.13}$$

Thus, A and B can be estimated by regressing $\ln \{P(t)/[1 - P(t)]\}$ on t.[12] (The natural logarithm of any number, say, Y, is designated $\ln Y$. Recall footnote 20, in Chapter 5.)

Given estimates of A and B, equation (8.11) can be used to forecast $P(t)$ for future values of t. On the basis of the interview data, the model forecasted that about 33 percent of the firms would be using numerically controlled machine tools. On the basis of mail-survey data, the model forecasted that about 37 percent of the firms would be using them.

To see how these forecasts compare with those obtained on the basis of other methods, two alternative types of forecasts were made. First, the firms—both in interviews with a carefully selected sample of industry executives and in the mail survey of the industry were asked whether they planned to begin using numerical control in the next two years. Since considerable lead time is required in obtaining numerical control, it seemed reasonable to suppose that their replies would have some forecasting value. The results of the interviews indicated that about 16 percent of nonusers planned to use numerical control; the results of the mail survey indicated that this was the case for 28 percent of the nonusers. Therefore, the forecast was 33 percent, based on the interview data, or 43 percent, based on the mail survey.

Second, forecasts were obtained from the machine tool builders, the firms presumably closest to and best informed about the market for numerically controlled machine tools. About 25 of the 150 members of the National Machine Tool Builders Association provided forecasts. The results showed a considerable amount of variation, but the median forecast was about 30 percent.

How accurate were these forecasts? Which forecasting approach was most accurate? Table 8.2 shows that the model's forecast based on the data from the mail survey was almost precisely correct and that the model's forecast based on the interview data was off by only 4 percentage points. Regardless of whether we look at results based on the interview data or the mail survey data, the

---

[12]This is only a rough estimation technique, but it is adequate for present purposes.

TABLE
8.2

Alternative Two-Year Forecasts of the Percentage of Firms in the U.S. Tool and Die Industry Using Numerical Control, and the Actual Percentage

Type of forecast	Based on interview data	Based on mail survey
Model	33	37
Plans of tool and die firms	33	43
Median forecast by machine tool builders	30	30
Actual percentage	37	37

model forecasts better than the other two techniques. Moreover, it forecasts better than simple extrapolation by "naive" models.[13] Certainly, this is encouraging. On the basis of these and other results, it appears that this simple model may be of use in forecasting the rate of diffusion. Of course, this does not mean that it is anything more than a crude device or that it can be applied in situations in which its basic assumptions do not hold. But it does mean that, used with caution, the model may perform at least as well as other commonly used forecasting devices.

Summary

1. Technological change is the advance of technology; it often results in a change in the production function for an existing product or in a new product. The rate of technological change is often measured by changes in productivity. Changes in total factor productivity are often used by firms to measure changes in efficiency.

2. Research and development can be regarded as a process of uncertainty reduction, or learning. Chance plays a large role in research and development, and many projects use parallel efforts to help cope with uncertainty. Techniques are presented in this chapter to indicate when parallel efforts should be used.

3. An R and D project's likelihood of economic success is the product of three factors: the probability of technical success, the probability of commer-

[13]Specifically, the model forecast better than naive models that assumed that the increase in the percentage of firms using numerical control would be the same amount, in absolute or relative terms, during the next two years as it had been during the previous two years.

ANALYZING MANAGERIAL DECISIONS

The Use of Technology in the Airbus A380

The Airbus A380 is scheduled to be the largest passenger aircraft ever flown. In planning since 1994, the aircraft's maiden voyage is scheduled for 2006. The plane is over 262 feet (73 m) in length, weighs over 250 tons, and has a wingspan of 240 feet (80 m). It will carry up to 555 passengers over a maximum distance of 9,380 miles (15,100 km). The challengers facing engineers in building such an aircraft are immense, compounded by the fact that the aircraft has to fly both safely and profitably for those airlines purchasing them.

Since the cost of fuel is a major component of an aircraft's cost structure, a major challenge for engineers is to reduce the aircraft's weight. By using new technologies and materials, they estimate a weight savings over 17 tons. Over 40% of the plane's components are constructed from synthetic materials that barely existed a decade ago. These materials not only reduce weight, they better withstand the enormous stresses aircraft are subject to better than the metals they replace.

The A380 extensively uses glass- and carbon-fiber reinforced mats. Because of the size of this project, these mats could not be produced by the previous process of manual labor. To automate this process, new machines and machines were developed. The mats on the A380 are automatically moulded on large machines using high levels of pressure and temperature. Airbus estimates that these new product and process technologies help reduce the cost of building the plane by over 20%.

The plane's design also incorporates the use of carbon-fiber reinforced plastics. These plastics are used to construct the control surfaces, the deck floors, the rear bulkhead, and the wing boxes. Compared to old metal technology used to construct these parts, engineers estimate a weight savings of approximately one ton.

The upper fuselage of the plane (which is subject to enormous stress) is also composed of a new material consisting of glass fiber reinforced aluminium. Not only does this material weigh less than metal, it holds up better when subjected to the stresses of flying. While the lower fuselage is still constructed from aluminium, it is welded, not riveted. These laser welds produce a stronger fuselage, and reduce the cost of building the fuselage.

Because the A380 has a maximum takeoff weight of 650 tons, the landing gear posed a huge manufacturing problem. Working with B.F. Goodrich, Airbus developed a gear that individually supports 175 tons (there are four on the plane). Theunis Botha, president of Goodrich's landing gear's division commented. "Most people don't realize just how much technology is embedded in landing gear, the tolerances have to be within thousandths of an inch. It is the equivalent of making a 14-foot long surgical instrument in terms of precision."

References: www.airbusnorthamerica.com/newsroom "Airbus employs new technology to drop weight from jumbo jet", (The Wall Street Journal Online, 1/19/2001) www.flug-revue.rotor.com

cialization (given technical success), and the probability of economic success (given commercialization). All three seem to be directly related to how quickly an R and D project is evaluated for its economic, as opposed to only technical, potential.

4. To promote successful R and D, there must be a strong link between R and D and marketing personnel and project selection techniques must be effective. However, this does not mean that more complicated quantitative selection techniques need be used.

5. For a particular innovation, there is likely to be a time-cost trade-off function. If the firm cuts the total time taken to develop and introduce the innovation, it incurs higher costs. Time-cost trade-off functions vary from firm to firm, because some firms are more adept and experienced than others in developing and introducing a particular innovation. The optimal duration of the project is the time interval where the discounted gross profits exceed the discounted cost by the maximum amount.

6. In many industries, there is a learning curve, which shows the extent to which the average cost of producing an item falls in response to increases in its cumulative total output. This learning curve plays an important role in pricing. For example, Texas Instruments successfully priced its product at less than its then-current average cost to move quickly down the learning curve. Regression techniques can be applied to estimate the learning curve for a particular product.

7. As the number of firms adopting a new process increases, the probability of its adoption by a nonuser increases. Also, the probability that a nonuser will adopt the innovation is higher for more-profitable innovations than for less-profitable innovations and for innovations requiring small investments than for those requiring large investments. A model based on these propositions can sometimes be of use in forecasting the rate of diffusion of an innovation.

Problems

1. The Monroe Corporation uses three inputs: labor, energy, and materials. In 2002, it used 20,000 hours of labor, 50,000 kilowatt-hours of energy, and 10,000 pounds of materials to produce 200,000 pounds of output. In 2003, it used 30,000 hours of labor, 100,000 kilowatt-hours of energy, and 14,000 pounds of materials to produce 300,000 pounds of output. In 2002, the price of labor was $10 per hour, the price of a kilowatt-hour of energy was $0.02, and the price of a pound of materials was $5.
   a. What was the total factor productivity in 2002?
   b. What was the total factor productivity in 2003?
   c. What is the base year in the preceding calculations?

2. The chief scientist at the Roosevelt Laboratories estimates that the cost (in millions of dollars) of developing and introducing a new type of antiulcer drug equals

$$C = 100 - 19t + 0.5t^2, \quad \text{for } 1 \le t \le 6$$

where t is the number of years taken to develop and introduce the new drug. The discounted profit (gross of innovation cost) from a new drug of this type (in millions of dollars) is estimated to equal

$$R = 110 - 15t, \quad \text{for } 1 \le t \le 6$$

a. The managers of the Roosevelt Laboratories are committed to developing and introducing this new drug within six years, and it is impossible to develop and introduce it in less than one year. What project duration would minimize cost?
b. Why does R decline as t increases?
c. What is the optimal project duration? Why?

3. The Flynn Company produces a particular type of commercial truck. Its chief engineer regresses the logarithm of the input cost of the Qth truck produced on the logarithm of Q, the result being

$$\log C = 5.1 = 0.25 \log Q$$

where C is input cost (in dollars).
a. What is the estimated input cost of the 100th truck produced?
b. What is the estimated input cost of the 200th truck produced?
c. By what percentage does unit input cost decline if output is doubled (from 100 to 200 trucks)?

4. The Martin Company's president wants to estimate the proportion of chemical firms that will be using a particular new process in 2004. One of her assistants regresses $\ln \{m(t)/[n - m(t)]\}$ on t where $m(t)$ is the number of chemical firms using this process in year t and n is the total number of chemical firms that can use this process. Measuring t in years from 1986, the regression is

$$\ln \left[\frac{m(t)}{n - m(t)} \right] = -4.0 + 0.22t$$

a. Prove that, if the proportion of chemical firms using the new process increases in accord with the logistic curve in equation (8.11), $\ln \{m(t)/[n - m(t)]\}$ is a linear function of t.
b. On the basis of the preceding regression, can you estimate A and B (the parameters of the logistic curve in equation (8.11))? If so, how?

    c. Forecast the percentage of chemical firms using the new process in 2004.

5. In the aircraft industry, many studies indicate that a doubling of cumulative output results in about a 20 percent reduction in cost. If the cost of the 30th unit produced of a particular aircraft is $12 million, what is the cost of the 60th unit produced? Of the 120th unit produced?

6. The Bureau of Labor Statistics produced data showing that output per hour of labor in blast furnaces using the most up-to-date techniques has sometimes been about twice as large as the industry average.

    a. How can such large differences exist at a given time? Why don't all firms continually adopt the most up-to-date techniques?

    b. Should firms always adopt techniques that maximize output per hour of labor? Why or why not?

    c. Should firms adopt techniques that maximize output per dollar of capital? Why or why not?

7. The Russell Corporation is trying to develop an engine that will emit fewer pollutants. There are two possible approaches to this technical problem. If either one is adopted, there is a 50–50 chance that it will cost $2 million to develop the engine and a 50–50 chance that it will cost $1 million to do so.

    a. If the firm chooses one of the approaches and carries it to completion, what is the expected cost of developing the engine?

    b. If the two approaches are run in parallel and the true cost of development using each approach can be determined after $150,000 has been spent on each approach, what is the expected cost of developing the engine? (Note that the total cost figure for each approach, if adopted, includes the $150,000.)

    c. Should parallel approaches be used?

8. To help decide whether particular R and D projects should be carried out, some firms compare the estimated cost of each project with the estimated profits it will earn. To carry out such an analysis, the firm's personnel must estimate how much the R and D project would cost if it were carried out. In one major drug firm, the frequency distribution of 49 projects by the ratio of actual to estimated cost is as follows:

Actual cost divided by estimated cost	Number of projects
Less than 1.01	6
1.01 and under 2.01	24
2.01 and under 3.01	16
3.01 and under 4.01	3

    a. If this firm were using this technique to help determine whether particular R and D projects should be carried out, what problems would be encountered?

    b. How might the firm try to cope with these problems?

9. The Monroe Corporation wants to develop a new process that would reduce its costs by 10 percent. There are two ways to go about developing such a process. If the first way is adopted, there is a 0.6 probability that it will cost $5 million to develop the process and a 0.4 probability that it will cost $3 million to do so. If the second way is adopted, there is a 0.7 probability that it will cost $3 million and a 0.3 probability that it will cost $5 million.

    a. If the first way is adopted, what is the expected cost of developing the new process?

    b. If the second way is adopted, what is the expected cost?

    c. If the two approaches can be run in parallel and the true cost of development using each approach can be determined after $500,000 has been spent on each approach, what is the expected cost? (Assume that the outcomes of the two approaches are independent. Also, note that the total cost figure for each approach, if adopted, includes the $500,000.)

10. On the basis of past growth of the percentage of firms in the machinery industry using robots, this percentage can be approximated by

$$P(t) = \frac{1}{1 + e^{-(-6.1 + 0.41t)}}$$

where $P(t)$ is this percentage and t is measured in years from 1970.

    a. During which year did about 25 percent of the firms in the machinery industry use robots?

    b. During which year did 50 percent of the firms in this industry use robots?

The Analysis
of Costs

Even a manager who fully understands the physical relationship between inputs and outputs still cannot make optimal (profit-maximizing) decisions without cost information. The key question managers must ponder is this: How are costs related to output? A full understanding of costs is a necessary managerial characteristic since virtually all business decisions require a comparison between costs and benefits. The marginal analysis of Chapter 2 highlights this importance. A manager wants to undertake an action if the additional (marginal) revenue attributable to that action exceeds the additional (marginal) cost attributable to that action. As we will see, to maximize profit, a manager wishes to produce when the marginal revenue equals the marginal cost. Obviously, this is not obtainable without a knowledge of costs.

Cost is a complex concept. As managers, you will find that what seems like a simple cost concept often provokes controversy over the nature of costs, how they are defined, and the scope and attribution of relevant costs for the decision (hence, the basis for a core course in cost accounting in virtually every MBA program). This means a thorough understanding of cost is necessary for a variety of basic managerial decisions—pricing output, transfer pricing within and among divisions of a firm, cost control, and planning for future production needs. Thus, costs have both a short- and a long-run component, and management decisions will differ in the short run and the long run in similar situations given the nature of costs.

This chapter includes the basics of cost analysis, examines the results of empirical studies relating costs and output for various firms and industries, and describes the nature and usefulness of breakeven analysis, which is commonly used by managers to analyze the effects of a variation in price or output on their profits and to decide whether or not to enter a market.

Opportunity Costs

Managerial economists define the cost of producing a particular product as the value of the other products that the resources used in its production could have produced instead. For example, the cost of producing locomotives is the value of the goods and services that could be obtained from the labor, equipment, and materials used currently in locomotive production. The costs of inputs to a firm are their values in their most valuable alternative uses. These costs, together with the firm's production function (which indicates how much of each input is required to produce various amounts of the product), determine the cost of producing the product. This is called the **opportunity cost doctrine**.

The opportunity cost of an input may not equal its **historical cost**, which is defined to be the amount the firm actually paid for it. For example, if a firm invests $1 million in a piece of equipment that is quickly outmoded and too inefficient relative to new equipment to be worth operating, its value is clearly not $1 million. Although conventional accounting rules place great emphasis on historical costs, managerial economists emphasize that historical costs can be misleading.

There are two types of costs, both of which are generally important. The first type is **explicit costs**, which are the ordinary items that accountants include as the firm's expenses. They are the firm's payroll, payments for raw materials, and so on. The second type is **implicit costs**, which include the costs of resources owned and used by the firm's owner. Unfortunately, accountants and managers, in calculating the costs of the firm, often omit the second type of costs.

Implicit costs arise because the opportunity cost doctrine must be applied to the inputs supplied by the owner of the firm. Consider John Harvey, the proprietor of a firm who invests his own labor and capital in the business. These inputs should be valued at the amount he would have received if he had used these inputs in another way. If he could have received a salary of $25,000 if he worked for someone else and he could have received dividends of $20,000 if he invested his money in someone else's firm, he should value his labor and his capital at these rates. To exclude these implicit costs can be a serious mistake.

CONCEPTS IN CONTEXT

How Harley-Davidson Reduced Costs

Harley-Davidson Motor Company, a producer of motorcycles, has experienced very tough competition, particularly from Japanese rivals. Faced with a decreasing share of the market and lower profits, it took a number of major steps to increase manufacturing efficiency and reduce costs. For one thing, it phased out many of its machining operations and began to purchase its metal from steel service centers, which are companies that supply steel products and provide just-in-time delivery.

According to Harley-Davidson officials, this program reduced its work-in-process inventory by nearly $24 million. This meant a substantial cost reduction. Why? Because it costs money to house inventories, tie up capital in inventories, and hire people to move materials in and out of inventory. If a firm can reduce its inventories, it can cut these costs significantly.

Specifically, suppose that Harley-Davidson had borrowed the money to finance its work-in-process inventory and the interest rate on its loan was 15 percent. By reducing the amount that it had to borrow by $24 million (the amount of the reduction in its work-in-process inventory), Harley-Davidson reduced its annual costs by $0.15 \times 24 = \$3.6$ million.

To some extent, Harley-Davidson adopted the sort of just-in-time system pioneered by Toyota and other Japanese firms (recall page 268). As pointed out by one Harley-Davidson executive, "The plant doesn't have enough real estate to physically accommodate the larger mill orders. Timely service center deliveries have enabled us to make more productive use of our floor space."* This story also illustrates the importance of fostering and maintaining good working relationships between firms and their suppliers. Often economies can be realized if relationships of this sort are improved.

*A. Sharkey, "Making Industry More Competitive," *Chicago Purchasor*, November–December 1986, pp. 11–12. Also, see "Revving up for Relief: Harley-Davidson at the ITC," a case in the Study Guide accompanying this textbook.

Short-Run Cost Functions

Given the firm's cost of producing each level of output, we can define the firm's cost functions, which play a very important role in managerial economics. A firm's **cost functions** show various relationships between its costs and its output rate. The firm's production function and the prices it pays for inputs determine the firm's cost functions, which can pertain to the short run or the long run.

The **short run** is a time period so short that the firm cannot alter the quantity of some of its inputs. As the length of the time period increases, the level of more and more inputs become variable. Any time span between one where the quantity of no input is variable and one where the quantity of all inputs is variable could reasonably be called the **short run**. However, a more restrictive

TABLE
9.1

Fixed, Variable, and Total Costs, Media Corporation

Units of output Q	Total fixed cost (dollars per day) TFC	Total variable cost (dollars per day) TVC	Total cost (dollars per day) TC
0	100	0	100
1	100	40	140
2	100	64	164
3	100	78	178
4	100	88	188
5	100	100	200
5.5	100	108.625	208.625
6	100	120	220
6.64	100	139.6	239.6
7	100	154	254
8	100	208	308
9	100	288	388
10	100	400	500

definition is generally employed: We say the short run is the time interval so brief that the firm cannot alter the quantities of plant and equipment. These are the firm's **fixed inputs**, and they determine the firm's **scale of plant**. Inputs like labor, which the firm can vary in quantity in the short run, are the firm's **variable inputs**.

Three concepts of total cost in the short run must be considered: total fixed cost, total variable cost, and total cost. **Total fixed costs** are the total costs per period of time incurred by the firm for fixed inputs. Since the amount of the fixed inputs is fixed (by definition), the total fixed costs are the same regardless of the firm's output rate. Examples of fixed costs may be depreciation of plant and equipment and property taxes. Table 9.1 shows the costs of the Media Corporation, a producer of sofas. According to Table 9.1, this firm's total fixed costs are $100 per day; the firm's total fixed cost function is shown graphically in Figure 9.1. The values in Table 9.1 (and in Table 9.2) come from the total cost relationship

$$TC = 100 + 50Q - 11Q^2 + Q^3$$

Total variable costs are the total costs incurred by the firm for variable inputs. They go up as the firm's output rate rises, since higher output rates require higher variable input rates, which mean bigger variable costs. For

TABLE
9.2

Average and Marginal Costs, Media Corporation

Units of output Q	Average fixed cost (dollars) TFC/Q	Average variable cost (dollars) TVC/Q	Average total cost (dollars) TC/Q	Marginal cost (dollars) ΔTC/ΔQ[a]	Marginal cost (dollars) dTC/dQ[a]
0	–	–	–	–	–
1	100	40	140	40	31
2	50	32	82	24	18
3	33.33	26	59.33	14	11
4	25	22	47	10	10
5	20	20	40	12	15
5.5	18.18	19.75	37.93		19.75
6	16.67	20	36.67	20	26
6.64	15.06	21.04	36.11		36.11
7	14.29	22	36.29	34	43
8	12.5	26	38.5	54	66
9	11.11	32	43.11	80	95
10	10	40	50	112	130

[a] The figures in the ΔTC/ΔQ column pertain to the interval between the indicated amount of quantity and one unit less than the indicated amount of quantity. The figures in the dTC/dQ column are the continuous marginal cost, that is $dTC/dQ = MC = 50 - 22Q + 3Q^2$.

example, the larger the output of a woolen mill, the larger is the quantity of wool that must be used and the higher is the total cost of the wool. The Media Corporation's total variable cost schedule is shown in Table 9.1. Figure 9.1 shows the corresponding total variable cost function. Up to a particular output rate (four units of output), total variable costs are shown to rise at a decreasing rate; beyond that output level, total variable costs rise at an increasing rate. This characteristic of the total variable cost function follows from the law of diminishing marginal returns. At low levels of output, increases in the variable inputs may result in increases in their productivity, with the result that total variable costs increase with output but at a decreasing rate. (More will be said on this score later.)

Finally, **total costs** are the sum of total fixed costs and total variable costs. To derive the total cost column in Table 9.1, add total fixed cost and total variable cost at each output. The total cost function for the Media Corporation is shown in Figure 9.1. The total cost function and the total variable cost function have the same shape, since they differ by only a constant amount, which is total fixed cost.

FIGURE
9.1

Fixed, Variable, and Total Costs, Media Corporation

Fixed costs do not vary with output and so the fixed cost curve is a horizontal line. Variable costs at first increase with output at a decreasing rate and then increase with output at an increasing rate. The total cost curve is the vertical summation of the fixed cost curve and the average variable cost curve. The total cost function and the total variable cost function have the same shape, since they differ by only a constant amount, which is total fixed cost.

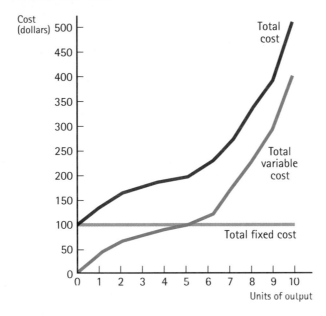

Average and Marginal Costs

While the total cost functions are of great importance, managers must be interested as well in the average cost functions and the marginal cost function. There are three average cost functions, corresponding to the three total cost functions. **Average fixed cost** is total fixed cost divided by output. Average fixed cost declines with increases in output; mathematically, the average fixed cost function is a rectangular hyperbola. Table 9.2 and Figure 9.2 show the average fixed cost function for the Media Corporation.

Average variable cost is total variable cost divided by output. For the Media Corporation, average variable cost function is shown in Table 9.2 and Figure 9.2. At first, output increases result in decreases in average variable cost, but beyond a point, they result in higher average variable cost. The theory of production in Chapter 7 leads us to expect this curvature of the average variable

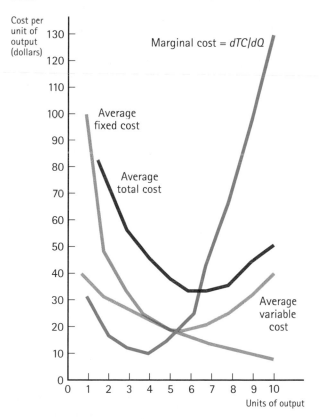

FIGURE 9.2

Average and Marginal Cost Curves, Media Corporation

Average fixed cost continually decreases as output increases. Average variable cost and average total cost at first decrease, reach a minimum, then increase as output increases. The minimum of the average total cost occurs at a higher output than the minimum of the average variable cost. The average total cost curve is the vertical summation of the average fixed cost and the average variable cost curves. Marginal cost passes through the minimum of both average cost curves, and when marginal cost is below the average cost, average cost falls and vice versa. Average total cost achieves its minimum at a higher output rate (6.64) than average variable cost (5.5), because the increases in average variable cost are, up to a point, more than offset by decreases in average fixed cost.

cost function. If AVC is the average variable cost, TVC is the total variable cost, Q is the quantity of output, U is the quantity of the variable input, and W is the price of the variable input, it must be true that

$$AVC = \frac{TVC}{Q} = W\frac{U}{Q}$$

Consequently, since Q/U is the average product of the variable input (AVP),

$$AVC = W \frac{1}{AVP} \tag{9.1}$$

Since AVP generally rises then falls with increases in output and W is constant, AVC must decrease then go up with increases in output.

Average total cost is total cost divided by output. For the Media Corporation, the average total cost function is shown in Table 9.2 and Figure 9.2. Average total cost equals the sum of average fixed cost and average variable cost, which helps account for the shape of the average total cost function. For those levels of output where both average fixed cost and average variable cost decrease, average total cost must decrease too. However, average total cost reaches its minimum after average variable cost, because the increases in average variable cost are for a time more than offset by decreases in average fixed cost.

Marginal cost is the addition to total cost resulting from the addition of the last unit of output. That is, if $C(Q)$ is the total cost of producing Q units of output, the marginal cost between Q and $(Q - 1)$ units of output is $C(Q) - C(Q - 1)$. For the Media Corporation, the marginal cost function is shown in Table 9.2 and Figure 9.2. At low output levels, marginal cost may decrease (as it does in Figure 9.2) with increases in output, but after reaching a minimum, it goes up with further increases in output. The reason for this behavior is found in the law of diminishing marginal returns. If ΔTVC is the change in total variable costs resulting from a change in output of ΔQ and if ΔTFC is the change in total fixed costs resulting from a change in output of ΔQ,

$$MC = \frac{\Delta TVC + \Delta TFC}{\Delta Q}$$

But ΔTFC is zero because fixed costs are fixed; therefore,

$$MC = \frac{\Delta TVC}{\Delta Q}$$

Moreover, if the price of the variable input is taken as given by the firm, $\Delta TVC = W(\Delta U)$, where ΔU is the change in the quantity of the variable input resulting from the increase of ΔQ in output. Consequently,

$$MC = W \frac{\Delta U}{\Delta Q} = W \frac{1}{MP} \tag{9.2}$$

where MP is the marginal product of the variable input. Because MP generally increases, attains a maximum, and declines with increases in output, marginal cost normally decreases, attains a minimum, and then increases.[1]

If the total cost function is continuous, marginal cost is defined as dTC/dQ, where TC is total cost (recall Chapter 2). Suppose, for example, using the Media Corporation's total cost function,

$$TC = 100 + 50Q - 11Q^2 + Q^3$$

where TC is expressed in thousands of dollars and Q is expressed in units of output. This firm's marginal cost function is

$$MC = \frac{\partial TC}{\partial Q} = 50 - 22Q + 3Q^2$$

Consider the previous definitions with the product function of the Thomas Machine Company ($Q = 30L + 20L^2 - L^3$) from Chapter 7. If the wage rate is 390, then Table 9.3 shows the relationship between average variable product and average variable cost and between marginal product and marginal cost. As you can see, when AVP is maximized, AVC is minimized. Likewise, it can be seen that marginal cost equals average variable cost when average variable cost is minimized. This is to be expected, because marginal product equals average variable product when average variable product is maximized. Average variable product is maximized when 10 units of labor are employed (at 130); average variable cost is minimized when 10 units of labor are employed (at 3); and marginal cost is also equal to 3 when 10 units of labor are employed.

Note that marginal cost always equals average variable cost when the latter is at a minimum. If AVC is this firm's average variable cost,

$$AVC = \frac{TVC}{Q} = 50 - 11Q + Q^2$$

Taking the derivative of AVC with respect to Q and setting it equal to zero, we find the value of Q where AVC is at a minimum:

$$\frac{dAVC}{dQ} = -11 + 2Q = 0$$
$$Q = 5.5$$

When Q equals 5.5, both marginal cost and average variable cost equal 19.75 thousand dollars. (Substitute 5.5 for Q in the preceding equations for MC and

---

[1]However, this is not always true, as indicated in Figure 9.6, in which short-run marginal cost always rises as output increases.

TABLE
9.3

Relationship of Average Variable Product and Marginal Product to Average Variable Cost and Marginal Cost for the Thomas Machine Company

L	Q	AVP_L	$MP_L = dQ/dL$	W	$AVC = W/AVP_L$	$MC = W/MP_L$
0	0	–	–	390	–	–
1	49	49	67	390	7.96	5.82
2	132	66	98	390	5.91	3.98
3	243	81	123	390	4.81	3.17
4	376	94	142	390	4.15	2.75
5	525	105	155	390	3.71	2.52
6	684	114	162	390	3.42	2.41
6.67	792.6	118.9	163.33	390	3.28	2.388 ← MP_L max,
7	847	121	163	390	3.22	2.393 so MC min
8	1008	126	158	390	3.10	2.47
9	1161	129	147	390	3.02	2.65
10	1300	130	130	390	3.00	3.00 ← AVP_L max,
11	1419	129	107	390	3.02	3.64 so AVC min
12	1512	126	78	390	3.10	5.00
13	1573	121	43	390	3.22	9.07
14	1596	114	2	390	3.42	195.00
15	1575	105	−45	390	3.71	–

AVC and see for yourself that this is true.) Therefore, as pointed out, marginal cost equals average variable cost when the latter is at a minimum. Note also that marginal cost equals average total cost when the latter is at a minimum. The firm's average total cost is

$$ATC = (100/Q) + 50 - 11Q + Q^2$$

Taking the derivative of ATC with respect to Q and setting it equal to zero, we find the value of Q where ATC is at a minimum:

$$dATC/dQ = (-100/Q^2) - 11 + 2Q = 0$$

or

$$2Q^3 - 11Q^2 - 100 = 0$$

ANALYZING MANAGERIAL DECISIONS

The Effects of Output on the Cost of Producing Aircraft

The National Research Council made a study of the U.S. aircraft industry that stressed the importance to airplane manufacturers of serving the entire world market. As evidence, the council presented the following graph.*

(a) As indicated in this graph, the cost per airplane of producing 525 aircraft of a particular type is about 10 percent higher than the cost per airplane of producing 700 aircraft of this type. Assuming that this graph pertains to the short run, by what percentage does average fixed cost increase if 525 rather than 700 aircraft are produced? (b) If average fixed cost is 30 percent of average total cost if 700 aircraft are produced and 36 percent of average total cost if 525 aircraft are produced, is it true that average total cost is about 10 percent higher if 525 rather than 700 aircraft are produced? (c) According to the

council, "If a foreign government elected to incur a cost penalty in order to establish a domestic [aircraft] industry that serves 25 percent of the world market, the effect would be to dramatically change the pricing and thus the profit prospects for a privately funded U.S. manufacturer." What sorts of changes in pricing and profit prospects would occur? Why? (d) The council goes on to say, "With the opportunity for profit reduced or destroyed due to a split market, the U.S. firm might well choose not to enter, and the foreign competitor would then have the total market available." Why?

SOLUTION (a) If the number of aircraft produced is 525 rather than 700, average fixed cost is $TFC/525$ rather than $TFC/700$, where TFC equals total fixed cost. Therefore, average fixed cost

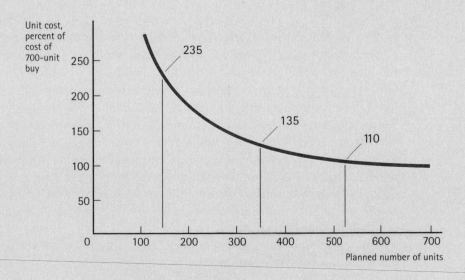

increases by 33 percent. (b) For 700 aircraft, average total cost equals $X/0.30 = 3.33X$, where X is average fixed cost when 700 aircraft are produced. For 525 aircraft, average total cost equals $1.33X/0.36 = 3.69X$, since average fixed cost equals $1.33X$ when 525 aircraft are produced. Therefore, average total cost increases by about 11 percent (from $3.33X$ to $3.69X$) if 525 rather than 700 aircraft are produced. (c) Because U.S. airplane manufacturers would be shut out of part of the market, they would be likely to sell fewer airplanes, the result being that their average total cost would be higher. Hence, their profits would be reduced or their prices would have to go up, or both. (d) If the U.S. airplane manufacturer felt that it was shut out of so large a part of the market that its average cost would be too high to enable it to make a reasonable profit, it would not build the airplane in question.

*National Research Council, *The Competitive Status of the U.S. Civil Aviation Manufacturing Industry* (Washington, DC: National Academy Press, 1985).

This can be solved for $Q = 6.64$. Substituting 6.64 into the ATC and MC equations yields $\text{MC} = \text{ATC} = 36.11$.

Note that we have two definitions of marginal cost. The first ($\Delta \text{TC}/\Delta Q$) assumes that we can produce only in discrete units, like a car or a cake. The second ($d\text{TC}/dQ$) assumes that we can produce on a continuous basis, as in 3.14 tons of grain or 10.33 gallons of gasoline. Which one you use depends on the situation you are in: Are you constrained to an integer number of the product or can you produce fractions of the product?

Long-Run Cost Functions

In the **long run**, all inputs arc variable and a firm can build any scale or type of plant that it wants. There are no fixed cost functions (total or average) in the long run, since no inputs are fixed. A useful way to look at the long run is to consider it a **planning horizon**. While operating in the short run, managers must continually plan ahead and decide strategy in the long run. Decisions concerning the long run determine the sort of short-run position the firm will occupy in the future. For example, before the IBM Corporation makes the decision to add a new type of product to its line, the firm is in a long-run situation, since it can choose among a wide variety of types and sizes of equipment to produce the new product. But, once the investment is made, IBM is confronted with a short-run situation, since the type and size of equipment are, to a considerable extent, frozen.

Assume it is possible for a firm to construct only three alternative scales of plant; the short-run average cost function for each scale of plant is represented by G_1G_1', G_2G_2', and G_3G_3' in Figure 9.3. In the long run, the firm can build (or

FIGURE

9.3

Short–Run Average Cost Functions for Various Scales of Plant

The long-run average cost function is the solid portion of the short-run average cost functions, G_1DEG_3'.

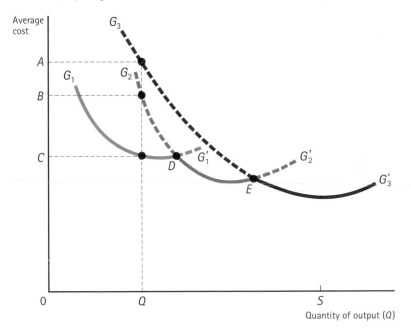

convert to) any one of these possible scales of plant. Which scale is most profitable? Obviously, the answer depends on the long-run output rate to be produced, since the firm wants to produce this output at a minimum average cost. For example, if the anticipated output rate is Q, the firm should pick the smallest plant, since it will produce Q units of output per period of time at a cost per unit, C, smaller than what the medium-sized plant (cost per unit B) or the large plant (cost per unit A) could. However, if the anticipated output rate is S, the firm should pick the largest plant.

The **long-run average cost function** shows the minimum cost per unit of producing each output level when any desired scale of plant can be built. In Figure 9.3, the long-run average cost function is the solid portion of the short-run average cost functions, G_1DEG_3'. The broken-line segments of the short-run functions are not included since they are not the lowest average costs, as is obvious from the figure.

Now, we must abandon the simplifying assumption that there are only three alternative scales of plant. In fact, there are many alternative scales, so the firm

FIGURE
9.4

Long–Run Average Cost Function

The long-run average cost function, which shows the minimum long-run cost per unit of producing each output level, is the envelope of the short-run functions.

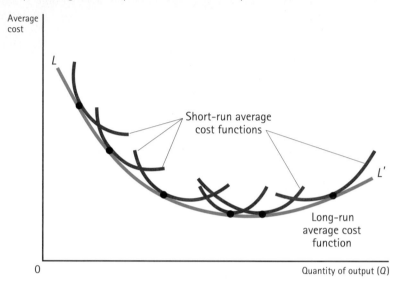

is confronted with a host of short-run average cost functions, as shown in Figure 9.4. The minimum cost per unit of producing each output level is given by the long-run average cost function, LL'. The long-run average cost function is tangent to each of the short-run average cost functions at the output where the plant corresponding to the short-run average cost function is optimal. (Mathematically, the long-run average cost function is the envelope of the short-run functions.)

If you have the long-run average cost of producing a given output, you can readily derive the long-run total cost of the output, since the latter is simply the product of long-run average cost and output. Figure 9.5 shows the relationship between long-run total cost and output; this relationship is called the **long-run total cost function.** Given the long-run total cost function, you can readily derive the **long-run marginal cost function,** which shows the relationship between output and the cost resulting from the production of the last unit of output if the firm has time to make the optimal changes in the quantities of all inputs used. Of course, long-run marginal cost must be less than long-run average cost when the latter is decreasing, equal to long-run average cost when the latter is at a minimum, and greater

FIGURE

9.5

Long-Run Total Cost Function

The long-run total cost of a given output equals the long-run average cost (given in Figure 9.4) times output.

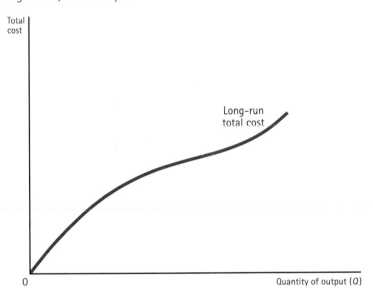

than long-run average cost when the latter is increasing. It can also be demonstrated that, when the firm has built the optimal scale of plant for producing a given level of output, the long-run marginal cost is equal to short-run marginal cost at that output.[2]

[2]Suppose that the long-run average cost of producing an output rate of Q is $L(Q)$ and the short-run average cost of producing this output with the ith scale of plant is $A_i(Q)$. Let $M(Q)$ be the long-run marginal cost and $R(Q)$ be the short-run marginal cost with the ith scale of plant. If the firm maximizes profit, it is operating where short-run and long-run average costs are equal; in other words, $L(Q) = A_i(Q)$. Also, the long-run average cost function is tangent to the short-run average cost function; this means that

$$\frac{dL(Q)}{dQ} = \frac{dA_i(Q)}{dQ} = \text{and } Q\frac{dL(Q)}{dQ} = Q\frac{dA_i(Q)}{dQ}$$

From these conditions, it is easy to prove that the long-run marginal cost, $M(Q)$, equals the short-run marginal cost, $R_i(Q)$.

$$M(Q) = \frac{d[QL(Q)]}{dQ} = L(Q) + \frac{QdL(Q)}{dQ}$$

$$R_i(Q) = \frac{d[QA(Q)]}{dQ} = A_iQ + \frac{QdA_i(Q)}{dQ}$$

Since we know from the previous paragraph that $L(Q) = A_i(Q)$ and $QdL(Q)/dQ = QdA_i(Q)/dQ$, it follows that $R_i(Q)$ must equal $M(Q)$.

The Crosby Corporation: A Numerical Example

To illustrate the relationship between a firm's long-run and short-run cost functions, consider the Crosby Corporation, a hypothetical producer of flashlights. Crosby's engineers have determined that the firm's production function is

$$Q = 4(KL)^{0.5} \tag{9.3}$$

where Q is output (in thousands of flashlights per month), K is the amount of capital used per month (in thousands of units), and L is the number of hours of labor employed per month (in thousands). Because Crosby must pay \$8 per hour for labor and \$2 per unit for capital, its total cost (in thousands of dollars per month) equals

$$TC = 8L + 2K = \frac{Q^2}{2K} + 2K \tag{9.4}$$

since equation (9.3) implies that

$$L = \frac{Q^2}{16K}$$

In the short run, which is a time period so brief that a firm cannot vary the quantity of its plant and equipment, K is fixed. Because the Crosby Corporation has 10 thousand units of capital, $K = 10$. Substituting 10 for K in equation (9.4), the short-run cost function is

$$TC_S = \frac{Q^2}{20} + 20 \tag{9.5}$$

where TC_S is short-run total cost. Therefore, the short-run average total cost function is

$$AC_S = \frac{TC_S}{Q} = \frac{Q}{20} + \frac{20}{Q}$$

and the short-run marginal cost function is

$$MC_S = \frac{dTC_S}{dQ} = \frac{Q}{10}$$

ANALYZING MANAGERIAL DECISIONS

Should We Continue to Make Autos from Steel?

In recent years, auto makers have begun to substitute synthetic materials for steel. Engineers at the Materials Systems Laboratory of the Massachusetts Institute of Technology made careful studies of the costs of producing an automobile fender. Assuming that the annual production volume of the fender is 100,000, the average cost of a fender is as in the table if sheet steel or four alternative plastics fabrication technologies (injection moulding, compression moulding, reaction injection moulding, and thermoplastic sheet stamping) are used to make the fender:

Cost	Sheet steel	Injection moulding	Compression moulding	Reaction injection moulding	Thermo-plastic sheet
Materials	$4.25	$8.50	$4.84	$4.89	$5.75
Labor	0.24	0.42	0.63	0.83	0.52
Capital	0.66	2.62	1.57	1.40	2.18
Tooling	2.57	0.86	0.71	0.57	0.71
Total[a]	$7.71	$12.39	$7.75	$7.70	$0.17

[a]Figures do not sum to totals because of rounding errors.

If the annual production volume is 200,000, rather than 100,000, the cost per fender, if sheet metal is used is less than $7—and less than the cost of any of the plastics fabrication technologies. (a) If 100,000 fenders are made per year, does the cost per fender differ significantly if sheet steel is used relative to reaction injection moulding (or compression moulding)? (b) Compared with reaction injection moulding (or compression moulding), sheet steel uses less (or less costly) materials, labor, and capital. Why then doesn't it have lower average total costs? (c) If sheet steel is used, are there economies of scale in fender production? (d) Steel is commonly thought to be the most advantageous material for high-volume production of auto fenders. Does this seem to be true?

SOLUTON (a) No. The cost is $7.71 for sheet steel versus $7.70 for reaction injection moulding (and $7.75 for compression moulding). (b) Sheet steel has much higher tooling costs per fender than reaction injection moulding (or compression moulding). (c) Yes. Whereas the cost per fender is $7.71 when 100,000 fenders are produced per year, it is less than $7 when 200,000 are produced per year. (d) Yes. For a production volume of 200,000 per year, sheet steel, according to the figures quoted, has a lower average cost than any of the plastics fabrication techniques.*

*For further discussion, see G. Amendola, "The Diffusion of Synthetic Materials in the Automobile Industry," *Research Policy*, 1990.

In the long run, no input is fixed. To determine the optimal amount of capital input to be used to produce an output of Q units per month, Crosby's managers should minimize total cost. On the basis of equation (9.4),

$$\frac{dTC}{dK} = -\frac{Q^2}{2K^2} + 2$$

Setting this derivative equal to zero, we find that the cost-minimizing value of K is

$$K = \frac{Q}{2}$$

Substituting $Q/2$ for K in equation (9.4), we see that the long-run cost function is

$$TC_L = 2Q \tag{9.6}$$

where TC_L is long-run total cost. Since $TC_L/Q = 2$, the long-run average cost equals $2 per flashlight.

Figure 9.6 shows the relationship between the Crosby Corporation's short-run average and marginal costs and its long-run average costs. As is always the case (recall page 333), the short-run marginal cost function intersects the short-run average cost function at its minimum point, where $Q = 20$ and $AC_S = 2$, in this case. Because it is horizontal (owing to constant returns to scale), the long-run average cost function is tangent to the short-run average cost function at the latter's minimum point. Note that the fact that the long-run average cost function is horizontal is unusual. Instead, as illustrated in the following section, there are economies of scale (over at least some range of output) in a wide variety of industries.

Economies of Scale in Nursing Homes

A long-run average cost curve is important for practical decision making by managers because it shows whether, and to what extent, larger plants have cost advantages over smaller ones. In cases in which this occurs, we often say that there are *economies of scale*. To illustrate, consider nursing homes, which is a huge industry with annual sales of over $70 billion. Figure 9.7 shows the long-run average cost curve for a nursing home, based on Texas data.

As you can see, there are substantial economies of scale. If a nursing home provides only 10,000 patient-days of service per year, the cost per patient-day is almost $29; if it provides about 50,000 patient-days of service per year, the cost per patient-day is under $26. Curves like Figure 9.7 are constructed by

FIGURE
9.6

Short-Run Average and Marginal Costs and Long-Run Average Cost, Crosby Corporation

Because the long-run average cost function is horizontal, it is tangent to the short-run average cost function at the latter's minimum point.

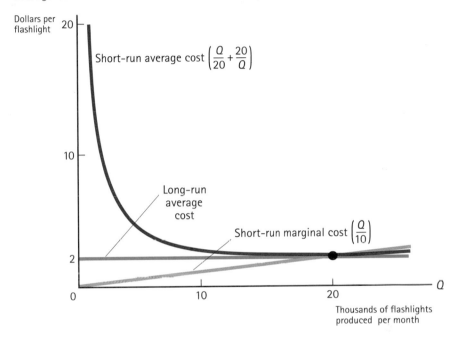

engineers and economists for a wide variety of plants and industrial processes. Without such information, managers could not make rational decisions concerning the size of plant they should build.

In many industries, firms can operate more than one plant, and there may be economies of scale at the firm (in contrast to the plant) level. In other words, holding the size of each plant constant, average cost may fall in response to increases in the number of plants operated by the firm. This seems to be true in the nursing home industry. Because of advantages due to centralized purchasing of inputs and a more specialized staff, firms with many nursing homes seem to have lower costs than those with only one nursing home.[3]

Beyond nursing homes, other examples of economies of scale exist. Mergers and alliances are happening in many industries, including oil, automotive, and airlines. While there are many reasons for firms to merge, one may be

[3]N. McKay, *Health Services Research*, April 1991. The average cost curve in Figure 9.7 is based on the assumption that a variety of factors influencing nursing home costs are held constant.

FIGURE
9.7

Long-Run Average Cost Curve for Texas Nursing Homes

For nursing homes with under 60,000 patient-days, there seem to be substantial economies of scale.

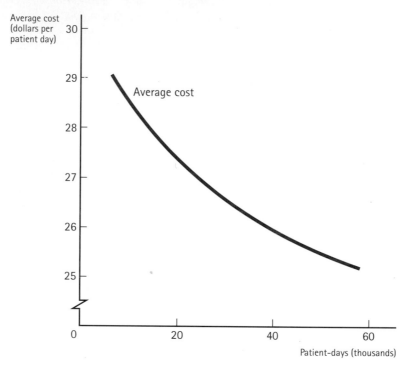

economies of scale—by becoming larger, average costs may become smaller. Consider the following three examples:

1. *Cruise ships.* The economies of scale created by the advent of huge ships have put pressure on smaller cruise lines prompting rapid industry consolidation in recent years.[4]
2. *UniDanmark.* The merger of UniDanmark and Tryg-Baltica (banking and insurance companies) in Denmark is expressed as a merger to exploit economies of scale.[5]
3. *DaimlerChrysler.* The creation of DaimlerChrysler is described as forcing the other auto companies to assess their previous assumptions about optimal size and economies of scale.[6]

[4]"Carnival Sails into Dominant Position in Cruise Holidays" *Financial Times*, March 19, 1998.
[5]"Merger Aims to Exploit Economies of Scale," *Financial Times*, May 19, 1999.
[6]"End of the Road for Independence?" *Financial Times*, February 5, 1999.

Managers must understand their cost relationships to know whether economies of scale exist. If scale exists, managers must then decide how to attain scale either by making it (through expansion of output and plant) or acquiring it (through a merger).

Measurement of Short-Run Cost Functions: The Choice of a Mathematical Form

To analyze many important problems, managers must estimate cost functions— or **cost curves**, as they are often called—in particular firms and industries. An initial step in estimating a cost function is to choose the mathematical form of the relationship between output and cost. As a first approximation, managers often assume that short-run total cost is a linear function of output, which means that marginal cost tends to be constant in the relevant output range (see Figure 9.8). In fact, as we shall see, a linear function often fits the data for particular firms and plants quite well in the short run. To some extent, this may

FIGURE
9.8

Average Cost and Marginal Cost, Linear Total Cost Function.

Marginal cost is constant.

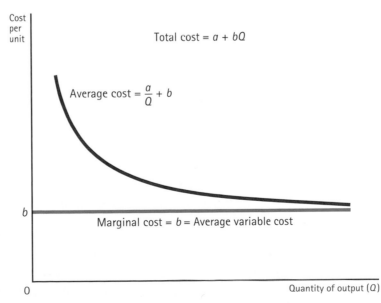

$$\text{Total cost} = a + bQ$$

$$\text{Average cost} = \frac{a}{Q} + b$$

Marginal cost = b = Average variable cost

Quantity of output (Q)

reflect the fact that some empirical studies are biased toward constant marginal cost by the nature of accounting data and the statistical methods used. Also, the data used in these studies often do not cover periods when the firm was operating close to the peak of its capacity, which is when marginal cost would be expected to increase substantially. Although marginal costs may well be relatively constant over a wide range, it is inconceivable that they do not eventually increase with increases in output. Therefore, a linear function is likely to be appropriate for only a restricted range of output.

It is also possible to assume that total cost is a quadratic or cubic function of output. If the quadratic form is chosen, marginal cost increases with output, as shown in Figure 9.9. If the cubic form is chosen (and c is large enough), marginal cost first decreases then increases with output, as shown in Figure 9.10. Whether these forms are better than the linear form depends on whether they fit the data better. In many cases, they seem to do no better in this regard than the linear form. However, before deciding that the linear form is satisfactory, you should be careful to inspect the residuals from the estimated cost function to see whether there is evidence of departures from linearity. (Recall the discussion on pages 185 to 186 of the appropriate inspection procedure.)

FIGURE
9.9

Average Cost and Marginal Cost, Quadratic Total Cost Function

Marginal cost increases as output rises.

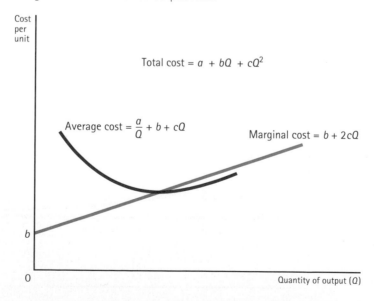

FIGURE
9.10

Average Cost and Marginal Cost, Cubic Total Cost Function

Marginal cost first falls then rises as output increases.

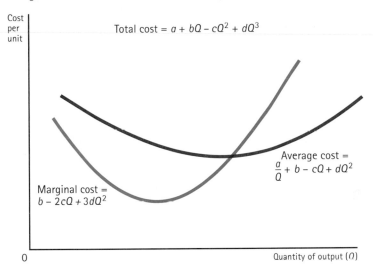

Nature and Limitations of Available Data

Having chosen a mathematical form, one must decide on the type of data to use in estimating a cost function. One possibility is to use time-series data and relate the total cost of a firm in each time period to its output level in that period. Regression analysis (described in Chapter 5) is frequently used to estimate this relationship. Another possibility is to use cross-section data and relate the total costs of a variety of firms (during the same period of time) to their output levels. Figure 9.11 plots the 2004 output of eight firms in a given industry against their 2004 total costs. Here, too, regression analysis can be used to estimate the relationship. A third possibility is to use engineering data to construct cost functions.

Regardless of which of these types of data are used, there are a number of important difficulties in estimating cost functions. Accounting data, which are generally the only cost data available, suffer from a number of deficiencies when used for this purpose. The time period used for accounting purposes generally is longer than the economist's short run. Accountants often use arbitrary allocations of overhead and joint costs. The depreciation of an asset over a period of time is determined largely by the tax laws rather than

FIGURE
9.11

Relationship between Total Cost and Output, Cross Section

Each firm's level of cost during 2004 is plotted against its output level during that year. Such a relationship generally is only a very rough approximation of the relevant cost function.

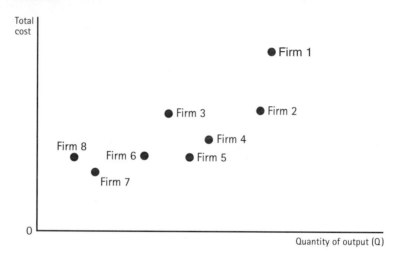

economic criteria. Many inputs are valued at historical, rather than opportunity cost.

Engineering data also suffer from important limitations. Engineering data, like cost accounting data, relate to processes within the firm. An inevitable arbitrariness is involved in allocating costs that are jointly attached to the production of more than one product in multiproduct firms. Also, a problem in using such data to estimate cost functions for an entire firm is that the costs of various processes may affect one another and not be additive.

If you are considering the use of cross-section data, it is important to watch out for the so-called regression fallacy. Because the output produced and sold by a firm is only partly under its control, actual and expected output often differ. When firms are classified by actual output, firms with very high output levels may produce at an unusually high level, and firms with very low output levels may produce at an unusually low level. Since firms producing at an unusually high level of output may be producing at lower average costs than firms producing at an unusually low level of output, cross-section studies may be biased, the observed cost of producing various output levels being different from the minimum cost of producing these output levels.

Key Steps in the Estimation Process

Having chosen a mathematical form and decided on the type of data to be used, the following six steps should be carried out before using the regression techniques described in Chapter 5 to estimate a short-run cost function.

1. *Definition of Cost.* As pointed out at the beginning of this chapter, the relevant concept of cost for managerial decision making ordinarily is opportunity cost, not cost based on accounting data. You must be careful to ensure that the accounting data—or engineering data, for that matter—on which an estimated cost function is based are reasonably indicative of opportunity costs. If not, they should be adjusted. For example, suppose that historical data regarding a firm's depreciation costs are based on the tax laws, rather than on opportunity costs of the relevant equipment. To remedy this problem, the cost data should be revised to reflect opportunity costs not tax conventions.

2. *Correction for Price Level Changes.* When using time-series data to estimate cost functions, it is important that changes over time in the prices of all inputs be recognized and measured. What we want is a cost function based on next year's input prices if next year is the period to which the analysis pertains. Since our historical data are based on input prices at various times in the past, we need a price index that will allow us to adjust our historical cost data for changes in the prices of various inputs. Moreover, since various inputs may experience quite different rates of inflation, we frequently must obtain or construct a separate price index for each of a number of major types of inputs. Using these price indexes, we must convert the available historical cost data into cost data reflecting next year's input prices, not those in the past.

3. *Relating Cost to Output.* If an estimated cost function is to be reasonably accurate, it is important that our cost data distinguish properly between costs that vary with output and those that do not. For many types of equipment, as well as other assets, depreciation depends on both the passage of time and the extent to which they are used, with the result that it is very difficult, if not impossible, to determine solely from accounting data how much the depreciation cost varies with output alone. Also, some costs do not vary with output so long as output does not exceed some critical level. Above this critical level, these costs may increase considerably. For example, up to some output level, a firm may be able to get along with one machine tool of a particular type, but beyond that output level, it may have to get an additional machine tool.

4. *Matching Time Periods.* Major errors sometimes occur because the cost data do not pertain to the same time periods as the output data. To see what mayhem this can cause, suppose that we were to plot a firm's 2003 cost

against its 2002 output, its 2002 cost against its 2001 output, and so on. Would the resulting plot of points be a good estimate of the firm's cost function? Of course not. Instead, we should relate a firm's costs in a particular period to its level of output in that same period. However, this rule must be modified in cases in which some of the costs of producing output in one period do not arise until subsequent periods. These delayed costs must be recognized, measured, and charged against the period in which the output occurred. For example, the costs of maintenance and repairs, when they are delayed, should be treated in this way.

5. *Controlling Product, Technology, and Plant.* As stressed earlier in this chapter, when we estimate a firm's cost function, we do so on the basis of a fixed definition of the firm's product, as well as on a fixed level of technology and (for short-run cost functions) a fixed scale of plant. This means that we must be careful to ensure that the product mix of the firm does not change over time if we are carrying out a time-series analysis. Also, the observations used in the analysis should not cover so long a period of time that they pertain to different levels of technology (or different scales of plant).

6. *Length of Period and Sample Size.* Since there are important advantages in having a reasonably large number of observations extending over a period that is not so long that technology has changed greatly, many analyses are based on observations of monthly cost and output, often with about 30 or 40 such observations. However, one problem with the use of monthly data is that one month's output may result in costs that occur in subsequent months. No simple rule can be used to specify the best length of period. Like so many aspects of this subject, the answer depends in considerable part on the quality and level of detail of the firm's accounting records.

A Hosiery Mill's Short-Run Cost Functions

If a conscientious effort is made to carry out each of the steps described in previous sections and one is careful to avoid the pitfalls cited, it generally is possible to estimate cost functions that are of considerable use in promoting better managerial decisions. To illustrate how cost functions have been estimated, we consider a pioneering study by the late Joel Dean of Columbia University of the cost behavior of a hosiery knitting mill that was a part of a large silk-hosiery manufacturing firm.[7] This mill began with the wound silk and carried the work up to the point at which the stockings were ready to be sent to other plants for dyeing and finishing. Therefore, this mill's operations were carried on by skilled labor and highly mechanized equipment.

---

[7]J. Dean, "Statistical Cost Functions of a Hosiery Mill," *Studies in Business Administration*, vol. 14, no. 3 (Chicago: University of Chicago Press, 1941).

In addition to studying total cost, Dean obtained cost functions for productive labor cost, nonproductive labor cost, and overhead cost. As a first step, he plotted each kind of monthly cost against monthly output. Then, he fitted a simple regression equation of the form $TC = a + bQ$ to the observations for combined (that is, total) cost and its three components. The resulting regression equations are shown in Table 9.4. (Total cost is in dollars and output is in dozens of pairs of stockings.)

The regression equation for combined cost is illustrated graphically in Figure 9.12. As you can see, the linear form of the equation fits quite well. The regression line is $TC = 2{,}935.59 + 1.998Q$. The slope of the regression line equals 1.998, which indicates that marginal cost was $1.998. Average cost (in dollars) was

$$AC = 1.998 + \frac{2{,}935.59}{Q}$$

Using this equation, the firm's managers could estimate average costs for any output level in the range covered by the data. For example, if they planned to produce 20,000 dozen pairs of stockings next month, their estimate of the total cost per dozen pairs of stockings would be

$$1.998 + \frac{2{,}935.59}{20{,}000} = 2.145$$

or about $2.15.

TABLE 9.4

Regressions of Combined Cost and Its Components on Output, Hosiery Mill

	Combined cost	Productive labor cost	Nonproductive labor cost	Overhead cost
		Monthly observations		
Simple regression equation	$TC = 2935.59$ $+ 1.998Q$	$TC = -1695.16$ $+ 1.780Q$	$TC = 992.23$ $+ 0.097Q$	$TC - 3638.30$ $+ 0.121Q$
Standard error of estimate	6109.83	5497.09	399.34	390.58
Correlation coefficient (r)	0.973	0.972	0.952	0.970

Source: Dean, "Statistical Cost Functions of a Hosiery Mill."

FIGURE
9.12

Regression of Total Cost on Output, Hosiery Mill

In the output range covered by these data, the total cost function seems to be approximately linear.

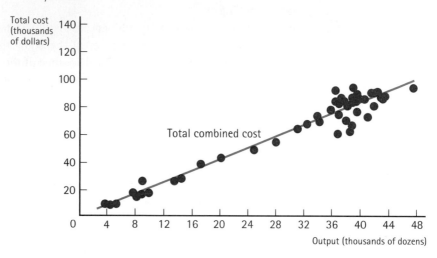

A Transportation Firm's Short-Run Cost Functions

In the six decades since Joel Dean's pioneering study of the hosiery mill, a great many studies of this sort have been carried out and statistical and economic techniques have advanced considerably. Nonetheless, the basic approach has not changed very much. To illustrate, consider one of the largest road passenger transport firms in the United Kingdom. Jack Johnston, a well-known econometrician, estimated this firm's cost functions.[8] To begin with, he broke down the firm's expenses into six categories: (1) vehicle operating expense, (2) maintenance and depreciation of vehicles and equipment, (3) other traffic costs, (4) maintenance and renewal of structures, (5) vehicle licenses, and (6) general expenses.

The largest and most-important element of cost is the vehicle operating expense, which consists of the wages, clothing, and national insurance of drivers and conductors, gasoline and fuel oil, tires, and lubricants. The second element of cost—maintenance and depreciation of vehicles and equipment—is also important. Maintenance cost, which consists of expenditure on labor and mate-

[8]J. Johnston, *Statistical Cost Analysis* (New York: McGraw-Hill, 1960).

FIGURE
9.13

Relationship between Total Costs and Car–Miles, Road Passenger Transportation Firm

As in Figure 9.12, the total cost function seems to be approximately linear.

Source: Johnston, *Statistical Cost Analysis.*

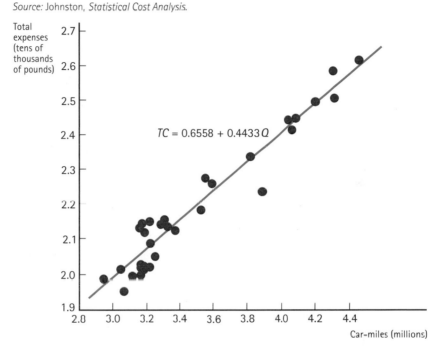

rials, varies directly with the number of car-miles run by the firm. The third element of cost—other traffic costs—consists of the wages of the traffic staff, bus cleaning, tickets, cost of tolls, insurance of vehicles, and other such miscellaneous expenses. These three categories account for over 90 percent of the firm's costs.

Figure 9.13 shows the relationship between the firm's total costs and its output, as measured by the number of car-miles. (Each point pertains to a four-week period.) Using more sophisticated statistical methods than were available to Dean, Johnston estimated the firm's total cost function; this estimate is included in Figure 9.13. The equation for this cost function is

$$TC = 0.6558 + 0.4433Q$$

where TC is total cost (in tens of thousands of British pounds) and Q is car-miles (in millions).

For values of car-miles ranging from 3.2 to 4.0 million, a 10 percent increase in the firm's output is associated with an increase of about 7 percent in its total cost. Therefore, the short-run average cost function slopes downward to the right, a 10 percent increase in output is associated, on the average, with about a 3 percent decrease in average cost per unit of output. Empirical results of this sort are of basic importance to a firm's managers. Any manager, to be effective, must have a good working knowledge of his or her firm's short-run cost structure.

Long-Run Statistical Cost Estimation

The same sorts of regression techniques used by Dean or Johnston to estimate short-run cost functions can also be used to estimate long-run cost functions. However, it is very difficult to find cases in which the scale of a firm has changed but technology and other relevant variables remain constant. Therefore, it is hard to use time-series data to estimate long-run cost functions. Generally, regression analyses based on cross-section data have been used instead. Specifically, a sample of firms (or plants) of various sizes is chosen, and a firm's (or plant's) total cost is regressed on its output, as well as other independent variables, such as regional differences in wage rates or other input prices.

Cross-section analysis of this sort, while useful, faces a number of difficulties, some of which have been noted already. (1) Firms may use different

---

FIGURE 9.14

Typical Long–Run Average Cost Curve

Its shape is L-shaped, not U-shaped (as in Figure 9.4). The minimum efficient scale is Q_m.

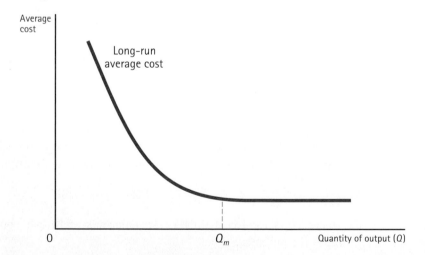

TABLE
9.5

Cost Disadvantage of Plants That Are 50 Percent of Minimum Efficient Scale

Industry	Cost disadvantage (percent)	Industry	Cost disadvantage (percent)
Flour mills	3.0	Synthetic rubber	15.0
Bread baking	7.5	Detergents	2.5
Paper printing	9.0	Bricks	25.0
Sulphuric acid	1.0	Machine tools	5.0

Source: F. M. Scherer, *Industrial Market Structure and Economic Performance* (2d ed; Chicago: Rand McNally, 1980).

accounting methods, with the result that their cost data are not comparable. Thus, the true relationship between cost and output may be obscured. (2) Firms in different regions of the country may pay quite different wage rates (and other input prices may differ considerably among regions). Unless input prices are held constant (by including them as independent variables in the regression), the estimated relationship between cost and output may be biased. (3) Whereas the long-run cost function is based on the assumption that firms minimize cost, the actual data used in the statistical analysis may pertain to firms that are not operating efficiently. Thus, the estimated cost function may exaggerate how much it would cost an efficient firm to produce a particular output.

Despite these difficulties, a great many valuable studies of long-run cost functions have been carried out. In general, these studies have found very significant economies of scale at low output levels but that these economies of scale tend to diminish as output increases and that the long-run average cost function eventually becomes close to horizontal at high output levels. In contrast to the U-shaped curve in Figure 9.4, which often is postulated in microeconomic theory, the long-run average cost curve tends to be L-shaped, as in Figure 9.14.

Given that this is the case, managers and others are particularly interested in estimating the minimum efficient scale of a plant or firm in a particular industry. The **minimum efficient scale** of a plant is defined as the smallest output at which the long-run average cost is at a minimum. If the long-run average cost curve is as shown in Figure 9.14, the minimum efficient scale of plant is Q_m. One reason why managers are so interested in the minimum efficient scale is that plants below this size are at a competitive disadvantage, since their costs are higher than those of their larger rivals. Table 9.5 shows, for various industries, the cost disadvantage of plants that are 50 percent of minimum efficient scale. In synthetic rubber, such plants have average costs that are 15 percent higher than those of plants of minimum efficient scale.

The minimum efficient scale of a plant or firm in a particular industry can be estimated from the long-run average cost function, which as we have seen, can be approximated on the basis of the regression techniques described earlier. Another way to estimate the minimum efficient scale of a plant or firm is through engineering analysis. Using their knowledge of the relevant production technology, engineers can determine the optimal input combination to produce each quantity of output. The long-run total cost function can then be estimated by multiplying the optimal quantity of each input by its price and summing to obtain the total cost. From the long-run total cost function, we can readily obtain the long-run average cost function, from which the minimum efficient scale can be determined.[9]

The Long-Run Average Cost Function for Electric Power: A Case Study

To illustrate the estimation of long-run cost functions, consider the study made of the U.S. electric power industry by Laurits Christenson and William Greene.[10] Using cross-section data for all investor-owned utilities with more than $1 million in revenues, they employed the regression techniques described in Chapter 5 to estimate the long-run average cost functions prevailing in 1955 and 1970, the results being shown in Figure 9.15. In accord with the previous section, the long-run cost curve in both years appears to have been L-shaped, not U-shaped.

The minimum efficient scale of a firm seems to have been at an output of about 12 billion kilowatt-hours in 1970. Figure 9.15 shows a substantial reduction in average costs between 1955 and 1970, as indicated by the fact that the 1970 average cost curve is well below the 1955 curve. In considerable part, this cost reduction was due to technological change of the sort we studied in Chapter 8.

The Survivor Technique

Still another way to estimate the minimum efficient scale is to use the **survivor technique** pioneered by the late Nobel laureate George Stigler. To use this

---

[9]For a case study, see L. Cookenboo, "Production Functions and Cost Functions in Oil Pipelines," in the Study Guide accompanying this textbook.

[10]L. Christenson and W. Greene, "Economies of Scale in U.S. Electric Power Generation," *Journal of Political Economy*, 1976. The mathematical form used in this study is the translog cost function, which is a more general (and more complex) relationship than those discussed previously.

FIGURE
9.15

Long-Run Average Cost Function, Electric Power

Between 1955 and 1970, the average cost function fell considerably. The minimum efficient scale of a firm seemed to have been at an output of about 12 billion kilowatt-hours in 1970.

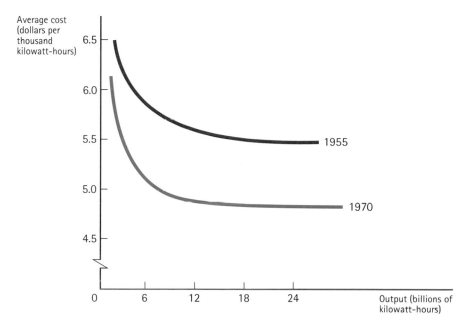

technique, we classify the firms in an industry by size and compute the percentage of the industry output coming from each size class at various times. If the share of one size class diminishes over time, it is assumed to be relatively inefficient, whereas if its share increases, it is assumed to be relatively efficient. Hence, if firms or plants below a particular size tend to account for a smaller share of industry output, this may indicate that they are below the minimum efficient scale. However, because of the effects of regulation, barriers to entry, collusion, and a variety of other factors, the average cost may not be as closely linked to survival as the survivor technique assumes. Therefore, this technique should be viewed with appropriate caution.

In Figure 9.16, we show Stigler's estimate of the long-run average cost function for ingot steel production. Apparently, firms with less than about 2.5 percent and greater than about 25 percent of the market had relatively high average costs. Firms in these size categories declined (as a percentage of industry output) during the period he studied. As you can see, a major limitation of the survivor technique is that it tells us nothing about the extent of the cost differentials

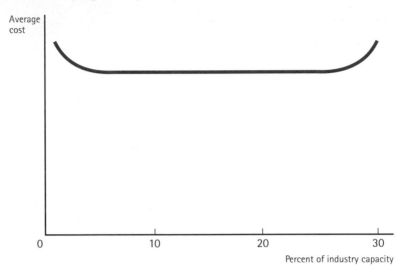

FIGURE
9.16

Long-Run Average Cost Function, Steel Ingot Production

Firms with less than about 2.5 and more than 25 percent of the market seem to have had relatively high average costs.

among firms of different sizes. This is reflected in the lack of scale on the vertical axis in Figure 9.16.

To illustrate the use of the survivor technique, consider the question of whether efficiencies might arise from common ownership of multiple radio stations within a market. Economists at the Federal Trade Commission carried out an analysis based on the survivor technique to see whether AM-FM radio combinations have increased in number relative to independently owned and operated stations. According to their results, this has been the case. They interpret these findings as suggesting that common ownership may result in significant economies.[11]

The Importance of Flexibility

On the basis of the measurement techniques described in previous sections, one can derive, for various types of plants, the relationship between output and average total cost. Suppose that the Marion Manufacturing Company is faced with the task of deciding which of two types of plant (type 1 or type 2) to build. The nature and quality of the output of one type of plant do not differ from

[11]K. Anderson and J. Woodbury, "Do Government-Imposed Ownership Restrictions Inhibit Efficiency?" Bureau of Economics, Federal Trade Commission, December 1988.

FIGURE
9.17

Average Cost Function, Type 1 and Type 2 Plants, and Two Probability Distributions of Output (*C* and *D*)

If the probability distribution of output is *D*, a type 2 plant is likely to be preferable to a type 1 plant.

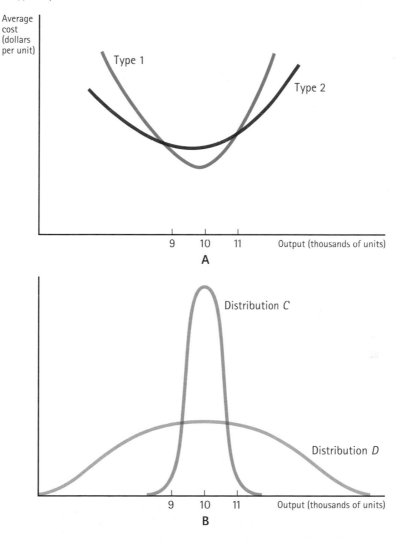

the nature and quality of the output of the other type of plant. The average total cost function for each type of plant is shown in panel A of Figure 9.17. Suppose the executives of the Marion Manufacturing Company believe that they will want to produce about 10,000 units of output per month. Which of the two types of plant should they build?

CONCEPTS IN CONTEXT

Economies of Scope in Advertising Agencies

In recent years, there has been considerable controversy over the extent to which there are economies of scope in the advertising industry. An advertising agency can provide many products. According to Alvin Silk and Ernst Berndt of MIT, these products (that is, types of advertising) can be categorized into the following nine categories: (1) network television, (2) spot television, (3) general magazines, (4) special print media (such as business publications), (5) newspapers, (6) direct response advertising, (7) radio, (8) outdoor and media services, and (9) non-media services. To what extent are an advertising agency's costs reduced by producing a mix of these products rather than producing them separately?

On the basis of a statistical analysis, Silk and Berndt estimated that the percentage cost reduction from joint production for 401 advertising agencies was as follows:

As you can see, the cost saving from joint production of these products ranged from essentially zero to about 86 percent, depending on which advertising agency is considered. On the average, this cost saving was about 26 percent.

Clearly, advertising has very substantial economies of scope. However, it is important to recognize that they are much more important for small advertising agencies than for large ones. For the handful of very large agencies with gross annual incomes of $100 million or more, economies of scope seem to be virtually nonexistent, according to the estimates provided by Silk and Berndt. But for small agencies with gross annual incomes of a few million dollars, economies of scope are very significant.*

*For further discussion, see A. Silk and E. Berndt, "Scale and Scope Effects on Advertising Agency Costs," Working Paper No. 3463, National Bureau of Economic Research, October 1990.

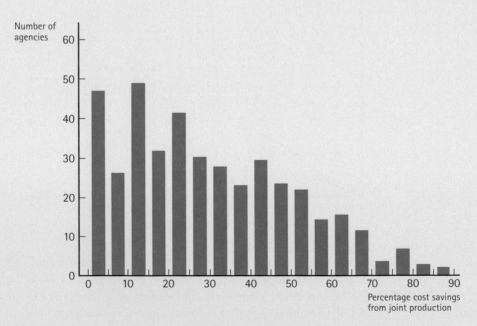

The answer depends on how certain they are of the output of the plant. Suppose that the probability distribution of the plant's output is distribution C (in panel B of Figure 9.17). In this case, a type 1 plant probably is preferable because it is very likely that the plant will be called on to produce 9,000 to 11,000 units per month; and in that range, the type 1 plant produces at a lower average cost than the type 2 plant. However, if the probability distribution of output is distribution D (in panel B of Figure 9.17), the type 2 plant is likely to be preferable, because it is very likely that the plant will be called on to produce fewer than 9,000 or more than 11,000 units; and in those ranges, the type 2 plant produces at lower average cost than the type 1 plant.

This case illustrates the importance of flexibility. While the type 1 plant is more economical if output is close to 10,000 units, the type 2 plant is more flexible. If output is likely to depart greatly from 10,000 units, the type 2 plant is the better choice.

Economies of Scope

Firms commonly produce more than one product. Oil firms like Exxon Mobil and BP Amoco produce both petroleum and chemical products; drug firms like Merck and SmithKline Beecham produce both vaccines and tranquilizers; and publishers like Random House and Simon and Schuster produce both mysteries and biographies. In many cases, a firm obtains production or cost advantages when it produces a combination of products rather than just one. These advantages sometimes arise because certain production facilities used to make one product can also be used to make another product or by products resulting from the making of one product are useful in making other products.

Economies of scope exist when the cost of producing two (or more) products jointly is less than the cost of producing each one alone. For example, suppose that the Martin Company produces 1,000 milling machines and 500 lathes per year at a cost of $15 million, whereas if a firm produced 1,000 milling machines only, the cost would be $12 million, and if it produced 500 lathes only, the cost would be $6 million. In this case, the cost of producing both the milling machines and the lathes is less than the total cost of producing each separately. Hence, there are economies of scope.

To gauge the extent of economies of scope, the following measure is sometimes calculated:

$$S = \frac{C(Q_1) + C(Q_2) - C(Q_1 + Q_2)}{C(Q_1 + Q_2)} \tag{9.7}$$

where S is the degree of economies of scope, $C(Q_1)$ is the cost of producing Q_1 units of the first product alone, $C(Q_2)$ is the cost of producing Q_2 units of the second product alone, and $C(Q_1 + Q_2)$ is the cost of producing Q_1 units of the first product in combination with Q_2 units of the second product. If there are economies of scope, S is greater than zero, because the cost of producing both products together—$C(Q_1 + Q_2)$—is less than the cost of producing each alone—$C(Q_1) + C(Q_2)$. Clearly, S measures the percentage saving as a result of producing them jointly rather than individually. In the case of the Martin Company,

$$S = \frac{\$12 \text{ million} + \$6 \text{ million} - \$15 \text{ million}}{\$15 \text{ million}} = 0.20$$

which means that there is a 20 percent saving of this sort. The larger is the value of S, the bigger the economies of scope.

To managers, it is very important that economies of scope be recognized and exploited. For example, a small airline may find that its regularly scheduled passenger service can be profitably supplemented by providing cargo services, since the cost of flying both passengers and cargo is much less than that of specializing in either passenger or cargo services. Similarly, in the trucking industry, there are substantial economies, particularly for small firms, in combining short hauls, intermediate hauls, and long hauls. A firm's managers must constantly be alert to the potential profitability of extending its product line or adding new product lines. Therefore, when the Xerox Corporation introduced its 9700 electronic printer, it had to consider whether and to what extent this new product line complemented its existing copier business and whether there were economies of scope.

Break-Even Analysis

An analytical tool frequently employed by managerial economists is the break-even chart, an important application of cost functions. Generally, a break-even chart assumes that firm's average variable costs are constant in the relevant output range; hence, the firm's total cost function is assumed to be a straight line. Since average variable cost is constant, the extra cost of an extra unit (marginal cost) must be constant too and equal to average variable cost. In Figure 9.18, we assume that the Carson Company's fixed costs are $600,000 per month and its variable costs are $2 per unit of output per month.

To construct a break-even chart, plot the firm's total revenue curve on the same chart with its total cost function. Typically, we assume that the price the firm receives for its product is not affected by the amount it sells, with the result that total revenue is proportional to output. Consequently, the total revenue curve is a straight line through the origin. Figure 9.18 shows the Carson Company's total revenue curve, assuming that the price of the product is $3 per unit. The break-even chart, which combines the total cost function and the total revenue curve, shows the monthly profit or loss resulting from each sales

FIGURE
9.18

Break-Even Chart, Carson Company

The break-even point, the output level that must be reached if the firm is to avoid losses, is 600,000 units of output per month.

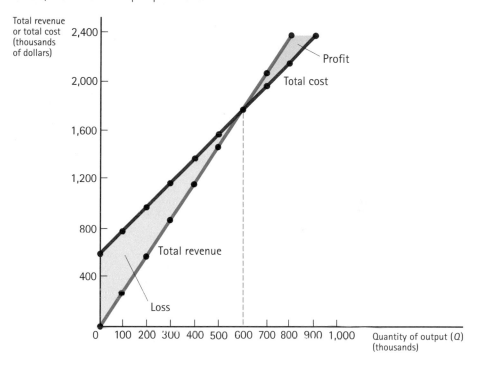

level. For example, Figure 9.18 shows that if the Carson Company sells 300,000 units per month, it will make a loss of $300,000 per month. The chart also shows the **break-even point**, the output level that must be reached if the firm is to avoid losses; in Figure 9.18, the break-even point is 600,000 units of output per month. In effect, a break-even chart can be regarded as a simplified version of Figure 2.12 for output levels up to about Q_0.

Under the right conditions, break-even charts can produce useful projections of the effect of the output rate on costs, receipts, and profits. For example, a firm may use a break-even chart to determine the effect of a projected decline in sales on profits. Or it may use it to determine how many units of a particular product it must sell to break even. However, break-even charts must be used with caution, since the assumptions underlying them may be inappropriate. If the product price is highly variable or costs are difficult to predict, the estimated total cost function and the estimated total revenue curve may be subject to substantial errors.

Break-even charts are used extensively. It is worth noting that although the total cost function generally is assumed to be a straight line in break-even charts, this assumption can easily be dropped and a curvilinear total cost function can be used instead. But, for fairly small changes in output, a linear approximation is probably good enough in many cases. Also, as was pointed out, empirical studies suggest that the total cost function is often close to linear, as long as the firm is not operating at or close to capacity.

Algebraic Break-Even Analysis

In the previous section, we showed how a break-even analysis can be carried out geometrically; now we see how such an analysis can be carried out algebraically. Let P be the price of the good, Q be the quantity produced and sold, AVC be the average variable cost, and TFC be the firm's total fixed cost. The break-even point is the output, Q_B, at which total revenue equals total cost.

Since total revenue equals PQ and total cost equals TFC + AVC (Q), it follows that

$$PQ_B = \text{TFC} + \text{AVC}(Q_B)$$
$$(P - \text{AVC})Q_B = \text{TFC}$$
$$Q_B = \frac{\text{TFC}}{P - \text{AVC}} \tag{9.8}$$

In the case of the Carson Company, $P = \$3$, AVC = $\$2$, and TFC = $\$600,000$. Consequently,

$$Q_B = \frac{\$600,000}{3 - 2} = 600,000$$

which agrees with our finding based on Figure 9.18. Of course, this algebraic procedure always produces the same results as the geometric procedure in the previous section.

Profit Contribution Analysis

In making short-run decisions, firms often find it useful to carry out various types of profit contribution analysis. The profit contribution is the difference between total revenue and total variable cost; on a per-unit basis, it is equal to price minus average variable cost. In the case of the Carson Company, where price is $3 and average variable cost is $2, the per-unit profit contribution is $3 − $2, or $1. This profit contribution can be used to help pay the firm's fixed costs and, once these costs are met, to build up the firm's profits.

To illustrate how profit contribution analysis can be used, suppose that the Carson Company wants to determine how many units of output it must produce and sell to earn a profit of $1 million per month. The required sales equals

$$Q = \frac{\text{total fixed cost} + \text{profit target}}{\text{profit contribution (per unit)}}$$
$$= \frac{\$600,000 + \$1,000,000}{\$1}$$
$$= 1,600,000 \text{ units}$$

As another example, suppose that the Carson Company sells only 500,000 units per month, which means that it loses $100,000 per month. The firm's marketing director hopes to land an order for 50,000 units of the firm's product. How much will this order reduce the firm's loss? To find out, multiply the order size (50,000 units) by the per-unit profit contribution ($1) to get the increase in profit (or reduction in loss, which is the case here); the result is $50,000.

Summary

1. Managerial economists define the cost of producing a particular product as the value of the other products that the resources used in its production could have produced instead. This, the product's opportunity cost, may differ from historical cost, which is generally the basis for accounting statements.

2. In the short run, it is important to distinguish between a firm's fixed and variable costs. The firm's total and average costs, total and average fixed costs, and total and average variable costs all can be plotted against output. So can the firm's marginal cost. The resulting cost functions, or cost curves (as they are often called), show how changes in output affect the firm's costs, a major concern of any firm.

3. The long-run average cost function shows the minimum cost per unit of producing each output level when any desired scale of plant can be built. The long-run average cost function is tangent to each of the short-run average cost functions at the output where the plant corresponding to the short-run average cost function is optimal. The long-run average cost curve is important to managers because it shows the extent to which larger plants have cost advantages over smaller ones.

4. Many studies based on the statistical analysis of cross-section and time-series data, as well as engineering studies, have been carried out to estimate the cost functions of particular firms. The regression techniques described in Chapter 5 play an important role here. Both short- and long-run cost functions can be estimated, as illustrated by the many examples considered. A detailed account of the relevant procedures and problems has been given.

5. In choosing among plants, a major consideration is flexibility if the output of the plant is highly uncertain. Some plants, while they have higher costs than others at the most likely output, have lower costs than the others over a wide range of output. If one cannot predict output reasonably well, flexible plants of this sort may be best.

6. Economies of scope occur when the cost of producing two (or more) products jointly is less than the cost of producing them separately. Such economies may arise because the production facilities used to make one product can also be used to make another product or by-products resulting from the making of one product can be useful in making other products.

7. Break-even analysis compares total revenue and total cost, graphically or algebraically. A break-even chart combines the total cost function and the

total revenue curve, both of which are generally assumed to be linear, and shows the profit or loss resulting from each sales level. The break-even point is the sales level that must be achieved if the firm is to avoid losses. Firms often find it useful to carry out various types of profit contribution analysis. The profit contribution is the difference between total revenue and total variable cost; on a per-unit basis, it is equal to price minus average variable cost.

Problems

1. In 1985, the National Academy of Engineering, using data developed at the Massachusetts Institute of Technology, estimated the costs of producing steel with three different technologies: (1) coke, blast furnace, basic oxygen furnace, ingots, and finishing mills, (2) coke, blast furnace, basic oxygen furnace, continuous casting, and finishing mills, and (3) steel scrap, electric arc furnace, continuous casting, and finishing mills. Under reasonable assumptions concerning input prices, the estimated average costs per ton were as follows:

Cost category	Coke, blast furnaces, basic oxygen furnace, ingots, finishing mills	Coke, blast furnaces, basic oxygen furnace, continuous casting, finishing mills	Steel scrap, electric arc furnace, continuous casting, finishing mills
Process materials	$148.34	$136.19	$122.78
Energy	21.15	15.98	41.58
Direct labor	83.43	75.09	67.43
Capital	102.06	99.93	54.08
Other	46.74	41.67	24.47
Total	$401.72	$368.86	$310.34

a. The academy's report concludes that "unless significant changes occur in other technologies, the electric-furnace continuous-casting route will dominate domestic production." Why?

b. At the same time, the report notes that the price of scrap (which is used in this route) "could increase as electric furnace production expands because of the increased demand." Why is this relevant?

c. The academy also concludes that, regardless of which of these technologies is used, cost per ton is about 25 to 30 percent higher if wages are $26 per hour rather than $2 per hour. What does this imply concerning the competitiveness of U.S. steel producers relative to producers in other countries that pay wages far below U.S. levels?

d. If the above cost figures are long-run average costs, under what circumstances would they also equal long-run marginal costs?

2. The Haverford Company is considering three types of plants to make a particular electronic device. Plant A is much more highly automated than plant B, which in turn is more highly automated than plant C. For each type of plant, average variable cost is constant so long as output is less than capacity, which is the maximum output of the plant. The cost structure for each type of plant is as follows:

	Plant A	Plant B	Plant C
Average Variable Costs			
Labor	$1.10	$2.40	$3.70
Materials	0.90	1.20	1.80
Other	0.50	2.40	2.00
Total	$2.50	$6.00	$7.50
Total fixed costs	$300,000	$75,000	$25,000
Annual capacity	200,000	100,000	50,000

a. Derive the average cost of producing 100,000, 200,000, 300,000, and 400,000 devices per year with plant A. (For outputs exceeding the capacity of a single plant, assume that more than one plant of this type is built.)

b. Derive the average cost of producing 100,000, 200,000, 300,000, and 400,000 devices per year with plant B.

c. Derive the average cost of producing 100,000, 200,000, 300,000, and 400,000 devices per year with plant C.

d. Using the results of parts a through c, plot the points on the long-run average cost curve for the production of these electronic devices for outputs of 100,000, 200,000, and 400,000 devices per year.

3. The Abner Corporation, a retail seller of television sets, wants to determine how many television sets it must sell in order to earn a profit of $10,000 per month. The price of each television set is $300, and the average variable cost is $100.

a. What is the required sales volume if the Abner Corporation's monthly fixed costs are $5,000 per month?

b. If the firm were to sell each television set at a price of $350 rather than $300, what would be the required sales volume?

c. If the price is $350, and if average variable cost is $85 rather than $100, what would be the required sales volume?

4. According to a statistical study, the following relationship exists between an electric light and power plant's fuel costs (C) and its eight-hour output as a percent of capacity (Q):

$$C = 16.68 + 0.125Q + 0.00439Q^2.$$

    a. When Q increases from 50 to 51, what is the increase in the cost of fuel for this electric plant?

    b. Of what use might the result in part a be to the plant's managers?

    c. Derive the marginal (fuel) cost curve for this plant, and indicate how it might be used by the plant's managers.

5. The following table pertains to the Lincoln Company. Fill in the blanks:

Output	Total cost	Total fixed cost	Total variable cost	Average fixed cost	Average variable cost
0	50	_____	_____	_____	_____
1	75	_____	_____	_____	_____
2	100	_____	_____	_____	_____
3	120	_____	_____	_____	_____
4	135	_____	_____	_____	_____
5	150	_____	_____	_____	_____
6	190	_____	_____	_____	_____
7	260	_____	_____	_____	_____

6. The Deering Manufacturing Company's short-run average cost function in 2004 is

$$AC = 3 + 4Q,$$

where AC is the firm's average cost (in dollars per pound of the product), and Q is its output rate.

    a. Obtain an equation for the firm's short-run total cost function.

    b. Does the firm have any fixed costs? Explain.

    c. If the price of the Deering Manufacturing Company's product (per pound) is $3, is the firm making profits or losses? Explain.

    d. Derive an equation for the firm's marginal cost function.

7. The president of the Tacke Corporation believes that statistical research by his staff shows that the firm's long-run total cost curve can be represented as:

$$TC = \alpha_0 Q^{\alpha_1} P_L^{\alpha_2} P_K^{\alpha_3}$$

where TC is the firm's total cost, Q is its output, P_L is the price of labor, and P_K is the price of capital.

    a. Tacke's president says that α_1 measures the elasticity of cost with respect to output—that is, the percentage change in total cost resulting from a 1 percent change in output. Is he correct? Why or why not?

b. He also says that if $\alpha_1 < 1$, economies of scale are indicated, whereas if $\alpha_1 > 1$, diseconomies of scale are indicated. Is he correct? Why or why not?

c. According to Tacke's president, the $\alpha3$ can be estimated by regressing $\log (TC/P_K)$ on $\log Q$ and $\log (P_L/P_K)$. Is he correct? Why or why not?

8. Engineers sometimes rely on the "0.6 rule," which states that the increase in cost is given by the increase in capacity raised to the 0.6 power; that is,

$$C_2 = C_1(X_2/X_1)^{0.6},$$

where C_1 and C_2 are the costs of two pieces of equipment, and X_1 and X_2 are their respective capacities.

a. Does the 0.6 rule suggest economies of scale?

b. Some experts have stated that in the chemical and metal industries, the 0.6 rule can be applied to entire plants rather than individual pieces of equipment. If so, will the long-run average cost curve in these industries tend to be negatively sloped?

c. Can you think of a way to test whether this rule is correct?

9. The Dijon Company's total variable cost function is:

$$TVC = 50Q - 10Q^2 + Q^3,$$

where Q is the number of units of output produced.

a. What is the output level where marginal cost is a minimum?

b. What is the output level where average variable cost is a minimum?

c. What is the value of average variable cost and marginal cost at the output specified in the answer to part b?

10. The Berwyn Company is considering the addition of a new product to its product line. The firm has plenty of excess manufacturing capacity to produce the new product, and its total fixed costs would be unaffected if the new product were added to its line. Nonetheless, the firm's accountants decide that a reasonable share of the firm's present fixed costs should be allocated to the new product. Specifically, they decide that a $300,000 fixed charge will be absorbed by the new product. The variable cost per unit of making and selling the new product is $14, which is composed of the following:

Direct labor	$8.20
Direct materials	1.90
Other	3.90
Total	$14.00

a. Should the Berwyn Company add the new product to its line if it can sell about 10,000 units of this product at a price of $25?

b. Should it add the new product if it can sell about 10,000 units at a price of $20?

c. Should it add the new product if it can sell about 10,000 units at a price of $15?

d. What is the minimum price (that the firm can get for the new product) that will make it worthwhile to add the new product to its line?

11. The Jolson Corporation produces 1,000 wood cabinets and 500 wood desks per year, the total cost being $30,000. If the firm produced 1,000 wood cabinets only, the cost would be $23,000. If the firm produced 500 wood desks only, the cost would be $11,000.

a. Calculate the degree of economies of scope.

b. Why do economies of scope exist?

12. The Smith Company made and sold 10,000 metal tables last year. When output was between 5,000 and 10,000 tables, its average variable cost was $24. In this output range, each table contributed 60 percent of its revenue to fixed costs and profits.

a. What was the price per table?

b. If the Smith Company increases its price by 10 percent, how many tables will it have to sell next year to obtain the same profit as last year?

c. If the Smith Company increases its price by 10 percent, and if its average variable cost increases by 8 percent as a result of wage increases, how many tables will it have to sell next year to obtain the same profit as last year?

Appendix: Break-Even Analysis and Operating Leverage

Managers must continually make comparisons among alternative systems of production. Should one type of plant be replaced by another? How does your plant stack up against your competitor's? Break-even analysis can be extended to help make such comparisons more effective. In this appendix, we show how you can analyze how total costs and profits vary with output, depending on how automated or mechanized the plant may be. This is an important topic, since top-level managers often have to make such comparisons.

At the outset, it is essential to recognize that some plants, because they are much more mechanized than others, have relatively high fixed costs but relatively low average variable costs. Consider firms I, II, and III in Figure 9.19. Firm I's plant has fixed costs of $100,000 per month, which are much higher

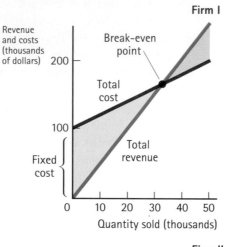

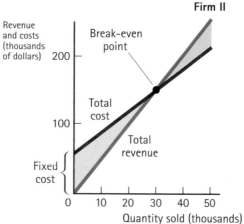

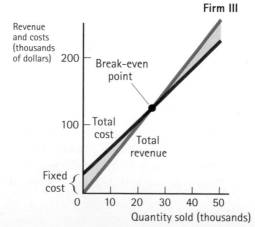

FIGURE
9.19

Break–Even Analysis and Operating Leverage

Firm I has relatively high fixed costs and low variable costs; firm III has relatively low fixed costs and high variable costs; and firm II is in the middle.

Firm I

Total fixed cost = $100,000
Average variable cost = $2
Selling price = $5

Quantity sold	Total revenue	Total cost	Total profit
10,000	$ 50,000	$120,000	$-70,000
20,000	100,000	140,000	-40,000
30,000	150,000	160,000	-10,000
40,000	200,000	180,000	20,000
50,000	250,000	200,000	50,000

Firm II

Total fixed cost = $60,000
Average variable cost = $3
Selling price = $5

Quantity sold	Total revenue	Total cost	Total profit
10,000	$ 50,000	$ 90,000	$-40,000
20,000	100,000	120,000	-20,000
30,000	150,000	150,000	0
40,000	200,000	180,000	20,000
50,000	250,000	210,000	40,000

Firm III

Total fixed cost = $25,000
Average variable cost = $4
Selling price = $5

Quantity sold	Total revenue	Total cost	Total profit
10,000	$ 50,000	$ 65,000	$-15,000
20,000	100,000	105,000	-5,000
30,000	150,000	145,000	5,000
40,000	200,000	185,000	15,000
50,000	250,000	225,000	25,000

than those of the plants operated by firm II or III; however, its average variable cost of $2 is much lower than that of firm II or III. Essentially, firm I has substituted capital for labor and materials. It has built a highly automated plant with high fixed costs, but low average variable cost.

At the opposite extreme, firm III has built a plant with low fixed costs but high average variable cost. Because it has not invested a great deal in plant and equipment, its total fixed costs are only $25,000 per month, which is much less than for firm I or II. However, because of the relatively low level of mechanization at its plant, firm III's average variable cost is $4, considerably higher than at the other two firms. Relative to firm I, firm III uses more labor and materials and less capital.

Firm II's plant occupies a middle position (between firms I and III) in this regard. Its total fixed cost of $60,000 is less than firm I's but more than firm III's, and its average variable cost of $3 is greater than firm I's but less than firm III's. It has not automated its plant to the extent that firm I has, but it has done more in this regard than firm III.

In comparing these plants, one of the important things to consider is the degree of operating leverage, which is defined as the percentage change in profit resulting from a 1 percent change in the number of units of product sold. Specifically,

$$\text{Degree of operating leverage} = \frac{\text{percentage change in profit}}{\text{percentage change in quantity sold}}$$

$$= \frac{\Delta\pi/\pi}{\Delta Q/Q}$$

$$= \frac{\Delta\pi}{\Delta Q}\left(\frac{Q}{\pi}\right) \quad \text{or} \quad \frac{d\pi}{dQ}\left(\frac{Q}{\pi}\right), \quad (9.9)$$

where π is the firm's profits, and Q is the quantity sold.

The degree of operating leverage, because it measures how a given change in sales volume affects profits, is of great importance. If firm I is selling 40,000 units per month, and if we let $\Delta Q = 10,000$ units, the degree of operating leverage equals

$$\frac{\Delta\pi}{\Delta Q}\left(\frac{Q}{\pi}\right) = \frac{\$50,000 - \$20,000}{10,000}\left(\frac{40,000}{\$20,000}\right) = 6,$$

since Figure 9.19 shows that if $\Delta Q = 10,000$ units, $\Delta\pi = \$50,000 - \$20,000$. (Why? Because if Q changes from 40,000 to 50,000 units, π changes from $20,000 to $50,000.) Thus, a 1 percent increase in quantity sold results in a 6 percent increase in profits.

If both the total revenue curve and the total cost function are linear, as in Figure 9.19, a simple way to calculate the degree of operating leverage when output equals Q is to use the following formula:

$$\text{Degree of operating leverage} = \frac{Q(P - AVC)}{Q(P - AVC) - TFC}, \tag{9.10}$$

where P equals selling price, AVC equals average variable cost, and TFC equals total fixed cost. It can be shown that if both the total revenue curve and the total cost function are linear, equation (9.10) yields the same result as equation (9.9). Thus, for firm I, if $Q = 40{,}000$, equation (9.10) says that the degree of operating leverage equals

$$\frac{Q(P - AVC)}{Q(P - AVC) - TFC} = \frac{\$40{,}000(\$5 - \$2)}{40{,}000(\$5 - \$2) - \$100{,}000}$$
$$= \frac{\$120{,}000}{\$120{,}000 - \$100{,}000} = 6$$

since P equals $5, AVC equals $2, and TFC equals $100,000. The result is the same as in the previous paragraph. (In both cases, it is 6.)

It is interesting and important to compare the degree of operating leverage of the three firms, since this comparison reveals a great deal about how these plants differ. If $Q = 40{,}000$, the degree of operating leverage for firm II equals

$$\frac{Q(P - AVC)}{Q(P - AVC) - TFC} = \frac{\$40{,}000(\$5 - \$3)}{40{,}000(\$5 - \$3) - \$60{,}000} = 4.$$

For firm III, it equals

$$\frac{Q(P - AVC)}{Q(P - AVC) - TFC} = \frac{\$40{,}000(\$5 - \$4)}{40{,}000(\$5 - \$4) - \$25{,}000} = 2.67$$

Thus, a 1 percent increase in sales volume results in a 6 percent increase in profit at firm I, a 4 percent increase in profit at firm II, and a 2.67 percent increase in profit at firm III. Clearly, firm I's profits are much more sensitive to changes in sales volume than firm III's profits; firm II is in the middle in this regard.

Market Structure, Strategic Behavior, and Pricing

Perfect Competition

CHAPTER 10

Sometimes managers find themselves in situations where they have no control over the price of their product; for example, they are a small participant in a large market where the market supply and demand curves determine the price and the manager maximizes the firm's profit *given that the market determines the price.* Other examples occur when the government sets the price (either via price controls or by virtue of being in a regulated industry) or where the firm is a follower firm in a situation where a price leader sets the price for the industry.

The polar case of perfect competition shows us the optimal behavior of a manager where the manager takes the price as a given. It is often suggested that the small farmer is in this position. While not controlling price, the farmer does decide on quantity, that is, how much of crop X to plant. This decision must be made Y months before the crop actually comes to market. To minimize risk, the farmer may sell his crop now for future delivery, but most do not. After the crop is planted, the price may change as conditions influencing demand (tastes, income) and supply (weather, crop disease) change. The farmer makes a second quantity decision at harvest time; how much of the crop to harvest. Farmers may also stop growing a crop before it matures, replow, and plant another crop because of changes in the market prices. What is common in all these cases is that the farmer makes *quantity* decisions only, and they are based on a price over which he has no control.

How, then, should a manager choose the profit maximizing quantity when the price is a given? Note the manager still faces all the challenges outlined in earlier chapters with respect to producing the product in the most efficient manner and controlling costs. While the analysis is couched in terms of a market determined price, the behavioral rules developed for the firm hold if the price is set by government or a dominant firm (more on the latter in Chapter 13).

Market Structure

This situation of a price-taking producer is one of four general categories of market structure that we investigate. We preview all four categories in this section, then spend the rest of the chapter on the perfect competition (price taker) category. As pointed out in Chapter 1, a **market** consists of a group of firms and individuals that are in touch with each other in order to buy or sell some good or service. Economists have generally found it useful to classify markets into four broad types: perfect competition, monopoly, monopolistic competition, and oligopoly. In **perfect competition** and **monopolistic competition**, there are *many* sellers, each of which produces only a small part of the industry's output. In **monopoly**, on the other hand, the industry consists of only a *single* seller. **Oligopoly** is an intermediate case, where there are a *few* sellers. It is the most prevalent category. Hence, Baltimore Gas and Electric, if it is the only supplier of electricity in a particular market, is a monopoly. And since there are only a small number of automobile manufacturers, the market for automobiles is an oligopoly.

Market structures vary substantially in the extent to which an individual firm controls its price. A firm under perfect competition has *no control* over price. For example, a farm producing corn (which for present purposes can be regarded as a perfectly competitive firm) has no control over the price of corn. On the other hand, a monopolist is likely to have *considerable control* over price. In the absence of public regulation, Baltimore Gas and Electric would have considerable control over the price of electricity in Baltimore. A firm under monopolistic competition or oligopoly is likely to have *less* control over price than a monopolist and *more* control over price than a perfectly competitive market.

These market structures also vary in the extent to which the firms in an industry produce standardized (that is, identical) products. Firms in a perfectly competitive market all produce *identical* products. One farmer's wheat is essentially the same as another farmer's. In a monopolistically competitive industry like shirt manufacturing, firms produce *somewhat different* products. One firm's shirts differ in style and quality from another firm's shirts. In an oligopoly, firms *sometimes*, but not always, produce identical products; for example, in steel and aluminum they do, while in autos, they do not. And, in a monopoly, there can be *no difference* among firms in their products, since the industry contains only one firm.

How easily firms can enter the industry differs from one market structure to another. In perfect competition, **barriers to entry** are *low*. Only a small investment is required to enter many parts of agriculture. Similarly, there are *low* barriers to entry in monopolistic competition. But, in oligopolies such as auto manufacturing and oil refining, there tends to be *very considerable* barriers to entry because it is so expensive to build an auto plant or an oil refinery (and for many other reasons, too). In a monopoly, entry is *blocked*; once entry occurs, the monopoly no longer exists.

Market structures also differ in the extent to which firms compete on the basis of advertising, public relations, and differences in product characteristics, rather than price. In perfect competition, there is *no* nonprice competition. (If every farmer produces identical corn and has to take the market price, why devote some of the proceeds to advertising?) In monopolistic competition, *considerable emphasis* is placed on nonprice competition. Shirt manufacturers compete by trying to develop better styles and by advertising to accentuate the advantages of their product lines. Oligopolies that produce differentiated products also tend to rely heavily on nonprice competition, while oligopolies that produce nondifferentiated products do not. For example, computer firms try to increase their sales by building better computers and by advertising, while steel companies do very little. Monopolists also engage in advertising and public relations, although these activities are directed not at capturing the sales of other firms in the industry, since no other firms exist, but rather at increasing total market demand and insulating the firm from the negative connotations sometimes associated with monopoly.

Table 10.1 provides a summary of many of the key features of each market structure. Be sure to look over this table before proceeding further. This chapter discusses perfect competition. Chapter 11 covers monopoly and monopolistic competition. Chapter 12 extends the monopoly model to consider sophisticated monopoly pricing strategies. Chapter 13 considers oligopoly.

Market Price under Perfect Competition

In a perfectly competitive industry, market price, as we saw in Chapter 1, is determined by the intersection of the market demand and supply curves: The market demand curve shows the total amount that individual buyers of the commodity will purchase at any price; the market supply curve shows the total

| | | Number | | Power of | Barriers | |
Market structure	Examples	of producers	Type of product	firm over price	to entry	Nonprice competition
Perfect competition	Parts of agriculture are reasonably close	Many	Standardized	None	Low	None
Monopolistic competition	Retail trade	Many	Differentiated	Some	Low	Advertising and product differentiation
Oligopoly	Computers, oil, steel	Few	Standardized or differentiated	Some	High	Advertising and product differentiation
Monopoly	Public utilities	One	Unique product	Considerable	Very high	Advertising

TABLE 10.1 Characteristics of Perfect Competition, Monopolistic Competition, Oligopoly, and Monopoly

amount that individual suppliers of the commodity will supply at any price. Figure 10.1 shows the market demand and supply curves for a good produced in a perfectly competitive market. As is ordinarily the case, the market supply curve slopes upward to the right. That is, increases in price generally result in higher industry output because managers find it profitable to expand production. Also, in accord with Chapters 1 and 3, the market demand curve slopes downward to the right. That is, increases in price generally result in less of the product being demanded.

To determine the equilibrium price, which is the price that will eventually prevail in this market, we must find the price where market supply equals market demand.[1] The demand curve in Figure 10.1 is

$$P = 22 - 0.5Q_D \qquad (10.1)$$

where P is the price (in dollars) of this good and Q_D is the quantity demanded (in thousands of units). The supply curve in Figure 10.1 is

$$P = 4 + 0.25Q_S \qquad (10.2)$$

---

[1] Recall from Chapter 1 that an equilibrium price is a price that can be maintained. If conditions do not change, the actual price tends to equal the equilibrium price.

FIGURE
10.1

Determination of Price in a Perfectly Competitive Market

Equilibrium price is $10, and equilibrium quantity is 24 thousand units.

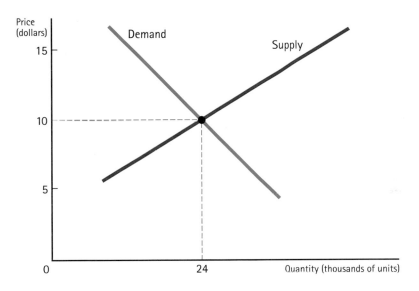

where Q_S is the quantity supplied in thousands of units. Since the equilibrium price is at the level where Q_D (the quantity demanded) equals Q_S (the quantity supplied),

$$P = 22 - 0.5Q = 4 + 0.25Q = P$$
$$0.75Q = 18$$
$$Q = 24$$

Substituting 24 for Q_D in equation (10.1), we find that $P = \$10$. (If we substitute 24 for Q_S in equation (10.2), we get the same result.) Therefore, as shown in Figure 10.1, price would be expected to equal $10, and output would be expected to equal 24 thousand units.

While Figure 10.1 shows that both total quantity demanded and total quantity supplied depend on price, this does not mean that an individual firm can affect price. According to the market demand curve in equation (10.1),

$$P = 22 - 0.5Q_D$$

If 1,000 firms are in this market, each produces, on the average, only 24 units of the product. Even if an individual firm doubles its output (from 24 to 48 units), the effect on price is minuscule. Specifically, an increase in output of 24 units results in a price reduction of only 1.2 cents, or about 0.1 percent.[2] What this means is that the demand curve for the output of an individual firm under perfect competition is essentially *horizontal*. Whereas the demand curve for the output of the entire industry slopes downward to the right (as shown in Figure 10.1), the demand curve for the output of any single firm can be regarded as horizontal (at price $10 in this case).

Shifts in Supply and Demand Curves

Shifts in the market supply or demand curves result in changes in price (recall Chapter 1). For example, if the supply curve in Figure 10.1 shifts to the left, the price would be expected to rise. Shifts in market supply and demand curves have significant consequences for firm performance, and managers must try to anticipate them and respond as best they can. Consider the increase in the United States for the price of natural gas in 2003. Due to the lack of drilling activity and low inventories, natural gas prices in mid 2003 were around $6 per million British thermal units. This price was about twice the historical norm. The *Wall Street Journal*[3] reported how, at one time, the United States had the cheapest natural gas prices in the world. Because natural gas is the main raw material in the manufacture of many chemicals, U.S. chemical producers exported more chemicals than were imported. In 1999, the chemical industry had a foreign trade surplus of over $8 billion. Because of the increase in the price of natural gas, that trade surplus had changed to an expected deficit of $9 billion in 2003. As Greg Lebedev, a top executive of the American Chemistry Council, put it, "The competitiveness of the U.S. chemical industry is predicated on natural-gas pricing. It is an absolute sea of change."

Managers took several actions to counteract the increase in the price of natural gas due to decreases in its supply. Many chemical producing plants were shut down. Analysts estimated that over a dozen large chemical plants in the United States were closed in 2003. Managers also tried to recoup some of their additional costs by passing them on to buyers. For example, in the choline chloride market (also dependent on natural gas for production), prices increased 75 percent. Prices also increased in the methanol, caustic soda, and titanium dioxide markets. Finally, some production was moved to countries where the price of natural gas was cheaper. For example, in 2003, the price of natural gas in Saudi Arabia was around $1 per million British thermal units.

---

[2]If output increases by 24 units, Q increases by 0.024, since Q is measured in thousands of units. If Q increases by 0.024, P falls by 0.5(0.024) = 0.012, according to the demand curve in equation (10.1). Since P is measured in dollars, this amounts to 1.2 cents.

[3]T. Herrick, "Natural Gas Cooks Chemical Sector—Rising Prices Force Firms to Cut Jobs, Shut Plants as Output Moves Abroad," *Wall Street Journal*, June 18, 2003, A2.

For present purposes, the point is that managers must understand the factors affecting the supply and demand curves of the products they buy and sell. There is no need here to dwell at length on the factors causing shifts in demand curves, since they have been discussed in Chapter 3. But it is worth recalling from Chapter 1 that two of the most important factors causing shifts in supply curves are improvements in technology (discussed in Chapter 8) and changes in input prices. Improvements in technology tend to shift a product's supply curve to the right, since they permit firms to reduce their costs. On the other hand, increases in input prices tend to shift a product's supply curve to the left, since they push up the firm's costs. For agricultural products, the supply curve also shifts in response to weather conditions. For example, in 1986, a drought in Brazil cut the coffee crop by about 60 percent; this caused a significant shift to the left of the supply curve for coffee.

The Output Decision of a Perfectly Competitive Firm

How much output should a perfectly competitive firm produce? As we saw in the section before last, a perfectly competitive firm cannot affect the market price of its product and it can sell any amount of its product that it wants (within its capabilities) at the market price. To illustrate the firm's situation, consider the example in Table 10.2. The market price is $10 a unit and the firm

TABLE 10.2

Cost and Revenues of a Perfectly Competitive Firm

Units of output period	Price (dollars)	Total revenue (dollars)	Total fixed costs (dollars)	Total variable costs (dollars)	Total cost (dollars)	Total profit (dollars)
0	10	0	1	0	1	−1
1	10	10	1	3	4	6
2	10	20	1	8	9	11
3	10	30	1	15	16	14
4	10	40	1	24	25	15
5	10	50	1	35	36	14
6	10	60	1	48	49	11
7	10	70	1	63	64	6
8	10	80	1	80	81	−1
9	10	90	1	99	100	−10

FIGURE
10.2

Relationship between Total Cost and Total Revenue of a Perfectly Competitive Firm

The output rate that would maximize the firm's profit is four units per time period. The profit (total revenue minus total cost) equals $15.

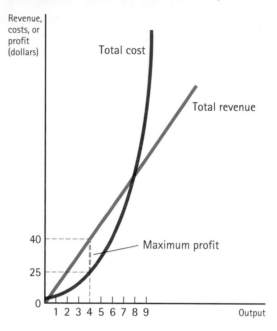

can produce as much as it chooses. Hence, the firm's total revenue at various output rates is given in column 3 of Table 10.2. The firm's total fixed cost (1), total variable cost $(2Q + Q^2)$, and total cost $(1 + 2Q + Q^2)$ are given in columns 4, 5, and 6 of Table 10.2. Finally, the last column shows the firm's total profit.

Figure 10.2 shows the relationship between total revenue and total cost, on the one hand, and output, on the other. The vertical distance between the total revenue and the total cost curve is the profit at the corresponding output rate. Below one unit of output and above seven units of output, this distance is negative. Since the firm can sell either large or small volumes of output at the same price per unit, the total revenue curve is a straight line through the origin with a slope equal to the fixed price. (Specifically, total revenue = price times quantity, so since the price is constant, total revenue is proportional to quantity.) Since a perfectly competitive firm takes the price as a given, the slope of the total revenue *always* is the market price.

The firm's profit (Π) is expressed as total revenue (TR) minus total cost (TC); that is, $\Pi = TR - TC$. It follows that $d\Pi/dQ - dTR/dQ - dTC/dQ$. If $d\Pi/dQ = 0$, then $dTR/dQ - dTC/dQ$ must also equal zero, that is, $dTR/dQ = dTC/dQ$.

Here dTR/dQ is the firm's marginal revenue. It represents a change in the total revenue when the output changes by a small amount (usually, by $dQ = 1$). The firm's total revenue is price times quantity or PQ. Therefore, marginal revenue is $dTR/dQ = P$. So the firm's marginal revenue is the product's price. This is not surprising. If the firm sells five units, then its total revenue is $5P$; if it sells six units, then its total revenue is $6P$; if it sells seven units, its total revenue is $7P$; and so on. Every time another unit is sold, total revenue goes up by P. In this case, $P = \$10$, so the firm's marginal revenue (always equal to price for a price taker) is $\$10$.

Consider the firm's total cost ($TC = 1 + 2Q + Q^2$). Therefore, $dTC/dQ = 2 + 2Q$, and dTC/dQ is called the firm's marginal cost. It represents a change in the total cost (or variable cost) when output changes by a small amount.

The condition $dTR/dQ = dTC/dQ$ is restated as MR = MC; that is, to maximize profits, the manager must set marginal revenue equal to marginal cost. In the case of a price taker, the profit maximizing condition reads $P = MC$ (since $P = MR$). Hence,

$$P = 10 = 2 + 2Q = MC \quad \text{or} \quad Q - 4 \tag{10.3}$$

Table 10.2, Figures 10.2 and 10.3, and equation (10.3) show that manaagers maximize the firm's profit at four units per time period. At this output, the profit figure in the last column of Table 10.2 is the highest, the vertical distance between the total revenue and cost curves in Figure 10.2 is the largest, and the profit curve in Figure 10.3 is the highest.

It is worthwhile to present the marginal revenue and marginal cost curves as well as the total revenue and total cost curves. Table 10.3 shows the firm's marginal revenue and marginal costs at each output rate.

Figure 10.4 shows the resulting marginal revenue and marginal cost at each output rate. Because the firm takes the price as given, it is a constant for all output levels, since marginal revenue equals price. Hence, the marginal revenue curve is also the firm's demand curve, which (for the reasons discussed already) is horizontal.

The central point to note is that we maximize profit at the output rate where *the price (= marginal revenue) equals the marginal cost*. Both the numbers in Table 10.3 and the curves in Figure 10.4 indicate that the price equals the marginal cost at an output rate of four units, which we know from Table 10.2, Figures 10.2 and 10.3, and equation (10.3) to be the profit maximizing output.

FIGURE
10.3

Relationship of Profit and Output of a Perfectly Competitive Firm

The output rate that maximizes profit is four units per time period. To maximize profits, the slope of the profit function ($d\Pi/dQ$) must be zero.

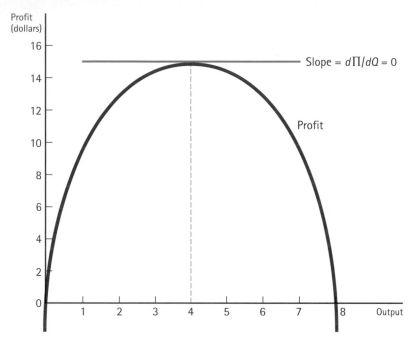

Setting the Marginal Cost Equal to the Price

Earlier we showed that price equal to marginal cost is required for a firm to maximize profit. But that is not quite enough. Recall from Chapter 2 that a second condition has to hold for maximization to occur. The condition in this case requires that

$$d(d\Pi/dQ)/dQ < 0$$

that is, for maximum to occur, the sign of the second derivative must be negative.

Note that $d(d\Pi/dQ)/dQ = d(d\,TR/dQ)/dQ - d(d\,TC/dQ)/dQ = d\text{MR}/dQ - d\text{MC}/dQ$. The second required condition is that $d\text{MR}/dQ - d\text{MC}/dQ < 0$. Since $\text{MR} = P$ and does not change as Q changes, $d\text{MR}/dQ = 0$. This implies that $d\text{MC}/dQ > 0$;

TABLE
10.3

Marginal Revenue and Marginal Cost, Perfectly Competitive Firm

Output per period	Marginal revenue	Marginal cost[4]
0	10	2
1	10	4
2	10	6
3	10	8
4	10	10
5	10	12
6	10	14
7	10	16
8	10	18

[4]This column was calculated from $MC = 2 + 2Q$. This assumes that output can be sold and produced in noninteger, continuous amounts. Many goods meet this criteria, for example, gasoline, deli meats, and bulk agricultural products. While these goods are priced on a per unit basis (by the gallon, per pound), seldom do we purchase integer units. Other goods are produced and consumed only in integer units, such as cars, televisions, and compact discs. In this case, the marginal cost for output level n is calculated as the total cost at output level n minus the total cost for output level $n - 1$. For instance, the total cost at $Q = 3$ is 16, at $Q = 4$ is 25, at $Q = 5$ is 36 (see Table 10.2). Therefore, the marginal cost at $Q = 4$ is 9 and at $Q = 5$ is 11 (as opposed to 10 and 12 shown in this table). Under these conditions, the manager wants to produce the fourth unit because the marginal revenue from doing so ($10) exceeds the marginal cost ($9). However, the manager would not produce the fifth unit because the marginal cost of doing so ($11) exceeds the marginal revenue ($10). Therefore, the manager produces four units in the integer output case and in the continuous output case.

that is, the slope of the marginal cost must be positive for profits to be at a maximum. As can be seen in Table 10.3 and Figure 10.4, this is true.[5]

Even if a firm is doing its best, it still might not earn a profit, that is, even if it satisfies the preceding rules ($P = MC$ and MC is rising). If the price is P_2 in Figure 10.5, the short-run average total cost exceeds the price at all possible outputs. Because the short run is too short (by definition) to permit the firm to alter the scale of plant, all the firm can do is to produce at a loss or discontinue production. Its decision should depend on whether the product's price covers the average variable costs. If there is an output rate at which price exceeds average variable costs, it pays the firm to produce, even though the price does not cover average total costs. If there is no output rate at which price exceeds

[5]Recall from Chapter 9 that, in the short run, $MC = W/MP$, where W is the fixed wage of labor and MP is the marginal product of labor. Therefore, if the marginal cost is increasing, the marginal product of labor must be decreasing. A price-taking situation, therefore, implies diminishing marginal productivity of labor in the short run.

FIGURE
10.4

Marginal Revenue and Marginal Cost of a Perfectly Competitive Firm

When output is at the profit maximizing level of four units, price (=marginal revenue) equals marginal cost.

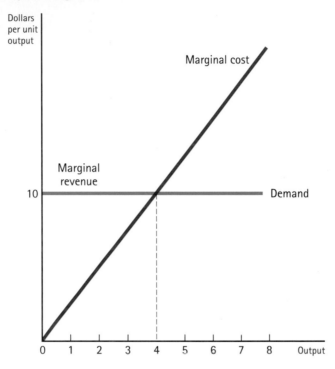

the average variable cost, the firm is better off producing nothing at all. Hence, if the average variable cost curve is as shown in Figure 10.5, the firm will produce if the price is P_2 but not if it is P_1.

It is essential to recognize that, if the firm produces nothing, it still must pay its fixed costs. Therefore, if the loss from producing is less than the firm's fixed costs (the loss of shutting down), it is more profitable (a smaller deficit) to produce than to discontinue production. Another way of expressing this is if the loss per production unit is less than average fixed cost; that is, if ATC − $P <$ AFC, where ATC is average total cost, P is price, and AFC is average fixed cost. This is true if ATC $<$ AFC $+ P$, since P is merely added to both sides of the inequality. Subtracting AFC from both sides, results in ATC − AFC $< P$.

FIGURE

10.5

Short–Run Average and Marginal Cost Curves

If the price is P_0, the firm will produce an output of X; if price is P_2, it will produce an output of Y; and if price is less than P_3 (i.e., when P_3 equals the minimum of average variable cost), the firm will produce nothing.

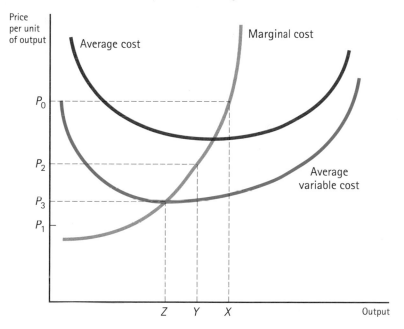

ATC − AFC is the average variable cost, hence it is better to produce than to discontinue production if the price exceeds the average variable cost.

The point (Z, P_3) is called the *shutdown point* of the firm, since at that point, the price equals the average variable cost and the firm loses a fixed cost if it produces or loses fixed cost if it shuts down. Managers are indifferent between producing or not producing. At any price below P_3, the firm shuts down. Therefore, the marginal cost curve (above the minimum average variable cost) is the supply curve of the price taking firm; that is, if the price is P_2, the firm produces Y, and if the price is P_3, the firm produces X. These points (Y, P_2) and (X, P_3) are also points on the firm's marginal cost curve.

To summarize, if the manager maximizes profit or minimizes loss, the output is set so the short-run marginal cost equals the price and the marginal cost is rising. But this proposition has an exception: If the market price is below the firm's average variable costs at every output level, the firm minimizes losses by discontinuing production.

Forecasting the Price of Salmon

A major producer of consumer goods set out to forecast the price of fresh salmon three years ahead. Such a forecast was needed in deciding whether the firm should enter the business of supplying salmon. Its analysts estimated the quantity of fresh salmon that would be supplied three years ahead. Because of substantial plans to expand the production of farmed Atlantic and Pacific salmon in Canada, Chile, Japan, and Ireland, this projected supply was considerably greater than the actual supply at the time the forecast was made. In addition, the firm's analysts estimated the quantity of fresh salmon that would be demanded three years ahead, using the sorts of techniques described in previous chapters. Their results showed that, if the price of salmon remained unchanged over the next three years, the quantity supplied would exceed the quantity demanded by about 15 percent at the end of the three-year period.

The firm's analysts also estimated the price elasticity of demand for fresh salmon to be about 1.5. This estimate, too, was based on the sorts of techniques described in previous chapters. Like the other estimates presented here, it was regarded as rough but useful.

If you were a consultant to this firm and were asked to use these estimates to forecast the change in the salmon price over the next three years, what would be your forecast? (The firm's analysts believed that the quantity supplied three years hence would be approximately equal to their estimates, regardless of whatever changes occurred in price during this three-year period.)

This section is based on an actual case, although the numbers and situation have been disguised somewhat.

The Kadda Company: A Numerical Example

As an illustration, consider the Kadda Company, a perfectly competitive firm with the following total cost function:

$$TC = 800 + 6Q + 2Q^2$$

where TC is the total cost (in dollars) and Q is the firm's output per day. The firm's marginal cost is therefore

$$dTC/dQ = MC = 6 + 4Q$$

If the price of Kadda's product equals $30, then the firm should set its output so that

$$MC = dTC/dQ = 6 + 4Q = 30 = P \qquad (10.4)$$

In other words, it should set marginal cost equal to price ($30). Solving equation (10.4) for Q, we find that the firm should set output equal to six units per day. To make sure that the price not less than average variable cost at that output, we note that, since the firm's total variable cost equals $6Q + 2Q^2$, its average variable cost (AVC) equals

$$AVC = (6Q + 2Q^2)/Q = 6 + 2Q$$

Therefore, if $Q = 6$, average variable costs equals $6 + 2(6)$ or $18, which is less than the price of $30.

Producer Surplus in the Short Run

In Chapter 4, we examined consumer surplus and saw that it equals the difference between the market price and the price consumers are *willing* to pay (their reservation price). Now, we introduce a parallel idea, called *producer surplus*, which derives from the supply side of the market. Producer surplus is the difference between the market price and the price the producer is *willing* to receive for the good or service (the producer's reservation price). As just shown in our analysis of a perfectly competitive market, a producer's reservation price is the marginal cost of producing the good or service (above the break-even point of the firm). Panel A of Figure 10.6 shows this surplus (the shaded area). The firm's profit before accounting for fixed cost (its variable cost profit = $P^*BC'D' = P^*BE$) is just total revenue (P^*Q^*) minus variable cost ($D'C'Q^*0$). But, the variable cost is also just the area under the marginal cost up to output Q^*, that is, EBQ^*0. This variable cost profit is also the shaded area in Panel A of Figure 10.6, that is, P^*BE. Note the difference between profit (P^*BCD) and producer surplus. To arrive at a producer surplus, managers subtract only the variable cost from the total revenue, while to get their profit, they subtract both the fixed and variable costs from total revenue. Hence, the variable cost profit is larger than profit (by the level of fixed cost). Thus, producer surplus and variable cost profit are the same. Because the perfectly competitive firm's marginal cost represents its supply curve, we can view producer surplus as the difference between the supply curve and the price received for the good (area b in Panel B of Figure 10.6).

Figure 10.7 shows the market equilibrium. Just as market demand is the horizontal summation of individuals' demand curves for the product, market supply is the horizontal summation of individual firms' supply curves for the

FIGURE
10.6

Producer Surplus and Variable Cost Profit

Producer surplus for the firm is its variable cost profit, or total revenue minus variable cost. Producer surplus for the market is the area above the supply curve but below the price received for the good, since the supply curve is the horizontal summation of the competitive firms' marginal cost curves.

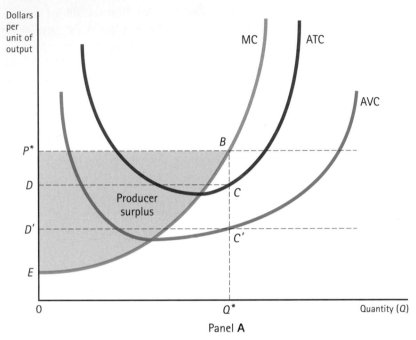

Panel **A**

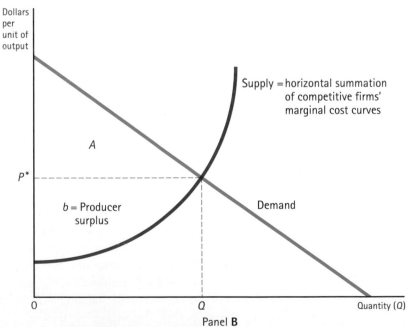

Panel **B**

FIGURE
10.7

Market Social Welfare (A + B) of a Perfectly Competitive Price Policy, P*

Societal welfare at a given price (P*) is measured by the sum of the consumer surplus (A) and the producer surplus (B).

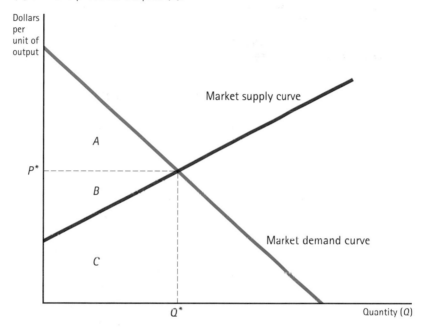

product. Using the results for consumer surplus (Chapter 4), we can see from Figure 10.7 that the market equilibrium price of P* yields a consumer surplus of A and a producer surplus of B.

The sum of A and B, the total surplus, is the economist's measure of social welfare at the price P* and the quantity Q*. To understand this idea, think about the total benefit and cost that consumers and producers assign to the goods in the market. For consumers, this is the area beneath the demand curve, left of the equilibrium quantity, that is, the total amount consumers are willing to pay for the goods (areas A, B, and C in Figure 10.7). For producers, the total variable cost of supplying quantity Q* is the area beneath the supply curve left of the equilibrium quantity (area C in Figure 10.7). In the market, consumers pay and producers receive P*. Yet P* is less than the total benefit and greater than the variable cost of the goods. In this sense, the market exchange generates value for participants, represented by consumer, producer, and total surplus. In this case, the difference between what the demanders are willing to spend (A, B, and C) and what the suppliers are willing to receive (C), is the measure of social welfare, that is, $A + B$. Clearly, the magnitude of the total surplus and its distribution between consumers and producers depend on the shape of the demand and supply curves. For instance, keeping the equilibrium at P^*, Q^*, a more gently sloped supply curve reduces producer surplus, while a more gently sloped demand curve reduces consumer surplus. But, the thing to remember is that market exchanges, generally speaking, provide opportunities for gains, and as we see later, savvy managers can devise ways to capture a greater share of those gains for their firms.

We use this measure of social welfare to show the rationale of antitrust policy in Chapter 19 and the gains from trade in Chapter 20.

Long-Run Equilibrium of the Firm

In the long run, how much will managers of a competitive firm produce? The long-run equilibrium position of the firm is at the point where its long-run average total cost curve[6] equals the price. If price is in excess of the average total cost for any firm, economic profits are earned and new firms enter the industry. This increases supply, thereby driving down price and hence profits. If the price is less than the average total costs for any firm, that firm will exit the industry. As firms exit, supply falls, causing price and profits to rise. Only when economic profits are zero (which means that long-run average cost equals price) is a firm in long-run equilibrium.

Recall from Chapter 1 that economic profits are not the same as accounting profits. Economic profits are profits above and beyond what the owners could obtain elsewhere from the resources they invest in the firm. Therefore, long-run equilibrium occurs when the owners receive no more (and no less) than they could obtain elsewhere from these resources.

More specifically, the price must be equal to the *lowest value* of the long run average total cost. That is, firms must produce at the minimum point on their long-run average cost curves. To see why, note that, if firms maximize their profits, they must operate where price equals long-run marginal cost. Also, we just saw that they must operate where price equals long-run average cost. But, if both of these conditions are satisfied, it follows that long-run marginal cost must equal long-run average cost. And, we know from Chapter 9 that long-run marginal cost is equal to long-run average cost only at the point at which long-run average cost is a minimum. Consequently, this point must be the equilibrium position of the firm.

---

[6]This is also called the *long-run average cost curve*. Since all costs are *variable* in the long run, there is no need for an adjective in front of average costs, as there is in the short run, to distinguish between average total, average variable, and average fixed costs. There are only average costs in the long run.

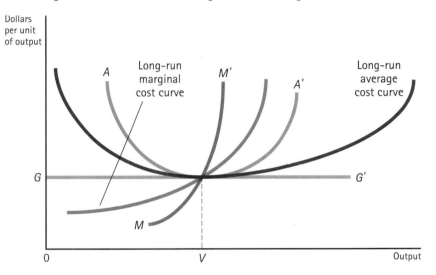

FIGURE
10.8

Long-Run Equilibrium of a Perfectly Competitive Firm

In long-run equilibrium, the firm produces an output of V, and price = marginal cost (both long-run and short-run) − average cost (both long-run and short-run).

To illustrate this equilibrium position, consider Figure 10.8. When all the adjustments are made, price equals G. Since price is constant, the demand curve is horizontal and, therefore, the marginal revenue curve is the same as the demand curve, both being GG'. The equilibrium output of the firm is V, and its optimal-sized plant is described by the short-run average and marginal cost curves AA' and MM'. At this output and with this plant, we see that long-run marginal cost equals short-run marginal cost equals price. This ensures that the firm maximizes profit. Also, long-run average cost equals the short-run average cost equals price; this ensures that economic profits are zero. Because long-run marginal cost and long-run average cost must be equal, the equilibrium point is at the bottom of the long-run average cost curve.

The Bergey Company: A Numerical Example

For example, suppose that the Bergey Company's long-run average cost curve is

$$AC = 200 - 4Q + 0.05Q^2 \tag{10.5}$$

where AC is long-run average cost (in dollars) and Q is the firm's output per day. Since the Bergey Company is a perfectly competitive firm, its output in the long run equals the value of Q that minimizes AC. Note from Figure 10.8, that the slope of the long-run average total cost curve when it is a minimum is $dAC/dQ = 0$; that is, GG' is tangent to AC at the output level V in Figure 10.8.

Differentiating equation (10.5) gives $dAC/dQ = -4 + 0.1Q = 0$, which implies that $Q = 40$. Therefore, if Bergey maximizes profit, its output in the long-run will equal 40 units per day.

As indicated previously, the average cost equals the marginal cost at this output. To see this, note that, since total cost equals Q times AC,

$$TC = Q(200 - 4Q + 0.05Q^2)$$
$$= 200Q - 4Q^2 + 0.05Q^3$$

where TC is total cost.

The firm's marginal cost is $MC = dTC/dQ$. Therefore, $MC = dTC/dQ = 200 - 8Q + 0.15Q^2$. Since $Q = 40$,

$$MC = 200 - 8(40) + 0.15(40)^2 = 120$$

Also, inserting 40 for Q in equation (10.5),

$$AC = 200 - 4(40) + 0.05(40)^2 = 120$$

Therefore, marginal cost equals average cost when $Q = 40$. (Both marginal cost and average cost equals \$120. This means that the long-run equilibrium price is \$120.)

The Long-Run Adjustment Process:
A Constant-Cost Industry

Having looked at the behavior of the perfectly competitive firm in the short and long runs, we turn to the long-run adjustment process of a perfectly competitive industry. We assume that the industry is a *constant-cost industry*, which means that expansion of the industry does not increase input prices. Figure 10.9 shows long-run equilibrium under conditions of constant cost. The top panel shows the short- and long-run cost curves of a typical firm in the industry. The bottom panel shows the demand and supply curves in the market as a whole, D being the original demand curve and S the original short-run supply curve. It is assumed the industry is in long-run equilibrium, with the result that the

FIGURE
10.9

Long-Run Equilibrium in a Constant-Cost Industry

A constant-cost industry has a horizontal long-run supply curve, as shown in panel *B*. If demand shifts upward from *D* to D_1, the consequent increase in price (to $7 per unit) results in the entry of firms, which shifts the supply curve to the right (to S_1), thus pushing the price back to its original level ($6 per unit).

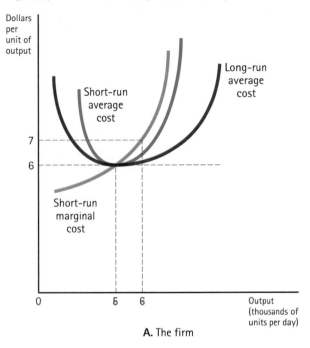

A. The firm

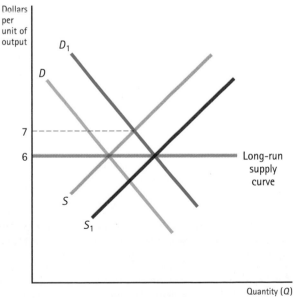

B. The industry

price ($6 per unit) equals the minimum value of the long-run (and short-run) average cost.

Suppose now that the demand curve shifts to D_1. In the short-run, with the number of firms fixed, the product price rises from $6 to $7 per unit; each firm expands its output from 5,000 to 6,000 units per day; and each firm makes economic profits, since the new price, $7, exceeds the short-run average costs of the firm when the output is 6,000 units per day. The result is that firms enter the industry and the supply curve shifts to the right. In the case of a constant-cost industry, the entrance of the new firms does not influence the costs of the existing firms. The inputs used by this industry are used by other industries as well, and new firms in this industry do not bid up the price of inputs and hence raise the costs of existing firms. Neither does the entry of the new firms reduce the existing firms' costs.

Hence, a constant-cost industry has a horizontal long-run supply curve. Since output can be increased by increasing the number of firms producing 5,000 units of output per day at an average cost of $6 per unit, the long-run supply curve is horizontal at $6 per unit. So long as the industry remains in a state of constant costs, its output can be increased indefinitely. If price exceeds $6 per unit, firms enter the industry; if price were less than $6 per unit, firms leave the industry. Therefore, long-run equilibrium can occur in this industry only when price is $6 per unit. And, industry output can be raised or lowered, in accord with demand conditions, without changing this long-run equilibrium price.

The Long-Run Adjustment Process:
An Increasing-Cost Industry

Not all industries are constant-cost industries. Next, we consider the case of an *increasing-cost industry*, which occurs when industry expansion results in an increase in input prices.[7] An increasing-cost industry is shown in Figure 10.10. The original conditions are the same as in Figure 10.9, D is the original demand curve, S is the original supply curve, $6 per unit is the equilibrium price, and LL' and AA' in the top panel are the long- and short-run average cost curves of each firm. As in Figure 10.9, the original position is one of long-run equilibrium, since price equals the minimum value of long-run (and short-run) average cost.

[7]In addition to constant-cost and increasing-cost industries, there are also decreasing-cost industries, which are the most unusual case, although quite young industries may fall into the category. External economies, which are cost reductions that occur when the industry expands, may be responsible for the existence of decreasing-cost industries. For example, the expansion of an industry may lead to an improvement in transportation that reduces the costs of each firm in the industry. A decreasing-cost industry has a negatively sloped long-run supply curve.

FIGURE

10.10

Long-Run Equilibrium in an Increasing-Cost Industry

An increasing-cost industry has a positively sloped long-run supply curve, as shown in panel *B*. After long-run equilibrium is achieved, increases in output require increases in the price of the product.

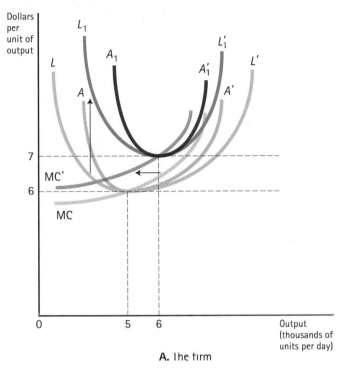

A. The firm

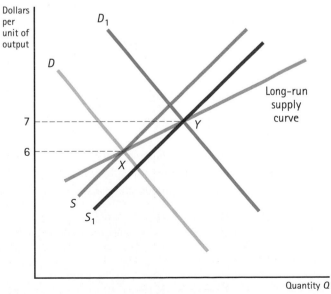

B. The industry

Assume now that the demand curve shifts to D_1, with the result that the price of the product goes up and the firms earn economic profits, attracting new entrants. More and more inputs are needed by the industry and, in an increasing-cost industry, the price of the inputs goes up with the amount used by the industry. Therefore, the cost of inputs increases for the established firms as well as the entrants and the average cost curves are pushed up to L_1L_1' and A_1A_1'.

If each firm's marginal cost curve is shifted to the left by the increase in input prices, the industry supply curve tends to shift to the left. But this tendency is more than counterbalanced by the effects of the increase in the number of firms, which shifts the industry supply curve to the right. The latter effect must more than offset the former effect, because otherwise, there would be no expansion in total industry output. (No new resources would be attracted to the industry). The process of adjustment must go on until a new point of long-run equilibrium is reached. In Figure 10.10, this point is where the price of the product is $7 per unit and each firm produces 6,000 units per day.[8]

An increasing-cost industry has a *positively sloped long-run supply curve*. That is, after long-run equilibrium is achieved, increases in output require increases in the price of the product. For example, points X and Y in Figure 10.10 are on the long-run supply curve for the industry. The difference between constant-cost and increasing-cost industries is as follows: *In constant-cost industries, new firms enter in response to an increase in demand until the price returns to its original level; whereas in increasing-cost industries, new firms enter until the minimum point on the long-run average cost curve has increased to the point where it equals the new, higher price.*[9]

Finally, some industries are neither constant-cost nor increasing-cost industries: They are decreasing-cost industries. Their long-run supply curve is negatively sloped. For further discussion of these industries, which are encountered less frequently than constant-cost or increasing-cost industries, see footnote 7.

How a Perfectly Competitive Economy Allocates Resources

It is important for managers to understand how a competitive economy allocates resources. Without such an understanding, they cannot interpret or anticipate the fundamental changes that may occur. To illustrate this allocation

[8]We cannot be sure that the firm's new output exceeds its old output as shown in Figure 10.10. It is possible for its new output to be less than or equal to its old output.

[9]This is not the only way in which equilibrium can be achieved in increasing-cost industries. It is also possible that the increase in input prices (due to the expansion of industry output) raises average cost more than the increase in demand raises average revenue. Therefore, firms may experience losses, some may leave the industry, and the remaining firms may produce at a bigger scale.

process, we take a simple case: Consumers become more favorably disposed toward corn and less favorably disposed toward rice than in the past. What happens in the short run? The increase in the demand for corn increases its price and results in some increase in the output of corn. However, the output cannot be increased very substantially because the capacity of the industry cannot be expanded in the short run. Similarly, the fall in the demand for rice reduces its price and results in some reduction in the output of rice. But the output of rice cannot be curtailed greatly because firms continue to produce as long as they can cover their variable costs. Because of the increase in the price of corn and the decrease in the price of rice, corn producers earn economic profits and rice producers show economic losses. Producers reallocate resources to correct this imbalance.

When short-run equilibrium is achieved in both the corn and rice industries, the reallocation of resources is not yet complete since there has not been enough time for producers to build new capacity or liquidate old capacity. In particular, neither industry operates at minimum average cost. The corn producers may operate at greater than the output level where average cost is a minimum; and the rice producers may operate at less than the output level where average cost is a minimum.

What occurs in the long run? The shift in consumer demand from rice to corn results in greater adjustments in output and smaller adjustments in price than in the short run. In the long run, existing firms can leave rice production and new firms can enter corn production. As firms leave rice production, the supply curve shifts to the left, causing the price to rise above its short-run level. The transfer of resources out of rice production ceases when the price has increased and costs have decreased to the point where losses no longer occur.

Whereas rice production loses resources, corn production gains them. The short-run profits in corn production stimulates the entry of new firms. The increased demand for inputs raises input prices and cost curves in corn production, and the price of corn is depressed by the movement to the right of the supply curve because of the entry of new firms. Entry stops when economic profits are no longer being earned. At that point, when long-run equilibrium is achieved, more firms and more resources are used in the corn industry than in the short run.

Summary

1. Managers of a perfectly competitive firm set output so that price equals marginal cost. If there is an output level where price exceeds average variable cost, it pays the firm to produce in the short run, even though price does not cover average total costs. But, if there is no output level where price exceeds average variable cost, the firm is better off to produce nothing at all. In the long run, the firm produces at the minimum point on its

long-run average total cost curve. The price tends to be at the level where the market demand curve intersects the market supply curve. The short-run supply curve of a perfectly competitive firm is its marginal cost curve above the point of the minimum average variable cost.

2. Producer surplus is equivalent to the firm's variable cost profit, that is, total revenue less variable costs. The producer surplus is the difference between the price a seller receives for its product less the seller's reservation price (the minimum price at which it would sell its product). This is measure of welfare from a producer's perspective. When combined with the consumer surplus introduced in Chapter 4, the sum of the producer and consumer surpluses gives a measure of societal welfare. This measure is used to compare the benefits of different pricing proposals and the benefits of trade (as shown in Chapters 19 and 20).

3. A constant-cost industry has a horizontal long-run supply curve; an increasing-cost industry has a positively sloped long-run supply curve. If a constant-cost industry expands, there is no increase (or decrease) in input prices; if an increasing-cost industry expands, there is an increase in input prices.

Problems

1. The Hamilton Company is a member of a perfectly competitive industry. Like all members of the industry, its total cost function is

$$TC = 25,000 + 150Q + 3Q^2$$

where TC is the firm's monthly total cost (in dollars) and Q is the firm's monthly output.

   a. If the industry is in long-run equilibrium, what is the price of the Hamilton Company's product?

   b. What is the firm's monthly output?

2. In 2001, the box industry was perfectly competitive. The lowest point on the long-run average cost curve of each of the identical box producers was $4, and this minimum point occured at an output of 1,000 boxes per month. The market demand curve for boxes was

$$Q_D = 140,000 - 10,000P$$

where P is the price of a box (in dollars per box) and Q_D is the quantity of boxes demanded per month. The market supply curve for boxes was

$$Q_S = 80,000 + 5,000P$$

where Q_S is the quantity of boxes supplied per month.

   a. What is the equilibrium price of a box? Is this the long-run equilibrium price?

   b. How many firms are in this industry when it is in long-run equilibrium?

3. The Burr Corporation's total cost function (where TC is the total cost in dollars and Q is quantity) is

$$TC = 200 + 4Q + 2Q^2$$

   a. If the firm is perfectly competitive and the price of its product is $24, what is its optimal output rate?

   b. At this output rate, what are its profits?

4. The supply and demand curves for pears are

$$Q_S = 10,000P$$
$$Q_D = 25,000 - 15,000P$$

where Q_S is the quantity (tons) supplied, Q_D is the quantity (tons) demanded, and P is the price per pear (in hundreds of dollars per ton).

   a. Plot the supply and demand curves.

   b. What is the equilibrium price?

   c. What is the equilibrium quantity?

5. The White Company is a member of the lamp industry, which is perfectly competitive. The price of a lamp is $50. The firm's total cost function is

$$TC = 1,000 + 20Q + 5Q^2$$

where TC is total cost (in dollars) and Q is hourly output.

   a. What output maximizes profit?

   b. What is the firm's economic profit at this output?

   c. What is the firm's average cost at this output?

   d. If other firms in the lamp industry have the same cost function as this firm, is the industry in equilibrium? Why or why not?

6. The long-run supply curve for a particular type of kitchen knife is a horizontal line at a price of $3 per knife. The demand curve for such a kitchen knife is

$$Q_D = 50 - 2P$$

where Q_D is the quantity of knives demanded (in millions per year) and P is the price per knife (in dollars).

   a. What is the equilibrium output of such knives?

   b. If a tax of $1 is imposed on each knife, what is the equilibrium output of such knives? (Assume that the tax is collected by the government from the suppliers of knives.)

   c. After the tax is imposed, you buy such a knife for $3.75. Is this the long-run equilibrium price?

Monopoly and Monopolistic Competition

How does one manage a monopoly? US Airways is the only carrier flying between Ithaca, New York, and Philadelphia, Pennsylvania. In the winter, Kubel's Restaurant is the only restaurant open in Barnegat Light, New Jersey. Only one supermarket may be open all night long in your area. The Philadelphia Gas Works is the only supplier of natural gas in Philadelphia, Pennsylvania.

The market demand curve for air travel between Ithaca and Philadelphia *is* the demand curve for US Airways. The market demand for winter restaurant meals in Barnegat Light *is* the demand curve that Kubel's sees. Likewise, the market demand and the firm demand for overnight supermarket shopping and natural gas in Philadelphia are the same. The demand faced by these managers is downward sloping; that is, as price increases, quantity demanded decreases. The manager controls the market price (and quantity). Given this control, what price (quantity) should the manager choose to maximize profit?

This is the situation faced by monopolists. As one, you are the only game in town. But, this does not give you carte blanche; you need to consider whether others want your product. If no one wants to fly between Ithaca and Philadelphia or shop at 3 AM or eat in a restaurant in the winter in Barnegat Light, your monopoly is worthless. In addition, even if there is high demand for your product, you are unlikely to be successful if you do not manage your costs and resources efficiently. Last, monopolists still must worry about potential competitors. It is only 183 miles between Ithaca and Philadelphia, so driving or taking a bus may be an option. While Barnegat Light only has one winter restaurant, a restaurant exists in a town four miles away and home-cooked meals are a substitute. Many grocery stores are open all day and in the early evening, so that customers can easily shop at times other than 3 AM. Finally, you need not heat your home or hot water with gas but could use oil or electric. Cross elasticities (see Chapter 3) can tell us what goods, locations, and times are substitutes for the "monopoly" product.

So, although you are a monopolist in your market, substitute products, locations, and times exist. If you do not take account of product, spatial, and temporal competition, you are likely to make serious managerial mistakes. And, high profit may attract entry into your specific market. Finally, concern about you making excess profits may prompt the authorities to regulate your business.

In this chapter, we answer the question of how much output the monopolist should produce and at what price to sell this output. The impact of substitute products are subsumed in the intercept of the demand curve (see Chapter 3).

We also show the profit maximizing rule for managers in monopolistic competitive markets. Here, each manager faces a downward-sloping demand curve but a lack of entry barriers allows others into the market. Industries such as shirt manufacturing and personal computers approximate the model of monopolistic competition.

In the cases of both pure monopoly and monopolistic competition, the rule derived in Chapter 10 of marginal revenue equals marginal cost dictates profit maximization. We see that this is a powerful rule and it dictates all behavior in our market structure analysis.

Pricing and Output Decisions under Monopoly

The monopolist behaves differently than the perfect competitor of Chapter 10. An unregulated monopolist maximizes profit by choosing the price and output where the difference between total revenue and cost is the largest. For example, consider a monopolist with a demand curve of

$$P = 10 - Q$$

where P is the price per unit of the product and Q is the number of units demanded at that price. The monopolist has a total cost curve of

$$TC = 1 + Q + 0.5Q^2$$

Cost, Revenue, and Profit of a Monopolist

Output	Price (dollars)	Total revenue (dollars)	Variable cost (dollars)	Total cost (dollars)	Total profit (dollars)	Variable cost profit (dollars)
0	10	0	0	1	−1	0
1	9	9	1.5	2.5	6.5	7.5
2	8	16	4	5	11	12
3	7	21	7.5	8.5	12.5	13.5
4	6	24	12	13	11	12
4.5	5.5	24.75	14.625	15.625	9.125	10.125
5	5	25	17.5	18.5	6.5	7.5
6	4	24	24	25	−1	0
7	3	21	31.5	32.5	−11.5	−10.5
8	2	16	40	41	−25	−24
9	1	9	49.5	50.5	−41.5	−40.5
10	0	0	60	61	−61	−60

The monopolist's total revenue is $TR = PQ$, or

$$TR = (10 - Q)Q = 10Q - Q^2$$

The total revenue and total cost for the monopolist at various levels of output are shown in Table 11.1. The firm maximizes profit at the output where total revenue exceeds total cost by the greatest amount. Figures 11.1 and 11.2 show the situation graphically.

Under monopoly, as under perfect competition, the firm maximizes profit if it sets the output rate at the point at which marginal cost equals marginal revenue. As can be seen by Figure 11.2, profits are maximized when $d\Pi/dQ = 0$. Recall from Chapter 10 that $\Pi = TR - TC$, that is, profit equals total revenue minus total cost, and that $d\Pi/dQ = d\,TR/dQ - d\,TC/dQ = 0$, which implies that $MR - MC = 0$ or that $MR = MC$.

Let us investigate the situation in Table 11.1 and Figures 11.1 and 11.2 in greater detail. The marginal revenue $= MR = d\,TR/dQ = 10 - 2Q$.

Note that, with a linear demand curve, the marginal revenue curve has the same dollar intercept as the demand curve (10) but it falls twice as fast as the demand curve; that is, the marginal revenue curve has twice the slope of the demand curve. This is always true for linear demand curves (which we almost always use for illustrative purposes—of course, in the real world, demand curves

FIGURE

11.1

Total Revenue, Total Cost, and Total Profit of a Monopolist

To maximize profit, the monopolist chooses an output rate of three units per period of time and a price of $7.

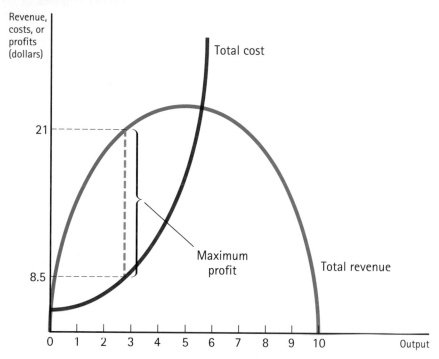

could take any form that shows an inverse relationship of price and quantity). Therefore, if the demand curve had been $P = 250 - 12.5Q^2$, the marginal revenue would be $MR = 250 - 25Q$.[1]

The total cost function is $TC = 1 + Q + 0.5Q^2$. Therefore, marginal cost = $MC = dTC/dQ = 1 + Q$.

Setting marginal revenue equal to marginal cost gives

$$MR = 10 - 2Q = 1 + Q = MC, \quad \text{or } Q = 3 \tag{11.1}$$

and hence $P = 10 - 3 = \$7$.

---

[1]Total revenue would be $TR = (250 - 12.5Q)Q = 250Q - 12.5Q^2$ and so $MR = dTR/dQ = 250 - 25Q$.

FIGURE
11.2

Profit and Output of a Monopolist

To maximize profit, the monopolist chooses an output rate of three units per time period and makes a profit of $12.5.

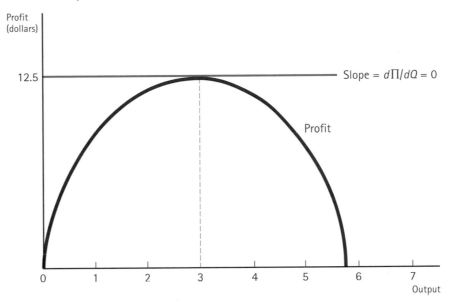

Note that the firm's marginal revenue is no longer constant nor is it equal to price. Recall from Chapter 3 that

$$\text{MR} = P[1 + (1/\eta)] = P[1 - (1/|\eta|)] = P + (P/\eta) = P - (P/|\eta|) \qquad (11.2)$$

where MR is marginal revenue, P is price, and η is the price elasticity of demand. Since $\eta < 0$, the marginal revenue equals price *minus* $P/|\eta|$. Hence, marginal revenue is price *minus* something positive so price must exceed marginal revenue. In addition, no rational manager produces where marginal revenue is negative (i.e., this would imply that selling another unit decreases total revenue; since producing another unit would increase the total costs, the firm would move away from its objective of maximizing profits). In addition, if marginal revenue were negative, equating it to marginal cost implies that marginal cost is negative. Total costs *increase* when the firm increases production, not decrease. If marginal revenue is positive, then from equation (11.2), $\eta < -1$ (i.e., $|\eta| > 1$), which implies an elastic demand.[2] Thus, a monopolist will *not* produce in the inelastic range of its demand curve *if* it is maximizing profit.

[2]From equation (11.2), if $|\eta| > 1$, then $1/|\eta| < 1$ and $[1 - (1/|\eta|)] > 0$. This makes MR > 0, since P must be positive.

TABLE
11.2

Marginal Cost and Marginal Revenue of a Monopolist

Price	Output	Marginal cost[a]	Marginal revenue[b]	Total profit[c]	Elasticity
10	0	1	10	−1	−∞
9	1	2	8	6.5	−9
8	2	3	6	11	−4
7	**3**	**4**	**4**	**12.5**	**−2.33**
6	4	5	2	11	−1.5
5.5	4.5	5.5	1	9.125	−1.22
5	5	6	0	6.5	−1
4	6	7	−2	−1	−0.67
3	7	8	−4	−11.5	−0.43
2	8	9	−6	−25	−0.25
1	9	10	−8	−41.5	−0.11
0	10	11	−10	−61	0

[a]The marginal cost is calculated from the equation $MC = 1 + Q$. This assumes that the product is produced in continuous amounts, such as gasoline. If the product can be produced only in discrete amounts, such as cars, the marginal cost for output n is defined as the total cost of producing n units minus the total cost of producing $n − 1$ units. Using the total cost information from Table 11.1, the marginal cost of producing two units is $2.5, that is, $5–$2.5; the marginal cost of producing three units is $3.5, that is, $8.5–$5; and the marginal cost of producing four units is $4.5, that is, $13–$8.5. Why does this differ from the marginal cost of $5 shown for output 4 in the table? Because the costs differ if you can produce continuously as opposed to only in discrete integer units.

[b]The marginal revenue is calculated from the equation $MR = 10 − 2Q$. This assumes that the product can be sold in continuous amounts, such as gasoline. If the product can be sold only in discrete amounts, such as cars, the marginal revenue for output n is defined as the total revenue from selling n units minus the total revenue of selling $n − 1$ units. Using the total revenue information from Table 11.1, the marginal revenue of selling two units is $7, that is, $16 − $9; the marginal revenue of selling three units is $5, that is, $21 − $16; and the marginal revenue of selling four units is $3, that is, $24 − $21.

[c]Note that using the discrete marginal revenue and the marginal cost gives the same result as the continuous analysis; that is, the profit maximizing output is three units. In the discrete case, the firm would clearly produce the second unit, since the marginal revenue exceeds the marginal cost (i.e., $7 > $2.5) and, hence, would increase profits. Likewise, it would produce the third item, since the marginal revenue exceeds the marginal cost (i.e., $5 > $3.5) and, hence, would increase profits. However, the firm would not produce the fourth item, because the marginal revenue is exceeded by the marginal cost (i.e., $3 < $4.5) and, hence, would decrease profits.

Table 11.2 and Figure 11.3 present the marginal revenue and marginal cost numbers for these functions, graph those functions, and substantiate that profits are maximized when marginal revenue equals marginal cost.

Note that, at the optimal output of three units (price = $7), the demand is elastic (−2.33) and the marginal revenue is positive ($4). It is also the case that, in a monopoly, the price must exceed average variable cost if the monopolist maximizes profits (and from Table 11.1, it can be calculated that AVC = $2.5; i.e., AVC = VC/Q = $7.5/3 = $2.5).

FIGURE
11.3

Marginal Revenue and Marginal Cost of a Monopolist

At the monopolist's profit maximizing output (three units), the marginal cost equals the marginal revenue (at $4).

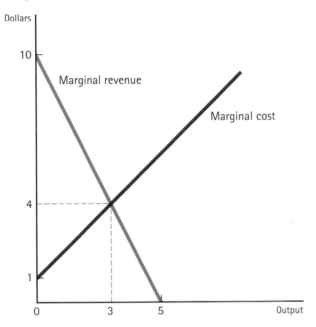

It is easy to represent graphically the price and output decision of the monopolist. Figure 11.4 shows the demand curve, the marginal revenue curve, the marginal cost curve, the average total cost curve, and the average variable cost curve faced by the firm. To maximize profit, it should produce the output Q_M where the marginal cost curve intersects that of marginal revenue. If the monopolist produces Q_M, she will set a price of P_M. Since she is the only member of the industry, the firm's demand curve is the industry demand curve. This is in contrast to perfect competition, where the demand curve for a firm's output is horizontal. The demand curve for the monopolist's output slopes downward to the right, as shown in Figure 11.4.

In Figure 11.4, the firm's profit per unit is $P_M - \text{ATC}$. This, multiplied by the number of units, Q_M, is the shaded area of the diagram. Note also that $P > \text{AVC}$, and so our second condition for profit maximization is satisfied.

If an industry is monopolized, it generally sets a higher price and a lower output than if it were perfectly competitive. In the preceding example, if the firm were forced to behave as a perfect competitor, it would set price equal to marginal cost; that is, $P = 10 - Q = 1 + Q = \text{MC}$. This yields $2Q = 9$ or an output of 4.5 and a price of 5.5; that is, $P = 10 - 4.5$. Therefore, output is cur-

FIGURE
11.4

Output and Price Decisions of a Monopolist

In equilibrium, the monopolist produces Q_M units of output and sets a price of P_M. (Note that, in contrast to perfect competition, the demand curve slopes downward to the right.)

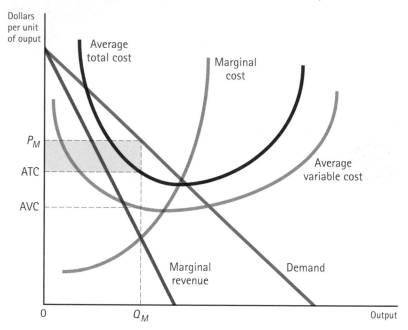

tailed under monopoly (from 4.5 to 3), price is increased (from $5.5 to $7), and profits are increased from $9.125 to $12.5)—see Table 11.1.

The perfectly competitive firm operates at the point at which price equals marginal cost, whereas the monopolist operates at the point at which price exceeds marginal cost. To see that the monopolist's price exceeds marginal cost, recall that

$$MR = P[1 + (1/\eta)]$$

and that the monopolist sets marginal revenue equal to marginal cost. Therefore,

$$MC = P[1 + (1/\eta)] \tag{11.3}$$
$$P = MC/[1 + (1/\eta)]$$

Since $\eta < 0$, it follows that $[1 + (1/\eta)] < 1$, which means that P must exceed MC.

The secret to the monopolist is that it marks the price above its marginal cost, whereas the perfect competitor merely charges the marginal cost. Of course, both types of firms must make sure that price exceeds average variable cost.

The Newspaper Industry in Detroit

Relatively few cities in the United States have rival newspapers that are separately owned and commercially independent. Take the case of Detroit. In early 1989, the *Detroit Free Press* and the *Detroit News* obtained approval from the U.S. Court of Appeals to establish a newspaper monopoly in Detroit. Arguing that the *Free Press* was a failing newspaper, they took advantage of a special exemption from antitrust law, permitted under the Newspaper Preservation Act of 1970. (This exemption was created to keep alive competing editorial voices in major cities). The two newspapers were allowed to continue to print newspapers under their own names. But all commercial operations would be merged.

Because the merged newspapers were legally permitted to fix prices and allocate markets as they pleased, they constituted a monopoly, even though their newspapers were printed under two different names. The result was a very substantial increase in profit. Before they combined, each lost more than $10 million a year; after they combined, experts estimated that they would make more than $150 million a year. This is eloquent testimony to the effect of monopoly on profit.

The reasons for this increase in profit were summarized as follows by the *New York Times*: "The formation of the monopoly enterprise would end an all-out war for control of advertising and circulation dollars, sending, . . . rates skyrocketing for readers and advertisers."[3] This, of course, is entirely consistent with the discussion in the previous section. A monopolist, free from the constraints imposed by direct competition, can set a higher price—and obtain a higher profit level—than it could if it had to compete with rival firms.

However, even a monopoly is not guaranteed a profit. In July 1995, about 2,500 reporters, editors, press operators, drivers, and other workers of the *Detroit Free Press* and *Detroit News* struck over job cuts, wages, and work rules. This strike continued for over 18 months and cut heavily into the profits of the merged newspapers.[4]

The McComb Company: A Numerical Example

To illustrate how price and output can be chosen to maximize profit, consider the McComb Company, a monopolist producing and selling a product with the demand curve

$$P = 30 - 6Q \tag{11.4}$$

[3]*New York Times*, September 18, 1988.
[4]*New York Times*, February 20, 1997.

ANALYZING MANAGERIAL DECISIONS

Franchiser versus Franchisee?

What happens when a franchiser with monopoly power has a different objective from a franchisee's? Consider the case of McDonald's, where the franchiser makes its money by collecting a percentage of each store's sales, or total revenues. Therefore, the franchiser wants to maximize the total revenue from the sales of its hamburgers by having each store maximize its total revenues (and by adding more stores). We assume that franchisees wish to maximize their profits. To do so, the franchisee would set $MR = MC$ (in the elastic range of demand where $\eta_D < -1$). But maximizing total revenue requires that $MR = 0$ (and that $\eta_D = -1$). Since the objectives of the franchiser

and the franchisee cannot be accomplished with the same pricing policy, they are in conflict. The situation is depicted in the figure.*

Note that this conflict exists in other situations such as book publishing. Authors generally receive a percentage of book sales as a royalty. Therefore, authors would like publishers to maximize total revenues. Publishers, on the other hand, want to maximize profits.

*Business Week, June 2, 1997.

A monopolist produces at $P_{Franchisee}$, $Q_{Franchisee}$ as dictated by marginal revenue equals marginal cost. A revenue maximizer produces where marginal revenue is zero ($P_{Franchiser}$, $Q_{Franchiser}$), that is, where $\eta = -1$.

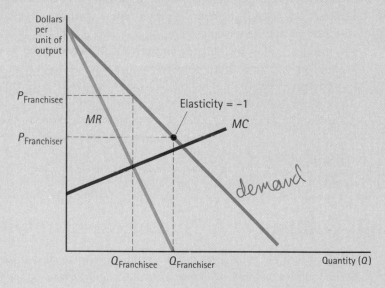

where P is price (in thousands of dollars) and Q is the firm's output (in thousands of units). The firm's total cost function is

$$TC = 14 + 3Q + 3Q^2 \tag{11.5}$$

where TC is total cost (in millions of dollars).

CONCEPTS IN CONTEXT

Using Patents to Maintain Market Power

The U.S. government often tries to break up monopolies, but one government institution, the patent system, is designed to grant firms monopoly power on their inventions and product innovations. The government grants companies patents for 20 years. This gives the patent holder the exclusive rights to their invention or new product for the life of the patent. Because companies apply for a patent before the product is on the market, the effective life of a patent can be significantly less than 20 years. For drugs, the effective patent protection is about 12 years.

Because of the monopoly granted by the patent system (and the anticipated monopoly profits from a popular product), drug companies are willing to invest significant funds in research and development (R and D). It is estimated that a successful new drug averages approximately $350 million in development costs. Without patent protection, it is doubtful whether drug companies would undertake highly problematic and expensive R and D.

What do drug companies do pricewise with their patent-generated monopoly power? One test is to compare the price of drugs just as drugs come off patent with the price of the generics that presently appear on the market. Bristol-Meyers Squibbs's heart drug Capoten sold for 57 cents per pill and the generic sold for 3 cents. This suggests at least a 19-times markup.

Source: "With Patents Expiring on Big Prescription Drugs, Drug Industry Quakes," *Wall Street Journal,* August 12, 1997.

From the demand curve in equation (11.4), we can determine the firm's total revenue (in millions of dollars), which is

$$TR = PQ = (30 - 6Q)Q = 30Q - 6Q^2$$

Therefore, marginal revenue equals $dTR/dQ = 30 - 12Q$.

From the total cost function in equation (11.5), we can determine that their marginal cost is

$$dTC/dQ = 3 + 6Q$$

Setting marginal revenue equal to marginal cost,

$$MR = 30 - 12Q = 3 + 6Q = MC$$

This means that $Q = 1.5$. Inserting 1.5 for Q in the demand equation (10.3), we find that $P = 30 - 6(1.5)$, or $21. So, to maximize profits, the McComb Company should set a price of $21,000 and produce and sell 1,500 units. If it does so, its profit equals $[30(1.5) - 6(1.5)^2] - [14 + 3(1.5) + 3(1.5)^2] = 6.25$ million dollars.

Cost-Plus Pricing

Academic studies of pricing behavior consistently suggest the wide use of a cost–plus heuristic (see the "Pricing Behavior of Managers" box). Managers act as if cost is the primary driver of price. Although the behavior has many variations, they all follow a guiding principal: Price is set as a function of cost. Managers first allocate unit costs conditional on a given output level (e.g., 70-percent capacity). Then, they add a profit margin. This margin is generally a percentage of costs and is added to the estimated average costs. The markup is meant to cover costs that are difficult to allocate to specific products and as a return on firm investment.

In terms of basic algebra, the percentage markup can be expressed:

$$\text{Markup} = (\text{price} - \text{cost})/\text{cost} \tag{11.6}$$

where the numerator–that is, (price − cost)–is the **profit margin**. If the cost of a paperback book is $4 and its price is $6, the markup is

$$\text{Markup} = (6 - 4)/4 = 0.50$$

or 50 percent. If we solve equation (11.6) for price, the result is

$$\text{Price} = \text{cost} (1 + \text{markup}) \tag{11.7}$$

which is the pricing formula described in the previous paragraph. In the case of the paperback book,

$$\text{Price} = 4(1 + 0.5) = \$6$$

since the markup is 50 percent.

Some firms have set up a **target return** figure that they hope to earn, which determines the markup. For example, General Electric at times has established a target rate of return of 20 percent. Under target rate-of-return pricing, price is set equal to

$$P = L + M + K + (F/Q) + (\pi A/Q) \tag{11.8}$$

where P is price, L is unit labor cost, M is unit material cost, K is unit marketing cost, F is total fixed or indirect costs, Q is the number of units the firm plans to produce during the relevant planning period, A is total gross operating assets, and π is the desired profit rate on those assets. If a firm believes that its labor cost is $2, its unit material cost is $1, its unit marketing cost is $3, its total fixed cost is $10,000, its output will be 1,000 units,

ANALYZING MANAGERIAL DECISIONS

Pricing Behavior of Managers

Surveys of financial officers of large manufacturing companies suggest behavioral differences that vary across countries. When asked to rank factors that influence market price, the majority of officers in U.S. companies said product cost was the primary driver of price. These managers were also more likely to use full unit cost, instead of variable cost. Managers in Japan, Ireland, and the United Kingdom showed different behavior. They listed market factors as the primary driver of price.

The use of a cost-plus heuristic explains the behavior of American managers. The heuristic requires greater knowledge of cost. Hence, managers focus on product cost to set price. The nature of competition is an afterthought. In contrast, behavior in Japan, Ireland, and the United Kingdom suggest managers first focus on market competition and then on cost. It is as if managers in Japan, Ireland, and the United Kingdom backwardly induct, and those in the United States do not.

This market focus is more refined by Japanese managers. Surveys find Japanese managers are more likely to use value engineering in the pricing

decision. In value engineering, managers first go to the market and look at the products of rivals. They determine a price they think must be received in the market for their product to succeed. Then, they go back to the design engineers, and ask whether the product can be built within the price constraint.

While it is arguable that a cost-plus policy is not consistent with a market focus, the use of the heuristic is widely used. For example, an entire software industry provides programs to help managers optimize their cost-plus pricing decisions (e.g., www.acornsys.com/products). Cost-plus purchase programs are even seen as a competitive advantage (e.g., www.monettech.com/products).

Sources: P. Blayney and I. Yokoyama, "Corporate Analysis of Japanese and Australian Cost Accounting and Management Practices," *Abacus* 6, 1997, 33–50; M. Cornick, W. Cooper, and S. Wilson, "How Do Companies Analyze Their Overhead?" *Management Accounting,* June 1988, 41–43; C. Drury, S. Braund, P. Osborne, and M. Tayles, "A Survey of Management Accounting Practices in UK Manufacturing Companies," Association of Chartered Certified Accountants publication, London, 1993.

its assets are $100,000, and its target rate of return is 15 percent, its price would be set at

$$P = 2 + 1 + 3 + (10,000/1,000) + [0.15(100,000)/1,000] = \$31$$

For firms that produce more than one product, the charge for indirect cost, or overhead, is often established by allocating this cost among the firm's products on the basis of their average variable costs. If a firm's total annual indirect costs (for all products) are estimated to be $3 million and the total annual variable costs (for all products) are estimated to be $2 million, then indirect costs would be allocated to products at a rate of 150 percent of variable costs.

For example, if the average variable cost of product Y is estimated to be $10, the firm would add a charge of 1.50 × $10, or $15, for indirect cost. Adding this charge to the average variable cost, the firm obtains an estimated fully allocated cost of $10 + $15, or $25. This figure would then be marked up to allow for profit. For example, if the markup is 40 percent, then the price is 1.40 × $25, or $35.

Cost-Plus Pricing at Therma-Stent

Cost-plus pricing is widely used in medical group purchasing organizations. Therma-Stent is a producer of graft stents. Managers set price by estimating the average production costs (including indirect ones). They then add a 40 percent markup to set the product's market price:

$$\text{Factory cost/unit} = \$2,300 \text{ (at production of 20,000)}$$
$$40 \text{ percent markup} = 920$$
$$\text{U.S. list price} = \$3,220$$

The use of the heuristic eases the complexity of setting price by ignoring market considerations. For instance, price is set without considering prices of rival products. This pricing scheme works better when products are differentiated. Therma-Stent produces graft stents that are fairly unique in form and surface structure.

Cost-Plus Pricing at Internet Companies and Government-Regulated Industries

Many online companies seem to have adopted a cost-plus pricing scheme. Consider Onsale, an online computer store. Its pricing policy is called "At Cost" and the claim is that they sell products based at the wholesale price plus a fixed transaction fee (the markup).[5]

Online sellers in other product lines have adopted the same pricing scheme. 4Cost.com claims to sell major household appliances (GE, Hotpoint washers, dryers, refrigerators, and ovens) and electronics (RCA, Sony, TVs, and camcorders) on a cost-plus basis, where the purchaser is shown the wholesale price of the item they are interested in.[6]

Many automobile dealers also use this approach. However, auto dealer invoices contain some items such as "area allowances," which are hard for the novice consumer to interpret, and manufacturer givebacks are not included in

[5]"Egghead Whips up a $400 Million Deal with Onsale," *San Francisco Chronicle*, July 15, 1997.
[6]Cost Appliances and Electronics: Lowest Prices on the Web, found at www.4cost.com/.

the invoice. Therefore, the consumers are not seeing the true price the dealer paid for the car. In addition, many customers trade in their old vehicles. In dealing with a customer, the dealers are concerned with how much money they can make in the package—the trade-in plus the sale of the new vehicle. This makes dealing with the auto dealer harder than dealing with the appliance dealer (where trade-ins are nonexistent).

Government regulators have also used cost-plus pricing in industries that they regulate or control. For instance, the Coal Ministry in India recently allowed "Rajmahal" coal to be priced at cost plus Rs143 per tonne after meeting production costs.[7] The danger of such a pricing scheme in a government-controlled industry is that, when the profit is guaranteed, the firm may lose the incentive to be cost efficient. This tends to create a larger government regulatory bureaucracy to monitor costs.

Does Cost-Plus Pricing Maximize Profit?

On the basis of the previous discussion, it seems extremely unlikely that cost-plus pricing will result in the maximization of profits. Indeed, this pricing technique seems naïve, because it takes no account, explicitly at least, of the extent or elasticity of demand or of the size of marginal, rather than average, cost. Nevertheless, if applied properly, cost-plus pricing may result in managers coming close to maximizing profits. To see this, it is important to note how little has been said about the factors determining the size of the percentage markup. (Even in the case of target-rate-of-return pricing, no explanation has been given for the target rate of return that a firm chooses). For example, why was the paperback book cited on page 416 marked up by 50 percent? Why not 25 percent, or 150 percent? If the bookseller maximizes profit, the markup is determined by the price elasticity of demand for the book.

To understand why this is true, recall from equation (11.3) that

$$MC = P[1 + (1/\eta)]$$

Dividing both sides of the equation by $1 + (1/\eta)$, we get

$$P = MC\{1/[1 + (1/\eta)]\}$$

which means that, to maximize profit, the firm should set the product's price so that it equals its marginal cost multiplied by

$$\{1/[1 + (1/\eta)]\}$$

[7]Badal Sanyal, "Cost Plus Pricing Helps Rajmahal Expansion," August 26, 1996 found at www.hindubusinessline.com/1996/08/26/BLFP.08.html.

TABLE 11.3

Relationship between Optimal Markup and Price Elasticity of Demand

Price elasticity of demand	Optimal percentage markup of marginal cost
−1.2	500
−1.4	250
−1.8	125
−2.5	66.67
−5.0	25
−11.0	10
−21.0	5
−51.0	2

Looking back at equation (11.6), you can see that, according to cost-plus pricing, the price is set equal to cost multiplied by (1 + markup). If marginal (not average) cost is the cost concept really used here and

$$\text{Markup} = -1/(\eta + 1) \tag{11.9}$$

cost-plus pricing results in the maximization of profit.

Put differently, a firm maximizes profit if it marks up marginal (not average) cost and the markup equals the value specified in equation (11.9). As equation (11.9) shows clearly, the markup, under these circumstances, depends entirely on the product's price elasticity of demand. Table 11.3 provides the profit-maximizing markup corresponding to particular values of the elasticity. If a product's price elasticity of demand equals −1.2, the optimal markup is 500 percent. If its price elasticity is −21, the optimal markup is only 5 percent. Table 11.3 should be studied carefully, since it provides interesting and useful information that can help managers formulate and maintain an effective pricing policy.

Note that the optimal markup goes up as the price elasticity of demand (in absolute value) for the product goes down. Table 11.3 shows this very clearly. In managerial economics, as in other things, you ought to check whenever possible to make sure that what you are told makes sense. To see that the inverse relationship in Table 11.3 between the markup and the price elasticity is eminently reasonable, ask yourself the following question: If the quantity demanded of a product is not very sensitive to its price, should I set a relatively high or low price for this product? Obviously, you should set a high price if you want to make as much money as possible. Since this is what Table 11.3 tells us, it accords with common sense.

The Humphrey Corporation: A Numerical Example

To illustrate how cost-plus pricing can be used to maximize a firm's profits, consider the Humphrey Corporation, a seller of office furniture. One of Humphrey's major products is a metal desk for which the company pays $76 per desk, including transportation and related costs. Although Humphrey has a variety of overhead and marketing costs, these costs essentially are fixed, so marginal cost is approximately $76. Given that many firms in Humphrey's geographic area sell reasonably comparable desks, Humphrey's marketing managers believe that the price elasticity of demand for desks is fairly elastic–about −2.5. On the basis of Table 11.3, it should establish a markup of 66.67 percent if it wants to maximize profit.

According to equation (11.7), the optimal price is

$$\text{Price} = \text{cost}(1 + \text{markup})$$
$$= 76(1 + 0.6667)$$
$$= \$126.67$$

Consequently, to maximize profit, Humphrey should set a price of approximately $127 per desk. However, this is spuriously precise. In fact, as we saw in Chapters 5 and 9, firms very seldom can estimate their marginal costs with great precision. Nor is it worth what it would cost them to try to do so. Since Humphrey's estimates are only approximate, so is the $127 figure. Recognizing that this is the case, Humphrey's managers set a price of $127, but are prepared to push it up or down a bit in accord with their sense of what is most profitable.

The Multiple-Product Firm: Demand Interrelationships

Having discussed cost-plus pricing, we turn to the pricing problems of the multiproduct firm. If a firm makes more than one product, it must recognize that a change in the price or quantity sold of one of its products may influence the demand for its other products. For example, if the Akkina Company produces and sells two products, X and Y, its total revenue (that is, sales) can be represented as

$$TR = TR_X + TR_Y \qquad (11.10)$$

ANALYZING MANAGERIAL DECISIONS

Pricing Steaks at the Palm Restaurant

If you want a steak in New York, a top-notch place to go is the Palm restaurant, owned by the Palm Management Corporation, which has 11 Palm restaurants in 10 cities, all with the same menu. The price of a steak at each of these 11 restaurants in 1993 was as follows:

New York (2 restaurants)	$27.00	Chicago	$22.00
East Hampton	26.00	Houston	23.00
Philadelphia	24.00	Dallas	23.00
Washington	24.00	Las Vegas	25.00
Miami	24.50	Los Angeles	26.00

(a) According to Bruce Bozzi, the co-owner of the Palm Management Corporation, "People are very price-conscious in Chicago, and our manager there knows what we have to charge to be competitive." Assuming that the market for restaurant food is monopolistically competitive in each of these cities, is the demand curve for steak at the Palm restaurant in Chicago the same as at the Palm restaurant in New York? If not, how does it differ? (b) Mr. Bozzi also states that, "Our labor costs are highest in New York. We figure labor at around $8 per customer. That's nearly double what we pay in some other cities. Utilities are also high. It costs us $7,000 a month for garbage removal for the two restaurants." Is the marginal cost curve for steak at the Palm restaurant in New York the same as at the Palm restaurant in Chicago? If not, how does it differ? (c) Why is the price higher in New York than in Chicago? (d) If marginal cost is 20 percent higher in New York than in Chicago and the price elasticity of demand is −3 in New York and −4 in Chicago, what would you expect to be the percentage price differential between New York and Chicago?

SOLUTION (a) No. On the basis of Mr. Bozzi's statement, the demand curve is more price elastic in Chicago than in New York. A 1 percent price increase is likely to reduce the quantity demanded by a larger percentage in Chicago than in New York. (b) No. The marginal cost curve is lower in Chicago than in New York. (c) As pointed out on page 419, the profit-maximizing price equals

$$P = MC \div \left(1 + \frac{1}{\eta}\right)$$

where MC equals marginal cost and η equals the price elasticity of demand. (This is true under any market structure.) Since MC is higher and η is less elastic in New York than in Chicago, the profit-maximizing price is higher in New York than in Chicago. (d) If P_C is the price in Chicago and P_N is the price in New York, MC_C is the marginal cost in

Chicago and MC_N is the marginal cost in New York, and η_C is the price elasticity of demand in Chicago and η_N is the price elasticity of demand in New York,

$$\frac{P_C}{P_N} = \frac{MC_C \div \left(1 + \frac{1}{\eta_C}\right)}{MC_N \div \left(1 + \frac{1}{\eta_N}\right)}$$

$$= \frac{MC_C \div \left(1 + \frac{1}{-4}\right)}{1.2 MC_C \div \left(1 + \frac{1}{-3}\right)} = 0.74.$$

Therefore, the price in Chicago would be expected to be about 26 percent below the price in New York.

For further discussion, see *New York Times*, April 28, 1993. All prices refer to filet mignon.

where TR_X is its total revenue from product X and TR_Y is the total revenue from product Y. The marginal revenue from product X is

$$MR_X = (\partial TR_X / \partial Q_X) - (\partial TR_Y / \partial Q_X) \qquad (11.11a)$$

and the marginal revenue from product Y is

$$MR_Y = (\partial TR_Y / \partial Q_Y) - (\partial TR_X / \partial Q_Y) \qquad (11.11b)$$

The last term in each of these equations represents the demand interrelationship between the two products. In equation (11.11a), the last term shows the effect of an increase in the quantity sold of product X on the total revenue from product Y. This effect can be positive or negative. If products X and Y are complements, this effect is positive, since an increase in the quantity sold of one product increases the total revenue from the other product. On the other hand, if products X and Y are substitutes, this effect is negative, since an increase in the quantity sold of one product reduces the total revenue from the other product.

If you do not understand or pay proper attention to demand interrelationships of this sort, serious error can result. For example, if product X is a fairly close substitute for product Y and the division of the Akkina Company producing product X launches a campaign to increase its sales, the results may be good for the division but bad for the company as a whole. Why? Because the resulting increase in product X's sales may be largely at the expense of product Y's sales.

Pricing of Joint Products: Fixed Proportions

In addition to being interrelated on the demand side, a firm's products are often interrelated in production. For example, products sometimes are produced in a fixed ratio, as is the case of cattle, where beef and hide are obtained from each animal. In such a situation, there is no reason to distinguish between the products from the point of view of production or costs. Since they must be produced in fixed proportions, they are not separate products from a production point of view but should be regarded as a bundle. One hide and two sides of beef might be such a bundle in the case of cattle, since they are produced from each animal. Because the products are produced jointly, there is no economically correct way to allocate the cost of producing each such bundle to the individual products.

To determine the optimal price and output of each such product, compare the marginal revenue of the output bundle with its marginal cost of production. If the marginal revenue—that is, the sum of the marginal revenues obtained from each product in the package—is greater than its marginal cost, expand your output. Assuming there are two joint products (A and B), Figure 11.5 shows the demand and marginal revenue curves for each, as well as the marginal cost for the bundle composed of these products in the fixed proportion in which they are produced.[8] The **total marginal revenue** curve is the **vertical** summation of the two marginal revenue curves for the individual products, since each bundle of output yields revenues from the sale of both products. Consequently, the profit-maximizing output in Figure 11.5 is Q, where the total marginal revenue equals marginal cost. The optimal price for product A is P_A, and the optimal price for product B is P_B.

It is important to note that the total marginal revenue curve coincides with the marginal revenue curve for product A at all outputs beyond Q_0 in Figure 11.5. This is because the firm would never sell product B at a level where its marginal revenue is negative. This would mean that greater revenues are obtained if less were sold. Therefore, if the total output exceeds Q_0, the firm would sell only part of the product B produced; specifically, it would sell the amount corresponding to an output of Q_0 product bundles. Consequently, if output exceeds Q_0, the total marginal revenue equals the marginal revenue of product A alone.

What if the marginal cost curve intersects the total marginal revenue curve to the right of Q_0, in Figure 11.5? In particular, suppose that the situation is as

[8]For simplicity, we assume that the demand curve for product A is not influenced by the price of product B and vice versa.

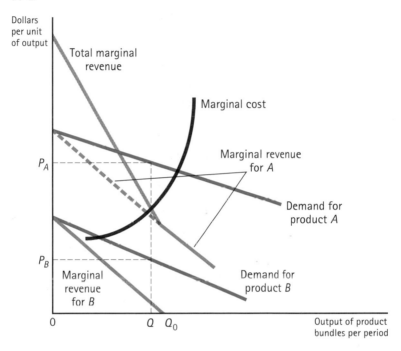

FIGURE 11.5

Optimal Pricing for Joint Products Produced in Fixed Proportions (Case 1)

The price of product A is set at P_A, the price of product B is set at P_B, and output is set at Q.

shown in Figure 11.6, where the marginal cost curve is lower than in Figure 11.5 (but the other curves are the same). The profit maximizing output is Q_1, where the marginal cost and total marginal revenue curves intersect. All of product A produced is sold, the price being P_A, but not all of product B is sold. Instead, the amount sold is limited to the amount of output Q_0, so that the price of product B is P_B. The "surplus" amount of product B, that is, $Q_1 - Q_0$, must be thrown away and kept off the market to avoid depressing its price.

The Warmingham Company: A Numerical Example

To illustrate the technique discussed in the previous section, consider the Warmingham Company, which manufactures two goods, A and B, that are jointly produced in equal quantities. That is, for every unit of product A produced, the

FIGURE
11.6

Optimal Pricing for Joint Products Produced in Fixed Proportions (Case 2)

The price of product A is set at P_A, the price of product B is set at P_B, and not all of product B is sold.

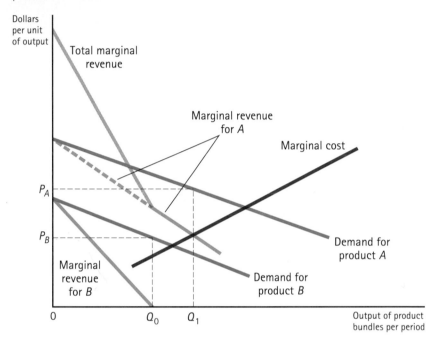

firm also produces a unit of product B (whether it wants it or not). Warmingham's total cost function is

$$TC = 100 + Q + 2Q^2 \qquad (11.12)$$

where Q is the number of units of output. (Each unit contains one unit of product A and one unit of product B). The demand curves for the firm's two products are

$$P_A = 200 - Q_A \qquad (11.13)$$
$$P_B = 150 - 2Q_B \qquad (11.14)$$

where P_A and Q_A are the price and output of product A and P_B and Q_B are the price and output of product B.

How much of each product should Warmingham produce and sell per period? What price should it charge for each? Warmingham's total revenue equals the sum of the total revenues from its two products:

$$TR = P_A Q_A + P_B Q_B \qquad (11.15)$$

Substituting the right-hand sides of equations (11.13) and (11.14) for P_A and P_B, respectively, it follows that

$$TR = (200 - Q_A)Q_A + (150 - 2Q_B)Q_B$$
$$= 200Q_A - Q_A^2 + 150Q_B - 2Q_B^2$$

Assuming that Warmingham sells all it produces of both products, $Q_A = Q_B = Q$, since, as stressed, a unit of one product is produced whenever a unit of the other product is produced. Therefore,

$$TR = 200Q - Q^2 + 150Q - 2Q^2 = 350Q - 3Q^2 \qquad (11.16)$$

To obtain Warmingham's profit, Π, we must subtract its total cost in equation (11.12) from its total revenue in equation (11.16).

$$\underset{TR}{\Pi = (350Q - 3Q^2)} - \underset{TC}{(100 + Q + 2Q^2)}$$
$$= -100 + 349Q \quad 5Q^2$$

To maximize profit, we need to set $d\Pi/dQ = 0$:

$$d\Pi/dQ = 349 - 10Q = 0$$

or

$$10Q = 349$$

or

$$Q = 34.9$$

In other words, to maximize profit, Warmingham should produce 34.9 units of each product per period of time.[9] To sell this amount, equation (11.13) tells us that the price of product A must be

$$P_A = 200 - 34.9 = \$165.10$$

---

[9]Note that there is no reason why Q must be an integer. Warmingham can produce 34.9 units per period of time. How? By producing a total of 349 units during 10 periods.

and equation (11.14) tells us that the price of product B must be

$$P_B = 150 - 2(34.9) = \$80.20$$

At this point, it may seem that the analysis is finished—but it is not. As indicated, we have assumed that Warmingham sells all it produces of both products. To see whether this is true, we must see whether, if $Q = 34.9$, the marginal revenues of both products are nonnegative. Only then will Warmingham sell all it produces of both products (recall Figure 11.6). From equations (11.13) and (11.14), we find that TR_A, the total revenue from product A, equals

$$TR_A = P_A Q_A = (200 - Q_A)Q_A = 200Q_A - Q_A^2$$

and that TR_B, the total revenue from product B, equals

$$TR_B = P_B Q_B = (150 - 2Q_B)Q_B = 150Q_B - 2Q_B^2$$

Hence, the marginal revenue of product A is

$$MR_A = dTR_A/dQ_A = 200 - 2Q_A = 130.2 \qquad \text{(when } Q_A = 34.9)$$

And, the marginal revenue of product B is

$$MR_B = dTR_B/dQ_B = 150 - 4Q_B = 10.4 \qquad \text{(when } Q_B = 34.9)$$

Since both marginal revenues (MR_A and MR_B) are nonnegative when Q_A and $Q_B = 34.9$, the assumption underlying the analysis is valid.[10]

Output of Joint Products: Variable Proportions

Having discussed the case where two joint products are produced in fixed proportions, we turn to the case in which they are produced in variable proportions. This generally is the more realistic case, particularly if one is considering a fairly long period of time. Even in the case of cattle, the proportions of hides and beef can be altered because cattle can be bred to produce more or less beef relative to hide.

---

[10]If one product's marginal revenue had been negative when Q_A and Q_B equaled 34.9, the optimal solution would have involved producing more of this product than is sold, as indicated in Figure 11.6. The firm would sell only the amount of this product where the marginal revenue is zero. The marginal revenue for the other product would be used to determine its optimal amount level, as shown in Figure 11.6.

FIGURE
11.7

Optimal Outputs for Joint Products Produced in Variable Proportions

The optimal point, which must be at a point where an isorevenue line is tangent to an isocost curve, is at point *M*, where profit per day is $7,000.

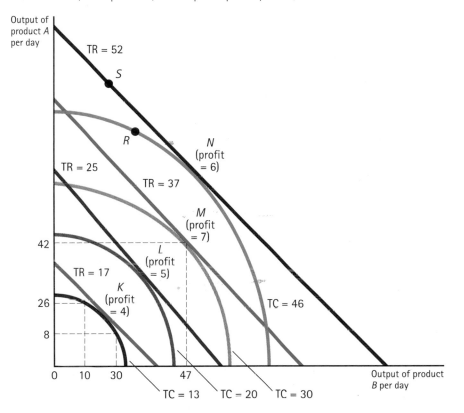

Suppose a firm produces and sells two products, *A* and *B*, and that each isocost curve (labeled TC in Figure 11.7) shows the amounts of these goods that can be produced at the same total cost. The isocost curve labeled TC = 13 shows the various combinations of outputs—for example, 26 units of product *A* and 10 units of product *B* or 8 units of product *A* and 30 units of product *B*—that can be produced at a total cost of $13.00 per day.

Also included in Figure 11.7 are isorevenue lines (labeled TR), each of which shows the combinations of outputs of the two products that yield the same total revenue. For example, the isorevenue line labeled TR = 52 shows the various combinations of outputs, such as those corresponding to points *S* or *N*—that yield a total revenue of $52,000 per day. Other isorevenue lines show the output combinations that yield total revenues of $17,000, $25,000, and $37,000, respectively.

The problem facing the manager is to determine how much of products *A* and *B* to produce. The first step toward solving this problem is to observe that, if an output combination is at a point where an isorevenue line is *not* tangent to an isocost curve, it *cannot* be the optimal output combination. To see this, note that, if an output combination is at a point where an isorevenue line is not tangent to an isocost curve (say, point *R*), it is possible to increase revenue (without changing cost) by moving to a point (on the same isocost curve) where an isorevenue line *is* tangent to the isocost curve (say point *N*). Therefore, any output combination that is not at a tangency point cannot be the profit-maximizing output combination, since we indicated how profit can be increased if the firm is at such a nontangency point.

Given that this is the case, we find the optimal output combination by comparing the profit level at each tangency point and choosing the point where the profit level is the highest. For example, four tangency points are shown in Figure 11.7—points *K*, *L*, *M*, and *N*. As indicated in Figure 11.7, the profit levels corresponding to these four points are $4,000, $5,000, $7,000, and $6,000, respectively. So, if we must choose among the output combinations on the isocost curves in Figure 11.7, the optimal output combination for this firm is point *M*, where the firm produces and sells 42 units of product *A* and 47 units of product *B* per day and makes profits of $7,000.

Monopolistic Competition

Having taken up perfect competition and monopoly, we turn to monopolistic competition. The central feature of monopolistic competition is *product differentiation*. Unlike perfect competition, in which all firms sell an identical product, firms under monopolistic competition sell somewhat different products. In many parts of retail trade, producers try to make their product a little different, by altering the product's physical makeup, the services they offer, and other variables. Eddie Bauer's shirts are not *exactly* the same as those from Land's End, but they are not too dissimilar either. Because of the differences among their products, producers have some control over their price, but it usually is small, because the products of other firms are very similar to their own.

Under perfect competition, the firms included in an industry are easy to determine because all produce an identical product. But if product differentiation exists, it is no longer simple to define an industry, because each firm produces a somewhat different product. Nevertheless, it may be useful to group together firms that produce similar products and call them a *product group*. We can formulate a product group called *neckties*, or *toothbrushes*, or *shirts*. The process by which we combine firms into product groups must be somewhat arbitrary, since there is no way to decide how close a pair of substitutes must be to belong to the same product group. But it is assumed that meaningful product groups can be established. Clearly, the broader is the definition of the product group, the greater the number of firms included.

In addition to product differentiation, other conditions must be met for an industry to qualify as a case of monopolistic competition.

1. *There must be a large number of firms in the product group*. The product must be produced by perhaps 50 to 100 or more firms, with each firm's product a fairly close substitute for the products of the other firms in the product group.

2. *The number of firms in the product group must be large enough that each firm expects its actions to go unheeded by its rivals and unimpeded by possible retaliatory moves on their part*. Hence, when formulating their own policies with regard to price and output, they do not explicitly concern themselves with their rivals' responses. If there are a large number of firms, this condition normally is met.

3. *Entry into the product group must be relatively easy, and there must be no collusion, such as price fixing or market sharing, among firms in the product group*. If there are a large number of firms, it generally is difficult, if not impossible, for them to collude.

Price and Output Decisions under Monopolistic Competition

If each firm produces a somewhat different product, it follows that the demand curve facing each firm slopes downward to the right. That is, if the firm raises its price slightly, it will lose some, but by no means all, its customers to other firms. And, if it lowers its price slightly, it will gain some, but by no means all, of its competitors' customers.

Figure 11.8 shows the short-run equilibrium of a monopolistically competitive firm. The firm, in the short run, will set its price at P_0 and its output rate at Q_0, since this combination of price and output maximizes its profits. We can be sure that this combination of price and output maximizes profits because marginal cost equals marginal revenue at this output level. Economic profits are earned because price, P_0, exceeds average total cost, C_0, at this output level. As in the case of monopoly and prefect competition, price must exceed average variable cost for profits to be maximized (which they clearly do in Figure 11.8, since average variable cost lies below average total cost).

One condition for long-run equilibrium is that each firm makes no economic profits or losses, since entry or exit of firms occur otherwise—and entry and

FIGURE
11.8

Short–Run Equilibrium in Monopolistic Competition

The firm will set its price at P_0 and its output rate at Q_0, since marginal cost equals marginal revenue at this output. It will earn a profit of P_0C_0 per unit of output.

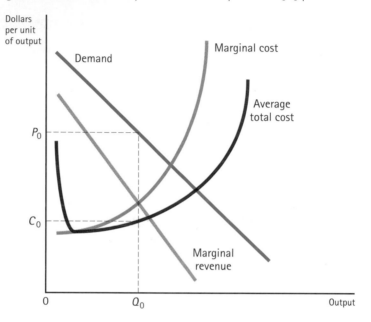

exit are incompatible with long-run equilibrium. Another condition for long-run equilibrium is that each firm maximize its profits. At what price and output are both these conditions fulfilled? Figure 11.9 shows that the long run equilibrium is at a price of P_1 and an output of Q_1. The zero-economic-profit condition is met at this combination of price and output, since the firm's average cost at this output equals the price, P_1. And the profit maximization condition is met, since the marginal revenue curve intersects the marginal cost curve at this output rate.[11]

Advertising Expenditures: A Simple Rule

Firms under monopolistic competition, as well as other market structures, spend huge amounts on advertising. How much should a profit-maximizing firm spend on advertising? In this section, a simple rule is derived that helps a manager

[11]The seminal work in the theory of monopolistic competition was E. Chamberlin, *The Theory of Monopolistic Competition* (Cambridge, MA: Harvard University Press, 1933).

FIGURE
11.9

Long-Run Equilibrium in Monopolistic Competition

The long-run equilibrium is at price P_1 and output Q_1. There are zero profits, since long-run average cost equals price. Profits are maximized, since marginal cost equals marginal revenue at this output.

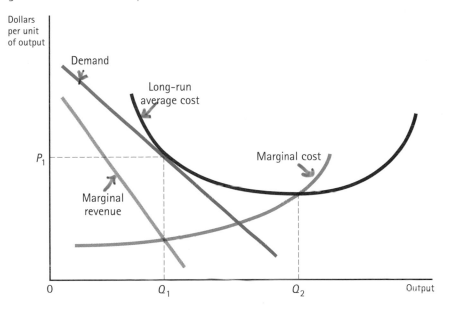

answer this question.[12] The quantity a firm sells of its product is assumed to be a function of its price and the level of its advertising expenditures. There are assumed to be diminishing marginal returns to advertising expenditures, which means that, beyond some point, successive increments of advertising outlays yield smaller and smaller increases in additional sales. (Table 11.4 shows an illustrative case in which successive increments of $100,000 in advertising outlays result in smaller and smaller increases in quantity sold. For example, the quantity sold increases by 2 million units when advertising expenditures rise from $800,000 to $900,000, but by only 1.5 million units when they rise from $900,000 to $1 million).

Let P be the price of a unit of the product and MC the marginal cost of production. If we assume that neither price nor marginal cost is altered by small changes in advertising expenditure, the firm receives an increase in gross profit of $(P - MC)$ from each additional unit of product that it makes and sells. Why

[12]This rule, put forth by R. Dorfman and P. Steiner, applies to monopolistic or oligopolistic (see Chapter 13) firms as well as monopolistically competitive firms.

TABLE
11.4

Relationship between Advertising Expenditures and Quantity

Advertising expenditures (millions of dollars)	Quantity sold of product (millions of units)
0.8	15.0
0.9	17.0
1.0	18.5
1.1	19.5
1.2	20.0

is this the *gross* profit of making and selling an additional unit of output? Because it takes no account of whatever additional advertising expenditures are required to sell this extra unit of output. To obtain the net profit, the firm must deduct these additional advertising outlays from the gross profit.

To maximize total net profits a manager must set advertising expenditures at the level where an extra dollar of advertising results in extra gross profit equal to the extra dollar of advertising cost. Unless this is the case, the firm's total net profits can be increased by changing its advertising outlays. If an extra dollar of advertising results in more than a dollar increase in gross profit, the extra dollar should be spent on advertising (since this raises the total net profits). If the extra dollar (as well as the last dollar) of advertising results in less than a dollar increase in gross profit, advertising outlays should be cut.[13] Therefore, if ΔQ is the number of extra units of output sold as a result of an extra dollar of advertising, the firm should set its advertising expenditures so that

$$\Delta Q(P - MC) = 1 \tag{11.17}$$

because the right-hand side of this equation equals the extra dollar of advertising cost and the left-hand side equals the extra gross profit resulting from this advertising dollar.

If we multiply both sides of equation (11.17) by $P/(P - MC)$, we obtain

$$P\Delta Q = P/(P - MC) \tag{11.18}$$

---

[13]For simplicity, we assume that the gross profit resulting from an extra dollar spent on advertising is essentially equal to the gross profit resulting from the last dollar spent. This is an innocuous assumption.

Because the firm is maximizing profit, it is producing an output where marginal cost (MC) equals marginal revenue (MR). Therefore, we can substitute MR for MC in equation (11.18), the result being

$$P\Delta Q = P/(P - MR) \tag{11.19}$$

Using equation (3.16), it can be shown that the right-hand side of equation (11.19) equals $-\eta$, the negative of the price elasticity of demand for the firm's product.[14] The left-hand side of equation (11.19) is the marginal revenue from an extra dollar of advertising (since it equals the price times the extra number of units sold as a result of an extra dollar of advertising). To maximize profit, the manager should set advertising expenditure so that

$$\text{Marginal revenue from an extra dollar of advertising} = -\eta \tag{11.20}$$

This rule can be very helpful to managers.[15] Consider the Ishimine Corporation, which knows that the price elasticity of demand for its product equals -1.6. To maximize profit, this firm must set the marginal revenue from an extra dollar of advertising equal to 1.6, according to the rule in equation (11.20). Suppose Ishimine's managers believe that an extra $100,000 of advertising would increase the firm's sales by $200,000, which implies that the marginal revenue from an extra dollar of advertising is about $200,000/$100,000, or 2.0 rather than 1.6. Because the marginal revenue exceeds the negative of the price elasticity, Ishimine increases its profit if it does more advertising.[16] To maximize profit, it should increase its advertising up to the point where the marginal revenue from an extra dollar of advertising falls to 1.6, that is, the negative of the value of the price elasticity of demand.

Using Graphs to Help Determine Advertising Expenditure

A simple graphical technique can be used to see how much a firm, if it uses the preceding rule, should spend on advertising. Take the case of the Hertzfeld

---

[14]Recall from equation (3.16) that $MR = P[1 + (1/\eta)]$. Therefore, $[1 + (1/\eta)] = MR/P$ and $-1/\eta = 1 - (MR/P)$; this means that

$$-\eta = 1/[1 - (MR/P)] = P/(P - MR)$$

which is the right-hand side of equation (11.19).

[15]However, this rule is based on many simplifying assumptions and is not a complete solution to this complex problem.

[16]Had Ishimine's managers believed that the marginal revenue from an extra dollar of advertising was *less* than the price elasticity of demand, a *reduction* in the firms' advertising expenditures would increase profit.

FIGURE 11.10

Optimal Advertising Expenditure

The firm's optimal advertising expenditure is *R* if the marginal revenue curve is *B* (or *S* if the marginal revenue curve is *B'*).

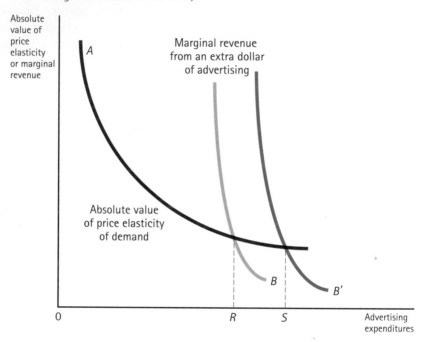

Chemical Company. Curve *A* in Figure 11.10 shows the relationship between the price elasticity of demand of this firm's product and the amount it spends on advertising. With little or no advertising, this firm's product would be regarded by consumers as similar to lots of other products; hence, its price elasticity of demand would be very high (in absolute value).

But, since appropriate advertising can induce consumers to attach importance to this product's distinguishing features, increases in advertising expenditure reduce its price elasticity (in absolute value) considerably (by decreasing the product's perceived substitutability with other goods).[17] At each level of advertising expenditure, the *B* curve shows the marginal revenue from an extra dollar of advertising. Since the *A* curve intersects the *B* curve when Hertzfeld's advertising expenditure is *R* dollars, this, on the basis of equation (11.20), is the level of advertising expenditures that maximizes Hertzfeld's profits.

---

[17]This is true for some products, but not for others. In some cases, the absolute value of price elasticity of demand is directly, not inversely related to the amount spent on advertising.

A firm's optimal advertising expenditure depends on the position and shape of its B curve and its A curve. For example, suppose Hertzfeld's B curve shifts rightward to B^*, as shown in Figure 11.10. Such a shift might occur if the firm or its advertising agency found ways to increase the effectiveness of its advertisements. An increase in the optimal level of the firm's advertising expenditures (to S dollars in Figure 11.10) would be the result.

Advertising, Price Elasticity, and Brand Equity: Evidence on Managerial Behavior

Promotions and advertising tend to be two sides of the same coin. While they both seek to improve market performance, promotions appeal to the price sensitive, while ads build brand loyalty. Promotions use a price-oriented message to test the limits of brand loyalty; advertising illuminates brand worth and does not mention price. Both strategies persuade purchase by influencing the price sensitivities of consumers. Promotions increase price elasticity and, in the long run, work to limit the price consumers are willing to pay for brand quality. Understanding their effects on consumer behavior certainly helps managers better understand the consequences of their actions.

So, can we find "real-world" evidence on the effectiveness of these strategies? Yes. A large body of evidence shows that promotions do increase the price elasticities of consumers.[18] These studies also show the change in elasticities varies across consumers and time. Brand loyalty does protect against promotions. Promotional strategies have less of an effect on the elasticities of brand loyalists relative to the nonloyalists. And, promotion is characterized as decaying in time. Short-term change is greater, as if consumers operate with a high discount rate. Or, they may have short memories. Like Pavlov's dog, they respond to promotion but only if prompted.

Mela et al. report on a mature good market where the ratio of advertising to promotions shifted from spending $250 million on advertising and offering promotions less than 10 percent of the time to spending less than $100 million on advertising and giving discounts more than 25 percent of the time. They found the price elasticity of the average nonloyalist was twice that of the average brand loyalist. Loyalty is measured as frequency of repeat purchases. A drop in advertising messages, affects all consumers, but the effect is much greater on the nonloyal crowd. In fact, a drop in advertising leads to a larger number

---

[18]K. Pauwells, D. Hanssens, and S. Siddarth. "The Long-Term Effects of Price Promotions on Category Incidence, Brand Choice, and Purchase Quantity," *Journal of Marketing Research*, Vol. 39, November 2002, 421–436. C. Mela, S. Gupta, and D. Lehmann. "The Long-Term Impact of Promotion and Advertising on Consumer Brand Choice," *Journal of Marketing Research*, Vol. 34, May 1997, 248–262.

of nonloyalists. Without reinforcement, the brand is eroded by the price. Frequent promotions encourage the nonloyalists to look for them, so their price sensitivities increase. The effect of promotions on the price sensitivity of nonloyalists is four times that of loyalists.

Pauwels et al. report on the soup and yogurt markets. They study buying habits over a two-year period by analyzing the purchase of over 690,000 ounces of yogurt and 535,000 ounces of soup. In both markets, they find the effects of promotion on price sensitivities is the greatest within the two-week period following its announcement. After this initial time period, the effect gets weaker. The frequency of promotions also varies across firms, as does the amount of the discount. The findings indicated that promotions are used more frequently by managers whose brand is weaker.

Summary

1. Under monopoly, a firm maximizes profit if it sets its output rate at the point where marginal revenue equals marginal cost. It does not follow that a firm that holds a monopoly over the production of a particular product must make a profit. If the monopolist cannot cover its variable costs, it, like a perfectly competitive firm, will shut down, even in the short run.

2. An industry that is monopolized generally sets a higher price and a lower output than if it were perfectly competitive. The perfectly competitive firm operates at a point at which price equals marginal cost, whereas the monopolist operates at a point at which marginal revenue equals marginal cost (and price exceeds marginal cost).

3. Empirical studies indicate that cost-plus pricing is used by many firms. In this approach, the firm estimates the cost per unit of output of the product (based on some assumed output level) and adds a markup to include costs that cannot be allocated to any specific product and to provide a return on the firm's investment. On the surface, it is questionable whether this approach can maximize profit, but if marginal cost (not average cost) is really what is being marked up and the size of the markup is determined (in the appropriate way) by the product's price elasticity of demand, cost-plus pricing can result in profit maximization.

4. Firms generally sell more than one product. It is important for managers to recognize the demand interrelationships among the products they sell. Also, a firm's products are often interrelated in production. If two products are produced jointly in fixed proportions, the profit maximizing output is where the total marginal revenue curve (the vertical summation of the marginal revenue curves for the individual products) intersects the marginal cost curve for the bundle of products, assuming that the marginal revenue of each product is nonnegative.

MANAGERIAL ECONOMICS IN CONTEXT

A Rocky Road for Caterpillar Tractor

For decades, Caterpillar Tractor Company has been regarded as the leader in the world market for earth-moving equipment, a market dominated by relatively few firms. It makes products of very high quality. As one of its vice presidents once said, "Market share for us is not an objective. Building sophisticated, durable, reliable products and providing good support is." The firm also invests heavily in advanced automation to reduce its costs. Noted for its conservative financial policies, it has been well respected by Wall Street, its customers, and its competitors.

With regard to its pricing, Caterpillar traditionally charged more than its rivals. For example, in 1981, Lee Morgan, Caterpillar's chairman, compared his firm's prices with those of Komatsu (Caterpillar's leading rival) in the following terms: "Komatsu's products are priced at least 10 to 15 percent below Caterpillar's. That says clearly what they believe our value is versus theirs." In other words, Caterpillar's managers felt that their products were sufficiently superior to that of their rivals to warrant their charging a premium price.

In the early 1980s, the dollar became very strong relative to the Japanese yen, and as a result Komatsu, a Japanese firm, could sell its products at prices that Caterpillar found difficult to meet. Moreover, the recession in the United States caused Caterpillar's U.S. customers to emphasize its price disadvantage. As one of Caterpillar's customers stated in 1982, "Work's going cheap in our business, so we're looking particularly hard at costs." For these and other reasons, Caterpillar's sales fell by about 29 percent in 1982, and it experienced a $180 million loss. As Lee Morgan put it, "It seemed like we were in a free fall. If I had any personal despair, it was coming in every morning and wondering if we would ever hit bottom."

In 1983, Caterpillar began to change its pricing policy. To become more competitive, it offered price discounts. Its rival, Komatsu, priced to expand its market share and operated with very tight profit margins (about 4 to 5 percent of sales). Caterpillar felt it had to become more competitive with respect to price. To do so, the firm embarked on a major cost-reduction program, including cuts in blue-collar and white-collar employment. During 1983–84, plans were announced to close six plants. By 1985, the company was back in the black (see the table).

In 1987, Caterpillar's chairman stated:

We recognized that our industry was faced with substantial overcapacity, and that there would be tremendous price pressure on our products. . . . We've priced our products competitively on a value basis and offered special incentive programs to enhance the marketing effects of our dealers—perhaps at the sacrifice of some short-term profitability for longer-term improved results.

Sales and Profits, Caterpillar Tractor Company, 1981–1996 (Billions of Dollars)

	1996	1995	1993	1991	1989	1987	1985	1983	1981
Sales	16.5	16.0	11.6	10.2	11.1	8.2	6.7	5.4	9.2
Profits	1.4	1.1	0.7	−0.4	0.6	0.3	0.2	−0.3	0.6

During the late 1980s, Caterpillar continued its worldwide effort to improve productivity and cut costs. In 1987, the company started a $2.1 billion program to modernize its production facilities, called Plant with a Future. Flexible manufacturing systems (recall page 439) were installed. In 1990, Caterpillar eliminated layers of managers and organized itself into 17 profit centers. Nonetheless, because of the recession in the United States and elsewhere, as well as a strike and lockout at the firm, Caterpillar lost money in 1991 and 1992.

In 1993, the firm's sales rose considerably as a weak dollar made it hard for Komatsu to compete and as the U.S. economy recovered. Profits at Caterpillar increased greatly from 1993 to 1996. However, labor relations at the firm were a problem. Although the union (the United Auto Workers) returned to work in late 1995 after a tough 18-month strike, its members did not ratify the contract Caterpillar offered and in 1997 were working without a contract.

(a) What sort of market structure exists in the tractor industry?

(b) Does Caterpillar use cost-plus pricing? Why or why not?

(c) In 1981, did Caterpillar set its prices to deter entry?

(d) Was Caterpillar minimizing its cost in 1981 and 1982?

(e) According to Caterpillar's chairman, "New designs, new materials, new technology, and increased attention to 'manufacturability' are providing substantial cost reduction with further gains in quality and performance." Up to what point is it worthwhile to spend money on such technical improvements?

(f) As pointed out, Caterpillar's chairman also stated that, in its pricing and marketing strategy, the company may have sacrificed "some short-term profitability for longer-term improved results." Is this always wise? Under what conditions is it wise policy?

(g) In 1991, the average hourly worker represented by the United Auto Workers at Caterpillar earned $31.74 per hour. The firm asked for wage concessions to reduce its costs. On November 4, 1991, the union struck two of the firm's plants; four days later, the firm closed several more. In April 1992, after a five-month strike, the workers agreed to return to work on terms regarded as favorable to the firm. In 1994, the union struck once again, and managers, supervisors, and other white-collar employees began working on Caterpillar's assembly lines. Some observers said that the firm was trying to exert pressure on union leaders to force them to negotiate issues that would lower labor costs. What effect would this have on the firm's pricing?*

*For further discussion, see H. Bartlett, *Cases in Strategic Management for Business* (Fort Worth, TX: Dryden Press, 1988); Caterpillar's Annual Reports; *New York Times,* April 16, 1992, and June 24, 1994; and *Business Week,* July 4, 1994, and January 20, 1997.

5. If two products are produced jointly in variable proportions, one can construct isocost curves, each of which shows the combinations of outputs that can be produced at the same total cost. Also, isorevenue lines can be constructed, each of which shows the combination of outputs that yield the same total revenue. For an output combination to be optimal, it must be at a point where an isorevenue line is tangent to an isocost curve. To deter-

mine which output combination is optimal, one compares the profit levels at the tangency points. The tangency point where profit is the highest is the optimal output combination.

6. In contrast to perfect competition, where all firms sell an identical product, firms under monopolistic competition sell somewhat different products. Producers differentiate their product from that of other producers. Therefore, the demand curve facing each firm slopes downward to the right—and is not horizontal, as it would be under perfect competition. Each firm sets marginal revenue equal to marginal cost if it maximizes profit.

7. Monopolistically competitive firms spend very large amounts on advertising. To maximize its profits, a firm should set its advertising so that the marginal revenue from an extra dollar of advertising equals the negative of its price elasticity of demand (under the conditions discussed).

8. Advertising of price changes may make the price elasticity of demand for the product whose price has changed more elastic. This is because the advertising makes consumers more aware of the price changes. Measures of brand loyalty are useful in guiding decisions concerning promotional activities to increase sales of particular brands.

Problems

1. Harry Smith is the owner of a metals-producing firm that is an unregulated monopoly. After considerable experimentation and research, he finds that its marginal cost curve can be approximated by a straight line, $MC = 60 + 2Q$, where MC is marginal cost (in dollars), and Q is output. The demand curve for the product is $P - 100 - Q$, where P is the product price (in dollars) and Q is output.

   a. If he wants to maximize profit, what output should he choose?

   b. What price should he charge?

2. The Wilson Company's marketing manager has determined that the price elasticity of demand for its product equals -2.2. According to studies he carried out, the relationship between the amount spent by the firm on advertising and its sales is as follows:

Advertising expenditure	Sales
$100,000	$1.0 million
200,000	1.3 million
300,000	1.5 million
400,000	1.6 million

   a. If the Wilson Company spends $200,000 on advertising, what is the marginal revenue from an extra dollar of advertising?

442 | Chapter 11   Monopoly and Monopolistic Competition

b. Is $200,000 the optimal amount for the firm to spend on advertising?

c. If $200,000 is not the optimal amount, would you recommend that the firm spend more or less on advertising?

3. The Coolidge Corporation is the only producer of a particular type of laser. The demand curve for its product is

$$Q_D = 8,300 - 2.1P$$

and its total cost function is

$$TC = 2,200 + 480Q + 20Q^2$$

where P is price (in dollars), TC is total cost (in dollars), and Q is monthly output.

a. Derive an expression for the firm's marginal revenue curve.

b. To maximize profit, how many lasers should the firm produce and sell per month?

c. If this number were produced and sold, what would be the firm's monthly profit?

4. The Madison Corporation, a monopolist, receives a report from a consulting firm concluding that the demand function for its product is

$$Q = 78 - 1.1P + 2.3Y + 0.9A$$

where Q is the number of units sold, P is the price of its product (in dollars), Y is per capita income (in thousands of dollars), and A is the firm's advertising expenditure (in thousands of dollars). The firm's average variable cost function is

$$AVC - 42 \quad 8Q + 1.5Q^2$$

where AVC is average variable cost (in dollars).

a. Can one determine the firm's marginal cost curve?

b. Can one determine the firm's marginal revenue curve?

c. If per capita income is $4,000 and advertising expenditure is $200,000, can one determine the price and output where marginal revenue equals marginal cost? If so, what are they?

5. The Wilcox Company has two plants with the marginal cost functions[19]

$$MC_1 = 20 + 2Q_1$$
$$MC_2 = 10 + 5Q_2$$

---

[19]This question pertains to the chapter appendix.

where MC_1 is marginal cost in the first plant, MC_2 is marginal cost in the second plant, Q_1 is output in the first plant, and Q_2 is output in the second plant.

    a. If the Wilcox Company minimizes its costs and produces five units of output in the first plant, how many units of output does it produce in the second plant? Explain.

    b. What is the marginal cost function for the firm as a whole?

    c. Can you determine from these data the average cost function for each plant? Why or why not?

6. If the Rhine Company ignores the possibility that other firms may enter its market, it should set a price of $10,000 for its product, which is a power tool. But, if it does so, other firms will begin to enter the market. During the next two years, it will earn $4 million per year, but in the following two years, it will earn $1 million per year. On the other hand, if it sets a price of $7,000, it will earn $2.5 million in each of the next four years, since no entrants will appear.

    a. If the interest rate is 10 percent, should the Rhine Company set a price of $7,000 or $10,000? Why? (Consider only the next four years.)

    b. If the interest rate is 8 percent, should the Rhine Company set a price of $7,000 or $10,000? Why? (Consider only the next four years.)

    c. The results in parts a and b pertain to only the next four years. How can the firm's managers extend the planning horizon?

7. During recessions and economic hard times, many people—particularly those who have difficulty getting bank loans—turn to pawnshops to raise cash. But, even during boom years, pawnshops can be very profitable. Because the collateral that customers put up (such as jewelry, guns, or electric guitars) is generally worth at least double what is lent, it generally can be sold at a profit. And because the usury laws allow higher interest ceilings for pawnshops than for other lending institutions, pawnshops often charge spectacularly high rates of interest. For example, Florida's pawnshops charge interest rates of 20 percent or more *per month*. According to Steven Kent, an analyst at Goldman, Sachs, pawnshops make 20 percent gross profit on defaulted loans and 205 percent interest on loans repaid.

    a. In late 1991, there were about 8,000 pawnshops in the United States, according to American Business Information. This was much higher than in 1986, when the number was about 5,000. Indeed, in late 1991 alone, the number jumped by about 1,000. Why did the number increase?

    b. In a particular small city, do the pawnshops constitute a perfectly competitive industry? If not, what is the market structure of the industry?

    c. Are there considerable barriers to entry in the pawnshop industry? (Note: A pawnshop can be opened for less than $125,000, but a number of states have tightened licensing requirements for pawnshops.)

8. In 1996, dairy farmers, hurt by a decade of low milk prices, began reducing their herds. Subsequently, Kenneth Hein, a Wisconsin farmer, said he was getting $16 per 100 pounds of milk, rather than $12, which he had gotten earlier.[20]
   a. Why did the price increase?
   b. Dairy cattle are often fed corn. When Mr. Hein got $16 per 100 pounds of milk, he paid $5 a bushel for corn; but when he got $12 per 100 pounds of milk, he paid $2.50 a bushel for corn. Does this mean that Mr. Hein made less money when the price of milk was $16 than when it was $12?

9. The demand for diamonds is given by

$$P_Z = 980 - 2Q_Z$$

where Q_Z is the number of diamonds demanded if the price is P_Z per diamond. The total cost (TC_Z) of the De Beers Company (a monopolist) is given by

$$TC_Z = 100 + 50Q_Z + 0.5Q_Z^2$$

where Q_Z is the number of diamonds produced and put on the market by the De Beers Company. Suppose that the government could force De Beers to behave as if it were a perfect competitor; that is, via regulation, force the firm to price diamonds at marginal cost.
   a. What is social welfare when De Beers acts as a single price monopolist?
   b. What is social welfare when De Beers acts as a perfect competitor?
   c. How much does social welfare increase when De Beers moves from monopoly to competition?

10. The Hassman Company produces two joint products, X and Y. The isocost curve corresponding to a total cost of $500,000 is

$$Q_Y = 1,000 - 10Q_X - 5Q_X^2$$

where Q_Y is the quantity of product Y produced by the firm and Q_X is the quantity of product X produced. The price of product X is 50 times that of product Y.
   a. If the optimum output combination lies on this isocost curve, what is the optimal output of product X?
   b. What is the optimal output of product Y?
   c. Can you be sure that the optimum output combination lies on this isocost curve? Why or why not?

[20]*Philadelphia Inquirer*, September 14, 1996.

11. The McDermott Company estimates its average total cost to be $10 per unit of output when it produces 10,000 units, which it regards as 80 percent of capacity. Its goal is to earn 20 percent on its total investment, which is $250,000.
    a. If the company uses cost-plus pricing, what price should it set?
    b. Can it be sure of selling 10,000 units if it sets this price?
    c. What are the arguments for and against a pricing policy of this sort?

12. The Morrison Company produces tennis rackets, the marginal cost of a racket being $20. Since there are many substitutes for the firm's rackets, the price elasticity of demand for its rackets equals about −2. In the relevant range of output, average variable cost is very close to marginal cost.
    a. The president of the Morrison Company feels that cost-plus pricing is appropriate for his firm. He marks up average variable cost by 100 percent to get price. Comment on this procedure.
    b. Because of heightened competition, the price elasticity of demand for the firm's rackets increases to −3. The president continues to use the same cost-plus pricing formula as before. Comment on its adequacy.

13. The Backus Corporation makes two products, X and Y. For every unit of good X that the firm produces, it produces two units of good Y. Backus's total cost function is

$$TC = 500 + 3Q + 9Q^2$$

where Q is the number of units of output (where each unit contains one unit of good X and two units of good Y) and TC is total cost (in dollars). The demand curves for the firm's two products are

$$P_X = 400 - Q_X$$
$$P_Y = 300 - 3Q_Y$$

where P_X and Q_X are the price and output of product X and P_Y and Q_Y are the price and output of product Y.
    a. How much of each product should the Backus Corporation produce and sell per period of time?
    b. What price should it charge for each product?

Appendix: Allocation of Output among Plants

Many firms own and operate more than one plant. In this appendix, we show how the managers of these firms should allocate output among various plants. This is an important decision, and our results have major direct practical value. We consider the case of the Johnson Company, a monopolist, but our results are valid for any firm that exercises market power.

The Johnson Company, a monopolist that makes a particular type of fixture, operates two plants with marginal cost curves shown in columns 2 and 3

TABLE
11.5

Costs of the Johnson Company

Output per hour	Marginal cost[a]		Marginal cost for firm[a] (dollars)	Price (dollars)	Marginal revenue[a] (dollars)
	Plant I (dollars)	Plant II (dollars)			
1	10	14	10	40	—
2	12	18	12	30	20
3	14	22	14	26	18
4	20	26	14	23	14
5	24	30	18	20.8	12

[a]These figures pertain to the interval between the indicated output and one unit less than the indicated output.

of Table 11.5, output being shown in column 1. Clearly, if the firm decides to produce only one unit of output per hour, it should use plant I, since the marginal cost between 0 and 1 unit of output is lower in plant I than in plant II. Hence, for the firm as a whole, the marginal cost between 0 and 1 unit of output is $10 (the marginal cost between 0 and 1 unit for plant I). Similarly, if the plant decides to produce two units of output per hour, both should be produced in plant I, and the marginal cost between the first and second unit of output for the firm as a whole is $12 (the marginal cost between the first and second unit in plant I). If the firm decides to produce three units of output per hour, two should be produced in plant I and one in plant II, and the marginal cost between the second and third unit of output for the firm as a whole is $14 (the marginal cost between 0 and 1 unit of output for plant II). Alternatively, all three could be produced at plant I (as the marginal cost between the second unit and the third unit of output in plant I is also $14).

Going on in this way, we can derive the marginal cost curve for the firm as a whole, shown in column 4 of Table 11.5. To maximize profits, the manager should find that output at which marginal revenue equals the marginal cost of the firm as a whole. This is the profit-maximizing output level. In this case, it is three or four units per hour. Suppose that the firm picks four units.[21]

---

[21]The firm is indifferent between producing three or four units. If it produces four, its total revenue is $92,000 (i.e., 23 × 4) and its variable cost is $50,000 (i.e., 10 + 12 + 14 + 14), yielding a variable cost profit of $42,000. If it produces three, then the total revenue is $78,000 (i.e., 26 × 3) and the variable cost is $36,000 (i.e., 10 + 12 + 14), yielding a variable cost profit of $42,000. Since both plants already exist, their fixed costs must be paid and, therefore, are irrelevant in the short run. In the long run (if demand were predicted to remain constant), the firm could divest itself of plant II.

To determine what price to charge, the firm must see what price corresponds to this output on the demand curve. In this case, the answer is $23.

At this point, we solved most of the Johnson Company's problems, but not quite all. Given that it will produce four units of output per hour, how should it divide this production between the two plants? The answer is that it should set the marginal cost in plant I equal to the marginal cost in plant II. Table 11.5 shows this means that plant I would produce three units per hour and plant II would produce one unit per hour. The common value of the marginal costs of the two plants is the marginal cost of the firm as a whole: this common value must be set equal to the marginal revenue if the firm maximizes profit.

Many firms use this technique to allocate output among plants. For example, electric power companies developed computer programs to facilitate the actual job of allocating electricity demand (or "load") among plants in accord with this theoretical rule. These programs allow a central dispatcher, who is in constant communication with the plants, to compute quickly the optimal allocation among plants. The result has been millions of dollars of savings.

As a further illustration, consider the Chou Company, which has plants at Altoona, Pennsylvania, and at High Point, North Carolina. The total cost function for the Altoona plant is

$$TC_A = 5 + 9Q_A + Q_A^2$$

where TC_A is the daily total cost (in thousands of dollars) at this plant and Q_A is its output (in units per day). The total cost curve for the High Point plant is

$$TC_H = 4 + 10Q_H + 0.5Q_{H}^2$$

where TC_H is the daily total cost (in thousands of dollars) at this plant, and Q_H is its output (in units per day).

The Chou Company's demand curve is

$$P = 31 - Q$$

and its total revenue is

$$TR = PQ = (31 - Q)Q = 31Q - Q^2$$

Therefore, the Chou Company's marginal revenue curve is

$$MR = dTR/dQ = 31 - 2Q$$

Note that $Q = Q_A + Q_H$, P is price, and MR is the marginal revenue (both in thousands of dollars per unit).

To maximize profit, the firm must choose its price and output such that

$$MC_A = MC_H = MR \qquad (11.21)$$

where MC_A is the marginal cost (in thousands of dollars) at the Altoona plant and MC_H is the marginal cost (in thousands of dollars) at the High Point plant. The Altoona plant's marginal cost is

$$MC_A = dTC_A/dQ_A = 9 + 2Q_A$$

The High Point plant's marginal cost is

$$MC_H = dTC_H/dQ_H = 10 + Q_H$$

According to equation (11.21), MC_A must equal MC_H. Therefore,

$$9 + 2Q_A = 10 + Q_H$$

or

$$Q_H = -1 + 2Q_A$$

Also, because equation (11.21) states that MC_A must equal MR,

$$\begin{aligned} 9 + 2Q_A &= 31 - 2(Q_A + Q_H) \\ &= 31 - 2(Q_A - 1 + 2Q_A) \\ &= 33 - 6Q_A \end{aligned}$$

or

$$8Q_A = 24$$

Consequently, $Q_A = 3$. And, since $Q_H = -1 + 2Q_A$, it follows that $Q_H = 5$. Moreover, $P = 23$, because $P = 31 - (Q_A + Q_H)$. Put in a nutshell, the Chou Company should charge a price of \$23,000 per unit and produce three units per day at its Altoona plant and five units per day at its High Point plant.

Sophisticated
Monopoly Pricing

The market demand curve is the monopolist's demand curve. It would seem that the monopolist, with full reign over this demand curve, could come up with a better strategy than charging just one price. Indeed, monopolists have. While Chapter 11 shows the best single price for a monopolist to charge *if* it is charging one price, this chapter explores the profit enhancing possibilities if the monopolist charges *multiple* prices, bundles its product so it sells multiple units, or prices the product internally to other divisions of the same firm. Monopolists may not choose to sell their product for multiple prices because the costs of doing so exceed the generated additional revenues. However, given the incidence of sophisticated pricing by firms and our assumption of firm rationality, we can assume that the benefits of following these sophisticated pricing policies exceed the costs in a number of cases.

A car dealership (except Saturn) aims to sell each vehicle for the highest price it can get (subject to that price being higher than its reservation price). Airlines segment their markets and sell the same seats at vastly different prices depending on when you purchase, whether you stay over Saturday night, whether the tickets are refundable, whether you can change your travel plans, and the like. In general, they separate their demand function into classes—

roughly, a relatively price-insensitive business class and a relatively price-sensitive leisure class. The car dealership is an example of first-degree price discrimination, where the dealer attempts to extract the reservation price of each buyer. Airlines are an example of third-degree price discrimination, where the airline tries to extract the "average" reservation price of each of a group of buyers. The airline pricing model is compromised somewhat by Internet firms, such as Expedia, that search airline databases for the lowest fares. This provides the consumer with more information about the range of fares available and enables the consumer to potentially get a lower fare than that available from dealing directly with the carrier.

Another way of operationalizing first-degree price discrimination is through a two-part tariff. Monopolists get the consumer to pay an "entry fee" for the privilege of paying a "use fee" for the purchase of each unit of the product they wish to consume. Membership fees for clubs are the entry fee and a "greens fee" for playing a round of golf at the country club, court fees for a tennis match, or the price of a meal are the use fees. Hardwire telephone company services charge a hookup fee and monthly fees so that you can access the network that are independent of your use of the system, then charge you use fees for each message unit consumed. It is a neat, efficient method to extract consumer surplus. A very innovative recent use of a two-part tariff is the personal seat license for sports tickets. To purchase a ticket to see a game (the game price ticket being the use fee), one must purchase a personal seat license (the entry fee). One generally then owns the right to purchase individual game tickets for an extended period of time. This pricing method has been used to raise funds to finance new sports stadiums.

Managers also developed a pricing technique called *bundling*. In this technique, the firm bundles together products whose demands are not positively correlated. In general, in bundling situations, we have negative correlation; that is, some group of customers have higher reservation prices for one item in the bundle but lower reservation prices for another item in the bundle, whereas another group of customers has just the reverse preferences. By bundling together the products, the firm (under certain conditions) can make a greater profit than by selling the products separately. McDonald's practices what is known as *mixed bundling*. It offers the same items for sale separately and as a bundle, such as Happy Meals 1 through 8. Columbia Music, on the other hand, offers only a pure bundle. Even if you like only one or two songs by artist X, you must purchase the compact disc that contains eight other songs you do not wish to own. They sell their product only as a bundle.

In some cases, transactions occur where markets do not exist. This could happen between two divisions of a firm, where a product required as an input is produced exclusively in an upstream plant for use in the production of a product in a downstream plant. Transfer pricing results from creating an internal market that simulates an external market and allows for optimal profit maximizing decisions by both divisions of the firm. For instance, auto companies purchase inputs from their components' divisions so that they can produce automobiles. When an external market exists for the product of the upstream division, the rules for the optimal transfer price determination differ, because now the upstream division has the option of selling the product in the external market and the downstream division has the option of purchasing the upstream product in the external market.

This chapter explores the details of these more-sophisticated extensions of monopoly pricing. First-degree and third-degree discrimination and transfer pricing are shown to be extensions of the now familiar marginal revenue equals marginal cost profit-maximizing rule.

Motivation for Price Discrimination

Consider Figure 12.1, which shows the profit maximizing price and quantity for a single-price monopolist. By charging price P_M, the monopolist sells Q_M units. But, aside from the customer whose reservation price was P_M, all other purchasing customers value the good at higher than P_M, but were asked to pay only P_M for it, that is, those in area AB of the demand curve. Consumers can retain a significant amount of consumer surplus—money they are willing to leave with the producer but are not asked to do so. The amount of that consumer surplus is V.

Consumers in area BC of the demand curve are unwilling to spend P_M for the good but have reservation prices that exceed the marginal cost of producing the good and hence represent potential profitable sales. These sales are not made by the single-price monopolist, who curtails output at Q_M, whereas profitable sales could continue up to Q_C. The amount of profit represented by those potential sales is $X + Z$.

Instead, the single-price monopolist settles for a variable cost profit of $W + Y$ (where total revenue is $P_M Q_M = W + Y + U$ and variable cost is the area under the marginal cost curve U (as shown in Chapter 11).

If the monopolist raises the price above P_M to capture some of the consumer surplus in area V, area $X + Z$ becomes greater. If it lowers the price below P_M to capture some of the potential profit in area $X + Z$, area V becomes bigger. We know that it cannot gain by raising or lowering the price because we showed in Chapter 11 that P_M is the profit-maximizing price for the single-price monopolist. If the producer is going to capture some (or all) of region V and some (or all) of region $X + Z$, it cannot do it with a single-price strategy. It must think of a strategy that involves two or more prices. We now explore what those strategies should be. The motivation is capturing areas V and area $X + Z$. If the

FIGURE
12.1

Single-Price Monopolist Profit-Maximizing Outcome

The single-price monopolist prices at P_M and produces and sells Q_M units. Consumers in region AB are willing to pay a higher price than P_M, yet are not asked to do so. Consumers in region BC are unwilling to pay a price as high as P_M but will pay a price higher than it costs the producer to make the good. Both these situations are potentially profitable sales that are not made.

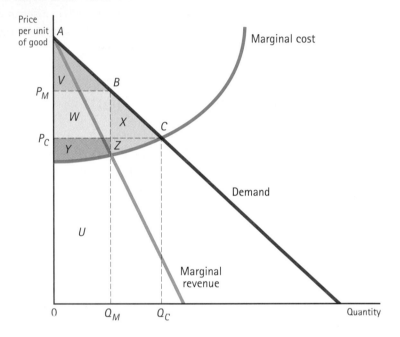

benefit of capturing some or all of those areas exceeds the costs of doing so (and sophisticated pricing is more costly to implement and monitor than simple single pricing), then our producer should do so.

Price Discrimination

Price discrimination occurs when the same product is sold at more than one price. For example, an airline may sell tickets on a particular flight at a higher price to business travelers than to college students. An automobile dealer may sell the exactly equipped make and model at vastly different prices on the same day to different buyers. Even if the products are not precisely the same, price discrimination is said to occur if very similar products are sold at prices that are in different ratios to their marginal costs. If a firm sells boxes of candy with a label (cost of the label is 2 cents) saying "Premium Quality" in rich neighborhoods for $12 and sells the same boxes of candy without this label in poor neighborhoods for $5, this is price discrimination. The mere fact that differences in price exist among similar products is not evidence of discrimination; only if these differences do not reflect cost differences is there evidence of this kind.

First-Degree Price Discrimination

There are three basic **types of price discrimination**: first, second, and third degree. The auto dealer is indicative of first degree, while the airline and candy firm are indicative of third degree. Selling electricity (to certain customers) is an example of second degree. By examining price discrimination in a bit more detail, we can get a handle on all three types.

Consider again the diagram of a simple monopoly (single-price) profit maximizer shown in Figure 12.1. To reiterate what was said, consumers in segment AB of the demand curve are willing to pay more than the single monopoly price of P_M. Consumers in the segment BC of the demand curve are willing to pay more for the good than it costs the producer to produce it, that is, the firm's marginal cost.

The simple monopolist makes a variable cost profit of $W + Y$, as shown in Figure 12.1 and leaves the consumer surplus of V with the consumers of segment AB. If the firm could **perfectly price discriminate** (another name for **first-degree price discrimination**), it could charge each of the consumers in segment AB their reservation prices and capture all the consumer surplus and turn it into producer surplus. By perfectly discriminating in segment AB, the firm's variable cost profit would become $V + W + Y$.

But the firm can do even better. By perfectly discriminating in segment BC, the firm can add an additional variable cost profit of $X + Z$, since the reservation price of the consumers in segment BC exceeds the additional cost of producing the units involved, $Q_C - Q_M$. Therefore, by perfectly discriminating in both the AB and the BC segments, the firm has increased its variable cost profits (and hence its profits) by $V + X + Z$. This is precisely all the area we saw that the simple monopolist was not exploiting in Figure 12.1. The potential for these additional profits gets creative managers thinking about pricing strategies to capture them.

If the firm is able to capture all of $V + X + Z$, we say that it is practicing *discrimination of the first degree*. In essence, the firm is charging the reservation price for each unit of the good. Clearly, the firm is willing to do this up to Q_C units in Figure 12.1. The additional revenue the firm earns by selling an additional unit of product is the reservation price of the consumer. Managers sell to a consumer as long as the reservation price (which the firm can charge and the consumer is willing to pay) exceeds the marginal cost of the firm to produce the good. In essence, under perfect discrimination, the firm's demand curve becomes the firm's marginal revenue curve. Therefore, the firm will not sell the Q_C + 1st item, because the marginal cost of producing it exceeds the revenue that it would generate for the firm, that is, the reservation price of the Q_C + 1st good.

Therefore, the profit maximizing rule developed in Chapters 10 and 11 holds. The perfectly discriminating firm maximizes profit by setting its marginal revenue (its demand curve) equal to its marginal cost.

One other interesting outcome of first-degree price discrimination is that it results in the same output that would be produced if the monopolist were forced to behave as if it operated in a perfectly competitive market, that is, Q_C. The difference is in the distribution of consumer and producer surplus in Figure 12.1. Under perfectly competitive pricing (P_C), consumer surplus is $V + W + X$ and producer surplus is $Y + Z$. Since total welfare is the sum of consumer and producer surplus, social welfare would be V through Z. Under first-degree discrimination, consumer surplus is zero (it has all been captured) and producer surplus is V through Z. Therefore, the welfare is the same under both pricing mechanisms, V through Z, but consumers benefit under perfect competition and producers get *all* the benefit under first-degree price discrimination. Because the output is the same under each pricing scheme, the social welfare is the same under each pricing scheme.

For first-degree price discrimination, a firm must have a relatively small number of buyers and must be able to estimate the maximum prices they are willing to accept. In addition, other conditions must hold that are elaborated on when we treat third-degree price discrimination. For these reasons, the two-part tariff method of pricing, to be discussed later, is a way of operationalizing first-degree price discrimination.

Honest Sam's Used Cars: A Numerical Example of First-Degree Price Discrimination

We now view an example of first-degree price discrimination versus simple monopoly pricing. Honest Sam sells used cars. The demand for Sam's used cars is $P = 12 - Q$, where P is the price in thousands and Q is the quantity of cars per month.

Sam has two ways of selling cars. He can set a price (like the Saturn Motor Company) and merely pay a general manager to write up the paperwork. The total cost of selling each car under such an arrangement is $2 (thousand), so Sam's marginal cost is $2 (thousand). This is also Sam's average variable cost of selling a car. Sam has fixed costs of $5 (thousand) per month.

To maximize profit under simple monopoly pricing would entail setting marginal revenue equal to marginal cost. Sam's total revenue is $TR = PQ = (12 - Q)Q = 12Q - Q^2$. Sam's marginal revenue, $MR = dTR/dQ$ is

$$MR = 12 - 2Q$$

Setting Sam's marginal revenue equal to Sam's marginal cost,

$$MR = 12 - 2Q = 2 = MC$$

gives $Q = 5$, which implies that the price of cars is $P = 12 - 5 = 7$ or $7,000.

Sam's total revenue per month is $35 (i.e., $PQ = (\$7)(5) = \$35$ thousand), variable costs are $10 (i.e., $(AVC)Q = (\$2)(5) = \$10$ thousand), and fixed costs are $5 (thousand), resulting in a monthly profit of $20 (thousand) by following simple monopoly pricing.

Sam could also sell cars the old-fashioned way—customers haggle with salespeople. Sam can hire a sales force that is pretty slick. By "chit-chatting" with customers, the salesperson can pretty well estimate the customer's reservation price of a car; for example, salespeople often come right out and ask the customer how much the customer is looking to spend or are more subtle by asking, say, "What do you do for a living? Do you want to drive the car home tonight?" Salespeople who are not very good at estimating customers' reservation prices tend not to be employed very long in the automobile business. A general manager is still needed to write up the paperwork, and the salespeople are paid strictly on commission, $1 (thousand) for each car they sell. Under this model of sales, Sam's marginal cost is $3 (thousand) per car. The haggle model is first-degree price discrimination in action. As mentioned, practicing price discrimination often is more costly than charging a single price.

Under this model, Sam sells cars up to the point where the reservation price equals marginal cost, or

$$P = 12 - Q = \$3 = MC \quad \text{or} \quad Q = 9$$

All consumer surplus (J in Figure 12.2) is captured. Sam's profit is total revenue ($J + K$) less total cost (variable cost, K, plus fixed cost). In this case, total revenue is $67.5[1] (thousand), variable cost is $27 $((AVC)(Q) = (\$3)(9) = \$27$ thousand), and fixed cost is $5 (thousand), resulting in a profit of $35.5 (thousand).

Sam prefers the haggle model over the simple-monopoly posted-price model (since $35.5 > $20). Presumably, this explains why most auto dealers have not

---

[1] The area of trapezoid $J + K$ is one-half the height (9) times the sum of the trapezoid's two sides $(12 + 3)$. Therefore $0.5(9)(15) = 67.5$.

FIGURE

12.2

First-Degree Price Discrimination

The first-degree price discriminator captures all consumer surplus *J* and turns it into producer surplus (variable cost profit).

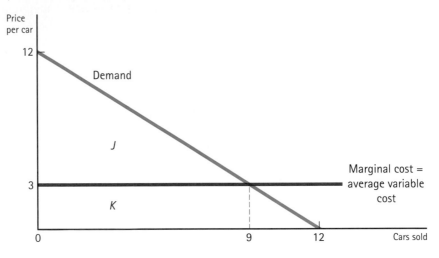

switched to the Saturn-posted price model and continue with the haggling method of selling cars.

Second-Degree Price Discrimination

Second-degree price discrimination is more common. Take the case of a gas company, *each* of whose customers has the demand curve shown in Figure 12.3. The company charges a high price, P_0, if the consumer purchases less than X units of gas per month. For an amount beyond X units per month, the company charges a medium price, P_1. For purchases beyond Y, the company charges an even lower price, P_2. Consequently, the company's total revenues from each consumer are equal to the shaded area in Figure 12.3, since the consumer purchases X units at a price of P_0, $(Y - X)$ units at a price of P_1, and $(Z - Y)$ units at a price of P_2.[2]

The gas company, by charging different prices for various amounts of the commodity, is able to increase its revenues and profits considerably. After all,

---

[2] Of course, this assumes for simplicity that each consumer purchases Z units and that each price considered exceeds the firm's marginal cost. Also, other simplifying assumptions (which need not concern us here) are made in this and the next paragraph.

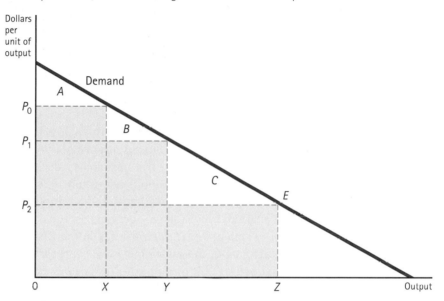

FIGURE 12.3

Second-Degree Price Discrimination

The company charges a different price (P_0, P_1, or P_2) depending on how much the consumer purchases, thus increasing its total revenue and profits.

if it were permitted to charge only one price and wanted to sell Z units, it would have to charge a price of P_2. Thus, the firm's total revenue would equal only the rectangle $0P_2EZ$, which is considerably less than the shaded area in Figure 12.3. By charging different prices, the firm raises its profits over those available under a single-price strategy. However, note that the firm also leaves a consumer surplus of $A + B + C$ on the table; that is, consumers retain money that they are willing to pay for the product. According to some authorities, second-degree price discrimination plays an important role in the schedule of rates charged by many public utilities—gas, water, electricity, and others.[3]

Third-Degree Price Discrimination

We now consider the most prevalent form of price discrimination—**third-degree price discrimination**—in greater detail. For a firm to be able and willing to

[3] R. Davidson, *Price Discrimination in Selling Gas and Electricity* (Baltimore: Johns Hopkins University Press, 1955) and C. Cicchetti and J. Jurewitz, *Studies in Electric Utility Regulation* (Cambridge, MA: Ballinger, 1975).

engage in price discrimination, the buyers of the firm's product must fall into classes with considerable differences among those classes in price elasticity of demand for the product, and it must be possible to identify and segregate these classes at moderate cost. Also, buyers must be unable to transfer the product easily from one class to another, since otherwise, persons could make money by buying the product from the low-price classes and selling it to the high-price classes, making it difficult to maintain the price differentials among classes. We call these latter two conditions the ability to *segment* and *seal* the market.[4] The differences among classes of buyers in the price elasticity of demand may be due to differences among classes in income levels, tastes, or the availability of substitutes. For example, the price elasticity of demand for the boxes of candy discussed earlier may be lower (in absolute value) for the rich than for the poor.

If a firm practices discrimination of this sort, it must decide two questions: How much output should it allocate to each class of buyer, and what price should it charge each class? Suppose there are only two classes of buyers. Also, for the moment, assume the firm has already decided on its total output; consequently, the only real question is allocation between the two classes. The firm maximizes its profits by allocating the total output between the two in such a way that marginal revenue in one class is equal to marginal revenue in the other. For example, if marginal revenue in the first class is \$25 and that in the second class is \$10, the allocation is not optimal. Profits can be increased by allocating one less unit of output to the second class and one more unit to the first class. Only if the two marginal revenues are equal is the allocation optimal. And, if the marginal revenues in the two classes are equal, the ratio of the price in the first class to that in the second class equals

$$(P_1/P_2) = [1 + (1/\eta_2)]/[1 + (1/\eta_1)] \tag{12.1}$$

where η_1 is the price elasticity of demand in the first class and η_2 is that in the second class.[5] Therefore, it does not pay to discriminate if the two price elasticities are equal, since $\eta_1 = \eta_2$ implies that $P_1 = P_2$. Moreover, if discrimination does pay, the price is *higher* in the class in which the demand is *less elastic*.

---

[4]Segmenting and sealing can have another meaning. In 2000, customers of Amazon.com discovered (via an Internet chat room) that they had been charged significantly different prices by Amazon for the same DVD. When they expressed their displeasure and made the price differences public, Amazon announced that it no longer would engage in such a pricing practice. If the customers had not discovered the price differences, they would have been satisfied (as revealed by their purchase of the DVD) and Amazon could have continued selling the same product at different prices. See David Streitfeld, "On the Web, Price Tags Blur," *Washington Post*, September 27, 2000.

[5]Recall from equation (3.16) that marginal revenue equals $P[1 + (1/\eta)]$ where P is price and η is the price elasticity of demand. Therefore, if marginal revenue is the same in the two classes, $P_1[1 + (1/\eta_1)] = P_2[1 + (1/\eta_2)]$. Hence, $P_1/P_2 = [1 + (1/\eta_2)]/[1 + (1/\eta_1)]$.

Turning to the more realistic case in which a firm must also decide on its total output, it is obvious that the firm must look at its costs as well as demand in the two classes. Specifically, the firm chooses the output where the marginal cost of its entire output is equal to the common value of the marginal revenue in the two classes. The firm's profits (π) are

$$\pi = TR_1 + TR_2 - TC$$

where TR_1 is the total revenue from class 1, TR_2 is the total revenue from class 2, and TC is the total cost. The total cost is a function of the total amount of the good (Q) produced and sold, and is allocated Q_1 to class 1 and Q_2 to class 2.

The monopolist has two output choices, and so profits are maximized when $\partial\pi/\partial Q_1 = 0$ and $\partial\pi/\partial Q_2 = 0$. Note that $\partial\pi/\partial Q_1 = (\partial TR_1/\partial Q_1) - (\partial TC/\partial Q_1)$, since $(\partial TR_2/\partial Q_1) = 0$ because revenues in class 2 are independent of sales in class 1. Likewise, $\partial\pi/\partial Q_2 = (\partial TR_2/\partial Q_2) - (\partial TC/\partial Q_2)$, since $(\partial TR_1/\partial Q_2) = 0$ because revenues in class 1 are independent of sales in class 2. These two relationships are rewritten as

$$\partial\pi/\partial Q_1 = MR_1 - MC = 0$$
$$\partial\pi/\partial Q_2 = MR_2 - MC = 0$$

(12.2)

Note that both $\partial TC/\partial Q_1$ and $\partial TC/\partial Q_2$ equal MC (and not MC_1 and MC_2) because the plant manager knows only that, when producing another unit, additional costs are incurred. It is the marketing or sales department's job to decide whether the good is destined for class 1 or class 2 demanders.

The equations in (12.2) state that, to maximize profits, the firm must set $MR_1 = MC$ and $MR_2 = MC$, implying that $MR_1 = MR_2 = MC$. Had there been n classes of demanders, the profit maximizing rule would become $MR_1 = MR_2 = \ldots = MR_n = MC$. To see this in the two class case, consider Figure 12.4, which shows D_1, the demand curve in class 1; D_2, the demand curve in class 2; R_1, the marginal revenue curve in class 1; R_2, the marginal revenue curve in class 2; and the firm's marginal cost curve. The curve representing the horizontal summation of the two marginal revenue curves is G. This curve shows, for each level of marginal revenue, the total output needed if marginal revenue in each class is to be maintained at this level. The optimal output is shown by the point where the G curve intersects the marginal cost curve, since marginal cost must be equal to the common value of the marginal revenue in each class. If this were not true, profits could be increased by expanding output (if marginal cost were less than marginal revenue) or contracting output (if marginal cost were greater than the revenue). Therefore, the firm produces an output of Q units and sells Q_1 units in the class 1 market and Q_2 units in the class 2 market. The price is P_1 in the class 1 market and P_2 in the class 2 market. This results in higher profits than if the firm quoted the same price in both markets.

FIGURE
12.4

Third-Degree Price Discrimination

To maximize profit, the firm produces a total output of Q units and sets a price of P_1 in the class 1 market and P_2 in the class 2 market.

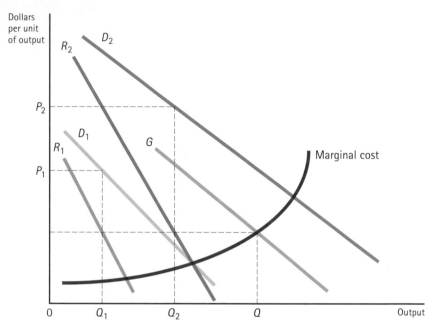

Airline Travel: A Case Study

Perhaps the most frequently cited example of price discrimination is the case of airline tickets. The airlines often charge a lower fare for essentially the same ticket if it is purchased well in advance, if there is a penalty if the trip is canceled or changed, and if the trip includes a Saturday night stay. For example, in 2001, the price of a round-trip coach ticket from New York to San Francisco ranged from about $301 to $850 for flights leaving and returning on similar dates.

One reason for these price differences is that the price elasticity of demand for business travel is much less elastic than that for vacation travel. Business travelers must meet with clients, suppliers, and associates at particular times, often as soon as possible. Regardless of the price of an airline ticket (so long as it remains within reasonable bounds), many of these trips would be well worth making. On the other hand, vacation travelers often plan their trips well in advance, are relatively flexible with regard to the timing of their trips, and are sensitive to moderate differences in ticket price. From the discussion in the previous section, it seems likely that the airlines, to maximize profit, would like to set higher prices for business travelers than for vacation travelers. And this is the effect of the price differences just cited, since business travelers are much less likely than vacation travelers to buy their tickets well in advance or to include a Saturday night stay[6] and they desire the flexibility of being able to change their flight schedule.

At the same time, it is also worth noting that, because the airlines can reduce their costs if demand is more predictable (as a result of better scheduling of equipment and personnel), they may enjoy savings if travelers buy their tickets well in advance. Also, if a ticket is not refundable, it clearly is not the same as a ticket that is refundable, even though the penalty involved in changing it may be relatively small. Therefore, the price differences are *not due entirely* to price discrimination, pure and simple.

In recent years, entrepreneurs stepped in with a business model that mitigates some of the airlines' ability to practice third-degree price discrimination. Internet firms such as Expedia scour airline databases continuously looking for cheap fares from *A* to *B*. Consumers, in turn, scour Expedia (and other competitors, such as CheapTicket or Travelocity, to view such fares). These additional information sources can lead to lower fares than if the customer dealt with the air carrier alone. This is not always the case, however. In addition, one has to take the time to search the sites. Since airlines change fares continuously, if the sites do not update frequently, the customer may not get the cheapest fare. A recent search of two such sites done within seconds of each other revealed a $500 difference between the cheapest fare from Philadelphia to Hyderabad, India. One must be careful not to be lulled into thinking that the fare one sees is the cheapest, despite the names and advertising claims of the sites. In addition, since the airlines release the sale of these seats to the sites, they are still falling into the airlines' overall pricing plan (that plan, however, would be different if the sites were not present). In addition, some sites, like Priceline, actually play into the airlines' hands. By naming your price (say *X*), you have revealed your reservation price. If the airline (Priceline) would be willing to sell to you at price *Y* (less than *X*), then you have paid too much (*X* − *Y*) for your ticket.

Third-Degree Price Discrimination: A Pharmaceutical Example

To illustrate how price discrimination can be used, suppose a drug manufacturer sells a major drug in Europe and the United States. Because of legal

[6] Because of the events of September 11, 2001, and a business recession that started in the second quarter of 2001, business travel on the airlines fell precipitously. Many airlines relaxed certain restrictions, including the Saturday night stay, in an attempt to woo back the business traveler.

restrictions, the drug cannot be bought in one country and sold in another. The demand curve for the drug in Europe is

$$P_E = 10 - Q_E \tag{12.3}$$

where P_E is the price (in dollars per pound) in Europe and Q_E is the amount (in millions of pounds) sold there. The demand curve for the drug in the United States is

$$P_U = 20 - 1.5Q_U \tag{12.4}$$

where P_U is the price (in dollars per pound) in the United States and Q_U is the amount (in millions of pounds) sold there. The total cost (in millions of dollars) of producing the drug for sale worldwide is

$$TC = 4 + 2(Q_E + Q_U) \tag{12.5}$$

The firm's total profit (π) from both Europe and the United States is

$$\begin{aligned}
\pi &= P_E Q_E + P_U Q_U - TC \\
&= (10 - Q_E)Q_E + (20 - 1.5Q_U)Q_U - [4 + 2(Q_E + Q_U)] \\
&= 10Q_E - Q_E^2 + 20Q_U - 1.5Q_U^2 - 4 - 2Q_E - 2Q_U \\
&= -4 + 8Q_E - Q_E^2 + 18Q_U - 1.5Q_U^2 \tag{12.6}
\end{aligned}$$

To maximize profit with respect to Q_E and Q_U, we must set $\partial\pi/\partial Q_E = 0$ and $\partial\pi/\partial Q_U = 0$. Hence, $\partial\pi/\partial Q_E = 8 - 2Q_E = 0$ and $\partial\pi/\partial Q_U = 18 - 3Q_U = 0$.

Solving these equations for Q_E and Q_U, we find that 4 million pounds of the drug should be sold in Europe and 6 million pounds should be sold in the United States.

To find the optimal prices in Europe and the United States, we substitute 4 for Q_E and 6 for Q_U in equations (12.3) and (12.4); the result is that the price in Europe should be $6 per pound and the price in the United States should be $11 per pound. Substituting these values of P_E and P_U, as well as the foregoing values of Q_E and Q_U, into equation (12.6), we find that the firm's profit equals

$$\pi = -4 + 8(4) - 4^2 + 18(6) - 1.5(6^2) = 66$$

or $66 million.

At this point, it is important to note that, if we had used the graphical technique in the previous section, we would have obtained precisely the same results. Whether the graphical technique or the mathematical technique is used, the answer is the same.

Having obtained these results, it is interesting and useful to determine how much additional profit the firm makes because it engages in third-degree price discrimination. If price discrimination were not possible (say, because the submarkets could not be segmented and sealed), P_E would have to equal P_U. Letting this common price be P, it follows from equation (12.3) that $Q_E = 10 - P$, and from equation (12.4) that $Q_U = (1/1.5)(20 - P) = (40/3) - (2/3)P$. Therefore, the firm's total amount sold in Europe and the United States combined is

$$Q = Q_E + Q_U = (30/3) - (3/3)P + (40/3) - (2/3)P = (70/3) - (5/3)P$$

which implies that[7]

$$P = 14 - 0.6Q \qquad (12.7)$$

for $P \le \$10$ or for $Q \ge 20/3$. (For $P \ge \$10$ or $Q \le 20/3$, $P = 20 - 1.5Q$, because only the United States purchases the drug if the price exceeds \$10). Hence, the firm's profit is

$$\begin{aligned}
\pi &= PQ - TC \\
&= (14 - 0.6Q)Q - (4 + 2Q) \\
&= 14Q - 0.6Q^2 - 4 - 2Q \\
&= -4 + 12Q - 0.6Q^2 \qquad (12.8)
\end{aligned}$$

because $Q = Q_E + Q_U$.

To maximize profit, the firm selects Q so that $d\pi/dQ = 0$. Therefore,

$$d\pi/dQ = 12 - 1.2Q$$

Solving for Q, we find that the firm, if it does not engage in price discrimination, produces a total of 10 million pounds of the drug (which is the same as the output produced when they discriminated).[8] Substituting 10 for Q in equations (12.7) and (12.8), it follows that

$$\begin{aligned}
P &= 14 - 0.6(10) = \$8 \\
\pi &= -4 + 12(10) - 0.6(10^2) = \$56
\end{aligned}$$

Therefore, if the firm does not engage in price discrimination, its profit is \$56 million, rather than the \$66 million it can earn by price discrimination.

[7]This means that $(5/3)P = (70/3) - (3/3)Q$ or $5P = 70 - 3Q$ or $P = 14 - 0.6Q$.

[8]If the demand curves are curvilinear, the output of the third-degree discriminator and the single-price monopolist are not necessarily the same.

Since 10 million pounds were produced under both pricing schemes, the cost of production is the same in both cases, $4 + 2(10) = \$24$. So, the total revenues are $80 (= 56 + 24)$ when there is no discrimination and $90 (= 66 + 24)$ when there is discrimination. With no discrimination, the average revenue per unit is just the price $(80/10 = \$8)$, but with discrimination, the average revenue per unit is $9 (90/10)$. The profit-enhancing property of third-degree discrimination is that it raises the average revenue above the price on the demand curve for a given amount of quantity.

If segmenting and sealing the market is possible but costly, the preceding example tells us that the firm would be willing to pay up to the difference in the profits of the two pricing schemes (but no more) to segment and seal, that is, up to $10 million in this case.

Finally, note that, at price $6, 4 million pounds of the drug are sold in Europe (from $Q_E = 10 - 6$) and that, at a price of $11, 6 million pounds are sold in the United States (from $Q_U = (40/3) - (2/3)11$). Also, note that $dQ_E/dP_E = -1$ and $dQ_U/dP_U = -2/3$. Recall from Chapter 3 that elasticity is $\eta = (P/Q)(dQ/dP)$. So $\eta_E = (6/4)(-1) = -1.5$ and $\eta_U = (11/6)(-2/3) = -1.22$. Therefore, the price is raised (from $8 to $11) to the less elastic demander and lowered (from $8 to $5) to the more elastic demander (just as we would expect from equation (12.1)).

Using Coupons and Rebates for Price Discrimination

One way of implementing a price discrimination strategy is with coupons and rebates. Basically, these devices reduce the price of products. But why don't managers simply reduce prices? Primarily, because coupons are used to price discriminate. Not all consumers use coupons. Of 291.9 billion coupons distributed in the United States in 1995, only 5.8 billion were redeemed. A certain segment of consumers (20 to 30 percent) regularly use coupons in buying goods and services. This demand segment is more price sensitive and on the more elastic part of their demand curve. Hence, managers use coupons and rebates to price discriminate, because other consumers (on the less elastic part of their demand curve) are willing to pay "higher prices," that is, buy the good without a coupon.

By estimating the elasticity of demand, managers can approximate how much coupons should be worth. Suppose the Barnegat Light Fish Company sells its product, a special blend of crab cake, in a market where it estimates two types of consumers exist: a more affluent group (R) with an estimated price elasticity for Barnegat Light crab cakes of -2 ($\eta_R = -2$) and a less affluent group (S)

CONCEPTS IN CONTEXT

Why Do Women Pay More?

Two individuals walk into a hair salon. They have equal length hair and want the same amount cut and the same hairstyle. Yet one pays more for the service than the other. The same two individuals walk into a dry cleaning establishment. One tenders a white silk dress shirt as does the other. Except in the latter case, the shirt is called a *blouse*. The bill for the first shirt is less than for the second. In some states, like Pennsylvania, Massachusetts, and California, state laws exist that prohibit price discrimination based on gender. A consumer advocacy group surveying Philadelphia business establishments found that women paid a premium at 4 of the 14 dry cleaners they randomly surveyed and at 18 of the 22 hair salons randomly surveyed. For the "same" shirt, the maximum difference for a standard shirt was $2.45. At hair salons, the difference could be double. A California study suggested that gender pricing could entail an additional expense of $1,351/woman/year for a total of $15 billion more than men.

The law, however, states that, if the price differs, it must be for a reason other than gender. We must then ask this question: Is the good or service exactly the same or not and, if not, do the price differences reflect the cost of service differences? Not surprisingly, those found not in compliance argued that women were more expensive to service than men—hence the price difference. Another explanation was that what currently is sold under a one-number rubric, like a haircut, is really a bundle of products. Were the law to be enforced, one hair salon owner stated that it would just unbundle the product and charge separately for the actual cutting of the hair, the gelling, the blow drying, and the styling. Since many men get nothing more than the cutting and since many women get more than just the cutting, women would pay more than men.

Source: "Being a Woman: It Can Cost You in PA," *Philadelphia Inquirer,* March 5, 1999.

with an estimated price elasticity for Barnegat Light crab cakes of -5 ($\eta_S = -5$). The Barnegat Light Fish Company puts a posted price of a particular amount (P) on its product but issues a $X-off coupon in the newspaper local to the consumer types. Every buyer pays the nominal price of P per unit for Barnegat Light crab cakes on the grocers' sales receipt, but at the bottom of the sales receipt, a $X credit appears for those who tender a coupon. Thus, while all buyers pay the same price, P, in reality the noncoupon tenderers pay P while the coupon tenderers pay $P - X$. What should the values of P and X be? As we saw, to maximize profits, marginal revenue in each market should be equal and they, in turn, should equal Barnegat Light's marginal cost (MC). Therefore,

$$P[1 + (1/\eta_R)] = (P - X)[1 + (1/\eta_S)] = MC$$

ANALYZING MANAGERIAL DECISIONS
Yield Management and Airline Performance

A recent survey shows that yield management is a major factor in airline profitability. The managers of American Airlines used yield models to generate over $1 billion in savings over a three-year period. Yield management models are a nice example of how mathematical models apparently capture the complexity of our social structure, using only a few variables. They also show how the intellectual effort of managers generates profits for the firm.

Yield management models are complex pricing mechanisms. They are dynamic in the sense that prices respond to customer behavior. At any one time, there are several classes of seats, which are priced at different levels. Prices at each level depend on a real-time demand forecasting model that analyzes market behavior then optimizes pricing behavior. The firm prices as if it were practicing third-degree price discrimination.

The models can handle the complexity of reality only by looking at a simplified version of it. It is as if life is abridged. Yield management models focus on a few key variables and ignore everything else. Most focus on overbooking, discount allocation, and traffic management. Managers build models that look at the revenue potential of a complex menu of price and itinerary pairs.

For example, consider overbooking. Airlines must overbook because some customers never claim their reservations. If they did not overbook, then some aircraft that should fly full based on demand (customer behavior) would fly with unused capacity. So managers build models that balance the trade-offs between the increased revenue of more passengers and the costs of having passengers take the next flight (ideally).

Modeling the situation is not easy. Clearly, reputational costs with customers are involved if overbooking becomes too common. There are also real economic costs. Passengers not permitted to board the plane because of overbooking must be paid certain costs. Many are given vouchers for discounts on future flights, some must be fed or given a hotel room.

Managers built the models to maximize expected net revenue. The optimal overbooking rule is to overbook until the expected marginal revenue from one more passenger on the flight is equal to the marginal cost of an additional overbooking. The actual point chosen reflects concerns for customer satisfaction, so it is constrained a bit.

Other variables are modeled using similar decision rules. For example, in discount allocation models, the objective is to balance the expected marginal revenue of a specific fare request against the expected marginal net revenue of all other fares. To help understand how sophisticated the models are, consider the inclusion of "sell-up" probabilities. These probabilities are used in discounting models to predict those customers who will buy the higher priced ticket, if not offered a low price.

The models require sophisticated hardware and software to operate efficiently. IT reservation systems like SABRE play an integral part in yield management. These systems interface with the market; their ability to capture and analyze data allows the models to constantly update pricing levels. They also control seat inventory.

Given the competitive nature of the airline market, airlines have not been able to keep all the surplus generated by yield management programs. The programs generate some benefits for airline customers, mainly in the form of lower ticket prices and more efficient use of equipment.

Sources: "Yield Management—A Growth Key Driver," www.airlinesgate.free.fr; "Airlines Ties Profitability Yield to Management," *The Travel Tightwad,* May 28, 2002, at www.elliot.org.

Suppose Barnegat Light's marginal cost was a constant $2:

$$P[1 + (1/ - 2)] = P[1 - (1/2)] = P/2 = 2, \quad \text{or } P = \$4$$
$$(4 - X)[1 + (1/-5)] = (4 - X)(0.8) = 2$$

or

$$3.2 - 0.8X = 2, \quad \text{or } X = \$1.5$$

Therefore, Barnegat Light should price its crab cakes at $4 per unit and offer a $1.50 off coupon. The more affluent pay $4/unit for the crab cakes and the less affluent clip the coupon and pay (net) $2.50/unit for the *same* crab cakes. More elastic people (the less affluent in this case) use coupons and the less elastic people (the affluent in this case) do not. So, by issuing coupons (and rebates, too) firms can price discriminate (and increase their profits).

As a regular reader of the local newspaper or the holder of a mailbox, you become acquainted with many coupon offers per year. More price elastic consumers take the time to sort through all the coupons and clip the ones they are interested in using. The less elastic consumers cannot be bothered with such activity for the $0.25 or $0.50 off the coupons yield. The "transaction costs" of taking the time to sort and clip outweigh the monetary value of the coupon for such individuals. For small rebates, there are even more transaction costs—clip the UPC code from the product, mail it (postage is your expense) and the cash register receipt, and wait six weeks for a very small check. As a result, the customer response rate to small dollar amount rebates is very low.

Tying at IBM, Xerox, and Microsoft

Tying is a pricing technique in which managers sell a product, the use of which requires the consumption of a complementary product. The consumer is required, generally by contract, to buy the complementary product from the firm selling the product itself. For example, during the 1950s, customers who leased a Xerox copying machine had to buy Xerox paper, and customers who leased an IBM computer had to buy paper computer cards made by IBM. More recently, both the United States and the European Union charged that Microsoft uses a tying strategy to force consumers to use its browser product (Internet Explorer) instead of a rival product (Netscape Navigator). Microsoft did this by tying the browser to the Windows operating system, then using its market power to force PC manufacturers to package only Internet Explorer on their products.

Successful implementation of a tying strategy generally requires the exercise of market power. For example, IBM, Xerox, and Microsoft all had market

CONCEPTS IN CONTEXT

Tying Up Your Printer

Tying is a concept that links products together for the economic gain of the producer. The market for printers is competitive; therefore, printers sell for relatively low prices. This is not where a printer manufacturer's profit is made. But try running your printer without an ink cartridge.

Once you have purchased company X's printer and your included-with-the-purchase ink cartridge runs out of ink, many consumers replace it with the same model cartridge from company X. That is where the printer manufacturers make their money. At Hewlett Packard in fiscal 2002, over half the printer group's revenues were from cartridges. One way that purchasers of company X's printers got around the high cost of company X's replacement cartridges was to have the original cartridge refilled. This created environmental savings (e.g., fewer cartridges in landfills), resource savings (e.g., less plastic needed to make new cartridges), and saved users lots of money when new cartridges did not have to be purchased. Printer manufacturers got wise to this practice and started building cartridges with a chip in them that prevented them from being refilled.

The European Union proposed a new law (to take effect in 2006) that bans companies from making products that cannot be reused because of specific design features (the chip in the case of the cartridges). Nonreusable cartridges make up approximately 90 percent of the market currently.

The tying has not been perfect, as "cloners" have begun to rapidly erode the printer manufacturers' share of the market in recent years with inexpensive "clone" cartridges. Still, allowing refilling of the printer manufacturer's cartridge (such refills sell at a fraction of the price of a manufacturer's cartridge) further erodes the tying profits of the printer manufacturers.

Source: "European Law May Hit Printer Makers," *Financial Times*, December 19, 2002.

shares above 85 percent in their respective markets. Firms engage in tying practices for several reasons. One reason is that it is a way of practicing price discrimination. By setting the price of the complementary product well above its cost, the firm can get, in effect, a much higher price from those who use it more often. For example, suppose that customer A uses a Hewlett-Packard printer to print 10,000 pages per month, whereas customer B uses an HP printer to print only 1,000 pages per month. It is hard for Hewlett-Packard to price its machines to obtain more revenue from customer A, the more intensive user, than from customer B. But, if HP can tie the sale of printer cartridges to the sale of its printer, it can get more profit from customer A than from customer B because it makes more on the selling of cartridges.

A 2003 notice from the Department of the Treasury warns wholesale liquor dealers that they cannot use tie-in sales when dealing with liquor retailers. Some examples of actual practices that were ruled illegal include[9]

- Requiring a retailer to purchase a regular case of distilled spirits to purchase the spirits in a special holiday container.
- Requiring a retailer to purchase 10 cases of a winery's Chardonnay to purchases 10 cases of the winery's Merlot.
- Requiring the retailer to purchase a two-bottle package of a winery's Merlot and Chardonnay to purchase cases of the winery's Merlot.

Another reason firms use the strategy is to maintain their monopoly position. For example, Microsoft has held a market share of above 90 percent in the PC operating system market since 1991. Even a competitor the size of IBM was forced to quickly withdraw from the market after spending hundreds of millions of dollars on the OS/2 operating system. Netscape was a concern for Microsoft because its product threatened to reduce the number of application programs written for Windows. So Microsoft wanted to exclude Netscape's product. When asked the following question by a government lawyer, a Microsoft executive agreed with the lawyer's assessment:

> And all I am trying to establish is that the reason for that [packaging Internet Browser with Windows] was because you believed that if the customer had a choice of the two browsers side by side, the user would, in the vast majority of cases or in the majority of cases, pick Netscape for the reasons that you've identified, correct?[10]

This belief was reiterated in an internal Microsoft e-mail presented at the trial:

> It seems clear that it will be very hard to increase browser share on the merits of Internet Explorer alone. It will be more important to leverage the OS asset to make people—to make people choose Explorer instead of Navigator.[11]

In addition, managers use a tying strategy to ensure that the firm's product works properly and its brand name is protected. To do so, the firm insists that customers use its complementary product. For example, Jerrold Electronics Corporation, which installed community antenna systems, required customers to accept five-year maintenance contracts to avoid breakdowns resulting from improper servicing of its equipment. And McDonald's franchises have had to buy their materials and food from McDonald's so that the hamburgers are uniform and the company's brand name is not tarnished. McDonald's is, in fact, protecting the franchise value of all franchisees by promoting a policy of "you know exactly what to expect" at every McDonald's.

[9]Department of the Treasury, Alcohol and Tobacco Tax and Trade Bureau, Industry Circular Number 2003–3, March 27, 2003.

[10]From www.microsoft/presspass/trial/transcript, September 21, 1999, trial transcript.

[11]Ibid.

Two–Part Tariffs

A **two-part tariff** is a way to operationalize first-degree price discrimination. The secret is to charge multiple prices to the consumer to allow the consumer to purchase, consume and use the product. A typical example is a country club (which actually practices a three-part tariff). Before you can play a round of golf, you must be approved for membership. With that comes a one-time initiation fee, then yearly dues. Both payments are made before you can play and are independent of the number of rounds you play. (Indeed, you may never play. You may have joined merely to improve your image—a resume enhancer!) In this sense, the initiation fee and the dues are like the fixed costs firms face. But, should you wish to play a round of golf, having been selected as a member (i.e., been chosen and paid your initiation fee) and are a member in good standing (i.e., you have paid your dues), you must pay a greens fee to play a round of golf (i.e., to use the service the club provides, a use fee). In this sense, the greens fee is analogous to the variable costs that firms face. Eating clubs, tennis clubs, health clubs, and amusement parks all practice similar pricing policies. In many amusement parks, one fee (the entry fee) gets you inside the park where the fee to go on the rides (the use fee) is zero (aside from the value of your time while waiting in line for the rides) for many rides, but some rides (the newest, the most popular) often require an additional fee for each ride taken. Businesses aside from the leisure market also use this pricing. Walmart's Sam's Club is one example. After paying a membership fee, you are admitted to a Sam's Club store where you pay individually for every item you purchase. Many Internet service providers practice such pricing. For a fixed monthly fee (the entry fee), you get access to the Internet. Then, you pay for each time unit you are online (the use fee). In many cases, the use fee may be zero for the first X minutes, but after those X minutes are over, a per minute fee is assessed. In some places, such as France, being connected entails X being zero; that is, you pay for each minute used. Most wireless phone plans, as well as hardwired phone service, also price this way.

We start with the simplest case to demonstrate the principle. Suppose that all demanders for a service are perfect clones; that is, *each* demander has the same demand curve for the services. We assume that the demand curve is linear of the form $P = a - bQ$, where P is the price per unit and Q is the number of units demanded at price P. In addition, we assume that the producing firm has a constant marginal cost (equals average variable cost) of production.

To maximize profits, the optimal two-part tariff charges the marginal cost as the use fee and the resulting consumer surplus as the entry fee. Consider the situation in Figure 12.5. The use fee (P^*) equals MC. At that use fee, the demander wishes to consume Q^* units. The resulting consumer surplus is A^* and that is the optimal entry fee. Note that the use fee covers the firm's variable cost of serving the consumer (since MC = AVC and (AVC)Q^* = VC), and the variable

FIGURE
12.5

Optimal Two–Part Tariff when All Demanders Are the Same

The optimal two-part tariff when all demanders are clones is a use fee equal to marginal cost ($P^* = MC$) and an entry fee equal to the consumer surplus resulting from such a use fee (i.e., A^*).

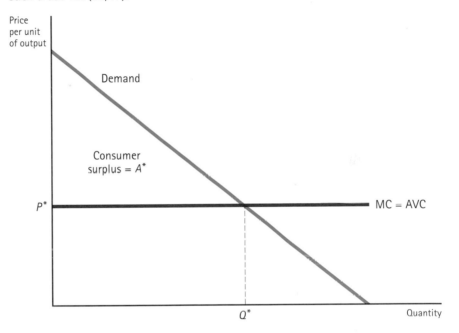

cost profit of the firm for serving this consumer is $A^* + P^*Q^* - (\text{AVC})Q^* = A^*$ (since $\text{AVC} = P^*$). Multiplying A^* by the number of clones and subtracting the firm's fixed cost gives the firm's profit.

Note that what the firm has done is the same that the first-degree discriminator did; that is, it captured all the consumer surplus (as the entry fee) and converted it into producer surplus (variable cost profit). It produced the output where price equals marginal cost.

The two-part tariff is simpler to administer than first-degree price discrimination because the firm need not charge the individual different prices for each unit of the good consumed. Because estimating the demand curve (and hence the consumer surplus) is difficult, what many firms have done is offered many different two-part tariffs and let the demanders self-select into the various plans, revealing what their demand curves look like. See the Concepts in Context box about a hardwired phone company (Verizon) later in this chapter and its various two-part tariffs.

A Numerical Example of a Two-Part Tariff: C-Pal Industries

This example demonstrates the two-part tariff. C-Pal Industries faces 100 identical individuals, each with a demand curve of $P = 10 - Q$. C-Pal has a constant marginal cost of $4 per unit produced and a fixed cost of $500. C-Pal's situation is depicted in Figure 12.6.

C-Pal charges a use fee of $4 (= MC) for each good a consumer purchases. Consumers purchase six goods (since the demand can be rewritten as $Q = 10 - P = 10 - 4 = 6$). C-Pal's total revenue from the use fee from one customer is $P^*Q^* = (\$4)(6) = \$24$ and C-Pal's variable cost for serving one customer is $(AVC)Q^* = (\$4)(6) = \$24$. The consumer surplus when six goods are demanded at price $4 for a customer is $0.5(10 - 4)6 = \$18$ and C-Pal charges this as an entry fee. C-Pal's total revenue from one customer is $\$24 + \$18 = \$42$ and C-Pal's variable cost of serving that customer is $24, yielding C-Pal a variable cost profit of serving that customer of $\$42 - \$24 = \$18$, the consumer surplus

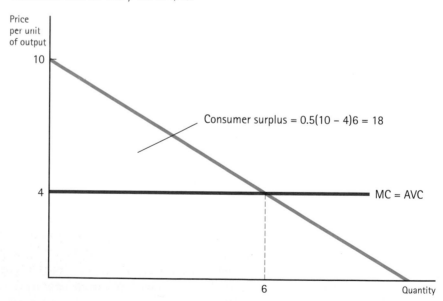

FIGURE

12.6

A Two-Part Tariff Example: C-Pal Industries

C-Pal's optimal two-part tariff entails charging a use fee of $4 (= MC) for each item consumed and an entry fee of $18.

Consumer surplus = 0.5(10 – 4)6 = 18

MC = AVC

captured from the consumer and converted into producer surplus. Since there are 100 clones, C-Pal's total variable cost profit is 100($18) = $1,800. C-Pal's profit is the variable cost profit minus the fixed costs, $1,300 = $1,800 − $500.

One point of confusion with respect to the two-part tariff is what happens when a demander conceives of a two-part tariff as a one-part tariff? Consider one of C-Pal's customers. He is paying (on average) $7 for each item he consumes, that is, $4 from the use fee and $3 (= $18/6) from the entry fee. But, if C-Pal had merely put a flat charge on each item sold of $7, its customers would purchase only three units ($Q = 10 − P = 10 − 7 = 3$). The individual demand curve derived in Chapter 4 shows the amount the consumer pays for *each* unit. Indeed, if C-Pal's customers are faced with a price of $7, they would take only three. But that is not the deal they have been offered. The *only* way they can buy the good is to pay an entry fee of $18 for the privilege of purchasing each unit they chose to purchase at price $4. They choose to purchase six, because the benefits of doing so just equal their costs of doing so. That is why the two-part tariff is so clever. It extracts all the consumer surplus from the consumer (which the single price does not).

A Two-Part Tariff with a Rising Marginal Cost

What if the situation first posited exists, but the marginal cost is upward sloping rather than constant? The optimal rule is still the same: charge a use fee equal to marginal cost and an entry fee equal to the resulting consumer surplus. The only difference here is that the firm now makes a profit off of the use fee (see area X^*) as well as their entry fee in Figure 12.7.

Charging a use fee of P^* results in selling Q^* to the consumer. This yields revenues of $P^*Q^* = X^* + Y^*$ from the use fee. The firm's variable cost of serving Q^* units to the customer is the area under the marginal cost curve (Y^*). Therefore, the revenue from the use fee more than cover the variable costs of serving the customer, and the firm earns a variable cost profit from serving the customer of X^* from the use fee. The entry fee is the consumer surplus that results from charging the use fee of P^* (i.e., A^*). Hence, the variable cost profit of serving this customer is $A^* + X^*$.

A Two-Part Tariff with Different Demand Curves

It is unrealistic to assume that each demander is the same. Consider the case when a strong demander (one who has a greater quantity demanded at any price) and a weak demander exist. This case presents two possibilities. If the strong demand is much stronger than the weak demand, it may be more

FIGURE
12.7

Optimal Two–Part Tariff when Marginal Cost Is Rising

The optimal two-part tariff is to charge a use fee P^* equal to marginal cost and an entry fee equal to the resulting consumer surplus (A^*). The firm's variable cost profit is now $A^* + X^*$, as the firm's use revenues now exceed its variable cost (of Y^*).

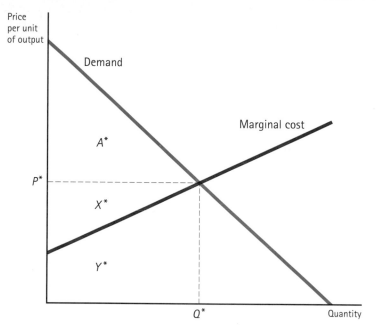

profitable to charge a use fee equal to marginal cost and an entry fee equal to the resulting consumer surplus of the strong demander. This possibility excludes the weak demander from the market. (The weak demander's consumer surplus is smaller than that of the strong demander, and so the weak demander cannot afford to pay the entry fee. Note that it is not unusual to exclude demanders from markets. In a single-pricing scenario, every consumer whose reservation price is below the price set in the market does not participate in that market.) The other possibility is that the strong demand is not that much stronger than the weak demand. Here, the use fee is set above the marginal cost and the entry fee is set at the resulting consumer surplus of the weak demander. Both consumer types participate in the market. The situation is depicted in Figure 12.8.

If the firm excludes the weak demander, it sets the use fee equal to marginal cost (= AVC) and the entry fee equal to the resulting consumer surplus of the strong demander. The revenue from the use fee equals the variable cost incurred serving the customer. The variable cost profit of the firm is the entry

FIGURE
12.8

Optimal Two-Part Tariff with Two Demand Types

The use fee should be set equal to marginal cost and the entry fee equal to the result-ing consumer surplus of the strong demander (areas A^* through F) if areas A^* through F exceed $2A^* + 2C + D + E$. The use fee should be set equal to P^* (>MC) and the entry fee equal to the resulting consumer surplus of the weak demander (A^*) if $2A^* + 2C + D + E$ exceed areas A^* through F.

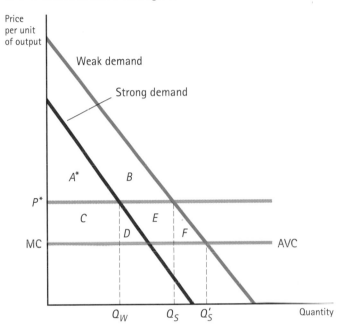

fee (areas A^* though F). If the firm includes the weak demander, it must choose the use fee P^*, which maximizes the area $2A^* + 2C + D + E$. Once P^* is cho-sen, it determines the consumer surplus A^*. Since both demanders are willing to pay A^*, the firm receives $2A^*$ in revenues. The revenues from the use fees more than cover the firm's variable cost from serving the consumers. At a use fee of P^*, the weak demander wants Q_W units of the good and the strong deman-der wants Q_S units of the good. Area C represents the variable cost profit the firm realizes from the user fee revenues from the weak demander, and area $C + D + E$ represents the variable cost profit the firm realizes from the strong deman-der. Therefore, the total variable cost profit is $2A^* + 2C + D + E$ from serving both demander types. If $2A^* + 2C + D + E$ exceeds areas A^* through F, then it is more profitable to serve both demanders. If the reverse occurs, then only the strong demander is served.

CONCEPTS IN CONTEXT

Making Them Pay Twice: Personal Seat Licenses for Sports Teams

Charlotte, North Carolina, is a city on the move. It is the banking capital of the southeastern United States. One way that many upcoming cities "get on the map" is to obtain a professional sports franchise. Charlotte acquired a National Football League franchise for the Charlotte Panthers. But it needed a stadium. How to finance such a large capital expense?

Enter Max Muhlemann. Charlotte was rabid about its new team. Fans were supportive. Muhlemann suggested that the Panthers sell personal seat licenses for the new stadium. The concept was that a fan would have to purchase a personal seat license to be able to purchase a ticket to see the Panthers play football. The personal seat license was an entry fee. The use fee is the price of a ticket for the game.

Demand for the licenses was very strong. They sold for prices that reflected the desirability of the seats. The average price of a personal seat license was $2,400. The Panthers sold 62,000 personal seat licenses. That's $149 million received by the team *before* a game was ever played in the stadium. That's $149 million in consumer surplus that fans were willing to spend just for the *right* to purchase tickets to see the games. After holding the personal seat license, the holder buys a game ticket at a price no different than other football teams charge. The big difference is that other teams were not collecting the consumer surplus as the Panthers were.

Other teams caught on to this application of the two-part tariff to professional sports, and the use of personal seat licenses to finance new stadiums and stadium improvements is growing. Muhlemann has become a busy consultant and is known as the "father" of the personal seat license.

Source: F. Klein, "Growing Plague: Buying the Right to Buy a Ticket," *Wall Street Journal.* Sept. 26, 1996.

A Two-Part Tariff with Different Demands: A Numerical Example

The Bruger Company has a strong demander (with a demand curve of $P_S = 8 - Q_S$) and a weak demander (with a demand curve of $P_W = 6 - Q_W$). It has a constant marginal cost of production of $2. It wants to consider a two-part tariff and calls in a consultant to make some pricing proposals. One proposal the consultant considers is charging a use fee of $2 (the firm's marginal cost) and an entry fee equal to the resulting consumer surplus of the strong market. Since the strong demand curve can be rewritten as $Q_S = 8 - P_S$, if the use fee is $2, the strong demander would purchase six units. The resulting consumer surplus would be $0.5(8 - 2)6 = \$18$. The consultant proposes this as the entry fee. Under this suggestion, the firm receives a variable cost profit of $18. Another possibility considered is charging a use fee of $2 and an entry fee equal to the consumer surplus of the weak demander. Since the weak demand can be rewritten as $Q_W = 6 - P_W$, if the use fee is $2, the weak demander would purchase four units. The resulting consumer surplus for the weak demander equals $0.5(6 - 2)4 = \$8$. If this is charged as the entry fee, both demand types would pay it, and the firm's variable cost profit would be $16.

The consultant then considers a use fee greater than marginal cost and an entry fee equal to the resulting consumer surplus of the weak demander. How would the consultant determine that P^* ($> MC$)? If the firm charges an entry fee of P^*, then the strong demander would purchase $Q_S = 8 - P^*$ units and the weak demander would purchase $Q_W = 6 - P^*$ units. Since $P^* > MC = AVC$, the firm makes a variable cost profit (of $P^* - 2$) from every unit it sells (and it sells $8 - P^* + 6 - P^* = 14 - 2P^*$ units). The variable cost profit from the use fee is $(P^* - 2)(14 - 2P^*) = -2P^{*2} + 18P^* - 28$. With $6 - P^*$ units sold in the weak market, the resulting consumer surplus in the weak market is $0.5(6 - P^*)(6 - P^*) = 18 - 6P^* + 0.5P^{*2}$. This is the entry fee, and since both demanders would pay it, variable cost profit from the entry fee would be $36 - 12P^* + P^{*2}$. Therefore, the total variable cost profit would be

$$VC\pi = -2P^{*2} + 18P^* - 28 + 36 - 12P^* + P^{*2} = -P^{*2} + 6P^* + 8 \quad (12.9)$$

The variable cost profit is maximized when $dVC\pi/dP^* = 0$. Therefore,

$$dVC\pi/dP^* = 0 = -2P^* + 6$$
$$\text{or } P^* = \$3.$$

Substituting $P^* = \$3$ in equation (12.9) gives

$$VC\pi = -(3^2) + 6(3) + 8 = \$17$$

Therefore, the best variable cost profit of the three considered is to serve only the strong demander and earn a variable cost profit of $18.[12]

The consultant has one last proposal to make. Suppose the firm combines both the concept of price discrimination and the two-part tariff. We saw from the preceding that the consumer surplus of the weak demander when the use fee is marginal cost (= $2) is $8, and the consumer surplus of the stronger demander when the use fee is marginal cost is $18. Therefore, the consultant

[12]If the strong demand had been $P_S = 7 - Q_S$, then serving only the strong demander yields a variable cost profit of $12.5, while serving both demand types with a use fee equal to marginal cost yields a variable cost profit of $16. If a use fee greater than marginal cost is chosen (optimal fee $2.5) and the resulting consumer surplus of the weak demander is the entry fee ($6.125), the variable cost profit is $16.25, which is the best of the three considered.

CONCEPTS IN CONTEXT

Verizon Local Calling Plans

Telephone service is a classic example of a two-part tariff. A subscriber pays the phone company a monthly fee for the privilege of receiving a dial tone. This fee must be paid regardless of whether there are zero, tens, or hundreds of incoming or outgoing calls per month. It is an entry fee for having the service available (although one could avoid this fee by using the pay phone on the corner, albeit at a higher use fee for outgoing calls).

Managers of phone companies are becoming more adept at using sophisticated pricing strategies. Consider Verizon's local calling plans in New Jersey. Because Verizon managers do not know, with certainty, the demand curve of individual consumers, they let the consumers reveal their preference function by offering a menu of pricing plans. Although most of the plans are primarily two-part tariff pricing, managers combine this pricing strategy with bundling and price discrimination.

In 2004, Verizon offered the following local calling plans in New Jersey.

- *Flat rate service*—price: $6.75–$8.19/month. This plan gives the consumer unlimited message units of local outgoing calls during the month. A message unit is a local call of five minutes.
- *Moderate message rate service*—price $5.44–$6.58/month. This plan includes 75 outgoing message units. Additional message units are billed at $0.065 each.
- *Low use message rate service*—price $4.40–$5.39/month. This plan includes 20 outgoing message units. Additional messages are billed at $0.10 each.
- *Verizon local package*—price $21.95/month. This plan gives the consumer unlimited message units of local outgoing calls per month. It also includes unlimited directory assistance and up to three calling features. Features include caller ID, three-way calling, and call waiting.

Source: www.verizon.com.

proposes that the use fee be set equal to marginal cost, the weak demander is charged an entry fee of $8, and the strong demander is charged an entry fee of $18. This yields the firm a variable cost profit of $26. Price discrimination does not take place on the use fees but on the entry fees.

Think about the latter pricing policy in light of the real world. Clubs have full members, associate members, junior members, and the like. Each has a different initiation and dues structure. Usually, there is some restriction on use (not all members can play golf on Wednesday afternoons, when the doctors play). But, can you see the motivation behind these different classes of membership?

Bundling

Consumers often encounter bundling when firms offer distinct goods or services together at a packaged price. Economists distinguish between pure bundling, when the goods are offered only in the package, and mixed bundling, when the goods have a packaged price as well as stand-alone prices. Examples abound. We previously mentioned the value meals of fast-food restaurants. Entertainers, as diverse as professional sports teams and opera companies, also commonly practice mixed bundling, offering tickets to individual performances as well as season tickets, subscriptions of tickets to multiple (but not all) performances, and other bundles. On the other hand, a record company bundles 12 songs of your favorite recording artist on a CD, and you must buy the CD (the bundle) to obtain the several songs you want (and hence obtain more songs that you do not want very much, if at all). They sell their product only as a pure bundle.

Why is bundling so common? One reason is that it can increase the seller's profits if the customers have varied tastes. In addition, it can be a way to accomplish or emulate perfect price discrimination when perfect price discrimination is not possible (either because knowing individual reservation prices is too difficult or expensive to pursue) or it is not legal to charge multiple prices for the same "product." With the bundle, you need not know the reservation price of each consumer for each good (as you do in perfect price discrimination) but only the distribution of all consumers' reservation prices over the goods. To keep the example simple, we consider the case of two goods.

As a further simplification, assume that the worth of the bundle of goods to a consumer is the sum of the consumer's reservation prices for each good; that is, the goods are independent of each other. One could envision cases of complementarity of the goods where the goods as a bundle would have a value to the individual greater than the sum of their separate reservation prices, such as items that have to be assembled, software and hardware. One could also envision cases of substitutability of the goods where the goods as a bundle would have a value to the individual less than the sum of their separate reservation prices, such as, a bundle of a Coke and a Pepsi. In addition, assume that there are no economies of scope in the production of these two goods. The costs of producing each good is the same regardless of whether the goods are produced for sale separately or as a bundle; that is, the cost of a bundle is the sum of the individual costs of the two goods. Also assume that consumers consume no more than one unit of any good or no more than one bundle. Finally, assume that the resale of goods by the consumer is not possible.

Of course, the seller could always sell the goods as separate items. If the seller cannot price discriminate but must charge a single price for each good, assume that price is the simple monopoly profit-maximizing one.

FIGURE

12.9

Price Separately

Whether consumers purchase goods separately depends on their reservation price of the good relative to the prices charged by the seller.

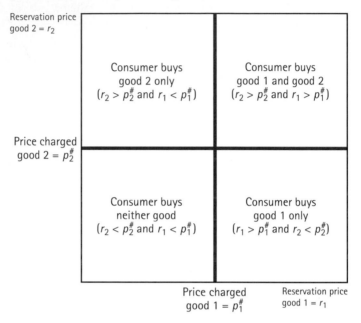

Reservation price good 2 = r_2

Consumer buys good 2 only $(r_2 > p_2^\# \text{ and } r_1 < p_1^\#)$

Consumer buys good 1 and good 2 $(r_2 > p_2^\# \text{ and } r_1 > p_1^\#)$

Price charged good 2 = $p_2^\#$

Consumer buys neither good $(r_2 < p_2^\# \text{ and } r_1 < p_1^\#)$

Consumer buys good 1 only $(r_1 > p_1^\# \text{ and } r_2 < p_2^\#)$

Price charged good 1 = $p_1^\#$

Reservation price good 1 = r_1

We can investigate the three possible pricing scenarios in the following three figures. Figure 12.9 shows the price separately situation. The firm chooses the optimal simple monopoly prices for good 1 and good 2 (the ones that maximize profits). Call them $p_1^\#$ and $p_2^\#$. Figure 12.9 shows the resulting consumption behavior of consumers depending on where they lie in reservation price space.

Figure 12.10 shows the situation of pure bundling. The firm chooses the optimal pure bundle price (the one that maximizes profits). Call it $p_B^\#$. Figure 12.10 shows the resulting consumption behavior of consumers depending on where they lie in the reservation price space.

Figure 12.11 shows the situation of mixed bundling. The firm chooses the optimal pure bundle price (p_B^*), the optimal separate price for good 1 (p_1^*), and the optimal separate price for good 2 (p_2^*) where these prices are set to maximize the firm's profit. Figure 12.11 shows the resulting consumption behavior of consumers depending on where they lie in the reservation price space.

The optimal solution is the greatest profit of the profit-maximizing solutions yielded by separate pricing, pure bundling, and mixed bundling. The manager

FIGURE
12.10

Pure Bundling

Whether consumers purchase the bundle depends on the sum of their reservation prices for the good relative to the bundled price charged by the seller.

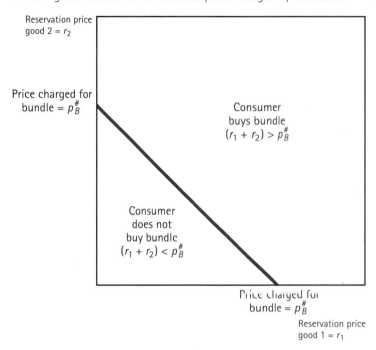

chooses the action that maximizes profit. These figures do not show the cost of producing the goods. This keeps the figures simple. Obviously, although the figures show the buyers' intentions, their realized transactions are a subset of those shown because certain pricing actions are precluded by the manager's profit-maximizing behavior. Solving for the profit-maximizing solutions for Figures 12.9 and 12.10 is easy, because one has to consider only individual reservation prices for the goods as candidate prices in Figure 12.9 and only the sum of each consumer's reservation prices as candidate prices for the pure bundle in Figure 12.10. Any other prices would unnecessarily leave consumer surplus on the table (and a profit-maximizing seller always wants to convert such consumer surplus into producer surplus).

The more difficult calculation is determining the best mixed bundle prices. As shown next in an example, the optimal prices do not have to be a reservation price of a good or a bundle. The solution is either one of "educated" trial and error or via a computer program that searches all separate prices and pure bundle prices and chooses the combination yielding the highest profits. Trial

FIGURE
12.11

Mixed Bundling

Whether the consumer purchases the goods separately or as a bundle depends on the consumer surplus (the difference between consumers' reservation price, or sum of their reservation prices, and the price charged by the seller). Consumers choose the goods or bundle that maximize their consumer surplus.

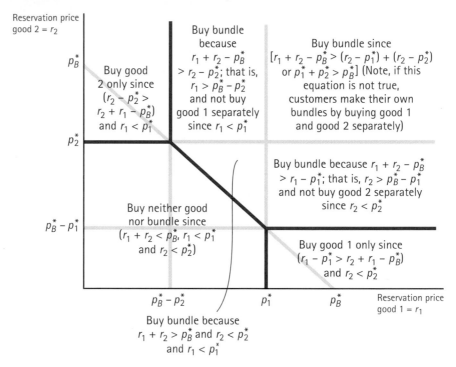

and error can be done in simple cases with few consumers and goods. Cases with many consumers and goods require a computer program. Critical to mixed bundling, is creating a "credible" mixed bundle. Credibility of the bundle means that customers who managers anticipate will purchase the bundle do, and those anticipated to purchase the goods separately do.

The following example shows the three types of pricing in a situation of perfectly negative correlation of consumer reservation prices; that is, all the reservation prices lie on a line of slope -1 in the reservation price space. Note that, while the customers have a negative correlation in their reservation prices for the two goods, they exhibit *no* variation in their valuation of the bundle: They all value the bundle at $100. The consumer reservation prices are shown in Table 12.1 and the situation is depicted in Figure 12.12.

TABLE 12.1

Reservation Prices of Good 1 and Good 2 of Consumers A, B, C, and D

Consumer	Reservation Price Good 1	Good 2	Bundle Price
A	90	10	100
B	60	40	100
C	50	50	100
D	10	90	100

FIGURE 12.12

Example of Perfect Negative Correlation of Consumers' Reservation Prices

Consumers A, B, C, and D value each good differently but all value the bundle of the two goods at $100.

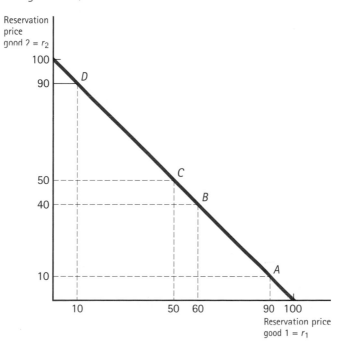

TABLE 12.2

Optimal Separate Price Prices for Good 1 and Good 2

Consumer	Price 1	Cost/unit	Profit/unit	Number of units	Profit
A	90	1	89	1	89
B	60	1	59	2	118
C	50	1	49	3	147
D	10	1	9	4	36

Consumer	Price 2	Cost/unit	Profit/unit	Number of units	Profit
A	10	1	9	4	36
B	40	1	39	3	117
C	50	1	49	2	98
D	90	1	89	1	89

The profit from the best separate price strategy of $P_1 = \$50$ and $P_2 = \$40$ is $264.

Suppose that the constant unit cost of production of each good is 1. The separate price, pure bundling, and mixed bundling cases are shown in Tables 12.2, 12.3, and 12.4.

Note that one can always come up with a mixed bundle by pricing the individual goods at prices at which no consumer purchases the good. In some cases, *but not this one*, it is possible to increase profits through mixed bundling. Mixed bundling, therefore, always *weakly dominates* pure bundling.

If we look at mixed bundles where customers actually consume the bundle and at least one of the goods is sold separately, the situation in Table 12.5 is the best mixed bundle.

Note that consumer A does not consume the bundle because, at price $100, she receives no consumer surplus. However, consumer A consumes good 1 at $89.99 because she receives a positive consumer surplus (of $0.01). Likewise, consumer D does not consume the bundle because at price $100, he receives no consumer surplus. However, consumer D consumes good 2 at $89.99 because

TABLE 12.3

Optimal Pure Bundle Price for Consumers A, B, C, and D

Consumer	Bundle price	Cost/bundle	Profit/bundle	Number bundles	Profit
A, B, C, D	100	2	98	4	392

The profit from the best pure bundling strategy of $P_{Bundle} = \$100$ is $392.

Optimal Mixed Bundle Prices

Consumer	Bundle price	Cost/bundle	Profit/bundle	Number of bundles	Profit
A, B, C, D	100	2	98	4	392

Consumer	Price 1	Cost/unit	Profit/unit	Number of units	Profit
None	90.01	1	89.01	0	0

Consumer	Price 2	Cost/unit	Profit/unit	Number of units	Profit
None	90.01	1	89.01	0	0

The profit from the best mixed bundling strategy of $P_{Bundle} = \$100$, $P_1 > \$90$, and $P_2 > \$90$ is $392.

he receives a positive consumer surplus (of $0.01). We discuss this logic further in another example.

In the preceding case, where pure bundling is the best pricing strategy, perfect price discrimination is completely replicated as the manager extracts *all* the consumer surplus from each customer. This goal is called **extraction**. In addition, a manager likes to practice **exclusion**, not selling a good to a customer who values the good at less than the cost of producing it. Finally, a seller likes to practice **inclusion**, selling a good to a customer who values the good at greater than the seller's cost of producing the good. Perfect price discrimination extracts all available consumer surplus, does not sell to anyone at below

Optimal Mixed Bundle Prices when Consumer Consumes Bundle and at Least One of the Separate Priced Goods

Consumer	Bundle price	Cost/bundle	Profit/bundle	Number of bundles	Profit
B, C	100	2	98	2	196

Consumer	Price 1	Cost/unit	Profit/unit	Number of units	Profit
A	89.99	1	88.99	1	88.99

Consumer	Price 2	Cost/unit	Profit/unit	Number of units	Profit
D	89.99	1	88.99	1	88.99

The profit from the best mixed bundling strategy where customers actually purchase the bundle and purchase at least one of the separately priced goods of $P_{Bundle} = \$100$, $P_1 = \$89.99$, and $P_2 = \$89.99$ is $373.98.

cost, and sells to everyone who values the good at greater than cost. Thus, perfect price discrimination perfectly satisfies all of the three bolded concepts. These three pricing mechanisms can be compared to perfect price discrimination on the three dimensions of extraction, exclusion, and inclusion.

Pricing separately should never entail exclusion, but because of its single price per good nature, it will not fulfill complete extraction or inclusion (for negatively sloped demand curves). Pure bundling can allow complete extraction (as in the preceding case), but when all demanders' sum of reservation prices for goods do not lie on a line with a slope of −1 (i.e., less than perfect negative correlation of reservation prices), extraction is less than complete. Mixed bundling falls someplace in between pricing separately and pure bundling.

Pure bundling can also fail inclusion and exclusion. Note how the best price strategy changes when the cost of producing the goods change. Consider the example just used but with the cost of production of each good now at $11 each. Tables 12.6, 12.7, and 12.8 show the solutions for price separately, pure bundling, and mixed bundling.

However, if we look at mixed bundles where customers actually consume the bundle and at least one of the goods sold separately, Table 12.9 shows the best mixed bundle.

In this case, the concept of exclusion dominates the concept of extraction. The pure bundle price of $100 completely extracts all consumer surplus. However, the seller sells (in the bundle) good 2 to consumer A and A values the good at only $10, whereas it costs the seller $11 to produce good 2. Likewise, the seller sells good 1 to consumer D in the bundle and D values the good at only $10, whereas it costs the seller $11 to produce good 1. It is better for the seller to exclude consumer A from buying good 2 and consumer D from

TABLE
12.6

Optimal Separate Price Prices for Good 1 and Good 2

Consumer	Price 1	Cost/unit	Profit/unit	Number of units	Profit
A	90	11	79	1	79
B	60	11	49	2	98
C	50	11	39	3	117
D	10	11	−1	4	−4

Consumer	Price 2	Cost/unit	Profit/unit	Number of units	Profit
A	10	11	−1	4	−4
B	40	11	29	3	87
C	50	11	39	2	78
D	90	11	79	1	79

The profit from the best separate price strategy of $P_1 = \$50$ and $P_2 = \$40$ is $204.

TABLE 12.7

Optimal Pure Bundle Prices for Consumers *A*, *B*, *C*, and *D*

Consumer	Bundle price	Cost/bundle	Profit/bundle	Number of bundles	Profit
A, B, C, D	100	22	78	4	312

The profit from the best pure bundling strategy of $P_{Bundle} = \$100$ is $312.

TABLE 12.8

Optimal Mixed Bundle Prices

Consumer	Bundle price	Cost/bundle	Profit/bundle	Number of bundles	Profit
A, B, C, D	100	22	78	4	312

Consumer	Price 1	Cost/unit	Profit/unit	Number of units	Profit
None	90.01	11	79.01	0	0

Consumer	Price 2	Cost/unit	Profit/unit	Number of units	Profit
None	90.01	11	79.01	0	0

The profit from the best mixed bundle strategy of $P_{Bundle} = \$100$, $P_1 > 90$, and $P_2 > 90$ is $312.

TABLE 12.9

Optimal Mixed Bundle Prices when Consumer Consumes Bundle and at Least One of the Separately Priced Goods

Consumer	Bundle price	Cost/bundle	Profit/bundle	Number of bundles	Profit
B, C	100	22	78	2	156

Consumer	Price 1	Cost/unit	Profit/unit	Number of units	Profit
A	89.99	11	78.99	1	78.99

Consumer	Price 2	Cost/unit	Profit/unit	Number of units	Profit
D	89.99	11	78.99	1	78.99

The profit from the best mixed bundle strategy where customers actually purchase the bundle and at least one of the separately priced goods of $P_{Bundle} = \$100$, $P_1 = \$89.99$, and $P_2 = \$89.99$ is $313.98. Therefore, mixed bundling is the best pricing strategy for the seller.

buying good 1. The seller can do that by practicing mixed bundling. The seller sacrifices $10.01 in consumer surplus from each of consumers A and D by switching those consumers from a price of $100 for the bundle to a price of $89.99 for the separate good (a total of $20.02). But the seller saves $22 in cost by not producing one unit of good 1 and one unit of good 2. This $1.98 difference is the difference in profits between the best pure bundle profit of $312 and the best mixed bundle profit of $313.98. Inclusion and exclusion are practiced perfectly in this case of mixed bundling but complete extraction is not. In general, optimal pricing solutions among these three methods entail a trade-off of the concepts of extraction, exclusion, and inclusion.

Suppose further that the cost of producing each good is now $55. Tables 12.10, 12.11, and 12.12 show the solutions for pricing separately, pure bundling, and mixed bundling.

The only reason that mixed bundling yielded the same profit as separate pricing is that a bundle price is selected so that no consumer would choose the bundle, that is, a price over $100. In cases where separate pricing is the best, one can always price the bundle at a price at which no one would consume it. Therefore, mixed bundling weakly dominates pricing separately. Since previously we established that mixed bundling weakly dominates pure bundling, *technically mixed bundling should be a part of any bundling strategy (because the profit from it is always better than or equal to that of pricing separately or pure bundling).*

While pure bundling perfectly extracts all consumer surplus in this perfectly negatively correlated reservation price example when the unit production cost is $55, it fails miserably on exclusion. Many units (five) are sold to customers who value the good at less than its cost of production. Mixed bundling, except at a price that excludes all from buying the pure bundle, can do no better than

TABLE 12.10

Optimal Price Separately Prices for Good 1 and Good 2

Consumer	Price 1	Cost/unit	Profit/unit	Number of units	Profit
A	**90**	55	35	1	**35**
B	60	55	5	2	10
C	50	55	−5	3	−15
D	10	55	−45	4	−180

Consumer	Price 2	Cost/unit	Profit/unit	Number of units	Profit
A	10	55	−45	4	−180
B	40	55	−15	3	−45
C	50	55	−5	2	−10
D	**90**	55	35	1	**35**

The profit from the best separate price strategy of $P_1 = \$90$ and $P_2 = \$90$ is $70.

TABLE
12.11

Optimal Pure Bundle Prices for Consumers A, B, C, and D

Consumer	Bundle price	Cost/bundle	Profit/bundle	Number of bundles	Profit
A, B, C, D	100	110	−10	4	−40

The best pure bundling strategy is any bundle price over $100. No one will buy the bundle and the profit is $0.

pricing separately. Pricing separately extracts much of the *profitable* consumer surplus, excludes the right consumer surplus, but does not include consumer *B* who values good 1 at $60 (the cost of production is $55).

The negative correlation of the reservation prices enables the manager to fully extract all the consumer surplus with the pure bundle when the cost of production is low. If we increase the production cost while keeping the reservation prices with perfectly negative correlation, initially mixed bundling is the profit-maximizing action; if production costs keep increasing, eventually separate pricing will maximize profit.

But, *negative correlation is not required to make bundling the best choice.* Suppose customers are uniformly distributed over reservation prices for good 1 from $0 to $100 and for good 2 from $0 to $100. This would be a case of **zero correlation** of reservation prices. There are 10,000 such consumers. To keep things simple, suppose that production costs of the goods are $0. Therefore, maximizing the total revenue is the same as maximizing profits.[13]

[13] The following examples are from "Bundling: Teaching Note," Harvard Business School, 5-795-168, rev. July 22, 1998.

TABLE
12.12

Optimal Mixed Bundle Prices at Any Pure Bundle Price over $100 (so No Bundle Is Purchased)

Consumer	Price 1	Cost/unit	Profit/unit	Number of units	Profit
A	90	55	35	1	35

Consumer	Price 2	Cost/unit	Profit/unit	Number of units	Profit
B	90	55	35	1	35

The profit from the best mixed bundle strategy of $P_{Bundle} > \$100$, $P_1 = \$90$, and $P_2 = \$90$ and is $70.

FIGURE
12.13

Optimal Separate Price Prices in the Case of Uniformly Distributed Consumer Reservation Prices

The optimal separate price prices when the uniform distribution of consumer reservation prices is between $0 and $100 for both goods is $50 for each good. Profits are $500,000.

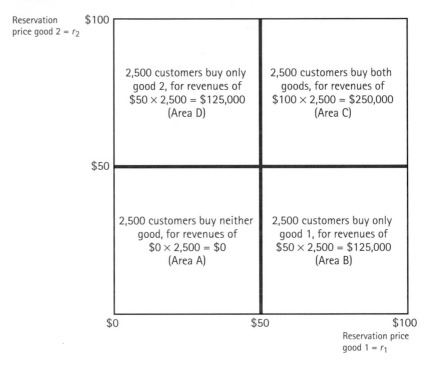

The best separate price is $P_1 = \$50$ and $P_2 = \$50$ and the profit is $500,000.[14] This is shown in Figure 12.13.

[14]Call the optimal price of good 1 x. Because of the uniform distribution, this also is the optimal price of good 2. When x is chosen, it determines how many customers consume each good. Consider choosing x on the horizontal axis. Everyone to the left of x does not consume good 1 and everyone on and to the right of x consumes good 1. Consider choosing x on the vertical axis. Everyone below x does not consume good 2 and everyone on and above x consumes good 2. The total area of Figure 12.13 is $100 \times 100 = 10,000$. Viewing each of the four areas created, we can calculate the percentage of the total area occupied by each of the subareas. For instance, Area A occupies $x^2/10,000$ amount of the total area. Area B occupies $(100 - x)x/10,000 = (100x - x^2)/10,000$ of the total area (as does Area D). Area C occupies $(100 - x)(100 - x)/10,000 = (10,000 - 200x + x^2)/10,000$ of the total area. The number of customers in each area is the percentage of the total area times 10,000. The revenue from each area is the number of customers times the price they

FIGURE
12.14

Optimal Pure Bundle Price in the Case of Uniformly Distributed Consumer Reservation Prices

The optimal pure bundle price when the uniform distribution of consumer reservation prices is between $0 and $100 for both goods is $81.65. Profits are $544,331.10.

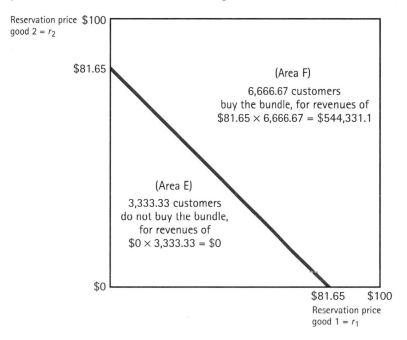

The best pure bundle price is approximately $81.65 and profits are approximately $544,331.1.[15] This is shown in Figure 12.14. Even without negative

pay. Therefore, Area A generates $0r^2$ in revenue, Area B generates $r(100r - r^2)$ in revenue, Area C generates

$2r(10,000 - 200r + r^2)$ in revenue, and Area D generates $r(100r - r^2)$ in revenue, yielding a total revenue (TR) of $20,000r - 200r^2$. We maximize TR by setting $d\text{TR}/dr = 20,000 - 400r = 0$ or $r = \$50$. Total revenues (profits) are $500,000.

[15]Call the optimal price of the bundle y. When the price of the bundle is chosen, it creates a line of slope -1 that connects the vertical axis from point y to the horizontal axis at point y. Area E has area of $0.5(y)(y) = 0.5y^2$. Its share of the whole area is $0.5y^2/10,000$ and hence has $0.5y^2$ customers in it. Area F has the remainder of the customers, that is, $10,000 - 0.5y^2$. The total revenue generated from Area E is $\$0(0.5y^2) = \$0$ and the total revenue generated from Area F is $y(10,000 - 0.5y^2)$. The total revenue (TR) from pure bundling is therefore $10,000y - 0.5y^3$. Maximize TR by setting $d\text{TR}/dy = 10,000 - 1.5y^2 = 0$ or $y \approx \$81.65$. Total revenues (profits) are approximately $544,331.10.

correlation, bundling can increase profits over simple monopoly pricing (i.e., pricing separately).

The best mixed bundle has a bundle price of approximately \$86.19, $P_1 =$ \$66.67, and $P_2 =$ \$66.67, yielding a profit of approximately \$549,201.[16] Therefore, mixed bundling is even better than pure bundling. This is shown in Figure 12.15. So, with no negative correlation of reservation prices, the best pricing policy is mixed bundling.[17]

We may also consider quantity discounting as mixed bundling. Suppose that the cost of producing the good is \$1. Table 12.13 represents consumers' reservation price for the first unit of the good and the second unit of the good. Consumers want (at most) two units of the good. Table 12.14 shows the case of separate pricing, and Table 12.15 shows the pure bundling strategy. Finally, Table 12.16 shows the best mixed bundling strategy.

We give one final example of bundling to demonstrate how tricky calculating the optimal mixed bundle pricing package can be. The example demonstrates the point made previously about having to consider only customers' reservation prices as candidates for optimal separate price prices and only the sum of customer's reservation prices as candidates for pure bundling. It also shows that, in mixed bundling, the optimal prices need not be any customer's

---

[16]Call y the bundle price and x the price of good 1 (and good 2 because of the symmetry). Areas $G + H + I = 0.5y^2$. As shown in the two previous footnotes, these areas represent the number of consumers in the area. Area $H =$ Area $I = 0.5(y - x)(y - x) = 0.5y^2 - xy + 0.5x^2$. Therefore, Area $G = 2xy - 0.5y^2 - x^2$. Area $I +$ Area $J =$ Area $H +$ Area $L = (100 - x)(y - x) = 100y - 100x + x^2 - xy$. Hence, Area $J =$ Area $L = 100y - 100x + x^2 - xy - (0.5y^2 - xy + 0.5x^2) = 100y - 100x - 0.5y^2 + 0.5x^2$. Area $J +$ Area $K +$ Area $L = 10,000 - 0.5y^2$. Area $K = 10,000 - 0.5y^2 - (200y - 200x - y^2 + x^2) = 10,000 - 200y + 200x + 0.5y^2 - x^2$. Consumers in Area $I +$ Area J purchase only good 2 and yield revenues of $x(100y - 100x + x^2 - xy) = 100xy - 100x^2 + x^3 - x^2y$. Consumers in Area $H +$ Area L purchase only good 1 and yield revenues of $x(100y - 100x + x^2 - xy) = 100xy - 100x^2 + x^3 - x^2y$. Consumers in Area K purchase the bundle and yield revenues of $y(10,000 - 200y + 200x + 0.5y^2 - x^2) = 10,000y - 200y^2 + 200xy + 0.5y^3 - x^2y$. Consumers in Area G buy nothing and yield no revenues. Total revenue (TR) is therefore $10,000y - 200y^2 + 400xy + 0.5y^3 - 3x^2y - 200x^2 + 2x^3$. Total revenues are maximized where $\partial TR/\partial x = 0$ and $\partial TR/\partial y = 0$; $\partial TR/\partial x = 400y - 6xy - 400x + 6x^2 = 0$.

This yields $400x - 400y = 6x^2 - 6xy$ or $400(x - y) = 6x(x - y)$, or $6x = 400$, which yields $x =$ \$66.67. $\partial TR/\partial y = 10,000 - 400y + 400x + 1.5y^2 - 3x^2 = 0$. Substituting $x =$ \$66.67 into $\partial TR/\partial y$ yields $10,000 - 400y + 26,666.67 + 1.5y^2 - 13,333.33 = 1.5y^2 - 400y + 23,333.33 = 0$. Solving via the quadratic formula yields $y =$ \$86.19. Substituting $y =$ \$86.19 and $x =$ \$66.67 into TR $= 10,000y - 200y^2 + 400xy + 0.5y^3 - 3x^2y - 200x^2 + 2x^3 =$ \$549,201.

[17]Bundling can also work if reservation prices are positively correlated. Consider the case where consumer A values good 1 at 11 and good 2 at 24, consumer B values good 1 at 15 and good 2 at 45, and consumer C values good 1 at 16 and good 2 at 15. The reservation prices are weakly positively correlated; that is, the slope of a linear regression is 0.006. The cost of good 1 is 5 and the cost of good 2 is 10. The best separately priced price is $P_1 = 15$ and $P_2 = 45$ and yields a profit of 55. The best pure bundle price is $P_B = 31$ yielding a profit of 48. But the best is a mixed bundle of $P_B = 60$, $P_1 = 16$, and not offering good 2 separately. Consumer B buys the bundle, consumer C buys good 1, and consumer A buys nothing. The profit is 56.

FIGURE
12.15

Optimal Mixed Bundle Pricing in the Case of Uniformly Distributed Consumer Reservation Prices

The optimal mixed bundle pricing when the uniform distribution of consumer reservation prices is between $0 and $100 for both goods is $P_1 = 66.67$, $P_2 = 66.67$, and $P_{Bundle} = 86.19$. Profit is $549,201.

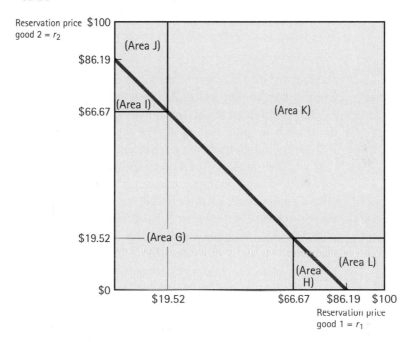

TABLE
12.13

Reservation Prices for the First and Second Units of a Good by Consumers A and B

| | Reservation price of good | |
Consumer	First unit	Second unit
A	4	1.5
B	3.99	3

TABLE
12.14

Optimal Separate Price Prices for the Good

Price of good	Cost/unit	Profit/unit	Number of units	Profit
4	1	3	1	3
3.99	1	2.99	2	5.98
3	1	2	3	**6**
1.5	1	0.5	4	2

So the best separately priced price is $3 and the profit is $6.

reservation price (or sum of reservation prices). And, the consumer chooses the good or bundle that leaves her with the greatest consumer surplus.

The complexity of solving for the optimal bundle is that managers have no $d\pi/dQ = 0$ formula to help derive the optimal pricing scheme. The procedure is more trial and error than derivation. The mixed bundle pricing package consists of prices for individual components, then a single price for the product (or service) bundle. A manager can maximize profit even if the prices of the individual components or the bundle are different from the reservation prices of the consumers. This cannot be true when considering just separate pricing or pure bundling. Whether we deal with prices different than reservation prices or their sums depends on trade-offs from the consumers' view of consumer surplus and from the producers' view of producer surplus. We again assume the reservation price of the goods as a bundle is the sum of the two reservation prices, that is, no positive or negative synergy, where the whole is worth more (or less) than the sum of its parts.

Consider the scenario in Table 12.17. There are three consumers (or consumer groups)—A, B, and C, for simplicity, with an equal number of consumers in each group and each wanting no more than one of each good at its reservation price or less—and two goods, X and Y. Both products cost a constant $4

TABLE
12.15

Optimal Pure Bundle Price for Two Units of the Same Good

Price of bundle	Cost/bundle	Profit/bundle	Number of bundles	Profit
5.5	2	3.5	2	**7**
6.99	2	4.99	1	4.99

So the best pure bundling strategy is a price of $5.5 and the profit is $7.

TABLE 12.16 Optimal Mixed Bundling Prices for the Case of a Single Good

Price of bundle	Cost/bundle	Profit/bundle	Number of bundles	Profit
6.99	2	4.99	1 (B)	4.99

Price of good	Cost/unit	Profit/unit	Number of units	Profit
4	1	3	1 (A)	3

So the best mixed bundle and the best overall pricing strategy is to price a unit of the good at $4 and a bundle of two goods at $6.99. This yields a profit of $7.99.

to produce. The best separate pricing prices are shown in bold in Table 12.18. Therefore, the best separate pricing strategy is price X at $12 and price Y at $8, which yields a profit of $16. The best pure bundling price is shown in Table 12.19 in bold. The best pure bundle price is $13.33, which yields a profit of $15.99.

Note the negative relationship (correlation) among the customer's reservation prices. Note also that, in considering separate price, you need never consider a nonreservation price as a pricing candidate. For instance, suppose you investigated pricing good X at $5. Two customers would purchase at that price (A and B, who have reservation prices of $5.33 and $12, respectively). Your profit with such a price is ($5 − $4)2 = $2. But, when you price at $5, you leave consumer surplus on the table. Consumer A is willing to pay $5.33 but you do not ask her to. As a result, you sacrifice $0.33 in profit (not only on customer A but also on customer B). By lowering your price to $5, you pick up no additional sales and sacrifice $0.66 in profit. If you do not charge the reservation prices of the customers, you cannot maximize profits using a separate price strategy.

TABLE 12.17 Consumer Reservation Prices for Good X and Good Y (in dollars)

	Reservation prices for goods by consumer		
	Good X	Good Y	Both X and Y
Consumer A	5.33	8	13.33
Consumer B	12	3	15
Consumer C	3	11	14

TABLE 12.18

Best Separate Price Strategy

	Cost/unit	Profit/unit	Number of units	Profit
Price of X				
5.33	4	1.33	2	2.66
12.00	4	8.00	1	**8.00**
3.00	4	−1.00	3	−3.00
Price of Y				
8.00	4	4.00	2	**8.00**
3.00	4	−1.00	3	−3.00
11.00	4	7.00	1	7.00

The same is true for pure bundling. Why shouldn't you consider pricing the bundle at $14.50 as one of your candidates? Because, at $14.50, you get only customer B to buy the bundle and she would have purchased the bundle at $15. You would leave consumer surplus on the table.

Consider now a mixed bundling strategy with a bundle price of $13.33, a price of good X at $10.32, and a price of good Y at $10.32. It first might appear that all customers would buy the bundle a $13.33 (because B gets consumer surplus of $15 − $13.33 = $1.67 and C gets consumer surplus of $14 − $13.33 = $0.67). But, if the price of X is $10.32, consumer B gets a higher consumer surplus of $12 − $10.32 = $1.68 > $1.67 if she buys good X alone, and if the price of good Y is $10.32, consumer C gets a higher consumer surplus of $11 − $10.32 = $0.68 > $0.67 if she buys good Y alone. But consumer B does not get to consume good Y if she does not buy the bundle, and consumer C does not get to consume good X if she does not buy the bundle—doesn't that count? Yes, but they are still better off with the larger consumer surplus from consuming just one good, as we shall see.

TABLE 12.19

Best Pure Bundling Strategy

Price of bundle	Cost/bundle	Profit of bundle	Number of bundles	Profit
13.33	8	5.33	3	**15.99**
15.00	8	7.00	1	7.00
14.00	8	6.00	2	12.00

Consider consumer B. Suppose consumer B has $15. If she buys the bundle for $13.33, she would have consumer surplus of $1.67 and both goods. But, if she buys just good X for $10.32, she would have good X and $4.68 left over. She has $1.68 in consumer surplus from good X and while she does not have good Y, she has $4.68 in cash ($3 of which is not part of the consumer surplus from good X). But $4.68 in cash instead of good Y is attractive to consumer B since good Y is worth only $3 to her (and she has the equivalent to good Y with the $3 in cash that is not associated with the consumer surplus for good X, as the definition of the reservation price entails that a person is exactly indifferent between the good and the amount of dollars of the reservation price). Therefore, $4.68 in cash and good X is a better position for consumer B than $1.67 in cash and both goods (which is worth only $4.67 to her). Analogously, consumer C, starting off with $14, is better off with $3.68 in cash and good Y rather than having $0.67 in cash and both goods (because good X is worth $3 to her).

How does the firm do with such a mixed bundle? Table 12.20 demonstrates the profit improvement on $17.97. The profit of $17.97 dominates the profit of $16 available from the best separate pricing strategy and the profit of $15.99 available from the best pure bundling strategy. The secret is to see if you could pull customers out of the best pure bundling strategy and increase profit with a credible bundle. The best pure bundle yields $5.33 profit per customer. We retain that net profit for customer A and pull customers B and C out at higher profit margins, thus increasing the firm's profit. In the case of separate pricing, we need to ask the question, Can we put some customer(s) in a bundle and do better? We sacrifice profit margin from consumer B (down from $8 in the best price separately situation), but we more than make up that loss with the tremendous gain we make on consumers A and C, who were yielding only $4 each

TABLE 12.20

Best Mixed Bundling Strategy

Price of bundle	Cost/bundle	Profit on each	Total number	Total profit
13.33	8	5.33	1 (consumer A)	5.33
Price of X	Cost/unit	Profit/unit	Total number	Total profit
10.32	4	6.32	1 (consumer B)	6.32
Price of Y	Cost/unit	Profit/unit	Total number	Total profit
10.32	4	6.32	1 (consumer C)	6.32
				Sum of profit
				17.97

under the best separate pricing strategy, increasing the firm's profits (i.e., we are down $1.68 from customer B but up $1.33 from customer A and up $2.32 from customer C, so up on net $1.97, the difference between the mixed bundle profit of $17.97 and the best price separately profit of $16).

If you price good X at $10.34, then customer B does not buy it (it yields a consumer surplus of only $12 − $10.34 = $1.66 and she can get $15 − $13.33 = $1.67 by buying the bundle). So pricing good X at $10.34 and the bundle at $13.33 is not a credible mixed bundle because someone you didn't want to buy the bundle (consumer B) would.

As you can see, mixed bundling need not charge the reservation prices of a consumer for the items. But, we see a lot of mixed bundling in the market— so it is important to know that experimentation plays an important role and pure bundling and separate pricing are not always the best strategies.

Despite the lack of an analytical solution, a few simple rules do exist, however:

1. If goods' reservation prices are positively correlated, pure bundling can do no better than separate pricing (but mixed bundles might).
2. If the marginal cost of producing a good exceeds its reservation price, in general, you should think carefully about selling it.[18]
3. If goods' reservation prices are correlated *perfectly* negatively and the marginal cost of production of the goods is zero, then pure bundling is best.
4. If goods' reservation prices are negatively correlated, as the marginal cost of production increases, mixed bundling is likely to be better than pure bundling, and as they increase further, separate pricing is likely to be better.

But, everything really depends on the reservation prices and the costs of production, so remember that intelligent experimentation is the way to solve bundling pricing. The other approach, especially when the numbers of demanders or goods is large, is to use a computer program to search all three types of pricing and every price in each type for the profit-maximizing result.

---

[18]Sometimes it may be more profitable to sell a good in a pure bundle even though the reservation price of a bundle buyer for a good in the bundle is less than the cost of producing the good. Consider a situation where the firm is choosing between only separate pricing and pure bundling. The reservation prices for good 1 and good 2 for consumers A through F are ($70, $30), ($80, $20), ($75, $25), ($75, $15), ($84, $16) and ($90, $10), respectively. The unit cost of production of good 1 is $70 and of good 2 is $20. The optimal separate pricing prices are $P_1 = \$80$ and P_2 either $30 or $25, to yield a profit of $40. The optimal pure bundling price is $100 and yields a profit of $50. Consumers E and F, who buy the bundle, value good 2 at less than its cost and are not excluded because that would decrease the firm's profit. If mixed bundling is allowed, the exclusion problem can be solved. The bundle would be priced at $100 and good 1 would be priced at $83.99. This yields a profit of $57.98, and E and F consume only the good (good 1) they value at greater than cost.

CONCEPTS IN CONTEXT

How the *New Yorker* Used Bundling

The *New Yorker* is a wonderfully written magazine with witty, informative, entertaining articles. But apparently the market for high-quality journalism has fallen on hard times as consumers have switched their preferences from culture to monster truck shows.

Magazines depend on subscriptions and newsstand sales, but most of all, advertising for their revenues. And advertising revenues are interdependent with the number of magazines sold, because advertisers pay more if the circulation to their demographic group is higher.

Over the years, circulation and advertising revenues fell. It appeared that the *New Yorker* could

not cover its costs with its revenues. Thus, the *New Yorker's* publisher (Conde Nast) came up with a bundling strategy. Conde Nast also publishes *Architectural Digest* and *Vanity Fair* (which are doing well). The bundling strategy? If a company wanted to advertise in *Architectural Digest* or *Vanity Fair*, it also had to advertise in the *New Yorker*. This proved to be a profitable strategy and the *New Yorker* is still publishing.

Source: "There's Less Buzz and Less Lunch at the *New Yorker*," *New York Times*, Monday, June 28, 1999.

Peak Load Pricing

The demand for goods or services may shift with the time of day (e.g., the demand for highway and transit services is greatest during the morning and evening rush hours, lower during midday, and lower still overnight), with the time of week (e.g., roads to resorts are likely to have a greater demand on the weekend than during the week), or with the time of year (e.g., Miami Beach hotels have a greater demand in February when it is cold in the northern United States than in the summer when it's warm almost everywhere in the United States, and the demand for electricity is higher in the summer, for air conditioning, and in the winter, for heating and fewer daylight hours, than in the spring or fall).

Because these temporal differences in demand are coupled with a plant capacity that does not change over the demand cycle, firms faced with these demand conditions (many times) charge different prices in the peak (high ones = P_P) and in the trough (low ones = P_T). The rule they follow is that marginal revenue equals marginal cost. The marginal revenue curves differ because the demand curves for the service differ between the peak and trough. The marginal cost is usually quite high in the peak, as the supplier is operating at or near capacity, and usually quite low in the trough, as much excess capacity

CONCEPTS IN CONTEXT

When Bundling Fails

AT&T customers have spoken. Would they want a cell phone, wireless service, or a free oil change bundled with their local and long distance service? The answer is a Jiffy Lube. Of the 149 bundles AT&T offers (talk about self selection into what consumer group you are in), the most popular bundle is the one with the free Jiffy Lube coupon.

This seems to be because many homeowners do not wish to be captive to one provider for their home phone, wireless, Internet, and TV service (a monopoly fear). In addition, consumers are concerned that the prices they pay for the component services of the bundle are not transparent, making comparison shopping difficult. So, one stop shopping, at least in this field, has yet to take off.

As Adam Quinton, an analyst at Merrill Lynch states, "Bundling works selectively. There are some bundles that are clearly very powerful, but the answer isn't necessarily to bundle everything."

Another reason for the failure of like-product bundling is that AT&T was unable to bill all services on one bill (although some phone providers are moving in this direction). The failure to do so helps in the transparency to consumers of their cost of services but hurts in the convenience fac-tor (two or three checks written, stamps, envelopes licked, etc., versus one of each). Other consumers, by "cherry picking" services from different providers, have been able to beat the bundled price. (Remember that there are transaction costs in wading through all the competing services in attempting to find the best).

Another factor is psychological. Writing one big check to one provider is perceived by some consumers as more expensive than writing four small checks to four different providers even if the sum of dollars to the four exceeds the sum of dollars to the one. This is something like "sticker shock"— with the one payment, you really see how expensive it is to be "tuned into the world." In Australia, Telstra (the communications giant) purposely does not put all services into one bill for that very reason.

The AT&T experience certainly shows that unrelated products can be bundled. But logic suggests that complementary products would seem to be more likely to make successful bundles.

Source: "Why 'Bundling' Its Consumers Services Hasn't Benefited AT&T," *Wall Street Journal*, October 24, 2000.

exists. Note that this is not the same as third-degree price discrimination. Both the third-degree price discrimination and peak-trough situations have separate marginal revenues for each demand class, but in the case of third-degree price discrimination, the demand classes share the *same* supplier capacity at the *same* time. Therefore, marginal cost in third-degree price discrimination is a function of $Q_1 + Q_2$; that is, the two demands are interdependent in the way they influence marginal cost. But, in the intertemporal demand case, the demanders use the *same* capacity but at *different* times. Therefore, there are separate levels of marginal cost for Q_1 and Q_2; that is, the demands are independent in their influence on the marginal cost. The optimal solution for third-degree price discrimination is $MR_1(Q_1) = MR_2(Q_2) = MC(Q_1 + Q_2)$, whereas the optimal solution for peak-trough pricing is $MR_1(Q_1) = MC_1(Q_1)$ and $MR_2(Q_2) = MC_2(Q_2)$. The parenthesis indicates "a function of." These conditions are shown in Figure 12.16.

The Concepts in Context box discusses peaks and troughs in electricity demand. Consider the situation on roadways. The Texas Transportation Institute reports that Americans suffered 3.6 million hours of delay on congested roadways in the 75 largest metropolitan areas of the United States in 2000.[19] This is indicative of severe auto congestion in some areas. The worst is in Los Angeles, where the typical driver could save 15 minutes on both the morning and afternoon commute if he or she could drive at the free flow rates on the roadway, that is, at the posted speed limit. One reason that such levels of congestion exist is that roadways, in general, are not peak-trough priced in the

[19]David Schrank and Tim Lomax, *2002 Urban Mobility Report* (College Station: Texas Transportation Institute, Texas A & M University, June 2002).

FIGURE
12.16

Determination of Peak and Trough Prices

The optimal peak price (P_P) is determined by locating where the peak marginal revenue equals the firm's marginal cost and the optimal trough price (P_T) is determined by where the trough marginal revenue equals the firm's marginal cost.

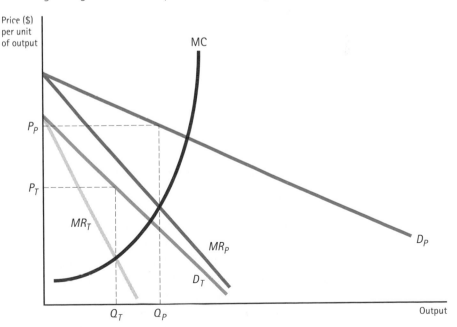

CONCEPTS IN CONTEXT

Why Do Your Laundry at 3 AM?

Gertrude Stein once wrote that "a rose is a rose is a rose." In most states, a kilowatt hour is a kilowatt hour is a kilowatt hour. But not in Florida, Pennsylvania, Washington, and Wisconsin. These states allow electric utilities to practice time-of-day pricing to residential customers if the customer opts to be charged in this way. Otherwise, consumers can stick with the traditional plan, where they pay the same flat rate per kilowatt hour all the time for power. In these pricing schemes, prices of a kilowatt hour can change every several hours. (A Pennsylvania utility, Allegheny Power, is experimenting with rates that change every hour.) Not surprisingly, in these states, it costs more to consume a kilowatt hour in the peak periods, when demand is greatest, and less during the trough periods, when demand is the lowest. In many states, time-of-day pricing has been allowed for commercial and industrial customers for quite some time.

In Florida, Gulf Power of Pensacola charges 4.2 cents per kilowatt hour at night, on weekends, and on holidays. Demand is less during those periods because the 9 to 5 workday, workweek crowd is not at work. Gulf charges 10 cents per kilowatt hour on weekday afternoons when residential and commercial power demand peaks because of air conditioning use. A third rate is a "critical rate" of 30.9 cents when supplies of kilowatt hours go extremely short (less than 1 percent of the time). These rates compare to the alternative residential plan of a flat 6.3 cents per kilowatt hour regardless of the time. A customer utilizing the plan estimates that he saved $600 off of his annual power bill by shifting a third of his power consumption to the off peak periods. In Washington, Puget Sound Energy, estimates that running the same dishwasher in the off-peak time saves the user 25 percent off of the peak rate. With about one third of the customers participating in the off-peak plan, Puget Energy Inc. (the biggest residential time-of-use provider) estimates that peak demand has been cut by 5 percent. This saves the energy company big money. If it cannot handle peak loads, it enters the power grid market to buy the required power at spot market rates (which are usually expensive) or brings its least efficient (hence, most expensive) capacity on line. By restricting the quantity demanded in the peak via pricing, it need not resort to these expensive alternatives. In addition, by bolstering trough demand, it gets to utilize its capital plants better.

Source: "Cut Your Electric Bill: Do Laundry at 3 a.m.," *Wall Street Journal*, August 22, 2002.

United States. Singapore has been peak-trough pricing its central cordon area (central city) since the 1970s. In 2003, London instituted a £5 (approximately $8) price for driving in central London. Initial reports are that driving has decreased by 20 percent. (Are you surprised by the direction of the change? Having studied managerial economics, we hope you are not.) State Route 91 in Orange County, California, has priced newly constructed lanes (where the price varies in real time to keep the lanes operating at free flow level) and kept the existing lanes free (where rush hour traffic moves at 10–25 mph). Many transit systems run 10 times as much equipment during the peak rush hours as compared to the off-peak period. However, many transport systems charge a flat fee to use the system, independent of the time of use. In fact, many systems actually reward peak use by selling weekly or monthly passes at a discount compared to purchasing single rides for each commute. Therefore, some peak riders actually pay less per ride compared with off-peak riders—just the opposite of what we stated was optimal.[20] Some systems, such as the Metro system in Washington, DC, practice peak-trough pricing.

Another version of intertemporal pricing exists. Some consumers have to read the best-selling book on the *New York Times* list as soon as it reaches that position (or perhaps before it reaches that position if they are truly trendsetters). Others must see the latest *Lord of the Rings* or *Star Wars* movie the first weekend it opens (or soon thereafter). Such individuals are able to discuss the book or movie at the next cocktail party or around the water cooler and judged to be "worthy" by their peers. These people have a high demand to be "with it" and hence pay a high price for hardcover books and first-run movies.

Others have an interest in such books or movies but not at the prices that the trendsetters will pay. By waiting a year, the paperback version of the best seller appears at 20–40 percent of the price of the hardcover book. By waiting a year, the DVD of the movie is available for purchase for approximately two admissions to the first-run movie theater (and you can see it again and again, pause while you do something else, rewind to see a favorite scene—or one that someone has talked over—and see lots of extras: interviews with the stars, deleted scenes, bloopers, alternative endings).

So book and movie suppliers realize that there are leaders and followers in the market for their services and figured out how to cater to both with high prices for those who cannot wait and low prices for those who can.

Transfer Pricing

Transfer pricing is prevalent. A recent survey shows that 91 percent of the Fortune 150 practice some form of transfer pricing and that one third of the firms engage in four or more instances of intrafirm transactions where transfer pricing is used.

Consider a conglomerate firm with a downstream monopoly and an upstream provider of a crucial input to the downstream product, such as an engine maker serving a downstream automaker. We assume initially that there is no external market for engines; that is, no other engine maker can supply engines to the downstream automaker nor can any other automaker use the engines of the upstream engine maker. Therefore, managers of this conglomerate firm must

---

[20]Such a pricing policy may be related to the fact that transit's competition (highway) has a policy of zero price during the peaks and troughs.

decide how many engines and autos to make (these are the same, since there is no external market for engines).[21] The downstream operation is subject to the discipline of the market, since autos are sold in an external market. But, since there is no external market for the upstream product, what price should change hands between the two divisions for payment for the upstream product? This payment, called a **transfer price**, simulates a market where no formal market exists.

Job 1 of the transfer price is to ensure that the profit-maximizing (from the point of view of the conglomerate) level of the downstream and the upstream output is produced. Job 2 of transfer pricing is to ensure that the upstream managers have the right incentive to produce the profit-maximizing amount of the upstream product in the most efficient way.

The following notation enables us to view the problem facing the conglomerate firm and show the solution to jobs 1 and 2. The demand curve for the downstream product is

$$P_D = P_D(Q_D)$$

where P_D is the price of the downstream product per unit and Q_D is in units of the downstream product. Recall that the impacts of complementary and substitute goods on this demand are subsumed in the intercept of the demand curve, as shown in Chapter 3.

The production function of the downstream operation is defined as

$$Q_D = f(L_D, K_D | Q_U)$$

The production function is like those of Chapter 7, but it is conditional; that is, it states that Q_D can be produced with labor (L_D) and capital (K_D) *given* the critical input Q_U.

This production function yields a downstream cost function of

$$TC_D = TC_D(Q_D | Q_U)$$

which is the total cost of the downstream division *exclusive* of the cost of the upstream operation.

Finally, the total cost of the upstream division is just a function of Q_U, and reads

$$TC_U = TC_U(Q_U)$$

and is typical of the cost functions we developed in Chapter 9.

---

[21]For simplicity, we assume that all the upstream product produced during the period must be sold then. In other words, no inventories of the upstream product can be carried over.

The profit of the conglomerate firm is

$$\pi = TR_D - TC_D - TC_U \tag{12.10}$$

To maximize profits, we must have $\partial\pi/\partial Q_U = 0$. Note that Q_U is the variable that controls what the firm does. Without the critical input produced by the upstream division, nothing can be produced in the downstream division. And whatever is produced upstream equals the amount produced downstream; that is, $Q_D = Q_U$, when transfer pricing is done correctly. While one might be tempted to put a total revenue for the upstream division in equation (12.10) (i.e., $TR_U = P_U Q_U$, where P_U would be the transfer price), it would be exactly offset by a cost item for the downstream firm (recall that TC_D is the downstream cost *exclusive* of the cost of the upstream product). Since this nets out to zero, it is not included in equation (12.10).

If we make the left-hand side of equation (12.10) $\partial\pi/\partial Q_U = 0$, we must make the following adjustments to the right-hand side of equation (12.10), so that

$$\partial\pi/\partial Q_U = (\partial TR_D/\partial Q_D)(\partial Q_D/\partial Q_U) - (\partial TC_D/\partial Q_D)(\partial Q_D/\partial Q_U) - dTC_U/dQ_U = 0$$

or

$$[(\partial TR_D/\partial Q_D) - (\partial TC_D/\partial Q_D)](\partial Q_D/\partial Q_U) = (dTC_U/dQ_U) \tag{12.11}$$

or

$$(MR_D - MC_D)MP_U = MC_U \tag{12.12}$$

Note that $(\partial Q_D/\partial Q_U)$ is the marginal product of the upstream product in producing the downstream product.

The intuition of equation (12.12) is straightforward. If the firm produces another unit in the upstream operation, it incurs an additional cost, MC_U. Producing that additional upstream product enables the conglomerate to produce MP_U more downstream units. Each additional downstream unit produced causes the firm to incur additional cost in the downstream plant (MC_D) but also enables the firm to earn additional revenue (MR_D). If the additional net revenue earned, $(MR_D - MC_D)MP_U$, which is produced as a result of incurring the additional cost upstream, MC_U, exceeds that additional upstream cost, then the firm should produce the additional unit upstream (since profits increase). If it does not, the firm should not produce the additional unit upstream (because the conglomerate's profit decreases). It maximizes profits when the additional net revenue earned downstream received as a result of producing an additional unit upstream just equals the additional cost incurred in producing another unit upstream.

But MP_U equals 1, since every time one more unit is produced upstream, one more unit can be produced downstream. In situations where it would appear that the upstream firm has to produce multiple units to enable one additional unit to be produced downstream, such as four tires are required to produce one car, we treat this by having one bundle (of four tires) produced upstream required to produce one car. Obviously, the situation can also go the other way, such as producing one extra steer on the upstream cattle ranch enables the downstream meat processing division to produce X (>1) steaks.

In the situation when $MP_U = 1$, equation (12.12) becomes

$$MR_D - MC_D = MC_U$$

or

$$MR_D = MC_D + MC_U \qquad (12.13)$$

and the rule becomes the familiar one of the marginal revenue of the product must equal the marginal cost of producing it; that is, the marginal cost of producing the downstream product is the marginal cost of the downstream operation (remember this excludes the cost of the upstream operation) plus the marginal cost of the upstream product.

Solving equation (12.13) for $Q_U^* = Q_D^* = Q^*$ gives the correct amount of the upstream product and downstream product produced. This is job 1.

Now, suppose that the managers of the conglomerate set the transfer price the downstream division pays and the upstream division receives for its upstream product. They tell the upstream division chief that she will receive P_U for every unit she produces. A profit-maximizing division chief (who is now a price taker) maximizes profits by setting $P_U = MC_U$, as was shown in Chapter 10. But what P_U should the conglomerate management set? Clearly, it is the P_U that results in Q_U^* units being produced. This is shown in Figure 12.17.

What difference does it make what P_U is chosen? Whatever it is, would it not merely cause the upstream division to have $P_U Q_U^*$ in revenues and the downstream division to have $P_U Q_U^*$ in costs? The two terms merely cancel each other out (which is the reason we left them out of equation (12.10). From the point of view of the conglomerate, profits are the same. However, *the profits of each division differ.* And, since managers' bonuses are often predicated on their division's profits, these managers care a lot about the transfer price. If the conglomerate's managers determine the optimal Q (i.e., Q^*) and order both divisions to produce it, then the conglomerate maximizes profits regardless of the transfer price.

But, if the conglomerate wishes to use the transfer price as a signal to let jobs 1 and 2 do their tasks, then it is critical that the correct P_U be chosen. If P_U is chosen too high, then the upstream division will produce too much of the product (recall that in price-taking situations, the marginal cost is rising). If P_U is chosen too high, then the downstream division will see its marginal cost of

FIGURE

12.17

Determination of the Transfer Price, Given No External Market for the Transferred Good

The optimal transfer price, P_U, equals the marginal cost at the optimal output, Q^*.

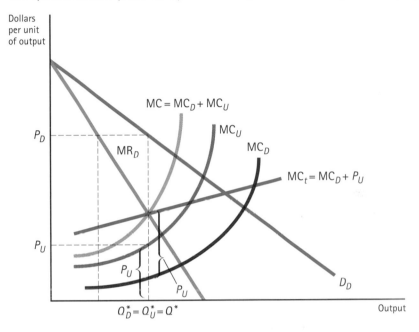

producing another unit (i.e., $MC_D + P_U = MC_t$) as too high and, therefore, produce too few of the downstream output. Therefore, profits are not maximized. The reverse would be true if P_U were set too low.

Transfer Pricing: A Perfectly Competitive Market for the Upstream Product

In many cases, there is a market outside the firm for the product transferred from one division to the other. If this is true, the output levels of the downstream division and the upstream division no longer need be equal. If the downstream division wants more of the upstream product than is produced by the upstream division, it can buy some from external suppliers. If the upstream division produces more of its product than the downstream division wants, it can sell to some external customers. Assuming that the market for the upstream

Determination of the Transfer Price, Given a Perfectly Competitive External Market for the Transferred Product

The optimal transfer price, P_U, equals the market price of the transferred product.

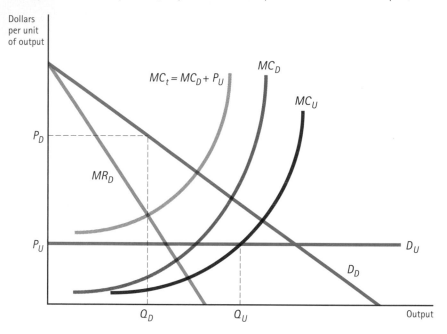

product is perfectly competitive, we can readily determine the way in which the firm should set the transfer price under these circumstances.

Figure 12.18 shows the optimal price and output for the firm as a whole. Since there is a perfectly competitive market for the upstream product, the upstream division is confronted with a horizontal demand curve, D_U, for its output, where the price is P_U, the price of the upstream product in the external market. To maximize profit, the upstream division should produce the output, Q_U, where the marginal cost of the upstream division, MC_U, equals the *externally* determined market price P_U. In this sense, the upstream division behaves like a perfectly competitive firm.

To maximize the firm's overall profit, the transfer price should equal P_U, the price of the upstream division in the perfectly competitive market outside the firm. Since the upstream division can sell as much of its product as it wants to external customers at a price of P_U, it has no incentive to sell it at a price below P_U to the downstream division. Similarly, since the downstream division can buy as much of the upstream product as it wants from external suppliers at a price of P_U, it has no incentive to buy it from the upstream division at a price above P_U.

The downstream division, which must buy the upstream product at price P_U regardless of where it comes from, has a marginal cost of MC_t, which is the sum of the downstream division's marginal cost, MC_D, and the market-determined price of the upstream product, P_U. To maximize its own profit, the downstream division must choose the output level, Q_D, where its marginal cost, MC_t $(= MC_D + P_U)$, equals its marginal revenue, MR_D. Since Figure 12.18 shows the output of the downstream division, Q_D, is less than the output of the upstream division, Q_U, the optimal solution in this case calls for the conglomerate's upstream division to sell part of its output (specifically, $Q_U - Q_D$ units) to outside customers.[22]

Transfer Pricing Around the World

Transfer pricing is widespread. Many firms have policies whereby one division can buy another division's product, with the transfer price determined by various means. This observation found support in a 1992 survey of transfer pricing that targeted Fortune 500 firms. For domestic interdivisional transfers, the most common methods were the use of market prices, actual or standard full production costs, full production costs plus a markup, and negotiated prices. For international transfers, market-based transfer prices and full production costs plus a markup were the most commonly reported methods. Comparing the results from an earlier survey conducted in 1977, the shift has been to market-based prices in both the domestic and international markets.[23]

Firms use transfer pricing to shift profits from division to division to minimize tax liability. This, done on a state-by-state and country-by-country basis, has caused government officials to investigate transfer pricing as a method to avoid taxation. A 1999 survey by Ernst and Young showed that the number 1 international tax issue is transfer pricing. Firms are concerned with double taxation and onerous penalties for noncompliance. Many countries have enacted legislation enabling their tax agencies to intensify their transfer pricing inquiries and regulation enforcement. These countries feel that firms use transfer prices to decrease profits in high-tax countries, transfering these profits to low-tax

---

[22]Of course, it is not always true that Q_D is less than Q_U. Whether this is the case depends on the shape and position of the marginal cost curves (MC_D and MC_U) and the demand curve as well as the price of the transferred product in the externally perfectly competitive market. If $Q_D > Q_U$, then the downstream division purchases the required $Q_D - Q_U$ units in the external market at the market determined price of P_U.

[23]Roger Tang, "Transfer Pricing in the 1990s," *Management Accounting*, 73(8), 22–26. This 1992 survey replicated one conducted in 1977.

countries. Items included in transfer pricing are goods, services, property, loans, and leases. Fortunately (and in line with the theory developed in this chapter), survey respondents note that "the most important factor shaping transfer pricing policies is maximization of operating performance, not optimizing tax arrangements."[24]

Just why have transfer prices become so important on the international level? Four basic reasons exist: increased globalization, different levels of taxation in various countries, increased scrutiny by tax authorities, and inconsistency in the rules and laws in the various tax jurisdictions. Transfer price policies that seem to cause the least degree of legal problems in the international scenario are (1) comparable uncontrolled price, in which the prices are the same or similar to "arms-length" transaction prices; (2) cost-plus prices, in which a markup used in arm's-length transactions is added to the seller's cost of the good or service; and (3) resale price, in which the resale price is used as a base for determining an arm's-length margin for the functions performed by the selling company.[25]

The Orion Corporation: A Numerical Example

Consider the Orion Corporation, where an upstream chemical division (P) produces a product that it transfers to a downstream marketing division (M), which packages the basic chemical into the final product and sells it to outside customers. To illustrate how a firm's managers can calculate the optimal output rates, assume that its demand and cost conditions are as follows. The demand for the finished product sold by Orion's downstream marketing division is

$$P_M = 100 - Q_M \tag{12.14}$$

where P_M is the price (in dollars per ton) of the finished product and Q_M is the quantity demanded (in millions of tons per year). Excluding the cost of the basic chemical, the marketing division's total cost function is

$$TC_M = 200 + 10Q_M \tag{12.15}$$

where TC_M is the division's total cost (in millions of dollars).

Turning to Orion's upstream production division, its total cost function is

$$TC_P = 10 + 2Q_P + 0.5Q_P^2 \tag{12.16}$$

[24]"Multinationals Face Greater Transfer Pricing Scrutiny According to New Ernst & Young Survey," *Business Wire*, November 3, 1999.

[25]Brenda Humphreys, "International Transfer Pricing: More Important than Ever Before!" *Cost & Management*, 68(4), 24–26.

where TC_P is total production cost (in millions of dollars) and Q_P is the total quantity produced of the basic chemical (in millions of tons per year). As studied in the section before last, we assume a perfectly competitive market for the basic chemical (the upstream output). Assume that its price in this market is $42 per ton.

Under these conditions, we can readily determine the optimal rate for each division as well as the proper transfer price for the basic chemical. The production division can sell all the basic chemical that it wants at $42 per ton. Therefore, its marginal revenue equals $42. From equation (12.16), we see that $d\,TC_P/dQ_P = MC_P = 2 + Q_P.$

To find the output that maximizes the production division's profits, we must set its marginal revenue equal to its marginal cost:

$$MR_P = 42 = 2 + Q_P = MC_P$$

or

$$Q_P = 40$$

Hence, the production division should produce 40 million tons per year of the basic chemical.

The transfer price of the basic chemical should be its price in the perfectly competitive market outside the firm. Since this market price is $42 per ton, the transfer price should be the same. Also, we know from the section before last that the marketing division's marginal cost, MC_t, is the sum of its own marginal marketing cost, MC_M, and the transfer price. That is,

$$MC_t = MC_M + P_U$$

where $P_U = \$42$ and its own marginal marketing cost equals $MC_M = d\,TC_M/dQ_M$. From equation (12.15), we see that $d\,TC_M/dQ_M = MC_M = 10$. Therefore,

$$MC_t = 10 + 42 = 52$$

To maximize the marketing division's profit, we must set its marginal cost equal to its marginal revenue. The marketing division's total revenue is

$$TR_M = P_M Q_M = (100 - Q_M)Q_M = 100Q_M - Q_M^2$$

The marketing division's marginal revenue is therefore

$$d\,TR_M/dQ_M = 100 - 2Q_M$$

CONCEPTS IN CONTEXT

Japan's Tax Man Leans on Foreign Firms

Japan's tax authority claims that foreign companies have a propensity to avoid the country's high corporate taxes by illegally shifting profits off their books in Japan.

The authority has filed claims against at least 50 multinationals totaling approximately $492.4 million in back taxes. Among the firms accused are Coca-Cola, Goodyear Tire and Rubber, Procter and Gamble, DaimlerChrysler, Roche Holding AG. DaimlerChrysler recently paid Japan an extra $45.87 million for taxes allegedly owed in Japan that were shifted to Germany via transfer payments.

Japanese activity in this regard has become so large that Arthur Anderson added 10 more transfer pricing specialists to its Tokyo office. While Japan is not the only country that goes after firms that allegedly hide profits from local tax authorities, Japan's high taxes make Japan a tempting country in which to dodge taxes. In Japan, about 50 percent of yearly earnings go to national and local governments. The comparable tax burden is estimated to be 41 percent in the United States and 33 percent in the United Kingdom.

Japan believes that the non-Japanese parent company of a Japanese subsidiary overcharge the subsidiary for use of its products or trademarks and hence transferred profits out of Japan.

But Japan is not the only one. In 1993, Nissan paid approximately $144 million to the United States Internal Revenue Service to settle a claim that Nissan had transferred part of its profits back to Japan. Nissan had a comparable problem in the United Kingdom. The auto industry has a reputation for using transfer pricing to minimize taxable profits.

The potential problem here is enormous. Approximately half the world's trade is estimated to involve goods that are subject to transfer pricing. Over two-thirds of the world's multinationals have been investigated by tax authorities regarding their transfer pricing policies.

Sources: "Japan's Tax Man Leans on Foreign Firms," *Wall Street Journal*, November 25, 1996; "Transfer Pricing: Confusion over Tax Treatment," *Financial Tiimes*, September 2, 1997; "Daimler-Chrysler Japan Forced to Pay More Tax," *Financial Times*, October 10, 2000; and "Nissan's UK Arm Hit by Tax Charges," *Financial Times*, November 8, 2000.

Setting this expression for its marginal revenue equal to its marginal cost, we find that

$$MR_M = 100 - 2Q_M = 52 = MC_t = MC_M + P_U$$

or

$$Q_M = 24$$

Hence, the marketing division should sell 24 million tons per year of the base chemical at a price of $76; that is, $P_M = 100 - 24$.

CONSULTANT'S CORNER

Settling Some Strife over a Pricing Formula

An oil company consists of two divisions, one involved in the production and sale of natural gas products and one involved in petrochemical production. The former division owns and operates about 10 plants containing extraction units, which take the gas liquids out of the natural gas stream, and fractionators, which separate the gas liquid stream into particular gas liquids. The latter division, which has a variety of petrochemical plants, buys about half of the ethane it uses from the former division.

The price that the gas products division charges the petrochemical division for ethane is determined by a formula designed to help the gas products division earn a 12 percent rate of return on its investment. This formula evolved from negotiations between the former heads of the two divi-

sions, but the present head of the gas products division feels that it should be abandoned because he could get much more for the ethane by selling it to buyers outside the firm. (The formula resulted in a price that was below the current market price of ethane.) On the other hand, the head of the petrochemical division pointed out that the ethane production facilities at the gas products division had been constructed to provide ethane for his division.

If you were a consultant to this firm, would you support the recommendation of the head of the gas products division? Explain why or why not.*

*For a much more complete account of a somewhat similar situation, see M. E. Barrett and M. P. Cormack, *Management Strategy in the Oil and Gas Industries: Cases and Readings* (Houston: Gulf, 1983).

To sum up, the Orion Corporation's production division should produce 40 million tons per year of the basic chemical. Of this amount, 24 million tons should be transferred to Orion's marketing division at the market price of $42 per ton and 16 million tons (40 − 24) sold externally at the market price of $42 per ton. The transfer price should be the same as the market price, that is $42 per ton.

Summary

1. Price discrimination occurs when the same product is sold at more than one price or similar products are sold at prices that are in different ratios to marginal cost. A firm is able and willing to practice price discrimination if various classes of buyers with different price elasticities of demand can be identified and segregated and the product cannot be transferred easily from one class to another. If the total market is divided into such classes, a firm that discriminates maximizes its profits by choosing prices

and outputs so that the marginal revenue in each class equals the marginal cost. This is called *third-degree price discrimination.* First-degree price discrimination entails selling each good at its reservation price. This practice captures all the consumer surplus and converts it to producer surplus. Second-degree price discrimination prices increments of output at different rates, charging a high price for the first increments of output then lower rates as the consumer's consumption increases.

2. Two-part tariffs are a way of operationizing first degree-price discrimination. The process entails charging the consumer an "entry" fee for the right to pay a "use" fee to actually purchase the product. In the simplest case, where all demanders are the same, the optimal use fee is the marginal cost of the product and the entry fee is the consumer surplus available when that use fee is charged. If consumers have different demand curves, the firm may exclude weaker demanders from the market and follow the preceding rule with the stronger demanders or the firm may include all demanders by pricing the use of the product above its marginal cost and choosing the entry fee to be the consumer surplus of the weak demander resulting from such a use fee. Practicing price discrimination on the entry fee, while charging all consumers the marginal cost as a use fee, yields the maximum profit.

3. Bundling is a way for firms to increase profits by selling two or more goods as if they were one in a bundle. To consider pure bundling as a pricing alternative, the reservation prices for the goods of different consumer types must not be positively correlated. In general, the reservation prices of goods must be negatively correlated; that is, one group must have a high reservation price for one good and a low reservation price for another good relative to another group. Even so, bundling may not be superior to pricing each good separately. A pure bundle occurs when the goods are sold only as a bundle. Mixed bundling occurs when goods are sold both as a bundle and at least one good sold separately. No analytical model is available to solve the bundling pricing problem, so experimentation or a computer model is used.

4. Demands tend to show temporal variation (by day, week, or season). To account for these variations in temporal demand, managers facing such demands many times charge high prices during the peaks and lower prices during the troughs (as opposed to a single price across the whole temporal cycle). The optimal rule is as always to set the relevant marginal revenue equal to marginal cost.

5. Many large firms are decentralized, and one division of the firm sells its product to another division of the firm. To maximize the firm's overall profit, it is important that the price at which this transfer takes place, the so-called transfer price, be set properly. If there is no market outside the firm for the transferred product, the transfer price should equal the marginal production

cost of the transferred product at the optimal output. If there is a perfectly competitive market for the transferred product outside the firm, the transfer price should equal the price of this product in that market.

Problems

1. The Ridgeway Corporation produces a medical device, which it sells in Japan, Europe, and the United States. Transportation costs are a negligible proportion of the product's total costs. The price elasticity of demand for the product is -4.0 in Japan, -2.0 in the United States, and -1.33 in Europe. Because of legal limitations, this medical device, once sold to a customer in one country, cannot be resold to a buyer in another country.
   a. The firm's vice president for marketing circulates a memo recommending that the price of the device be $1,000 in Japan, $2,000 in the United States, and $3,000 in Europe. Comment on his recommendations.
   b. His recommendations are accepted. Sales managers send reports to corporate headquarters saying that the quantity of the devices being sold in the United States is lower than expected. Comment on their reports.
   c. After considerable argument, the U.S. sales manager agrees to lower the price in the United States to $1,500. Is this a wise decision? Why or why not?
   d. Can you be sure that the firm is maximizing profit? Why or why not?
2. The Locust Corporation is composed of a marketing division and a production division. The marginal cost of producing a unit of the firm's product is $10 per unit, and the marginal cost of marketing it is $4 per unit. The demand curve for the firm's product is

$$P = 100 - 0.01Q$$

where P is the price per unit (in dollars) and Q is output (in units). There is no external market for the good made by the production division.
   a. What is the firm's optimal output?
   b. What price should the firm charge?
   c. How much should the production division charge the marketing division for each unit of the product?
3. Ann McCutcheon is hired as a consultant to a firm producing ball bearings. This firm sells in two distinct markets, one of which is completely sealed off from the other. The demand curve for the firm's output in the first market is $P_1 = 160 - 8Q_1$, where P_1 is the price of the product and Q_1 is the amount sold in the first market. The demand curve for the firm's output in the second market is $P_2 = 80 - 2Q_2$, where P_2 is the price of the product and Q_2 is the amount sold in the second market. The firm's marginal cost curve is

$5 + Q$, where Q is the firm's entire output (destined for either market). The firm asks Ann McCutcheon to suggest what its pricing policy should be.

a. How many units of output should the firm sell in the second market?

b. How many units of output should it sell in the first market?

c. What price should it establish in each market?

4. The Xerxes Company is composed of a marketing division and a production division. The marketing division packages and distributes a plastic item made by the production division. The demand curve for the finished product sold by the marketing division is

$$P_O = 200 - 3Q_O$$

where P_O is the price (in dollars per pound) of the finished product and Q_O is the quantity sold (in thousands of pounds). Excluding the production cost of the basic plastic item, the marketing division's total cost function is

$$TC_O = 100 + 15Q_O$$

where TC_O is the marketing division's total cost (in thousands of dollars). The production division's total cost function is

$$TC_1 = 5 + 3Q_1 + 0.4Q_1^2$$

where TC_1 is total production cost (in thousands of dollars) and Q_1 is the total quantity produced of the basic plastic item (in thousands of pounds). There is a perfectly competitive market for the basic plastic item, the price being $20 per pound.

a. What is the optimal output for the production division?

b. What is the optimal output for the marketing division?

c. What is the optimal transfer price for the basic plastic item?

d. At what price should the marketing division sell its product?

5. The Lone Star Transportation Company hauls coal and manufactured goods. The demand curve for its services by the coal producers is

$$P_C = 495 - 5Q_C$$

where P_C is the price (in dollars) per ton-mile of coal hauled and Q_C is the number of ton-miles of coal hauled (in thousands). The demand curve for its services by the producers of manufactured goods is

$$P_M = 750 - 10Q_M$$

where P_M is the price (in dollars) per ton-mile of manufactured goods hauled, and Q_M is the number of ton-miles of manufactured goods hauled (in thousands). The firm's total cost function is

$$TC = 410 + 8(Q_C + Q_M)$$

where TC is total cost (in thousands of dollars).

    a.   What price should the firm charge to haul coal?

    b.   What price should the firm charge to haul manufactured goods?

    c.   If a regulatory agency were to require the firm to charge the same price to haul both coal and manufactured goods, would this reduce the firm's profits? If so, by how much?

6.   Electric companies typically have 5–10 different rate schedules for their main customer groups. The average price charged large industrial users may differ substantially from that charged residences. Moreover, many consumers pay a price for electricity based on the time of day they use it. For example, the prices charged by Consolidated Edison, a large New York electric utility, and Pacific Gas and Electric, a major California electric utility, are as follows:

Company and time of day of electricity use	Price (cents per kilowatt-hour)
Consolidated Edison	
8 AM–10 PM (peak hours)	27
10 PM–8 AM (off-peak hours)	4[a]
Pacific Gas and Electric	
Summer	
Noon–6 PM (peak hours)	28.3
6 PM–noon (off-peak hours)	9.2
Winter	
Noon–6 PM (peak hours)	11.3
6 PM–noon (off-peak hours)	8.0

[a]Approximate figure.

Electric utilities utilize their cheapest generators continuously and start up their more costly ones as demand goes up. Consequently, at 3 AM, a utility might meet its requirements from a hydroelectric dam that produces electricity for 2 cents per kilowatt-hour. However, on a hot day in August, when air conditioners are running full blast, demand would be so great that the utility would be forced to use its most costly generators, perhaps an oil-fired plant where electricity costs 7 cents per kilowatt-hour.

    a.   Does price discrimination occur in the market for electricity?

    b.   Why have some state regulatory commissions, including the Public Service Commission of New York, ordered that time-of-day rates be phased in for residential consumers?

    c.   In many areas, both residential and industrial consumers tend to pay a lower price per kilowatt-hour if they use more rather than less electricity. Is this price discrimination? If so, what kind of price discrimination is it?

d. Explain why price discrimination is used by electric companies.[26]

7. Knox Chemical Corporation is one of the largest producers of isopropyl alcohol, or isopropanol, as it frequently is called. Isopropanol is used to produce acetone, an important industrial chemical; also, it is used to make various chemical intermediate products. Since Knox Chemical produces both acetone and these chemical intermediates, it uses much of the isopropanol it makes. One of the many tasks of Knox's product manager for isopropanol is to set transfer prices for isopropanol within the company.

a. Knox's product manager for isopropanol generally sets the transfer price equal to the prevailing market price. Is this a sensible procedure?

b. When the production of phenol expands rapidly, a great deal of acetone is produced because it was a by-product of the process leading to phenol. What effect do you think this has on the market price of isopropanol?

c. In producing a pound of phenol, 0.6 pound of acetone is produced. Are phenol and acetone joint products?

d. Are they produced in fixed proportions?[27]

8. The reservation prices (in dollars) of three classes of demanders (classes A, B, and C) for Ricky Parton's (a Latin country-western singer) compact discs are given in the table that follows:

Class	CD 1	CD 2
A	11	5
B	8	9
C	9	10

It costs $4 to produce and distribute each compact disc. The company can sell each CD separately, can put them together as a boxed set (i.e., as a pure bundle), or sell them in a mixed bundling format (i.e., offer the CDs both separately and as a boxed set). Assume that each demander wants only one of each of the CDs at their reservation price (or at any lower price) and that there are an equal number of demanders in each class. For simplicity, assume that the only costs are those mentioned here.

a. What pricing method would you advise Ricky's company to use?

b. How much better (profitwise) is the best pricing method than the second most-profitable pricing method?

---

[26]For further discussion, see W. Shepherd and C. Wilcox, *Public Policies toward Business* (Homewood, IL: Irwin, 1979); and *New York Times*, June 9, 1990.

[27]For further discussion, see E.R. Corey, *Industrial Marketing: Cases and Concepts* (3rd ed.; Englewood Cliffs, NJ: Prentice-Hall, 1983).

Oligopoly

CHAPTER 13

An oligopoly is a market structure with a small number of firms. A good example of an oligopoly is the U.S. petroleum industry, in which a few firms have accounted for much of the industry's refining capacity in recent years. Each of the major oil firms must take account of the reaction of the others when it formulates its price and output policy, since its policy is likely to affect theirs. Therefore, when Exxon Mobil raises its price of home heating oil by 1 or 2 cents per gallon, it has to anticipate the reaction of other firms in the industry. If its rivals decide against such a price increase, it is likely that the price increase will have to be rescinded; otherwise, its rivals will pull away a large number of Exxon Mobil customers. In addition, uncertainty exists because of supply disruptions due to world political tensions. For example, sanctions against Iraq initially affected the world supply by limiting the amount of Iraqi oil that could reach the market. Now, with a regime change in Iraq, infrastructure damage suffered during the recent conflict limits the flow of Iraqi oil to the world market. When Iraqi oil is able to flow to the marketplace again, significant adjustments will occur in the strategies of OPEC and non-OPEC oil companies because of the potentially large supply of oil that could enter the world market.

Oligopolies abound in most countries. In the United States, the automobile industry is dominated by three domestic firms—General Motors, Ford, and Daimler Chrysler—as well as a small number of foreign producers. There are many reasons for oligopoly, one being economies of scale. In some industries, the number of firms tend to be rather small because low costs cannot be achieved unless a firm is producing an output equal to a substantial percentage of the total available market.

We devote an entire chapter to oligopoly because of both its importance and the lack of a single theory of oligopoly. In contrast to perfect competition or monopoly, for which there is a single unified model, many types of oligopoly models exist and are used. Each of these theories may be appropriate, depending on the circumstances. In the following chapter, we take up game theory, which is also used to analyze oligopoly.

The Emergence of Oligopolistic Industries[1]

Oligopolistic industries, like others, often (but not always) pass through a number of stages: introduction, growth, maturity, and decline.[2] As indicated in Figure 13.1, the industry's sales grow very rapidly in the introduction phase, less rapidly in the growth phase, and even less rapidly during maturity. In the stage of decline, the industry's sales fall. As the industry goes through these stages, the nature of the competition shifts.

During the early stages when sales are growing relatively rapidly, there frequently is a great deal of uncertainty about the industry's technology. Which product configuration will turn out to be best? Which process technology will be most efficient? Because of small production volume and the newness of the product, production costs tend to be higher than those the industry eventually will achieve. The learning curve (recall Chapter 8) often is comparatively steep. Newly formed companies tend to be a larger percentage of the industry than in subsequent years. Many of these new firms may be started by personnel leaving other firms to start their own businesses. For example, many semiconductor firms were offshoots of Fairchild Camera and Instrument Corporation.

At these early stages of an industry's evolution, a major strategic question facing managers is this: Which markets for the industry's new product will tend to open up early, and which ones will open up relatively late? This question is important because firms should allocate marketing efforts and R and D resources

---

[1]The discussion in this and the following section is based on M. Porter, *Competitive Strategy* (New York: Free Press, 1980).

[2]Whether industries are perfectly competitive, monopolistic, monopolistically competitive, or oligopolistic, they often go through the stages discussed here. However, we focus, in this chapter, on the evolution of oligopolistic industries.

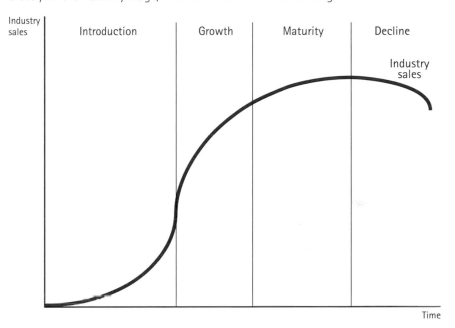

FIGURE 13.1

Typical Stages of the Evolution of an Industry

Industry sales grow at a rapid rate in the introduction and growth stages, more moderately in the maturity stage, and not at all in the decline stage.

to relatively receptive markets and the nature of the early markets can exert a significant influence on the way the industry evolves. To forecast which markets or market segments are likely to be the most receptive to a new product, one should consider the following three factors.

First, the most receptive buyers tend to be those for which the new product is most profitable. For example, if a new robot is much more profitable in the railroad industry than in the agricultural equipment industry, it is more likely to be used first by railroads, not by agricultural equipment firms. Second, buyers who face a relatively low cost of product failures are likely to be quicker to adopt a new product than those for which the potential costs are very high. If this new robot could cause millions of dollars of losses in the auto industry but only minor losses in the steel industry, it is more likely that steel producers will take a chance on it than that auto firms will do so. Third, buyers who would experience relatively low costs in switching from old products to the new one sold by this industry are likely to be more receptive to this industry's product than buyers who would experience high changeover costs.

Maturity and Decline of Oligopolistic Industries

Eventually, most industries enter the maturity phase, when industry sales grow much more modestly than before. This is a critical phase for many members of the industry. Since firms cannot maintain the growth rates to which they are accustomed merely by protecting their market share, there is often a tendency for firms to attack the market shares of their rivals in the same industry. For example, this occurred in the dishwasher business in the late 1970s, when GE and Maytag attacked Hobart in the higher-price segments of the market, which was becoming saturated. In this phase of an industry's evolution, firms often must alter their assumptions about how their competitors are likely to behave and react. The likelihood of interfirm warfare, based on price, service, or promotion, is high in this phase.

During the maturity phase, rivalry among firms often centers on cost and service, rather than on new or greatly improved products. Because of slower growth, more knowledgeable customers, and greater technological maturity, competition tends to focus on cost and service, which may prompt a significant reorientation of firms that have competed on other grounds in the past. Also, as the industry adjusts to slower growth, there generally is a reduction in the additions to productive capacity. Often, firms do not realize that they have entered this maturity phase until after they have installed more capacity than is required. Therefore, for some time, the industry suffers from overcapacity.

After the maturity phase, many industries enter a stage during which sales decline. One reason for such a decline may be that the product is being supplanted by a new one (as slide rules were supplanted by electronic calculators that have been supplanted by sophisticated palm pilots). Another reason may be a shrinkage in the size of the customer group that buys the product, perhaps because of demographic changes. Still another reason may be a change in buyers' tastes or needs.

Although firms in declining industries are often advised to curtail investment and get lots of cash out of the business as quickly as possible, this is not always the best strategy. Some industries, like some people, grow old more gracefully and profitably than others. Some firms have done well by investing heavily in a declining industry, making their business better "cash cows" later. Others have avoided losses subsequently experienced by their rivals by selling out before it was generally recognized that the industry was in decline.

Collusive Agreements

Conditions in oligopolistic industries tend to encourage collusion, since the number of firms is small and the firms are aware of their interdependence. The advantages to the firms of collusion seem clear: increased profits, decreased uncertainty, and a better opportunity to prevent entry. But, collusive arrangements are often hard to maintain, since once a collusive agreement is made, any of the firms can increase its profits by cheating on the agreement. Moreover, in the United States, collusive arrangements generally are illegal.

If a collusive arrangement is made openly and formally, it is called a **cartel.** In many countries, cartels have been common and legally acceptable; but in the United States, most collusive agreements, whether secret or open cartels, were declared illegal by the Sherman Antitrust Act (discussed in detail in Chapter 19), which dates back to 1890. But, this does not mean that such agreements do not exist. For instance, there was widespread collusion among U.S. electric equipment manufacturers during the 1950s. Also, trade associations and professional organizations may sometimes perform functions somewhat similar to those of a cartel. Further, some types of cartels have had the official sanction of the U.S. government. For example, airlines flying transatlantic routes have been members of the International Air Transport Association, which agreed on uniform prices for transatlantic flights.

If a cartel is established to set a uniform price for a particular (homogeneous) product, what price will it charge? To answer this question, the cartel must estimate the marginal cost curve for the cartel as a whole. If input prices do not increase as the cartel expands, the marginal cost curve is the horizontal summation of the marginal cost curves of the individual firms. Suppose that the resulting marginal cost curve for the cartel is as shown in Figure 13.2. If the demand curve for the industry's product and the relevant marginal revenue curve are as shown there, the output that maximizes the total profit of the cartel members is Q_0. Therefore, if it maximizes cartel profits, the cartel will choose a price of P_0, which is the monopoly price.

The cartel must also determine the industry's total sales among the firms belonging to the cartel. If the purpose of the cartel is to maximize cartel profits, it allocates sales to firms in such a way that marginal cost of all firms is equal (and, in turn, equal to the cartel's marginal revenue). Otherwise, the cartel could make more money by reallocating output among firms to reduce the cost of producing the cartel's total output. If the marginal cost at firm A is higher than that at firm B, the cartel can increase its total profits by transferring some production from firm A to firm B.

This allocation of output is unlikely to take place, however, since allocation decisions are the result of negotiation between firms with varying interests and varying capabilities. This is a political process in which firms have different amounts of influence. Those with the most influence and the shrewdest negotiators are likely to receive the largest sales quotas, even though this raises the total cartel costs. Also, high-cost firms are likely to receive bigger sales quotas than cost minimization requires, since they would be unwilling to accept the small quotas required by cost minimization. In practice, sales are often distributed in accord with a firm's level of sales in the past or the extent of its

FIGURE
13.2

Price and Output Determination by a Cartel

The cartel chooses a price of P_0 and an output of Q_0.

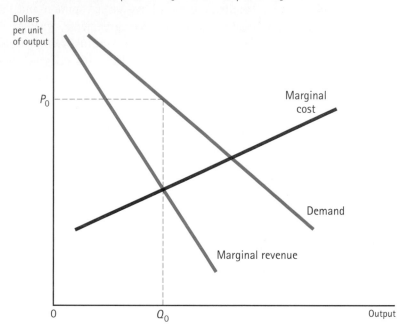

productive capacity. Also, a cartel sometimes divides a market geographically, with some firms being given particular countries or regions and other firms being given other countries or regions.

The Breakdown of Collusive Agreements

One of the most important things a manager should understand about collusive agreements is that they tend to break down. To understand why firms are tempted to leave the cartel, consider the case of the firm in Figure 13.3. If this firm were to leave the cartel, it would be faced with a demand curve of DD' as long as the other firms in the cartel maintained a price of P_0. This demand curve is very elastic; the firm can expand its sales considerably by small reductions in price. Even if the firm were unable to leave the cartel, but it granted secret price concessions, the same sort of demand curve would exist.

The firm's maximum profit, if it leaves the cartel or secretly lowers price, is attained if it sells an output of Q_1 at a price of P_1, since this is the output at

FIGURE

13.3

Instability of Cartels

If the firm leaves the cartel, profit equals $Q_1 \times P_1 B$, which is generally higher than it would be if the firm adhered to the price and sales quota established by the cartel.

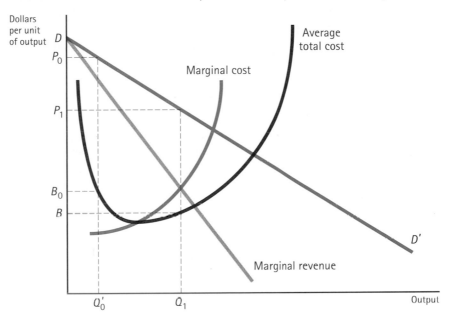

which marginal cost equals marginal revenue. This price would result in a profit of $Q_1 \times P_1 B$, which is generally higher than the profit would be if the firm conformed to the price and sales quota dictated by the cartel.[3] A firm that breaks away from a cartel—or secretly cheats—can raise its profits as long as other firms do not do the same thing and the cartel does not punish it in some way. But, if all firms do this, the cartel disintegrates.

Hence, there is a constant threat to the existence of a cartel. Its members have an incentive to cheat, and once a few do so, others may follow. Price concessions, made secretly by a few "chiselers" or openly by a few malcontents, cut into the sales of cooperative members of the cartel, who are then induced to match them. Ultimately, the cartel may fall apart.

[3]At price P_0, the firm will sell Q_0'. Its profit would be $Q_0' \times P_0 B_0$, which is less than $Q_1 \times P_1 B$. Because the demand curve is so elastic, total revenues increase significantly as price drops from P_0 to P_1. While the total costs increase as output increases from Q_0' to Q_1, unless they increase very rapidly, the increase in total revenue exceeds the increase in total cost.

Dissension in the OPEC Cartel

To illustrate the difficulties in maintaining an effective cartel, consider the Organization of Petroleum Exporting Countries (OPEC), which consists of 12 major oil-producing countries, including Saudi Arabia, Iran, Venezuela, Libya, Nigeria, and the United Arab Emirates. This cartel increased the price of crude oil dramatically during the 1970s, but by 1983, a decade after the first of its huge price increases, OPEC experienced problems in maintaining the price of oil, and by 1993, the price had fallen to below $15 per barrel. To some extent, the downward pressure on price was due to a leftward shift in the demand for oil brought about by conservation of oil and competition from other fuels (stemming partly from the great increases in the oil prices in earlier years). Also non-OPEC oil production (in Mexico and the North Sea, for example) soared, putting additional pressure on OPEC.

But, this is only part of the story. The price declines were also due to internal dissension, and individual members of the OPEC cartel refused to abide by the production quotas set by the cartel. Consider the meeting of OPEC oil ministers in early 1994. Iran and other OPEC countries criticized Saudi Arabia severely, arguing that it should reduce its huge output rate. The Saudis refused, saying that there would be little or no effect on price if it reduced production, because other OPEC members would cheat and raise their own output correspondingly. Clearly, in cartels, as in other families, harmony may be hard to achieve.

By the late 1990s, oil prices had fallen to about $12 a barrel, fostering another round of production cuts and price increases. This time, non-OPEC countries, such as Mexico and Norway, just as weary of low prices as the OPEC members, agreed to reduce production. Oil prices skyrocketed, reaching $40 per barrel in early 2000. This led to production increases aimed at restoring prices to about $24–$25 per barrel.

Price Leadership

In many oligopolistic industries, one firm sets the price and the rest follow its lead. Examples of industries that have been characterized by such **price leadership** are steel, nonferrous alloys, and agricultural implements. In this section, we show how the price leader should set its price and output. We assume that the industry is composed of a large dominant firm (the price leader) and a number of small firms. We also assume that the dominant firm sets the price for the industry but lets the small firms sell all they want at that price. Whatever amount the small firms do *not* supply at that price is provided by the dominant firm.

A new version of price leadership has arisen in the retail sector with the arrival of the "big box" stores. When Wal-Mart or Home Depot comes to town,

CONCEPTS IN CONTEXT

Cartels Come in Many Shapes and Sizes

In 1997, every two weeks in Rutherford, New Jersey, 20 shipping line managers met and discussed what they would charge to move cargo across the North Atlantic. While this meeting could be composed of the managers of a single ocean shipping line discussing pricing strategy, it was not. Rather, they were executives of 20 different companies. Exempt from the U.S. antitrust laws, they collusively set rates on tens of billions of dollars of cargo. This practice has since been declared illegal.

Their monopoly power was limited because the cartel was unable to control the shipping capacity of its members, and some ocean carriers were not members of the cartel. Nevertheless, it is estimated that the cartel was able to raise rates 18 to 19 percent above competitive rates.

Of course, the modern epitome of controlling supply and, hence, creating monopoly power is OPEC and the crude oil market. The ability to mark price over marginal cost is substantial. A product that costs the most efficient producer several dollars to take out of the ground is marked up as much as 15 times.

The monopoly power is so substantial because of the strong demand for the product, the inelasticity of demand for the product, and the fact that the low-cost producers are members of the cartel, and although the cartel is not perfect (not all producers are members), those nonmembers are high-cost producers.

Others have tried to emulate the behavior of OPEC. Brazil and Columbia, major coffee producers, attempted a coffee cartel that failed. The major problem was that coffee has a fairly elastic demand. So, when the Brazilians and Columbians withheld supply to raise prices, consumers switched to other beverages like tea and caffeinated colas. If you control the supply in a market that has many close substitutes, your monopoly power is not likely to be significant.

Cartels need not exist for goods only. They can exist for services, too. In Germany a wage-setting cartel is constitutionally sanctioned between unions and corporations. The cartel keeps wages high and labor strife low and ends up costing Germans jobs. This is exactly what we expect a monopoly to do—raise prices (wages) and restrict output (jobs).

Sources: "As U.S. Trade Grows, Shipping Cartels Get a Bit More Scrutiny," *Wall Street Journal,* October 7, 1997; "German Wage Pact Ends up Costing Jobs," *Wall Street Journal,* February 19, 1997.

the small retailers, hardware stores, lumber yards, and the like, are basically victims of the prices charged by those big stores. Small stores may try to differentiate with service and "high-end" items, but anyone who was selling the items sold by Wal-Mart and Home Depot before the arrival of the big box stores now must follow the prices of the big guys. Some do and survive, but the newspapers are full of stories of the demise of "ma and pa" businesses that just cannot compete with the prices (and variety) of the big box stores.

Under these circumstances, you can readily determine the price that the dominant firm sets if it maximizes profits. Since each small firm takes the price as

FIGURE
13.4

Price Leadership by a Dominant Firm

The dominant firm sets a price of P_1 and supplies Q_1 units of the product. The total industry output is D_1.

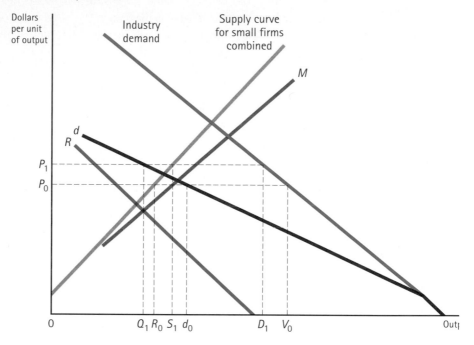

given, it produces the output at which price equals marginal cost. Therefore, a supply curve for all small firms combined can be drawn by summing *horizontally* their marginal cost curves. This supply curve is shown in Figure 13.4. The demand curve for the dominant firm can be derived by subtracting the amount supplied by the small firms at each price from the total amount demanded at that price. Thus, the demand curve for the output of the dominant firm, d, can be determined by finding the *horizontal* difference at each price between the industry demand curve and the supply curve for all small firms combined.

To illustrate how d is derived, suppose that the dominant firm sets a price of P_0. The small firms supply R_0, and the total amount demanded is V_0. Therefore, the amount to be supplied by the dominant firm is $V_0 - R_0$, which is the quantity d_0 on the d curve at price P_0. In other words, d_0 is set equal to $V_0 - R_0$. The process by which the other points on the d curve are determined is exactly the same; this procedure is repeated at various levels of price.

Knowing the demand curve for the output of the dominant firm, d, and the dominant firm's marginal cost curve, M, you can readily determine the price and output that maximizes the profits of the dominant firm. The dominant firm's

ANALYZING MANAGERIAL DECISIONS

Price Cuts for Breakfast

In April 1996, the Kraft Food Division of Philip Morris cut prices on its Post and Nabisco brands of breakfast cereal by 20 percent. According to industry observers, this was because the cereal producers had become frustrated with stagnating demand, and consumers had become annoyed by escalating prices of cereal. Before this price cut, the market shares of the leading cereal producers were as follows:

Producer	Share of market for 52 weeks ending February 25, 1996
Kellogg	36
General Mills	26
Philip Morris	16
Quaker	8
Ralston	4
Other	10
Total	100

(a) By June 1996, Philip Morris' share of the market was more than 20 percent. Does it appear that the price cut worked? (b) Kellogg had products that are relatively similar to Philip Morris'. By June 1996, Kellogg's share of the market was 32 percent. Was it particularly affected by Philip Morris' price cut? (c) Subsequently, Kellogg announced a 19 percent cut in its own prices. It was estimated that this would reduce the firm's revenues by about $350 million. Why then did the price cut seem worthwhile?

SOLUTION (a) Yes. (b) Yes. (c) Apparently, Kellogg believed that it would incur an even greater loss if it did not cut its prices.

Source: New York Times, June 11, 1996.

marginal revenue curve, R, can be derived from the dominant firm's demand curve, d, in the usual way. The optimal output for the dominant firm is the output, Q_1, where its marginal cost equals its marginal revenue. This output is achieved if the dominant firm sets a price of P_1. The total industry output is D_1, and the small firms supply S_1 $(= D_1 - Q_1)$.

Ghoshal, Inc.: A Numerical Example

To illustrate how a dominant firm can determine the price that will maximize its profits, consider Ghoshal, Inc., the dominant firm in a particular industry. The demand curve for this industry's product is

$$Q = 100 - 5P$$

where Q is the quantity demanded and P is the price. The supply curve for the small firms in this industry is

$$Q_S = 10 + P$$

where Q_S is the total amount supplied by all these small firms combined. Ghoshal's marginal cost is

$$MC = 2Q_A \tag{13.1}$$

where Q_A is Ghoshal's output.

To derive the demand curve for Ghoshal's output, we subtract Q_S from Q, the result being

$$Q_A = Q - Q_S = (100 - 5P) - (10 + P) = 90 - 6P$$
$$P = 15 - (1/6)Q_A \tag{13.2}$$

Remembering that Ghoshal's total revenue equals PQ_A, Ghoshal's total revenue equals

$$TR = [15 - (1/6)Q_A]Q_A = 15Q_A - (1/6)Q_A^2$$

Therefore, Ghoshal's marginal revenue is

$$dTR_A/dQ_A = MR_A = 15 - (1/3)Q_A \tag{13.3}$$

To maximize profit, Ghoshal must set marginal revenue, in equation (13.3) equal to marginal cost, in equation (13.1):

$$MR_A = 15 - (1/3)Q_A = 2Q_A = MC_A$$

so Q_A must equal $6\frac{3}{7}$. Consequently, from equation (13.2), it follows that $P = 13\frac{39}{42}$, or $\$13.93$.

To sum up, if you were chief executive officer of Ghoshal and wanted to maximize profit, you would be well advised to charge a price of $\$13.93$. This is the profit-maximizing price.

Possible Views of Competition among a Few Firms

We now take a different view of competition among a few firms. For simplicity, we view two firms, a duopoly, but as we subsequently show, the results are generalizable to more firms.

ANALYZING MANAGERIAL DECISIONS

Cranberries: Where 34 Percent of the Market Producers Are Price Takers

The cranberry, that marvelous red berry that helps prevent bladder infections, has a lot of vitamin C, and contains antioxidants, is dominated by a giant growers' cooperative—Ocean Spray.

Ocean Spray is the price setter. When Ocean Spray (with a 66 percent market share) sets its price for cranberries, the other (nonmember) producers fall into line. Each year, in late September and early October, Ocean Spray sets a price for sales to supermarkets per case of 24 12-ounce bags. This price is based on anticipated and actual supply and demand conditions in the market.

Given the price that Ocean Spray sets, other producers must decide how much of the product they wish to harvest for sale, harvest to inventory, harvest but for use in other products (e.g., juice and juice blends), or leave in the bogs.

Thus, Ocean Spray is the price leader and the remaining 34 percent of the producers are fol-

lowers. Whatever price is set by Ocean Spray, the followers take as given and optimize versus that price.

Source: "The Case of the Vanishing Berries," *New York Times,* November 12, 2000.

The two firms produce an identical product and make their output decisions simultaneously. Firms clearly face simultaneous move situations when they compete against one another in sealed bid auctions, when they must place advertising copy at the newspaper by Thursday afternoon for the Sunday special sales edition, when both are entering a market at the same time and planning their plant capacity, and in many other situations.

Later on, we consider sequential move strategies, where one firm moves first, then is followed by other firms. First movers or leaders occur in many situations, and the first mover may arise because of luck (it receives a franchise to enter the market first by lottery—the first mobile phone franchises in the United States and the allocation of landing slots into some airports in the United States were done in this manner), because of business acumen (it invented or patented the product), or because an entrepreneur decided that a market provided an opportunity before any other business decided to enter that market.

Competition among a Few Firms: Price Competition

Consider two firms, A and B, producing identical products in a simultaneous-move scenario. Suppose that both firms have identical total cost functions of the following form:

$$TC_i = 500 + 4q_i + 0.5q_i^2 \qquad (13.4)$$

where $i = A, B$ and q_i is the output of firm i.

The market demand as seen by both firms is

$$P = 100 - Q = 100 - q_A - q_B \qquad (13.5)$$

where P is the unit price of the product, Q is the quantity demanded at price P, and $Q = q_A + q_B$.

Under the scenario, we initially consider three options the duopolists might follow: compete against each other on the basis of price, collude and form a cartel, and compete against each other on the basis of quantity (the so-called **Cournot strategy**).

The marginal cost of firm i is

$$MC_i = dTC_i/dq_i = (4 + q_i) \qquad (13.6)$$

If the firms were to compete on the basis of price, they would be willing to lower their price until they reached the level of their marginal cost. They would never lower their price below marginal cost because the additional revenue made from making the last sale would be exceeded by the additional cost of making that sale.

The first good demanded has a reservation price of $99; that is, $100 - 1$. This good would cost each producer $5; that is, $4 + 1$, to produce. If they competed in price over this customer, while they could charge as high as $99, they would be willing to accept as low as $5. In fact, if there were just this one customer, and they competed on price to get its business, we expect the price to be $5. Suppose that firm A offered to sell to the customer at $99 (hoping for a profit of $99 - $5 = $94). Firm B would then offer to sell to it for $98 (hoping for a profit of $98 - $5 = $93). Then, firm A would counteroffer at $97. As you can see, in a series of counteroffers to outbid its rival, the price would be bid down to $5. After that point, the possibility of a profitable sale by a lower price disappears (since any lower price would be exceeded by the marginal cost of production).

So, we can expect that price equal to marginal cost is the ultimate resolution of this pricing contest. For firm A, this means that

$$P = 100 - Q = 100 - q_A - q_B = 4 + q_A = MC_A$$
$$2q_A = 96 - q_B$$
$$q_A = 48 - 0.5q_B \qquad (13.7)$$

For firm B, this means that

$$P = 100 - Q = 100 - q_A - q_B = 4 + q_B = MC_B$$
$$2q_B = 96 - q_A$$
$$q_B = 48 - 0.5q_A \qquad (13.8)$$

We can determine the ultimate result of this pricing game by substituting equation (13.8) into equation (13.7) and solving for q_A (or by substituting equation (13.7) into equation (13.8) and solving for q_B):

$$q_A = 48 - 0.5(48 - 0.5q_A) = 24 + 0.25q_A$$
$$0.75q_A = 24$$
$$q_A = 32$$

Substituting $q_A = 32$ into equation (13.8) gives $q_B = 48 - 0.5(32) = 32$, which should not be surprising (because each firm has identical cost functions). Since each produces 32, the total output is 64 ($= Q$). Substituting $Q = 64$ into the market demand function yields a price of \$36 ($=100 - 64$). This also equals each firm's marginal cost, \$36; that is, $4 + 32$. Each firm has a total revenue of \$1,152 ($\$36 \times 32$) and total costs of \$1,140 ($= 500 + 4(32) + 0.5(32^2)$), leaving each firm with a profit of \$12.

Competition among a Few Firms: Collusion

Since competing on price does not seem to be a very promising strategy from the point of view of profit,[4] suppose the two firms could legally form a cartel. Under these circumstances, the market demand curve would be the cartel's demand curve and the cartel's marginal cost curve would be the *horizontal*

[4]If each was a constant-cost firm with an identical marginal cost, then price competition would take the price down to that marginal cost and profits would be zero (or minus fixed costs if fixed costs exist). For example, if both firms had marginal cost of \$4, the cartel would produce 96; that is, $4 = 100 - Q$ or $Q = 96$ (with each producing 48). Each firm's total revenue would be \$192 ($= 4 \times 48$) and both firms would have variable cost of \$192 ($= 4 \times 48$). Thus, all profit would be lost to competition.

summation of each firm's marginal cost curve.[5] Rewriting each firm's marginal cost as

$$q_A = -4 + MC_A$$
$$q_B = -4 + MC_B$$

and adding q_A and q_B (i.e., summing the marginal costs horizontally—adding up the quantities produced at any given marginal cost), we get

$$Q = q_A + q_B = -4 + MC_A - 4 + MC_B = -8 + 2MC$$

and rearranging yields

$$2MC = 8 + Q$$
$$MC = 4 + 0.5Q$$

which is the cartel's marginal cost.

The cartel behaves as a monopolist (see Chapter 11 and earlier in this chapter) and sets its marginal revenue equal to its marginal cost. The cartel's total revenue is

$$TR = PQ = (100 - Q)Q = 100Q - Q^2$$

The cartel's marginal revenue is therefore

$$MR = dTR/dQ = 100 - 2Q$$

Setting the cartel's marginal revenue equal to the cartel's marginal cost yields

$$MR = 100 - 2Q = 4 + 0.5Q = MC$$
$$2.5Q = 96$$
$$Q = 38.4$$

Substituting $Q = 38.4$ into the cartel's demand curve gives a price of $61.6 (i.e., $100 - 38.4$). The cartel's total revenue is \$2,365.44 (i.e., \$61.6 \times 38.4$). Since each firm has the same marginal cost equation, each should produce the same

[5]It is the horizontal summation because we want to measure the additional cost of producing an additional unit of output in the cartel. To produce that additional unit in the cheapest possible way, the cartel would always want to have identical marginal costs for each producer. If the marginal costs were not the same, the cartel could lower its total cost of production by shifting production from the high-marginal-cost firm to the low-marginal-cost firm until their marginal costs were equalized. See appendix to Chapter 11 and the earlier discussion in this chapter.

amount, 19.2, so that both have a marginal cost of $23.2 (i.e., 4 + 19.2), which, of course, equals the cartel's marginal revenue of 23.2 (i.e., 100 − 2(38.4)). The two firms split the total revenue so that each receives $1,182.72. Each firm has a total cost of $761.12 (= 500 + 4(19.2) + 0.5(19.2²)); hence, each firm makes a profit of $421.6, a considerable improvement over the $12 made when the firms competed on price. Note that the cartel significantly restricted output (from 64 to 38.4) and significantly increased price (from $36 to $61.6), but as observed in Chapter 11, that is what monopolists do.

Competition among a Few Firms: Quantity (Capacity) Competition

In many situations, forming a cartel (or colluding to restrict output) is illegal. So, how can the two firms avoid the lose-lose situation (i.e., competing on price) and *approach* the win-win profits of a cartel? The solution lies in competition on quantity (or production capacity) as opposed to price, and the solution is attributed to Cournot.

Cournot analysis makes the following assumptions: The firms move simultaneously, have the same view of the market demand (i.e., both view the same market demand curve), know each other's cost functions, and optimize (i.e., make the profit-maximizing decision) their quantity decision assuming the other firm's quantity decision is given.

We already gave examples of firms moving simultaneously. Having the same view of the market demand is problematic, because each firm has its own analysts to estimate the market demand. In many situations, however, a somewhat similar conclusion about the market is possible because government- or trade-association-generated data (macroeconomic and industry-specific variables) are used by all analysts and the corporate intelligence of each firm observes the same economic landscape. Nevertheless, it is possible for two (or more) firms viewing the same economic data to come up with different conclusions or assessments. With respect to knowing each other's cost functions, in some cases, good approximations of adversaries' costs are likely. For instance, in the airline industry, only two manufacturers of large aircraft remain (Boeing and Airbus) and only several producers of small commercial aircraft (e.g., Bombardier and Embraer). The carriers are either flying the same aircraft as their adversaries or have "speced" the aircraft (i.e., received all the operating characteristics of that aircraft from the manufacturer when the carrier considered purchasing new aircraft). Personnel are unionized (for the most part) and wage rates are well known. All carriers buy fuel, meals, and other items from a limited set of suppliers. Therefore, carrier A has a fairly decent estimate of what it costs carrier B to operate its fleet (and vice versa). In addition, executive talent is mobile within the industry, and when executives leave carrier A, they carry knowledge of the company in their heads that can be useful to company B.[6]

The last assumption is that firm A optimizes their quantity (capacity) given that firm B's quantity (capacity) is fixed. This is not as restrictive as it sounds. We first formulate this situation as a series of "what-if" questions. *If* my adversary actually is going to produce quantity X, *what* quantity would I produce to maximize my profit? Which output you actually choose to produce of all the "what-if" possibilities depends on what you think your adversary will *actually* do (and your adversary is going through the same "what-if" process). By a process of deduction, you can figure out the most logical output for your adversary and it can figure out your most logical output. This is the Cournot solution, and we see that it yields the solution we would get from following game theory (see Chapter 14).

We now view the Cournot solution to the preceding case in two different ways. The first is by following a series of "what-if" scenarios. We deal with the decisions of firm A and treat this as your firm. Clearly, if you thought that your adversary (firm B) would abdicate the market to you, you would behave like a monopolist. Since the monopolist's marginal revenue is the same as the cartel's in the preceding situation (and now your marginal revenue, since you are the only producer in the market), and your marginal cost is $MC_A = 4 + q_A$, you maximize profits by setting MR = MC or

$$MR_A = 100 - 2q_A = 4 + q_A = MC_A$$
$$3q_A = 96$$
$$q_A = 32$$

So, if $q_B = 0$, your profit-maximizing optimal-quantity response is $q_A = 32$.

On the other hand, if you thought your adversary would produce 96 units, there would be only 4 for you to produce (at most). Rewrite the market demand curve as $Q = 100 - P$. Your *residual* demand curve (i.e., the market demand curve less what you assume firm B produces), what is left for you after firm B made its production decision, is

$$q_A = 100 - P - 96 = 4 - P$$
$$P = 4 - q_A$$

---

[6]We will leave it to your ethics course to debate about what information can be revealed. To see how information is obtained on competitors, see "They Snoop to Conquer," *Business Week*, October 28, 1996. In a classic case of crossing the line, Jose Ignacio Lopez left General Motors in 1992 allegedly carrying a briefcase of GM blueprints to his new job at Volkswagen. You need no ethics course to know that this is wrong. GM sued, and in 1996 the case was settled. Lopez was forced to resign from VW and VW was required to pay GM $100 million and purchase $1 billion worth of GM auto parts.

You would produce nothing under these circumstances, since the *highest* the price could be is $4 (when q_A is zero) and the lowest your marginal cost could be is $4 (when q_A is zero). Therefore, the price could never be equal to or exceed your marginal cost at a positive level of output (and so you produce nothing, since you would lose money if you produced a positive quantity). Therefore, if $q_B = 96$, your profit-maximizing optimal-quantity response is $q_A = 0$.

Suppose you thought your adversary would produce 50 units; that is, $q_B = 50$? Under these circumstances, your residual demand is

$$q_A = 100 - P - 50 = 50 - P$$
$$P = 50 - q_A$$

Your total revenue is $Pq_A = (50 - q_A)q_A = 50q_A - q_A^2$. Hence, your marginal revenue is

$$MR_A = dTR_A/dq_A = 50 - 2q_A$$

To maximize profit, you set $MR_A = MC_A$, or

$$MR_A = 50 - 2q_A = 4 + q_A = MC_A$$

$$3q_A = 46$$
$$q_A = 15.33$$

Therefore, if $q_B = 50$, your profit-maximizing optimal-quantity response is $q_A = 15.33$.

So, we know the optimal profit-maximizing responses for the "what-if" scenarios we investigated (see Table 13.1).

By doing more "what-if" situations, we could fill out Table 13.1 for all possible firm B outputs between 0 and 96. But, we can get the equivalent of a full table directly with the analysis that follows.

TABLE
13.1

Profit-Maximizing Output Responses of Firm *A* Given That Firm *A* Assumes What Quantity Firm *B* Produces

If firm B produces	Then firm A produces
0	32
50	15.33
96	0

Firm A (you) maximizes profit when your total revenue (Pq_A) exceeds your total cost ($500 + 4q_A + 0.5q_A^2$) by the maximal amount. Your total revenue is

$$TR = (100 - Q)q_A = (100 - q_A - q_B)q_A = 100q_A - q_A^2 - q_Aq_B$$

Your marginal revenue is

$$MR_A = \partial TR_A/\partial q_A = 100 - 2q_A - q_B \tag{13.9}$$

To maximize profit, you set $MR_A = MC_A$, or

$$MR_A = 100 - 2q_A - q_B = 4 + q_A = MC_A$$
$$3q_A = 96 - q_B$$
$$q_A = 32 - (1/3)q_B \tag{13.10}$$

Equation (13.10) is called firm A's **reaction function**; that is, it tells us the profit-maximizing amount of product to produce *given* the output of the adversary firm B. Every number in the right-hand column of Table 13.1 occurs when the corresponding number on the left-hand side of Table 13.1 is substituted into the reaction function (13.10).

Because firm B has the same cost function as firm A and both face the same market demand curve, firm B's reaction function is

$$q_B = 32 - (1/3)q_A \tag{13.11}$$

The optimal amount to produce that should be deduced by each firm is found by substituting firm A's reaction function (13.10) into firm B's reaction function (13.11) and solving for q_A. Alternatively, firm B's reaction function (13.11) could be substituted into firm A's reaction function (13.10) and solved for q_B. The former yields

$$q_A = 32 - (1/3)[32 - (1/3)q_A]$$
$$q_A = (96/3) - (32/3) + (1/9)q_A$$
$$(8/9)q_A = (64/3)$$
$$q_A = 24$$

Substituting $q_A = 24$ into firm B's reaction function (13.11) gives

$$q_B = 32 - (1/3)24 = 24$$

Therefore, $Q = q_A + q_B = 48$ and substituting $Q = 48$ into the market demand function gives a price of $52; that is, $100 - 48$. These are the only quantities where what one producer wants to do is mutually consistent with what the other

CONCEPTS IN CONTEXT

The Staples and Office Depot Nonmerger

In 1997, Staples proposed a merger with Office Depot. Both firms are "category killers" in the office supply business; that is, one can go to them for one-stop shopping and get everything one would need to outfit and supply an office. Staples estimated that the merged firm would control 4–6 percent of the office supply market. The government antitrust officials (the U.S. Department of Justice and the Federal Trade Commission) disagreed. Staples defined the market to include Wal-Mart, K-Mart, Dell Online, Radio Shack, stores that sold office furniture, and the like, basically anyplace you could purchase a subset of the products they sold. The government defined the market only as "category killers," that is, only stores where you could buy everything that Staples sold. The government rejected the proposed merger, partially based on studies it commissioned that showed markets with two "category killers" instead of three (the other major "category killer" was Office Max), had prices significantly higher. Likewise, markets that had one "category killer" instead of two had even higher prices. From these results, we can conclude that more competition, even when the number of competitors is quite small, can have a significant impact on prices (and, hence, customer well-being).

Source: W.J. Baer, director of competition, FTC, "Why the FTC Opposes the Staples Merger," *Wall Street Journal*, April 1997.

producer wants to do; that is, it is an equilibrium—known as a Nash equilibrium after Nobel-laureate John Nash; subject of the book and the movie *A Beautiful Mind.*

Under the Cournot scenario, each firm produces 24 units and the market price is $52. Each firm's total revenue is $1,248 (i.e., $52 × 24), and each firm's total cost is $884 (i.e., $500 + 4(24) + 0.5(24^2)$), so each firm earns a profit of $364. While this is less than each share of the monopoly (cartel) profit of $421.6, it is considerably better than they would make if they competed on price ($12). The significance of this is the powerful impact of adding just one more equal producer to a monopoly market. In this case, the price falls by 15.6 percent (from $61.6 to $52) and output increases by 25 percent (from 38.4 to 48). Hence, adding a competitor can have a significant impact on mitigating the power of a monopolist. Looked at from the other direction, the two firms acting as Cournot quantity competitors can retain 86.3 percent of the monopoly (cartel) profit and enhance the price-competitive profit slightly over 30-fold.

How can a firm get itself into a Cournot scenario and avoid a price-competitive scenario? Some firms cannot seem to avoid the latter; for example, the airlines constantly seem to engage in price wars, much to the detriment of their profit. On the other hand, firms that learn not to "rock the boat" or to

FIGURE
13.5

Cournot Reaction Functions for Firms A and B

A Cournot equilibrium occurs where the two firms' reaction functions intersect. This is the only output combination where both firms' expectations of what the other firm will produce is consistent with their own expectations of their own optimal output. In this case, both firms produce 24 units.

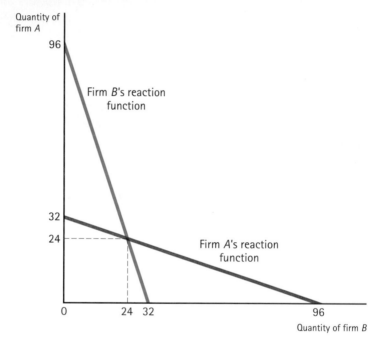

"kill the goose that lays the golden egg" learn to compete on quantity (capacity) and not price. Examples include General Electric and Westinghouse in the marketplace for steam turbine engines and Rockwell International and others in the market for water meters.[7] As can be seen from the preceding, the stakes are high, so this quantity (capacity) competition is a strategy worth learning for many firms playing the game of competition among the few. Figure 13.5 is a picture of the situation just discussed.

The Cournot Scenario with More than Two Firms

Table 13.2 shows the situation when multiple firms (each of which is identical to the two Cournot firms) compete on quantity. Adding a third equal (in cost)

[7]See Nancy Taubenslag, "Rockwell International," Harvard Business School Case, 9-383-019, July 1983.

How Seagoing Chemical Haulers May Have Tried to Divide the Market

Stolt-Nielsen SA and Odfjell ASA, two of the world's largest shipping companies, seem to have colluded to divide up a large amount of the maritime liquid chemical transport market. Company documents and previous employees suggest that the two maritime giants discussed which shipping business each would go after on a route-by-route basis and, at times, would exchange information on their bid prices. It is alleged that Stolt-Nielsen had gone as far as calculating a table that showed how much better off their revenue would be if they cooperated rather than competed.

The EFTA Surveillance Authority and the European Commission are investigating to see whether there is enough evidence of a cartel agreement and any violation of the European competition laws. Meanwhile, in the United States, a former general counsel of Stolt is bringing a lawsuit against the company accusing it of violating U.S. and international antitrust laws by fixing prices and colluding. Stolt and Odfjell claim they have violated no laws and are cooperating with authorities.

Whether the companies are guilty or not remains to be seen. But we should not be surprised that a company could calculate a table that showed their gains of cooperating rather than competing.

Source: "How Seagoing Chemical Haulers May Have Tried to Divide Market," *Wall Street Journal*, February 20, 2003.

TABLE
13.2

Price, Output, and Profits with Multiple Cournot Competitors

Number of competitors	Price	Percent decrease	Quantity/ firm	Profit/ firm	Total quantity	Percent increase
Cartel	61.6				38.4	
2	52	15.58	24	364	48	25
3	42.4	31.17	19.2	52.96	57.6	50
4	36	41.56	16	−116	64	66.67
5	31.43	48.98	13.71	−217.92	68.57	78.57
6	28	54.55	12	−284	72	87.5
7	25.33	58.88	10.67	−329.33	74.67	94.45
8	23.2	62.34	9.6	−360.8	76.8	100
9	21.45	65.18	8.73	−385.77	78.55	104.56
10	20	67.53	8	−404	80	108.33
n	$\dfrac{4n + 200}{n + 2}$		$\dfrac{96}{n + 2}$	$(11{,}824 - 2{,}000n - 500n^2)/(n + 2)^2$	$\dfrac{96n}{n + 2}$	
∞	4	93.51	0	−500	96	150

CONCEPTS IN CONTEXT

The Impact of More Sellers in the Market

In October 2002, Judge Barbara Jones of the Federal District Court in Manhattan upheld two AstraZeneca patents on Prilosec, a popular ulcer drug (in fact, the world's best-selling drug) that had generated $5.7 billion for AstraZeneca. The patents are valid until 2007. However, the judge also allowed KUDco, an American unit of Schwarz Pharma, a German pharmaceutical firm, the opportunity to make a lower-cost version of Prilosec long before 2007. KUDco introduced its generic version of the drug in 2002.

An important point for this ruling is its impact on pricing. "With only one generic competitor for Prilosec, there will probably be a shallower dis-

count from AstraZeneca's price of $4 a pill, perhaps to $3 rather than $1 or $2, which would be typical under full-blown competition."

The important conclusion is that adding just one competitor to a monopoly market can substantially reduce price (by 25 percent in this case). While full competition (as many generics as wish to enter) would lower prices by 50 to 75 percent, a 25-percent decrease is not trivial. It shows the power of one.

Source: U. Ruling, "Prilosec May Still Face Generic Rival," *New York Times Online,* http://www.nytimes.com/2002/10/14/business/14PLAC.html.

competitor to our duopoly drops the price 31.17 percent from the cartel monopoly price and increases output by 50 percent. Having eight equal-in-cost competitors in this Cournot situation drops the price by 62.34 percent relative to the cartel monopoly price and increases output by 100 percent. Profits become negative after three Cournot competitors because of the high level of fixed costs ($500). If the fixed cost were lower (say $50), all situations depicted (except for high values of *n*) would entail positive profit.

This analysis shows just how the addition of a few firms in a Cournot situation can bring significant price competition into the market. Even if the firms brought in have higher costs, significant downward pressure still is placed on price.

The Stackelberg Case: The First-Mover Advantage

Now consider a situation in which one firm gets to move before the other firm. This situation and its solution is called the **Stackelberg problem**. As mentioned, this can occur due to luck or skill. Suppose firm *A* can go first. Firm *A* knows how firm *B* will react to Firm *A*'s chosen output; that is, firm *B* follows *B*'s reaction function since doing so maximizes B's profit given A's choice of output (and A chooses first).

Therefore, the demand curve firm A faces reads (after substituting firm B's reaction function, equation (13.11), for q_B in the market demand curve, since we know firm B will produce that much)

$$P = 100 - q_A - q_B = 100 - q_A - [32 - (1/3)q_A] = 68 - (2/3)q_A$$

Firm A's total revenue is $Pq_A = [68 - (2/3)q_A]q_A = 68q_A - (2/3)q_A^2$. The firm's marginal revenue is

$$MR_A = dTR_A/dq_A = 68 - (4/3)q_A$$

Firm A sets its marginal revenue equal to its marginal cost to maximize profit:

$$MR_A = 68 - (4/3)q_A = 4 + q_A = MC_A$$
$$(7/3)q_A = 64$$
$$q_A = 27.43$$

Substituting $q_A = 27.43$ into firm B's reaction function yields

$$q_B = 32 - (1/3)27.43 = 22.86$$

Therefore, $Q = q_A + q_B = 50.29$ and substituting $Q = 50.29$ into the market demand curve gives a price of $49.71 (i.e., $100 - 50.29$). Firm A's total revenue is $1,363.59 (i.e., 49.71×27.43), and firm A's total cost is $985.88 (i.e., $500 + 4(27.43) + 0.5(27.43^2)$); therefore, the profits are $377.71 (which is $13.71 better than under Cournot, so it is better to go first if you can). Firm B's total revenue is $1,136.33 (i.e., 49.71×22.86), and firm B's total cost is $852.65 (i.e., $500 + 4(22.86) + 0.5(22.86^2)$); therefore, the profits are $283.67 (which is $80.33 worse than under Cournot, so, it is bad to go second).

The situation would be exactly reversed if firm B went first. In this case, where the firms have the same costs, it is worth the same amount for each firm to go first, $94.04 i.e., the gain from going first plus the loss if you went second. In situations where the firms have different cost functions, the low-cost firm has a greater advantage than the high-cost firm in all the pricing schemes discussed here, including the first-mover situation. The low-cost firm has the most to gain by moving first. The low-cost firm can afford to "purchase" the first-mover advantage, such as buy the first move from the lucky lottery winner, outbid the high-cost firm for the patent on the product, build a bigger plant than the high-cost firm to preempt the output decision of the second mover.

We change the situation a little and see what the impact is when firms A and B face the demand curve $P = 100 - q_A - q_B$, firm A has the cost function

$TC_A = 500 + 4q_A + 0.5q_A^2$, but firm B has the cost function $TC_B = 500 + 10q_B + 0.5q_B^2$ (i.e., firm B has higher costs than firm A). Firm A's reaction function is $q_A = 32 - (1/3)q_B$, and firm B's reaction function is $q_B = 30 - (1/3)q_A$. If you solve for the Stackelberg solution with firm A going first, $P = \$51.143$, $q_A = 28.286$, $q_B = 20.571$, $\pi_A = \$433.429$, and $\pi_B = \$134.776$. If you solve for a Stackelberg solution with firm B going first, $P = \$51.429$, $q_A = 23.714$, $q_B = 24.857$, $\pi_A = \$343.551$, and $\pi_B = \$220.857$.

Now, we can see the advantage of going first over going second when costs differ. If firm A goes first, it gets $\pi_A = \$433.429$, whereas if it goes second, it gets $\pi_A = \$343.551$. Therefore, firm A gains $\$433.429 - \$343.551 = \$89.878$ by going first. If firm B goes first, it gets $\pi_B = \$220.857$, whereas if it goes second, it gets $\pi_B = \$134.776$. Therefore, firm B gains $\$220.857 - \$134.776 = \$86.081$ by going first. Firm A gains the most from going first. If it were a question of acquiring the patent rights from an inventor that would enable a firm to go first, firm A could afford to outbid firm B for the patent (since firm A could afford to bid up to $\$89.878$ while firm B could afford to bid up to only $\$86.081$ for the patent). We would expect that firm A would acquire the patent and pay a little more than $\$86.081$ for it (since it has to beat out just the firm that values the patent second most to win the patent).

Since oligopoly and competition among the few is so prevalent, these conditions should be studied carefully. For the first time in our analysis of firm behavior, *your optimal strategy depends on what your adversary does*; that is, in equation (13.9), your marginal revenue depends not only on what you do, *but also* on what your adversary does. Hence, the price you receive for your product depends on both your and your adversary's decisions. This is the chain of reciprocal decisions; that is, my actions depend on your actions, which, in turn, depend on my actions, and so forth. The interdependence of business decisions is typical of most of the economy. This mutual dependence is the basis of the management strategy formulation discussed in the game theory chapter (Chapter 14).

The Kinked Demand Curve and "Sticky" Prices

The Cournot model explains why price might be "sticky"; that is, firms learn the optimal solution and have no incentive to deviate from it in the case of homogeneous products. This is especially true in industries when the cost and demand has been stable or easily predicted and the decision makers have faced each other many times before. Another theory of oligopoly also explains prices that do not change in the competition among the few when products are somewhat differentiated.

Consider a firm facing a limited number of competitors. It currently prices at P_0 and produces Q_0. Should the firm increase its price, its demand will be quite elastic (but not perfectly elastic, because with a differentiated product, the other goods are not *perfect* substitutes). Many customers will leave the firm, but some will stay because they like the characteristics of the product (or the seller) and are willing to pay more for them.

On the other hand, should the firm drop its price, it is assumed that the demand will be much less elastic because other producers will also drop their prices to protect the sales of their product. While lowering the price, *if* no other firm followed suit, would probably lead to a large increase in the lowering firm's quantity, when other firms do follow suit, only a slight increase in the firm's quantity demanded is observed (because they share the increase generated by the lower price with all other firms).

FIGURE
13.6

The Situation of the Kinked Demand Curve

The demand curve kinks at (Q_0, P_0), with the curve being relatively elastic above the kink and relatively less elastic below the kink. The marginal revenue curve is discontinuous at Q_0 (gap BC) and the marginal cost curves intersect the marginal revenue in the gap, leading to marginal revenue equal to marginal cost, yielding an optimal price of P_0 and an optimal quantity of Q_0, despite major shifts in the marginal cost curve.

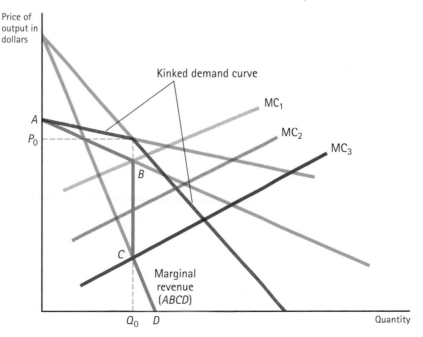

Hence, the firm's demand curve kinks at point (Q_0, P_0), being gently sloped above it and steeply sloped below it. This pattern yields a discontinuous marginal revenue curve (see gap BC in Figure 13.6) at Q_0 (recall that for linear demand curves, the marginal revenue curves have the same dollar axis intercept but fall twice as fast).

Therefore, the marginal cost curves MC_1 and MC_3 (and anything in-between, such as MC_2) yield the same price P_0 and quantity Q_0 for the profit-maximizing profit when they intersect the marginal revenue ($ABCD$) in the discontinuity. Thus, costs can shift around quite a bit without changing the profit-maximizing price (making it "sticky").

What Strategies Seem to Pay off Best?

Having described various models of oligopolistic behavior, we conclude this chapter by considering the question that is perhaps the most important of all for managers: What business strategies seem to have been the most successful? On the basis of the PIMS (profit impact of market strategy) data pertaining to 450 companies and 3,000 business units since 1972, Harvard's Robert Buzzell and Bradley Gale have concluded that *the most important single factor influencing a business unit's profitability is the quality of its products and services relative to those of its rivals.*[8] In the short run, better quality enhances profits because the firm is able to charge premium prices. In the long run, superior quality leads to both a gain in market share and the expansion of the relevant market. Therefore, despite short-term costs associated with rising quality, over a period of time, they may be offset by economies of scale.

Of course, this does not mean that any or all attempts to improve quality are worthwhile. Before making such attempts, it is important that a firm's managers evaluate carefully whether the prospective benefits outweigh the costs. Firms generally achieve quality advantages first by innovations in product (and service) design and subsequently by product and process improvements. In Chapter 8, we discussed many of the factors that influence the success or failure of innovative activities.

Buzzell and Gale also stress that *market share and profitability are strongly related.* As shown in Figure 13.7, a business unit's return on investment is directly related to its share of the market. As they are quick to point out, this relationship may be spurious in part, since both market share and profitability

[8]R. Buzzell and B. Gale, *The PIMS Principles Linking Strategy to Performance* (New York, Free Press, 1987). Also see National Academy of Sciences, "Competition in the Pharmaceutical Industry," and National Research Council, "Corporate Strategies in the Auto Industry." Both are in E. Mansfield, ed., *Managerial Economics and Operations Research* (4th ed.; New York: Norton, 1980).

ANALYZING MANAGERIAL DECISIONS

Global Oligopoly in the Disposable Syringe Market

A disposable plastic syringe (a single-use hypo-dermic needle and vacuum container for the injec-tion of drugs) is a major advance over the glass syringe.

Becton, Dickinson, which produced glass syringes before the advent of the plastic syringe, is a large seller of such syringes in the world. In the early 1980s, its market share ranged from 94 percent in Mexico to 51 percent in the United States to only about 10 percent in Germany. A few producers—Becton, Dickinson; Turumo (a Japanese firm); and Sherwood/Brunswick—dominate the market, their worldwide market shares having been 31 percent, 18 percent, and 16 percent, respec-tively.

(a) The minimum economic scale of production for a firm in this industry has been estimated to be at least 60 percent of the combined sales of the two key national markets (the United States and Japan). Is this fact related to the oligopolistic struc-ture of the industry? If so, how? (b) A doubling of volume has been estimated to lower the average cost of production by 20 percent. Is this fact related to the industry's structure? If so, how? (c) Becton, Dickinson's strategy "was to be the world's lowest-cost producer through selling a wide line of mass-produced syringes in all the important country markets worldwide, employing large-scale plants and aggressive marketing efforts to con-vince doctors of the merits of disposables."* Why did it want to sell abroad as well as in the United

States? (d) In each market, local competitors tended to set higher prices than Becton Dickinson and its global competitors. Why?

SOLUTION (a) Yes. Given that the minimum economic scale of production is so large a pro-portion of total sales, one would expect that there would be only a relatively few producers. (b) Yes. Given that economies of scale are substantial, one would expect relatively few producers. (c) One important reason was to reap the benefits of economies of scale. (d) Because local competitors tended to be small, their average costs tended to be higher than those of Becton, Dickinson and its global competitors.

*M. Cvar, "Case Studies in Global Competition: Patterns of Suc-cess and Failure," in M. Porter, ed., *Competition in Global Indus-tries* (Boston: Harvard Business School, 1986).

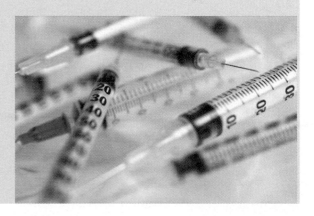

FIGURE
13.7

Relationship between Profitability and the Market Share of Business Units

In general, profitability seems to be directly related to market share.

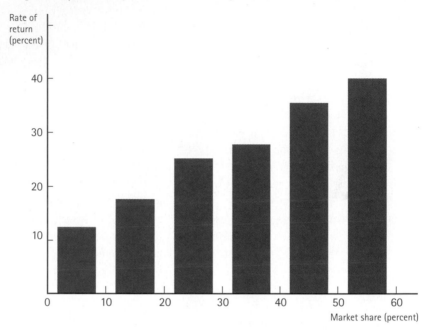

are likely to reflect other factors, such as management skill or luck. But, they argue, even when a wide variety of other market and strategic factors are taken into account, market share still seems to have a positive impact on profitability. Why? Because businesses with high market shares tend to enjoy economies of scale. In addition, businesses with large market shares are survivors, and firms do not survive unless they are profitable.

Although these results suggest that it is often wise to attempt to increase a firm's market share, this is not always the case. Take the case of Yamaha, which made a dramatic attack on Honda, the world leader in motorcycles. Yamaha cut prices, introduced new models, and advertised heavily in an attempt to increase its market share at Honda's expense. Honda counterattacked with ferocity, the result being that Yamaha's motorcycle sales fell by more than 50 percent and the company incurred heavy losses. Subsequently, Yamaha's president admitted: "We cannot match Honda's product development and sales strength. . . . I would like to end the Honda-Yamaha war."

Summary

1. Oligopoly is characterized by a small number of firms with a great deal of interdependence, actual and perceived, among them. A good example of an oligopoly is the U.S. oil industry, in which a small number of firms account for the bulk of the industry's capacity.

2. Oligopolistic industries, like others, usually pass through a number of phases: introduction, growth, maturity, and decline. As an industry goes through these phases, the nature of firm behavior often shifts. During the early stages, there often is considerable uncertainty regarding the industry's technology and which markets will open up soonest. During the maturity phase, there frequently is a tendency for firms to attack the market shares of their rivals.

3. There is no single model of oligopoly but many models, depending on the circumstances. Conditions in oligopolistic industries tend to promote collusion, since the number of firms is small, and the firms recognize their interdependence. The advantages to be derived by the firms from collusion seem obvious: increased profits, decreased uncertainty, and a better opportunity to control the entry of new firms. However, collusive arrangements are often hard to maintain, since once a collusive agreement is made, any firm can increase its profits by cheating on the agreement. Also, firms may find it difficult to identify a course of action that is agreeable to all members of the industry.

4. Another model of oligopolistic behavior is based on the supposition that one of the firms in the industry is a price leader, because it is the dominant firm. We show how, under these circumstances, this firm should set its price to maximize profits. This is also the model that explains pricing in the imperfect (one where not all producers are members) cartel.

5. When competition among a few firms exists, the firms may engage in price competition. This is usually a lose-lose situation, as they compete prices down to their marginal costs, with severe impact on profits. While forming a cartel and monopolizing the market is a theoretical possibility that maximizes profit, it many times is illegal. Cournot competition (competition on quantity or capacity) is a way to capture a significant share of the level of cartel profits and avoids the negative impact on profits brought about by price competition. The Cournot scenario is a simultaneous move, noncooperative situation, where participants initially strategize "what-if" moves; that is, what would be my profit-maximizing output response given an output by my adversary(ies). By logically tracing out all your profit-maximizing responses to your opponents' output choices, then putting yourself in their position and doing the same analysis for them, all participants performing the same analysis can deduce their best output of all the "what-if" scenarios considered, because only one is consistent with what your

adversaries want to do. The key to competition among the few is interdependence, where your optimal output is not only a function of what you wish to do but what your adversaries wish to do (and vice versa).

6. If one firm can act before another firm, the Stackelberg model explains the optimal (profit-maximizing) behavior for the first mover and all subsequent movers in this sequential game. In general, first movers see their profits improve relative to the simultaneous-move Cournot situation, and subsequent movers see their profits decrease (relative to the Cournot situation). If low-cost firms move first, they receive a bigger advantage than if high-cost firms move first. One can purchase the right to move first from the firm with the right to move first; for example, buy the patent rights from the holder. The value of the right to go first to the firm is the firm's profits if it goes first minus the firm's profits if it follows.

7. Prices may be "sticky" (i.e., tend to be stable) in oligopolies with differentiated products. This occurs because the demand curve kinks at the current price (being very elastic above the current price, as competitors do not follow any price increase of the firm and the firm is likely to lose a significant number of sales because of the price increase, whereas it is much less elastic below the current price, as competitors are likely to meet any price decrease by the firm to protect their sales). The kink in the demand curve leads to a discontinuity in the firm's marginal revenue curve. Therefore, the marginal cost can shift upward or downward considerably but still meet the marginal-revenue-equals-marginal-cost condition for profit maximization in the marginal revenue discontinuity and, thus, not change the profit-maximizing price and quantity.

8. Statistical studies based on the data pertaining to hundreds of firms suggest that the single most important factor influencing a business unit's profitability is the quality of its products and services, relative to those of rivals, and market share and profitability are strongly related.

Problems

1. The Bergen Company and the Gutenberg Company are the only two firms that produce and sell a particular kind of machinery. The demand curve for their product is

$$P = 580 - 3Q$$

where P is the price (in dollars) of the product, and Q is the total amount demanded. The total cost function of the Bergen Company is

$$TC_B = 410Q_B$$

where TC_B is its total cost (in dollars) and Q_B is its output. The total cost function of the Gutenberg Company is

$$TC_G = 460Q_G$$

where TC_G is its total cost (in dollars) and Q_G is its output.
   a. If these two firms collude and they want to maximize their combined profits, how much will the Bergen Company produce?
   b. How much will the Gutenberg Company produce?
   c. Will the Gutenberg Company agree to such an arrangement? Why or why not?

2. The can industry is composed of two firms. Suppose that the demand curve for cans is

$$P = 100 - Q$$

where P is the price (in cents) of a can and Q is the quantity demanded (in millions per month) of cans. Suppose that the total cost function of each firm is

$$TC = 2 + 15q$$

where TC is total cost (in tens of thousands of dollars) per month and q is the quantity produced (in millions) per month by the firm.
   a. What are the price and output if the firms set price equal to marginal cost?
   b. What are the profit-maximizing price and output if the firms collude and act like a monopolist?
   c. Do the firms make a higher combined profit if they collude than if they set price equal to marginal cost? If so, how much higher is their combined profit?

3. An oligopolistic industry selling a particular type of machine tool is composed of two firms. The two firms set the same price and share the total market equally. The demand curve confronting each firm (assuming that the other firm sets the same price as this firm) follows, as well as each firm's total cost function.

Price (thousands of dollars)	Quantity demanded per day	Daily output	Total cost (thousands of dollars)
10	5	5	45
9	6	6	47
8	7	7	50
7	8	8	55
6	9	9	65

a. Assuming that each firm is correct in believing that the other firm will charge the same price as it does, what is the price that each should charge?

b. Under the assumptions in part a, what daily output rate should each firm set?

4. James Pizzo is president of a firm that is the price leader in the industry; that is, it sets the price and the other firms sell all they want at that price. In other words, the other firms act as perfect competitors. The demand curve for the industry's product is $P = 300 - Q$, where P is the price of the product and Q is the total quantity demanded. The total amount supplied by the other firms is equal to Q_r, where $Q_r = 49P$. (P is measured in dollars per barrel; Q, Q_r, and Q_b are measured in millions of barrels per week.)

a. If Pizzo's firm's marginal cost curve is $2.96Q_b$, where Q_b is the output of his firm, at what output level should he operate to maximize profit?

b. What price should he charge?

c. How much does the industry as a whole produce at this price?

d. Is Pizzo's firm the dominant firm in the industry?

5. The International Air Transport Association (IATA) has been composed of 108 U.S. and European airlines that fly transatlantic routes. For many years, IATA acted as a cartel: It fixed and enforced uniform prices.

a. If IATA wanted to maximize the total profit of all member airlines, what uniform price would it charge?

b. How would the total amount of traffic be allocated among the member airlines?

c. Would IATA set price equal to marginal cost? Why or why not?

6. In late 1991, two firms, Delta Airlines and the Trump Shuttle, provided air shuttle service between New York and Boston or Washington. The one-way price charged by both firms was $142 on weekdays and $92 on weekends, with lower off-peak advance-purchase fares. In September 1991, Delta increased the per-trip shuttle mileage given to members of the Delta frequent-flier program from 1,000 to 2,000 miles, even though actual mileage from New York to either Boston or Washington is about 200 miles. Moreover, Delta also offered an extra 1,000 miles to frequent fliers who made a round-trip on the same day, raising a possible day's total to 5,000 miles. Almost simultaneously, Trump changed the frequent-flier mileage it gave shuttle passengers. (It participated in the One Pass frequent-flier program with Continental Airlines and some foreign carriers.) What sorts of changes do you think Trump made? Why?

7. Two firms, the Alliance Company and the Bangor Corporation, produce vision systems. The demand curve for vision systems is

$$P = 200,000 - 6(Q_1 + Q_2)$$

where P is the price (in dollars) of a vision system, Q_1 is the number of vision systems produced and sold per month by Alliance, and Q_2 is the number of vision systems produced and sold per month by Bangor. Alliance's total cost (in dollars) is

$$TC_1 = 8,000Q_1$$

Bangor's total cost (in dollars) is

$$TC_2 = 12,000Q_2$$

    a. If each of these two firms sets its own output level to maximize its profits, assuming that the other firm holds constant its output level, what is the equilibrium price?

    b. What is the output of each firm?

    c. What is the profit of each firm?

8. In Britain, price competition among bookshops has been suppressed for over 100 years by the Net Book Agreement (of 1900), which was aimed at the prevention of price wars. However, in October 1991, Waterstone and Company began cutting book prices at its 85 British shops. According to Richard Barker, Waterstone's operations director, the decision to reduce the price of about 40 titles by about 25 percent was due to price cuts by Dillons, Waterstone's principal rival.

    a. According to the president of Britain's Publishers Association, the price-cutting was "an enormous pity" that will "damage many booksellers who operate on very slim margins."[9] Does this mean that price-cutting of this sort is contrary to the public interest?

    b. Why would Dillons want to cut price? Under what circumstances would this be a good strategy? Under what circumstances would it be a mistake?

9. In the 1960s, Procter and Gamble recognized that disposable diapers could be made a mass-market product and developed techniques to produce diapers at high speed and correspondingly low cost. The result is that it dominated the market. According to Harvard's Michael Porter, who made a careful study of this industry, the following were some ways in which Procter and Gamble might have signaled other firms to deter entry.[10]

---

[9]"British Book Shops in Price Skirmishes," *New York Times*, October 7, 1991.

[10]M. Porter, "Strategic Interaction: Some Lessons from Industry Histories for Theory and Antitrust Policy," in S. Salop, ed., *Strategy, Predation, and Antitrust Analysis*, (Washington, DC: Federal Trade Commission, 1981); *New York Times*, April 15, 1993, and March 25, 1995; and *Business Week*, April 26, 1993, and September 19, 1994.

Tactic	Cost to Procter and Gamble	Cost to an entrant
1. Signal a commitment to defend position in diapers through public statements, comments to retailers, etc.	None	Raises expected cost of entry by increasing probability and extent of retaliation.
2. File a patent suit	Legal fees	Incurs legal fees plus probability that P and G wins the suit with subsequent cost to the competitor.
3. Announce planned capacity expansion.	None	Raises expected risk of price-cutting and the probability of P and G's retaliation to entry.
4. Announce a new generation of diapers to be introduced in the future.	None	Raises the expected cost of entry by forcing entrant to bear possible product development and changeover costs contingent on the ultimate configuration of the new generation.

    a. In considering these possible tactics, why should Procter and Gamble be concerned about the costs to itself?

    b. Why should it be concerned with the costs to an entrant?

    c. By the 1990s, Procter and Gamble had to compete with high-quality, private-label diapers (as well as with Kimberly-Clark, which successfully entered the market in the 1970s). In March 1993, its Pampers brand had about 30 percent of the market, and its Luvs brand had about 10 percent. The price of Luvs and Pampers exceeded that of discount brands by over 30 percent. Should Procter and Gamble have cut its price?

    d. In 1993, Procter and Gamble sued Paragon Trade Brands, a private-label producer, alleging infringement of two patents. Are lawsuits of this kind a part of the process of oligopolistic rivalry and struggle?

10. Under which circumstances do firms find it profitable to increase the quality of their products? Do the benefits always exceed the costs? Why or why not?

11. The West Chester Corporation believes that the demand curve for its product is

$$P = 28 - 0.14Q$$

where P is price (in dollars) and Q is output (in thousands of units). The firm's board of directors, after a lengthy meeting, concludes that the firm should attempt, at least for a while, to increase its total revenue, even if this means lower profit.

a. Why might a firm adopt such a policy?
b. What price should the firm set if it wants to maximize its total revenue?
c. If the firm's marginal cost equals $14, does the firm produce a larger or smaller output than it would if it maximized profit? How much larger or smaller?

12. Steve Win has purchased land (an old landfill—from rags to riches) from the city of Atlantic City in the Marina section of the city. There are stories of a new casino building boom in Atlantic City (MGeeM is also talking about entering and Gump is opening his fourth casino). Some talk is circulating that Win will subdivide his new land purchase and perhaps three casinos will be built on the site.

   Suppose that Win subdivides his land into two parcels. He builds on one site and sells the other to another gambling entrepreneur. Win estimates that the demand for gambling in the Marina area of Atlantic City (*After* accounting for the presence of two existing casinos in the Marina and adjusting for the rest of the casinos in Atlantic City) to be

$$P = 750 - 5Q$$

where P is the price associated with gambling and Q is the quantity of gambling (think of P as the average amount that a typical patron will net the casino, an amount paid for the entertainment of gambling, and Q as the number of gamblers).

   Win, of course, does not sell the other parcel until his casino is built (or is significantly far along); thus, he has a first-mover advantage.

   Win's total cost (TC_W) of producing gambling is

$$TC_W = 20 + 40Q_W + 15.5Q_W^2$$

where Q_W is the number of gamblers in Win's casino and the total cost (TC_R) of producing gambling for Win's rival is

$$TC_R = 10 + 50Q_R + 20Q_R^2$$

where Q_R is the number of gamblers in the rival's casino and

$$Q_W + Q_R = Q$$

Would Atlantic City have done better to sell the land as two separate parcels rather than as a single parcel to Win (given that Win was going to subdivide, Win and his rival could not collude, and Win did not have the ability to produce as a monopolist)? You may assume that Win and his rival could have been Cournot duopolists. If Atlantic City could do better, show why and by how much? Carry all calculations to the thousandths decimal point.

Game Theory

Strategic Decisions and Game Theory

A goal of this book is to help managers make better decisions. Decisions can be classified as either nonstrategic or strategic. Nonstrategic ones do not involve others, so their actions need not be considered. For example, a shipping company can map the most efficient shipping route without considering what other shipping companies are doing. Strategic decisions are fundamentally different. They are characterized by interactive payoffs, hence require a different mindset. Interactive payoffs mean the outcome of your decision depends on both your actions and the actions of others. For example, your firm decides to enter a new market. If others follow you into the market, your payoff will be different than if they do not follow you. Or, you tell your current romantic interest how you enjoy his company. His response certainly affects your mental being.

So, when you ponder strategic decisions, you must explicitly consider what actions others will take. And, your optimal choice may change, depending on what you believe others will do. But that is not all. Complicating the situation is the thought that all others are sitting there thinking the same of you. And, this is just the first link of the expectation chain. Would you change a decision because you think others expect you to do something? Making a strategic

563

decision is like looking at oneself in a hall of mirrors, except in strategy, there are others with you.

A characteristic of strategic decisions is the direct result of interactive payoffs. This is the lack of an unconditional optimal strategy. There is no "best" strategy for all situations; optimality is always conditional. It is conditional on situational parameters, many of which are controlled by managers. So, although a strategic situation offers challenges to the decision-making skills of managers, it also offers opportunities. Managers might change the parameters to increase their payoffs. For example, changing a relationship to the long term from the short can alter the behavior of others (as we show later in this chapter).

In an effort to bring some order to the complexity of strategic decisions, mathematicians in the last century developed an organizing framework, now known as **game theory**. As we shall see, one hallmark of game theory is the capacity to help better understand any strategic decision. Through its use, you increase your ability to correctly anticipate the actions of others. This, in turn, makes you a better decision maker.

Like any long-standing theory, the theory of games furthers our understanding of a phenomenon on several levels. Gravity is a theory that most of us understand, although few can cite its mathematical formula. Game theory is similar, in that it can help us better understand strategic decisions, even if we cannot formally solve for the equilibrium (although we are better off if we can). Much of this greater clarity comes from the visual identification and organization of game parameters.

The mathematics of game theory also bring greater clarity to our understanding of strategic principles. Managers who follow these principles make better business decisions. The most important principle to remember is that "you control your strategic environment." Because of interactive payoffs, as you move, you can induce others to move. Like we said, optimality is conditional.

Finally, the theory offers decision rules for managers to follow. Many of the situations we discuss combine conflict with mutual dependence. Such situations are common in the business world—price wars, negotiations, intrafirm relations—and better managers understand the relevant considerations. A better grasp of game theoretical thinking improves these decision-making skills.

Strategy Basics

Before one plays a game, one needs to understand its rules. For example, take the game of poker. There are many ways to play poker, the rules determine the specific game being played. Game parameters, like how many cards will be dealt, what is the betting procedure, which hands are better than others, define the particular game being played. The same is true for any strategic situation, the rules (i.e., parameters) define the game being played. Hence, before one acts, one needs to assess and understand the rules, for strategically they define the situation.

All game theoretic models are defined by a common set of five parameters. Additional parameters may affect the strategically setting, and game theory usually recognizes these. The defining, and common, five factors are these:

1. *The players.* You cannot know who is playing without a scorecard. A *player* is defined as the entity making the decision. Entities can be either individuals or groups. The decisions of all players determine the outcome. These other entities are in the hall of mirrors with you, looking at the same situation as you, but from their viewpoints. Models describe both the identity of the players and their number, as changes in either can alter play. Identities are important because of the diversity of the universe. You need to know exactly who is in the hall of mirrors with you. For example, does your behavior change when you are with your parents rather than roommates? How about a total stranger? Most of us act differently as the individual (or group of individuals) with whom we interact changes. The model explicitly recognizes this, so it requires identification. Changes in the number of players can also alter strategies. Few of us act the same when alone with our current significant other as when we are part of a larger group.

2. *The feasible strategy set.* One cannot anticipate, much less assess, an action he or she believes is impossible. So, only actions given a nonzero probability of occurring are assessed within the model. These actions constitute the feasible strategy set. Think of it as the potential behavior of others. Behavior not in this set is outside the analytic limits of the particular game model.

3. *The outcomes or consequences.* Game models visually represent the intersection of the first two parameters as outcomes. Each player has a feasible strategy set (i.e., behavior) comprising individual potential strategies. Each strategy of a player intersects all combinations of the strategies of others to form the outcome matrix. A particular outcome is defined by the strategy choice of each player. Think of the matrix as a crystal ball that contains all possible future states. After all players have selected and played their strategy, we end up in one of these states. Like a fortune-teller, a goal of game theory is to predict which state will occur before it is actually realized.

4. *The payoffs.* The model assigns a payoff for each player onto all outcomes. So the payoff for an outcome is expressed as a vector of individual payoffs. And, each possible outcome has a corresponding payoff. A player's payoff is based on his or her preferences. An inherent assumption of game theory is that players are rational, in the sense they do not wish to harm themselves. Given the choice and all others things equal, they would prefer a higher payoff to a lower one. This is another reason why player identities are important. Preferences are subjective: A payoff not highly valued

by one player can be highly valued by others. So, like the real world, players may not have identical preferences.

5. *The order of play*. Timing is important in both love and war. The model specifies the order in which players reveal their chosen strategy. Models are **simultaneous** if all players reveal their strategy without knowing the strategy of others. Simultaneous play is not entirely time dependent. All players need not announce their decisions at precisely the same moment. It is more a matter of information. If all players commit to a strategy before learning the strategies of others, then the game is simultaneous. Nonsimultaneous games are, by definition, **sequential**. In any sequential game, the model specifies the order of play.

One way to measure the usefulness of a model is to examine how congruent it is with the real world. So, we summarize the framework represented by the mathematics, and you decide whether it captures the nature of strategic situations. Before making a strategic decision do you consider the following factors:

- How the outcome depends on your action and the actions of others.
- The identities of others involved in the decision.
- The order of play.
- How others will react to your decision.
- The goal to achieve outcomes favorable to your preferences.

If you answered these questions in the affirmative, then your framework is similar to that of game theory. Game theory takes what most intuitively consider when making decisions and analyzes it more formally. The building of a game model requires information we already know and think about. It asks for a finer partition of the information, a sharpening of our strategic focus. And, as we shall see, the theory's visual representations are tools to help us with that focus.

Visual Representation

Game models visualize interactive payoffs (i.e., outcomes) as the intersection of individual strategies across players. The visuals of these payoffs take one of two forms—matrix or extensive. The two represent the same information, although sequential games are more easily shown in the extensive form. The matrix form summarizes all possible outcomes; the extensive form provides a roadmap of player decisions.

Figure 14.1 represents a matrix form game of the following situation. Two firms, Allied and Barkley, discover they both are planning to launch a product development program for what will essentially be competing products. They can

FIGURE
14.1

A Two-Person Simultaneous Game

Barkley's strategy

		Spend at current level	Increase spending
Allied's strategy	Spend at current level	3, 4	2, 3
	Increase spending	4, 3	3, 2

choose to either keep spending at the currently planned level or increase it in hopes of speeding up product development and getting to market first. Expected profits are a function of the expected development costs and revenues.

Let us see how the matrix addresses the five common parameters:

1. *Players:* There are two players, Allied and Barkley.
2. *Order of play.* Simultaneous, each must reach a decision without knowing that of the other.
3. *Feasible strategy set:* Each player can choose to either maintain the current spending or increase it.
4. *Outcomes:* Because there are two players, and each has two strategic options, there are four possible outcomes.
5. *Payoffs:* The payoffs are listed for each player within every possible outcome. The convention in game theory is to list the row player's (Allied) payoff first in each cell and the column player's (Barkley) second. So, if Allied increases spending but Barkely does not, then Allied's expected profit is $4 million and Barkley's is $3 million.

Extensive form games are also called *game trees*. These are akin to the decision trees we visit in Chapter 15 and are figuratively the same. The fundamental difference between a game tree and a decision tree is one of strategy. A game tree is of a strategic nature, a decision tree is not. Decision trees have no interactive payoffs; payoffs are a function of the single individual and nature.

Think of any extensive form game as a decision road map. Just start at the beginning and you cannot get lost. The extensive form gives more details than the matrix form by explicitly stating the timing of choices among players. Extensive form games represent when players must reveal choices with **decision nodes**.

The node specifies who the player is and his or her feasible strategy set (i.e., behavior). The first node (decision) of the game is represented by an open square, all other nodes are shown by a solid square. Arrows from each node represent the elements of the feasible strategy set. If other players reveal strategies later in the game, then the arrows lead from one node to another, to show the order of play. If the player is the last to reveal his or her strategy, then the arrows lead from the node to a payoff schedule.

Figure 14.2 shows an extensive form game that represents the following situation. Managers at Allied and Barkley must now decide on a pricing policy for the new product. They know that the other will introduce a similar competing product. Because Barkley is expected to enter the market slightly sooner than Allied, Barkley announces its price first (note the clear square). Barkley can choose one of three prices: $1.00, $1.35, or $1.65. Allied will reveal its price later. Because it is second to market, its possible price points are $0.95, $1.30, and $1.55. Payoffs, which represent profits, are a function of costs and revenues.

FIGURE
14.2

Allied–Barkley Pricing—Sequential

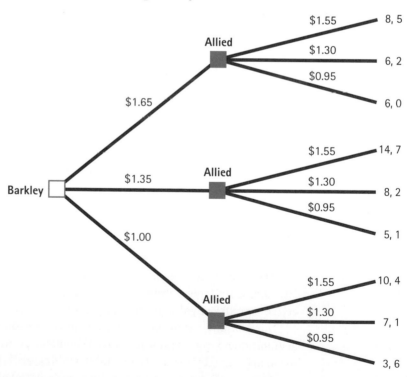

FIGURE

14.3

Allied–Barkley Pricing—Simultaneous

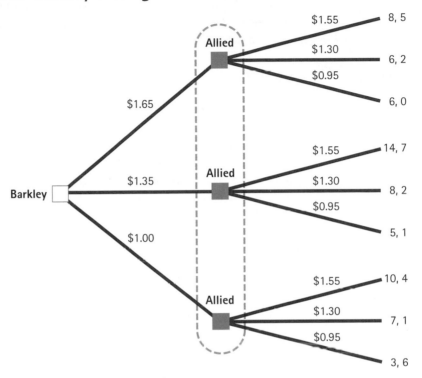

The extensive form can also show simultaneous games. It does this with so-called information sets. All simultaneous games are played with imperfect information. That is, when revealing his strategy, a player does not know the strategies of all others. That is the nature of simultaneous situations. Figure 14.3 shows the simultaneous version of the situation depicted in Figure 14.2. The only difference between the two figures is the dotted line drawn around the Allied decision nodes. It represents Allied's information set, or knowledge at the time it reveals its strategy. The dotted line signifies that Allied managers know they were at one of the three nodes, but not which one, because Barkley has not revealed its strategy.

These two types of game models show how the theory represents strategic situations. As you see, the information required is not voluminous. But, it does require some thought and reflection. The models provide a good organizing framework. They allow managers to communicate more clearly, providing a common language. The models are very good at examining "what-if" scenarios, a favorite (and helpful) pastime, of managers. If this is all they offer, we think the marginal benefits of learning them would far outweigh the marginal costs. But, the best is yet to come. These models allow you to see the future (i.e., anticipate). They do so by predicting the future actions of others (and yourself). It is important to understand their underlying strategic principles. This knowledge gives you greater insights into the behavior of others.

Solution Concepts

How does game theory let you see the future? It anticipates (correctly) the behavior of others. The knowledge of how to do so is part of ancient history. What the theory of games adds is a formalization of ideas and parameters. How do models anticipate behavior? Well, unlike crystal balls and tarot cards, the theory provides details of the underlying logic of its predictive power. We now examine that logic.

Much of the theory's predictive power comes from solution concepts. These concepts are basically rules of behavior. The theory anticipates behavior because it believes individuals act according to prescribed rules. The theory of gravity follows similar thinking; although humans are not planets, so our behavior may sometimes stray outside the rules. Before we examine some of these rules, we need to understand the concept of an equilibrium.

Equilibria

Equilibria predict behavior in the following way. In an equilibrium, no player has an incentive to unilaterally change his or her strategy. This rule of behavior says little about how individuals arrive at this point, but once there, none move unilaterally. So game models predict individual behavior for each player and identify the future (outcome). The concept of an equilibrium "holds" this behavior in place.

CONCEPTS IN CONTEXT

The Use of Game Theory in Business

The use of game theory in the corporate world continues to increase. One example of its use is illustrated by Freight Traders Ltd., a division of Mars, Inc. Mars, Inc., is a confectionery company that holds a worldwide market share of 7.2 percent, second only to the 7.3 percent market share of Nestlé. Freight Traders is an online service (www.freight-traders.com) that uses game theoretic concepts to help match shippers with carriers. The service is used by over 800 carriers and 150 manufacturers.

One game theoretic principle used by Freight Traders is incentive compatibility. To create more efficient markets, a market organizer (like Freight Traders) wants participants to truthfully reveal their reservation prices. Of course, many participants do not want to reveal this information, because they want to maximize their profits. So, how does one induce participants to tell the truth? Well, one way is to make it in their best interest to be truthful. Then, they will be truthful, because if they are not, they suffer the consequences. This is the idea underlying incentive compatible mechanisms. By using these mechanisms, you actually encourage truth-telling.

For example, Freight Traders conducts markets that use second-price auctions. This type of auction is incentive compatible in that it induces participants to truthfully reveal their reservation prices (we see why in Chapter 16). Carriers know they can bid their reservation price and still make a profit, while manufacturers know they are obtaining the best-possible price, given the current market conditions.

Managers at Freight Traders also use game theory to help clients decide the number of bidding rounds, reserve prices (minimum acceptable prices), and whether to allow negotiations between bidding rounds. Evidence of the benefits to clients are easy to find. Numico, a manufacturer of baby food and infant nutrition products, annually ships over 80,000 tons of goods. Using these game theory principles, managers at Freight Traders helped the firm achieve an estimated cost savings of 12 percent. And, the benefits did not end there. As John Coles, the operations director, put it: "People are immediately drawn to the financial savings, but for me, one of the biggest pluses of using Freight Traders was that it ensured a consistent approach across our company, whilst retaining our flexibility and control. When this is rewarded with a 12 percent reduction to our freight bill, it makes it even more worthwhile."

Game theory is also being used by insurers to estimate the risk of terrorism and the subsequent pricing of policies to cover these acts. Dr. Gordon Woo of Risk Management Solutions believes game theory can help insurers better recognize the potential targets of terrorists.

Woo argues that current models used by insurers to predict losses from natural causes are inadequate in assessing the risks of terrorist acts. Clearly, insurers act as if their current models are inadequate since most exclude terrorist acts from their commercial coverage. While some insurers offer coverage of terrorist acts, the premiums are so expensive that most businesses simply go without it.

One result of these initial game theoretic models showed that the probability of monetary losses at well-known landmark buildings (like the Empire State Building) is very similar to those of ordinary office buildings. While the landmark buildings are more likely to be attacked, they are also more likely to be better defended against attacks. This finding is counterintuitive to the industry's conventional wisdom, which dictates that landmark buildings pay higher premiums for coverage against terrorist acts.

Other game theory models appear to support this above finding. Game theorists have shown why it is rational for authorities to increase security at probable terrorist targets and, in turn, why rational terrorists will then target softer, less well-protected targets.

Sources: "Web-Based Freight Trading Tastes sweet," *Wall Street Journal*, November 29–December 1 2002, R2; www.freight-traders.com; "Can the Risk of Terrorism Be Calculated by Insurers? Game Theory Might Do It," *Wall Street Journal*, April 8, 2002, C1; "How to Bomb Friends and Alienate People," *Sydney Morning Herald* (online version) May 30, 2003.

Players do not change their behavior because they cannot increase their payoff. In an equilibrium, of all possible choices (i.e., the feasible strategy set), what we are presently doing rewards us with the highest payoff, given that no other player changes behavior. Basically, we are doing the best we can (remember, payoffs are interactive). So, implicitly, we assume behavior is directed by our preferences. We are rational in the sense that we do not want to hurt ourselves and accept a lower payoff. Hence, an equilibrium is rational, optimal, and stable. A player's behavior is directed by a preference function. Each player tries to obtain the highest payoff possible, given the actions of others. Once an equilibrium is reached, no player has an incentive to unilaterally change behavior.

Dominant Strategies

One way to tame the complexity of strategic thinking is to make it more nonstrategic in nature. That basically takes you out of the hall of mirrors and puts you in front of one mirror. Looking back at you is the only person responsible for payoffs in nonstrategy land, you. If you do not choose the optimal strategy, you only have yourself to blame. But, mathematicians do not ignore the interactive nature of the game, that would be like cheating on a math test. So they looked at life, and life suggests there are times when one possesses an option that is strategically strong relative to all others. From love, "Tis better to have loved and lost than never to have loved at all" to war, "Damn the torpedoes, full speed ahead," we all face situations where one strategy dominates our thoughts.

Mathematicians represent these as dominant strategies. A **dominant strategy** is one whose payoff in any outcome, relative to all other feasible strategies, is strictly higher.[1] So, if you are rational, you choose your dominant strategy. While the strategy choices of others still affect your payoff, you care less about them, because when you choose your dominant strategy you are doing the best you can. Thinking about others offers little strategic value, the marginal benefit is extremely low. Consider this, any time spent thinking about the strategies of others will not change your decision. You should always choose the dominant strategy.

It is easier to visually represent dominant strategies using the matrix form. Look at Figure 14.1 again. For Barkley, the dominant strategy is to maintain the current spending level (left column). If Allied also maintains current spending, then Barkley receives a payoff of $4 million; if Allied increases spending, the payoff is $3 million. The dominated strategy is increase spending (right

---

[1] A strategy is weakly dominant if it does at least as well as any other strategy for some outcomes (it is tied with another for the highest payoff) and better than any strategy for the remaining outcomes. Even if a strategy is only weakly dominant, the player would choose it.

column). Should Barkley choose this strategy and Allied maintain current spending, then Barkley would receive $3 million; if Allied increased spending, Barkley would receive $2 million. So whatever strategy Allied chooses, Barkley is better off to maintain current spending.

So, one rule of behavior on which game theory predicts is if you have a dominant strategy, you will choose it. Put another way, you never choose a dominated strategy. Why would you? No matter what others choose, you are always better off with the dominant one.

Barkley will maintain current spending. How about Allied? It turns out it also has a dominant strategy. Allied should increase spending. No matter what Barkley chooses, Allied is better off with increased spending.

We can now predict that Barkley will maintain current spending and Allied will increase it. We have a dominant strategy equilibrium. Why will this outcome prevail? Because each player has a dominant strategy and each is always better off playing it. Why won't they change their strategy? See the preceding: Any change in strategy leads to guaranteed lower payoffs. Domination is the minimum hurdle required of rationality. If you choose dominated strategies when you know dominant ones exist, then you are truly hurting yourself.

So, dominant strategies are a wonder of the strategic world. They ease the mental cost of decision making and simplify the analytic process. With them, you can ignore the actions of others. Given the hectic schedule of managers, they are a great time saver. For example, in Chapter 16 we discuss auctions. Auction parameters affect whether a dominant strategy exists for the particular auction. In those with no dominant strategy, you must consider the bids of others, in choosing your bid. In ones with a dominant strategy you need not. Good strategic managers understand the difference and do not waste time thinking about something irrelevant to the decision.

Not surprising, it is dominant to first look for dominant strategies in matrix games. Even if the game is not solvable through dominance, this process eliminates those outcomes mapped to dominated strategies. We essentially reduce the set of playable strategies. Recall that no player should ever play a dominated strategy, because he or she is always better off playing the dominant one. So we can eliminate dominated strategies from any future consideration. We never "reach" those outcomes, because the dominated strategy is not played. Visually, our outcome matrix is reduced by rows or columns. Mentally, the analysis is simplified, since we consider fewer outcomes.

More important strategically, when you eliminate a strategy, you reduce the set of possible outcomes. This, in turn, may change a formerly nondominated strategy into a dominated one. This iterative process may proceed until each player is left with only one playable strategy (i.e., dominance solvable).

Figure 14.4 is the matrix form of the game shown in Figure 14.2. All extensive form games can be shown in the matrix form and vice versa. Note that players, outcomes, and payoffs are identical across the two figures.

FIGURE
14.4

Matrix Form Representation of Figure 14.2

Allied's pricing strategies

		$0.95	$1.30	$1.55
Barkley's pricing strategies	**$1.00**	3, 6	7, 1	10, 4
	$1.35	5, 1	8, 2	14, 7
	$1.65	6, 0	6, 2	8, 5

We now look at the strategies for Allied and Barkley. Allied's strategies are nondominated, but Barkley has a dominated strategy—$1.35 dominates $1.00. Barkley will never choose $1.00, so we need not further consider its outcomes. Effectively, this reduces the figure's matrix to that shown in part A of Figure 14.5.

Since we could eliminate Barkley's $1.00 strategy as a playable strategy, Allied now has a dominated strategy, two in fact: $1.55 dominates both $0.95 and $1.30. Hence, the matrix is reduced to that shown in part B. Allied has only one playable strategy, to charge $1.55. Because of this, Barkley now has another dominated strategy. Since 14 is greater than 8, Barkley will charge $1.35. So this game has a dominant strategy equilibrium: Allied will price at $1.55 and Barkley will price at $1.35.

While both this game and the one represented in Figure 14.1 have dominant strategy equilibriums, they are solved using different degrees of rationality. Most view rationality as dichotomous: If you are not rational, you are irrational. But rationality has continuous measures. One such measure is the degree of rationality required to reach an equilibrium. Because of interactive payoffs, we have to worry not only about our own rationality but the rationality of others. So the degree of rationality measures the number of conjectures required to reach an equilibrium.

For example, in Figure 14.1 you can solve the game simply by knowing you are rational. If rational, choose your dominant strategy. No matter what others do, that is your best response. But, this single degree of rationality does not get

FIGURE
14.5

Iterative Dominance

A. Barkley's $1.00 strategy is eliminated.

Allied's pricing strategies

		$0.95	$1.30	$1.55
Barkley's pricing strategies	$1.35	5, 1	8, 2	14, 7
	$1.65	6, 0	6, 2	8, 5

B. Allied's $0.95 and $1.30 strategies are eliminated.

Allied's pricing strategies

		$1.55
Barkley's pricing strategies	$1.35	14, 7
	$1.65	8, 5

you to the game equilibrium in Figure 14.4. Because dominance is of the iterative variety, you need to consider the rationality of others.

Let us view the game from Barkley's viewpoint. Okay, I know I am rational. I see that $1.00 is dominated, so I will not play it. Hmm, how about Allied? Will it figure out that my $1.00 is dominated and I will not play it? If it does, then its $1.55 strategy is dominant.

In matrix form games, we measure the degree of rationality by the rounds of iterative dominance needed to reach the equilibrium. The game in Figure 14.4 requires three rounds. An individual may be rational for games with few degrees of rationality but not for those requiring many degrees.

So, solving games with domination principles is straightforward enough. Why use anything else? Unfortunately, life is not that simple. Too few games have a dominant strategy equilibrium. Interaction with others is more complex. How can we predict behavior in a game without dominant strategies?

Nash Equilibrium

That is the question John Nash asked himself in the early 1950s. His answer is our most widely used solution concept, the **Nash equilibrium**. Similar to dominance, Nash had to develop a concept that was rational, optimal, and stable. And, it had to go one step further than dominance, by predicting the future and anticipating the actions of others. Basically, Nash had to conceive the rule of behavior players would follow if they lacked a strategy that dominated all others. The intuition underlying Nash's idea is the following.

A player's objective remains the same whether he has one or more playable strategies, to maximize his payoff. If he must choose among two or more playable strategies, he selects the optimal one. And, since payoffs are interactive, he must choose conditional on what he thinks of others. So, what rule are the others following? If they are the same (i.e., rational), their goal is identical, to maximize payoffs relative to what others will choose. Hence, each will choose the strategy that maximizes his or her payoff, conditional on others doing the same. That is John Nash's prescribed behavior for players with more than one playable strategy.

Not surprising, Nash's concept is more transparent in its mathematical form. Let each of N players identify a strategy s_i^*, where $i = 1, 2, 3, \ldots N$. An outcome then represents an array of strategies $s^* = (s_1^*, s_2^*, s_3^*, \ldots, s_N^*)$. Let $B_i(s^*)$ be the payoff to player i when s^* is chosen, with i being any player, $i = 1, 2, 3, \ldots, N$. Then, a Nash equilibrium is an array a strategies such that

$$B_i (s_1^*, s_2^*, s_3^*, \ldots, s_N^*) \geq B_i (s_1^*, s_2^*, s_3^*, \ldots, s_N^*) \qquad \text{for all outcomes}$$

The left side states the existence of an outcome(s), defined by the array of player strategies, where all have a best response to the best responses of others. The right side states that, if any player unilaterally changes strategy, she realizes a lower payoff. That is, she chooses a dominated outcome. For a rather complex and messy process, the Nash is an elegant solution. It treats all with equal rationality and so limits behavior. Dominance is still present, although now conditional. The solution exists for all games with a finite number of players and outcomes.

Dominance is unconditional in dominance-solvable games. One need not speculate on the behavior of others, because it makes no difference. But, anything less than unconditional requires anticipation. And, because payoffs are interactive, this anticipation requires a common vision with others. So the Nash prescribes a behavioral rule. Maximize your payoff, conditional on all others doing the same. A Nash solution is dominant, conditional on this rule being followed.

Recall that an equilibrium needs to be rational, optimal, and stable. Nash's solution is rational in the sense that all players follow the prescribed behavior. It is optimal in that all try to maximize their payoffs. And, it is stable because no player can unilaterally change strategy and realize a higher payoff.

Figure 14.6 illustrates the following. The numbers represent profits (in millions of dollars). Recall that Barkley entered the market first, followed by Allied. Both firms must now introduce new products. Each can choose one of several, but because of financial constraints, only one can be supported. Managers at both firms understand this. Their choice to introduce a product is conditional on how they think the other will behave. Nash says, we all behave identically, we maximize payoffs conditional on others doing the same. We will change behavior to obtain a higher payoff but not a lower one.

Look at Figure 14.6. Remember our decision rule: Look for dominated strategies. This is quickly done. Confirm that neither firm has a dominated strategy. Now, use the following algorithm. For each strategy, indicate the behavior of the other. For example, if Barkley managers knew (with certainty) that Allied will introduce alpha, what will they do? Well, Barkley receives 4 if it introduces lambda, 6 if pi, and 9 if sigma (the first numbers in each cell of the product alpha column). Since 9 is the highest of the three payoffs, Barkley managers will introduce pi, if they know Allied will introduce alpha. Mark a B in the alpha-pi outcome. Do the same for strategies beta and zeta. Now, follow the same procedure for Allied (the sequence of players makes no difference). For example, if Barkley introduces sigma, what should Allied managers choose? If Allied produces alpha it receives 8, if beta 7, and if zeta 5. So Allied managers will introduce alpha, if they know Barkley will introduce sigma. Mark an A in this outcome. Do the same for strategies lambda and pi. The resulting matrix is illustrated in Figure 14.7.

Any cell with an A and B is a Nash equilibrium. In this game, the Nash is for Barkley to introduce sigma (and receive 9) and Allied to introduce alpha (and receive 8). Let us understand why this outcome is predicted by Nash. An

New Product Introduction

		Allied		
		Product alpha	Product beta	Product zeta
Barkley	Product lamda	4, 6	9, 8	6, 10
	Product pi	6, 8	8, 9	7, 8
	Product sigma	9, 8	7, 7	5, 5

FIGURE
14.7

New Product Introduction with Other's Behavior

		Allied		
		Product alpha	Product beta	Product zeta
Barkley	Product lamda	4, 6	(B) 9, 8	6, 10 (A)
	Product pi	6, 8	8, 9 (A)	(B) 7, 8
	Product sigma	(B) 9, 8 (A)	7, 7	5, 5

A or B represents a conditional dominant strategy. A best response to a specific strategy of others. A Nash equilibrium is a meeting of the best responses—an outcome where all play conditionally dominant strategies. Beyond the reach of an individual, it is attained by the group.

Each player acts in his or her own best interest and maximizes payoffs. A player not choosing the Nash strategy is playing a dominated one (assuming others play their Nash strategies). Hence, no player has the incentive to unilaterally change behavior. For example, as long as Allied produces alpha, Barkley managers want to produce sigma and receive $9 million. If they produce pi they receive only $6 million and if lambda only $4 million. Allied managers face the same scenario, lower payoffs for any change in behavior. Interactive payoffs make the two hostage to each other.

Strategic Foresight: The Use of Backward Induction

Good managers use strategic foresight in making decisions. We define *strategic foresight* as the ability to make decisions today that are rational given what is anticipated will happen in the future. For example, a manager builds extra capacity today because she believes (correctly) that the demand will increase in the near future. Strategic foresight is a principle that should always be used. Remember, the decisions of today can never affect your past, only your future. In decision making you always want to have a forward-looking outlook. Using strategic foresight also helps managers understand that decisions have both short- and long-term consequences.

Game theory formally models strategic foresight through what is called **backward induction**. In game theory, we use backward induction to solve games by looking to the future, determining what strategy players will choose (anticipation), then choosing an action that is rational, based on these beliefs. Backward induction is most easily seen in extensive-form games, because of their ability to map out the choices of players.

Figure 14.8 shows a game in extensive form. Recall from Figure 14.7 that Barkley has chosen to introduce sigma, and Allied has chosen to introduce alpha. They must now decide whether to expand their product lines. Either firm has the choice to expand or not. Since Barkley is the market leader, assume it will reach its decision first. After seeing the decision of Barkley, Allied managers then decide whether or not to expand. Payoffs for the four possible outcomes are given in Figure 14.8.

Let us see how a manager with strategic foresight can use backward induction to solve this game. The decision node farthest left represents the decision of Barkley's managers to expand or not. If they decide to expand, then Allied's managers are faced with the situation represented by Allied's botom decision node. If Barkley does not expand, Allied faces the situation represented by the top decision node. Barkley managers use strategic foresight. They want to make a decision today that maximizes their payoff, given their vision of the future.

FIGURE 14.8

Allied–Barkley Expansion Decision

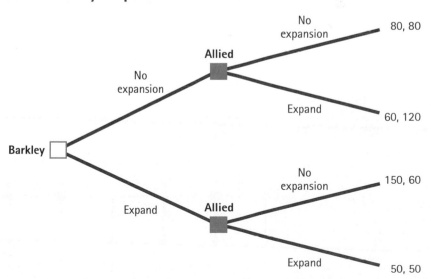

Barkley managers realize if they expand, Allied will receive a payoff of $50 million if it expands, and $60 million if it does not.

Hence, Barkley managers anticipate that, if they expand, then Allied will not. What if Barkley decides not to expand? Allied receives a payoff of $120 million for line expansion and $80 million if it does not expand. Hence, Barkley managers anticipate Allied will expand if they choose not to. So, if they expand, they anticipate a payoff of $150 million (since Allied will not expand). If Barkley does not expand, its managers should anticipate a payoff of $60 million (since Allied will expand). Since $150 million is greater than $60 million, the managers at Barkley know to expand their product line.

To use backward induction one must come back from the future. We anticipate the future actions of others, then choose actions that are rational, conditioned on our expected behavior of others.

Backward Induction and the Centipede Game

The usefulness of backward induction in strategic thinking is clearly shown in a simple game known as the *centipede game*. Many studies have used the game to study whether subjects use and understand backward induction thinking. The game is shown in Figure 14.9.

Two players (*A* and *B*) participate in this sequential game. Player *A* moves first and can either choose down (*D*) or right (*R*). If Player *A* chooses *D*, the game is over and both players receive a payoff of $1. If Player *A* chooses *R*, then Player *B* faces a similar choice. She can choose *d* or *r*. If Player *B* chooses *d*, the game is over; *A* receives a payoff of $0 and *B* receives a payoff of $3. If Player B chooses *r*, the game continues and Player *A* chooses either *D* or *R* again. The game continues until one player chooses down or Player *B* is asked to choose for a third time. At this point, if Player *B* chooses *d*, *A* receives $3 and *B* receives $6. If Player *B* chooses *r* at this point, both players receive $5. Look at Figure 14.9 and assume you are Player *A*. What strategy would you choose?

FIGURE

14.9

The Centipede Game

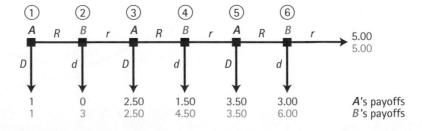

						A's payoffs
1	0	2.50	1.50	3.50	3.00	A's payoffs
1	3	2.50	4.50	3.50	6.00	B's payoffs

We solve the game using backward induction. The game is actually a series of six decisions. Player *A* chooses at stages 1, 3, and 5; and Player *B* chooses at stages 2, 4, and 6. We need to go to the end of the game and work from the future. Look at stage 6: Player B can choose down and receive $6 or choose right and receive $5. Since $6 is greater than $5, we anticipate Player B will choose down. Move forward to stage 5, for we know now the future. Player A faces the following. If *A* chooses right, he knows (anticipates correctly) *B* will choose down giving *A* a $3 payoff. Or, *A* can choose down and receive a payoff of $3.50. Since $3.50 is greater than $3, *A* will choose down at stage 5. What should Player B choose at stage 4 knowing this? *B* can choose down and receive a payoff of $4.50 or choose right and receive a payoff of $3.50 (since we know *A* will choose down at stage 5). Since $4.50 is greater than $3.50, Player *B* will choose down at stage 4. We move backward in the future to stage 3. Player *A* can choose down and receive a payoff of $2.50 or choose right and receive a payoff of $1.50 (since we anticipate *B* chooses down at stage 4). Since $2.50 is greater than $1.50, Player *A* will choose down at stage 3. We are now only one step beyond, at stage 2. Player *B* can choose down and receive a payoff of $3 or choose right and receive a payoff of $2.50 (since Player *A* will choose down at stage 3). So, Player B will choose down at stage 2. Finally, we find ourselves in the present, this is decision time. At Stage 1, Player *A* can choose down and receive $1 or choose right and receive $0 (since *B* will choose down at stage 2). Player *A* will choose down at stage 1. This is the only rational choice, given our view of the future. Player *A* will choose down at stage 1 and both players will realize a payoff of $1. What the ancients called foresight, game theorists model as backward induction.

Now comes the real question. How do subjects behave in playing the game? Initially, relatively few subjects appear to use foresight (or they have a distorted view of the future). Subjects appear to focus on the growing size of the payoffs and try to move down this path. At some late stage, either they choose down or the person they are playing with chooses it. The next time they play, most subjects tend to choose down at an earlier stage (especially those whose partners chose down in the earlier game). By the third or fourth time of play, most *A* players are resigned to the fact they should choose down at stage 1. They do so hesitantly, because they still see the path of greater payoffs. But, they also know the future. Experience has shown the wisdom of backward induction.

The Credibility of Commitments

Backward induction has many uses. One is to test the credibility of commitments. From threats to promises, epithet slinging to love's rhapsody, we want to know, Should we believe others? When faced with these situations, always check credibility first. That is a dominant strategy. Only consider credible commitments. A commitment is credible if the costs of falsely sending one are greater than the associated benefits. A company that proclaims its product is best is not credible. There is little cost to it and high associated benefits. The company can make that claim credible by offering a product warranty. A warranty increases the commitment cost (if it is falsely sent). Robin and Styne succinctly defined credibility when they wrote, "A kiss on the hand may be quite continental, but diamonds are a girl's best friend."

Consider the following. Recall that Barkley has expanded its product line but Allied has not. Allied's managers decide to counter Barkley's product line extension by dropping the price of their product. However, they are concerned that, if they drop their prices, then Barkley will follow with a price cut of its own. In fact, Barkley's managers told a common supplier of both firms that if Allied drops its price, they will drop theirs. What should Allied do?

Allied's managers first must consider whether the threat by Barkley to drop prices is credible. They can do so by looking at Figure 14.10 and solving the game using backward induction. Barkley can either keep prices high or drop prices. Allied has the same two strategies available to it. What happens if Allied drops prices? Then Barkley can either keep prices high and earn $30 million or also drop its price and earn $20 million. Since $30 million is greater than $20 million, Barkley should keep its price high if Allied drops its prices. What if Allied maintains its prices? Then Barkley could keep its price high and earn $50 million or drop prices and earn $70 million. Hence, Barkley will drop its price

FIGURE

14.10

Does Barkley Have a Credible Threat?

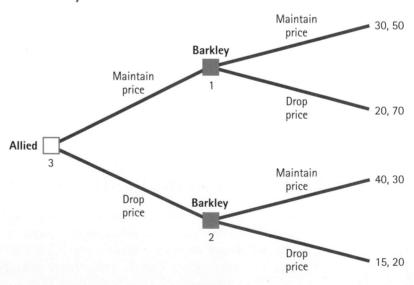

if Allied keeps its prices high. Given that Allied can anticipate these actions from Barkley, what should Allied do? It should drop its prices. Clearly, Barkley will not drop its prices. In fact, it is a dominant strategy for Barkley to maintain high prices. The threat by Barkley to lower prices is not credible, so it should be ignored. If forced to carry out the threat, Barkley managers will refuse. To do so would cost them $10 million in lost profits.

The equilibrium just described is a **subgame perfect equilibrium**. A subgame is defined as being a segment of a larger game. The subgames are marked in Figure 14.10. As you can see, within the overall game, the three constitute three separate subgames. In repeated games, all subgame perfect equilibria are also Nash equilibria, although not all Nash equilibria are subgame perfect. Those Nash equilibria based on noncredible threats are not subgame perfect. Formally, we define a subgame perfect equilibrium as a strategy profile s^* in the overall game (Δ) such that for any history h, the profile $s^*|_h$ is a Nash equilibrium for the subgame $\Delta(h)$. Intuitively, this says the equilibrium for any subgame is rational, conditional on equilibrium play in the future. For example, in the centipede game, the strategy profile of A choosing D (down) at stage 1 is rational, conditional on what we know will happen in future subgames. So, that is a subgame perfect equilibrium.

Repeated Games

The business world is characterized by repeated interactions. In many markets, firms compete against each other for decades. Within firms, managers interact with each other over long periods of time. Managers need to understand how the prospect of a future together can change player actions. Again, we turn to backward induction to help us understand the implications of repeated play.

We illustrate the strategic effect of repeated play using a stylized example from a class of games known as **prisoner's dilemmas**. Suppose Allied and Barkley produce an identical product. They also have similar cost structures. Both must decide whether to price the product at a high price or a low price. This situation is shown in Figure 14.11.

The Nash equilibrium of this game is for both firms to sell their products at a low price (and earn $3 million). Although both realize they are better off if each maintains a high price, they are afraid that the other firm will then drop its price and steal the market. Hence, both firms price low. If Allied and Barkley are going to compete in only one market for a single instance, then we expect both of them to keep prices low. After all, that is the rational choice. But, what if they are rivals for a long period of time? Instead of playing this pricing game once, they play it multiple times. Should we still expect both firms to price low, for each can see it is forfeiting $2 million per period, simply because neither can trust the other to maintain the high price. As Emerson commented, "Distrust is expensive."

FIGURE
14.11

Pricing as a Prisoner's Dilemma

		Allied's pricing strategies	
		Price high	Price low
Barkley's pricing strategies	Price high	5, 5	1, 20
	Price low	20, 1	3, 3

Strategically, the key difference between one-shot games and those that are repeated is the presence of a future. A future introduces behavior not possible in a one-shot world. Trust, reputation, promises, threats, and reciprocity need a future to exist. A future also means that payoffs are no longer relegated to the short term, for we now face longer-term implications. A betrayal of trust may lead to gains in the present, but these may be outweighed by future losses.

Models of repeated games reflect and account for this wider range of feasible behavior. They use the idea of a future to construct norms that let players reach mutually beneficial outcomes. For example, in the preceding situation, these norms help maintain an equilibrium where both firms price high. The risk of one firm undercutting the other is mitigated through the threat of future punishment. Of course, these threats must be credible. Let us see how these models work.

The first distinction these models make is whether or not the time horizon is finite. Cooperative behavior is easier to maintain in an infinite horizon game because the future always looms. In finite horizon games, the future grows smaller as we approach the last period. So, consider an infinite horizon in the game shown in Figure 14.11. If Allied and Barkley cooperate and price high, each receives a payoff of 5 per period. One can defect, price low, and earn 20 for a single period. The other will then price low and each will receive 3 for the rest of the game. So the incremental earnings of 15 (20 − 5) is lost within 8 periods ((5 − 3) × 8). In fact, in an infinite horizon game, no single period non-cooperative payoff will be larger than the sum of cooperative future payoffs.

The long shadow of a future in an infinite horizon game causes the well-known result called the *folk theorem*. This theorem basically states that any type of behavior can be supported by an equilibrium (as long as the discount rate is sufficiently close to 1). The support for a wide range of behaviors is because the future always matters in these games; hence, credible threats and promises can alter the current behavior of players. Of course, this makes it much harder to accurately predict behavior in games with infinite horizons.

Finite horizon games are fundamentally different, because as the game progresses, the future necessarily grows shorter. Because behavior in these games is predicated on the use of credible signals of future behavior, their power diminishes as the future grows shorter. And, in the last period, signals hold no power since there is no future (the last period of a repeated game is akin to a one-shot one). Hence, the Nash equilibrium is identical to that of a one-shot game. In the pricing game, this means that both firms price low. Without the restraint of credible signals and a future, one should expect others to act opportunistically. This is why the beginnings of romances are so blissful and the breakups so painful.

But, wait, if we know both firms will price low in the last period, how should this affect their actions in the prior-to-last period? Let us again use backward induction. Is there any strategy either firm can follow to change the outcome of the last period, to price low? No, regardless of the strategies played, both firms will price low. Their strategic fate is sealed. If this is true, the rational strategy is to price low in this period, too. And, just as we saw in the centipede game, similar reasoning extends forward to the first period. So, the equilibrium in a repeated version of the game is identical to that of a one-shot game. Both firms should price low.

That does not seem to make too much sense. What about the looming future and the use of credible commitments? Shouldn't that change behavior? Game theorists had similar thoughts, so they developed the theory to account for these factors. This was a more difficult task relative to the infinite horizon game because they had to account for the final period.

One insight recognized by game theorists is not everyone is opportunistic. Some like Mother Teresa do exist. So, what would happen if nonopportunistic individuals were in the population and you do not know (with certainty) whether you are playing with one? How would that change predicted behavior?

Incomplete Information Games

This question established a branch of game theory called **incomplete information games** (IIG). These games loosen the restrictive assumption that all players have the same information. The introduction of incomplete information makes it possible to derive cooperation (price high in Figure 14.11) as an equilibrium behavior. Now, when we backwardly induct, pricing low is not necessarily the predicted strategy in the last period. Nonopportunistic players may still price high in the last period because they obtain satisfaction from cooperating. They do not care that there is no future, they just want to cooperate.

Instead of pricing low from the initial period, players may want to "experiment" in early periods and price high, to determine whether they are playing with a nonopportunistic type.

One possible strategy players may use to experiment is commonly referred to as *tit for tat*. Players using tit for tat cooperate in the first period. In all succeeding periods, they mimic the preceding period's strategy of the other player. For example, assume Barkley is using a tit-for-tat strategy. In period 1, Barkley prices high. In period 2, Barkley mimics Allied's period 1 strategy. In period 3, Barkley mimics Allied's period 2 strategy. This means that Barkley begins the game by pricing high. Barkley continues to price high as long as Allied prices high. If Allied prices low, then Barkley prices low in the following period and continues to price low until Allied prices high again. Using this strategy, Barkley determines whether Allied is opportunistic, and if Allied is opportunistic, it suffers only one period of low payoffs.

FIGURE
14.12

Tough or Soft Barkley Managers

A. Barkley managers are tough.

		Allied's strategies	
		Enter the market	Do not enter the market
Barkley's strategies	Fight (price low)	6, 2	8, 3
	No fight (price high)	5, 4	2, 3

B. Barkley managers are soft.

		Allied's strategies	
		Enter the market	Do not enter the market
Barkley's strategies	Fight (price low)	2, 2	3, 3
	No fight (price high)	8, 4	4, 3

In IIG models, players possess asymmetric information. For example, Barkley may know more about its cost function than Allied. IIG models summarize this asymmetric information in the form of player "types." A type consists of player characteristics that are unknown to others. In business, types may consist of competitive attributes, like cost functions. In personal relationships, they may consist of personality traits, like the trustworthiness of a significant other.

Specific types are represented by different payoff (preference) functions. So, a low-cost type has a different payoff function relative to a high-cost type. A simple IIG model is shown in Figure 14.12. Allied needs to decide whether it should enter a product market where Barkley is an incumbent. Allied managers are uncertain of the reaction of Barkley managers if Allied decides to enter the market. If Barkley managers are "tough," then Allied expects them to lower price and defend their market. If Barkley managers are "soft," then Allied expects them to keep their prices high, allow Allied to enter the market, and share it with them.

When Barkley managers are actually tough (part A), the Nash equilibrium is for Allied not to enter the market and for Barkley to price low. Of course, Barkley will not have to price low because Allied will never enter the market. When Barkley managers are actually soft (part B), the Nash equilibrium is for Allied to enter the market and for Barkley to price high (allowing entry). Note that the payoffs for Allied are identical across parts A and B. The incomplete information is about Barkley, not Allied. Only the payoffs of Barkley change.

So, if Allied managers know the true type of Barkley managers, their decision is easy. If Barkley managers are soft, they enter the market; if Barkley managers are tough, they stay out of the market. The problem is that they do not know the true type of Barkley managers. And, knowing this, Barkley managers can take action to influence their beliefs.

Reputation Building

The presence of a future and incomplete information are the necessary ingredients for building reputations. In their presence, a reputation is a rent-generating asset. In the example here, if Barkley managers convince Allied managers they are tough in the early periods of the repeated game, then Allied will stay out of the market in the later stages.

In game theory, a reputation is simply the history of past behavior. Intuitively, reputation-building models parallel the human thought process. When we are unsure about the traits of others, we look to past behavior for clues. We use this information to form probabilistic beliefs regarding the traits of others. "I think I can trust him, but I wouldn't bet my life on it." In effect, we use a reputation model to infer future actions from past behavior. For example, assume a friend asks you to lend her $100. If you have previously loaned money to the friend, you will recall whether the friend paid you back. You are more likely to lend money to a friend who repaid a previous debt. Why? Well, since the friend paid back the earlier debt, you place a higher probability he or she will pay back this new debt. If the previous debt was not repaid, you are less likely to lend that person money again.

So, in situations with futures and incomplete information, your reputation is an intangible asset that earns future rents. In all such situations, you must consider how the current situation affects the future. Reneging on a debt has immediate payoffs (the debtor gains the amount you lent) and long-term consequences (you are less likely to loan money in the future). While these reputation models are too complex to explain here, the underlying idea is simple. In games with a future, players must consider both the present and the future. The payoff you receive today has two components, the immediate gain and its effect on the future.

For example, suppose Barkley's managers are actually soft. They still have an incentive to act tough in early periods. Of course, this will give them a lower payoff in these early periods than playing their true type, soft (price high, weakly dominates). But if they act tough early, then Allied might not enter later because it is convinced (at least enough) that Barkley is truly tough. Note though, as the future gets shorter (as it necessarily does in finite horizon games), the value of maintaining a false reputation gets smaller and smaller. So, in these later periods, there is an increasing probability that Barkley will reveal its true type to be soft. And, in the final period, Barkley managers will reveal they are truly soft with a probability of 1. Remember the pattern of romances and breakups.

Examples of reputation building in business are easily found. From product quality to entry deterrence, corporate culture to honest auditors, these models help explain behavior. For example, long before the recent corporate fraud scandals, game theorists modeled auditing firms as renting their reputation for being honest. The models predicted that those accounting firms involved in fraudulent activities would lose their "high-quality" reputation and the value of their name would decrease toward zero. This is exactly what we saw with the implosion of Arthur Anderson and Co. after the recent accounting scandals.

Coordination Games

Coordination games contain more than one Nash equilibrium. Recognizing the Nash equilibria (i.e., outcomes on which we want to coordinate) is generally not an issue but choosing which one to select is. After all, I want to be where the other is, and she with me, so my thoughts are on her thoughts as her thoughts are on mine. The question is more where will she be than where I want to be. As we shall see, as game parameters change, the impediments to coordination shift slightly. Game theory visualizes these shifts with changes in the payoff structure. As managers you will face many coordination games. It is essential to understand how payoffs affect behavior if one is to promote coordination.

Matching Games

In matching games, players generally have the same preferences (in terms of the outcome they prefer). However, there may be impediments to them reaching this outcome. Impediments may include the inability to communicate, different ideas on how to reach an objective, or asymmetric information. The game we show in Figure 14.13 concerns coordination in product attributes.

This game has two Nash equilibria. We expect one firm to produce for the consumer market and one for the industry. Though 7, 7 is clearly inferior to 12, 12, it is not ruled out as a Nash equilibrium. However, note that both Allied and Barkley prefer a payoff of 12 to that of 7.

Battle of the Sexes

In this coordination game, players still want to coordinate but on different outcomes. Because of different preferences, each prefers a payoff not favored by the other. If this game is repeated, players often switch between equilibria so both gain. However, in one-shot games like Figure 14.14, it is more difficult to predict the outcome.

Similar to the matching game, each wants to enter the submarket not entered by the other, but now the payoffs are not equal. Both Allied and Barkley are better off if they produce a high-end product, so it is not clear on which outcome they will coordinate.

FIGURE
14.13

Product Coordination Game

		Allied's strategies	
		Produce for consumer market	Produce for industrial market
Barkley's strategies	Produce for consumer market	0, 0	7, 7
	Produce for industrial market	12, 12	0, 0

FIGURE
14.14

Battle of the Sexes

		Allied's strategies	
		High-end product	Low-end product
Barkley's strategies	High-end product	0, 0	11, 6
	Low-end product	6, 11	0, 0

Assurance Games

Coordination games like that in Figure 14.15 are also known as *stag hunt games*. The French philosopher Rosseau tells the story of two hunters (actually poachers) who could coordinate efforts and catch a stag or renege on the agreement and each catch rabbits for himself. While each prefers to catch the stag, that strategy has the risk that the other reneges and the first hunter will catch nothing. So, players have similar preferences over outcomes but with an associated risk.

Here, we model a decision whether to shift to new standards. While both firms prefer to shift, there is a risk if one shifts and the other does not. We say

FIGURE
14.15

Stag Hunt or Assurance Game

		Allied's strategies	
		Stay with old standard	Shift to new standard
Barkley's strategies	Stay with old standard	6, 6	6, 0
	Shift to new standard	0, 6	12, 12

the outcome 12, 12 is *pareto dominate* (both players are better off) though risk dominated (if one chooses to shift and the other does not, the firm shifting receives 0).

First-Mover Games

We can also use coordination games to show the benefits of moving first. Figure 14.16 shows a sequential game where both firms want to coordinate but each has an incentive to produce a superior product (similar to the battle of the sexes). However, in this game, it is possible to move first by speeding up the product development process. The game shows which firm will move first and how much the firm is willing to pay to speed up the process.

In this game, both firms want to introduce the superior product first. There are two Nash equilibria. Allied produces a superior product, and Barkley produces an inferior one or vice versa. Once one has produced a superior product, then the other is resigned to producing an inferior product. The question is who is willing to pay a higher price to produce the superior product? We can answer this question by looking at the incremental benefits of moving first. The incremental benefit to Allied of producing the superior product is the difference in payoff between producing the superior product ($140) and the inferior product ($70). This is a difference of $70. The incremental benefit to Barkley of moving first is $110 − 30 or $80. We would predict that Barkley will move first since it is willing to spend up to $80 to move first, while Allied will spend only up to $70.

Hawks and Doves

This interesting coordination game has been applied to behavior in both the human and animal world. Assume two players are locked in a conflict. If both players

---

FIGURE 14.16

First-Mover Advantage

		Allied's strategies	
		Produce superior product	Produce inferior product
Barkley's strategies	Produce superior product	25, 50	110, 70
	Produce inferior product	30, 140	20, 30

FIGURE
14.17
Hawks and Doves

		Country 1 strategy	
		Act like a hawk	Act like a dove
Country 2 strategy	Act like a hawk	−1, −1	10, 0
	Act like a dove	0, 10	5, 5

act like hawks, conflict is inevitable. However, if one acts like a hawk and the other backs down (acting like a dove) then conflict is avoided. If both are doves, then conflict is not even threatened. The game is shown in Figure 14.17.

There are two Nash equilibria, they require one country to act like a hawk and the other to act like a dove. The issue is which country will back down and act like a dove, since this country will suffer a lower payoff.

John Maynard Smith applied similar models to the animal kingdom to model when animals fight among themselves. One interesting example of his concerns the behavior of spiders in New Mexico. Webs are a scarce commodity within the spider community because they are difficult to build in the desert. However, a female spider needs a web to lay her eggs. Therefore, female spiders fight (or threaten to fight) over existing webs. They do so by approaching the web and violently shaking it. After each has this show of force, one spider (the dove) generally leaves the web to the other spider. Rarely do the spiders actually engage in a physical fight. Smith and other biologists noted that certain physical traits account for which spider is the hawk and which is the dove. In the case of the spiders, the two most important traits appear to be incumbency and weight. The heavier spider usually claims the web, while the lighter spider backs down. Smith believes that the violent shaking of the web is actually a signal (credible) of which spider is the heaviest.

Strictly Competitive Games

The games we looked at have mixed motives in the sense that conflict interfaces with mutual dependence. However, some games are strictly competitive,

FIGURE
14.18 **Advertising Campaigns**

any gain by a player means a loss by another player. The net gain is always zero. What one gains, the other loses. These games are also known as *zero-sum games*. For example, slow growth (mature) markets can be characterized as zero sum. Since the market size remains fairly constant, any increase in the share of one firm means an identical decrease in the share of another firm. Figure 14.18 shows one such example.

Zero-sum games are still solvable using the Nash equilibrium. In Figure 14.18, the Nash equilibrium is for Allied to use campaign *A* and Barkley to use campaign 2.

Summary

1. Strategic decisions involve interactive payoffs. Since a player's payoff depends on his or her decision and the decisions of others, that player must anticipate the actions of others in formulating an optimal strategy.
2. Game theory is a mathematical framework that can help managers anticipate the actions of others. The theory helps managers represent the strategic issues by focusing on the players involved, their feasible set of strategies, the possible outcomes, and the payoffs associated with those outcomes.
3. In solving games, managers first need to look for dominant strategies. If they exist, one need not consider the actions of others. Rational players always play their dominant strategy.

4. If dominant strategies do not exist, one wants to predict the behavior of others using the solution concept of the Nash equilibrium. This concept assumes that all players do the best they can, conditional on all others doing the best they can. It is the most widely used solution concept in game theory.

5. Managers want to use strategic foresight; this is the ability to make decisions today that are rational, conditional on the anticipated future behavior of others. Game theory models this foresight through backward induction. In using backward induction, one goes to the end of the game to determine what strategies players will use, then chooses an action for the current period that is rational given these future beliefs.

6. You want to pay attention only to signals that are credible. One can use game models to determine the credibility of threats, promises, commitments, and the like.

7. Games with a future are called *repeated games*. When a future exists, players may change the strategy they select. Generally speaking, gaining cooperation from others is much easier in a repeated game.

8. Game theorists developed incomplete information models to look at situations where there is a future and some uncertainty exists regarding the traits of others. Under these conditions, building a reputation is important, because reputations can generate future rents.

9. The ability to coordinate is an important managerial trait. Coordination models help managers better understand the impediments to coordination and the action necessary to decrease the coordination costs.

Problems

1. Two soap producers, the Fortnum Company and the Maison Company, can stress either newspapers or magazines in their forthcoming advertising campaigns. The payoff matrix is as follows:

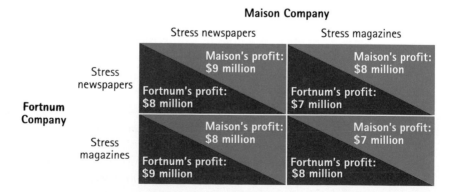

    a. Is there a dominant strategy for each firm? If so, what is it?

    b. What will be the profit of each firm?

    c. Is this game an example of the prisoner's dilemma?

2. The Ulysses Corporation and the Xenophon Company are the only producers of a very sophisticated type of camera. They each can engage in either a high or a low level of advertising in trade journals. The payoff matrix is as follows:

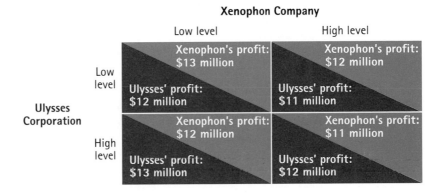

    a. Will Ulysses engage in a high or a low level of advertising in trade journals?

    b. Will Xenophon engage in a high or a low level of advertising in trade journals?

    c. Is there a dominant strategy for each firm?

3. The New York Times reports that Wal-Mart has decided to challenge Netflix and enter the online DVD by mail market. Because of economies of scale, Wal-Mart has a slight cost advantage relative to Netflix. Wal-Mart is considering the use of a limit pricing strategy. They can enter the market by matching Netflix on price. If they do, and Netflix maintains it price, then both firms would earn $5 million. But, if Netflix drops its price in response, then WM would have to follow and WM would earn $2 million and Netflix $3 million. Or, WM could enter the market with a price that is below Netflix's current price, but above WM's marginal cost. If it does, WM will earn profits of $0 and Netflix will earn profits of $2 million. Or it could keep its present price. If Netflix keeps its present price, then WM will either keep its present price and earn $6 million (while Netflix earns $4 million). Or, WM will increase its price and earn $2 million, while Netflix would earn $6 million.

    a. draw the extensive form of this game and solve it.

    b. Draw the game's matrix form and identify any Nash equilibrium(s).

4. Two rival bookstores are trying to locate in one of two locations. The locations are near to each other. Each would like to avoid a bidding war against one another since that will drive up each of their rents. Payoffs are given in the following table:

		Borders	
		Location 1	Location 2
Barnes and Nobles	location 1	10, 10	60, 40
	Location 2	25, 55	20, 20

Does either player have an incentive to bid higher for a location, and if so, by how much?

5. Two soft drink producers, York Cola and Reno Cola, secretly collude to fix prices. Each firm must decide whether to abide by the agreement or to cheat on it. The payoff matrix is as follows:

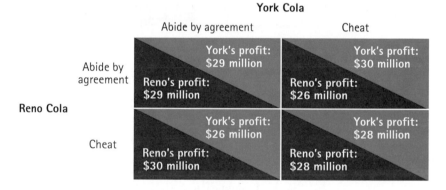

a. What strategy will each firm choose, and what will be each firm's profit?
b. Does it matter whether this agreement is for one period or for 2.5 periods?
c. Is this game an example of the prisoner's dilemma?

6. GD Capital and RK Leasing are engaged in multi-stage negotiations to form a joint venture for the leasing of large commercial aircraft. GD Capital has obtained the right to either accept or reject the terms of the venture. If GD accepts, then RK must decide whether to accept or reject. However, if GD rejects, then RK can either also reject the plan, or make slight changes to it and accept it. If RK accepts the revised plan, then GD must decide whether to accept or reject the revised plan. The situation is illustrated in the FIGURE below. Payoffs are for the length of the joint venture. Predict the outcome of these negotiations, and support your prediction by showing why your predicted outcome is an equilibrium.

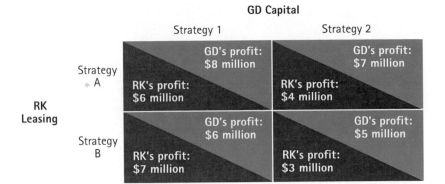

GD Capital

	Strategy 1	Strategy 2
Strategy A	GD's profit: $8 million RK's profit: $6 million	GD's profit: $7 million RK's profit: $4 million
Strategy B	GD's profit: $6 million RK's profit: $7 million	GD's profit: $5 million RK's profit: $3 million

RK Leasing

7. The Rose Corporation is one of two sellers of paint. It pursues a tit-for-tat strategy. However, it has great difficulty in telling whether its rival is secretly cutting its price. What problems is this likely to cause?

8. Consider a father who is trying to discipline his child. The father insists the child must go with the rest of the family to visit their grandmother. The child prefers to go to the movies with a friend. The father threatens to punish the child if the child doesn't visit the grandmother. If the child goes with the family to visit the grandmother, both child and father receive 1 unit of utility. If the child refuses to go to granny's house, and the father punishes the child, the child receives −1, and the father receives −1 units of utility. If the child refuses to go and the father relents (does not punish) the child receives 2 units of utility, and the father receives 0.
   a. Draw the game in matrix form
   b. Draw the game in extensive form
   c. Solve the game via backward induction

9. The Boca Raton Company announces that, if it reduces its price subsequent to a purchase, the early customer will get a rebate so that he or she will pay no more than those buying after the price reduction.
   a. If the Boca Raton Company has only one rival, and if its rival too makes such an announcement, does this change the payoff matrix? If so, in what way?
   b. Do these announcements tend to discourage price cutting? Why or why not?

PART

5

Risk, Uncertainty, and Incentives

Risk Analysis

Most business decisions involve some risk or uncertainty. Having made a decision, the manager cannot be sure of its outcome. Chance or the actions of others may play a role. For example, marketing a new product involves risk, since we cannot be sure of the level of demand. If the demand is high, profits can be high; but if demand is lower than expected, profits may be negative. Investing in research and development for a new drug or new software is risky. Can we be sure that the investment will eventually result in a product that can be brought to market? The answer is usually, "no." More innovative ideas offer the tantalizing possibility of high reward but they also offer great risk. Drilling a well for oil is risky. We cannot be sure in advance whether we will strike oil, how much we will strike, or exactly what are the costs of extraction of any oil we find. The inability to see the future can sometimes paralyze decision makers. However, some managerial techniques can help us see through the maze of possibilities and come to sensible decisions.

In this chapter, we present a variety of tools for helping to make decisions in the face of risk. We start with the concept of expected value, which summarizes a set of possible outcomes into a single representative value. We look at decision trees. Many decisions involve a myriad of possible outcomes, many of which are conditional on pure chance or the actions of others. For example, a manager might pose questions such as, "If interest rates are low and my competitor keeps prices high, then demand for my new product will be high—but what if interest rates rise, competitors' prices fall, or new entrants come into the market?" Decision trees give us a visual and intuitive guide through the web of possible consequences and allow us to structure decisions in a simple, sequential way.

We also examine techniques to reduce uncertainty. Techniques and databases are available that enable us to improve our ability to forecast the future. For example, the designer of a new product can conduct market research on consumer acceptance and analyze the performance of comparable products to provide more information about the likely demand. The oil company can use geological models and satellite surveys to give a clearer picture of the drilling site and its likelihood of holding oil. In short, we can invest in information about the future. We show how valuable such information is and how its quality depends on its reliability.

The other major concept we introduce here is that of expected utility. People react differently to risk, much as they have differing preferences for real goods. Given a choice between a safe investment with a low rate of return and a risky investment with a high expected return, some would choose the former, others the latter. This reflects their tolerance for risk. We see how expected utility analysis can be used to reflect risk tolerance in managerial decisions.

Risk and Probability

In ordinary parlance, risk is a hazard or a chance of loss. If you invest $10,000 in a firm carrying out research and development in biotechnology and there is a very substantial chance that you will lose your money because the firm will not come up with a successful new product, such an investment is risky. Moreover, in ordinary parlance, the bigger is the chance of loss, the more risky a particular course of action is. Therefore, an investment in a firm doing biotechnology research is riskier than an investment in Treasury notes, since there is a relatively greater chance of loss from the former investment.

To analyze risk, it is necessary to define a probability. Suppose a situation exists in which one of a number of possible outcomes can occur. For example, if a gambler throws a single die, the number that comes up may be 1, 2, 3, 4, 5, or 6. A probability is the number attached to each outcome. It is the proportion of times that this outcome occurs over the long run if this situation exists repeatedly. The probability that a particular die will come up a 1 is the proportion of times this will occur if the die is thrown many, many times; and the probability that the same die will come up a 2 is the proportion of times this will occur if the die is thrown many, many times; and so on.

If a situation exists a very large number of times, R, and if outcome A occurs r times, the probability of A is

$$P(A) = \frac{r}{R} \qquad (15.1)$$

Thus, if a die is "true" (meaning that each of its sides is equally likely to come up when the die is rolled), the probability of its coming up a 1 is 1/6, or 0.167, because if it is rolled many, many times, this will occur one-sixth of the time.

What we have just provided is the so-called **frequency definition of probability**. In some situations, this concept of probability may be difficult to apply because these situations cannot be repeated over and over. When the IBM Corporation introduced Warp, a new software package, in October 1994, this was an "experiment" that could not be repeated over and over again under essentially the same set of circumstances. Market and other conditions vary from month to month. If Warp had not been introduced that month, the types of software packages available from other firms (like Microsoft), the prices of these competing products, the advertising campaigns of other firms, and a host of other relevant factors would probably have been different.

In dealing with situations of this sort, managerial economists sometimes use a **subjective definition of probability**. According to this definition, the probability of an event is the degree of confidence or belief on the part of the decision maker that the event will occur. If the decision maker believes that outcome X is more likely to occur than outcome Y, the probability of X occurring is higher than the probability of Y doing so. If the decision maker believes that it is equally likely that a particular outcome will or will not occur, the probability attached to the occurrence of this outcome equals 0.50. The important factor in this concept of probability is what the decision maker believes.

Probability Distributions and Expected Values

In a particular situation, if all possible outcomes are listed and the probability of occurrence is assigned to each outcome, the resulting table is called a **probability distribution**. For example, suppose that Adept Technology, a San Jose, California, manufacturer of robots, believes that the probability is 0.6 that it can develop a new type of robot in one year and the probability is 0.4 that it cannot do so in this length of time. The probability distribution is as follows:

Event	Probability of occurrence
New robot is developed in one year	0.6
New robot is not developed in one year	0.4
	1.0

Note that the probabilities sum to 1, which must be the case if all possible outcomes or events are listed.

If Adept Technology will earn a profit of $1 million if it develops the new robot in one year and lose $600,000 if it does not develop the robot in one year, we can readily calculate the probability distribution of its profit from the new robot, which is:

Profit	Probability
$1,000,000	0.6
(−$600,000)	0.4

Moreover, we can also calculate the expected value of the profit, which is

$$\$1,000,000(0.6) + (-\$600,000)(0.4) = \$360,000$$

The expected value is the weighted average of the profits corresponding to the various outcomes, each of these profit figures being weighted by its probability of occurrence.

In general, the expected profit can be expressed by the equation

$$\text{Expected profit} = E(\pi) = \sum_{1}^{N} \pi_i P_i \tag{15.2}$$

where π_i is the level of profit associated with the ith outcome, P_i is the probability that the ith outcome will take place, and N is the number of possible outcomes. Since $N = 2$, $\pi_1 = \$1,000,000$, $\pi_2 = -\$600,000$, $P_1 = 0.6$, and $P_2 = 0.4$ in the case of Adept Technology, equation (15.2) says precisely the same thing as the equation that precedes it.

Comparisons of Expected Profit

To decide which of a number of courses of action to take, managers can compare the expected profit resulting from each one. For example, suppose that the Jones Corporation, a producer of automobile tires, is thinking of raising the price of its product by $1 per tire. On the basis of the firm's estimates, if it raises its price, it will experience an $800,000 profit if its current advertising campaign is successful and a $600,000 loss if the campaign is not successful. The firm believes that there is a 0.5 probability that its current advertising campaign will be successful and a 0.5 probability that it will not be successful.

Under these circumstances, the expected profit to the firm if it raises its price equals

$$\$800,000(0.5) + (-\$600,000)(0.5) = \$100,000$$

As indicated, the expected profit is the sum of the amount of money gained (or lost) if each outcome occurs times the probability of occurrence of the outcome. In this case, there are two possible outcomes: (1) the firm's current advertising campaign is successful or (2) it is unsuccessful. If we multiply the amount of money gained (or lost) if the first outcome occurs times its probability of occurrence, the result is $\$800,000(0.5)$. If we multiply the amount of money gained (or lost) if the second outcome occurs times its probability of occurrence, the result is $-\$600,000(0.5)$. Summing these two results, we get $\$100,000$, which is the expected profit if the firm raises its price.

What would be the expected profit if the Jones Corporation did not increase its price? Suppose that the firm's executives believe that, if there were no price increase, the firm's profits would be $\$200,000$. And, for simplicity, we assume that this profit level is regarded as certain if the price is not increased. Then, if the firm wants to maximize the expected profit, it should not increase its price, because its expected profit equals $\$200,000$ if it does not do so but only $\$100,000$ if it does. Later in this chapter, we discuss at length the circumstances under which it is rational to maximize the expected profit—and how to proceed if it is not rational to do so.

How to Construct a Decision Tree

Any situation involving decision making under conditions of risk has the following characteristics. First, the decision maker must make a choice or perhaps a series of choices among alternative courses of action. Second, this choice leads to some consequence, but the decision maker cannot tell in advance the exact nature of this consequence, because it depends on some unpredictable event or series of events as well as on the choice itself. For example, consider the case of the Jones Corporation, which must decide whether to increase the price of its automobile tires. The choice is between two alternatives: increase the price or do not. The consequence of increasing price is uncertain, since the firm cannot be sure that its current advertising campaign will be successful.

To analyze any such problem, a decision tree is useful. A **decision tree** is a diagram that helps you visualize the relevant choices. It represents a decision problem as a series of choices, each of which is depicted by a fork (sometimes called a *juncture* or *branching point*). A decision fork represents a choice where the decision maker is in control of the outcome; a chance fork represents a point where "chance" controls the outcome. To differentiate between a decision fork and a chance fork, we place a small square at the former juncture but not at the latter.

In Figure 15.1, we show the decision tree for the problem facing the Jones Corporation. Starting at the left-hand side of the diagram, the first choice is up to the firm, which can either follow the branch representing a price increase or the branch representing no such increase. Since this fork is a decision fork, it is represented by a square. If the branch representing no price increase is followed, the consequence is certain: The firm will have a profit of $200,000. Therefore, $200,000 is shown at the end of this branch. If the branch representing a price increase is followed, we come to a chance fork, since it is uncertain whether the firm's current advertising campaign will be successful. The upper branch following this chance fork represents the consequence that it is successful, in which case the firm will have a profit of $800,000, shown at the end of this branch. The lower branch following this chance fork represents the consequence that it is not successful, in which case the outcome is −$600,000 (a loss), shown at the end of this branch. The probability that "chance" will choose each of these branches is shown above the end of each branch; in both cases, this probability equals 0.50.

FIGURE

15.1

Decision Tree, Jones Corporation

If the Jones Corporation increases its price, the expected profit is $100,000. If it does not increase its price, the expected profit is $200,000.

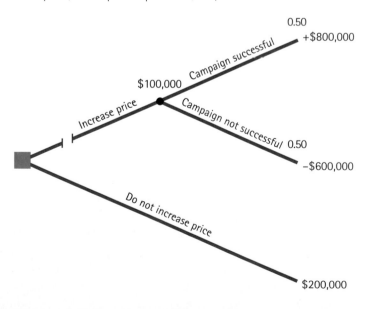

On the basis of such a decision tree, you can readily determine which branch the firm should choose to maximize the expected profit. As shown in Chapter 14, we use backward induction to solve this problem. We begin at the right-hand side of the decision tree, where the profit figures are located. The first step is to calculate the expected profit when the firm is situated at the chance fork immediately to the left of these payoff figures. In other words, this is the expected profit to the firm given that "chance" will choose which subsequent branch will be followed. Because there is a 0.50 probability that the branch culminating in a profit of $800,000 will be followed and a 0.50 probability that the branch culminating in a loss of $600,000 will be followed, the expected profit when situated at this chance fork is

$$0.50(\$800,000) + 0.50(-\$600,000) = \$100,000$$

This number is written above the chance fork in question to show that this is the expected profit when the firm is located at that fork. Moving farther to the left along the decision tree, it is clear that the firm has a choice of two branches, one of which leads to an expected profit of $100,000, the other of which leads to a $200,000 expected profit. If the firm wants to maximize the expected profit, it should choose the latter branch. In other words, it should not increase its price. Since the former branch (increase price) is nonoptimal, you place two vertical lines through it.

Of course, this graphic procedure for analyzing the Jones Corporation's pricing problem amounts to precisely the same thing as the calculations we made in the previous section. Recall that we compared the expected profit if the price was increased ($100,000) with the expected profit if it was not increased ($200,000) and followed the course of action that resulted in the larger of the two. Our procedure in Figure 15.1 is exactly the same.

Should Tomco Oil Corporation Drill a Well?

One major area where the concepts presented in the previous sections have been applied is oil exploration. Very large amounts of money have been and are being invested in oil exploration. Oil firms use these analytical tools as an aid to decision making. To illustrate how these concepts can be applied, consider the actual case of Tomco Oil Corporation, an oil producer that had to decide whether to drill a well at Blair West, a site in Kansas.[1] The firm had information concerning the

---

[1]This case is described in detail in J. Hosseini, "Decision Analysis and Its Application in the Choice between Two Wildcat Oil Ventures," *Interfaces*, March–April 1986. For pedagogical reasons, we simplified the analysis and the numbers involved. A general account of the use of decision trees in oil exploration is found in J. Pratt, H. Raiffa, and R. Schlaifer, "Introduction to Statistical Decision Theory," in E. Mansfield, ed., *Managerial Economics and Operations Research* (4th ed.; New York: Norton, 1980).

cost of drilling and the price of oil as well as geologists' reports concerning the likelihood of striking oil. Suppose the geologists' reports led the firm to believe that, if the well were drilled, there was a 0.60 probability that no oil would be found, a 0.15 probability that 10,000 barrels would be found, a 0.15 probability that 20,000 barrels would be found, and a 0.10 probability that 30,000 barrels would be found.

Using these probabilities alone, the firm cannot decide whether to drill the well. In addition, information is needed concerning the profit (or loss) that would accrue to the firm if each of these outcomes occurs. Suppose the firm believes that, if it drills the well, it will incur a $90,000 loss if it finds no oil, a $100,000 profit if it finds 10,000 barrels of oil, a $300,000 profit if it finds 20,000 barrels, and a $500,000 profit if it finds 30,000 barrels. Should the firm drill the well?

Assuming that the firm wants to maximize its expected profit, it can answer this question by constructing the decision tree shown in Figure 15.2. Starting at the left-hand side of the diagram, the first choice is up to the firm, which can follow the branch representing drilling the well or the branch representing not drilling. If the branch representing not drilling is followed, the expected profit is zero, which is shown at the end of this branch. (Why? Because the firm neither gains nor loses

FIGURE
15.2

Decision Tree, Tomco Oil Corporation

If Tomco Oil drills the well, the expected profit is $56,000. If it does not, the expected profit is zero.

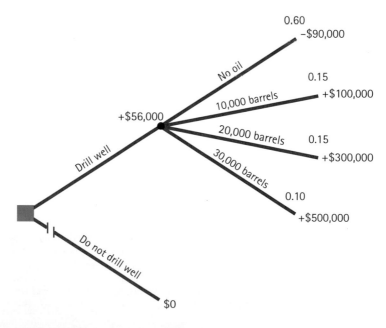

if it does not drill.) If the branch representing drilling the well is followed, we come to a chance fork, since it is uncertain whether the firm will strike oil and, if it does, how much oil it will find. The highest branch following this chance fork represents the consequence that no oil is found, in which case the firm loses $90,000, shown at the end of this branch. The second highest branch following this chance fork represents the consequence that 10,000 barrels are found, in which case the firm gains $100,000, shown at the end of this branch. Similarly, the second lowest and lowest branches following this chance fork represent respectively the consequences that 20,000 and 30,000 barrels are found; the number at the end of each of these branches is the corresponding profit to the firm.

Having constructed this decision tree, the firm's managers can compute the expected profit to the firm if it is situated at the chance fork immediately to the left of the profit (or loss) figures. If the firm is at this fork, there is a 0.60 probability that the branch culminating in a $90,000 loss will be followed, a 0.15 probability that the branch culminating in a $100,000 profit will be followed, a 0.15 probability that the branch culminating in a $300,000 profit will be followed, and a 0.10 probability that the branch culminating in a $500,000 profit will be followed. To obtain the expected profit if the firm is situated at this fork, the firm's managers should multiply each possible value of profit (or loss) by its probability, and sum the results. The expected profit if the firm is situated at this fork equals

$$0.60(-\$90,000) + 0.15(\$100,000) + 0.15(\$300,000) + 0.10(\$500,000) = \$56,000$$

In Figure 15.2, this result is written above the chance fork in question to show that this is the expected profit if the firm is located at that fork.

Going farther along the decision tree to the left, the firm has a choice of two branches, one of which leads to an expected profit of $56,000, the other of which leads to an expected profit of zero. If the firm wants to maximize its expected profit, it should choose the former branch; that is, it should drill the well.

The Expected Value of Perfect Information

Frequently, the decision maker can obtain information that will dispel (at least some of) the relevant risk. If the decision maker can get perfect information, how much is it worth? To answer this question, we define the expected value of perfect information as the increase in expected profit if the decision maker could obtain completely accurate information concerning the outcome of the relevant situation (but if he or she does not yet know what this information will be). In the case of the Jones Corporation (the firm that must decide whether to increase its tire price), this expected value is the increase in expected profit

CONCEPTS IN CONTEXT

Bidding for the SS *Kuniang*

Prudent application of decision tree analysis can make you a winning manager even if your bid is second best, as one utility discovered. The New England Electric System was a public utility holding company that generated and delivered electricity to over 1 million customers in Massachusetts, Rhode Island, and New Hampshire. Because some of its oil-fired power stations were converted to coal, it decided to obtain ships to bring coal from Virginia to New England. In 1981, the SS *Kuniang* ran aground, and the ship's owners offered to sell the salvage rights by means of a sealed bid auction. The New England Electric System was interested in making a bid, since, if the *Kuniang* could be restored, it would meet the company's needs very well.

To determine how much to bid, the company carried out a detailed analysis, based on a decision tree like that in Figure 15.1 or 15.2. It calculated the expected net present value of its earnings, given each amount it might bid. For example, if it bid $5 million, it calculated that the expected net present value would be $2.85 million. On the other hand, if it bid $7 million, it calculated that the net present value would be $3.05 million.

Why was the net present value higher if it bid $7 million rather than $5 million? Because the probability was higher that its bid would win. Obviously, the company could not be sure of this probability, but according to its best estimates, this probability would increase from about 1/6 to 1/2 if it bid $7 million rather than $5 million.

As a result of this analysis, the New England Electric System bid $6.7 million for the *Kuniang*, since this was the bid that maximized expected net present value. It came in second. The winning bid was $10 million. Of course, the fact that the company did not make the winning bid does not mean that the analysis was not useful. The point of the analysis was to determine how much it was worthwhile to bid. (If the company had made a high enough bid, it could have been reasonably sure of winning, but it would have lost money by doing so, the so-called winner's curse.) According to Guy W. Nichols, the company's chairman at that time, the analysis "was a useful contribution to our deliberations and to our decision regarding an appropriate bid for the ship."

D. Bell, "Bidding for the S.S. *Kuniang*," *Interfaces*, March–April 1984, 17–23.

if the firm could obtain perfectly accurate information indicating whether its current advertising campaign will be successful.

To illustrate how one can compute the expected value of perfect information, we return to the Jones case. We begin by evaluating the expected monetary value to the Jones Corporation if it can obtain access to perfectly accurate information of this sort. If it can obtain perfect information, it will be able to make the correct decision, regardless of whether or not its current advertising campaign is successful. If it is successful, the firm will be aware of this fact and increase the price. If it is not successful, the firm will be aware of this fact also and will not increase the price. Therefore, given that the firm has access to perfect information, the expected profit is

$$0.50(\$800,000) + 0.50(\$200,000) = \$500,000$$

To understand why this is the expected profit if the Jones Corporation has access to perfect information, it is important to recognize that, although it is assumed that the firm has access to perfect information, it *does not yet know what this information will be.* There is a 0.50 probability that this information will show that its advertising campaign would be successful, in which case the Jones Corporation will increase its price and the profit will be $800,000. There is also a 0.50 probability that the information will show that it would not be successful, in which case the Jones Corporation will not increase its price and its profit will be $200,000. So, as shown, the expected profit if the firm has access to perfect information (that is not yet revealed to the firm) is $500,000.

At this point, we must recall that the expected profit if the firm bases its decision on existing information is $200,000 (as we saw on pages 604–607), not $500,000. The difference between these two figures—$500,000 minus $200,000, or $300,000—is the expected value of perfect information. It is a measure of the value of perfect information: *It shows the amount by which the expected profit increases as a consequence of the firm having access to perfect information.*

In many circumstances, it is very important that the decision maker know how much perfect information would be worth. Business executives are continually being offered information by testing services, research organizations, news bureaus, and a variety of other organizations. Unless you know how much particular types of information are worth, it is difficult to decide rationally whether they should be bought. The sort of analysis presented in this section is useful to guide such decisions, since it shows the maximum amount that the firm should pay to obtain perfect information. The calculation of what to pay for less-than-perfect information is very complex and is not presented here. Needless to say, the amount is less than what one would pay if the information is perfect. And, when the accuracy of the information falls below a certain level (this level is generally well above that for information with zero accuracy), you would not pay anything for it.

Evaluating an Investment in a New Chemical Plant: A Case Study

To illustrate the usefulness of the expected value of perfect information, consider an actual case in which a decision tree was constructed to determine whether a major U.S. corporation should invest in a new plant. The major product of the new plant would be a brightener, but by using new processing methods, a valuable by-product could be made as well. The exact amounts of both

TABLE
15.1

Expected Value of Perfect Information Concerning Factors Influencing Whether to Build New Chemical Plant

Factor	Expected value of perfect information (millions of dollars)
By-product quantity	6.2
Level of impurities	3.9
Raw material costs	0.3
Plant efficiency	0.0

Source: Spetzler and Zamora, "Facilities Investment and Expansion Problem."

products that would be produced were uncertain. Very small quantities of impurities in the raw materials used in the process could greatly influence the amounts of brightener and by-product produced. Also, there were uncertainties concerning the costs of raw materials and plant efficiency.

Table 15.1 shows the expected value of perfect information concerning by-product quantity, impurities, raw material costs, and plant efficiency. As you can see, the critical uncertainties were those regarding by-product quantity and the level of impurities. For example, perfect information concerning by-product quantity would have been worth up to $6.2 million. On the other hand, information regarding raw materials and plant efficiency was of much less importance for this decision. Indeed, the expected value of perfect information concerning plant efficiency was close to zero. On the basis of these results, the analysts advised the company to do some research to reduce the uncertainties regarding by-product quantity and the level of impurities before committing itself to the construction of the new plant.[2]

Measuring Attitudes toward Risk: The Utility Approach

In discussing both the Jones Corporation's pricing decision and the Tomco Oil Corporation's drilling decision, we assume that the decision maker wants to maximize the expected profit. In this and the following sections, we formulate

---

[2]C. Spetzler and R. Zamora, "Decision Analysis of a Facilities Investment and Expansion Problem," in R. Howard and J. Matheson, eds. *The Principles and Applications of Decision Analysis* (Menlo Park, CA: Strategic Decision Group, 1984).

CONSULTANT'S CORNER

Choosing Areas for Research Regarding Pollution Costs

The National Academy of Sciences sponsored a study to examine emission control strategies for power plants. One purpose of this study was to determine the value of reducing the uncertainty concerning the pollution costs of various strategies. Efforts to reduce harmful emissions from coal-burning power plants focus on at least four strategies: (1) treating the coal to reduce its sulfur content, (2) using premium-priced, low-sulfur coal, (3) employing a tall stack and intermittent control systems, and (4) adopting a flue-gas desulfurization process. This study was concerned with the effects of various control alternatives on the total cost of electricity. Choosing among them is not easy, partly because it has been difficult to establish, with any certainty, the pollution costs of each strategy.

Because of the limitations on existing knowledge, the study found that there was considerable uncertainty regarding which of the alternative strategies was least costly. The expected value of perfect information, shown in the table, depended on whether the plant was in an urban or a remote area and whether low-sulfur coal was available.

	Low-sulfur coal available	Low-sulfur coal not available
Remote plant	$3.7 million	$2.4 million
Urban plant	1.3 million	2.8 million

If you were a consultant to the National Academy of Sciences, what conclusions could you draw concerning the kinds of plants for which further research of this sort would be most valuable?

This section is based on an actual case. For further discussion, see S. Watson and D. Buede, *Decision Synthesis* (Cambridge, U.K.: Cambridge University Press, 1987) (which summarizes the work of D. North and M. Merkhofer).

a more realistic criterion. To understand why a decision maker may not want to maximize the expected profit, consider a situation where a firm is given a choice between (1) a profit of $2,000,000 for certain and (2) a gamble in which there is a 50–50 chance of a $4,100,000 profit and a $60,000 loss. The expected profit for the gamble is

$$0.50(\$4,100,000) + 0.50(-\$60,000) = \$2,020,000$$

so the firm should choose the gamble over the certainty of $2,000,000 if it wants to maximize expected profit. However, it seems likely that many firms, particularly small ones, would prefer the certainty of $2,000,000, since the gamble entails a 50 percent chance that the firm will lose $60,000, a substantial sum for a very small firm. Moreover, many people may feel that they can do almost as much with $2,000,000 as with $4,100,000, and therefore the extra profit is not worth the risk of losing $60,000.

Whether the firm's managers will want to maximize the expected profit in this situation depends on their attitude toward risk. If they are elderly people of modest means, they may be overwhelmed at the thought of taking a 50 percent chance of losing $60,000. On the other hand, if they are the heads of a big corporation, the prospect of a $60,000 loss may be not the least bit unsettling; and they may prefer the gamble to the certainty of a mere $2,000,000 gain.

Fortunately, we need not assume that the decision maker wants to maximize the expected profit. Instead, we can construct a **utility function** for the decision maker that measures his or her attitudes toward risk. This concept of utility should not be confused with that discussed in Chapter 4. As we shall see, it is a quite different sort of concept. From this utility function, we can then go on to find the alternative that is best for the decision maker, given his or her attitudes toward risk.

Constructing a Utility Function

A rational decision maker *maximizes the expected utility*. In other words, the decision maker chooses the course of action with the highest expected utility. But what (in this context) is a utility? It is a number that is attached to a possible outcome of the decision. Each outcome has a utility. The decision maker's utility function shows the utility that he or she attaches to each possible outcome. This utility function, as we shall see, shows the decision maker's preferences with respect to risk. What is **expected utility?** It is the sum of the utility if each outcome occurs times the probability of occurrence of the outcome. For example, if a situation has two possible outcomes, *A* and *B*, if the utility of outcome A is 2 and the utility of outcome B is 8, and if the probability of each outcome is 0.50, the expected utility equals

$$0.50(2) + 0.50(8) = 5$$

What is the expected utility if the Tomco Oil Corporation drills the well under the circumstances described on pages 607–609? It equals

$$0.60U(-90) + 0.15U(100) + 0.15U(300) + 0.10U(500)$$

where $U(-90)$ is the utility that the decision maker attaches to a monetary loss of $90,000, $U(100)$ is the utility attached to a gain of $100,000, $U(300)$ is the utility attached to a gain of $300,000, and so on. Since there is a 0.60 probability of a $90,000 loss, a 0.15 probability of a $100,000 gain, a 0.15 probability of a $300,000 gain, and a 0.10 probability of a $500,000 gain, this is the expected utility. What is the expected utility if the firm does not drill the well? It equals $U(0)$, since under these circumstances, it is certain that the gain is zero.

To find the utility the decision maker attaches to each possible outcome, we begin by setting the utility attached to two levels of profit arbitrarily. The utility of the better consequence is set higher than the utility of the worse one. In the case of the decision maker in the oil-drilling problem, we might set $U(-90)$ equal to 0 and $U(500)$ equal to 50. It turns out that the ultimate results of the analysis do not depend on which two numbers we choose, as long as the utility of the better consequence is set higher than the utility of the worse one. Therefore, we could set $U(-90)$ equal to 1 and $U(500)$ equal to 10. It would make no difference to the ultimate outcome of the analysis.[3]

Next, we present the decision maker with a choice between the certainty of one of the other levels of profit and a gamble where the possible outcomes are the two profit levels whose utilities we set arbitrarily. In the oil-drilling case, suppose we want to find $U(100)$. To do so, we ask the decision maker whether he or she would prefer the certainty of a $100,000 gain to a gamble where there is a probability of P that the gain is $500,000 and a probability of $(1 - P)$ that the loss is $90,000. We then try various values of P until we find the one at which the decision maker is indifferent between the certainty of a $100,000 gain and this gamble. Suppose that this value of P is 0.40.

If the decision maker is indifferent between the certain gain of $100,000 and this gamble, it must be that the expected utility of the certain gain of

---

[3]The utility function we construct is not unique. Because we set the two utilities arbitrarily, the results vary, depending on the values of the utilities chosen. If $X_1, X_2, \ldots, X_n$ are the utilities attached to n possible monetary values, $(\alpha + \beta X_1), (\alpha + \beta X_2), \ldots, (\alpha + \beta X_n)$ can also be utilities attached to them (where α and β are constants, and $\beta > 0$).

$100,000 equals the expected utility of the gamble. (Why? Because the decision maker maximizes the expected utility.) Therefore,

$$U(100) = 0.40U(500) + 0.60U(-90)$$

And since we set $U(500)$ equal to 50 and $U(-90)$ equal to 0, it follows that

$$U(100) = 0.40(50) + 0.60(0) = 20$$

That is, the utility attached to a gain of $100,000 is 20.

Using the same procedure, we can find $U(300)$ and $U(0)$, the other utilities required to calculate the expected utility if the oil company drills the well and the expected utility if it does not drill it. For example, to obtain $U(300)$, we ask the decision maker whether he or she would prefer the certainty of a $300,000 gain to a gamble where there is a probability of P that the gain is $500,000 and a probability of $(1 - P)$ that the loss is $90,000. Then, we try various values of P until we find the one where the decision maker is indifferent between the certainty of a $300,000 gain and this gamble. Suppose this value of P is 0.80. Then, the expected utility of a certain gain of $300,000 must equal the expected utility of this gamble; this means that

$$U(300) = 0.80U(500) + 0.20U(-90)$$

And, since $U(500)$ equals 50 and $U(-90)$ equals 0, it follows that $U(300)$ equals 40.

The decision maker's utility function is the relationship between his or her utility and the amount of his or her profit (or loss). On the basis of our evaluation of $U(-90)$, $U(100)$, $U(300)$, and $U(500)$ in the previous paragraphs, we can identify four points on the decision maker's utility function, as shown in Figure 15.3. By the repeated use of the procedure just described, we can obtain as many such points as we like. (According to Figure 15.3, $U(0) = 10$.)

Using a Utility Function

Once a manager's utility function has been constructed, it can be used to indicate whether he or she should accept or reject particular gambles. Consider the actual case of Thomas Blair, president of the Tomco Oil Corporation. Using the previous procedures, a managerial economist constructed Mr. Blair's utility function.[4] Suppose the result is as shown in Figure 15.3 and Mr. Blair must decide whether to drill the well described on pages 607–609. He should drill the well if his expected utility if the well is drilled exceeds his expected utility if it is

---

[4]Hosseini, "Decision Analysis." The utility function in Figure 15.3 is hypothetical but adequate for present purposes. As noted, this case has been simplified in various ways for pedagogical reasons.

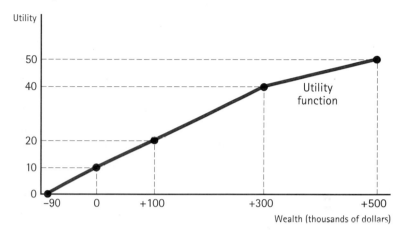

FIGURE 15.3

Utility Function

The decision maker's utility function is useful in indicating whether particular gambles should be accepted.

not drilled. As pointed out in the previous section, his expected utility if the well is drilled equals

$$0.60U(-90) + 0.15U(100) + 0.15U(300) + 0.10U(500)$$

If his utility function is as shown in Figure 15.3, this expression can be evaluated. Since $U(-90)$ equals 0, $U(100)$ equals 20, $U(300)$ equals 40, and $U(500)$ equals 50, his expected utility if the well is drilled is

$$0.60(0) + 0.15(20) + 0.15(40) + 0.10(50) = 14$$

It is important to note that we measure utility of "wealth" or "net worth" and not the utility of "changes in income." For example suppose my wealth is $100 and I am facing a choice about gambling as follows. If the coin come up heads, I win $10 and I lose $10 if tails. We must pose the choice in the following form.

GAMBLE − EXPECTED UTILITY = 0.5 U($100 + $10) + 0.50 ($100 − $10)
versus
NOT GAMBLE − EXPECTED UTILITY = 1.0 U($100).

With this in mind, as we return to Tomco Oil, we should think of values, −90, 100, 300, or 500 as the wealth or net worth of the firm under the different scenarios.

ANALYZING MANAGERIAL DECISIONS
Should Maxwell House Have Increased Its Price?

Some years ago, Maxwell House, the coffee producer, changed the design of its coffee cans. The idea was to appeal to consumers with a can that was easier to open. One important decision that Maxwell House had to make before introducing its new can was whether to raise the per-pound price of coffee in the new can by 2 cents. Coffee in the quick-strip can was expected to cost an average of 0.7 cent per pound more than in the old container.

According to Joseph Newman, who studied this case, if Maxwell House raised its price by 2 cents per pound, it might have been reasonable to expect (1) a 0.25 probability that its market share would decline by 1.5 percentage points, (2) a 0.25 probability that its market share would remain constant, (3) a 0.25 probability that its market share would increase by 1.0 percentage point, and (4) a 0.25 probability that its market share would increase by 2.5 percentage points. The change in Maxwell House's profits corresponding to each change in its market share is given in the table that follows.

According to Newman, if Maxwell House did not raise its price, it might have been reasonable to expect (1) a 0.1 probability that its market share would decline by 0.6 percentage point, (2) a 0.2 probability that its market share would remain constant, (3) a 0.5 probability that its market share would increase by 1.0 percentage point, and (4) a 0.2 probability that its market share would increase by 2.8 percentage points. The change in Maxwell House's profits corresponding to each of these market-share changes is provided in the table.

Price per pound held constant		Price per pound increased by 2 cents	
Change in market share (percentage points)	Change in profit (thousands of dollars)	Change in market share (percentage points)	Change in profit (thousands of dollars)
+2.8	4,104	+2.5	11,939
+1.0	−591	+1.0	6,489
0	−840	0	2,856
−0.6	−1,218	−1.5	−1,050

If the well is not drilled, Mr. Blair's expected utility equals $U(0)$, which is 10, according to Figure 15.3. Therefore, he should drill the well. Why? Because if he does not drill it, his expected utility is 10, whereas if he drills it, his expected utility is 14. Since he should maximize the expected utility, he should choose the action with the higher expected utility, which is to drill.

In fact, Tomco Oil Corporation did drill a well at Blair West. Subsequently, Mr. Blair stated, "Before we actually used decision-tree analysis to aid in our

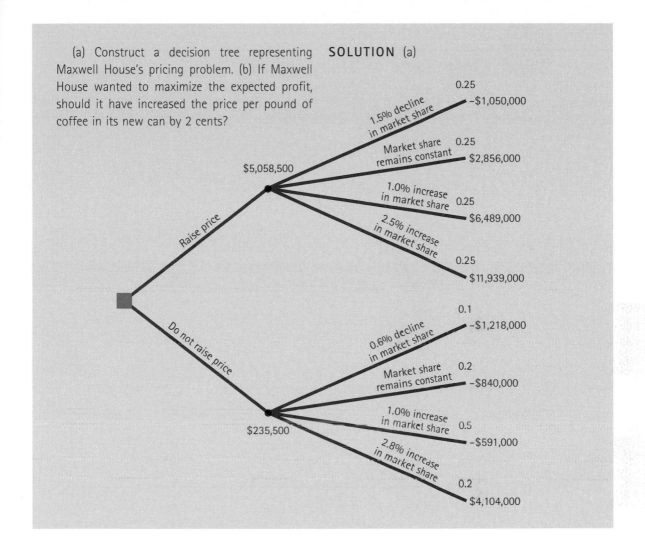

(a) Construct a decision tree representing Maxwell House's pricing problem. (b) If Maxwell House wanted to maximize the expected profit, should it have increased the price per pound of coffee in its new can by 2 cents?

SOLUTION (a)

selection of drilling sites, we were skeptical as to the application of decision-tree analysis in oil exploration and field development decisions. Now we find it helpful, not only in choosing between two or more drilling sites, but also in making decisions subsequent to the choice of a drilling site."[5]

Attitudes toward Risk: Three Types

Although one can expect that utility increases with monetary gain, the shape of the utility function can vary greatly, depending on the preferences of the decision maker. Figure 15.4 shows three general types of utility functions. The

[5]Hosseini, "Decision Analysis."

FIGURE
15.4

Three Types of Utility Functions

Utility functions assume a variety of shapes. In panel A, the decision maker is a risk averter; in panel B, he or she is a risk lover; and in panel C, he or she is risk neutral.

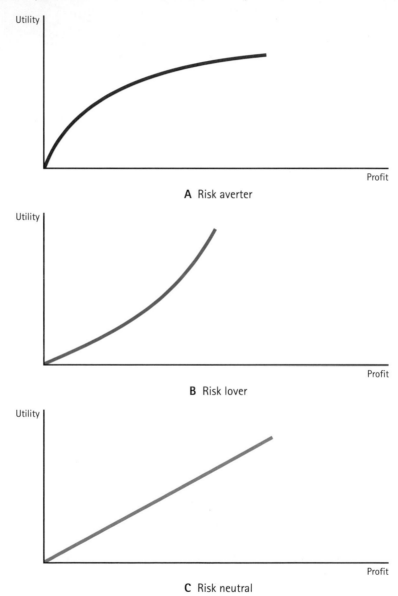

A Risk averter

B Risk lover

C Risk neutral

one in panel A is like that in Figure 15.3 in the sense that utility increases with wealth but at a *decreasing rate*. In other words, an increase in monetary gain of $1 is associated with *smaller and smaller* increases in utility as the wealth increases in size. Managers with utility functions of this sort are **risk averters**. That is, when confronted with gambles with equal expected wealth, they prefer a gamble with a more certain outcome to one with a less certain outcome.[6]

Panel B of Figure 15.4 shows a case in which utility increases with wealth but at *an increasing rate*. In other words, an increase in monetary gain of $1 is associated with *larger and larger increases* in utility as the wealth increases in size. Managers with utility functions of this sort are **risk lovers**. That is, when confronted with gambles with equal expected wealth, they prefer a gamble with a less certain outcome to one with a more certain outcome.[7]

Finally, panel C shows a case where utility increases with wealth and at a constant rate. In other words, an increase of $1 in monetary gain is associated with a constant increase in utility as wealth grows larger and larger. Stated differently, utility in this case is a linear function of wealth:

$$U = a + b\pi \tag{15.3}$$

where U is utility, π is wealth, and a and b are constants (of course, $b > 0$). People with utility functions of this sort are **risk neutral**.[8] In other words, they maximize expected wealth, regardless of risk. It is easy to prove that this is true. If equation (15.3) holds,

$$E(U) = a + bE(\pi) \tag{15.4}$$

where $E(U)$ is expected utility and $E(\pi)$ is expected wealth.[9] Consequently, since expected utility is directly related to expected wealth, it can be a maximum only when expected wealth is a maximum.

---

[6]Consider a gamble in which there is a probability of P that the gain is π_1 and a probability of $(1 - P)$ that the loss is π_2. A person is a risk averter if the utility of the gamble's expected profit, $U[P\pi_1 + (1 - P)\pi_2]$, is greater than the expected utility of the gamble, $PU(\pi_1) + (1 - P)U(\pi_2)$.

[7]Consider the gamble described in footnote 6. A person is a risk lover if the utility of the gamble's expected profit, $U[P\pi_1 + (1 - P)\pi_2]$, is less than the expected utility of the gamble, $PU(\pi_1) + (1 - P)U(\pi_2)$.

[8]A person can be a risk averter under some circumstances, a risk lover under other circumstances, and risk neutral under still other circumstances. The utility functions in Figure 15.4 are "pure" cases in which the person is always only one of these types, at least in the range covered by the graphs.

[9]To illustrate that equation (15.4) is correct, suppose that π can assume two possible values, π_1 and π_2, and that the probability that π_1 occurs is P and the probability that π_2 occurs is $(1 - P)$. Then, if $U = a + b\pi$,

$$\begin{aligned} E(U) &= P(a + b\pi_1) + (1 - P)(a + b/\pi_2) \\ &= a + b[P\pi_1 + (1 - P)\pi_2] \\ &= a + bE(\pi) \end{aligned}$$

since $E(\pi)$ equals $P\pi_1 + (1 - P)\pi_2$.

The Standard Deviation and Coefficient of Variation: Measures of Risk

The concept of risk is not easy to measure, but it is generally agreed that the riskiness of a given decision is directly related to the extent of the dispersion of the probability distribution of profit resulting from the decision. For exam-

---

FIGURE

15.5

Probability Distribution of the Profit from an Investment in a New Plant

The probability distribution in panel A shows more dispersion than that in panel B.

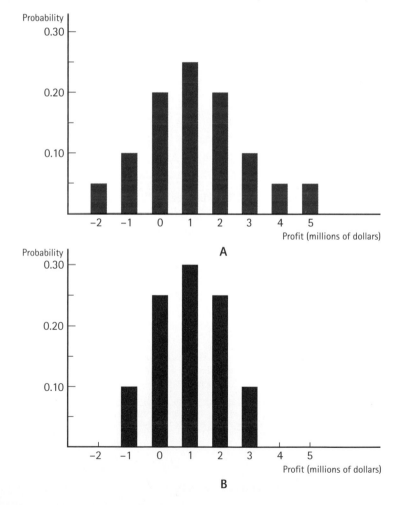

ple, suppose the Jones Corporation must decide whether to invest in a new plant. If the probability distribution of profit resulting from the new plant is as shown in panel A of Figure 15.5, the decision to invest in the new plant is more risky than it would be if this probability distribution were as shown in panel B. Why? Because the profit resulting from the new plant is more uncertain and variable in panel A than panel B.

As a measure of risk, we often use the **standard deviation**, σ, which is the most frequently used measure of the dispersion in a probability distribution.[10] To calculate the standard deviation of profit, we begin by computing the expected value of profit, $E(\pi)$ (recall equation (15.2)). Next, we subtract this expected value from each possible profit level to obtain a set of deviations about this expected value. (The ith such deviation is $\pi_i - E(\pi)$.) Then, we square each deviation, multiply the squared deviation by its probability of occurrence (P_i), and sum these products:

$$\sigma^2 = \sum_{i=1}^{N} [\pi_i - E(\pi)]^2 P_i$$

Taking the square root of this result, we obtain the standard deviation

$$\sigma = \left(\sum_{i=1}^{N} [\pi_i - E(\pi)]^2 P_i \right)^{0.5} \tag{15.5}$$

As an illustration, consider a company that must decide whether to invest in a flexible manufacturing system. According to the company's engineers, there is a 0.3 probability that such an investment will result in a $1 million profit, a 0.4 probability that it will result in a $0.2 million profit, and a 0.3 probability that it will result in a $0.6 million loss. Therefore, the expected value of the profit from this investment is

$$E(\pi) = 1(0.3) + 0.2(0.4) + (-0.6)(0.3) = 0.2$$

or $0.2 million. And, based on equation (15.5), the standard deviation is

$$\sigma = [(1 - 0.2)^2(0.3) + (0.2 - 0.2)^2(0.4) + (-0.6 - 0.2)^2(0.3)]^{0.5}$$
$$= (0.384)^{0.5} = 0.62$$

or $0.62 million.

A larger standard deviation tends to mean a larger amount of risk. If the standard deviation of the levels of profit resulting from the investment in the flexible manufacturing system were $2 million, rather than $0.62 million, there would be

---

[10]While the standard deviation often is a useful measure of risk, it may not always be the best measure. Our discussion here and in subsequent sections of this chapter is necessarily simplified. The measures and techniques we describe are rough, but many analysts have found them useful.

less certainty concerning its profitability. In other words, there would be a greater likelihood that its profitability would depart greatly from its expected value.

However, when we use the standard deviation as a measure of risk, we implicitly assume that the scale of the project is held constant. If one investment is twice as big as another, we would expect that the standard deviation of its profits would be greater than that of the other investment. To take account of the scale of the project, a measure of relative risk is required. Such a measure is the **coefficient of variation**, defined as

$$V = \frac{\sigma}{E(\pi)} \tag{15.6}$$

For example, in the case of the investment in the flexible manufacturing system, the coefficient of variation for the profit levels is 0.62/0.2, or 3.1.

ANALYZING MANAGERIAL DECISIONS

Deciding Whether to Buy an Option on a New Flight-Safety System

Cutler-Hammer, Inc., an electronic equipment manufacturer in Milwaukee, Wisconsin, was offered the option to purchase a license to produce and sell a new flight-safety system. Because of pending legislative action, the market for the product was very uncertain. A team of Cutler-Hammer personnel and outside analysts carried out an analysis to help the company decide whether to purchase the option to obtain this license.

According to this team, if Cutler-Hammer purchased this option, there was a 0.29 probability that it would not obtain the license, in which case it would lose $125,000, and a 0.71 probability that it would obtain the license. If the company obtained such a license, the team estimated that there was a 0.85 probability that it would not obtain a defense contract, in which case it would lose $700,000, and a 0.15 probability that it would obtain a defense contract, in which case it would gain $5.25 million.

(a) Construct the decision tree. (b) If Cutler-Hammer wanted to maximize expected profit, should it have purchased the option? (c) Cutler-Hammer also analyzed the consequences of another course of action: waiting and seeking a sublicense. The team estimated that such a course of action would result in the following probability distribution of profit:

Probability	Profit (thousands of dollars)
0.94	0
0.06	830

After considerable discussion, a unanimous decision was made by the firm's decision-making group (the president and his vice presidents for business development and operations) to adopt this course of action. Can you rationalize this graph decision?

SOLUTION (a) See the following graph. (b) Yes. (c) The expected profit from this course of action is $49,800, which is considerably less than it would be if the firm purchased the option ($100,425 according to part a). If the option is purchased, Cutler-Hammer has a 10.65 percent chance of making a large profit but an 89.35 percent chance of actually losing money. If it waits, the profit may be smaller but they cannot lose money. So if Cutler-Hammer is sufficiently averse to the downside risk, it is preferable to wait and seek the sublicense.

For further discussion, see J. Ulvila and R. Brown, "Decision Analysis Comes of Age," *Harvard Business Review*, reprinted in *Managerial Economics and Operations Research*, ed. Mansfield.

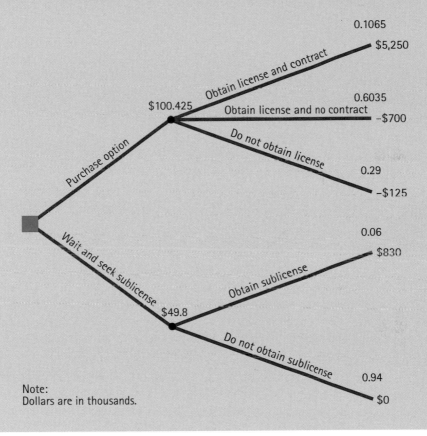

Note:
Dollars are in thousands.

Adjusting the Valuation Model for Risk

According to the basic valuation model discussed in Chapter 1, a firm's managers must continually be concerned with the effects of their decisions on the present value of the firm's future profits, defined as

$$PV = \sum_{t=1}^{n} \frac{\pi_t}{(1 + i)^t} \qquad (15.7)$$

But the firm's managers do not know with certainty what the firm's profits in year t (that is, π_t) will be. The best they can do is use the expected profit (that is, $E(\pi_t)$) instead. How can they adjust the formula in equation (15.7) to take account of risk?

One way is to use the so-called certainty equivalent approach, which is related to the utility theory developed in the previous sections. For example, consider the manager of the firm considering an investment in the flexible manufacturing system. Suppose she is indifferent between the certainty of a $100,000 net worth (i.e., the net worth is the wealth of the firm) and the gamble involved in investing in this system. If so, the certainty equivalent ($100,000), rather than the expected profit ($200,000), should be used as π_t in equation (15.7). If the certainty equivalent is less than the expected net worth, the decision maker is a risk averter; if it is more than the expected net worth, she is a risk lover; and if it equals the expected net worth, she is risk neutral.

On the basis of the decision maker's utility function, one can construct indifference curves of the sort shown in Figure 15.6. Each such indifference curve shows the certainty equivalent corresponding to various uncertain outcomes. Figure 15.6 shows that the manager is indifferent between the certainty of

---

FIGURE 15.6

Manager's Indifference Curve between Expected Profit and Risk

The manager is indifferent between gambles with the expected profit and risk shown here. Therefore, she is indifferent between the certainty of $100,000 and a gamble where the expected profit is $200,000 and the coefficient of variation is 3.1. Similar indifference curves exist for riskless amounts other than $100,000.

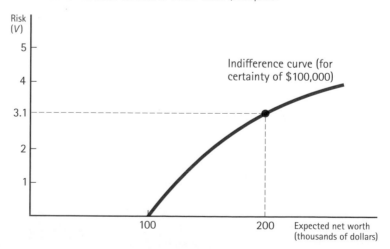

$100,000 and a gamble where the expected net worth is $200,000 and the coefficient of variation is 3.1. Using such indifference curves, one can estimate the certainty equivalent of any uncertain situation. (In contrast to the indifference curves in Chapter 4 other than on page 147, these indifference curves slope upward to the right. Why? Because the manager prefers less to more risk. In Chapter 4, the consumer preferred more of each commodity to less.)

In practice, of course, it is not easy to obtain such indifference curves, just as it is not easy to obtain the utility functions on which they are based. Because managers lack unlimited time and patience, it may not be feasible to get more than a limited amount of information concerning their utility functions. Nor is it always clear which of a number of managers is the relevant one. If many managers play an important role in coming to a particular decision and they have very divergent utility curves, they may come to quite different conclusions. But this, of course, should be expected. Indeed, it would be strange if managers with diverse attitudes toward risk did not come to divergent conclusions when faced with a choice among alternatives entailing quite different amounts of risk.

Certainty Equivalence and the Market for Insurance

Consider an individual with initial wealth (W) of $900. This individual faces a 25 percent chance of a catastrophic event that will leave him with wealth of $400 (and likewise faces a 75 percent chance that nothing happens and his wealth remains at $900). This is referred to as his *gamble against nature*. His expected wealth is therefore

$$0.25(400) + 0.75(900) = 100 + 675 = 775$$

The individual is risk averse with a utility (U) function of

$$U = W^{0.5}$$

Hence, his expected utility from the situation he faces is

$$0.25(400)^{0.5} + 0.75(900)^{0.5} = 0.25(20) + 0.75(30) = 5 + 22.5 = 27.5$$

The certainty equivalent in this case is the amount of wealth the individual must have with perfect certainty that would render the individual the same expected utility as the gamble against nature he faces, that is, 27.5,

$$U = W^{0.5} = 27.5$$

Squaring both sides yields $W = \$756.25$. So, if the individual had wealth of $756.25 with perfect certainty, he would have a utility of 27.5, which is the same as his expected utility in the gamble against nature. So 756.25 is his certainty equivalent.

The LBI Insurance Company provides coverage to protect individuals against such catastrophic events. LBI offers full coverage insurance—it will cover the insured's entire loss (500 in this case). LBI is risk neutral.

What premium should LBI charge for this full coverage policy? LBI's expected payout is $125. They have a 25 percent chance of paying out $500 and a 75 percent chance of paying out $0. Therefore, we expect a premium of at least $125, so that LBI could expect to at least break even on the policy.[11] What is the maximum that the individual would pay for such a policy? That is where the certainty equivalent becomes relevant. By charging $143.75 for the policy, the individual would be left with $756.25 ($900 − $143.75) for sure (since there is a 75-percent chance that nothing happens, in which case he would have $900 − $143.75 = $756.25 and a 25 percent chance that the catastrophic event occurs, in which case he would have $900 − $143.75 − $500 + $500 = $756.25). With the policy, he always will have the wealth of $756.25 or the utility of 27.5 for sure. Hence, he is indifferent between buying the full coverage insurance policy for $143.75 and facing the gamble against nature described earlier, because both give an expected utility of 27.5.

The difference between the premium that will just cover LBI's expected payout ($125) and the maximum that the individual would pay ($143.75) is called the individual's *risk premium*, or the amount the individual would be willing to pay the insurance company above the expected value of the loss. The risk premium is $18.75 in this case. A premium (P) between 125 and 143.75 yields a situation where the individual would buy insurance (because the utility of 900 − P > 27.5) and the insurance company would sell the policy (because the expected profit of P − 125 > 0). If LBI were a monopolist, it would charge $143.75 (or epsilon below) for the policy and extract all the consumer's surplus from purchasing it (by using the pricing policy, managers convert consumer surplus to expected variable profit).

---

[11]We are simplifying here. While the expected payout on this policy is $125, LBI incurs other costs that it must cover if it is to stay in business, such as agents who sell policies are paid commissions, back office staff process and pay or reject claims, and executives manage. However, insurance companies invest the premiums they receive and earn income from those investments. In this analysis, we implicitly assume that the costs other than the expected payout are covered by the earnings from the invested premiums. In addition, we assume that LBI is risk neutral. This is not an unreasonable assumption, because LBI insures many individuals and the probability of a catastrophic event occurring to their customers is very close to 25 percent (if all are clones of the individual analyzed here). Thus, LBI diffuses its risk by insuring many people.

The Use of Risk-Adjusted Discount Rates

Another way to introduce risk into the valuation model in equation (15.7) is to adjust the discount rate, i. This method, like that discussed in the previous section, is based on a manager's preferences with regard to risk. For example, suppose that Figure 15.7 shows a manager's indifference curve between expected rate of return and risk. As is evident from the fact that this curve slopes upward to the right, this manager is willing to accept greater risks if he obtains a higher expected rate of return. Specifically, he is indifferent between a riskless investment yielding an 8-percent return and a risky investment ($\sigma = 2$) yielding an expected 12-percent return. In other words, as the risk rises, bigger expected profits are required to compensate for the higher risk.

The difference between the expected rate of return on a particular (risky) investment and that on a riskless investment is called the **risk premium** on this (risky) investment. For example, if the manager in Figure 15.7 can obtain an

---

FIGURE

15.7

Manager's Indifference Curve between Expected Rate of Return and Risk

The manager is indifferent between a riskless rate of return of 8 percent and gambles with the expected rate of return and risk shown in the figure. Similar indifference curves exist for riskless rates of return other than 8 percent.

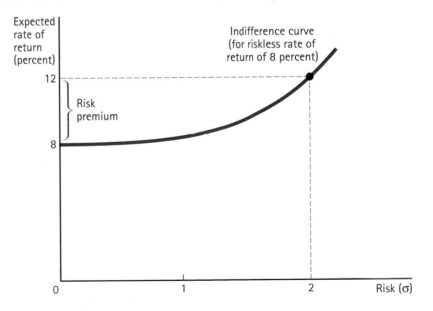

8-percent rate of return from a riskless investment, he will require a risk premium of 4 percent (that is, 12 percent minus 8 percent) to compensate for the level of risk corresponding to $\sigma = 2$. This is the extra rate of return required to induce him to make such a risky investment. If he is offered less than this 4-percent risk premium, he will not make the investment.

Because the required rate of return depends on how risky the investment is, we can adjust the basic valuation model in equation (15.7) to take account of risk by modifying the discount rate, i. The adjusted version of equation (15.7) is

$$PV = \sum_{t=1}^{n} \frac{\pi_j}{(1 + r)^t} \qquad (15.8)$$

where r is the risk-adjusted discount rate. The risk-adjusted discount rate is the sum of the riskless rate of return and the risk premium required to compensate for the investment's level of risk. If the risk is such that $\sigma = 2$, the risk-adjusted discount rate would be 12 percent for the manager in Figure 15.7. This risk-adjusted rate equals 8 percent (the riskless rate) plus 4 percent (the risk premium).[11]

Simulation Techniques

Confronted with decisions involving millions of dollars for which the risks are very substantial, managers frequently find simulation techniques to be useful. To illustrate the use of such techniques, suppose the officials of a chemical company must decide whether to build a new plant. The rate of return from the investment in this new plant depends on a number of factors: the capital cost of the plant, the plant's operating costs, the useful life of the plant, the size of the market for the product made by the plant, the price of this product, and this plant's share of the market. The firm's managers are uncertain concerning all these factors, but they and their staffs can provide probability distributions for the value of each factor. These probability distributions are shown in Figure 15.8.

Based on these probability distributions, a computer program can be developed to simulate what may occur. The computer picks one value at random from each of the probability distributions in Figure 15.8 and determines the rate of return from investing in the new plant (or the net present value) if these values prevail. For example, suppose that the computer picks a value of $2 million for the cost of the plant, $3 per pound for the plant's operating costs, five years for the useful life of the plant, $200 million for the market for the plant's product, $15 per pound for the price of this product, and 15 percent for this plant's share of the market. On the basis of these figures, the computer calculates the rate of return from the investment in the new plant.

This procedure is repeated over and over. The computer picks one set of values for the factors determining the rate of return from the investment, then a

FIGURE 15.8

Probability Distributions for Factors Determining the Rate of Return from Investment in a New Plant*

The computer picks one value at random from each of these probability distributions and calculates the rate of return. This is repeated over and over.

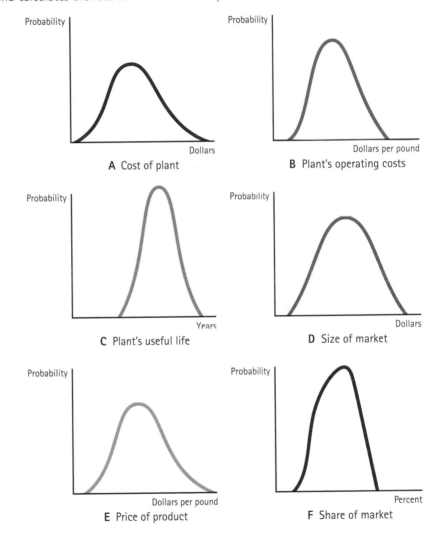

A Cost of plant

B Plant's operating costs

C Plant's useful life

D Size of market

E Price of product

F Share of market

*In contrast to Figure 15.5, these probability distributions are drawn as continuous curves. Depending on the circumstances, these variables can be regarded as continuous or discrete.

second set, then a third set, and so on. After picking each set of values, the computer calculates the rate of return on the investment. In this way, the computer builds a frequency distribution of the rate of return. For example, the frequency distribution of the rate of return from this investment may be as shown in Figure 15.9. This frequency distribution can be of great use to managers, because it summarizes concisely and effectively the extent of the risks involved in building the new plant. As pointed out in previous sections, the standard deviation (or coefficient of variation) of this frequency distribution can be used as a rough measure of risk and, together with the mean, can be used in the sorts of analyses discussed in previous sections.

While simulation techniques of this kind are of great value, it is important to recognize that the results are no better than the original probability distributions fed into the computer. So, if the probability distributions in Figure 15.8 are wildly in error, it is foolish to expect the results in Figure 15.9 to be dependable. Because it frequently is expensive to obtain good estimates of the original probability distributions, this means that simulation studies of this kind, if carried out well, tend to be done to shed light only on major decisions, not minor ones.

A rougher procedure, called **sensitivity analysis**, is also worth considering. Rather than deriving the probability distributions in Figure 15.8, some analysts

FIGURE
15.9

Frequency Distribution of Calculated Rate of Return from Investment in a New Plant

This is the frequency distribution resulting from the procedure described in Figure 15.8 being performed repeatedly.

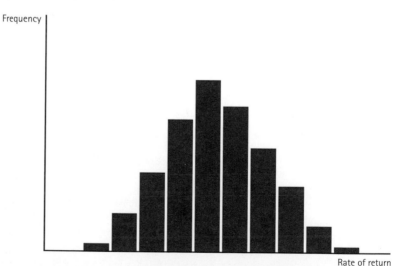

put together estimates of each factor (cost of plant, operating costs, and so on) that represent their best judgment of what will occur. Then, they vary each of these values (within reasonable limits) to see how sensitive the rate of return is to each one. The results indicate which factors are worth studying further, since there is little point in studying those factors that have only a minor effect on the results.

Application of the Maximin Rule

Throughout this chapter, we have been concerned with risk, not uncertainty. Risk occurs where the outcome is not certain but the probability of each possible outcome is known or can be estimated. **Uncertainty** refers to a situation where these probabilities are unknown. Although managerial economists have devised a number of types of rules to help a decision maker choose among alternative courses of action under conditions of uncertainty, none of these rules is universally considered to be preferable. All of them have disadvantages and difficulties. To illustrate the sorts of rules that have been proposed and their limitations, we take up the maximin rule.

According to this rule the decision maker should determine the worst outcome that could occur if each possible course of action is chosen and choose the course of action where this worst outcome is best. Consider a situation where the Jones Corporation, the hypothetical producer of automobile tires, must decide whether to move its production facilities from one location to another. The Jones Corporation is concerned that, if the tax authorities in the new location were to raise taxes, such a move might cut its profits considerably. As shown in Table 15.2, the Jones Corporation believes that if it moves its facilities and a tax increase occurs, it would lose $5 million. If it moves its facilities and a tax increase does not occur, it would gain $20 million. And, if it does not move its facilities, it would gain (and lose) nothing.

The Jones Corporation, if it applies the maximin rule, should determine the worst outcome under each course of action. There are two possible courses of

---

TABLE 15.2

Jones Corporation's Gains (or Losses), with or without a Tax Increase, If a Tax Increase Does or Does Not Occur

Course of action	Outcome	
	Tax increase	No tax increase
Firm moves facilities	−$5 million	$20 million
Firm does not move facilities	Zero	Zero

Using Simulation Techniques in the Computer Industry

In 1990, a major computer manufacturer was considering two investment projects. The first project involved a new technology requiring significant research. Because the technology was new and it was hard to know whether the project would result in the desired results, considerable risks were involved. The second project was based on existing technology. It called for incremental changes in technology and operations and was felt to be less risky than the first project.

To compare projects of this sort, this firm has generally used analytical techniques that pay limited attention to the riskiness of the project. Using these techniques, the firm's analysts found that the two projects seemed to be about equally attractive. However, the firm's management was concerned about the large number of unknowns hidden in the sales, cost, and profit estimates for the first project.

Eventually, it was decided to use a simulation study to compare the attractiveness of the two projects. For each project, probability distributions of sales and costs were estimated. The computer then picked one value of sales at random from the probability distribution of sales and one value of costs at random from the probability distribution

of costs. Then the computer calculated the discounted profit. This calculation was carried out repeatedly, first for one project then for the other. Based on these calculations, a frequency distribution of discounted profit for each project was constructed; the results are shown in the graph.

On the basis of these results, it was clear that the probability of a substantial loss was much higher with the first project than with the second project, as the firm's management had thought. Indeed, this probability was so high that the firm decided to reject the first project in favor of the second project. This is a good example of how the simulation techniques described on pages 630 to 633 have actually been used.

It is also a good illustration of the importance of taking proper account of risk. As Sandy Kurtzig, former head of ASK Computer Systems, put it, "Charting the future in business can be like one of those game shows where you have to choose from door #1, door #2, or door #3. You can as easily walk away with the set of carving knives as the trip to Hawaii."*

*S. Kurtzig, with T. Parker, *CEO: Building a $400 Million Company from the Ground Up* (New York: Norton, 1991).

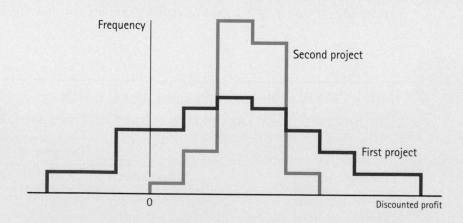

action: The firm can move its facilities or not move them. Regardless of which course of action is chosen, there are two possible outcomes: A tax increase can occur or not. If these facilities are moved, the worst outcome is a $5 million loss that will result if a tax increase occurs. If these facilities are not moved, the worst (and only) outcome is a zero gain. If the Jones Corporation applies the maximin rule, it should not move its facilities. Why? Because the worst outcome if these facilities are not moved is preferable to the worst outcome if they are moved.

Whether a tax increase will occur at the new location will not be determined by a rival or competitor who is out to inflict damages on the Jones Corporation. Instead, it will be determined by a host of political, economic, social, and other factors that have little to do with this particular firm. For this and other reasons, the maximin rule has been criticized as being overly conservative. Because there is no reason why the firm should assume that the relevant political, economic, social, and other factors are out to hurt it, there is no reason why it should pay attention only to the worst outcome that can occur if each course of action is taken.

Many rules other than the maximin rule have been proposed to help people make decisions under conditions of uncertainty.[12] However, each of these rules has its problems and limitations. Which, if any, is appropriate depends on the attitudes toward risk and the financial resources of the decision maker, as well as on the other aspects of the situation. No single rule can be applied universally to decision making under uncertainty. The truth is that, in situations in which the probability of each outcome cannot be estimated (even roughly), it is very difficult to provide managers with general guidelines for decision making.

Summary

1. The probability of an event is the proportion of times that this event occurs over the long run. Expected profit is the sum of the amount of money gained (or lost) if each outcome occurs times the probability of occurrence of the outcome.

2. A decision tree is a graphical representation of a decision problem as a series of choices, each of which is depicted by a decision fork or chance fork. A decision tree can be used to determine the course of action with the highest expected profit. A variety of examples were discussed, including Tomco Oil Corporation's decision on whether to drill an oil well at a site in Kansas.

3. The expected value of perfect information is the increase in expected profit if the decision maker could obtain completely accurate information con-

---

[12]Some examples are Bayes's rule, the maximax rule, the Hurwicz rule, and L. J. Savage's minimax regret rule. See W. Baumol, *Economic Theory and Operations Analysis* (2nd ed.; Englewood Cliffs, NJ: Prentice-Hall, 1965); and M. Shubik, "A Note on Decision-Making under Uncertainty," in *Managerial Economics and Operations Research*, ed. Mansfield.

cerning the outcome of the relevant situation (but he or she does not yet know what this information will be). This is the maximum amount that the decision maker should pay to obtain such information. Methods are provided to enable you to calculate the expected value of perfect information.

4. Risk is often measured by the standard deviation or coefficient of variation of the probability distribution of profit. Whether a decision maker wants to maximize expected profit depends on his or her attitude toward risk. The decision maker's attitude toward risk can be measured by his or her utility function.

5. To construct such a utility function, we begin by setting the utility attached to two monetary values arbitrarily. Then, we present the decision maker with a choice between the certainty of one of the other monetary values and a gamble in which the possible outcomes are the two monetary values whose utilities we set arbitrarily. Repeating this procedure over and over, we can construct the decision maker's utility function.

6. One way to adjust the basic valuation model for risk is to use certainty equivalents in place of the expected profit figures in equation (15.7). To do this, construct indifference curves (based on the decision maker's utility function) showing the certainty equivalent corresponding to various uncertain outcomes.

7. Another way to introduce risk into the valuation model is to adjust the discount rate. To do this, construct indifference curves between expected rate of return and risk, based on the decision maker's utility function. Using such indifference curves, you can estimate the risk premium (if any) that is appropriate.

8. *Uncertainty* refers to a situation in which the relevant probabilities cannot be estimated. According to the maximin rule, the decision maker under uncertainty should choose the course of action for which the worst possible outcome is least damaging. There are important problems with this rule, as well as with others proposed to handle the situation of uncertainty.

Problems

1. The president of the Martin Company is considering two alternative investments, X and Y. If each investment is carried out, there are four possible outcomes. The present value of net profit and probability of each outcome follows:

Investment X			Investment Y		
Outcome	Net present value	Probability	Outcome	Net present value	Probability
1	$20 million	0.2	A	$12 million	0.1
2	8 million	0.3	B	9 million	0.3
3	10 million	0.4	C	16 million	0.1
4	3 million	0.1	D	11 million	0.5

   a. What is the expected present value, standard deviation, and coefficient of variation of investment X?

   b. What is the expected present value, standard deviation, and coefficient of variation of investment Y?

   c. Which investment is riskier?

   d. The president of the Martin Company has the utility function

$$U = 10 + 5P - 0.01P^2$$

where U is utility and P is net present value. Which investment should she choose?

2. William J. Bryan is the general manager of an electrical equipment plant. He must decide whether to install a number of assembly robots in his plant. This investment would be quite risky, since both management and the work-force have no real experience with the introduction or operation of such robots. His indifference curve between expected rate of return and risk is as shown in the figure.

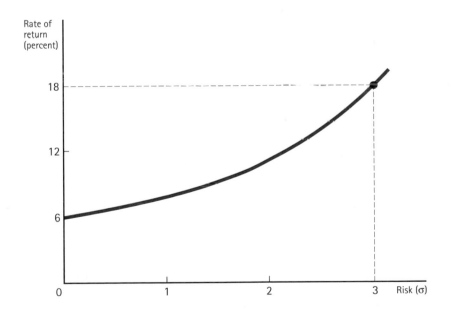

   a. If the riskiness (σ) of this investment equals 3, what risk premium does he require?

   b. What is the riskless rate of return?

   c. What is the risk-adjusted discount rate?

   d. In calculating the present value of future profits from this investment, what interest rate should be used?

3. The Zodiac Company is considering the development of a new type of plastic. Whether the plastic will be successful depends on the outcome of a research project being carried out at a major university. Zodiac's executives have no reasonably reliable means of estimating the university research team's probability of success. Zodiac's gains (or losses), depending on the outcome of the university research project, are as follows:

	Outcome of university research project	
Action	Success	Failure
Zodiac develops plastic	$50 million	−$8 million
Zodiac does not develop plastic	0	0

    a. If the firm's executives use the maximin rule, should they develop the new type of plastic?

    b. What are the disadvantages of the maximin rule?

    c. On the basis of the information given, can you calculate the expected value of perfect information? Why or why not?

4. The Electro Corporation, which manufactures television sets, has a fixed cost of $1 million per year. The gross profit from each TV set sold—that is, the price less the average variable cost—is $20. The expected value of the number of sets the company sells per year is 100,000. The standard deviation of the number of sets sold per year is 10,000.

    a. What is the expected value of the firm's annual profit?

    b. What is the standard deviation of the firm's annual profit?

    c. What is the coefficient of variation of the firm's annual profit?

5. Richard Miller, a Wall Street trader, says he is risk neutral. Suppose we let 0 be the utility he attaches to $100,000 and 1 be the utility he attaches to $200,000. If what he says is true, what is the utility he attaches to (a) $400,000? (b) $40,000? (c) −$20,000?

6. The chief executive officer of a publishing company says she is indifferent between the certainty of receiving $7,500 and a gamble where there is a 0.5 chance of receiving $5,000 and a 0.5 chance of receiving $10,000. Also, she says she is indifferent between the certainty of receiving $10,000 and a gamble where there is a 0.5 chance of receiving $7,500 and a 0.5 chance of receiving $12,500.

    a. Draw (on a piece of graph paper) four points on the utility function of this publishing executive.

    b. Does she seem to be a risk averter, a risk lover, or risk neutral? Explain.

7. The Oahu Trading Company is considering the purchase of a small firm that produces clocks. Oahu's management feels there is a 50–50 chance, if Oahu

buys the firm, that it can mold the firm into an effective producer of washing machine parts. If the firm can be transformed in this way, Oahu believes that it will make $500,000 if it buys the firm; if it cannot be transformed in this way, Oahu believes that it will lose $400,000.

a. Construct a decision tree to represent Oahu's problem.

b. What are the decision forks? (Is there more than one?)

c. What are the chance forks? (Is there more than one?)

d. Use the decision tree to solve Oahu's problem. In other words, assuming that the firm wants to maximize the expected extra profit, should Oahu buy the firm or not?

e. Before Oahu makes a decision concerning the purchase of the firm, Oahu's president learns that, if the clock producer cannot be made into an effective producer of washing machine parts, there is a 0.2 probability that it can be resold to a Saudi Arabian syndicate at a profit of $100,000. (If the firm cannot be resold, Oahu will lose $400,000.)

(1) Does this information alter the decision tree?

(2) Can you think of three mutually exclusive outcomes if Oahu buys the firm?

(3) What is the probability of each of these outcomes?

(4) What is the monetary value to Oahu of each of these outcomes?

f. Use your results in part e to solve Oahu's problem under this new set of conditions. In other words, on the basis of this new information, should Oahu buy the firm or not?

g. Oahu's executive vice president discovers an error in the estimate of how much Oahu will gain if it buys the clock manufacturer and turns it into an effective producer of washing machine parts.

(1) Under the circumstances in part d, how big would this error have to be to reverse the indicated decision?

(2) Under the circumstances in part e, how big would the error have to be to reverse the indicated decision?

8. According to Cal Tech's Nobel Prize–winning physicist the late Richard Feynman, the National Aeronautics and Space Administration (NASA) estimated the probability of a crash of the space shuttle to be 1 in 100,000, whereas the probability was in fact closer to about 0.01 to 0.02. If a decision tree had been used to determine whether to attempt a launch of the shuttle, what difference, if any, would this have made?

9. The *East Chester Tribune* must decide whether to publish a Sunday edition. The publisher thinks the probability is 0.6 that a Sunday edition would be a success and 0.4 that it would be a failure. If it is a success, she will gain $100,000. If it is a failure, she will lose $80,000.

a. Construct the decision tree corresponding to the problem, and use backward induction to solve the problem. (Assume that the publisher is risk neutral.)

b. List all forks in the decision tree you constructed, then indicate whether each is a decision fork or a chance fork and state why.

10. Roy Lamb has an option on a particular piece of land, and must decide whether to drill on the land before the expiration of the option or give up his rights. If he drills, he believes that the cost will be $200,000. If he finds oil, he expects to receive $1 million; if he does not find oil, he expects to receive nothing.

a. Construct a decision tree to represent Lamb's decision.

b. Can you tell whether he should drill on the basis of the available information? Why or why not?

   Mr. Lamb believes that the probability of finding oil if he drills on this piece of land is $\frac{1}{4}$, and the probability of not finding oil if he drills here is $\frac{3}{4}$.

c. Can you tell whether he should drill on the basis of the available information? Why or why not?

d. Suppose Mr. Lamb can be demonstrated to be a risk lover. Should he drill or not? Why?

e. Suppose Mr. Lamb is risk neutral. Should he drill or not?

Auctions

chapter 16

Revenues from online auctions increased from $6.5 billion in 2000 to over $30 billion in 2003. Experts expect revenue from online auctions to grow by 68 percent through 2006. This dramatic increase in auction usage has caught the attention of federal officials, who purchase over $200 billion worth of goods each year. They are currently experimenting with small online auctions, but want to create agencywide e-commerce acquisition processes whose centerpiece will be online markets, including auctions. But, like the private sector, the government is uncertain about how the use of these auctions will alter the procurement process. As Dennis Rabkin of acquisition policy at General Services Administration (GSA) says, "We don't know all the answers yet. We don't really know where you can't go or shouldn't go with the tool [online auctions]; and I don't know how far or broadly the tool should be defined. We want some feedback."[1]

To obtain this feedback, in October of 2000, the government issued Special Notice #2712, which asks private companies and individuals for their advice on

[1]Douglas Brown, "Feds Seek Advice on Reverse Auctions," *E-Commerce News*, November 16, 2000. See www.zdnet.com/e-commerce/stories.

an e-commerce acquisition process. Of particular interest to the government are issues of auction structure: mechanism, price transparency, auction length, and ownership. Or, as the report states, "How are pricing models, discounts, and volume pricing contracts established and maintained within an eCommerce/service provider/exchange relationship?"[2] These questions are echoed by managers in the private sector as they see the use of B2B auction sites explode in number. Over $30 billion in revenue was generated worldwide by these sites in 2003; some estimate this number will increase threefold by 2005.

B2C auction sites are following a similar growth trajectory. Online auction sales to consumers totaled over $11 billion in 2003 and are expected to grow to over $20 billion in 2005. The message is clear: Auction markets will play an integral role in the next 20 years, and those managers who understand them best will realize added value from their use. Managers who do not understand them run the risk of being closed out of these fast-growing markets or, even worse, seeing an erosion of firm value, as rivals use auctions to gain competitive advantages. And, e-commerce is not the only area experiencing an increase in auctions. Auction use is increasing in corporate acquisition activities and electronic trading markets.

This chapter examines structural parameters of auctions and shows how managers can manipulate them to affect revenue generation. All auctions, like markets, are governed by rules and procedures. Managers who understand these rules can design auctions to generate higher revenues. We focus on the auction mechanism, for as you will see, this parameter can significantly influence the behavior of auction participants. We also show that managers need not abandon the sophisticated pricing strategies discussed earlier just because they employ an auction format. Performance-enhancing strategies like price discrimination are still feasible even within auctions.

Also, managers will find a good understanding of auction theory is helpful in other areas. The theory is used to help develop behavioral implications in negotiations and monopoly markets. And, since much of auction theory is game theoretical in nature, many of the principles we discussed in Chapter 14 can be applied to auction settings.

A Short History of Auctions

The first written record of an auction was the annual Babylonian marriage market described by Herodotus, "the father of history." The socially aware Babylonians actually structured the auction to ensure that all women who wanted husbands found them. The most beautiful women were auctioned first, their bidders being the rich who could afford to pay for beauty. More modest-looking

---

[2]United States Department of Commerce, Special Notice #2712, October 24, 2000.

women then participated in a negative bid auction. The man with the lowest negative bid received the woman at his bid price. This price was then paid from funds generated by the beautiful women. Not only did this ensure that all willing women were married; it also provided the newlyweds with financial support.

Auctions were used in ancient Greece to award mineral rights and by Roman authorities to collect debts owed by individuals. Cicero reports a court case in 80 B.C. involving the auctioning of goods to satisfy a debt. In 1556, the French monarch appointed an officer to appraise and auction all property left by those executed by the state. Pepys reports on a candle auction of 1660. Candle auctions gave bidders a limited time to bid (until the candle burned out); they are the forerunner of today's timed auctions on eBay.

Auctions almost caused a continuation of the War of 1812. During the war, English goods were prohibited from being imported to the United States. The end of the war saw British merchants flooding the United States with goods to satisfy the pent-up demand. The goods were sold via auction because of the speed by which goods could be allocated (this also being one reason auctions and the Internet are such a good match). American manufacturers claimed the British were dumping the goods (selling below cost) and tried to get the auctions outlawed. Newspapers and U.S. trade organizations led a spirited fight to get state legislatures to abolish auctions. The fight even extended to the U.S. Congress, where the Ways and Means Committee actually introduced a bill to ban auctions. Fortunately, Congress never passed the bill.

Although markets grew quicker than auctions, auctions played a major role in the allocation of fruits and vegetables, fish, furs, tobacco, and livestock. By the 1980s, auctions were used to sell over $5 billion of goods yearly.

Auction use continued to increase and virtually exploded in the late 1990s with the increase in e-commerce. This exponential increase in use will continue, for the Internet is to auctions what mass retailing was to posted prices, a highly productive marriage of technology and allocation mechanism. Internet use significantly decreases organizational costs, a binding constraint on auction revenue. In most auctions, if I am the seller, "the more the merrier" (this idea is shown more formally later in the chapter). Expected revenue never decreases with increases in the number of bidders. So any technology that decreases the costs of bringing individuals together should increase auction use.

Types of Auction Mechanisms

All auctions involve a bidding process. In most auctions, a service or product is made available and buyers bid for the ownership rights. Reverse auctions occur when a buyer announces the need for a product or service and sellers bid for the right to sell the buyer the good or service. Whether using a normal or reverse auction, managers primarily use one of four auction mechanisms: the

English, or ascending-bid auction; the Dutch, or descending-bid auction; the sealed-bid auction; and the second-price, sealed-bid auction.

English, or Ascending-Bid, Auction

In English auctions, the initial price is set at the seller's reservation price (called the *reserve price*). Buyers then bid against each other with a succession of increasingly higher prices until only one bidder remains. This final bidder receives the good or service at his or her final stated price. There are several ways to manage this bidding procedure. An auctioneer can orally call out bids, bidders signal their acceptance of the price with a shake of their head or a wave of their bidding card. This method is used often by the large auction houses like Christie's and Sotheby's. Another method is for bidders themselves to call out their bids. This method is used by many commodity exchanges. Individual commodities are assigned their own area, called a *pit*; traders of a commodity gather in the pit and call out the price at which they are willing to buy (sell) the commodity. If others wish to sell (buy) at that price, they do so. English auctions are also conducted electronically. Here, the highest present bid is posted; others who want to bid higher are free to do so, and their bid then becomes the current high bid. Many Internet auction sites, including eBay, use this electronic format.

Two special cases of an ascending-bid auction are the Japanese auction and the ascending-bid timed auction. Much theoretical work has centered on the Japanese auction. In these auctions, bidders bid until the price exceeds their reservation price. They then drop out of the bidding process and do not return. Remaining bidders can thus determine who has dropped out and who remains. In the ascending-bid timed auction, the bidding continues for a specified period of time. The high bidder at the end of this period receives the good or service (assuming the bid is greater than the seller's reserve price). These timed auctions are used extensively by Internet auction sites.

Dutch, or Descending-Bid, Auction

In these auctions, initial prices are very high. This price is announced and then a set time passes (for example, 15 seconds). If no bidder accepts the good at that price, the price is lowered a set interval (for example, a dollar) and the procedure repeats itself. The price is lowered until one bidder accepts the announced price. The descending bid is often called a *Dutch auction* because it is used to sell flowers in the Netherlands. Here, auction halls larger than 10 football fields are used daily to auction thousands of flowers. Current offered prices are shown on a large screen, and bidders accept the price by pushing electronic buttons. The process is very quick, with over 500 transactions every hour.

Sealed-Bid Auction

In these auctions, bidders submit price bids known only to themselves. So, unlike an English auction, bidders do not know the valuation of others. In a first-price, sealed-bid auction, bids are opened at a preannounced time, and the high-valuation bidder receives the item at his or her stated price. Reverse sealed-bid auctions are often used for procurement of goods and services. So a state may submit a bid for highway construction, with the winning bidder being the one with the lowest bid.

Second-Price, Sealed-Bid Auction

This auction is a variant of the sealed-bid type of auction. In a second-price auction, the highest bidder receives the good or service at the bid of the second-highest bidder. These auctions are also called *Vickrey auctions*, after William Vickrey who wrote a seminal paper on the subject in the 1960s, which later led to his award of the 1996 Nobel Prize in economics. As we shall see, second-price auctions have characteristics conducive to bidders truthfully revealing their valuations.

Auction Mechanism and Revenue Generation

Similar to market settings, in auctions, managers want to maximize profit. And, as differences in structural parameters like differentiation, entry barriers, and location explain variance in market power (and profitability), auction rules explain variance in generated revenues. An advantage for auctions is that, relative to markets, it is easier (and less costly) for managers to influence structural parameters through auction rules. Hence, it pays for managers to recognize how auction design influences revenues. We examine the effect of auction rules on revenue by first looking at a simplified model. We then relax some model assumptions to show how rules affect revenue.

Our baseline case assumes that bidders are symmetric, risk neutral, and bids are based on independent signals drawn from a commonly known distribution. The behavioral implications of these assumptions are explained next:

- *Bidders are symmetric.* Think of a bidder as selecting a valuation (bid) from a distribution of possible bids. Symmetric bidders use similar distributions, commonly known to all. So, bidders with identical reservation prices and observing the same signal submit equivalent bids. We emphasize that (as in the real world) differences in reservation prices across bidders is not constrained by this symmetry.
- *Bidders are risk neutral.* That is, bidders bid to maximize expected values and not risk-adjusted utility. Most assume individuals are risk averse; how-

ever, evidence shows that when individuals "decide" as corporate agents, behavior resembles that of risk neutrality. That said, we later show how risk-averse bidders can be strategically exploited.

- *Signals are independent.* Signals are independent in one of two ways. In **private-value auctions**, reservation prices are a function of information and utility. Since signals depend on the information space, valuation is constrained to one's own signal. So, say, you find yourself standing next to me at an art auction. Are differences in how we value a painting a function of our own personal experience, or does what happens to you (but is unknown to me) affect my valuation? The former sounds more plausible. This describes a private-value auction with independent signals.

  In **common-value auctions**, all bidders value the good similarly. What is not known, though, is the true value of the good for which they bid. Consider the rights for minerals under a piece of land. Whatever is down there is worth about the same for all (given worldwide commodity markets), but none knows perfectly what is there. So each bidder measures and forms beliefs about the true value. If signals are independent, then what I estimate does not depend on the estimate of others, although the distribution of signals is commonly known.

For any auction format, let b = bid and p = price paid by the auction winner. So expected profit is simply $(b - p)(\text{Pr}_w)$, with Pr_w = the probability of winning the auction, conditioned on bid level. Since managers want to maximize profits, optimal bids depend on valuations (reservation prices). Therefore, expected profits for any b, Pr_w combination is given by

$$U(\text{Pr}_w, b, p) = (\text{Pr}_w)(b - p)$$

We can compare these profit functions across auction formats to determine how surplus $(b - p)$ is split between buyer and seller. We can show that the slope of the profit function equals the conditional probability of winning for any given bid. So, auction formats with identical surplus functions (conditioned on valuation) offer the same probability of winning at any given bid and hence recommend the same optimal strategies.

This relationship is the foundation for what is called the **revenue equivalence theorem**. The theorem shows that, whether a manager chooses an English, Dutch, sealed-bid, or second-price, sealed-bid auction, that choice does not affect the expected total surplus generated by the auction and hence does not affect the expected revenues of the seller. The theorem can even be extended to other auction formats. As long as the format ensures an efficient allocation of goods and gives zero profit to any bidder holding zero value ($0) for the good, then the surplus functions are identical and, hence, so are the recommended bidding strategies across formats. For example, lobbying efforts can be modeled as an "all-pay" auction. All bidders pay for the good but only the highest bidder receives it. Because this auction satisfies the stated conditions, its expected surplus is the same as any of the four standard auction formats.

Bidding Strategies

So what are the optimal bidding strategies across the four auction formats? Of the four standard formats, only English auctions give bidders an opportunity to learn more about the reservation price of others. In the sealed-bid format, bids of others are not revealed until after the bidding period is closed. In Dutch auctions, once a bidder reveals his or her reservation price (by accepting the current price) the auction is over. But, because of the ascending nature of the English auction and the public nature of bidding, bidders learn more about the reservation price of others. Unfortunately, this information is of limited value to the strategic bidder, for optimal behavior in these auctions is defined by a dominant strategy. And, if you remember, smart strategists do not worry about the behavior of others in using a dominant strategy, since it lacks strategic value. So optimal behavior in an ascending auction never changes. The bidder should always be willing to bid up to his or her reservation price.

Basically, this rule maximizes profit $(b - p)$. Clearly, you never bid above your reservation price unless you wish to suffer negative profit. Because profit always decreases with an increase in bid, why bid higher than necessary? After all, the winner in an ascending auction has to pay only the slightest bit (i.e., epsilon) higher than the reservation price of the second-highest bidder. Any bid above this amount is inefficient (and suggests badly trained managers, not to mention an inefficient format). The difference between the reservation prices of the top and second-highest bidders defines available surplus and, therefore, profits. If we want to maximize profits, then we must capture all available surplus.

The auction's dominant strategy helps managers reduce the complexity of strategic thought. Consider the strategy as a decision rule: You listen to any bid. If the bid is lower than your reservation price, you bid incrementally higher. If higher, do not bid. The simplicity of the procedure highlights one component of a dominant strategy's value: process efficiencies. Managers need not consider what others might do in choosing an optimal strategy. So managers can focus (and simplify) the strategic effort, trusting the completeness of dominance.

In any ascending-price auction be willing to bid to your reservation price. If everyone follows this strategy, then the item is sold at the reservation price of the second-highest bidder (well, actually, an epsilon higher). It is sold to the highest bidder, and his or her expected revenue is the total available surplus, defined as the reservation price differential between the two highest valuation bidders.

Now, some may ask, is it true, in first-price ascending auctions, that the highest bidder receives the item at the reservation price (plus epsilon) of the second-highest bidder? If the auction is efficient he or she does, and furthermore we shall show how this holds true across all four auction mechanisms.

So, in an ascending auction, the highest bidder claims the item at the reservation price of the second-highest bidder. We previously noted that this is the same prediction of the Vickrey auctions (those sealed-bid affairs in which the highest bidder claims the item at the reservation price of the second-highest bidder). So both English and second-price, sealed-bid auctions are ruled by the same dominant strategy. Though the two auctions differ in process, game theorists predict similar results. Of course, the latter format is more transparent than the former.

Anyway, let us see how the difference in bidding rules affects the decision rule of the dominant strategy. The two auctions differ in bidding rules. In English auctions, the rules allow you to publicly bid multiple times; in the sealed-bid auction, you bid once, privately. English auctions let you respond to the bids of others; sealed-bid auctions do not. Because the bidder in a sealed-bid auction has only one chance to bid, he or she should bid his or her reservation price. Negative payoffs are nonexistent, as zero becomes the bidder's worst possible payoff. And, the bidder who wins guarantees him- or herself all the available surplus. So, while the dominant strategy remains the same—be willing to bid up to your reservation price—the bidding rules of the second-price, sealed-bid auction require a slight revision of our managerial decision rule: *Bid your reservation price.* Managers who do so guarantee themselves the highest expected surplus. Do not worry about others (it does you no good); focus on your own preferences and think hard about your reservation price—then bid it.

Second-price, sealed-bid auctions are also a good example of how auction rules can change bidding behavior. The rules encourage all bidders to tell the truth. In fact, you are better off if you tell the truth. In a later discussion, we call such rules **incentive compatible**. These are rules that encourage individuals to reveal their true preferences.

Next, consider the descending (Dutch) and first-price, sealed-bid auctions. Although the two operate with different bidding rules, they are strategically similar. In fact, consider them identical twins that behave differently, for their behavior (as governed by their rules) is the only way to tell them apart. If we model them in their reduced normal form (matrix form), they have identical strategy sets and payoffs. That is, any given bid yields the same payoff in either auction, as a function of the bids of others. And, unlike the ascending or second-price formats, neither has a dominant strategy. In the Dutch or first-price, sealed-bid auctions, one must consider what others will bid. Let us see how this affects a manager's bid choice.

As explained earlier, bidders learn little about the valuations of others in either of these first-price auctions because bids are private until the auction is completed. But, because bidders are symmetric, all know the distribution of valuations. This information gives bidders the ability to anticipate the bidding strategy of others. Note that it does not give them the ability to predict the bids of others, just what others would bid conditional on some privately known information.

Each bidder is faced with an identical decision. If the bid is not the highest, he or she receives and pays nothing, so the surplus is zero. If he or she bids her reservation price and that bid is the highest, the surplus is still zero. A bid higher than his or her reservation price results in zero surplus (if the bidder is lucky and loses the auction) or negative surplus, if he or she wins. And, the bidder knows there is some positive probability that his or her bid is the highest. So what should he or she bid?

Unlike the previous types of auctions, the set of possible strategies approaches infinity in the descending and first-price, sealed-bid auctions. That is, dominant strategies exist for ascending and second-price, sealed-bid auctions, but not for Dutch or first-price, sealed-bid auctions. Managers now must consider what others will bid. Bidding strategies become conditional on bidding strategies of others. The world becomes more complex.

So how do you reduce the complexity? If you cannot get the feasible set reduced to one, how about at least a finite number? Since all bidders face the same complexity, can bidders help themselves via some constraint on bidding behavior? Well, economists believe they can by being rational. Rational players consider only those outcomes in which each player maximizes, given the actions of others. Unless we are all doing our best, given the actions of others, why should anyone agree to it? And, if we do adopt this rule, then no individual has an incentive to cheat by changing strategy.

As mentioned in Chapter 14, in **Nash equilibria**, all correctly anticipate the actions of others and choose those actions that maximize expected surplus. Often, its use reduces feasible strategies to a handful and aids in managerial efficiency. Note that the Nash equilibrium is not a promise that, under some conditions, your expected surplus is higher than that of all others. It simply states that, given your attributes and those of others, you are doing the best you possibly can.

What is the Nash solution to the descending and first-price, sealed auctions? What should we assume others are doing, and what is our optimal response to their actions? Well, we have already seen that we do not want to bid our reservation price because our highest possible payoff is then zero. But, what if everyone thinks about his or her reservation price and then discounts back from that? And, the discount is equal to what their expectations are of the reservation price of the second-highest bidder. Then, if our bid is the highest, we receive positive surplus; if it is not, we receive nothing and lose nothing. As in the ascending and second-price auctions, we must consider our reservation price, but in addition, we now must consider what others will bid and base our bid on this expectation. So our decision rule is to estimate the reservation price of the second-highest bidder and bid that.

Note that our beliefs about the reservation price of the second-highest bidder are influenced by the number of bidders. Basically, the greater is the number of bidders, the closer to our reservation price we should bid. We can be even more precise if we assume the distribution of bids is uniform. Then, our optimal bidding strategy is

$$B = v - [(v - L)/n]$$

where v is the bidder's reservation price, L is the lowest possible bid, and n is the number of bidders. For example, assume our own valuation of an item is $3, and we believe the bids will be evenly distributed between $0 and $15. Then, our optimal bid if there is only one other bidder is

$$b = 3 - [(3 - 0)/2], \quad \text{or } \$1.50$$

If there are two other bidders, then our optimal bid is

$$B = 3 - [(3 - 0)/3], \quad \text{or } \$2.00$$

And so we end where we began. It does not matter what auction format we use, because expected revenues are identical across them. The optimal response of bidders in each produces the same expected revenue. We bid up to our reservation price in ascending and second-price auctions, because the rules say, if we are the high bidder, then we have to pay only the reservation price of the second-highest bidder. In descending and first-price, sealed auctions, we consider our reservation price and discount, because the rules say the high bidder receives the item at his or her bid. But, the expected revenue is the same because the auction should yield revenue equal to the reservation price of the second-highest bidder.

Strategies for Sellers

Now, we turn to sellers. These days, many managers use auctions to sell goods, services, and assets. In these circumstances, good managerial decisions follow the standard economic rule: Maximize profits with marginal revenue equal to marginal cost. Of course, some adjustments for the bidding rules must be made.

In markets, managers want to produce where MR = MC. This is a quantity decision and it determines the pricing point. But auctions are used to sell items few in quantity (often, one). So the notion of quantity holds little strategic value when quantity is so limited. What does determine the optimal pricing point is the distribution of reservation prices across bidders. Therefore, managers want to focus on this distribution.

This is a subtle but important difference realized by the strategic manager. Consider an ascending auction. Managerial action in this format is similar to third-degree price discrimination in markets. Recall that *efficient allocation* is defined as the equality of marginal revenues across markets (the infamous $P_1/P_2 = [1 + (1/\eta_2)]/[1 + (1/\eta_1)]$. That is, managers maximize profits by ensuring sale to the consumers who value the product or service the most. Total output is determined by the horizontal summation of the marginal revenue curves and its intersection with marginal cost (see Figure 5.1).

Sellers want to use a similar strategy in auctions. Consider an auction selling a unique item. The seller maximizes profits by selling to the bidder with the highest reservation price. Because the seller's marginal costs remain constant to any change in price, the higher is the winning bid, the greater the surplus. The expected revenue generated by a given price is simply that price times the probability it is the winning bid. This, of course, is determined by the distribution of reservation prices across bidders. Consider bidder i, and the distribution $F(b)$. Given $F(b)$, we determine the probability that any bid b is the winning bid. This is simply $1 - F(b)$, as shown in Figure 16.1. Function b acts as a demand curve in the following way. Each point on b tells us the probability of that point being

FIGURE

16.1

Relationship between the Seller's Expected Revenue and the Winning Bidder's Expected Marginal Revenue

If b^* is the winning bid, the seller's expected revenue is equal to the horizontally shaded box. This is also equal to the expected marginal revenue of the bidder.

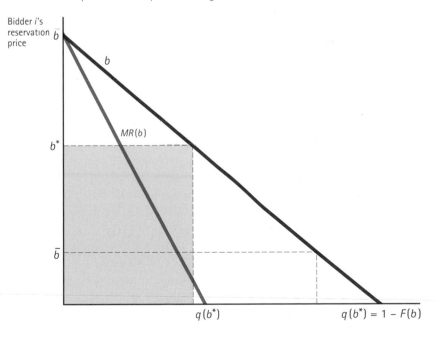

ANALYZING MANAGERIAL DECISIONS

Auction Design at FreeMarkets, Inc.

FreeMarkets is an example of how managers use online auctions to generate additional revenue. The company is a global provider of e-sourcing software and service solutions and operates the world's largest sourcing market. It is a major player in B2B Internet auctions and has been conducting them since 1995. As of December 2003, the firm has auctioned more than $70 billion worth of volume for goods and services. Managers estimate they have helped their customers identify over $14 billion in savings. Auctions are held for goods and services in over 190 supply verticals on a global basis. Firms, including Emerson Electric and Eaton Corp., use FreeMarkets as part of their purchasing process and report significant savings. For example, managers at global giant GlaxoSmithKline estimate cost savings of 10 percent. So how does FreeMarkets achieve such results?

The company combines Web-based software, in-depth supply market information, market operations, and expert sourcing services to create value-added markets for their customers. Let us examine more closely how they fashion markets to generate cost savings for their customers.

FreeMarkets e-source technology is designed to meet the needs of large industrial customers, many with global operations. These buyers use FreeMarkets to conduct real-time interactive auctions with selected suppliers. The auction format is that of descending price. Suppliers bid for the right to supply, generally, with the low bidder declared the winner (see the chart). The company identifies several areas of expertise: coordination, design, and services.

AUCTION COORDINATION All online markets are controlled from a central location. This guarantees that the markets operate correctly during the bidding process. FreeMarkets reduces software learning costs by using easily understood graphics and giving first-time bidders simulated trading sessions prior to the actual auction. Support is given to all bidders during the actual auction (in over 30 languages).

FreeMarkets has developed and enforces auction rules. For example, trade in many industrial markets is decided by factors other than low cost, like quality control or delivery logistics. FreeMarkets managers work with buyers to determine the qualification of the bidding pool. Its managers talk with those in the buying organizations about specifications, logistics, and quality. For example, all bidders could be required to be ISO-9000 certified and able to deliver within five days. Then, FreeMarkets handles bidder certification. This reduces the transaction costs to the buyer and the risk that winning (low-cost) suppliers cannot deliver promised supplies. This certification feature also helps bidders decide whether the auction is best suited to their resource base.

FreeMarkets creates a customer care center for all auctions. Here, bidders can find such services as surrogate bidding. By agreeing to act as if they were a bidder's agent, FreeMarkets eases the transaction costs of bidders.

AUCTION DESIGN The auction software is flexible to address the unique needs of different industrial markets. For example, some auctions are of the multicurrency type. This feature helps reduce the risks of both seller and buyer to currency fluctuations during the life of a long-term contract. The software is also easy to integrate into

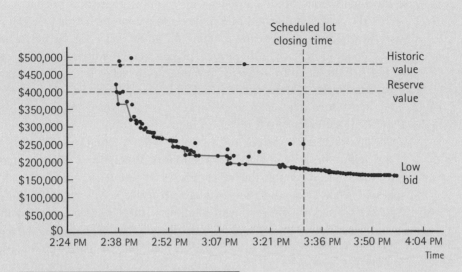

Lot summary	
Number of bidders:	16
Number of bids:	118
Historic value:	$481 thousand
Reserve value:	$397 thousand
Low bid:	$150 thousand
Potential savings:	$332 thousand (66.9%)
Savings in overtime:	$31 thousand (6.4%)

a buyer's ERP/MRP systems, which reduces the switching costs of buyers.

AUCTION SERVICES FreeMarkets gives advice to buyers about optimal auction lotting, strategies, and design. It identifies, recruits, and screens potential suppliers, reducing the risk that only qualified suppliers compete in the auction. Buyers are given postauction briefings by FreeMarkets to analyze results and make suggested changes for the future. Free-Markets has a global network of over 150,000 registered suppliers in 70 countries. It also supplies filters for searching its supplier database and maintains performance statistics on all suppliers.

Source: FreeMarkets OnLine, Inc. 1997

Note: Each dot represents a distinct bid for the lot by an individual supplier.

the winning bid. So, if the seller were to offer the item at price b, we could predict the expected demand at b. Expected revenue then is $b[1 - F(b)]$ or the area under the marginal revenue function for any b. Let b^* be the actual winning bid (the reservation price of the second-highest bidder). Mathematically, we can show that b^* represents the expected revenue to the seller and the expected marginal revenue to the winning bidder. That is, in ascending bid auctions, they are equal.

What does this mean to the seller? As in third-degree price discrimination markets, managers need to sell to high-reservation price-bidders (buyers). And, because they want to maximize surplus in both situations, they definitely cannot sell at any price below marginal costs. In auctions, consider marginal cost as the value at which the seller refuses to sell. The price at which the seller says, "If that's all others are willing to pay, I'll keep it myself." So sellers need to set a reserve price (or begin bidding at their reserve price) for the auction. And, what should this reserve price be? It should be the bid when the bidder's marginal revenue is equal to the seller's marginal cost. (Recall that the bidder's marginal revenue is also equal to the auction's expected revenue.) Hence, under general conditions, managers should consider the following decision rule in setting a reserve price:

optimal reserve price = the value of the object being auctioned off, if it does
       not sell, + (managerial estimates of the highest reservation price divided by 2)

For example, if the object's value is $0 if it is not sold, and a manager believes the highest reservation price is $300, then he or she should set a reserve price of $150. After that, sellers should sit back and relax. Let the ascending bid mechanism work, as it maximizes the expected surplus. Unlike monopoly pricing, but similar to third-degree price discrimination, auctions are often more efficient than a posted price scheme. Unlike a posted price scheme, auctions guarantee the highest reservation price at which consumers purchase the good. We note that the managerial similarity to third-degree price discrimination is not confined to ascending auctions. All formats that are revenue equivalent to ascending auctions share this feature. The following example illustrates the efficiency of auctions.

Assume a seller has four units of output at a marginal cost of $0. The market has six consumers with reservation prices of $90, $60, $50, $40, $20, and $15. Table 16.1 shows the total available surplus broken down into consumer and seller surplus if sellers use an auction. Table 16.2 shows the total surplus if sellers post a $40 price.

At any posted price other than $40, the total available surplus decreases. And, while the available surplus remains constant with a price of $40, sellers get a lower percentage of this relative to an auction ($160 versus $174). Auction usage increases seller surplus because of its price discriminatory property. The mechanism itself gets consumers to reveal their reservation prices.

TABLE 16.1

Auction

Consumers	Reservation price	Win bid
1	$40	$21
2	20	
3	15	
4	90	61
5	60	51
6	50	41
Total consumer surplus		66
Total seller surplus		174
Total available surplus		240

Value of Information

The preference-revealing nature of auctions not only guarantees the highest reservation price consumers buy (at their higher values), it also gets buyers to identify themselves when the demand is unknown. Managers can use auctions to gather more information about the demand before announcing a price schedule.

Repurchase Tender Offers

A primary example of this use of auctions is repurchase tender offers (RTO). The RTO is used by managers to buy back stock shares from current share-

TABLE 16.2

Posted Price

Consumers	Reservation price	Price paid
1	$40	$40
2	20	
3	15	
4	90	40
5	60	40
6	50	40
Total consumer surplus		80
Total seller surplus		160
Total available surplus		240

holders. Because shareholders are not required to sell, to induce selling, RTOs generally offer a premium above the current market price. Until 1981, just about every RTO was fixed in price. Managers would announce the buyback price per share and wait to see shareholder demand at that price. Since 1981, modified Dutch auction RTOs is the mechanism of managerial choice. And, it is easy to see why—relative to a fixed price RTO, the modified Dutch variety generally acquires shares at a lower total cost. Several studies show the average premium paid for fixed-price tendered shares is 15 to 20 percent while those in modified Dutch auctions average 10 to 15 percent.

Unlike a fixed-price RTO, where one price is announced, in a modified Dutch one, managers announce a price range at which they are willing to repurchase tendered shares. Generally, the minimum price is at a slight premium to market, while the maximum approaches that of a fixed price RTO. Any shareholder willing to tender reveals his or her valuations, as the seller sends managers a pricing schedule (how many shares to tender at $X). Managers then take the schedules of individual shareholders and construct a market supply schedule. They then determine how many shares they need and set the share price. All sellers who value the shares below that price receive the stated price. Again, note the timing differential between the fixed-price and modified Dutch auction RTO. In the fixed-price offer, managers set a price before knowing the supply schedule; in the modified Dutch auction, they set the price after seeing the supply schedule.

Citizens First Financial Corp. (CFFC) is a savings and loan holding company with headquarters in Bloomington, Illinois. The company has roughly $325 million in assets. Its managers wanted to repurchase 391,000 shares of its stock from shareholders. On October 31, 2000, managers announced a modified Dutch auction RTO. (The share price that day was $14.) They set a price range of $15 to $17 per share, a premium above the market of 7.1 to 21.4 percent. Shareholders had until December 1 to tender their shares. On December 11, 2000, CFFC managers announced they had purchased 391,096 shares at a price of $16 (a premium of 14.3 percent above the market).

We look at the situation as CFFC managers may have viewed it. Many times managers repurchase shares because they believe the stock is undervalued. An RTO is used by managers to distribute company value to shareholders. RTOs annually distribute over $4 billion to shareholders. Assume CFFC managers believe their stock will be worth $20 per share in the near future. They want to buy back some shares now but do not know the valuations of shareholders. After stating their beliefs, managers construct Table 16.3 to summarize them. It shows how many shares will be tendered at different prices in three possible supply scenarios—strong, medium, and weak—and the generated value associated with each price-supply scenario. The profit equals the difference between a tender price and the expected future value of $20.

| | TABLE 16.3 | Shareholder Supply Schedule | | | | | |

Shareholder Supply Schedule

Price	Strong	Profit	Medium	Profit	Weak	Profit
$15	400,000	$2,000,000	310,000	$1,550,000	280,000	$1,400,000
16	415,000	1,660,000	400,000	1,600,000	315,000	1,260,000
17	600,000	1,800,000	415,000	1,245,000	400,000	1,200,000
Probability of shareholder's willingness to tender						
	0.40		0.30		0.30	

If managers choose a fixed price RTO, they must set price before knowing the supply schedule. They might then choose a price based on an expected value basis (EV):

$$EV(\$15) = \$2,000,000(0.40) + \$1,550,000(0.30) + \$1,400,000(0.30) = \$1,685,000$$
$$EV(\$16) = \$1,660,000(0.40) + \$1,600,000(0.30) + \$1,260,000(0.30) = \$1,522,000$$
$$EV(\$17) = \$1,800,000(0.40) + \$1,245,000(0.30) + \$1,200,000(0.30) = \$1,453,500$$

If CFFC managers had used such an analysis, they might have set a tender price of $15 (and they would have fallen short of getting shareholders to tender 391,000 shares).

How might managers have increased firm value by structuring the RTO as a modified Dutch auction? If they use the auction, they will not select a tender price until after knowing the supply schedule. What is the expected value of the auction strategy? We use expected value because, when CFFC managers announce the Dutch RTO on October 11, they will not know the supply schedule. So, if the willingness to tender is strong, they will announce a price of $15; if it is medium, they will announce a price of $16; and if it is weak, a price of $15. Hence, the expected value of a modified Dutch auction RTO is

$$EV(auction) = \$2,000,000(0.40) + \$1,600,000(0.30) + \$1,400,000(0.30)$$
$$= \$1,700,000$$

So, managers are generally better off using a modified Dutch auction RTO. They get shareholders to reveal their valuations and, hence, can buy back shares at a lower price than if they used a fixed price. This creates value for the remaining shareholders, since some shares are retired at a lower cost. And, the expected number of shares tendered is

$$0.4(400,000) + 0.3(400,000) + 0.3(280,000) = 364,000$$

ANALYZING MANAGERIAL DECISIONS

The Use of Sophisticated Pricing within an Auction Format

Priceline.com is a good example of how managers can use sophisticated pricing policies within an auction format. The company was launched in April 1998 after Priceline managers helped develop software for a computer reservation system. The software gave airline managers the ability to make real-time adjustments to prices based on various factors, like unoccupied seats or competitor prices. Each airline sees only its own prices, but managers at Priceline are able to see prices across all member airlines.

Airline seats are perishable goods: Once the plane departs, empty seats are worthless, since they cannot be used again. And the marginal cost of flying a plane with one more passenger is almost zero, so any price is profitable for the airline. As Brian Ek of Priceline.com states, "The airlines fly with up to 700,000 empty seats a day. Naturally they would love to sell those seats if they could without affecting their retail fare structure." Priceline.com developed an auction mechanism to allow airlines to do just that. The company has sold over 5 million airline tickets since 1998.

Priceline.com uses a reverse auction mechanism. In reverse auctions, buyers name the price they are willing to pay for a good or service. The seller then decides whether to accept or reject this price. Priceline's auction operates as follows: A consumer specifies a departure date, the departing and destination airports, the price each is willing to pay for a ticket, and a credit card number. All sales are final. If Priceline finds a ticket at or below that price, the consumer is obligated to purchase it. After receiving a consumer's price, managers at Priceline examine their database to determine if any airline is offering tickets at or below that price. If there are tickets, Priceline buys them. The profit to Priceline is the difference between what the consumer is willing to pay for the ticket and the price Priceline was charged.

Although Priceline claims it has increased the market power of consumers (since they are free to name their own price), many disagree with the claim. Basically, Priceline's reverse auction allows the firm to practice price discrimination. Like airlines, Priceline sells tickets on the same airplane at different prices depending on the price quoted by the consumer. Say I submit a price of $300 for a ticket from New York to Chicago. If my friend submits a price of $250, she would buy an identical product at a cheaper price (assuming airlines were willing to sell tickets for $250). Basically, Priceline's reverse auction gets consumers to name their reservation price, then Priceline charges them this price. So the reverse auction does not guarantee that consumers receive a product at the lowest price, it simply guarantees them the chance to purchase a product at *their* reservation price.

Priceline's price-discriminating auction also improves on the traditional price discrimination schemes by making discounts less transparent to both consumers and rivals. Airlines need not post any special rates, which reduces the probability that rivals could engage in a disastrous price war. Also, the company is able to practice price discrimination selectively. For example, there is some evidence that Priceline will accept lower prices from first-time customers. When those consumers subsequently bid the same price for the same product, they find their bids are rejected.

Airlines that work with Priceline also receive demand information that helps them in their pricing decisions. The company compiles all bidding information (both successful and unsuccessful) and gives this information to airlines on a weekly basis. As Ek states, "They can see all of the demand, every consumer's price offer for every route, going all the way down to $1 . . . It's a great way for the airlines to privately move more inventory that was likely to go unsold through their retail sales channels."

Risk Aversion

As we've seen in Chapter 15, most individuals are risk averse. What are the effects of risk aversion on bidding behavior? In second-price auctions, risk preferences do not influence bidding strategy. Bidders in these auctions should always bid up to their reservation price. However, risk preference does affect bidding behavior in first-price auctions.

Consider the choices facing a risk-averse bidder in a first-price auction. The prevailing uncertainty in one's mind is this: Will my bid win the auction? Since first-price auctions have no dominant strategies, managers must anticipate the bids of others and, hence, only partially control this uncertainty. Their controlling mechanism is the bid price itself. Relative to any arbitrary benchmark, a higher bid increases the probability of winning. Since a risk-averse bidder will pay to avoid loss, he or she simply raises the bid by the amount of this "bidding insurance." So, risk-averse ones bid higher than risk-neutral bidders. Their rush toward certainty is tempered, however, as higher bids also reduce the expected surplus.

If bidders are risk averse, risk-neutral managers can increase performance through the use of auction rules. If bidders are likely to be risk averse, then managers want to use a first-price auction. This allows the seller to capture profits generated by risk preference differences.

What if the roles were reversed—bidders are risk neutral and sellers are risk averse—how should this affect managerial actions? Here, too, the seller prefers first-price auctions. Although we know that the expected revenues from the four auction formats are equal, there is more risk in second-price auctions. That is, even though the means of the revenue distribution are equal, there is greater spread in possible revenues for second-price auctions. Because risk-averse managers prefer to avoid risk, they should use first-price auctions.

Number of Bidders

We have seen that, in all auction formats, the expected bid is given by the reservation price of the second-highest bidder. Therefore, managers should consider actions to increase these prices, as they similarly do in market settings. One possible variable that seems easily controlled is the number of bidders.

Consider how markets work. As the number of sellers increases (other factors held constant), the equilibrium price is pushed downward toward the marginal cost (or the seller's reservation price). And, in perfectly competitive markets, the long-run equilibrium price is identical to the marginal cost. These markets have many sellers, selling the same good or service to consumers. Auctions are the reverse of this—many buyers and one (or few) sellers. What works on the supply side must also work on the demand side. The entry of more bidders (buyers) into a market must push the demand curve rightward and, hence, increases the price. So, the more bidders a manager can induce to enter the auction, the greater is the expected surplus.

Are 1,000,001 bidders better than 1,000,000? No, that is not quite the case, although it may be true. It turns out that auctions are efficient, under most conditions, so even a moderate number of bidders result in the seller's revenue approaching that expected for maximum valuation (conditioned on the probability function). You would not want to pay much to attract the 1,000,000th bidder to your auction, but the first 20 or so is important. The following example assumes the reservation price of bidders is uniformly distributed, with the highest price being $100. A seller's expected revenue in English auctions is then given by

$$B = [(N - 1)/(N + 1)] \text{ (reservation price of bidders)}$$

where $N =$ the number of bidders. Figure 16.2 shows how a seller's expected revenue increases as the number of bidders increase.

Intuitively, the expected revenue of the seller increases because of the increased competition caused by additional bidders. In placing bids, bidders must consider the trade-off between the probability of winning the auction and the level of consumer surplus (reservation price − bid price) they will realize. A lower bid gives a bidder higher surplus but a decreased probability of winning, for one loses an auction if only one bidder bids higher. As more bidders join the auction the probability of someone bidding higher increases quickly. Hence, as more bidders join the auction, bids must approach the reservation price of bidders (and seller revenue increases). Note, too, that a seller's expected revenue approaches its maximal level with less than 30 bidders.

Winner's Curse

In some auctions, the value of the object or service being auctioned off is not known with certainty, although it has a common value to all bidders. For example, the U.S. government auctions off the mineral rights to tracts of federally owned land. When the seller uses a sealed-bid first-price auction in these situations, bidders are exposed to what is known as the **winner's curse**. The bid-

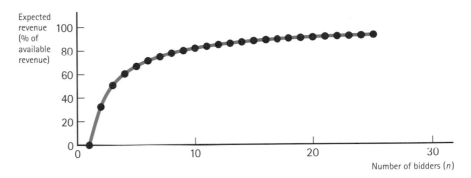

FIGURE
16.2

Expected Revenue versus Number of Bidders

As the number of bidders increases, the expected revenue of the seller increases.

der with the highest estimated value bids the highest and wins the auction, but the amount bid may be greater than the true value of the object. If this occurs, then the bidder wins the auction but pays a price higher than the object's true value. Let us see why this is true.

All bidders face the same decision problem. They must estimate the value of the object without knowing the estimates of others. Suppose each bidder makes an estimate, and on average, the estimates are approximately correct. Then the distribution of bids might resemble that shown in Figure 16.3. An unbiased estimate of the true value, if you knew the bids of others, would be the mean shown by the dashed line. Given this distribution of values across bidders, the distribution of bids would lie to the left, say, as distribution A. As you see, those bidders with extreme estimates (in the right tail of A) bid values that exceed the best estimate of the true value. The key is that they do not know their estimates are extreme (because they do not know the estimates of others). Hence, they are likely to win the auction but pay a price that is greater than the object's true value.

The winner's curse is a robust phenomenon; it has been documented in many situations (see the Analyzing Managerial Decisions box). While sophisticated algorithms for bidding behavior in these types of auctions are available, they are too complex to discuss in this text. However, managers should consider the following issues when contemplating their bids:

- *How much information do you have relative to others about the object's true value?* The less information you have relative to others, the more you want to lower your bid.

FIGURE

16.3

The Winner's Curse

If the value of the item being auctioned is uncertain, then bidders with extreme estimates of about the value can bid higher than the item's true value.

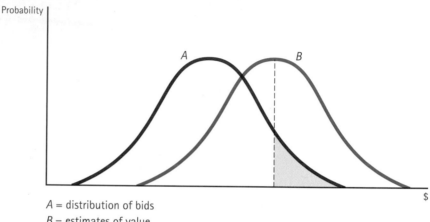

A = distribution of bids
B = estimates of value

- *How confident are you in your estimate of the object's true value?* The less confident you are, the more you want to lower your bid.
- *How many others are bidding against you?* The greater the number of bidders in the auction, the more you want to lower your bid.

Concerns in Auction Design

In designing auctions, managers must realize that no auction design is best suited for all situations. Managers need to carefully consider what is being auctioned off and the incentives an auction design gives bidders. However, there are two issues that managers must always address in choosing an auction's design: the ability of bidders to collude within the auction and the attractiveness of the auction to potential bidders.[3]

The ability of bidders to collude reduces the revenue of the seller and basically overpowers the efficiency of auctions. Bidders can collude in many ways. One common way is for a group of bidders to form a "ring," where the bidders do not bid against each other. A member of the ring is designated as the bidder, and this one person bids on the objects being auctioned. After the auction,

[3]See P. Klemperer, "What Really Matters in Auction Design," *Journal of Economic Perspectives*, Vol. 16, 2002, 169–189.

ANALYZING MANAGERIAL DECISIONS

The Winner's Curse in Bidding for Oil Rights

During their careers, many managers find themselves in a competitive bidding situation. These might entail bidding for the services of a qualified job applicant, for production inputs, to acquire another company, or to obtain a contract for corporate or personal services. When the bidding is conducted as a sealed-bid auction and it involves an object of common value, managers must be aware of the winner's curse.

An example of how costly this curse can be is shown in the following table, which compiles the **actual bids** (in millions of dollars) of oil companies for the right to drill for oil on two tracts of government-owned land. Bids are listed in descending order of magnitude.

The table clearly shows the range of estimates regarding how much oil is present within these tracts of land. For tract 1, the winning bid is 87 percent higher than the second-highest bid; for tract 2, this percentage increases to 181 percent. If we examine the ratio of the high bid to the low bid in each auction, we see, for tract 1, the high bid is 10 times that of the low bid; for tract 2, this ratio is 109.

The natural tendency for managers is to

Bids to drill for oil on federal land (in millions of dollars)

Tract 1	Tract 2
32.5	43.5
17.7	15.5
11.1	11.6
7.1	8.5
5.6	8.1
4.1	5.6
3.3	4.7
	2.8
	2.6
	0.7
	0.7
	0.4

increase their bids when more bidders enter the auction. But, in these types of auctions, managers need to reduce their bids, not increase them. Obviously, the manager who submitted the winning bid for tract 2 did not follow our recommendations. In both auctions, the winning bidder suffered the winner's curse. Neither firm realized a positive return from these tracts of land.

the members of the ring meet and distribute the objects from the auction. Many times, the form of the distribution is an auction among the members themselves.

Collusion is also possible in multiunit simultaneous auctions. In these auctions, multiple units of a good are auctioned off simultaneously. In the early stages of the auction, participants who collude signal each other what goods they desire. The colluding participants then do not bid up the prices of the identified objects. Klemperer claims this occurred in the auctioning off of spectrum rights in Germany. Two large telecoms—Mannesman and T-Mobile—split the 10 available blocks into 2. Each company acquired exactly half of the available blocks for the identical low price.

Managers also need to recognize that they want to make their auctions attractive to potential bidders. If the auction does not attract enough bidders, then the revenue raised by it can be lower than predicted. For example, if it is clear to bidders that one bidder will win the auction, then others may not enter because they are so sure they will not win. This happened in Glaxo's purchase of Wellcome. Though other firms were interested in Wellcome, none entered the bidding process because it was clear to them (and reinforced by Glaxo statements) that Glaxo would top any bid.

Bidders also may be deterred from entering an auction if the seller sets a reserve price that is too high or low. Setting a price that is too low can actually encourage collusion among bidders. If the price is set too low and there is a strong bidder, then that bidder may find it easier (and cheaper) to collude with others to keep the price low. Basically, if the bidder does not collude, then he or she is faced with the prospect of outbidding all other bidders, which is usually more expensive than colluding with others.

Summary

1. There are four types of auction mechanisms—English, Dutch, and first- and second-price sealed-bid auctions.

2. In common-value auctions with symmetric, risk-neutral bidders and independent signals, the auction mechanism chosen makes no difference. All mechanisms generate the same expected revenues.

3. There is no need to consider the bidding strategies of others in English and second-price auctions. In English auctions, managers should bid up to their reservation price. In second-price auctions, managers want to bid their reservation price.

4. Dutch and sealed-bid auctions have no dominant strategy. Optimal behavior in these auctions is conditioned on beliefs about the strategies of others. In each auction, bidders must consider the reservation price of the second-highest bidder (assuming you are the highest bidder). Then, bid this price.

5. Sellers want to set a reserve price according to the following rule:

   Optimal reserve price = the value of the object being auctioned off, if it does not sell + (managerial estimates of the highest reservation price divided by 2)

6. Auctions are often more efficient than posted pricing schemes because they can better discriminate among consumers with differing reservation prices.

Most auction designs ensure that consumers with the highest reservation price "win" the auction.

7. Auctions are useful if demand is unknown. They can be used to induce consumers to reveal their preferences before managers set a price. By knowing the demand before setting a price, managers increase revenues.

8. When bidding in sealed-bid, common-value auctions, managers need to recognize the tendency to bid too high. This tendency results in the winner's curse, where the high bidder wins the auction but pays a price higher than the object's true value.

Problems

1. Consultant.com is an Internet startup. The company employs business professors as virtual consultants who supply answers to other companies' problems. Consultant.com wants to raise funds via a private equity issue. Unfortunately, because of fluctuations in the stock market, it is uncertain about the demand for its offering. It hopes to issue the stock at either $45 or $50. The demand is categorized into four possible scenarios. The following table shows demand for each scenario-price combination along with the beliefs regarding the probability of each possible state. Consultant.com must pay 10 percent of the generated funds to the investment bank that helped it identify potential investors. The company wants to maximize the funds raised.

Price/share	State 1	State 2	State 3	State 4
$45	1,750	1,975	2,220	2,445
$50	1,200	1,415	2,001	2,305
Probability	0.35	0.20	0.30	0.15

What is the expected value of the stock offering if Consultant.com sets its price without knowing the future demand state? If Consultant.com can determine the future demand state by using a modified Dutch auction, what is its expected profit? If someone approached Consultant.com and told managers she could predict the future demand state, how much would that information be worth to them?

2. Your company is planning to auction off a manufacturing plant in Asia. You are asked to determine the auction design that will generate the highest revenues for the company. You believe that bidders will value the plant independently. Which design would you choose and why?

3. There are 100 bidders in an English auction. A random sample of 30 bidders shows the following reservation prices.

Number of bidders	Reservation price
1	$10
3	$20
6	$30
5	$40
8	$50
6	$60
7	$70
3	$80
1	$100

Assume the bidding distribution is normal.

a. What is the mean value of bids across the 100 bidders?

b. What is the probability of a bid being less than $80?

4. Your company is bidding for a service contract in a first-price, sealed-bid auction. You value the contract at $12 million. You believe the distribution of bids will be uniform, with a high value of $16 million and a low value of $3 million. What is your optimal bidding strategy with

a. 5 bidders?

b. 10 bidders?

c. 20 bidders?

5. The Philadelphia Eagles of the NFL built a new stadium. One revenue source during the construction of the stadium is a personal seat license (PSL), a one-time, up-front payment charged to season ticketholders before the stadium is built. It gives the buyer the right to purchase tickets for a particular seat.

The Eagles are uncertain about demand for seats in the new stadium. They have selected three price points for PSLs ($6,000, $7,000, and $8,000). Management also has estimated that demand for PSLs could be low, medium, or high. Their beliefs are reflected in this table:

Price	Low demand, probability = 0.4	Medium demand, probability = 0.35	High demand, probability, = 0.25
$6,000	24,500 PSLs sold	28,000 PSLs sold	40,000 PSLs sold
$7,000	21,500 PSLs sold	24,000 PSLs sold	32,000 PSLs sold
$8,000	17,500 PSLs sold	22,000 PSLs sold	25,000 PSLs sold

Some of the stadium funding is provided by the city of Philadelphia. Because Eagles fans view PSLs as an attempt to take away consumer surplus, they resent them and have put pressure on the city government to limit their use. Therefore, the city has set a target of 25,000 seats assigned to PSLs. If the Eagles sell less than 25,000 PSLs, the city will grant it a tax benefit of

$10/seat for each seat under 25,000. If the Eagles sell 25,000 or more PSLs, then no tax break is given. A consulting group has told the Eagles it is better off using a modified Dutch auction to sell the PSLs. The group has estimated the cost of running the auction as an additional $5.1 million. Eagles management has come to you for help. The managers want to know whether they should use an auction and what would be the expected benefits. What would you tell them?

6. Your company is bidding for a broadband spectrum license. You have been asked to submit an optimal bidding strategy. You expect that bidders will have independent private values for the licenses, since each bidder presently has a different structure in place. You believe the valuations for these licenses will be between $200 million and $700 million. Your own valuation is $650 million. There is some uncertainty about the auction design that will be used, so you must suggest an optimal bidding strategy for the following auction designs:

a. Second-price sealed-bid auction.

b. English auction.

c. Dutch auction.

Moral Hazard
and Principal-
Agent Problems

Principal-Agent Problems

For most of this book, we look at decision making in a firm as though the firm were a single person who wished to maximize personal wealth. For example, we assume that the firm makes a decision to maximize profit because profit is income to the firm's owner. Of course, *firms* do not make decisions; *people* make decisions. In practice, the firm's operating decisions are made by paid managers, with some supervision by the board of directors. Are the managers' decisions always best for the shareholders, or do the managers often make decisions for their own benefit? This is the **principal-agent**, or **moral hazard, problem:** a conflict of interest that arises when one person, the agent, makes decisions on behalf of another, the principal. For example, in publicly held firms, managers (agents) make decisions that affect the wealth of shareholders (principals).

When the interests of the principal and agent are identical, we do not worry about this problem. For example, the captain and sailors on a ship in a storm need each other to save the ship. Because the sailors know the captain wishes to save his own life, the sailors may be confident he will make decisions that are also in the best interests of the sailors. Problems arise when the interests are not identical. For example, will a general, who is not on the battlefield, devise strategies that best serve the soldiers under his command? Generals may wish to win battles; soldiers wish to stay alive. Can we be sure that elected politicians really serve their constituents and are not nudged away from that goal by interest groups? Will a plaintiff's lawyer be tempted to advise her client to go to trial (which enhances the visibility of the lawyer) rather than to accept a good settlement offer? Will a doctor prescribe treatment that is best for his patient, or might the doctor use the patient to further a research agenda or prescribe treatment that leads to the highest payment for the doctor?

In this chapter, we give examples of principal-agent problems and show how such incentive conflicts can make everybody worse off. We discuss how the problems can be anticipated and minimized. Many principal-agent problems arise under the umbrella of the firm. As mentioned, the most visible principal-agent problem we encounter here is between the firm's owners and its managers. In this chapter, we see how this problem is resolved through the use of bonuses, equity participation, and stock options. We also show how incentive conflicts can arise between shareholders and creditors, which, if not anticipated and controlled, can prevent a firm from adopting investment projects despite their positive net present values. Finally, we discuss how product liability law has evolved as a response to principal-agent problems between firms and their customers. In particular, these laws provide incentives for firms to produce safe products. However, we also show that, in the information age, product liability laws may not be necessary and the price mechanism may provide similar protections for consumers.

Owner-Manager Conflicts

One of the most important principal-agent problems encountered in business is that between the owners of a firm and its managers. The owners typically are shareholders who purchased the stock as an investment, investors who simply bought shares in a mutual fund, or pensioners whose assets are invested in a large number of companies. Most investors probably are interested in maximizing the value of their investment, which means either maximizing the income their assets yield or maximizing the value of those assets.

Shareholders are concerned about the value of their shares, but what are managers concerned with? It is reasonable to assume that they are interested in the performance of the firm, because their reputations are enhanced by high profits and a rising stock price. So, because both managers and owners prefer the same outcome, they share common interests. If we stop the story here, the principal-agent problem would disappear. We would conclude that incentives are aligned and managers act in the best interests of shareholders. What is good for the one is good for the other. The problem is that managers may have other objectives in mind. Let us make a plausible, though not necessarily complete, list of managers' objectives.

- *Minimizing effort.* Increasing profit often takes hard work. Many decisions involve a trade-off. How much harder is a manager prepared to work to make an extra dollar of profit for the owner? Given a choice between two activities, one involving a little more effort and the other a lot more effort, which would be chosen? The manager supplies the effort, while the owner reaps the profit. These examples suggest that many marginal decisions may tilt in favor of less effort rather than higher profit.
- *Maximizing job security.* Many decisions involve risk, but sometimes risk is accompanied by a high potential reward. Managers may be disinclined to make risky choices that could jeopardize their employment. Suppose an investment decision carries a large probability of very high returns and a small chance of failure that would cause the firm itself to fail. Shareholders, being diversified, might be inclined to accept this risk. Managers, however, might be more concerned with the downside (they do not share the upside profit and could lose their jobs given the downside risk), so they might be tempted to avoid such risky choices.
- *Avoiding Failure.* Managers can be rewarded for good performance and penalized for bad results. If a risky project is undertaken, the manager is rewarded if results (due somewhat to chance) are favorable and penalized if results are unfavorable. Often managers believe the bad results are much more likely to be noticed than good results. If so, they are disinclined to take risks.
- *Enhancing reputation and employment opportunities.* Although we argue that sometimes reputation is promoted by doing things that benefit shareholders, this is not always so. For example, a CEO with ambition to hold public office might be more concerned about showing himself to be a "good citizen" than maximizing the profits of the firm. Therefore, prices charged might be lowered below their profit-maximizing level. Alternatively, a manager might conduct contract negotiations with another firm partly with a view to establishing a personal relationship that could be a springboard to a new job.
- *Consuming perquisites.* Examples can include luxury travel, expensive artwork in the office, corporate donations to favorite charities, and employing favored people.
- *Pay.* Last, and not least, the manager presumably works for pay, and as we shall see, both the level and structure of the compensation package become important parts of the principal-agent story.

FIGURE
17.1

The Principal–Agent Problem

The principal employs an agent to undertake a task (produce output for the principal). The agent must expend effort to produce output; the more effort, the more output. Because the principal cannot observe (and therefore cannot reward) the effort, the agent tends to "shirk," or reduce effort, which, in turn, reduces the output for the principal.

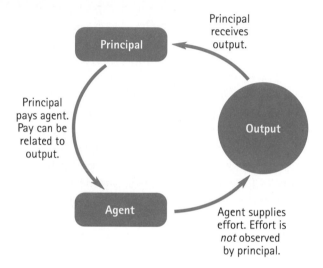

A Picture of the Principal-Agent Problem

Figure 17.1 shows a diagram of the principal-agent problem. The principal employs an agent who performs a task that results in a benefit to the principal. The benefit is called *output*. The principal must pay the agent. This compensation can be a fixed sum or can depend on the output. The level of output depends on the quantity and quality of the effort provided by the agent. If this effort were observable by the principal, the principal could simply require a certain level of effort, verify that this level of effort was provided, and compensate the agent accordingly. But effort is not always observable or measurable. The principal-agent problem is one in which effort cannot be monitored and measured by the principal and, therefore, cannot be directly rewarded. The solutions to this problem, as we will see, require some alignment of interests of the two parties. In this way, even if the principal cannot see what the agent is doing, the principal still can be assured that what is good for the agent is also good for the principal.

Examples of Principal-Agent Problems

Principal-agent problems arise from conflicting incentives; they involve a "separation of ownership and control." One party, the agent, has the control and makes the decisions. The other party, the principal, bears the consequences of those decisions (i.e., has a stake in or "owns" the outcome).

Principal-agent problems are sometimes referred to as **moral hazard**, a term usually associated with insurance. Suppose you have no insurance and visit your doctor for a damaged wrist. Your doctor says it may be sprained or broken and she can do an X-ray, which costs $200, or an MRI, which costs $1,500. She says the X-ray will almost certainly be sufficient to confirm a diagnosis and determine treatment, but there is a very small chance that the MRI will reveal something else that may cause a variation in treatment. Which do you choose? When paying ourselves, most would choose the X-ray, but what if you were insured? Many of us would also get the MRI because the insurance company, not us, foots the bill. This tendency for people to spend more on medical treatment when insured is well documented and another example of the separation of ownership and control. The agent, the patient, makes the decision, and the principal, the insurance company, pays the bill. Insurance also encounters prospective (ex ante) moral hazard. People who are insured may be tempted to take fewer precautions in protecting their homes (installation of burglar alarms, better locks, smoke alarms, and window shutters). Spending money on expensive safety devices saves the insurance company's money, rather than yours.

Returning to a more familiar theme in this book, we spend a lot of time assuming that firms maximize profit. This seems reasonable because the firm's owners (shareholders) are clearly interested in the value of their shares, and this value rests on the long-run profitability of the firm. We would expect the shareholders to appoint a board of directors and management team that pursued the profit objective. However, corporate governance is more complex. A subject of considerable research attention is whether boards really do control managers or vice versa. What is clear is that, although managers are accountable in the long run to the owners, they still have considerable discretion in making decisions. Consider some examples.

A life insurance company is thinking about selling its new products and has two choices about distribution channels. One alternative is to use an existing distribution channel: a network of independent agents who are paid commissions. This approach is safe but has a low expected profit. The other is to establish an electronic distribution system. This is new and untried but, if it succeeds, profits could be very high. If the expected profit is high enough for the e-business channel, one could argue that this system is best for the shareholders. Shareholders certainly benefit from the higher expected profit. Moreover, they probably are not too concerned about risk, because most shareholders hold a number of securities and can diversify the risk. However, managers might worry more about risk because, if the e-project is chosen and the firm has bad luck, the managers might lose their jobs. Therefore, managers might be tempted to use the existing distribution network even though electronic distribution could be better for shareholders.

Many firms make charitable contributions, and it can be argued that some level of charity benefits the shareholders. This visibility might stimulate demand for the firm's products and cast the firm in a favorable light with legislators and regulators. Charity also might bring some benefit in courts. For example, a car manufacturer that donates considerable sums to university research on safety might find that this charitable giving is an important signal of its commitment to safety, which helps in the defense of lawsuits. Now, consider a manager who has a personal agenda: He is a strong supporter of environmental causes. This manager not only increases the level of charitable giving above what is optimal for the shareholders but also redirects it to his favored environmental charity. This is a particularly stubborn problem because the firm might receive adverse publicity if it tried to discipline the manager and cut down on its charitable giving.

Finally, a firm that is inefficiently managed can become the target of a hostile takeover. Because the resources of the firm are not being managed effectively, the firm is generating lower profits than it otherwise would earn. If investors are aware of the inefficient management, it lowers the share price. This creates an opportunity for another firm to acquire the target firm and replace the management with one that is more competent or better motivated. If the new management is indeed better, or is perceived to be so by investors, the stock price rises. Thus, shareholders benefit from the takeover if there is a reasonable expectation that management quality will increase. The problem is that shareholders need advice on whether to sell their shares to the potential acquirer. The board normally provides this advice. Here, the problems start. If the board had been effective, it previously would have addressed the management issue. The problem might be that the board is influenced too much by the management. If so, the shareholders are hardly likely to get good advice from managers and board members, who will lose their positions if the takeover succeeds. More likely, shareholders will be advised to resist the takeover.

A Simple Model of the Principal–Agent Problem with No Risk

The Concept of "Effort"

We can summarize the idea of incentive conflict with the concept of effort. To achieve a target level of profit requires that managers incur some personal cost, which we call *effort*. This effort might simply be the manager's time required to attain that level of output, and the cost to the manager is the value of that time. But, time is not the only dimension. Certain tasks require less-pleasant work than others. Spending time with clients on the golf course may be valued differently by a manager than spending time bargaining with the union over wages. Managers may sacrifice other things to attain a profit goal. For example, to increase expected profits, a manager may cut down on perquisites and employ the best engineer, rather than giving the job to his favorite niece. In economist terms, the cost to the manager may be a direct cost or an opportunity cost. The personal cost to the manager of making a decision reflects the quantity and quality of effort required. Given a choice among activities, managers can be expected to exert some bias toward those tasks that require lower effort.

In the next few sections, we show how to resolve the principal-agent problem. To do so, we solve profit-maximizing equations similar to those in earlier chapters. We show that profit is simply revenue minus costs, and we try to maximize profit. However, in earlier chapters, we often try to choose a quantity (and a price) for a given product that would maximize the profit or perhaps some mix of inputs that would maximize profit. In the principal-agent problem, we choose the design of the manager's compensation to maximize profits. In doing this, we must recognize that how we compensate the manager, in turn, affects the manager's choice of effort.

We can now represent the principal-agent problem a little more precisely. The profit to the firm, π, depends on the manager's effort, e. We write this function as $\pi(e)$ to remind us of the impact of effort. We use this device quite a lot in the next few pages. We write a variable $y(x)$, which simply says that y depends on, or is a function of, x. For the moment, we pretend that the profit is not risky. Once the manager chooses effort, the profit can be forecast with certainty. However, profit is, of course, total revenue minus total costs, and the manager's effort affects profit by changing the total revenue. Therefore, we write revenue as $R(e)$, to show that revenue depends on effort. Finally, we divide total cost between the manager's compensation, S, and all other costs, C. So, profits can now be written as

$$\text{Profit} = \{\text{revenue}\} \text{ minus } \{\text{costs}\}$$
$$= \{\text{revenue}\} - \{\text{managerial compensation} + \text{other costs}\}$$
$$\pi = \{R(e)\} - \{S + C\}$$

More effort on the part of the manager results in higher revenue, so the derivative dR/de is positive. However, for the moment, we assume that S is a flat salary and cannot change. We also assume for simplification that other costs are not affected by the manager's effort. We could assume that managers could reduce costs if they tried harder. But, this would complicate our analysis, and all the main ideas we develop in this chapter would be substantially the same anyway. Therefore, we take the easiest route to our destination, which is to solve the principal-agent problem.

We can now state the profit before deducting the manager's salary as $R(e) = C$; and profit after deduction of salary, $\pi(e) = R(e) - S - C$, has the upward slope shown in Figure 17.2. If the owners were to choose the level of effort they wished the manager to supply, they would choose the highest feasible level. However, owners cannot simply choose the level of effort, e, to maximize profit. The manager, not the owners, must choose e. The manager has his (or her) own objectives and chooses a level of effort to maximize these personal objectives.

The objective of the manager is to maximize the net benefit of employment. The manager, first of all, obtains income from employment and wants this income to be high. To gain this income, the manager must supply effort. The cost to the manager of supplying effort is shown as the function $u(e)$. This can now be thought of as the **disutility of effort**. In Chapter 4, we talked of a basket of goods giving **utility** to the owner. In that context, the consumer enjoyed the goods, and the utility was a measure of the satisfaction derived from those goods. Here, the effort is not desirable; it is not a good to the manager but a bad. Therefore, the disutility of effort is a measure of the dissatisfaction to the manager from supplying effort. Naturally, more effort involves more cost, or disutility, to the manager, so $u(e)$ slopes upward. The net benefit to the manager of working at a given level of effort is now shown as

$$B(e) = S - u(e)$$

FIGURE
17.2

The Principal–Agent Problem with a Flat Salary

Because the net benefit to the agent is the salary minus the disutility of effort, this benefit declines as effort increases. Accordingly, the agent reduces effort, which reduces revenue.

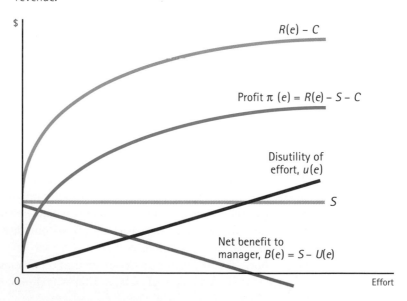

The Principal–Agent Problem with Flat Pay

The owner pays the manager a flat pay. The manager chooses to minimize effort; therefore, revenue and profits fall.

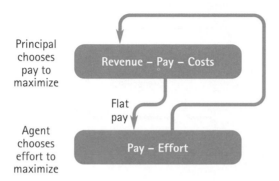

Principal chooses pay to maximize

Revenue − Pay − Costs

Flat pay

Agent chooses effort to maximize

Pay − Effort

Because the salary is constant and disutility increases with effort, the net benefit, $B(e)$, must slope downward, as in Figure 17.2. Therefore, the manager, who bears all of the cost of effort but gets none of the reward, is better off with as little effort as possible—in this case, zero effort. In contrast, the shareholders, who get all of the benefit of the manager's effort but pay none of the cost, want maximum effort from the manager.

The principal-agent problem with flat pay is summarized in Figure 17.3. At the top of the diagram, the principal wants to maximize profit but cannot control the manager's effort. The owner pays a flat salary. At the bottom of the picture, the manager wants to maximize the net benefit of employment, but because the pay is flat, maximizing this benefit can be achieved only by reducing effort. This reduction in effort reduces revenue and thereby reduces profit.

Resolving the Incentive Conflict If Effort Is Observable

Can we improve this sad state of affairs? If owners are able to observe the effort provided by managers, the owners can simply reward managers directly in relation to the effort. To see where we are going, look at Figure 17.4. This is similar to Figure 17.3, except for the inclusion of incentive pay. The pay by the owners is scaled to the manager's effort. Now, the manager's choice of effort is more complex. Although effort is unattractive in itself, it has the compensating advantage of increasing the manager's pay, so the manager is now persuaded to increase effort, which, in turn, increases revenue and profit.

FIGURE
17.4

Motivating Managers When Effort Is Observable

The owner pays incentive compensation based directly on effort. Because the agent's pay increases with effort, the agent increases his effort. This in turn increases the firm's revenue. If the increase in revenue exceeds the increase in pay, profit increases.

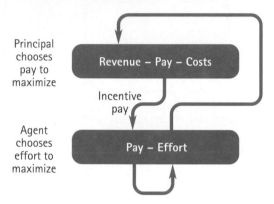

Principal chooses pay to maximize

Revenue − Pay − Costs

Incentive pay

Agent chooses effort to maximize

Pay − Effort

To see how this works in more detail, let the owners structure the compensation in two parts. The first part, K, is a fixed amount. $U(e)$ is an additional amount that varies with managerial effort. So, $U(e)$ represents the reward paid by the firm for managerial effort, while the lowercase $u(e)$, represents the money value of the disutility of effort to the manager. When $U(e) = u(e)$, the manager is fully compensated for effort, as we see shortly. Because compensation now is a function of effort, we write it as $S(e)$:

$$S(e) = K + U(e)$$

This is shown in Figure 17.5. The profit now is

$$\pi(e) = R(e) - S(e) - C$$
$$= R(e) - [K + U(e)] - C$$

which is shown in Figure 17.5. We can solve for the desired level of profit (and thus of effort) for the shareholders by maximizing the profit function. Note that only $R(e)$ and $U(e)$ depend on effort, so the maximum is obtained by

$$\frac{d\pi(e)}{de} = \frac{dR(e)}{de} - \frac{dU(e)}{de} = 0$$

which simply says that the marginal benefit from effort (in terms of increased revenue, $R(e)$) must equal the marginal cost of compensating the managers for

FIGURE

17.5

The Principal–Agent Problem with Pay as a Function of Effort

The manager is paid incentive compensation that increases with effort. Because this off-sets the disutility of effort for the manager, the manager now expends more effort, which increases revenue and profit.

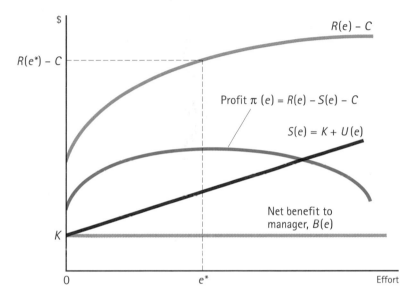

effort. Note that profit achieves a clear maximum in Figure 17.5 at effort level e^*. This is because profit reflects both the benefits to the shareholders and the costs to the manager for which the owners now have to pay him. The share-holders would wish to maximize profit at effort level e^*.

Now what does the manager wish to do? The manager receives a net ben-efit, $B(e)$, equal to compensation minus the cost of effort:

$$B(e) = S(e) - u(e)$$
$$= K + U(e) - u(e)$$

If that part of compensation designed to compensate the manager for effort, $U(e)$, is exactly equal to the disutility of effort, $u(e)$, then

$$B(e) = K$$

The manager now is fully compensated for the effort supplied and is quite happy to supply any effort level. How can we get the manager to choose exactly e^*, which maximizes profit for the shareholders? The simple answer is for the shareholders to tell the manager to produce e^* in effort. This is fine in our little example, because we make the assumption that the shareholders could observe the manager's effort. In practice, this assumption often is implausible.

In theory, the inherently different interests of managers and owners would be no problem if all managerial actions could be observed and evaluated without cost. If that were the case, the manager could be given very specific directions on what actions to take. For example, the owners allow a manager to consume some perquisites because they bring benefit to the owners, but he cannot consume other perks because they benefit the manager with no redeeming impact on profit. The manager is allowed to choose this risky investment project but not that one. He can lobby in Washington for this view but not for that one and so on. However, this ignores the main issue. Managers are appointed precisely because they, not the shareholders, have the time and skill to make decisions. Shareholders have no time to micromanage every firm in which they own some shares nor do they have the expertise to evaluate each decision. Nor can a board of directors micromanage every decision. Managers must be invested with considerable discretion. In the long run, the impact of their stewardship of a firm becomes visible. But the long run can be very long, and this permits managers considerable flexibility in balancing their own ambitions against those of the firm's owners. This discretion means that owners do not observe all the actions of the manager. In effect, the owners cannot always observe the manager's effort.

Resolving the Incentive Conflict If Effort Is Not Observable: Incentive Compatibility

The real nature of the principal-agent problem is that, when effort is not observable by the principal, that effort cannot be rewarded or penalized directly. Thus, the agent has a degree of freedom to pursue his or her own objectives, instead of acting in the best interest of the principal.

There may be a way around this problem if the firm's revenue, $R(e)$, is riskless and determined solely by the effort of the manager. The shareholders can ask the question, *What level of effort is necessary to produce this level of revenue?* In this way, shareholders deduce the level of effort by observing revenue. If $R(e)$ slopes upward, as we show in Figures 17.2 and 17.5, shareholders can read backward on the graph from a given R on the vertical axis to an implied level of e on the horizontal axis. For example, if shareholders observe output level, $R(e^*) - C$, then the effort level necessary to achieve this output must have been e^*.

Because shareholders can infer the level of effort, in this cosy little world, observing R is as good as observing e. We can now calculate what e must have been, so we can make the same compensation payment $S(e) = K + U(e)$ as before. However, there is one snag. This ensures that the manager gets a *retrospective* payment that fully compensates him for effort *already provided*. Anticipating this reward for effort, the manager is induced to work harder. But, how can we be sure that the manager will choose in advance exactly the level of effort, e^*, that the shareholders desire?

We now need to make a simple but very important change to the manager's compensation; we need to give him a share, α, of profits, $\pi(e)$. The new compensation is $S(e) = U(e) + \alpha\pi(e)$. We replaced the fixed amount K with a profit-sharing bonus.[1] Naturally, the manager has to wait until the end of the period before this element of pay is finally settled. Therefore, we decide on the level of bonus so that the overall package is competitive and attracts and retains skilled managers. We must be a little careful how we do our accounting here. First, let us divide the manager's compensation into two parts:

$$S(e) = (\text{salary}) + (\text{bonus})$$
$$= [U(e)] + [\alpha\pi(e)]$$

Moreover, the bonus is a share of profit after the salary is paid. So the profit is now

$$\pi(e) = R(e) - U(e) - C$$

This makes the bonus a real equity share in the firm.

The net benefit to the manager is now

$$B(e) = S(e) - u(e)$$
$$= U(e) + \alpha\pi(e) - u(e)$$
$$= \alpha\pi(e)$$

The last step was taken by setting the monetary compensation for effort, $U(e)$, at a level sufficient to offset the disutility of effort, $u(e)$. We have a clear alignment of the interests of the managers, who get a net benefit of $\alpha\pi(e)$, and the owners, who get the remainder $(1 - \alpha)[\pi(e)]$. Now, both are interested in maximizing the net profit, $\pi(e)$.

Consider what level of effort the owners would want and what level the manager will choose. The owners get a portion of the profit, $(1 - \alpha)\pi(e)$, and the manager gets $\alpha\pi(e)$, so whatever the level of α, both are most happy if $\pi(e)$ is maximized. We can think of the problem in two stages:

1. The manager chooses a level of effort to maximize $\pi(e)$. This is achieved where the marginal benefit of effort equals the marginal disutility of the cost of effort.

[1]Note that we have set part of the compensation, $U(e)$, in relation to effort. Although effort is not directly observed, the principal can infer effort from the actual level of profit.

2. The firm's owners choose a level of α such that the compensation package is competitive.

We have now introduced an important concept: **incentive compatibility**. Because the agent and the owner share in the profits of the firm, their incentives are aligned and compatible. We refer to contracts that have this alignment of interests as *incentive-compatible contracts*.

Illustration of Optimal Compensation When Output Is Not Risky and Effort Is Not Observable

The weekly revenue, $R(e)$, of a retail store called Sporting Goods depends on the manager's effort, e; the more effort she provides, the higher is the revenue. The effort is the number of hours worked. However, because many of the working hours are not in the store, the owner does not know directly how many hours the manager actually works. Assume that, even if the manager supplies no effort, revenues would equal 3,500. Effort by the manager causes revenue to increase by $100e^{0.5}$. Thus revenue can be written as

$$R(e) = 3,500 + 100e^{0.5}$$

But the manager incurs a disutility from supplying the effort of

$$u(e) = 853.55 + (7.07)e$$

In addition to paying the manager's salary, the store must pay production costs of 1,000. To be persuaded to work for the store, the manager must receive a net benefit, $B(e)$, of 1,000. If she receives less, she will leave and take another job.

How much effort, e, will the manager supply?
How much weekly profit, $\pi(e)$, will be made?
How much of this profit will be paid to the manager?

First, note that the owners of Sporting Goods can infer the level of effort provided by the manager from the week's revenue. This can be done by solving the revenue equation backward:

$$R(e) = 3,500 + 100e^{0.5}$$
$$\frac{R(e) - 3,500}{100} = e^{0.5}$$
$$e = \left(\frac{R(e) - 3,500}{100}\right)^2$$

The owner can pay the manager a compensation package that includes a component $U(e)$ to compensate indirectly for her effort and a bonus $\alpha\pi(e)$ related directly to profit.

The profit is now

$$\pi(e) = R(e) - U(e) - C = R(e) - u(e) - C$$

If the compensation component $U(e)$ is enough to compensate the manager for the disutility of her effort, $U(e) = u(e)$, she will choose to maximize her bonus, which is the same as maximizing profit:

$$\frac{d\pi(e)}{de} = \frac{dR(e)}{de} - \frac{du(e)}{de}$$

The solution to this type of problem is now familiar. The manager simply equates the marginal benefit and marginal cost:

$$\frac{dR(e)}{de} - 0.5(100)e^{-0.5} : \frac{du(e)}{de} = 7.07$$

Setting marginal benefit equal to marginal cost yields

$$0.5(100)(e)^{-0.5} = 7.07$$

so

$$e^{0.5} = 50/7.07$$
$$e = 50^2/7.07^2$$
$$= 2,500/50$$
$$= 50$$

The manager works 50 hours per week. We can plug this effort level into the profit equation to give weekly profit:

$$\begin{aligned}
\pi(e) &= R(e) - u(e) - C \\
&= (3,500 + 100e^{0.5}) - [853.55 + (7.07)e] - 1000 \\
&= [3,500 + 100(50)^{0.5}] - [853.55 + (7.07)(50)] - 1000 \\
&= (3,500 + 707) - (853.55 + 353.55) - 1000 \\
&= 2,000
\end{aligned}$$

If the manager is to receive a net benefit, $B(e)$, of 1,000, clearly she must receive 50 percent of the profit, so $\alpha = 0.5$.

The Principal-Agent Problem: Output Is Risky and Effort Is Not Observable

Many of the most interesting principal-agent problems involve risk, and the solutions are often compromises. These compromises are often summarized in the expression "there is a trade-off between risk sharing and efficiency." The main problems we have to deal with are how to account for risk and how to account for the effort not being observable by the principal. The second of these problems is the crux of the principal-agent issue and is aggravated by the presence of risk. With no risk, we could infer the level of effort from the firm's profit. However, when profit also is risky, we can never be sure whether high profits are due to high effort or simply good luck (a strong economy) and whether low profits are due to low effort or bad luck. Poor management can occasionally result in high profits due to Lady Luck. Similarly, determined effort can sometimes come unstuck due to the vagaries of the market.

Risk Sharing

Executive compensation is usually designed around two competing ideas: risk sharing and efficiency. The efficiency idea has been dealt with previously. The manager is inclined to attend to his or her own interests, so it becomes desirable for the firm's owners to align incentives with profit-sharing bonuses, equity participation, stock options, and similar instruments. However, the firm's profits and its equity value are uncertain. Moreover, this volatility is partly outside the control of the managers and owners. Profits and share prices are affected by macroeconomic factors, such as changes in interest rates, employment, inflation, foreign exchange rates, and movements in stock market indices. Thus, bonus plans impose some risk on managers.

A competing view of how to design executive compensation is based on who can tolerate risk at the least cost, or who is the least risk averse. In this view, there is some value to be divided among the stakeholders, and this value is inherently risky. The value can be expressed as the periodic profits or the value of the equity. As residual claimants, the shareholders normally get the risky profit or equity, but first they must pay the managers. Should the shareholders take out a fixed sum (a flat salary) and pay this to the managers, or should they simply give the managers a share in the risky profit or equity? For the shareholders, the riskiness of profit may not be too problematic. Most shares are owned by individual investors or institutions that are quite diversified. Many individual investors hold several assets in their portfolios and are concerned, not with the riskiness of each stock, but with the risk in their whole portfolio. Unless the stocks are highly correlated, the risk in the portfolio can be quite modest. Therefore, investors, being able to diversify, can tolerate the risk in an individual stock quite well. If, for example, the risk in one stock in her portfolio increased, the investor could offset this by spreading her capital over a few more stocks. Institutional investors are often much better diversified than individual investors and can very easily tolerate the risk for each individual stock.

In contrast, managers are usually much less well diversified. For the typical manager, the compensation received from an employer, and the equity stake in that employer, is a large proportion of his or her total wealth. Fluctuation in the value of bonuses or stock options can have a very big impact on the manager's net worth. Hence, we expect managers to be quite averse to risk in their compensation plan. This does not mean that they will not accept a risky compensation plan, rather they need to be compensated for the risk; they need a risk premium.

Comparing managers and shareholders, it seems that the riskiness of the firms' profit and equity values can be absorbed at lower cost by the shareholders than by the managers. In this view, it appears that the optimal executive-compensation plan would place all risk on the shareholders; that is, pay the managers a flat salary.

Two Executive-Compensation Schemes Based Solely on Risk Sharing

To illustrate this idea, the risky equity value of the firm (note that these values are before deduction of any compensation to the manager) is shown as

Equity = $10,000,000 (probability 0.5)   or $20,000,000 (probability 0.5)

The manager is risk averse. We represent the manager's attitude to risk by a utility function as shown in Chapter 15. To show risk aversion, we need to show a utility function such as that in part A of Figure 15.4, in which utility increases at a decreasing rate as wealth increases. This type of concave utility function can be represented by a square-root function as follows:

$$\text{Manager's utility} = \sqrt{(\text{wealth})^{0.5}}$$

The manager's only wealth is derived from employment. To be competitive, the firm must offer the manager a compensation package that has an expected utility of 1,000; otherwise, the manager will leave and find other employment. In contrast to the manager, the shareholders are risk neutral and interested only in the expected value of the equity.

FLAT SALARY OF $1,000,000   The manager has an expected utility sufficient to hold him or her in the job $(1,000,000)^{0.5}$. The shareholders have an expected equity stake, after paying the manager, of

$$0.5(\$10,000,000 - \$1,000,000) + 0.5(\$20,000,000 - \$1,000,000) = \$14,000,000$$

BONUS OF A PROPORTION, x, OF THE EQUITY   What proportion, x, of equity would be necessary to offer the manager an expected utility of 1,000? We can solve this by setting the expected utility from such a bonus equal to 1,000 (the manager will receive either x times 10 million or x times 20 million):

$$0.5(10,000,000x)^{0.5} + 0.5(20,000,000x)^{0.5} = 1,000$$
$$x^{0.5}[(10,000,000)^{0.5} + (20,000,000)^{0.5}] = 2,000$$
$$x^{0.5} = \frac{2,000}{7634.4}$$
$$x = 0.06863$$

Note that the expected dollar value of compensation is now 0.06863 times the expected value of equity:

$$\text{Expected value of compensation} = 0.06863(\$15,000,000) = \$1,029,450$$

This risky compensation offers the manager the same expected utility as a flat salary of $1 million, with the manager being paid a risk premium of $29,450 to compensate for bearing the risk.

The expected value of equity remaining for the shareholders is

$$\text{Expected equity to shareholders} = \$15,000,000 - \$1,029,450 = \$13,970,550$$

Comparing the two compensation plans, both offer the manager an expected utility of 1,000, so the manager is indifferent. However, the flat salary offers shareholders an expected residual equity of $14,000,000, whereas the bonus plan leaves them with an expected equity value of only $13,970,550. Therefore, looking only at risk sharing, the flat salary is clearly preferred.

Trading off Risk Sharing and Efficiency

We now have two competing ideas about principal-agent problems. One says that we should align the interests of the principal and the agent; that is, make the contract incentive compatible. The other says we should assign risk to the party that can bear it most easily. How do we reconcile these ideas? First, we need to account for the fact that the revenue of the firm is risky. We do this by dividing revenue into two parts. The first part, $R_1(e)$, depends on the effort of the manager: The higher is the manager's effort, the higher is this component of revenue. The second part is beyond the control of the manager and depends on factors such as interest rates, economic movements, and so forth; we call this $\tilde{R}_2$. The tilde over the R shows that this component of revenue is risky. Therefore,

$$R(e) = \underbrace{R_1(e)}_{\text{under manager's control}} + \underbrace{\tilde{R}_2}_{\text{outside manager's control}}$$

The compensation paid the manager needs some modification. Because the principal cannot observe the effort nor can it be inferred from profit, compensation cannot depend directly on effort. We restate compensation as combining a fixed element, E, which is independent of effort, and a bonus, $\alpha\pi(e)$, which depends on profit:

$$S = E + \alpha\pi(e)$$

and correspondingly, profit is (note that we deduct only the direct compensation from profit—the remaining compensation, the bonus, is a share of profit):

$$\pi(e) = R(e) - E - C$$
$$= R_1(e) + \tilde{R}_2 - E - C$$

The net benefit of employment for the manager also needs some changes because the manager is exposed to risk if he or she receives a bonus. The net benefit now comprises two parts. The first shows the expected utility of the manager from wealth. We show wealth as comprising only the manager's employment compensation, S.[2] The second element is the disutility of effort, $u(e)$:

$$B(e) = EU(S) - u(e)$$
$$= EU[E + \alpha\pi(e)] - u(e)$$

The principal-agent problem can be presented now as

1. *The principal's problem.* The principal must design a contract to offer to the agent. The contract will specify the compensation to the agent. However, the principal knows that he will not be able to observe the agent's effort. Compensation cannot depend directly on effort. However, the principal does anticipate that the agent will choose to make the effort after she

---

[2]It is easy to add in other components of wealth such as savings, financial assets, real assets, and so forth.

sees the contract terms. Therefore, the principal will try to fashion the compensation to align his interest with that of the agent.

2. *The agent's problem.* Having seen the contract terms (particularly, how she will be paid), the agent selects a level of effort.

3. *Wrap-up.* At the end of the contract, the output from the agent's activities is revealed. The agent is paid, and the remaining output is paid to the principal.

The overall effect is illustrated in Figure 17.6. The owner pays some flat pay to provide some certain income to the risk-averse manager. In addition, the manager is given a share of profits to ensure that she will increase her effort, which will increase expected revenue and profit. Note that no payment relates directly to effort because this is not observable by the firm's owner. Instead, the bonus motivates the manager, because higher effort yields higher expected profit.

Illustration: Running the Family Farm

You inherit the family farm when you are halfway through your MBA program. You plan to take a job in consulting and are not interested in, nor do you have the skills for, operating the farm yourself. However, because the farm has been in your family for generations, you do not wish to sell it. You want to pass it on to your children, so you decide to hire a manager. Your neighbors tell you

---

FIGURE
17.6

The Principal–Agent Problem When Effort Is Not Observable

The owner pays a bonus based on profit and flat pay. Because the expected value of the bonus increases with expected effort, the agent increases that effort, which, in turn, increases the revenue. If the increase in revenue exceeds the increase in pay, then profit increases.

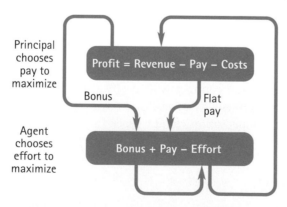

that the going salary for a good manager is \$50,000, but you are worried that such a salary will not motivate the manager to run the farm to its potential. You estimate that a properly motivated manager could change the profit of the farm as shown in Table 17.1. The figures shown in the table are gross, so the manager's compensation must be paid from the profit figure.

Note that, in addition to the manager's effort, profit is also sensitive to the price of grain. With low prices, profits are low, but profits increase if grain prices are higher. You have figured that, with your investments and your own career, the risk of the farm income is not critical to you, so you are interested in maximizing expected profit (after deducting the manager's compensation). The manager's only source of wealth is the compensation from the farm. Being undiversified, he is interested in maximizing expected utility. The manager's utility function if the manager supplies low effort is

$$U = W^{0.5}$$

If the manager supplies high effort, it is

$$U = W^{0.5} - u(e)$$
$$= W^{0.5} - 46.3$$

where U is utility and W is wealth. Note that utility is reduced by 46.3 for high effort. This represents the disutility of effort, $u(e)$.

Flat Salary

Consider first how the manager would behave if paid a flat salary:

$$\text{Utility with low effort} = (50,000)^{0.5} = 223.6$$
$$\text{Utility with high effort} = (50,000)^{0.5} - 46.3 = 177.3$$

Naturally, the manager's expected utility is higher if he supplies low effort. Because the manager is not rewarded for high effort, he will not work hard.

TABLE 17.1

Profit and Managerial Effort

	Grain, low–price (probability 0.5)	Grain, high–price (probability 0.5)
Low effort	\$ 50,000	\$150,000
High effort	\$100,000	\$200,000

Profit–Related Compensation

Because the local labor market for farm managers is competitive, you cannot offer the manager a package inferior to the flat salary of $50,000. Therefore, you must offer him at least 223.6 in expected utility. What portion x of profits would achieve this? To be competitive, x should satisfy

$$\text{Expected utility with flat salary and low effort} = \text{expected utility with bonus of } x \text{ profit and high effort}$$

$$223.6 = (0.5)(100{,}000x)^{0.5} + (0.5)(200{,}000x)^{0.5} - 46.3$$

$$2(223.6 + 46.3) = x^{0.5}[(100{,}000)^{0.5}1(200{,}000)^{0.5}]$$

$$\frac{539.8}{763.4} = x^{0.5}$$

$$x = 0.5$$

Note that the expected compensation would be $0.5[0.5(100{,}000) + 0.5(200{,}000)] = 75{,}000$. The extra $25,000 compensates the manager for both disutility of effort and risk.

We have simply said that, if the manager is paid 50 percent of profit and works hard, he will be just as happy as with a flat salary of $50,000 and low effort. We still do not know whether the manager will choose to work hard when he gets 50 percent of profit. To see whether he will, we need to see whether the 50 percent bonus leads to higher expected utility with high rather than with low effort:

$$\text{EU with high effort} = (0.5)[0.5(100{,}000)]^{0.5} + [0.5(200{,}000)]^{0.5} - 46.3 = 223.6$$

$$\text{EU with low effort} = (0.5)[0.5(50{,}000)]^{0.5} + [0.5(150{,}000)]^{0.5} = 216$$

Therefore, the manager will choose to work hard.

The final question that needs answering is whether you, as owner, are better off paying the manager a flat $50,000 or 50 percent of profits. This is not a trivial question. If you pay the bonus, he will work harder and that will increase revenues. On the other hand, you will end up paying him more on average if you give the 50 percent bonus recall that average earnings with this bonus is $75,000. To increase net profit, the extra expected revenue from high effort must exceed the additional expected compensation.

Your expected net profits will be as follows:

$$\text{Flat salary:} \quad E(\text{profit}) = 0.5(50{,}000) + 0.5(150{,}000) - 50{,}000$$
$$= 50{,}000$$

$$\text{Earnings related:} \quad E(\text{profit}) = 0.5(100{,}000) + 0.5(200{,}000) - 75{,}000$$
$$= 75{,}000$$

CONCEPTS IN CONTEXT

Call Options

A call option is a contract that gives the holder the right (but not an obligation) to purchase a given number of shares of stock in a firm at a preagreed price from a counterparty (the seller of the option). The fixed price is called the *striking price* or *exercise price*.

For example, suppose you have the right to buy *x* shares in six months' time (known as *maturity*) at a striking price of $50 per share. Suppose now that the actual market price of the stock in six months is $42 per share. You can, if you wish, *exercise your option* to buy the stock (which is now worth $42) for the striking price of $50, but that would be a silly thing to do. You can simply go to your broker and buy the stock anyway at the going market price of $42. Why use the option to pay more than the stock is worth?

Now, suppose the stock rises in price so that, in six-months, it is worth $74. You are sitting on a contract that allows you to buy the stock for $50, even though it is now worth $74. You would *exercise your option* to buy the stock for $50, thus clearing a profit of $24 per share.

The value of a call option, hence its price, depends on several features. Most important are

1. The lower is the striking price, the higher the value of the option. The holder gets paid the difference between the market price at maturity and the striking price (if this difference is positive), thus a lower striking price increases the payoff and, therefore, increases the current value of the call option.

2. The higher is the current price of the stock, the higher its value. The higher is the current stock price, the more likely the price at maturity will be above the striking price.

3. The higher is the risk or volatility of the stock price, the higher the option value. Increased risk enhances the possibility that the price at maturity will be very low (downside risk) or very high (upside risk). Increased downside risk does not hurt the option holder because the option will not be exercised, but increased upside risk enhances the payoff at maturity. Therefore, the risk has a one-sided positive effect.

The methodology for pricing options was developed largely by Robert Merton and Myron Scholes, who won the 1998 Nobel Prize for their work.

In summary, the call option allows you to make a profit if the stock price rises above the striking price at the maturity date. However, if the stock price at maturity falls below the striking price, you can throw away the option and not lose anything. Hence, the option gives you the chance of gain without the risk of loss. Naturally, such options are valuable, and you must pay a price to buy the option from the seller.

Therefore, the new 50 percent of profits plan works for both the principal and for the agent.

Some Refinements to Executive Compensation

Figures 17.7 and 17.8 show how different compensation plans can be developed to motivate managers to supply high effort while imposing different levels of risk on them. In Figure 17.7, the higher utility function shows the utility of wealth of the manager who supplies low effort. The lower utility function represents the utility when managers exert high effort. It is shifted downward to show that, for any level of wealth, high effort lowers the utility. Thus, with a flat salary of B, the manager chooses low effort and has a utility level shown as $U(B)$.

MOTIVATING THE MANAGER WITH PROFIT SHARING   Figure 17.7 shows how profit-sharing schemes can affect managerial effort. This is like that

FIGURE 17.7

The Effect of Compensation Schemes on Managerial Effort

The profit sharing gives the manager a 40–60 chance of pay levels A and C, which has an expected utility of EU when the manager supplies high effort. This profit-sharing plan is so designed that working hard gives the manager the same expected utility as a flat salary of B while supplying low effort.

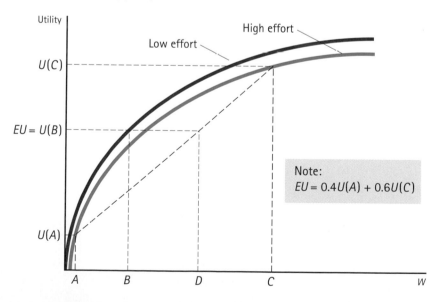

Note:
$EU = 0.4U(A) + 0.6U(C)$

in the farm example; that is, a straight percentage of the firm's profits. The profits of the firm are

50 times *A* with probability 0.4
50 times *C* with probability 0.6

In this case, the manager is paid 2 percent of profits, so his or her income is either

A with probability 0.4
C with probability 0.6

The expected value of this compensation is $(0.4)(A) + (0.6)(C) = D$ in the diagram. The purpose of this compensation is to get the manager to work hard. Note that the expected utility of this compensation with high effort (the lower utility curve) is $(0.4)U(A) + (0.6)U(C)$, which is labeled EU in the figure. This offers exactly the same expected utility as the flat salary of *B* and low effort, so the manager would be just as well off receiving the incentive compensation and working hard as having a flat salary and shirking. However, the expected compensation has been increased from a flat value of *B* to an expected value of *D*. The difference, $D - B$, is the combined premium necessary to compensate the manager for the risk and disutility of effort.

MOTIVATING THE MANAGER WITH AN INCOME GUARANTEE AND STOCK OPTIONS   Note in Figure 17.7 that the manager is risking a 40 percent chance of a fall in income from *B* to *A* in accepting the profit-sharing plan. Can we achieve the same effect while protecting the manager from downside risk? Figure 17.8 shows how we can use stock options. Suppose we replace the incentive plan with a salary floor (i.e., a guaranteed minimum income) of *E* and a stock option, which has a small chance of paying a large amount of money, *F*.

The chances of the stock option paying off are 35 percent. Now the manager's income is either

E with probability 0.65
F with probability 0.35

which has an expected value of *D* (i.e., exactly the same as the profit-sharing plan in Figure 17.7). Note that the expected utility from this plan (if the manager works hard) is $0.65U(E)10.35U(F)$, which is exactly the same expected utility as from the flat salary of *B* and shirking.

Why does this scheme reduce the downside risk? First, the manager is paid a flat salary of *E*. This salary is riskless; it is paid regardless of performance. Second, the manager receives a call option on the firm's stock, which is at risk.

FIGURE
17.8

Reducing Managerial Risk with Stock Options

The manager can be provided minimum compensation and strong incentives for efficiency. A flat salary of *E* is paid together with a stock option, which secures a gain of *F* minus *E* if the stock price rises sufficiently. This combination offers the manager the same expected utility as the simple profit-sharing plan in Figure 17.7.

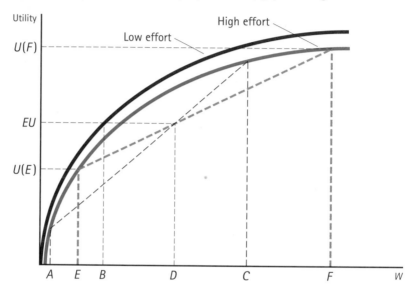

This option gives managers the right to purchase the firm's shares at some future date. Moreover, the price at which the stock can be purchased (the striking price or exercise price) is fixed in advance (see the Concepts in Context box). These call options may have a fairly modest value now but can be worth either nothing or a lot of money at maturity. Therefore, they offer the firm a way of paying the manager a bonus that has modest current value and high risk, with fabulous payoffs to the manager if the stock price rises significantly.

INDEXED STOCK OPTIONS   Both profit-sharing and stock-option plans motivate managers to give high effort; but even if they exert this greater effort, they are not guaranteed high payments. Factors they cannot control (e.g., interest rates) can affect firm performance. Hence, in introducing risk into executive compensation, the manager can be penalized for poor profit performance outside his or her control or rewarded simply because the market as a whole takes an upturn. Indeed, much of the impressive performance of executive compensation plans in the 1990s is as much due to the bull economy as to managerial effort and competence. Can we purge the performance yardstick of this external or exogenous risk?

One plan that has recently attracted attention is the indexed stock option.[3] Here, the manager is given stock options, but the striking price is not fixed. Rather, it is expressed in relation to an index of stock prices, such as the Dow Jones. As the index rises, so does the striking price of the option. This ensures the manager is not rewarded simply because the market performs well. On the downside, the striking price falls as the market index falls. This ensures the manager is not penalized for poor market performance. The net effect of all this is that the manager is handsomely rewarded if the stock price rises relative to the market. This ensures the manager's compensation is more closely related to factors under his or her control.

Insurance and Moral Hazard

In insurance, the principal-agent problem is called **moral hazard**. If you are not insured against fire, car crashes, illness, and other of life's contingencies, you face the possibility of sudden and possibly crippling financial losses. These uninsured risks should make you cautious. You should take care in your driving, look after your health, and protect your home by installing smoke detectors and burglar alarms. Although these safety practices can be costly or inconvenient, you are rewarded by lowering the probability, or intensity, of a financial loss. You bear the cost of safety (you pay for the smoke alarm) and reap the reward (you avoid the costs of a fire). If you are insured, there is a separation of the costs and benefits of safety. The policyholder may incur the cost and inconvenience of safety devices and preventative behavior, but the main beneficiary is the insurance firm, which now faces lower expected losses.

Insurance moral hazard can be divided into two types: ex-ante moral hazard and ex-post moral hazard. Ex-ante moral hazard refers to the tendency of insured people and firms to take less care to prevent future losses when they have insurance. The example of the previous paragraph (absence of smoke alarms) relates to ex-ante moral hazard. Ex-post moral hazard is equally important; this refers to the reluctance of policyholders who have already suffered some misfortune to keep the cost of the event under control. Consider a firm that has bought liability insurance against defective products and has now been sued by injured customers. The policy covers both the legal cost of defending the firm against the suit and the cost of compensating the victims. Because the insurer is paying both these costs, some managerial defendants want the settlement to be very generous. They see this as a way of buying back customer goodwill at the insurer's expense. Other defendants take the opposite view.

[3]These are discussed in Nicholas G. Carr, "Compensation: Refining CEO Stock Options," *Harvard Business Review*, vol. 76, 1998, 15–18.

Because the insurer is paying legal costs, they want the insurer to spend virtually unlimited amounts to defend the producer's reputation, even if it seems that liability is fairly clear.[4] Had the firm been without insurance, it might well have sought to balance the incremental costs of defending a claim with the costs of making a settlement offer to the injured customers.

Principal–Agent Problems between Shareholders and Creditors

Asset Substitution[5]

Our discussion has centered on the stakeholders in a firm: the shareholders and the managers. But, there are other stakeholders under the corporate umbrella, and other principal-agent problems can arise. We consider now the problems that can occur between equity holders and creditors. To focus our attention, we will assume that the board of directors has taken control of managerial compensation and aligned the interests of the shareholders and managers. Therefore, we can be reasonably assured that the managers act on behalf of the firm's owners. The new problem arises because shareholders have gained control (via their incentive-compatible schemes) of the decision-making process but creditors have not.

Consider a drug company with an existing product line that exposes the firm to some risk. Future earnings have an expected present value (PV) of either 100 or 200, each with a probability of 0.5. This risk could reflect different possible scenarios about consumer demand, or it could reflect the potential for the drug to have unforeseen side effects, which would result in a major lawsuit from injured customers. The firm has borrowed money under a bond issue, and this debt has a face value of 100 (the face value is the principal amount of the bond, also called the *par value*). Even under the worst-case scenario, the firm is worth 100 and can pay back its debt. Therefore, there is no chance the firm will default. We can now see how much the equity and the bonds are worth:

The overall value of the firm = 0.5(100) + 0.5(200) = 150

This value can be divided between the shareholders and the bondholders, with the bondholders' obligations being met first and only what is left (the residual

---

[4]Although almost all insurance policies have limits on what they will pay for damages, some policies carry an unlimited obligation on the part of the insurer for legal defense costs.

[5]See Hayne Leland, "Agency Costs, Risk Management and Capital Structure," *Finance*, 53, 1213–1243; and Neil Doherty, *Integrated Risk Management*, chaps. 7 and 8 (New York: McGraw-Hill, 2000).

TABLE 17.2	Project Selection Using NPV		
	Capital cost	Present value of earnings	Expected net present value
Project A	200	220	20
Project B	200	20; probability 0.5	−35
		310; probability 0.5	

claim) going to the shareholders. Therefore, if the firm is worth 100, the debt is paid off and nothing is left for equity. If the firm is worth 200, the debt is paid off, leaving the remaining 100 for the shareholders:

$$\text{Value of bonds} = 0.5(100) + 0.5(100) = 100$$
$$\text{Value of equity} = 0.5(0) + 0.5(100) = 50$$

The firm now faces a new investment decision. It can introduce a new hypertension drug. Its research has come up with two possible formulas. Formula A is moderately effective, has no adverse side effects, and is therefore unlikely to result in any consumer lawsuits. Formula B is a much more effective drug but has greater potential for unwanted side effects. If things go well, the firm could make much more money with formula B. However, if there were a lawsuit, the firm could lose a lot of money. The firm must choose which formula to produce. The capital cost of each project is 200 (as shown in Table 17.2), which will be financed by new borrowing. The third column shows the possible value that can be created. With project A, the present value, PV, of future earnings will be a certain 220. Therefore, the net gain (net present value, or NPV) is $220 - 200 = 20$. In contrast, project B could earn a total of only 20 (if there were a lawsuit) or 310 (if there were no lawsuit).[6] The expected NPV is

$$0.5(20) + 0.5(310) - 200 = -35$$

Which project should the firm choose? Well, clearly project A looks better because its NPV is a positive 20, whereas the NPV of B is a *negative* 35. However, the shareholders might look at the decision very differently.

[6]The earnings from the projects are independent of those from existing operations.

ANALYZING MANAGERIAL DECISIONS

Do Directors Act on Behalf of Shareholders or Managers?

The board of directors should act on behalf of shareholders in resolving the principal-agent problem. However, there is an ongoing debate about how much influence CEOs exert over the directors. The focus is on inside directors, who might be more easily influenced by the CEO. Recent studies show that agency problems are more severe in firms with inside directors. Newman and Moses found that when insiders are on the compensation committee (which designs the compensation for executives), the relationship between firm performance and CEO compensation is weaker.

Further work by Core, Holthausen, and Larcker is more specific. Their evidence shows that, when the governance structure of the firm is weak, the CEO earns greater compensation and the firm's performance tends to be worse. These results stress the importance of the governance structures and the composition of the board of directors in resolv-

ing the agency problem. Influential CEOs can block efforts to resolve the agency problem and can redirect the focus of the board from protecting shareholders to favoring the management.

Sources: John E. Core, Robert W. Holthausen, and David F. Larcker, "Corporate Governance, Chief Executive Officer Compensation and Firm Performance," *Journal of Financial Economics*, Vol. 51, 1999, 371–406; and Harry A. Newman and Haim A. Moses, "Does the Composition of the Board Influence CEO Compensation Practices?" *Financial Management*, Vol. 28, 1999, 41–53.

Value of the Firm If Project *A* Is Chosen

Consider the total value of the firm with each project choice. With project *A*, the firm has either 100 or 200 from existing operations plus an additional 220 from the project. This gives a total value of either 320 or 420. The total value is divided between the bondholders, to whom the firm owes a total of 300 (the original debt was 100, plus the firm borrowed 200 for the new project), and the shareholders. We assume that the original 100 must be paid first (it is called *senior debt*) because it was borrowed first. The debt raised to fund the new project is junior and can be paid only after the original debt is paid.

Note in Table 17.3 that the minimum value of the firm is 320, but it owes a total of 300. Therefore, there is always enough value to pay off the debt in full.

Firm Value If Project A Is Chosen

Value of the firm	0.5(320 + 420)	= 370
Old debt	0.5(100 + 100)	= 100
New debt	0.5(200 + 200)	= 200
Equity	0.5(20 + 120)	= 70

Value of the Firm If Project *B* Is Chosen

If project *B* is chosen, the total value can be either 100 or 200 from existing operations plus either 20 or 310 from the project. This leaves possible total values of

$$100 + 20 = 120$$
$$100 + 310 = 410$$
$$200 + 20 = 220$$
$$200 + 310 = 510$$

The values of the firm and of debt and equity are as shown in Table 17.4.

Here is the problem. The firm borrows 200 to spend on one of these two projects. Then, shareholders must choose which project to undertake. The choice should be clear. Shareholders are better off with project *B*, where their equity is worth 80, than with *A*, where their equity is worth only 70. How can this be? What seems like the worse project actually makes shareholders better off? The problem has to do with limited liability. If the firm undertakes *A*, it creates no risk of defaulting on the debt. Shareholders gain the full NPV of the new project of 20 (note that, before the project is undertaken, equity is worth 50; after project *A*, equity is worth 70). But, if *B* is undertaken, there is a 50 percent chance that the project will fail, resulting in a value of only 20. If that happens, the firm is bankrupt and unable to fully pay off the debt. On the other

Firm Value If Project B Is Chosen

Value of the firm	0.25(120 + 220 + 410 + 510)	= 315
Old debt	0.25(100 + 100 + 100 + 100)	= 100
New debt	0.25(20 + 120 + 200 + 200)	= 135
Equity	0.25(0 + 0 + 110 + 210)	= 80

hand, if the project succeeds (is worth 310), the shareholders reap a big reward. Therefore, when things go well, the shareholders keep all the upside risk; but when things go badly, the shareholders walk away from the debt. Shareholders are playing a "heads we win, tails bondholders lose" strategy.

This illustrates an important principal-agent problem. When firms have a significant amount of debt, the shareholders tend to favor unusually risky investment decisions. It seems that the bondholders are the unwilling victims of these games. But, let us look at the bondholders for a moment. Are they totally helpless? The answer is no. Bondholders must make the decisions of whether to lend to the firm and how much they wish to pay for the bonds. In this case, the firm is trying to issue bonds with a face value of 200 (the bonds contain a "promise" to pay back 200, assuming the firm is still solvent). If you were an investor looking at this firm, your thoughts might progress as follows:

> If I were to pay 200 to buy these bonds, what would the shareholders choose to do with the money? Well, the rational thing for the shareholders to do once they have my money is to choose project B, because the shares would then be worth 80 (compared with 70 for project A). In that case, I should anticipate that B would be chosen, and my new bonds would be very risky and worth only 135 (see the value of "new debt" in Table 17.4 when B is chosen). Consequently, I would be unwilling to buy these bonds for 200, rather I would pay only 135 for them, which is what they are worth.

If we follow the logic a little further, we see that the firm is unable to undertake either project. Because rational bondholders anticipate that B would be chosen, they are willing to pay only 135 for the new debt issue, even though the face value is 200. Because the capital cost of project B is 200, the amount raised from the debt issue would be insufficient to fund the project. Therefore, the firm is unable to finance project B. Does that mean that A would be chosen? Suppose, indeed, that the managers announced their intention to choose A. Unfortunately, investors buying the new debt issue would still rationally assume that, if they subscribed 200 for the issue, the shareholders would change their minds and use the 200 to fund project B. Hence, investors still would subscribe only 135 for the new bond issue. The firm is snookered. It is unable to undertake either project. Because bondholders anticipate the shareholders' temptation to choose the risky negative NPV project, the firm is unable to fund either project. It is forced to sacrifice not only the expropriatory project B but also a project with a genuine positive NPV.

Representing the "Bait and Switch" in Game Theory

Figure 17.9 shows this problem in a game theory form. The shareholders must choose A or B. Bondholders must choose either to pay the full 200 for the new debt or only 135. Because the firm cannot undertake either project unless bond-

FIGURE

17.9

Will Shareholders Pull the Bait and Switch?

If bondholders pay 200, they anticipate that shareholders will choose project B. These bondholders will pay only $135 for the debt. Note the first number at the end of each branch in the payoff for the bondholder and the second number is the payoff for the shareholder.

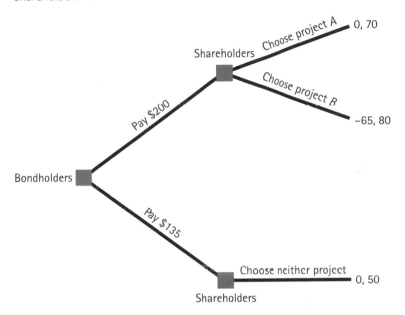

holders pay the full 200, shareholders have only the original equity value of 50 (from the existing product line). However, if the bondholders pay the full 200 to cover the project costs, the shareholders have equity value of 70 from choosing A and 80 from choosing B. The bondholders' payoff is the difference between what they pay for the bonds when they are issued and what they are worth. If the bondholders pay 200 and the firm chooses A, then the bonds are worth 200 and the net payoff is 0. If the bondholders pay 200 and the firm chooses B, then bonds are only worth 135, leaving a net payoff of −65. If the bondholders anticipate the bait and switch, they pay only what the bonds are worth and have a net payoff of zero.

The game is sequential, with the bondholders making the first move. Bondholders anticipate that shareholders will choose B if they pay 200. Therefore, bondholders pay only 135, and shareholders cannot undertake either project and are left with equity of 50. Shareholders would like to make the following promise to bondholders: If you pay 200, then we promise to undertake project A. The problem is that the promise is not credible. Having received the 200, the shareholders would then have the incentive to change their minds. There is a credibility problem; shareholders have an incentive to pull a "bait and switch."

Possible Solutions to the Asset Substitution Problem

There are several ways managers can avoid or minimize this problem:

- *Fund with equity.* The problem arose because managers tried to use debt to fund the project. If they can pay for the project by using internal funds or by making a new issue of shares, then the problem is mitigated or disappears.
- *Establish a reputation for protecting creditors.* If the firm makes a consistent habit of making decisions that preserve the interests of creditors, then a promise not to undertake risky projects in the future might be viewed as credible.
- *Precommit to hedge or insure risk.* Another way this problem is sometimes tackled is that the firm voluntarily commits itself to insure the risks. The problem arose because project *B* was risky, and this risk caused the possibility of default on the debt. If the risk were insured, then bondholders would be protected. Many debt instruments carry a legal obligation for the firm to insure assets.

Product Liability and the Safety of Consumer Goods

Many countries have laws that protect consumers against the risks of injury from defective products. These laws serve two purposes. First, they provide compensation for the injured consumer. If a consumer is injured by a defective product, the firm has to pay compensation. Second, because the firm must pay compensation if products are defective, there is an incentive for the firm to make safer products. Safer products result in fewer costly lawsuits. These laws are the solution to a principal-agent problem. The firm makes decisions on safety, but the consumer bears the costs if the product causes injury. The product liability law is incentive compatible because it aligns the interests of the principal (the consumer) and the agent (the producer).

How Safe Would Projects Be without a Product Liability Law?

We thought of the principal-agent problem earlier as one in which the agent chose a level of effort. The effort to consider here is how much the firm invests to make its products safer. We use s to denote the expenditure undertaken by the firm to make its products safer. Therefore, the cost of safety is s, and the marginal cost is simply 1:

$$\text{Total cost of safety} = s$$
$$\text{Marginal cost of safety} = \frac{ds}{ds} = 1$$

The benefit of safety is that it reduces the expected cost of injuries to consumers. Assume the expected cost of such injuries is

$$\text{Expected cost of accidents} = 4{,}000 - 20s^{0.5}$$

It can be seen that the expected costs of accidents depend on the firm's choice of s. Moreover, as s increases, the expected costs fall. This can be represented as the marginal benefit of safety (because the benefit of safety is a reduction in a cost, we must remember to change the sign):

$$\text{Expected marginal benefit of safety} = \frac{d[-(4{,}000 - 20s^{0.5})]}{ds} = \frac{10}{s^{0.5}}$$

However, in the absence of a product liability law, the firm is not required to compensate consumers for injuries suffered, and these costs fall directly on customers. The expected benefit *to the firm* from safety is zero. Hence, the firm pays all the costs of safety and receives none of the benefits. The profit-maximizing firm chooses $s = 0$. In this case, products are unusually dangerous.

Safety under a Product Liability Law

The product liability law can be rationalized as providing an incentive to managers to make safer products. To achieve this, the costs of accidents are borne by the firm, which now must compensate the victims. Therefore, the expected benefit to the firm from spending s on safety is now the reduction in the expected accident cost. The level of safety now optimal for the firm is that which equates marginal cost and marginal benefit:

$$\text{Marginal cost} = \text{marginal benefit}$$
$$1 = \frac{10}{s^{0.5}}$$
$$s = 100$$

The introduction of the law increases the firm's choice of safety from 0 to 100. Consequently, the expected cost of accidents declines from 4,000 to

[4,000 − 20(10)] = 3,800. This clearly looks like a social benefit, but was the law really necessary to achieve this?

Optimal Safety under a Market Mechanism

Clearly, the product liability law was incentive compatible, but would an incentive-compatible solution evolve under private-market incentives? There is a market-place for information. Specifically, information on the safety of products is widely disseminated in subscription magazines, newspaper articles, and television news shows. The volume of such information is increasing, and cost and access to information are improving as it becomes available over the Internet. Moreover, one might imagine that if there were no product liability law, such information would be more valuable and more widely available. Without a product liability law, consumers would bear the costs of accidents themselves, and safety would be reflected in the demand for, and therefore the price of, products.

Suppose our firm sells a product in a quantity of 1,000, and, to provide a reference point, customers would be willing to pay a price of 30 if they knew the product was perfectly safe. The firm's revenue would then be $30 \times 1,000 = 30,000$. However, information is available about the safety of the product and customers are willing only to pay a price of

$$Price = 30 − (4 − 0.02s^{0.5})$$

The total revenue is now

$$Total\ revenue = 1,000[30 − (4 − 0.02s^{0.5})] = 30,000 − (4,000 − 20s^{0.5})$$

Note that the revenue is now discounted by exactly the expected cost of accidents. Further assume the firm has other costs of production of 10,000. The profit of the firm is now

$$\pi = total\ revenue − cost\ of\ safety − other\ production\ costs$$
$$\pi = 30,000 − (4,000 − 20s^{0.5}) − s − 10,000$$

Now, the firm must choose the level of safety that maximizes profit, so we can set the derivative to zero:

$$\frac{d\pi}{ds} = \frac{10}{s^{0.5}} − 1 = 0$$

Of course, this is exactly the same result we got with the product liability law. This should not be a surprise. With product liability, the firm ended up paying the full expected cost of accidents directly in lawsuits. Under the mar-

MANAGERIAL ECONOMICS IN CONTEXT

The Composition of CEO Pay

The composition of CEO pay is changing with increasing focus on incentives. In a survey of CEO compensation compiled for the *Wall Street Journal*, William M. Mercer Inc. found that, in 1999, salary and bonus represented just over one-third of total compensation, the other 63 percent being long-term incentives and notable stock options (another survey by Pearl Meyer and Partners put the proportion of long-term incentive compensation at 70 percent for the largest 50 companies). These figures compared with roughly 50 percent in salary and bonus and 50 percent in long-term incentives five years earlier. Mercer's Peter Chingos attributes this to companies working to bring pay and performance into closer alignment.

At the very top end of the CEO compensation scale, *Forbes* magazine examined 12 CEOs with pay packages worth more than $100 million. The interesting fact is how little of this was salary and bonus. For example, Robert Knowling, who joined the then-private Covad Communications, accepted a salary and bonus of $650,000. In addition, he received stock shares equal to 5 percent of total equity. After six months on the job, Covac went public through an IPO (initial public offering). Following this IPO, Knowling's shares had a market value of $310 million.

Certainly, the 1990s bull market had an enormous influence on these figures. However, they do illustrate dramatically the importance of incentive compensation.

Sources: Fay Hansen, "Currents in Compensation and Benefits," *Compensation and Benefits Review*, Vol. 35, September/October 2000, 6-14; and *Forbes*, April 3, 2000, 122-128.

ket mechanism, the firm ended up having its revenue reduced by the full expected cost of accidents. Either way, the firm internalized the full cost of accidents and had an incentive to reduce these costs by investing in safety.

What this example shows is that there might be very different ways of solving principal-agent problems. One way can be through the force of civil law, making firms responsible for defective products and, therefore, aligning interests of firms and their customers. The other way is by appealing to market mechanisms by which self-interested customers seek out information and use this information in their purchasing decisions. Customers reward (or punish) firms by varying the price they are willing to pay according to the level of product safety. Therefore, the price mechanism becomes a way of aligning the interest of the firm and its customers.

Summary

1. A principal-agent relationship is one in which a principal employs an agent to undertake a task (shareholders employ managers to run a firm). The

objectives of the principal and agent may be quite different. Shareholders like a high profit and high share price. Managers like such things as prestige, income, pleasant work, and perquisites. More simply, managers may wish to do as little as possible for the greatest possible reward. Therefore, we use the term *effort* to describe when a manager forgoes his or her own objectives (the manager does not shirk) to attend the wishes of the shareholders. Higher effort on the part of the manager can usually increase a firm's profit.

2. The problem for the principal is to motivate the agent to work, not on his or her own behalf but for the benefit of the principal. Shareholders seek to get managers to supply high effort and maximize the firm's profits. If the shareholders could observe the effort of managers, this would be no problem. The managers' compensation could be scaled to the managers' effort. However, if the shareholders do not know how hard managers work, they are hard-pressed to reward them for effort.

3. The full principal-agent problem arises because the firm's owners lack the time or skill to observe all the actions of the manager. In other words, owners cannot observe the manager's effort. Nor can they infer the effort from the firm's revenue or profit if that profit is risky. The solution recognizes that, on average, higher effort results in higher profit. Managers are motivated by being given a share of the profit or an equity stake in the firm. However, this incentive compensation is risky for the manager. Profits can vary for reasons outside the manager's control. Therefore, compensation usually has a fixed component and a profit-related portion.

4. A particularly powerful type of incentive compensation is the stock option. The manager is given an option to buy the firm's stock at some future date at a preagreed-on price. These options are very risky for the manager. If the stock price falls, the options are worth nothing, but a big increase in the stock price can bring fabulous returns. The manager is penalized severely for bad firm performance and rewarded handsomely for good performance. Given the bull stock market of the 1990s, stock option plans brought great wealth to many CEOs.

5. Another type of principal-agent problem arises between shareholders and the firm's creditors. This is known as *asset substitution. Limited liability* means that, when a firm is bankrupt, the shareholders can walk away rather than pay the creditors. This gives an incentive for the shareholders to take on very risky investments. Risk implies a chance of a large upside gain and a chance of a large downside loss. If luck is favorable, the creditors can be paid off, and all the upside gain goes to the shareholders. But if things turn out badly, the shareholders can use bankruptcy law to default on the debt. Thus, high-risk projects have a "heads I win; tails you lose" quality for the shareholders. Of course, the risky projects hurt the creditors. This tension may lead the firm into dysfunctional investment decisions, and the firm may be forced to limit its debt financing to resolve this type of agency problem.

6. The provision of an optimal level of safety can be viewed as a principal-agent problem. Product liability laws require firms to pay for damages caused by their products. The probability of making these payments creates an incentive for firms to make their products safer. We also show that the same level of safety provided by these laws can be attained by the marketplace if consumers can be cheaply informed as to a product's safety level. Unsafe products would then sell at a discount relative to safe ones. Firms would be motivated to improve safety to improve their profits.

Problems

1. Your business generates the following profits (these are stated before compensation is paid to the manager):

	Low demand (0.3)	Medium demand (0.4)	High demand (0.3)
Low effort	$5 million	$10 million	$15 million
High effort	$7 million	$12 million	$17 million

You see that profit depends both on the level of effort chosen by the manager and the level of demand. The demand level is random, and probabilities of each demand level are shown. So, with low effort, expected profit is $10 million; with high effort, $12 million. The manager has a utility function that is either

$$\text{Utility} = (\text{Wealth})^{0.5}, \text{ if effort is low, or}$$
$$\text{Utility} = -100 + (\text{Wealth})^{0.5}, \text{ if effort is high.}$$

Therefore "minus 100" is the disutility of effort. You are interested in maximizing the expected profit after deduction of compensation. You consider three different compensation packages:

- A flat salary of $575,000.
- A payment of 6 percent of profits.
- A flat payment of $500,000 plus half of any profits in excess of $15 million.

Which compensation do you choose?

2. Suppose the typical Florida resident has wealth of $500,000, of which his or her home is worth $100,000. Unfortunately, Florida is in hurricane alley, and it is believed there is a 10 percent chance of a hurricane that could totally destroy the house (i.e., a loss of $100,000). However, it is possible to retrofit the house with various protective devices (shutters, roof bolts,

etc.) for a cost of $2,000. This reduces the size of loss from a 10 percent chance of loss of $100,000 to a 5 percent chance of a loss of $50,000. The homeowner must decide whether to retrofit and thereby reduce the expected loss. The problem for an insurance company is that it does not know whether the retrofit will be chosen and therefore cannot quote a premium conditioned on the policyholder choosing this action. Nevertheless, the insurance company offers the following two policies from which the homeowner can choose: (1) The premium for insurance covering total loss is $12,000 or (2) the premium for insurance covering only 50 percent of loss is $1,500. The typical homeowner has a utility function equal to the square root of wealth. Will the homeowner retrofit the house, and which insurance policy will the homeowner buy? Will the insurance company make a profit (on average) given the homeowner's choice?

3. The expected profit of your firm is 1,000, plus 500 if the manager works hard. The value of the firm's equity (it has no debt) is the expected value of these profits discounted at 10 percent. The manager receives a flat salary of 100 plus a portion x of any equity value in excess of 13,000. The manager's utility function is

$$EU - (\text{compensation})^{0.5} \text{ if she does not work hard}$$
$$EU - [(\text{compensation})^{0.5}21], \text{ if she works hard}$$

What portion x must be paid to the manager to ensure that she chooses to work hard? This new compensation package must be competitive with the 100 flat salary.

4. A firm used to have productive assets that generated an income stream with a present value (PV) of 3,000. However, fire occurred and most of those assets were destroyed. The remaining, undamaged assets produce an income stream that has a present value of only 1,000. Therefore, the fire has led to reduction in the value of the firm from 3,000 to 1,000. The firm could undertake a reconstruction of the damaged assets for a capital cost of 1,500, which would restore the income stream to its preloss level (PV = 3,000). The firm has existing debt of 2,000, which is a senior claim. Would the shareholders choose to reinvest by issuing new equity to pay for the loss or are they better off walking away from the firm? Would the decision made by the shareholders be in the best interests of the bondholders? In answering this question remember that the shareholders have limited liability and therefore the share value cannot be negative.

5. CareLess Industries has two divisions. Division 1 makes cleaning products, and the net worth of this division (PV of cash flows) is 500. Division 2 makes a chemical product. The net worth of division 2 is 300, absent any potential liability. However, there is a chance that division 2 could have a 700 liability for pollution damage. The potential victims have no contractual relationship with the firm. The probability of such a loss is $0.2/(1 + s)$,

where s is the amount the firm spends on safety. The firm must choose the level of s. If you could sell off division 2, would you do so? What is the gain from splitting the firm in this way? Assume a separated division 2 (as a stand-alone firm) is protected by limited liability. Note also the derivative of $a/(1 + s)$ with respect to s is $-a/(1 + s)^2$.

6. SubAquatics (SA) sells scuba diving equipment. Its clients typically read specialist journals and are very well informed about the price, reliability, and safety of SA Products and competitors' products. SA has estimated that, of 100,000 units sold each year at a price of $100 each, there is $4/(1 - s)$ or (4 divided by $1 - s$) fatal accidents due to defective equipment. The value s is the amount spent by SA on safety in millions of dollars.

   a. Assuming that SA is fully liable for such accidents and that the average settlement of each fatal accident is $1 million, how much should SA spend on safety?

   Now assume that SA can escape this liability by selling its product at a lower price under a sale contract that allocates all responsibility for accidents to the purchaser (assume that courts enforce such contracts). Now, if SA spends s (expressed in millions of dollars) on safety, the expected cost of accidents to any consumer is $[4/(1 - s)](\$1m/100,000) = \$40/(1 + s)$. Note that consumers are willing to pay $100 when all liability is assumed by SA (and assuming consumers are risk neutral),

   b. How much would consumers be willing to pay when they bear the cost of accidents?

   c. How much would SA spend on safety?

   d. Assuming that customers cannot observe the level of safety and there is no liability law, how much would SA spend on safety and how much would customers pay for the product?

7. A firm has existing operations that generate an earnings stream with a present value, PV, of 300 or 600, each with 0.5 probability. The firm has 250 in existing debt. The firm wishes to undertake one of the following mutually exclusive new investments:

	Capital cost	PV of earnings	NPV
Project A	400	420	20
Project B	400	0; probability 0.5	-50
		or	
		700; probability 0.5	

The capital cost of each project (400) is financed with new junior debt (face value 400). Is there an asset-substitution problem? (Will shareholders try to choose the lower net-present-value project?) Now, show whether any asset substitution problem would disappear if the new project were to be financed with an equity issue of 400 instead of new debt.

Adverse Selection

CHAPTER

18

We live in the information age as epitomized by the Internet. Buyers can get immediate access to information about the rival products, and sellers can reach millions of potential customers. Consider an enterprise such as the electronic auction eBay. If you wish to buy an antique clock of which only a handful may be for sale across the globe, you have a good chance of finding one of those rare sellers in this vast electronic market. If you wish to sell a used car, you want to expand the number of potential buyers to find one with a particularly high reservation price. Ebay gives you such wide access. This unprecedented access to information has profound effects on markets. Monopolies tend to break down as consumers can search and compare across many sellers. The geographical boundaries of markets are expanding and some markets are truly global. Information fosters competition.

But information can have more subtle effects on how we do business, and we consider some of these in the chapter. In particular, look at *differences* in information between buyers and sellers. In many transactions, selling a car, securing a mortgage, buying health insurance, or investing in a company's stock, the buyer and seller have different information. For example, the seller of a used car usually knows more about the quality of the car than the buyer. The borrower often knows more about his or her credit risk than the lender. The policyholder knows more about his or her state of health than the insurer. And "insiders" in the firm issuing shares of stock know more about the firm's prospects than the investors who may buy the stock. In these transactions, we are not really on a level informational playing field. Does this give the informed party some advantage? Can the party with more information secure a better price when selling the car? Can the informed firm sell its shares to uninformed investors for more than they are truly worth? Is the ignorant party at the mercy of the informed? Or are there any clever defenses the ignorant party can put in place to compensate for its lack of information?

The Market for "Lemons"

Some years ago the Nobel Prize–winning economist George Ackerlof wrote a famous paper on the market for "lemons." A "lemon" is a used car that turns out to have many faults that were not apparent at the time of sale, hence, the bitter taste. Let us call used cars that are virtually free of hidden defects "gems." The fact that some cars are lemons and some are gems may simply be random. But, what Ackerlof had in mind was something a little more disturbing. There may be a systematic process that ensures that a disproportionate number of lemons turn up in the used car market. This process arises from information differences between the buyer and seller. The basic idea is very simple. Sellers know more about the hidden qualities of the cars they are selling than buyers. If I have been driving a car, I know its defects; I know its mechanical record, and whether it has been involved in accidents. Therefore, I know whether I am selling a lemon or a gem. The buyer can invest some time inspecting the car but is never going to be as well informed as the seller. The hidden qualities, good or bad, remain hidden.

Let us try to get into the mind of the buyer. How much is she willing to pay for a used car? She knows some cars are worse than average and some are better than average but does not know where the particular car she considers buying lies on this spectrum. So it seems safe to assume that she is willing to pay, at most, the value of a car of average quality. If the seller has a car that is a gem, he will be most unwilling to sell at this average price since, known only to him, the car is really worth more than average. On the contrary, the seller of the lemon is in rapture. He has a worse-than-average car and a buyer who is willing to pay a price based on average quality. If he does not blow the sale by appearing too eager, he can get a great deal on his banger. Therefore, we find that, at this average price, people tend to hold on to their gems and the cars being offered for sale are predominantly worse than average; they are lemons. And it is all because buyers are uninformed.

It gets worse. Buyers may not know whether a particular car is good or bad, but they can figure out what is happening. They can reason that only owners of lemons would offer their cars for sale at a price reflecting the average quality. Therefore, the selection of cars coming onto the secondhand market is not a true reflection of the overall population of cars but is mostly lemons. So, buyers would not be willing to offer a price that reflects the average quality. Indeed, because they can anticipate that only lemons would be sold, they are willing to buy only at a price appropriate to a lemon. Consequently, no high-quality are cars are offered for sale, only lemons, and the price reflects this low quality. The market for high-quality used cars has disappeared.

You might object to this analysis—surely the seller of a high-quality car can tell the buyer, "My car is better than average and you should pay high price." The problem is that this statement is not credible. The buyer cannot verify this statement, so the owners of lemons have every reason to declare that their cars also are wonderful. Cheap talk is simply not convincing as it can be mimicked by the owners of lemons. Later, we show that there are mechanisms to separate the gems from the lemons but these involve more sophisticated signaling. We have to find a way in which the owner of the gem can send a signal that cannot be mimicked by the owner of the lemon. But, this is for later.

Economists often describe a lemons market as a "market failure." It is certainly desirable from everybody's viewpoint to have a vigorous market in high-quality used cars. But, due to asymmetric information, this market is stunted or killed completely. As we go through this chapter, we look at how the uninformed parties can compensate for their ignorance and how these damaged markets might be restored. But, first, we try to capture the lemons problem a little more formally by working through an example.

A Lemons Example

Of course there are many types of used cars so let us narrow things down to the market for 2000 Toyota Camrys. Some are better than average and, *if consumers knew they were buying one of these gems*, they would be willing to pay $10,000 for it. Other are lemons and, *if consumers knew they were buying a lemon*, they would be willing to offer only $5,000. The problem is that consumers do not know which car is a lemon and which a gem. So, at first blush, they are willing to pay a price of $7,500 reflecting the average quality.[1] Sellers do, of course know the quality of what they are selling.

At a price of $7,500,

1. Owners of gems that really are worth $10,000 would not sell for $7,500.
2. Owners of lemons that are worth $5,000 would be happy to sell for $7,500.

---

[1] We assume there are equal numbers of lemons and gems. For example, with 100 lemons and 100 gems, the average price is [100($10,000) + 100($5,000)]/200 = $7,500. If there were different numbers, then the average price would differ. For example, with 150 gems and 50 lemons, [150($10,000) + 50($5,000)]/200 = $8,750.

Therefore, only the lemons would be sold. Now, consumers, even though they do not know whether any particular car is a lemon or gem, know that only the owners of lemons choose to sell. Therefore, buyers assume that all cars being offered are lemons and are willing to pay only $5,000. The lemon owners should still be willing to sell at $5,000 since they know this is all their cars are worth.

Is the market really that simple? Of course, we oversimplify things somewhat. Buyers are not totally ignorant, and sellers do not know everything. For example, some sellers really do not know the quality of their cars and it is possible that some owners of high-quality vehicles sell at the "average" price. Other sellers may believe their car to be of high-quality but be willing to sell because they have an urgent need for money. Some buyers may believe they have better information or a "nose" for a good deal. The market is not as simple as we portrayed here, and some high-quality cars are sold in the secondhand market. But, the basic ideas of adverse selection still hold in this more realistic world. If it is generally true that sellers on average are more informed than buyers, then there may be some dispersion in secondhand prices, but these prices tend to converge toward the average price. Consequently, while a few people may sell gems at this price, the cars offered for sale are mostly lemons. So, we still get a used car market predominantly stocked with lemons and relatively few high-quality cars.

We can now see why the term **adverse selection** is used. Where buyers are unable to distinguish quality, the price averages across quality groups. However, at this common price, the *selection* of cars being offered for sale is not representative; rather it is weighted toward the low quality, or it is *adverse.*

Adverse Selection in Automobile Insurance

While the expression *lemons* was first used for cars, the term *adverse selection* was first used in insurance. We look now at how adverse selection arises in various insurance markets. To segue from cars to insurance, we first look at automobile insurance. After that, we look at annuities and life insurance.

If the insurance firm, the *insurer,* can distinguish drivers according to their respective loss characteristics, each policyholder can be charged a premium that precisely matches his or her expected loss. Good drivers pay low premiums and bad drivers pay higher premiums. Insurers take some trouble to try to tailor premiums in this way. They ask questions on observable characteristics, such as automobile type, location, or age and gender of the policyholder. And, by careful statistical analysis of their databases, they determine how far each of these characteristics goes in predicting accident rates.[2] This information is then

---

[2]Note that we are not saying that features such as age and gender differences *cause* differences in accident rates, only that there may be a statistical association.

used to set premiums. But, even after classifying in this way, there may still be remaining differences in risk between policyholders. For example, the insurer may determine a premium based on age, gender, vehicle type, and location. But not all 22-year-old men driving sedans in Philadelphia have the same loss potential. The skill levels and behavioral characteristics can vary substantially. So, there is an effective subsidy from low-risk drivers to high-risk drivers within each class. This subsidy can have an unsettling effect.

In Figure 18.1, we consider a category of drivers in the insurance pool, say, the 22-year-old men driving sedans in Philadelphia. Some are worse drivers than others. We call these respectively *high-* and *low-risk drivers*. Each policyholder has a wealth level of 125, but a loss can reduce the wealth to 25; that is, drivers can lose 100 of their wealth should the loss occur. For the high-risk group, the probability of loss is 0.75, resulting in an expected loss of 0.75 (100) = 75. For the low-risk group, the probability of loss is 0.25, resulting in an expected loss of 0.25 (100) = 25.

Perfect Information

First, we show that, if the insurer could distinguish between the two groups, competitive premiums would be charged and each group would buy insurance.

FIGURE
18.1

Adverse Selection in Automobile Insurance

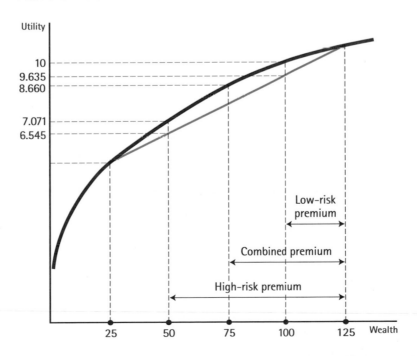

The competitive premiums for each group would be their respective expected losses of 75 and 25 (in practice, the insurer would add an allowance for transaction costs and profit). Using expected utility, we can now show that each person would buy insurance. We need a utility function that reflects risk aversion (if the people were not risk averse why would they buy insurance?):

$$\text{Utility} = (\text{wealth})^{0.5}$$

For the low-risk group, the utility of insuring and having wealth of 100 with certainty (this is derived by subtracting the premium of 25 from the initial wealth of 125; that is, $U(100)$, is higher than the expected utility of not insuring (where wealth stays at the initial 125 without loss but falls by 100 to 25 if a loss occurs).

Low-risk group

$$\text{Utility with insurance} = (125 - 25)^{0.5} = 10$$
$$\text{Utility with no insurance} = (0.75)(125)^{0.5} + (0.25)(25)^{0.5} = 9.635$$

and similarly, for the high-risk group,

$$\text{Utility with insurance} = (125 - 75)^{0.5} = 7.071$$
$$\text{Utility with no insurance} = (0.25)(125)^{0.5} + (0.75)(25)^{0.5} = 6.545$$

The respective positions are shown on the vertical axis of Figure 18.1.

Asymmetric Information

Now suppose that the insurer is unable to distinguish between high- and low-risk drivers. If there are equal numbers of low- and high-risk drivers, the insurer can break even by charging the average premium of $\frac{1}{2}(25 + 75) = 50$. But, will each group now continue to buy insurance? It is clear that the high-risk drivers will buy insurance. If they would have bought insurance at a premium of 75, then surely they still will buy if the premium is reduced to 50.

So, high-risk drivers

$$\text{Utility with insurance} = (125 - 50)^{0.5} = 8.660$$
$$\text{Utility with no insurance} = (0.25)(125)^{0.5} + (0.75)(25)^{0.5} = 6.545$$

But, for the low-risk group, the insurance premium has increased from 25 to 50. We can compare the expected utility with, and without, insurance for this group:

$$\text{Utility with insurance} = (125 - 50)^{0.5} = 8.660$$
$$\text{Utility with no insurance} = (0.75)(125)^{0.5} + (25)^{0.5} = 9.635$$

So the low-risk group would not buy the insurance. The only people who would buy insurance at the common price of 50 are the high-risk drivers. If you think one step ahead, you realize that this pricing structure is not tenable for the insurer. If only high-risk drivers buy the insurance, then each policyholder costs 75 (on average) in claims but pays a premium of 50. The insurer loses 25 on average for each policy and cannot stay in business unless premiums are increased to 75. The insurer offers full insurance only at a premium of 75. Now, who will buy this policy? We saw that the high-risk drivers get utility of 7.071 from buying this policy but have expected utility of 6.545 if they buy no insurance. So high-risk drivers buy the insurance. Good drivers do not buy the policy as now shown:

$$\text{Utility with no insurance} = (0.75)(125)^{0.5} + (0.25)(25)^{0.5} = 9.635$$
$$\text{Utility with insurance} = (125 - 75)^{0.5} = 7.071$$

This illustration is a perfect "lemons" market. Because of the inability of the insurer to discriminate between high- and low-risk drivers, it offers only one type of policy, which appeals to only the high-risk drivers. An *adverse selection* of drivers choose to purchase insurance. The people who suffer from the information problem are the low-risk drivers, who are priced out of the market.

We can restore the market so that the low-risk drivers have an appropriate choice of policies in two ways. Competition between insurers may help reduce the problem. Information on loss expectancies of individual drivers is of economic value to an insurer. Armed with such information, an insurer can selectively attract low-risk drivers from a rival who is unable to discriminate simply by offering a lower price and admitting only low-risk drivers. Thus, competition induces insurers to seek and compile information that enables them to use premium structures that discriminate to some extent among risk groups. Of course, information is never perfect, and adverse selection never disappears. But, in an actively competitive market, adverse selection is reduced to a level that reflects the cost of information.

The second way that markets might be restored calls for a little strategic thinking on the part of the insurer. We get to this later, but we offer a teaser here. Is there any way to induce the policyholders to reveal information about themselves in a credible way? Suppose we offered a choice to each driver; choose *A* or choose *B*. Can we design these alternatives such that only a low-risk driver would choose *A* and only a high-risk driver would choose *B*? If we can come up with such a menu, then we can infer what risk type each person is from what item he or she selects from the menu. This idea of *self-selecting menus* is discussed shortly.

The Market for Annuities

Another interesting adverse selection illustration is the market for annuities. Many people now have defined-contribution retirement plans. Under these plans, the employer or the employee (or both) make explicit contributions to a pension plan. The money is invested in some investment vehicle, and the value of the invested assets at retirement is available to the retiree. There is no guarantee of an income in retirement (unlike defined-benefit plans). So, suppose that someone wishes to take this sum of money and convert it into an income stream that will last until he or she dies. For example, if I knew I would live for 10 years, I could take my cash, divide it by 10 (with a little adjustment for investment income), and have a constant income stream for the rest of my life. The problem is that I cannot predict when I will die. In this savings scheme, I run out of money if I live for more than 10 years. I then sponge off my kids.

An annuity can solve my problem. Even though I do not know how long I am going to live, I can buy an annuity that converts my principle into a constant income stream for the remainder of my life. Essentially, I give my cash to an annuity firm (usually a life insurance company) that, in return, promises to pay me a constant annual sum for as long as I live. Thus, I "insure" against living too long and running out of money. Let us consider the annuity firm for a moment. This firm sells many annuities. But, take a block of 1,000 65-year-old women all of whom buy annuities. We work through two simple examples of how annuity markets work. In the first case, the health status of each individual is known both to that person and to the annuity firm—perfect information. In the second case, there is asymmetric information—the person knows her health status but the annuity firm does not. After we work through these two examples, we show some evidence to settle the score.

Annuity Markets when There Is Full Information

Our 65-year-old women differ. All are not in the same state of health, and consequently, they have different life expectations. For example, consider that

- $\frac{1}{4}$ of our population is in poor health and expected to live for only five years.
- $\frac{1}{2}$ is in average health and has a life expectation of 15 years.
- A further $\frac{1}{4}$ is in excellent health, with a life expectancy of 25 years.

Each person has $300,000 in capital and wishes to buy an annuity. Because the annuity firm knows each person's life expectation, it can make the following deals (to keep things very simple, we ignore interest and allow the annuity firm to break even):

- Those with a life expectation of five years are offered an annuity of $60,000 per year. The firm receives $300,000 up front and pays five annuity payments of $60,000 = $300,000.

- Those with a life expectation of 15 years are offered an annuity of $20,000 per year. The firm receives $300,000 up front and pays 15 annuity payments of $20,000 = $300,000.
- Those with a life expectation of 25 years are offered an annuity of $12,000 per year. The firm receives $300,000 up front and pays 25 annuity payments of $12,000 = $300,000.

In an economic sense, this is a "nondiscrimination" case. Each receives an annuity based on her own health status and no one subsidizes anyone else. Moreover, if annuity markets were perfectly competitive, this is the result that would occur.

Annuity Markets with Asymmetric Information—Adverse Selection

To start this, assume that the annuity firm now charges everyone a premium of $300,000 and pays $20,000 per year until the person dies. This same annuity can be purchased by anyone. To see what adverse selection does to this market, we have to ask who knows what about each person's health. Annuity firms can often find out something about health; they can ask for a medical test.[3] But, what are the annuity firms worried about when they ask for a test? They are certainly not worried about people being ill and having a five-year life expectancy. For each of these people, the firm receives $300,000, and pays five installments of $20,000, thus clearing a profit of $200,000 on each of these people. On the contrary, they are worried about people being too healthy and living too long. The annuity firm loses $200,000 on each of these (i.e., it receives $300,000 and pays 25 installments of $20,000). In testing people, the firm tries to spot those who are too healthy and will live too long. This is not so easy. Verifying that people are ill is one thing. Verifying that people who may wish to pretend they are ill but are indeed healthy is quite difficult. So the annuity firm usually lacks good information on the respective health status of its customers.[4] On the other hand, the persons know a lot about their own health sta-

---

[3]There are some restrictions on their ability to seek this information. For example, they are often not entitled to ask for genetic information.

[4]Contrast this with life insurance. Here, customers wish to pretend they are healthy so they can get good rates. And the insurance firm's task is to weed out those who are less healthy.

tus; they know their medical history, their dietary and exercise habits, and so forth. So, we have the classic information asymmetry that can lead to adverse selection. Finding health problems is a lot easier than finding the absence of them.

Now imagine that the annuity firm knows from its records that

- $\frac{1}{4}$ of the population is in poor health and expected to live for only five years.
- $\frac{1}{2}$ is in average health and has a life expectation of 15 years.
- A further $\frac{1}{4}$ is in excellent health, with a life expectancy of 25 years.

What it does not know is the particular health status of each particular applicant. So the firm figures it can break even if it receives $300,000 from each applicant and offers each an annuity of $20,000. To see this, the total income for the annuity firm is

$$1000 \times \$300{,}000 = \$300{,}000 \text{ m}$$

The total annuity payments[5] are

250 people ($\frac{1}{4}$ of 1,000) die after 5 years
$$= 250 \text{ times } \$20{,}000 \times 5 \text{ years} = \$\ 25{,}000 \text{ m}$$
500 people ($\frac{1}{2}$ of 1,000) die after 15 years
$$= 500 \text{ times } \$20{,}000 \times 15 \text{ years} = \$150{,}000 \text{ m}$$
250 people ($\frac{1}{4}$ of 1,000) die after 25 years
$$= 250 \text{ times } \$20{,}000 \times 25 \text{ years} = \$125{,}000 \text{ m}$$
$$\text{Total payments} \qquad\qquad\qquad \$300{,}000 \text{ m}$$

Another way to see this example is to look at the after-the-fact income statement for each group.

Those dying after 5 years pay $300,000 for the annuity and
$$\text{receive } (5)(\$20{,}000) = \$100{,}000$$

The annuity firm makes a profit of $200,000 on each of these individuals.

Those dying after 15 years pay $300,000 for the annuity
$$\text{and receive } (15)(\$20{,}000) = \$300{,}000$$

The annuity firm breaks even on each of these individuals.

Those dying after 25 years pay $300,000 for the annuity
$$\text{and receive } (25)(\$20{,}000) = \$500{,}000$$

The annuity firm loses $200,000 on each of these individuals.

[5]In practice, the annuity sum reflects both some markup for the firm's profit and also accounts for investment income.

Who buys the annuity? If those in poor health believe they have a life expectation of only five years, then five annual payments of $20,000 at an up front cost of $300,000 is (in annuity jargon) a lousy deal. These people would probably be much better off simply drawing down their capital. For example, if they allow themselves $30,000 a year, they will not run out of money until after 10 years (twice their life expectancy). So those in poor health are very unlikely to buy the annuity paying $20,000. Those in average health may be inclined to buy since they remove any uncertainty and get a reasonable financial deal (remember we are ignoring interest). Those in excellent health find the annuity of $20,000 per year to be a fabulous deal—they pay $300,000 and get back $500,000. So this deal appeals to only some of our 1,000 65-year-olds. Only those in average or better than average health buy the annuity.

Of course, the annuity firm can anticipate that only those in average or better-than-average health buy the policy, and if it offered an annuity of $20,000, it would lose money. To see this, note that it would break even on each of the 500 people in average health and lose $200,000 on each of the people in excellent health. Therefore, it would have to *reduce* the value of the annuity such that it breaks even on those choosing to buy at this reduced value.

Here is an open question. Suppose that the annuity firm reasons as follows. If it gets 500 people in average health and 250 in excellent health, the average life expectation is:

$$\frac{500}{750} \ (15 \ \text{years}) + \frac{250}{750} \ (25 \ \text{years}) = 18.333 \ \text{years}$$

So, the firm estimates that it can offer an annuity to everybody of $16,364. This is calculated by dividing the upfront price of $300,000 by the life expectation of 18.333 years. Will the firm really break even? If you answer no, then figure out what break even annuity the firm can offer and who will buy an annuity at this price. (Clue: Do not forget that the firm may know the proportions of the population with different health status, but it still does not know the health of each individual.)

Evidence of Adverse Selection in the Annuity and Life Insurance Markets

A very simple test can be used to see whether annuity markets are subject to adverse selection. Recall that, in the preceding illustration, the *population* held 1,000 people and the average life expectation was 15 years, calculated as follows

$$\frac{1}{4} \ (5 \ \text{years}) + \frac{1}{2} \ (15 \ \text{years}) + \frac{1}{4} \ (25 \ \text{years}) = 15 \ \text{years}$$

If the annuity was offered at $20,000, then only the 750 people in average or better-than-average health would actually buy it. Therefore, the life expectation of the annuitants is now

$$\frac{500}{750} \text{ (15 years)} + \frac{250}{750} = 18.333 \text{ years}$$

If we could observe life expectation, we could see whether it was greater for the annuitants than for the population as a whole. The problem is that we cannot observe life expectation. However, we can observe the actual mortality rates of the two populations. If the average life expectation of annuitants is indeed higher than that for the populations as a whole, we should find that those buying annuities would, on average, live longer than the population as a whole. We draw on some evidence from two colleagues at Wharton comparing the life span of annuitants with the population in the United States.[6] Figure 18.2 shows the distribution of age of death for those buying annuities and for the whole U.S. male population. The distribution for annuitants is clearly shifted to the right, indicating that they do indeed live longer on average.

The Absence of Adverse Selection in Life Insurance

While annuities "insure" people against living too long and running out of money, life insurance protects the survivors of people who die too soon. If life insurance firms have less information about the health status of each of their policyholders than the policyholders themselves, we would expect adverse selection here, too. But, do insurance companies indeed have less information?

Recall that, when we discussed annuities, we suggested that it might be quite difficult for the annuity firm to exclude those in good health; establishing the "absence" of poor health is difficult. Well, the evidence on annuities showed that there indeed seems to be an information asymmetry. Now the life insurance firm's task is to seek out those in poor health. And, life insurers routinely conduct medical examinations on those seeking life insurance and turn down (or charge higher premiums to) those who do not perform well on the medical exam. Does this suggest that there should be no information asymmetry and therefore no adverse selection? Let us see.

In Figure 18.3, we show some evidence drawn from the United States both for men and women. These figures show the histograms of mortality; that is, how many people die in different age groups. If insurance companies did not conduct effective medical exams and there was adverse selection, we would

---

[6]This is taken from David McCarthy and Olivia Mitchell, "International Adverse Selection in Life Insurance and Annuities," 2003.

FIGURE
18.2

Mortality Distributions for the U.S. Population and Annuitants

Source: O.S. Mitchell and D. McCarthy. "Annuities for an Ageing World," in E. Fornero and E. Luciano, eds., *Developing an Annuities Market in Europe* (Northhampton, MA: Edward Elgar, 2003).

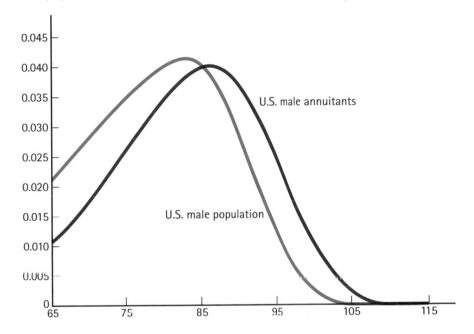

expect that the more healthy people would be less inclined to buy insurance and that the mortality rates for the insured population would be higher than for the population as a whole. But this is *not* what we see. The distribution for the insured population is clearly shifted to the *right*, indicating that mortality rates are *lower* among those who have life insurance. The same pattern can be seen for both men and women, but it is less dramatic for women. The same pattern has been observed in the United Kingdom. It appears that, far from having an information disadvantage, life insurance firms have been very effective in establishing the health status of their policyholders and offering insurance predominantly to those in good health.[7] There seem to be no traceable adverse selection here.

[7]There is another possible explanation for these results. People who buy life insurance probably have higher than average wealth. And, wealth is also associated with health and longevity. Therefore, the reason that insured people live longer may have more to do with their wealth rather than the insurance company screening.

FIGURE
18.3

Distribution of Age at Death Conditional on Attaining Age 25

Red line shows the distribution of age of death for the population and the blue line shows the distribution of age of death for those purchasing life insurance.

Source: D. McCarthy and O.S. Mitchell, "International Adverse Selection in Life Insurance and Annuities," S. Tuljapurkar, ed., in *Population Aging in the Industrialized Countries: Challenges and Explorations* (forthcoming), Figures 4 and 5. Derived using data provided by the Society of Actuaries. *Basic Mortality Table 1990–1995* (Schaumberg, IL: Society of Actuaries, 1997).

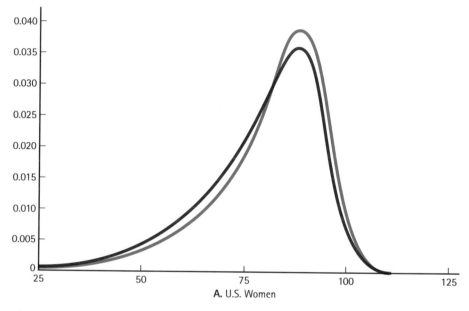

A. U.S. Women

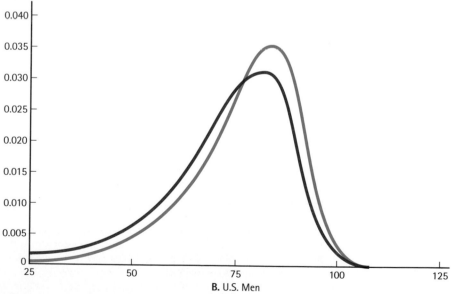

B. U.S. Men

Resolving Adverse Selection through Self-Selection

While Ackerloff laid out the adverse selection problem, Michael Rothschild and Joseph Stiglitz laid out an elegant solution to adverse selection. (Stiglitz was later awarded a Nobel Prize.) The idea behind the solution is simple. If the buyer of the secondhand car simply asks about quality, the answer is not really credible. If the insurance firm simply asks how bad a driver you are, you are certainly going to embellish your answer. Simply asking is not enough. How can the uninformed party get credible information? Consider, for example, the insurance company. The insurer does not know whether any driver is a high or low risk. But the insurer does know the following:

1. That some drivers are high risk and some are low risk.
2. That the drivers themselves know whether they are good or bad drivers.

The insurer can reason that, because individuals know their own risk type, they might sometimes use this private information to reach different decisions. Can the insurer design a problem to present to all drivers such that the good drivers will choose one solution to the problem and the bad drivers will choose another? An insurer that can come up with such a problem can observe each driver's decision and infer what type of driver he or she is. What the insurer is trying to achieve here is to induce the drivers to sort themselves into their risk types by the choices they make.

Well, this is all abstract. Let us think of a problem that does the trick. The insurance company offers every driver that seeks insurance a choice between two policies, full insurance or a high deductible:

- Policy A has a high premium (designed to break even if bought only by high-risk drivers) and offers full insurance. Full insurance means that every loss is paid in full.
- Policy B has a much lower premium but a big deductible. A deductible means that the insurer does not pay the full loss but pays the loss minus some fixed amount. For example, suppose that the policy has a $2,000 deductible. If there is a $20,000 loss, the insurer will pay $20,000 − $2,000 = $18,000. With a $5,000 loss the insurer pays $5,000 − $2,000 = $3,000, and so forth. If the loss is less than $2,000, the insurance firm pays nothing.

If you know you are a bad driver, you know that you are likely to have a claim, so the deductible is a big deterrent. It is much better to pay the higher premium and avoid the deductible. But, if you know you are a good driver, you reason that the premium saving is more important since you are unlikely to have a claim and, therefore, unlikely to be faced with the deductible. So good drivers select the cheaper deductible policy and bad drivers select the more expensive, full coverage.

Let us try another problem that induces this type of self-sorting: flat premiums or experience-related premiums:

- Policy A has a relatively high price. Furthermore, the driver can buy the policy next year, and the year after, and so on, at the same price. The premium does not go up (except for inflation) even if the driver has claims under the policy.
- In the first year, the premium for policy B is higher than for policy A. However, the premium changes in future years according to the number of accidents the driver has. If there are no claims, the premium falls to a level far below that for policy A. If there are claims, the premium stays at the high level, that is, a little higher than A.

Now put yourself in the bad driver's position. You can choose either policy. You know yourself there is a high chance you will crash your car and make an insurance claim. Therefore, policy B should look very unattractive. The potential premium reduction for having no claim is not really relevant given your self-knowledge. So, you come to the conclusion that, if you buy policy B, you always (or at least often) pay a higher premium. But, good drivers see the choice differently. For them, the chance of a very big premium reduction is attractive because they believe they are unlikely to have a claim. For them, the high likelihood of a big premium reduction more than makes up for a slightly higher premium in the first year.

Solving a Simple Adverse Selection Problem

We work through an illustration of the second problem. In the earlier example, each driver had an initial wealth of 125 and could lose 100 with a crash. The probabilities of a crash were

$$\text{Probability that bad drivers crash} = 0.75$$
$$\text{Probability that good drivers crash} = 0.25$$

We know from this example that the market for good drivers collapses altogether. Indeed, the only policy that would be offered is a policy offering full insurance at a premium of 0.75 (100) = 75, designed to break even for high-risk drivers. Only bad drivers buy insurance at this price. No insurance policy is offered that would appeal to good drivers. Can we do better?

Suppose we now offer the following two policies and each driver can choose which, if any, to buy:

- Policy 1 charges a premium of 75 but the policy fully pays for the loss of 100 if a crash occurs. Anyone buying this policy will have a wealth of 125 minus the premium of 75 = 50. Note that, because of the full insurance, the wealth of the individual is unaffected by whether the loss occurs.

- Policy 2 pays a fixed sum of 10 if the loss occurs and the premium is 2.5. Anyone buying this policy will have a wealth of

With no loss: 125 minus the premium of 2.5 = 122.5
With a loss: 125 minus the premium of 2.5,
minus loss of 100, plus the payment of 10 = 32.5

Clearly policy 2 is not a prefect insurance policy, but it offers some compensation for loss. Let us examine the choice facing each type of policyholder. First, look at the high-risk, bad drivers. Note that high-risk drivers (and low-risk drivers later) know their probability of loss so they use this probability when taking expected utility:

No insurance utility $= (0.25)(125)^{0.5} + (0.75)(125 - 100)^{0.5} = 6.545$
    Policy 1 utility $= (125 - 75)^{0.5} = 7.071$
    Policy 2 utility $= (0.25)(125 - 2.5)^{0.5} + (0.75)(125 - 100 - 2.5 + 10)^{0.5}$
        $= 7.043$

For the low-risk drivers, the expected utilities are taken using the low-risk probabilities:

No insurance utility $= (0.75)(125)^{0.5} + (0.25)(125 - 100)^{0.5} = 9.635$
    Policy 1 utility $= (125 - 75)^{0.5} = 7.071$
    Policy 2 utility $= (0.75)(125 - 2.5)^{0.5} + (0.25)(125 - 100 - 2.5 + 10)^{0.5}$
        $= 9.726$

Note that the two types of drivers choose different policies. For high-risk drivers, the best choice is policy 1 which offers them a utility of 7.071 (versus 7.043 for policy 2 and 6.545 for buying no insurance). But, for low-risk drivers, policy 2 is the best choice, offering them a utility of 9.726 (versus 7.071 for policy 1 and 9.635 for no insurance). In making these choices, individual policyholders act entirely in their self-interest (i.e., maximizing expected utility) and use their private information about their loss probabilities. Note also that this self-selection has taken place without the insurance firm being able to identify which policyholder is at low risk and which is at high risk of accidents. Hence, we can call this a **self-selection menu.**

There are other interesting features about this solution. When we introduced this adverse selection problem earlier in the chapter, only one policy survived, policy 1. In that earlier analysis, the good drivers prefer self-insurance to buying policy 1. Now with the self-selection menu comprising policies 1 and 2, we have made the good drivers better off (they prefer the newly introduced policy 2 to self-insurance) while bad drivers are in the same position (they continue to buy policy 2). This is a clear improvement, we improved the lot of good drivers at no cost to the bad drivers. So, the offer of this menu has at least partly salvaged the marketplace by enabling low-risk drivers to get at least some insurance.

Finally, we need to know whether such a menu is feasible. The most immediate worry is whether the insurance company will want to offer both policies. Because the policyholders self-select, the insurer, in fact, breaks even with each policy.

- Only high-risk drivers buy policy 1. The expected claims are 0.75 (100), which matches the premium of 75.
- Only low-risk drivers buy policy 2. Hence, expected claims are 0.25 (10), which matches the premium of 2.5.

Therefore, a competitive insurer can offer this choice and survive.

This solution to the adverse selection problem is called a **separating equilibrium**. It is in the interests of the uninformed insurer to offer such a choice; and the choice induces self-selection by the policyholders into their respective risk types. But, note that information asymmetry still imposes a cost. The insurance coverage in policy 2 does not offer complete protection to the low-risk drivers. While clearly better than no insurance, the coverage is rationed.

The Rothschild–Stiglitz Model

The problem we just solved is an illustration of the Rothschild-Stiglitz model, named after its inventors. In Figure 18.4, we illustrate this model as applied to the insurance problem we just looked at. There are still two risk types, who we will identify simply as high risks (with a high probability of loss) and low risks (with a low loss probability). As before, the individuals know their particular risk type but the insurance firm does not. The diagram illustrates the choice of contracts and shows how a separating equilibrium is reached.

The horizontal axis shows the amount of coverage purchased. People can buy insurance to reimburse them for some portion of their loss; they can buy full coverage, which covers the full replacement cost of the car, or they can scale their coverage to some percentage of the loss. In the extreme, they may buy no coverage at all. The premium is scaled according to the level of coverage. We show two premium lines. The higher, green, line shows a premium designed to just cover expected losses for high risks. For example, for a premium of P_H, policy H can be purchased, which provides full coverage. A second, blue premium schedule, designed to cover just the expected losses of low risks, is shown. For a premium of P_L, the policy labeled L can be bought, which provides about 70 percent coverage. The two policies, H and L, are offered to all policyholders, who may choose freely.

Who will choose which policy? To help us, we have shown indifference curves for the two risk types. Recall that indifference curves were described in earlier chapters. These devices show different combinations of two economic

FIGURE

18.4

The Rothschild–Stiglitz Model

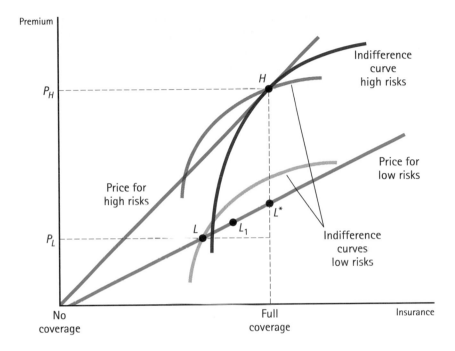

items that yield the same level of satisfaction to the individual. These curves slope upward at a decreasing rate, showing that people have a liking for insurance but dislike paying the premium. In econ-talk, insurance is a "good" and the premium is a "bad." We show only one indifference curve for the high risks and two curves for the low risks. Any points to the northwest of a person's indifference curve leave the individual worse off (they imply higher premiums or less coverage) and points to the southeast of the indifference curve improve the person's welfare. The red indifference curve for the high risks is steeper at any point than the orange indifference curves for the low risks. This difference in slope reflects the fact that high risks, knowing their risk type, are willing to pay more for coverage.

The two policies lie almost on the same indifference curve for the bad risks; policy H is right on the red indifference curve but policy L is slightly below. Therefore, high-risk policyholders just prefer policy H to L and, if offered the choice, choose H. For low-risk drivers, the choice is more pronounced. Policy L lies on a much better (i.e., southeasterly) yellow indifference curve than policy H. Thus, we now have the two types of policyholder choosing different policies. Moreover, although the insurer does not know which person is of which risk type, it has carefully designed the policy choice so that the high risks choose the policy priced to break even if held by high risks, and the low risks choose the policy priced to break even when held by low risks. Thus, the insurer does not lose money.

Note again that the low risk policy, L, does not offer full insurance. Any policy that offers more insurance coverage at the low-risk price lies along the low-risk price line to the right of L. More coverage clearly benefits the low-risk driver because they are risk averse. However, if we increased the coverage of policy L to say L_1 or even to L^*, we would run into a problem with the high risks. If offered a choice between H and L_1, the high risks would clearly prefer policy L_1. Now both risk types would choose L_1 over H. There is no self-sorting of the policyholders into their risk groups. But, recall that the policy L_1 breaks even only if purchased by low risks—the insurer loses money selling this policy to high risks. So any insurer offering the menu H and L_1 loses money and is unable to sustain this offering.

This model is designed to show how adverse selection can be resolved with a competitive insurance market. There are various extensions of this approach. The most important of these build in profit for the producer and look at how markets evolve over time with adverse selection. A caution is needed. It may not always be possible to find a choice for every possible situation that induces self-selection into different consumer types. Nonetheless, these separating choices can be found for many situations, and we look at one or two more examples.

Using Education as a Signal: Adverse Selection in the Job Market

An early, and somewhat surprising, application of this approach was presented by the economist Michael Spence. The problem he had in mind is straightforward enough; the solution is quite clever. Like other examples, we make the point by presenting an oversimplified example. We show that people use education to send a signal to potential employers of certain labor market skills that cannot be easily measured by employers. Of course, schools and universities also teach something. We are not denying this but simply pointing out that they serve a second purpose.[8]

You do not know everything about your job market skills, but you probably know a lot. You know how ambitious you are, how organized you are, whether you are prepared to work hard and long hours. You know something

---

[8]All the authors are professors, and their jobs might depend on this caveat.

about your "people" skills and your intellectual skills. These are initially not known to a potential employer, who may learn of your abilities only gradually and over a long time period. So, there is an information asymmetry. As in the insurance and annuity markets, simply asking people to reveal their private information does not work. Of course, I have learned how to best prepare my vita and have honed my interview techniques to present myself in the best possible light. In other words, we all try to deceive the employer into believing that we are better than we are. So we need a credible method for separating those who know they have good job skills from those who lack them.

The technique relies on there being a relationship between good job skills and good academic performance. This need not be a perfect relationship; only that, on average, people with good job skills have an easier time overcoming academic hurdles. We take an undergraduate degree that requires you to pass 30 courses. Many people do this in four years, but some take three years and others may take five or six, because they have to repeat courses or have a smaller course load. The cost of getting the degree, therefore, varies according to the length of time it takes. These costs include the direct costs of paying for education and the opportunity costs of losing wages because you are not working. Directs costs mount as courses are repeated and the lost wages climb as you take longer to finish.

Consider the following example. Average direct and indirect costs per course are

$$\text{High-quality job skills} = \$2,000 \text{ per course}$$
$$\text{Low-quality job skills} = \$3,450 \text{ per course}$$

Now, assume that, if employers knew the different job skills up front, they would pay the following wages:

$$\text{High-quality job skills} = \$50,000 \text{ per year for 5 years}$$
$$\text{Low-quality job skills} = \$30,000 \text{ per year for 5 years}$$

After five years, the employer is able to figure out your job skills.

Suppose that employers make the following offer. *All those that have taken at least x courses are paid a salary of $50,000 and those that took less than x courses are paid $30,000.* The trick for the employers is to choose the value of x to separate the high- and low-skilled workers.

Students know this offer stands, and they have to decide how many courses to take. So, they rationally look at the costs and benefits of different degree programs. The *benefit* of completing x courses to any student, of high or low skill, is that they increase their wage from $30,000 to $50,000 for five years giving a total benefit of $100,000 (we ignore the time value of money, i.e., discounting, here). But, the costs differ, being $2,000 per course and $3,450 per course for the high- and low-skilled people.

High skill: Benefit of achieving x courses = $100,000
Costs of achieving x courses = $2,000 times x

The benefit exceeds the costs if x is less than 50.

Low skill: Benefit of achieving x courses = $100,000
Costs of achieving x courses = $3,450 times x

The benefit exceeds the costs if x is less than 29.

So the employers now choose a level of x between 29 and 50. Say, they choose $x = 30$, which is the typical four-year degree program. People with low-quality skills do not choose to take the 30-course degree (the costs are $3,450 \times 30 = \$103,500$, and the benefit is only $100,000). But high-skilled types take the 30-course degree (cost is $2,000 \times 30 = \$60,000$, and the benefit is $100,000).

So, by cleverly setting the 30-course standard, employers persuade people to reveal their hidden information in the way they choose their education. Universities now provide two functions. In addition to actual teaching, they *screen* people according to employment skills and endorse these skills to potential employers. Another way of thinking about this is provided by our MBA students. When asked why they go for the MBA, many reply, "Because employers pay more for an MBA because they know that anyone accepted to this program and obtaining the degree must be good." Therefore, if a university wishes to signal to the market that its graduates are of high quality, it must set the standards sufficiently high to discourage low-skilled people.

Of course, education has other functions in addition to sorting people according to job skills. Ideally, people learn something as well.

Induced Adverse Selection and Social Policy: The Case of Genetic Testing

Adverse selection does not always result from the lack of information. Sometimes adverse selection is deliberately chosen as a social policy. We have many laws that prevent people or firms using information that is readily available. For example, we cannot use race as a factor in deciding who we employ or to whom we sell particular products.[9] We cannot use gender as a factor in some

[9]This is the thrust of antidiscrimination laws. However, affirmative action laws require that race be used as a matter of social policy as an instrument of reverse discrimination.

economic transactions. Many states have laws prohibiting the use of genetic tests in making employment decisions or underwriting life or health insurance. And, some states prevent insurance firms from charging different automobile insurance premiums to people who live in certain high-risk areas. These laws are passed because some particular group feels that the use of that particular information will place them at an economic disadvantage or we decide that the use of the information is morally wrong.

Scientific knowledge about the human genome has advanced by leaps and bounds in the 50 years since Watson and Crick cracked the structure of DNA. The pace has accelerated more recently with the mapping of the genome. As a result of this ongoing research, we improve diagnoses and develop new treatments and cures for some conditions and diseases. But, there is another important effect. Genetic tests reveal who is at risk for many diseases, such as breast cancer or Huntington's disease. And this information has economic value. For example, take health insurance or life insurance. As we have seen, in a competitive market, insurance companies classify people on the basis of information that helps predict their probability of having a claim. Thus, given positive test results for certain genetic diseases, insurance firms might choose to decline to offer insurance or to charge higher premiums. Let us ask two questions. First, would the use of such information by insurers be fair? Second, would the use of such information make the market more efficient?

The question of fairness is often posed like this. People cannot choose their genes. Through no fault of their own, some people may be unable to get insurance or forced to pay high premiums. Some of the same people might also have low income and be unable to pay the high premiums. Their genetic condition might also make it difficult to hold down a full-time job. Why should these people be discriminated against? This argument certainly has appeal and is often promoted by patient advocacy groups and the medical profession (two of the stakeholders). This appeal has been sufficiently compelling that some states have restricted the use of genetic tests in insurance underwriting and pricing.

But does the fairness question have more dimensions? We can use the type of reasoning of this chapter to pursue the issue a little further. First, let us take a simple version of the adverse selection model depicted in Figure 18.1. We reproduce this idea in Figure 18.5. Suppose that all people have initial wealth of W, which falls to $W - L$ if the disease caused by the genetic defect occurs, as shown on the horizontal axis. First, consider that the insurer is allowed to charge different premiums according to risk. The insurer charges premium P_{GT} if the policyholder has a positive result (indicative of a genetic defect) from a genetic test, and the policyholder has the utility denoted U_{GTI} (the subscript GTI suggests genetic test and insurance). If this type of policyholder had no insurance, the utility would be EU_{GT} which is lower than U_{GTI}, so insurance would be purchased. Now consider another policyholder, without adverse genetic test

FIGURE
18.5

Adverse Selection Model

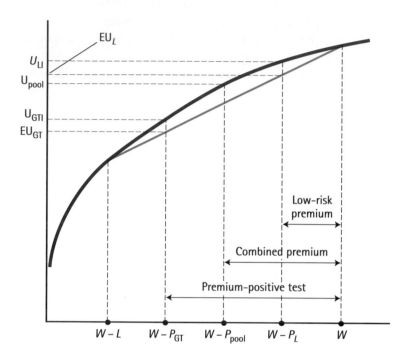

results. This person's risk is lower on average[10] and the appropriate premium is P_L. The utility for buying insurance for this type is U_{LI}, which is greater than the utility for not buying insurance, EU_L, so they would buy insurance.

Now, the state passes a law stating that genetic tests results cannot be used by insurers. Therefore, everyone must pay a pooled premium of P_{pool}. At this premium, the utility for buying insurance is U_{pool}. This is a good deal for those with positive test results, $U_{pool} > EU_{GT}$. But, it is unattractive for those without positive test results, $U_{pool} < EU_L$. So the low-risk people prefer not to have insurance. Let us now discuss these results a little further.

If health insurance is voluntary, then the law forbidding use of genetic test results increases the number of uninsured. In this simple model, this does not seem too bad because the uninsured are the low-risk people, and you could argue that they are less in need of insurance than those with adverse genetic inheritance. However, this seems a high price to pay when the model also pre-

---

[10] It may be that there are some untested people among this group who do, nevertheless, have an adverse genetic condition. However, there are lots of others with no such condition. Therefore, the average risk is lower than for the group testing positive.

dicts that there is no gain to those the law was supposed to protect. Because those at low risks have been priced out of the pool, the insurer has to charge the premium P_{GT} to break even. Thus, the law has not made those with positive genetic tests any better off but made everyone else worse off.

If health insurance is compulsory, then one can retain the low-risk group in the pool and subsidize those with positive test results. However, some arguments suggest that this may be an inefficient way to protect the high-risk people. Many economists would argue that it would be better to supplement the income of the high-risk people so they could afford the high insurance premiums, rather than distort insurance prices and consumption decisions. With this solution, the pattern of consumption does not match consumer preferences.

In practice, health care systems are compulsory in some countries and voluntary in others. In the United States, health care is usually provided with employment, but nevertheless, an estimated 40 million people are without health insurance. Those that are uninsured in the United States are not all at low risk and typically have lower than average incomes. These are usually the unemployed and low-wage workers. As health insurance costs rise, the number of uninsured will tend to rise. Thus, subsidizing those with positive test results tends to increase insurance premiums, raise the cost of health care, and increase the number of uninsured. Therefore, the fairness question is quite complex. In the current design of health care, one might be forced to choose between those with genetic defects and the uninsured.

Induced Adverse Selection and Wharton MBAS

A very similar type of induced adverse selection is chosen by various universities and student groups. The Wharton MBA students have a policy of nondisclosure of grades to prospective employers.[11] There has been much emotional debate on this issue, and being a little too close to this debate, we are not really brave enough to address it head on. But, we argue that the issue is very similar in structure to other adverse selection problems. In Table 18.1, we present the usual arguments made for and against grade disclosure. We ask that you look at these arguments and ask the following questions: Who gains and loses with, and without, grade disclosure? Will employers seek to obtain the information (e.g., ability to solve tasks, knowledge of subjects, ability to display that under pressure) conveyed in grades in other ways? If so, will these alternative ways of acquiring information be more or less efficient than through grades? If employers do not seek alternative ways of obtaining this information, will this affect the matching of people with particular abilities to jobs that demand those abilities?

---

[11]This is a policy adopted by the students themselves, and is not a school administrative policy.

TABLE
18.1

Argument For and Against Grade Disclosure

Pros	Cons
Grades convey some useful information about potential workplace productivity and, therefore, help employers recruit the most suitable people for each job.	Grades do not convey all the information needed by employers to assess value in the workplace; therefore, they are misleading. It encourages employers to ignore other important job skills.
Competition for grades motivates better performance in school and, thus, enhances learning.	Students in an MBA program are highly motivated and can direct their own learning more effectively if they are not competing for grades.
Individual performance and team performance are constantly measured in the real world and not regarded as mutually exclusive. An individual's contribution to a team is an important performance measure.	Many student tasks are graded in teams, which requires cooperation among team members. Grade disclosure makes people more competitive and, thus, less-effective team members.
Grade disclosure is fair, since it rewards people who spend more time on their studies to communicate the fruits of their effort to potential employers.	Grade disclosure is unfair, since it penalizes people who choose to spend time on extracurricular tasks such as student politics or community service.

Summary

Adverse selection arises when one party to a contractual or economic relationship knows more than the other. For example, the seller of a used car knows more than the buyer, the policyholder knows more than the insurance company, and the borrower knows more than the lender. This puts the uninformed party at a disadvantage. For example, insurance companies are unable to distinguish between safe and unsafe drivers; therefore, premiums are averaged over both types. This means that good drivers end up subsidizing the bad, and many good drivers may be tempted to cancel their insurance to avoid this subsidy. In the extreme case, adverse selection may bring a market crashing down as all the low-risk people are priced out of the market. Similarly, all sellers of high-quality used cars might decide to keep them rather than sell at a price reflecting average quality.

There are defenses against adverse selection. The obvious one is to become informed. We saw that, while adverse selection exists in the annuity market, life insurance companies seem to have been successful in removing the information problem by medical examinations. But, what if full information is not always obtainable? An ingenious strategy was derived by Rothschild and Stiglitz that induces people to reveal their private information in the self-interested choices they make. The uninformed party designs a menu of contracts designed so that the contracts have differential appeal to the different types. For example, in insurance, the offer might be a high-priced policy offering full insurance versus a low-priced policy to cover only part of the damage. Bad drivers get very worried about the partial coverage, since they know they are likely to have an accident. On the other hand, good drivers might like the partial coverage, since it is cheap and they figure they are unlikely to be in a crash. Games like the insurance menu are seen elsewhere. In labor markets, education is used as a signal of worker productivity, and producers might use warranties to distinguish their products from those of rivals.

References

G. Ackerlof. 1970. "The Market for Lemons: Quality Uncertainty and the Market Mechanism." *Quarterly Journal of Economics*, Vol. 84, 488–500.

M. Rothschild and J. Stiglitz. 1976. "Equilibrium in Competitive Insurance Markets: An Essay on the Economics of Imperfect Information." *Quarterly Journal of Economics*, Vol. 90, 950–958.

M. Spence. 1974. *Market Signaling*. Cambridge, MA: Harvard University Press. For a review of adverse selection theory, see "Adverse Selection in Insurance Markets." 2000. In G. Dionne, ed., *Handbook of Insurance*, Boston, MA: Kluwer.

And, for a review of empirical test of adverse selection, see P.-A. Chiappori and B. Salanie. 2000. "Testing for Asymmetric Information in Insurance Markets." *Journal of Political Economy*, Vol. 108(1), 56–78.

Problems

1. Sellers of used cars know the quality but buyers do not. So imagine that used Toyota Corollas are worth $10,000 if high quality and $5,000 if of poor quality. While buyers may not know the quality of any car, they do know that 25% will be of poor quality. In such a market, what cars will be sold on the second hand market and at what price?

2. The market for digital cameras is relatively new. Ajax Inc. produces what they regard as a high quality digital camera. Knockoff Inc. produces what they regard as a low quality digital camera. However, since the market is so new, reputations for quality have not yet developed and consumers can-

not tell the difference between an Ajax digital and a Knockoff digital just by looking at them.

If consumers knew the difference, they'd be willing to pay $200 for a high quality camera (i.e., their reservation price for a high quality camera) and they'd be willing to pay $100 for a low quality camera. It costs Ajax $60 to produce a high quality camera and it costs Knockoff $25 to produce a low quality camera.

A recent MBA hire at Ajax suggests that Ajax could differnetiate its camera from Knockoff's by offering a full coverage warranty (i.e., one which would fully cover any defect in their camera at no cost to the customer). The MBA estimates that it would cost Ajax $20 per year to offer such a warranty. The MBA also estimates that it would cost Knockoff $40 per year should Knockoff attempt to copy Ajax's warrenty strategy. Consumers will feel that the camera with the longest warranty is high quality and that with the shortest warranty is low quality. The camera companies want to maximize the profit per camera.

What's Ajax's profit per camera in the digital camera market?

3. No-State Insurance Company has made the following estimate of auto damage for several groups of potential customers who own cars worth 10,000. There are an equal number of customers in each group. No-State is risk neutral.

Group	Initial Value of Car	Probability of Accident That Devalues Car to 5,000
A	10,000	0.2
B	10,000	0.3
C	10,000	0.4

State regulation mandates every customer must pay the same premium regardless of their group and this premium must be sufficient to cover all expected claims from those who purchase insurance from No-State. There are no additional costs to the company other than the paying off of claims. All consumers have the following utility function (U) where

$$U = W^{0.5}$$

and where W is the consumer's wealth as represented by the value of their car.

What premium would No-State offer for full coverage insurance?

4. Some people are good drivers and others bad drivers. The former have a 10% chance of crashing their cars and the latter have a 30% chance. All have a total wealth of 400 but this will fall to 100 if they crash their cars. In other words, each will lose 300 of wealth if the crash. You are an insurance company who wishes to offer a pair of policies to all drivers. Each policy is designed to break even (zero profit) given the people that choose

to buy that policy. The first policy has a premium of 90 and covers all losses (i.e., will pay 300 in the event of a crash. The second policy has a premium of 5 and will pay 50 in the event of a crash. Who will buy which policy? Will the insurance company, (a) make a profit, (b) break even or (c) lose money?

Each person has a utility function as follows

$$\text{Utility} = (\text{wealth})^{0.5}$$

5. Consider a market for annuities for 70 year old males in which people differ both in terms of their expected remaining years of life and their risk preferences. Of the population of 200, half (i.e., 100) have a life expectancy of 9 years and the remaining half have a life expectancy of 11 years. We can express risk preference in the following way. The risk people are worried about is the risk of living too long and running out of wealth. The more risk averse you are, the higher the up-front price you are willing to pay for the annuity. The more risk-averse people are willing to pay 1.3 times "x" times the "A" where "x" is the expected years of life remaining and "A" is the dollar amount paid each year to the annuitant. Less risk-averse people are only willing to pay 1.1 times "x" times "A"/ Assume of the 100 people in each health group, half are more risk averse and half less risk averse.

Now the annuity firm sells and annuity of $50,000 per year for as long as the buyer lives and the price of the annuity is $50,000. Because the annuity firm cannot tell whether each applicanat is high or low life expectancy, it must accept any application for its product. What is the expected profit of the annuity firm? (You may if ignore discounting in this example.)

PART

6

Government-Business Relations and the Global Market

Government
and Business

CHAPTER

19

Bill Gates, chairman of Microsoft, the computer software giant, is a billionaire, yet he and other top executives of Microsoft had to be concerned with the U.S. Department of Justice's investigation of the firm's competitive practices. The government prevailed, and Microsoft was found guily of antitrust violations. This set in motion appeals of the verdict. The government and Microsoft ultimately reached a compromise.

The government is a major player for business. Managers must be aware not only of the antitrust laws but also laws for fair trade, employment, safety, environmental issues, and securities. U.S. companies, who often complain of excessive government interference with their activities, are now complaining about a lack of rules in the developing countries of the world. The game of business cannot be played without rules, and the government sets the rules.

In general, economic regulation has decreased in the United States in the last 25 years. Transportation and banking are two prime examples. Previously, government agencies controlled which carriers could enter and exit the transportation industries, the prices they charged, and whether they could merge or not. In banking, the range of services banks could provide was once heavily regulated; banks could provide banking services but not insurance or brokerage. After deregulation, transportation became like the restaurant industry—any company could enter and charge what it wished.

Yet, noneconomic regulation (which can have major economic costs) has grown in recent years. For instance, safety regulation and hours of service (number of hours on duty) regulation continue in the transportation industry. Laws are passed each year that affect how business is conducted.

Governments collect taxes that affect disposable income and the final prices of goods. Governments spend money that affects the demand for goods. Tax laws affect corporate investment policy. Governments subsidize certain goods, like agricultural products, that increase their production. Governments certify whether and when certain goods can appear in the market, as in the case of drugs, both legal and illegal. Governments provide infrastructure, like roadways, which are an important part of many firms' production functions.

Thus, government activity is pervasive. It accounts for over a third of our gross domestic product. If you plan to move to the top of the executive ranks, be prepared to interact not only with your colleagues and rivals but also with government agencies.

In this chapter, we discuss the nature and effects of public regulation, antitrust policy, and the patent system. Managers must not only understand the nature of public policy in these areas, they must understand what public policy is designed to achieve. Too frequently business executives lack the breadth of view and knowledge required to act effectively to promote their firms' interests in the public arena (even though over 20,000 registered lobbyists, many of them corporate, are in Washington).

Competition versus Monopoly

The Supreme Court has stated that "competition is our fundamental national policy." Many economists agree that competition is preferable to monopoly (or other serious departures from perfect competition), because it is likely to result in a better allocation of resources. As we saw in Chapter 11, a monopolist tends to restrict output, driving up the price. These economists argue that, from the point of view of social welfare, it would be better if the monopolist raised its output to the competitive level. (Also, in their view, monopolists are likely to be less efficient than competitive firms.) While economists are by no means unanimous on this score, the majority seem to prefer competition over monopoly.

One way our society has tried to deal with these problems has been to establish government commissions like the Federal Communications Commission and the Interstate Commerce Commission (now abolished but with some residual authority retained in the Surface Transportation Board) to regulate the behavior of monopolists. In this way, as we see in subsequent sections of this chapter, the government has tried to reduce the harmful effects of monopoly. In addition, Congress has enacted antitrust laws meant to promote competition and control monopoly. These laws, too, are discussed at length in this chapter. Any manager must be aware of the nature of these laws, since violating them may mean fines and jail sentences.

Although the United States has gone further in promoting competition than other major industrialized countries, this does not mean that our dedication to competition is complete. National policies are too ambiguous and rich in contradictions to be characterized so simply. The truth is that we, as a nation, have adopted many measures to promote monopoly and limit competition. For example, this is the effect of the patent system, which is designed to promote invention and innovation. In later sections of this chapter, we see why it is felt that the patent system is beneficial, even though it creates temporary monopolies.

Regulation of Monopoly

In some areas of the economy, such as the distribution of water, it is not economical for more than one firm to exist due to important economies of scale. In such industries, the single firm, a so-called natural monopolist, is in a position to charge a higher-than-competitive price for its product. Since such a price may lead to an inefficient allocation of society's resources, as well as to monopolistic profits regarded by the public as excessive and unjustifiable, government regulatory commissions often are established to set limits on the prices that a monopolist of this sort can charge.

Consider the Acme Water Company, whose demand curve, marginal revenue curve, average cost curve, and marginal cost curve are shown in Figure 19.1. Without regulation, the firm would charge a price of P_0 and produce Q_0 units of the product. By setting a maximum price of P_1, the commission can make the monopolist increase output, pushing the price and output to what they would be if the industry were organized competitively. If the commission imposes a maximum price of P_1, the firm's demand curve becomes P_1AD', its marginal revenue curve becomes P_1ABR', its optimum output becomes Q_1, and it charges the maximum price of P_1. By setting the maximum price, the commission aids consumers, who pay a lower price for more of the product. By the same token, the commission takes away some of the Acme Water Company's monopoly power.

Regulatory commissions often establish the price—or the maximum price—at the level at which it equals average total cost, including a "fair" rate of return on the company's investment. In Figure 19.2, the price would be set by the commission at P_2, where the demand curve intersects the average total cost curve. The latter curve includes what the commission regards as a fair profit per unit of output. Considerable controversy arises over what constitutes a fair rate of return as well as what should be included in the company's investment on which the fair rate of return is to be earned.

FIGURE
19.1

Regulation of Acme Water Company: Maximum Price

By setting a maximum price of P_1, a regulatory commission can make Acme increase output to Q_1.

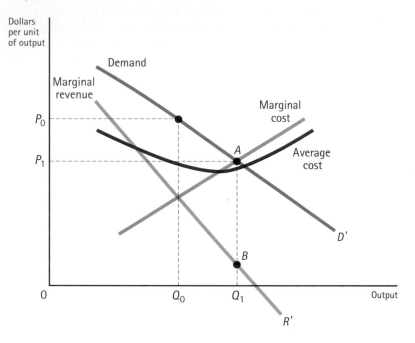

To illustrate the workings of the regulatory process, consider the telephone industry in Michigan. The two organizations that played a key role in the regulation of the telephone industry there are a firm, SBC Michigan (a subsidiary of SBC Corporation), and a commission, the Public Service Commission in Michigan.[1] Although SBC Michigan is not the sole telephone company in the state, it is the dominant firm, and there is no direct competition between firms in the industry. The commission, composed of three people appointed by the governor, has had authority over the telephone industry for over half a century.

General-rate cases play an important role in the regulatory process. Such cases are initiated by the firms, based on company claims that earnings are too small and a higher price level is needed. Demand is generally assumed to be price inelastic; consequently, higher prices are assumed to result in greater revenues. The industry usually receives less than it requests (and commission

---

[1]Ameritech (American Information Technologies Corporation) is one of seven regional holding companies resulting from the breakup of the American Telephone and Telegraph Company (AT&T), which is discussed on pages 760–761.

FIGURE
19.2

Regulation of Acme Water Company:
Fair Rate of Return

The regulated price is P_2, where the demand curve intersects the average total cost curve, which includes what the commission regards as a fair profit per unit of output.

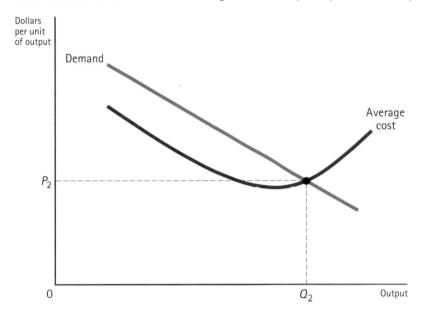

decisions lag behind the industry's revenue requests). However, the fact that the commission does not approve all requests does not imply that the company is constrained much by the commission, since the company may have asked for more than it thought it would receive.

The commission tries to regulate the industry so that earnings equal a "reasonable return on the value of a firm's existing plant." Yet a host of questions concern what constitutes a "reasonable return" and the "value of a firm's existing plant." The original cost or historical cost of the plant is the measure on which most commissions base their estimates of the value of the plant; but some permit firms to use replacement-cost valuations instead. In the early 1980s, regulated firms often asked for a rate of return of about 10 to 15 percent; commissions in recent years have approved rates of return of about 6 to 10 percent.[2]

[2]See R. Noll and B. Owen, eds., *The Political Economy of Regulation* (Washington, DC: American Enterprise Institute, 1983); W. Shepherd and C. Wilcox, *Public Policies toward Business* (6th ed.; Homewood, IL: Irwin, 1979); and W. Shepherd, ed., *Public Policies toward Business: Readings and Cases* (Homewood, IL: Irwin, 1979).

ANALYZING MANAGERIAL DECISIONS

The Social Cost of Monopoly

Consider the following figure. A monopolist would set price at P_M and output at Q_M. Consumer surplus under a monopoly would be A; producer surplus under a monopoly would be $B + C$; hence, the social welfare under a monopoly would be $A + B + C$.

If the market were perfectly competitive, price would equal marginal cost (P_C) and quantity would be Q_C. The consumer surplus under perfect competition would be $A + B + D$. The producer surplus would be $C + E$, and the social welfare $A + B + C + D + E$.

Therefore, the social welfare under perfect com-

petition is $D + E$ greater than under a monopoly. This is often called the *social welfare triangle* or *deadweight loss triangle*. The rationale for this welfare cost of monopoly is that the demanders along segment XY of the demand curve are willing to pay more than the marginal cost (ZY) of producing the goods (between the quantites $Q_C - Q_M$), yet the monopolist does not produce such socially beneficial goods (restricting output at Q_M).

Part of the rationale of antitrust policy and regulation is to ensure that society captures part or all of this $D + E$ triangle.

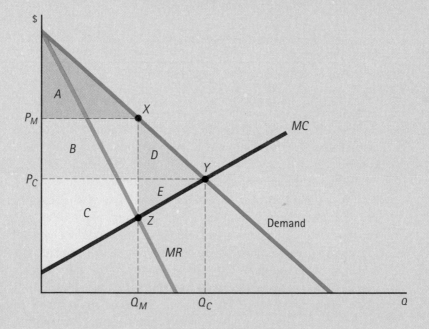

The Trenton Gas Company:
A Numerical Example

To illustrate the workings of public utility regulation, consider the Trenton Gas Company, which has assets of $300 million. The state Public Utility Commission, after considering the extent of the risks assumed by the firm and conditions in the financial markets, decides that a fair rate of return for the firm would be 10 percent. Trenton Gas is allowed to earn profits of 0.10($300 million) = $30 million per year. These profits are not economic profits; they are accounting profits. As stressed already, commissions try to allow firms to earn only a normal or fair rate of return, which tends to rule out economic profits (recall Chapter 1).

What price will the firm set, and what will its output be? To answer these questions, it is important to note that the demand curve for gas provided by the firm is

$$P = 30 - 0.1Q \tag{19.1}$$

where P is the price per customer (in dollars) and Q is the number of customers served (in millions). The firm's total cost equals

$$TC = 10 + 5Q + 0.9Q^2 \tag{19.2}$$

where TC is total cost (in millions of dollars). Note that this concept of total cost does not include the opportunity cost of the capital invested in the firm by its owners. Therefore, the firm's accounting profit equals

$$\pi = (30 - 0.1Q)Q - (10 + 5Q + 0.9Q^2)$$
$$= -Q^2 + 25Q - 10 \tag{19.3}$$

where π is the firm's profit (in millions of dollars).

Since the commission has decided that the firm's accounting profit should equal $30 million, we set π equal to 30, which implies that

$$30 = -Q^2 + 25Q - 10$$
$$Q^2 - 25Q + 40 = 0 \tag{19.4}$$

which is an equation of the form $aQ^2 + bQ + c = 0$. We can use the following equation to solve for the roots of this equation:

$$Q = \frac{-b \pm (b^2 - 4ac)^{0.5}}{2a}$$

$$= \frac{25 \pm [(-25)^2 - 4(1)(40)]^{0.5}}{2(1)}$$

$$= \frac{25 \pm (465)^{0.5}}{2}$$

$$= \frac{25 \pm 21.56}{2}$$

$$= 1.72, \quad \text{or} \quad 23.28$$

Because commissions generally want public utilities to serve as many customers as possible, the larger figure, $Q = 23.28$, is the relevant one. Therefore, the price is set as follows:

$$P = 30 - 0.1(23.28)$$
$$= 27.67$$

To sum up, the Trenton Gas Company's price will be $27.67, and it will serve 23.28 million customers.

The Lone Star Gas Company: A Case Study

As a further illustration of how regulatory commissions work, we look at an actual case. In 1978, the Lone Star Gas Company, which provided gas to 1.1 million residential and commercial customers in the Dallas–Fort Worth area, requested an increase in its price. The Texas Railroad Commission is the state regulatory body with authority over the rates that gas companies can charge. To decide whether an increase should be granted, the commission began by determining the appropriate rate base. The company's assets that were "used and useful" were identified and valued at their historical cost. After allowing for accumulated depreciation, the original cost of invested capital was calculated to be $185 million.

To establish the rate of return that Lone Star Gas should earn on this invested capital, the cost of both debt and equity capital and the percent of each to total capitalization were estimated. The cost of capital was estimated to be 13.87 percent for common equity, 9.75 percent for preferred equity, 8.59 percent for long-term debt, and 9.98 percent for short-term debt. After weighting each of these costs of capital by the percent of total capitalization it represented, the result was 11.1 percent. Thus, the commission concluded that Lone Star Gas should earn an 11.1 percent return on its invested capital of $185 million.

To earn this return, the firm should make an annual profit of 0.111 × $185 million, or $20.535 million. Since the firm's actual profit was only about $9.8 million, the commission decided to allow the firm to raise its price to the extent necessary to bring its profit up to the "reasonable" level of $20.535 million.[3]

Effects of Regulation on Efficiency

Regulators try to prevent a monopoly from earning excessive profits. As we saw in previous sections, the firm is permitted only a "fair" rate of return on its investment. A difficulty with this arrangement is that the firm is guaranteed this rate of return, regardless of how well it performs. If the regulators decide that the Acme Water Company should get a 9-percent rate of return on its investment, it will get this rate of return regardless of whether the Acme Water Company is managed well or poorly. Why is this a problem? Because, unlike a competitive firm, there is no incentive for the firm to increase its efficiency.

The regulatory process is characterized by long delays, which, ironically, may go partway toward encouraging efficiency in regulated firms. In many regulated industries, a proposed rate increase or decrease may be under review for months before a decision is made by the commission. In cases in which such a price change is hotly contested, it may take years for the required hearings to take place before the commission and for appeals to be made subsequently to the courts. Such a delay between a proposed price change and its ultimate disposition is called a **regulatory lag**. Long regulatory lags are often criticized by people who would like the regulatory process to adapt more quickly to changing conditions and yield more timely decisions. But an advantage of regulatory lags is that they result in some penalties for inefficiency and rewards for efficiency.

To illustrate, consider a regulated company whose price is established so that the firm can earn a rate of return of 9 percent (which the commission regards as a "fair" rate of return). The firm develops and introduces some improved manufacturing processes that cut the firm's costs, allowing it to earn 11 percent. If it takes 15 months for the commission to review the prices it approved before and modify them to take account of the new (lower) cost levels, the firm earns a higher rate of return (11 percent rather than 9 percent) during these 15 months than it would if it had not developed and introduced the improved manufacturing processes.

While the regulatory lag does restore some of the incentives for efficiency (and some of the penalties for inefficiency), it does not result in as strong a set of incentives as competitive markets. A fundamental problem with regulation is that, if a regulatory commission prevents a firm from earning higher-than-

[3]For further discussion, see M. E. Barrett and M. P. Cormack, *Management Strategy in the Oil and Gas Industries: Cases and Readings* (Houston: Gulf, 1983). The present treatment is simplified for pedagogical reasons.

CONSULTANT'S CORNER

A Dispute over a Requested Gas Rate Increase

The Boston Gas Company's request for a $17 million rate increase was examined at hearings conducted by the Massachusetts Department of Public Utilities. One consumers' group, which opposed the rate increase, argued that the gas company should be allowed a 10.5-percent rate of return, while the company asked for a 12.46-percent rate of return. The company also argued that, because of the regulatory lag, it was receiving considerably less than the 12-percent return it was allowed by the commission. Since the previous rate increases had not become effective until almost a year after they were requested, the company earned about 9 percent, not 12 percent.

At the hearing, an economist testifying for the consumers' group argued that the company's cost of equity capital was about 12 percent, whereas an economist hired by the company testified that it was about 16 percent. This was an important issue in the case. Both economists used the following equation:

$$k_t = \frac{D_1}{W} + g$$

where k_t is the required cost of capital at time t, D_1 is the dividend paid next year, W is the firm's capitalized value, and g is the annual rate of growth in the corporate dividend, to estimate the company's cost of equity capital; but the economist hired by the consumers' group assumed that the annual rate of dividend growth, g, would equal 0.01, whereas the company's economist assumed that it would equal 0.05.

If asked to advise this firm, what suggestions would you make concerning ways to reduce the adverse effects of the regulatory lag on the company's earnings? What sorts of analyses would you carry out to determine which of the two estimates of the cost of equity capital is closer to the truth?*

*For further discussion, see Barrett and Cormack, *Management Strategy in the Oil and Gas Industries.*

average profits, there may be little incentive for the firm to increase its efficiency and introduce innovations.

The Concentration of Economic Power

Government regulatory commissions are not the only device used by society to deal with the problem of monopoly; another device is the nation's antitrust laws. The antitrust laws reflect a feeling that excessive power lies in the hands of relatively few firms. According to the latest Census of Manufacturing (1997), manufacturing firms have a total book value of assets over $1.55 trillion. The 100 largest firms employ 16.1 percent of the manufacturing workforce, pay 22.6 percent of the manufacturing payroll, use 14.8 percent of the manufacturing production workers, create 31.7 percent of the value added in manufacturing, purchase 30.6 percent of the raw materials used in manufacturing, and make 28.6 percent of all the capital expenditures made by manufacturing firms. These percentages seem to have increased considerably since the end of World War II. Although bigness is not necessarily the same as monopoly power, there is a widespread feeling that economic power is concentrated in a relatively few hands.

The antitrust laws are aimed at promoting competition and limiting monopoly. As stressed, many economists believe that competition is preferable to monopoly because competition tends to result in a more effective allocation of resources. To measure how close a particular industry is to being perfectly competitive (or monopolized), economists devised the market concentration ratio, which shows the percentage of total sales or production accounted for by the industry's four largest firms. The higher the percentage, the more concentrated the industry.

Table 19.1 shows market concentration ratios for selected industries. These ratios vary widely from industry to industry. In the cigarette industry, the concentration ratio is very high, 98.9 percent. In the retail bakery industry, it is very low, 2.5 percent. The concentration ratio is only a rough measure of an industry's market structure, which must be supplemented with data on the extent and type of product differentiation in the industry, as well as on barriers to entry. Even with these supplements, it is still a crude measure because, for one thing, it takes no account of competition from foreign suppliers. Nonetheless, the concentration ratio has proven to be a valuable tool, although its limitations must be recognized.

Another measure of concentration shown in Table 19.1 is the **Herfindahl–Hirschman index** (HHI), which equals the sum of the squared market shares of all the firms in the market. This index is used by the U.S. Department of Justice, Antitrust Division, and the Federal Trade Commission as a guide to determine whether they should investigate proposed mergers.[4] For example, if two firms exist in a market and each has a 50 percent share of the market, this index equals $50^2 + 50^2 = 5,000$. The HHI can range from 10,000 (a monopolist would lead to an HHI of 100^2) to 0 (an infinite number of atomistic competitors each with a market share approaching 0). According to the merger guidelines, if the HHI (after the merger) would be less than 1,000, the merger is unlikely to be challenged by the government. If the postmerger HHI would be between 1,000 and 1,800 and the index changed by less than 100 points as a result of the merger, the merger is unlikely to be challenged. Finally, if the postmerger HHI would be greater than 1,800 and the index changed by less than 50 points as a result of the merger, the government is unlikely to challenge the merger. Note that this last requirement may be hard to satisfy. For instance, if firm with a 49 percent share wanted to merge with a firm with a 1

---

[4]See United States Department of Justice, Antitrust Division, *1997 Merger Guidelines* at www.usdoj.gov/atr/hmerger/11251.htm.

TABLE
19.1

Concentration Ratios and Herfindahl–Hirschman Indexes in Selected Manufacturing Product Markets

Industry[a]	Market share of four largest firms (percent)	Herfindahl–Hirschman index (for 50 largest firms)
312221 Cigarettes	98.9	D
311411 Primary smelting and copper refining	94.5	2,392.3
327213 Glass containers	91.1	2,959.9
312120 Breweries	89.7	D
326192 Resilient floor coverings	86.9	2,983.5
336411 Aircraft	84.8	D
311230 Breakfast food	82.9	2,445.9
336111 Auto and light-duty motor vehicles	79.5	2,349.7
325611 Soap and other detergents	65.6	1,618.6
315291 Infant's cut and sew material	60.9	1,300.1
311111 Dog and cat food	58.4	1,266.5
334220 Radio and TV broadcasting and wireless communication equipment	48.9	971.9
312111 Soft drinks	47.2	800.4
334111 Electronic computers	45.4	727.9
333295 Semiconductor machinery	43.5	818.4
322121 Paper (except newsprint)	37.6	541.7
325412 Pharmaceutical preparations	35.6	462.4
311513 Cheese	34.6	524.6
324110 Petroleum refining	28.5	422.1
333294 Food product machinery	19.1	139.8
321113 Sawmills	16.8	112.3
314912 Canvas and related products	10.4	56.9
327320 Ready-mix concrete	7.0	29.4
311811 Retail bakeries	2.5	3.7

[a]The six-digit numbers refer to industries classified by the North American Industry Classification System, a system used by Canada, Mexico, and the United States. D = The number can't be disclosed because it violates the U.S. Department of Commerce disclosure rules.

Source: U.S. Census Bureau, Concentration Ratios in Manufacturing, 1997 Economic Census, U.S. Department of Commerce, EC97M313-CR, June 2001, available at www.landview.census.gov/prod/ec97/m31s-cr.pdf.

percent share, the HHI would increase by 99 points. A firm with a 25 percent share merging with a firm with a 1 percent share would raise the HHI by 51 points. Table 19.1 shows that firms with low four-firm concentration ratio tend to have low HHIs (where the HHI is not calculated for all firms here but rather the largest 50, thus the HHI understates the true HHI). For instance, the HHI for the retail bakery industry is just 3.7, while the HHI for the glass container industry is 2,959.9. Note that the cigarette, brewery, and aircraft industries have no published HHIs. This is because the government has rules about disclosing information about firms. If both the four-firm concentration ratio and the HHI were given, clever people could discern which firms had what share (and hence what sales levels, etc.). With so few firms in each of these industries, we can presume that their 50 firm HHIs are quite high (if not 10,000).

The Sherman Act

The first federal antitrust law, the Sherman Act, was passed by Congress in 1890. While the common law had long outlawed monopolistic practices, it seemed to many Americans in the latter part of the 19th century that legislation was needed to discourage monopoly and to preserve and encourage competition. The formation of trusts (monopolistic combines that colluded to raise prices and restrict output) brought the matter to a head. The essence of the Sherman Act lies in the following two sections:

> Sec. 1. Every contract, combination in the form of trust or otherwise, or conspiracy, in restraint of trade or commerce among the several states or with foreign nations, is hereby declared to be illegal. Every person who shall make any such contract or engage in any such combination or conspiracy, shall be deemed guilty of a misdemeanor. . . .
>
> Sec. 2. Every person who shall monopolize, or attempt to monopolize or combine or conspire with any other person or persons, to monopolize any part of the trade or commerce among the several States, or with foreign nations shall be deemed guilty of a misdemeanor.

In 1974, the Sherman Act was amended, making violations felonies rather than misdemeanors. Corporations can now be fined up to $1 million, and individuals can be fined up to $100,000 and receive prison terms of up to three years. In addition to criminal fines and jail sentences, firms and individuals can be sued for triple damages in civil suits brought by those hurt by an antitrust violation.

It is important to recognize that, if executives of two or more firms in a particular industry talk about prices and agree to fix them, this is a violation of Section 1 of the Sherman Act. To illustrate this point, consider Robert Crandall, former chief executive officer of American Airlines. He called Howard

Putnam, chief executive officer of Braniff Airways, on February 21, 1982, and proposed that they raise prices. The telephone call, which (unknown to Crandall) was taped, went as follows:

Putnam: Do you have a suggestion for me?

Crandall: Yes, I have a suggestion for you. Raise your goddamn fares 20 percent. I'll raise mine the next morning.

Putnam: Robert, we . . .

Crandall: You'll make more money and I will, too.

Putnam: We can't talk about pricing!

Crandall: Oh [expletive deleted], Howard. We can talk about any goddamn thing we want to talk about.[5]

After finding out about the call, the Justice Department filed a suit accusing Robert Crandall of breaking the antitrust laws by proposing to fix prices. But, because there had been no agreement to fix prices, Section 1 had not been violated. Nonetheless, the court decided that a proposal of this sort could be an attempt to monopolize part of the airline industry, which is forbidden by Section 2 of the Sherman Act. American Airlines said that it would not do such a thing again.

The Clayton Act, the Robinson–Patman Act, and the Federal Trade Commission Act

During its first 20 years, the Sherman Act was not regarded by its supporters as being very effective. The ineffectiveness of the Sherman Act led Congress in 1914 to pass two other laws, the Clayton Act and the Federal Trade Commission Act. The Clayton Act attempted to be more specific than the Sherman Act in identifying certain practices that were illegal because they would "substantially lessen competition or tend to create a monopoly."

The Clayton Act outlawed unjustified price discrimination, which (as you recall from Chapter 12) is a practice whereby one buyer is charged more than another buyer for the same product. However, discrimination resulting from differences in the quality or quantity of the product sold or resulting from differences in cost or competitive pressures was allowed. In 1936, the Robinson-Patman Act amended the Clayton Act. It prohibited charging different prices to different purchasers of "goods of like grade and quality" where the effect "may be substantially to lessen competition or tend to create a monopoly in any line of commerce, or to injure, destroy, or prevent competition with any person who either grants or knowingly receives the benefit of such

---

[5]*New York Times*, February 24, 1983.

discrimination, or with customers of either of them." The Robinson-Patman Act was aimed at preventing price discrimination in favor of chain stores that buy goods in large quantities. The small independent retailers felt threatened by the chain stores and pushed hard for this law.

The Clayton Act also outlawed the use of tying contracts that reduce competition. As Chapter 12 indicated, tying contracts make buyers purchase other items to get the product they want. For a long time, IBM rented, but would not sell, its machines and insisted that customers buy IBM punch cards and use IBM maintenance services. The Supreme Court required IBM to end its tying contracts. However, not all tying contracts have been prohibited. If a firm needs to maintain control over complementary goods and services to make sure that its product works properly, this can be an adequate justification for a tying contract. Also, if the tying arrangements are voluntary and informal, there is no violation of the law. Thus, if a customer bought IBM punch cards because that firm felt that it worked best on IBM equipment, this was no violation of the law, so long as this customer did not have to buy IBM punch cards.

Further, the Clayton Act outlawed mergers that substantially lessen competition; but since it did not prohibit one firm purchasing a competitor's plant and equipment, it really could not stop mergers. In 1950, this loophole was closed by the Celler-Kefauver Antimerger Act. However, this does not mean that mergers have become less prevalent. On the contrary, there was an epidemic of mergers in the 1980s, as we shall see.

The Federal Trade Commission Act was aimed at preventing undesirable and unfair competitive practices. It established the Federal Trade Commission to investigate unfair and predatory practices and issue cease-and-desist orders. The act stated that "unfair methods of competition in commerce are hereby declared unlawful." The commission—composed of five commissioners, each appointed by the president for a term of seven years—was given the formidable task of defining exactly what was "unfair." Eventually, the courts took away much of the commission's power; but in 1938, the commission acquired the function of outlawing untrue and deceptive advertising. Also, the commission has authority to investigate various aspects of the structure of the U.S. economy.

Interpretation of the Antitrust Laws

The real impact of the antitrust laws depends on how the courts interpret them, and the judicial interpretation of these laws has varied substantially from one period of time to another. Typically, charges are brought against a firm or group of firms by the Antitrust Division of the Department of Justice, a trial is held, and a decision is reached by the judge. In major cases, appeals are made that eventually could reach the Supreme Court.

In 1911, as a consequence of the first major set of antitrust cases, the Standard Oil Company and the American Tobacco Company were forced to give up a large share of their holdings of other firms. The Supreme Court, in deciding these cases, put forth and used the famous **rule of reason**—that only unreasonable combinations in restraint of trade, not all trusts, required conviction under the Sherman Act. In 1920, the rule of reason was employed by the Supreme Court in its finding that U.S. Steel had not violated the antitrust laws even though it had tried to monopolize the industry, since the court said the company had not succeeded. U.S. Steel's large size and its potential monopoly power were ruled beside the point, since "the law does not make mere size an offense. It . . . requires overt acts."

In the 1920s and 1930s, the courts, including the conservative Supreme Court, interpreted the antitrust laws in such a way that they had little impact. While Eastman Kodak and International Harvester controlled very substantial shares of their markets, the Court, using the rule of reason, found them innocent on the grounds that they had not built up their near-monopoly position through overt coercion or predatory practices.

During the late 1930s, this situation changed dramatically, with the prosecution of the Aluminum Company of America (Alcoa). This case, decided in 1945 (but begun in 1937), reversed the decisions in the U.S. Steel and International Harvester cases. Alcoa achieved its 90 percent of the market by means that would have been regarded as "reasonable" in earlier cases—keeping its price low enough to discourage entry, adding capacity to take care of increases in the market, and so forth. Nonetheless, the court decided that Alcoa, because it controlled practically all the industry's output, violated the antitrust laws.

Frustrating as it sometimes may be to managers, the antitrust laws are rather vague and ambiguous; consequently, it is not easy to tell whether certain actions are permissible. Take the case of two breweries, Pabst and Blatz, which wanted to merge in 1958. The government objected to this merger even though the two firms together accounted for less than 5 percent of the nation's beer sales. What troubled the government was that they accounted for about 24 percent of beer sales in Wisconsin. The district court judge, agreeing with Pabst and Blatz that Wisconsin should be viewed as only part of the relevant market, dismissed the complaint, but the Supreme Court ruled against the firms. This case shows how difficult it can be to establish even the boundaries of the relevant market.

Antitrust Policy during the 1960s and 1970s

The 1960s and 1970s generally were vigorous decades from the viewpoint of antitrust. In 1961, the major electrical equipment manufacturers were convicted of collusive price agreements. Executives of General Electric, Westinghouse, and other firms in the industry admitted that they met secretly and communicated to maintain prices, share the market, and eliminate competition. Some of the executives were sentenced to jail on criminal charges, and the firms had to pay large amounts to customers to make up for the overcharges. The 1,800 triple-damage suits against the firms resulted in payments estimated at about $0.5 billion.

During the 1960s, horizontal mergers—mergers of firms making essentially the same good—became increasingly likely to run afoul of the antitrust laws. In the Von's Grocery case in 1965, the court disallowed a merger between two supermarkets that together had less than 8 percent of the Los Angeles market. Also, vertical mergers—mergers of firms that supply or sell to one another—were viewed with suspicion by the courts. For example, in the Brown Shoe case, the Supreme Court said that the merger of Brown with R. G. Kinney would mean that other shoe manufacturers would be frozen out of a substantial part of the retail shoe market. Another leading problem confronting the Justice Department was conglomerate mergers—mergers of firms in unrelated industries. However, this problem diminished in importance in the late 1960s, when the conglomerates began to show relatively disappointing earnings.

In 1969, the Antitrust Division sued IBM Corporation under Section 2 of the Sherman Act, beginning one of the biggest and most expensive antitrust cases in history. The government alleged that IBM held a monopoly and the firm's 360 line of computers was introduced in 1965 in a way that eliminated competition. IBM's defense was that its market position resulted from its innovative performance and economies of scale, its pricing was competitive, and its profit rate really had not been high. After the trial began in 1975, it took the government almost three years to present its case. In early 1982, the Reagan administration dropped the IBM case, on the grounds that it was "without merit and should be dismissed."

In 1974, the government brought an antitrust suit against the American Telephone and Telegraph Company (AT&T), which was settled on the same day in 1982 as the IBM case. According to the settlement, AT&T divested itself of 22 companies that provide most of the nation's local telephone service and kept its Long Lines Division, Western Electric, and the Bell Laboratories. The Federal Communications Commission estimated that long-distance rates dropped 38 percent after the divestiture. (For example, the cost of a 10-minute call from New York to Boston fell from $4.09 in December 1983 to $2.34 in December 1988.) But the cost of local telephone service rose substantially, according to some estimates, and divestiture seemed to cause a great deal of confusion among customers and costly adjustments within AT&T.

Antitrust Policy during the 1980s and 1990s

The 1980s were not a period of intense antitrust activity. Antitrust officials felt they should attack conspiracies to fix prices, but they were less concerned than their predecessors about many kinds of mergers. While critics argued that antitrust enforcement was too lax, the Reagan administration maintained that it was enforcing the laws in ways that advanced, rather than hindered, competition.

An epidemic of mergers took place during the 1980s. For example, Chevron took over Gulf Oil and General Electric took over RCA. In many cases, the acquiring firm bypassed the target corporation's management and tried to purchase a controlling interest directly from the target's stockholders. For example, Saul Steinberg, a prominent investor, tried to acquire the Walt Disney Company (page 5) in this way. A continuing debate has gone on concerning the social costs and benefits of this wave of takeovers. Without question, mergers can have substantial benefits; for example, they can result in economies of scale, a more accurate valuation of particular resources, or the substitution of a more efficient management for a less efficient one. However, these benefits are not assured. A firm may be less efficient, not more so, after a merger.

The George H. Bush administration was more actively involved in antitrust than its predecessor. The Justice Department filed suit against the American Institute of Architects on the grounds that it unreasonably restrained price competition among architects. Also, the Federal Trade Commission complained that Capital Cities—ABC Inc. and the College Football Association illegally conspired to limit the number of football games shown on television. Nonetheless, many observers feel that, for better or worse, antitrust activity during the early 1990s was not particularly aggressive.

The Clinton administration promised to put more emphasis on antitrust enforcement. It indicated that the Justice Department would look closely at mergers, business conduct, alleged price fixing, and foreign compliance with U.S. antitrust laws. Cases were brought against firms in the flat-glass, milk, cellular communications, and computer software industries, among others. One of the most prominent actions was taken against General Electric and deBeers, described in problem 13.

Du Pont's Titanium Dioxide Pigments: A Case Study

To understand the nature of antitrust law, it is useful to look closely at particular cases. Consider the case involving the chemical giant Du Pont, which produces titanium dioxide, a white chemical pigment used to make paint. In 1970, because of its development of the ilmenite chloride process for manufacturing titanium oxide, Du Pont held a substantial cost advantage (16 cents per pound versus 21 cents per pound) over its rivals. From 1972 to 1977, Du Pont increased its capacity and raised its market share from about 30 to 42 percent. In 1978, the government charged that Du Pont had used unfair methods of competition and unfair acts and practices by using its dominant position in an attempt to monopolize the production of titanium dioxide (TiO_2) pigments. The Federal Trade Commission described the situation as follows:

> Du Pont's growth strategy consists of three interrelated elements: a) expansion of capacity by construction of a large-scale plant; b) exploitation of its cost advantage by pricing its products high enough to finance its own expanded capacity, yet low enough to discourage rivals from expanding; and c) refusal to license its cost-saving ilmenite chloride technology with which rivals could learn to take advantage of the economies of scale inherent in the low-grade ore technology. In addition, the allegedly strategic behavior of Du Pont consisted of premature expansion of its TiO_2 capacity and exaggerated announcements of its expansion intentions, all for the primary purpose of preempting competitors' expansion plans.
>
> Complaint counsel contend that this conduct amounted to exclusionary and anticompetitive behavior insulating Du Pont's cost advantage from competitive erosion since the ilmenite chloride technology actually changes as the scale of operation increases and, without large-scale operations, no competitor will be able to reduce or eliminate Du Pont's cost advantage through "learning-by-doing" ilmenite chloride technology. The inevitable result of this strategy, according to complaint counsel, will be to give Du Pont the power to raise prices at will, restrict output, and prevent competition. Indeed, complaint counsel argue that Du Pont's expansion plan "made no sense unless it results in a monopoly."
>
> Du Pont admits that it sought to capitalize on its cost advantage in order to capture or serve the major portion of the growth in demand for TiO_2 well into the 1980s. Even so, it denies that the cost advantage was "fortuitous," claiming instead that it was due to its costly innovations in low-grade ilmenite chloride technology in earlier years. It further denies that its capacity expansion had any purpose other than to satisfy the expected increase in demand for TiO_2. Du Pont also denies that it engaged in an unlawful strategic pricing strategy, contending that its pricing during the period was attributable to market forces beyond its control. Indeed, Du Pont asserts that complaint counsel failed to prove that its prices were not profit-maximizing under the prevailing economic conditions.
>
> Furthermore, Du Pont claims that it was under no duty to license its ilmenite chloride technology to any competitor, and contends that its competitors, all large corporations engaged in TiO_2 manufacture, are not prevented from developing their own low-grade ore technology or constructing large-scale plants if they choose to make such investments. Finally, Du Pont points to its failure to achieve the anticipated growth in its market share and denies that it could attain monopoly power in the TiO_2 market.[6]

---

[6]Federal Trade Commission, *In the Matter of E. I. Du Pont de Nemours and Company*, docket no. 9108, October 20, 1980.

What was the outcome of this case? In 1980, the complaint was dismissed on the following grounds:

> Du Pont engaged in conduct consistent with its own technological capacity and market opportunities. It did not attempt to build excess capacity or to expand temporarily as a means of deterring entry. Nor did respondent engage in other conduct that might tip the scales in the direction of liability, such as pricing below cost, making false announcements about future expansion plans, or attempting to lock up customers in requirements contracts to assure the success of its growth plans. In short, we find Du Pont's conduct to be reasonable.[7]

One point that should be recognized is that Du Pont's strategy did not work very well, since demand did not grow as rapidly as the company had forecast, with the result that there was considerable excess capacity in the industry. But whether or not Du Pont's strategy worked, it won the antitrust case, which is our primary interest here.

The Patent System

While the antitrust laws are designed to limit monopoly, not all public policies have this effect. The patent system is a good example. The United States patent laws have granted the inventor exclusive control over the use of an invention for 20 years (from initial filing), in exchange for his or her making the invention public knowledge. Not all new knowledge is patentable. In separate cases, courts have ruled that a patentable invention "is not a revelation of something which existed and was unknown, but the creation of something which did not exist before,"[8] and that there "can be no patent upon an abstract philosophical principle."[9] A patentable invention must have as its subject matter a physical result or a physical means of attaining some result, not a purely human means of attaining it. Moreover, it must contain a certain minimum degree of novelty. "'Improvement' and 'invention' are not convertible terms. . . . Where the most favorable construction that can be given . . . is that the article constitutes an improvement over prior inventions, but it embodies no new principle or mode of operation not utilized before by other inventors, there is no invention."[10]

Three principal arguments are used to justify the existence of the patent laws. First, these laws are regarded as an important incentive to induce the inventor to put in the work required to produce an invention. Particularly in

[7]Ibid., p. 51.

[8]*Pyrene Mfg. Co.* v. *Boyce*, C.C.A.N.J., 292 F.480.

[9]*Boyd* v. *Cherry*, 50 F.279, 282.

[10]*William Schwarzwaelder and Co.* v. *City of Detroit*, 77 F.886, 891.

the case of the individual inventor, it is claimed that patent protection is a strong incentive. Second, patents are regarded as a necessary incentive to induce firms to carry out the further work and make the necessary investment in the pilot plants and other items required to bring the invention to commercial use. If an invention became public property when made, why should a firm incur the costs and risks involved in experimenting with a new process or product? Another firm could watch, take no risks, and duplicate the process or product if it is successful. Third, it is argued that, because of the patent laws, inventions are disclosed earlier than otherwise, the consequence being that other inventions are facilitated by the earlier dissemination of the information.

Unlike most other goods, new technological knowledge cannot be used up. A person or firm can use an idea repeatedly without wearing it out, and the same idea can serve many users at the same time. No one need be getting less of the idea because others are using it, too. This fact creates an important difficulty for any firm that would like to make a business of producing knowledge. For an investment in research and development to be profitable, a firm must be able to sell its results, directly or indirectly, for a price. But potential customers would be unwilling to pay for a commodity that, once produced, becomes available to all in unlimited quantity. There is a tendency to let someone else pay for it, since then it would become available for nothing.

The patent laws, which are a way of addressing this problem, make it possible for firms to produce new knowledge and sell or use it profitably. But the patent system has the disadvantage that new knowledge is not used as widely as it should be, because the patent holder, who attempts to make a profit, sets a price sufficiently high that some people who could make productive use of the patented item are discouraged from doing so. From society's point of view, all who can use the idea should be allowed to do so at a very low cost, since the marginal cost of their doing so is often practically zero. However, this would be a rather shortsighted policy, because it would provide little incentive for invention.

Without question, the patent system enables innovators to appropriate a larger portion of the social benefits from their innovations than would be the case without it, but this does not mean that patents are very effective in this regard. Contrary to popular opinion, patent protection does not make entry impossible or even unlikely. Within four years of their introduction, 60 percent of the patented successful innovations included in one study were imitated.[11] Nonetheless, patent protection generally increases imitation costs. In that study, the median estimated increase in imitation cost (the cost of developing and commercially introducing an imitative product) was 11 percent. In the drug industry, patents had a bigger impact on imitation costs than in the other

[11]E. Mansfield, M. Schwartz, and S. Wagner, "Imitation Costs and Patents: An Empirical Study," *Economic Journal*, December 1981.

industries, which helps to account for the fact that patents are regarded as more important in drugs than elsewhere. The median increase in imitation cost was about 30 percent in drugs, in contrast to about 10 percent in chemicals and about 7 percent in electronics and machinery.

Patents and the Rate of Innovation

One of the most important and controversial questions concerning the patent system is this: What proportion of innovations would be delayed or not introduced at all if they could not be patented? To shed light on the question, carefully designed surveys have been carried out to determine the proportion of their patented innovations that firms report they would have introduced (with no appreciable delay) if patent protection had not been available. According to the firms in one such study, about one-half of the patented innovations would not have been introduced without patent protection. The bulk of these innovations occurred in the drug industry. Excluding drug innovations, the lack of patent protection would have affected less than one-fourth of the patented innovations in the sample.

Patents frequently are not regarded as crucial because they often have only a limited effect on the rate at which imitators enter the market. For about half the innovations in the cited study, the firms believed that patents had delayed the entry of imitators by less than a few months. Although patents generally increased the imitation costs, they did not increase the costs enough in these cases to have an appreciable effect on the rate of entry. But, although patent protection seems to have only a limited effect on entry in about half of the cases, it seems to have a very important effect in a minority of them. For about 15 percent of the innovations, patent protection was estimated to have delayed the time when the first imitator entered the market by four years or more.

In another study based on a random sample of 100 firms from 12 industries (excluding very small firms) in the United States, the results indicate that patent protection was judged by the firms to have been essential for the development or introduction of 30 percent or more of the inventions commercialized in two industries, pharmaceuticals and chemicals.[12] In another three industries (petroleum, machinery, and fabricated metal products), patent protection was estimated to be essential for the development and introduction of about 10 to 20 percent of their inventions. In the remaining seven industries (electrical equipment, office equipment, motor vehicles, instruments, primary metals, rubber, and textiles), patent protection was estimated to be of much more limited importance in this regard. Indeed, in office equipment, motor vehicles, rubber, and textiles, the firms were unanimous in reporting that patent

[12]E. Mansfield, "Patents and Innovation: An Empirical Study," *Management Science*, February 1986.

protection was not essential for the development or introduction of any of their inventions during the period studied.

This does not mean, however, that firms make little use of the patent system. On the contrary, even in those industries in which practically all inventions would be introduced without patent protection, the bulk of the patentable inventions seem to be patented. And, in such industries as pharmaceuticals and chemicals, in which patents are important, over 80 percent of the patentable inventions are reported to have been patented. Clearly, firms generally prefer not to rely on trade secret protection when patent protection is possible. Even in industries like motor vehicles, in which patents are frequently said to be relatively unimportant, about 60 percent of the patentable inventions seem to be patented.

Regulation of Environmental Pollution

Having looked briefly at antitrust policy and the patent system, we return to the topic of government regulation. Government agencies regulate many aspects of economic life, not just the prices charged by electric, telephone, or transportation companies. Managers of firms in a wide variety of industries, ranging from steel or chemicals to paper or petroleum, must understand and cope with a huge number of government regulations to protect the environment. To illustrate the situation, consider the Reserve Mining Company (now Northshore Mining), which produces iron pellets from taconite rock. For every ton of iron pellets it manufactures, Reserve also produces two tons of waste taconite tailings, which for over a decade were dumped into Lake Superior. In 1969, Reserve found itself in a court battle, one of the most hotly debated matters being the discovery of asbestoslike fibers in the water supply of Duluth, Minnesota. When the legal battle was resolved in 1977, Reserve was granted the necessary permits to begin construction of a new dumping facility, which cost about $400 million. The price was high, but asbestos levels in Lake Superior have dropped substantially.

In the following sections, we explain why our economy, in the absence of government action, is likely to generate too much pollution. Then, we discuss the optimal level of pollution control and describe the various forms of government regulation. In view of the importance of the environment both to managers and to the public at large, this discussion should be of considerable interest.

External Economies and Diseconomies

To understand why our economy is likely to generate too much pollution, you must know what is meant by an *external economy* and an *external diseconomy*.

An **external economy** occurs when an action taken by a firm or individual results in uncompensated benefits to others. For example, a firm may train workers who eventually go to work for other firms, which need not pay the training costs. Or, a firm may carry out research that benefits other firms, which need not pay for the research. In general, there is a tendency for activities resulting in external economies to be underperformed from society's point of view. A firm or individual that takes an action that contributes to society's welfare but receives no payment for it is likely to take this action less frequently than would be socially desirable.

An **external diseconomy** occurs when an action taken by a firm or individual results in uncompensated costs or harm to others. For example, a firm may generate smoke that harms neighboring families and businesses, or a person may fail to keep up his or her property, reducing the value of neighboring houses. In general, there is a tendency for activities resulting in external diseconomies to be overperformed from society's point of view. A firm or individual that takes an action that results in costs borne by others is likely to take this action more frequently than is socially desirable.

The Genesis of the Pollution Problem

The key to understanding why our economy generates too much pollution (from society's point of view) is the concept of an external diseconomy. Firms and individuals that pollute our waterways and atmosphere are engaged in activities resulting in external diseconomies. For example, a firm may pollute a river by pumping out waste materials, or it may pollute the air with smoke or materials. These activities generate external diseconomies, and as pointed out, they are likely to be overperformed from a social viewpoint.

In a competitive economy, resources tend to be used in their socially most-valuable way, because they are allocated to the people and firms that find it worthwhile to bid most for them, assuming that prices reflect the true social costs. Suppose, however, that because of the presence of external diseconomies, people and firms do not pay the true social costs for certain resources. In particular, suppose that some firms or people can use water or air for nothing, but other firms or people incur costs as a consequence of this prior use. In this case, the price paid by the user of water or air is less than the true cost to society. In a case like this, users of water and air are guided in their decisions by the prices they pay. Since they pay less than the true social costs, water and air are artificially cheap for them, so that they use too much of these resources, from society's point of view.

The Optimal Level of Pollution Control

Managers, like other members of society, should be able to look at matters from a social, as well as private, standpoint. They should be sensitive to the effects of their actions on society as a whole, as well as on their firm's interests. An industry generally can vary, at each level of output, the amount of pollution it generates. For instance, it may install pollution control devices like scrubbers to lower the amount of pollution it generates at each level of output. In this section, we determine the socially optimal level of pollution control.

The total social cost of each level of discharge of an industry's wastes, holding constant the industry's output, is shown in Figure 19.3. The more untreated waste the industry discharges into the environment, the greater are the total costs. Figure 19.4 shows the costs of pollution control at each level of discharge of the industry's wastes. The more the industry reduces the amount of wastes it discharges, the higher are its costs of pollution control. Figure 19.5 shows the sum of these two costs (the cost of pollution and the cost of pollution control) at each level of discharge of the industry's wastes.

From society's point of view, the industry should lower its discharge of pollution to the point where the sum of these two costs (the cost of pollution and

FIGURE **19.3**

Pollution Cost

The cost of pollution increases as larger quantities of pollutants are emitted.

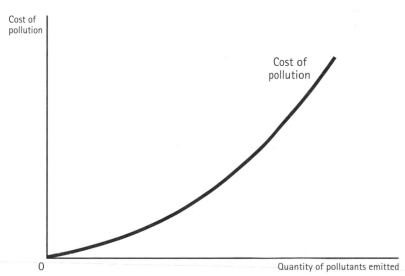

FIGURE
19.4

Pollution Control Cost

The cost of pollution control decreases as larger quantities of pollutants are emitted.

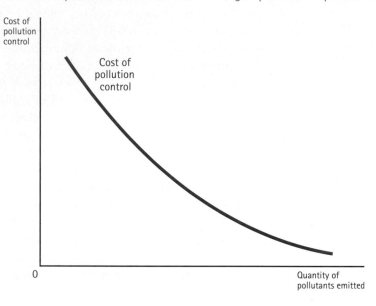

FIGURE
19.5

Sum of the Pollution Cost and the Pollution Control Cost

From the point of view of society as a whole, the optimal level of pollution in this industry is *B*.

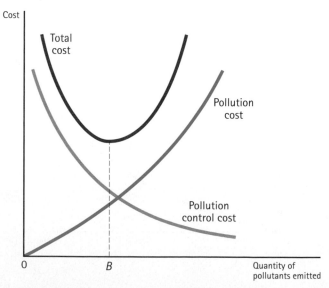

the cost of pollution control) is at a minimum. Specifically, the optimal level of pollution in the industry is *B* in Figure 19.5. To see why this is the optimal level, note that, if the industry discharges less than this amount of pollution, a one-unit increase in pollution lowers the cost of pollution control by more than it increases the cost of pollution; whereas if the industry discharges more than this amount of pollution, a one-unit reduction in pollution lowers the cost of pollution by more than it increases the cost of pollution control.

Figure 19.6 shows the marginal cost of an extra unit of discharge of waste at each level of discharge of the industry's wastes; this is designated *UU'*. Figure 19.6 also shows the marginal cost of reducing the industry's discharge of waste by one unit; this is designated by *VV'*. The socially optimal level of pollution for the industry is at the point where the two curves intersect. At this point, the cost of an extra unit of pollution is just equal to the cost of reducing pollution by an extra unit. Regardless of whether we look at Figure 19.5 or 19.6, the answer is the same: *B* is the socially optimal level of pollution.

Forms of Government Regulation

Because it does not pay all the social costs of its pollution, the industry in Figure 19.6 does not find it profitable to reduce its pollution level to *B*. One way the government can establish incentives for firms to reduce their pollution is

---

Marginal Cost of Pollution and Marginal Cost of Pollution Control

At the socially optimal level of pollution, *B*, the cost of an extra unit of pollution is equal to the cost of reducing pollution by an extra unit.

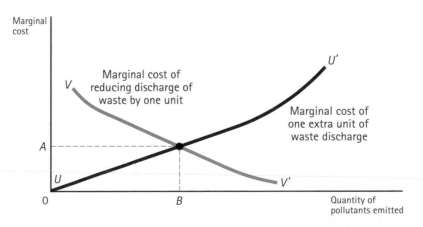

by direct regulation. For example, the government may decree that this industry is to limit its pollution to B units. Direct regulation of this sort is relied on in many sectors of the U.S. economy.

Another way to induce firms to reduce pollution is to establish effluent fees. An **effluent fee** is the fee a polluter must pay to the government for discharging waste. For instance, in Figure 19.6, an effluent fee of A per unit of pollution discharge might be charged. If so, the marginal cost of an additional unit of pollution discharge to the industry is A, with the result that it cuts back its pollution to the socially optimal level, B units. To maximize their profits, the firms in the industry reduce pollution to B units, because it is profitable to cut back pollution so long as the marginal cost of reducing pollution by a unit is less than A—and, as we see from Figure 19.6, this is the case when the pollution discharge exceeds B.

To illustrate the usefulness of effluent fees, take the case of Germany's Ruhr Valley, a highly industrialized area with limited water supplies. Effluent fees have been used in the Ruhr to help maintain the quality of the local rivers, and the results have been highly successful. But this does not mean, of course, that direct regulation is not useful, too. Some ways of disposing of certain types of waste are so dangerous that the only sensible thing to do is to ban them. Also, it sometimes is not feasible to impose effluent fees; for example, in cases in which it is very difficult to meter the amount of pollutants emitted by various firms and households.

Yet another way that the government can reduce the amount of pollution is to issue **transferable emissions permits**, which are permits to generate a particular amount of pollution. These permits, which are limited in total number so that the aggregate amount of pollution equals the level the government decides on, are allocated among firms. They can be bought and sold. Firms that find it very expensive to curb pollution are likely to buy these permits; firms that find it cheap to do so are likely to sell them. The Clean Air Act of 1990 called for the use of such permits to reduce the emission of sulfur dioxide, and the Chicago Board of Trade voted to create a market for these permits (see problem 2).

Consider another way of solving the problem, attributable to Ronald Coase, who won the 1991 Nobel Prize in Economics for his contributions (including this one) to economics. The Haddonfield Brewery (a microbrewery) is located downstream from the Cherry Hill Chemical Company. Cherry Hill dumps its effluent into the river. Haddonfield requires clean water to brew its beer and must, therefore, filter the river water before using it. This filtering costs Haddonfield $50,000 and its current profits are $200,000. Cherry Hill's current profits are $500,000. It is possible for Cherry Hill to refine the effluent before discharging it into the river so that the river water meets all standards for beer brewing. To install and operate such a refining system would cost Cherry Hill $40,000. Coase viewed the process on controlling pollution and its costs as one that could be solved without government intervention.

Suppose there are no government laws regarding pollution. Cherry Hill can pollute at will. The value of society's output as we initially view the situation above is $700,000, or $200,000 + $500,000.

Note that, if Haddonfield paid $40,000 to Cherry Hill to refine its outflowing water, Haddonfield could save $10,000 and increase its profits to $210,000 and, hence, increase the societal welfare to $710,000. Pollution would be eliminated and the societal welfare would be increased, and only private entities would be involved.

However, such a solution could be thwarted by negotiation costs. Suppose negotiation costs for an agreement between Haddonfield and Cherry Hill are $11,000. Cherry Hill has no reason to negotiate or pay negotiation costs. Haddonfield has $10,000 to gain but, if it must bear $11,000 in negotiation costs, it will choose not to do so.

Suppose we impose the basic common law on this situation—not a law against pollution per se, but a law that says one is liable for the damage one causes to another. Cherry Hill's effluent causes $50,000 in damages to Haddonfield (if Haddonfield had clean water, it would not have to spend $50,000 on filtering and its profit would increase to $250,000). Given liability for the damages it causes, Cherry Hill could shut down and stop polluting. But, it is very profitable, and shutting down would be foolish because it would deprive society of its output. A better solution would be to pay Haddonfield $50,000 for the damages caused to Haddonfield—it would still have $450,000. Still a better solution is to install the refining system and incur a cost of $40,000—it would still have $460,000. This eliminates any liability on Cherry Hill's part (because the water is now not polluted).

Note, in the first case, where there was no law (and no negotiation costs) and Cherry Hill could do as it wished, the ultimate solution was for Haddonfield to pay Cherry Hill to put in water refining equipment. In the latter situation, where there was a liability law, the ultimate solution was for Cherry Hill to install the refining equipment with no payment from Haddonfield. With or without the law, the private sector installs the cheapest method to eliminate the pollution problem. In either case, the societal welfare is $710,000.

The difference between the two situations is the distribution of welfare between Haddonfield and Cherry Hill. Under liability, Cherry Hill gets $500,000 − $40,000 = $460,000 and Haddonfield gets $250,000. With no liability, Cherry Hill gets $500,000 + $P − $40,000 = $460,000 + $P and Haddonfield gets $250,000 − $P, where $50,000 > $P > $40,000. Previously, we assumed that Haddonfield paid Cherry Hill's cost of installing the refining equipment, but with no liability laws, Cherry Hill need not abate its pollution. Clearly, Cherry Hill must receive at least $40,000 (the cost of the refining equipment) from Haddonfield; since getting rid of the pollution is worth $50,000 to Haddonfield, Cherry Hill could hold out for a payment P greater than $40,000 (but Haddonfield would never pay more than $50,000).

Therefore, under the nonlaw scenario, Cherry Hill would get between $500,000 and $510,000, and Haddonfield would get between $210,000 and $200,000. Cherry Hill prefers the nonliable scenario and Haddonfield prefers liability.

Effects of the Regulation–Induced Cost Increase on Price and Output

Regardless of how the government induces firms to reduce pollution, the result is an increase in the firms' costs, as in the case of the Reserve Mining Company discussed earlier. (Du Pont is reported to have spent about $500 million on environmental equipment in 1991 alone.[13]) It is important to recognize this and see how to determine the extent to which this cost increase is passed on to consumers in the form of a price increase—and the extent it will be borne by the firms. In this section, we learn how this can be done.

Suppose a new regulation is enacted that says that paper mills must use new methods to reduce water pollution. Assuming that the paper industry is perfectly competitive, we can compare the situation in the industry after the regulation's enactment with that prior to its enactment. Before the regulation, the marginal cost function of each paper producer is assumed to be

$$MC = 20 + 40Q \tag{19.5}$$

where Q equals the number (in thousands) of tons of paper produced per week. If the price is P, the firm, to maximize profit, sets price equal to marginal cost, which means that

$$P = 20 + 40Q$$

or

$$Q = -0.5 + 0.025P$$

If there are 1,000 paper producers, all with the same cost function, the industry's supply curve is

$$Q_S = 1,000(-0.5 + 0.025P) = -500 + 25P \tag{19.6}$$

---

[13]"How Clean-Air Bill Will Force Du Pont into Costly Moves," *Wall Street Journal*, May 25, 1990.

CONCEPTS IN CONTEXT

Buying and Selling the Right to Emit Nitrogen Oxides

Nitrogen oxides help produce smog and aggravate asthma and other respiratory problems. On March 16, 1994, Public Service Electric and Gas, headquartered in Newark, New Jersey, announced that it would reduce its emissions of nitrogen oxides by 1999 by 2,400 more tons than the law requires, probably by altering a coal-fired plant in Jersey City. Northeast Utilities, which operates in Connecticut, Massachusetts, and New Hampshire, said it would purchase the rights to emit 500 of those tons. This was the first use of transferable emissions permits for an air pollutant that affects human health directly. Previous deals of this sort centered on sulfur dioxide, which helps cause acid rain.

The Clean Air Act of 1990 authorized a market in emissions permits. Firms finding it relatively expensive to cut down on their nitrogen oxide emissions are likely to buy pollution permits because such permits cost less than cutting down on their emissions. On the other hand, firms finding it relatively cheap to cut down on their nitrogen oxide emissions are likely to sell pollution permits because their costs of reducing the emissions are less than what they can sell the permits

for. Therefore, the reduction in the total emission of nitrogen oxides occurs at relatively low cost.

For such a scheme to work, firms must be able to buy and sell permits. In this case, Public Service Electric and Gas sells the permits to a broker, the Clean Air Action Corporation of Tulsa, Oklahoma, at cost. The Clean Air Action Corporation sells them to Northeast Utilities and others at whatever the market price turns out to be. This price is set by the supply and demand curves for permits.*

*For further discussion, see *New York Times*, March 16, 1994; and *Philadelphia Inquirer*, March 16, 1994.

Assuming that the market demand curve for paper is

$$Q_D = 3,500 - 15P \qquad (19.7)$$

we can find the equilibrium price and output of paper by setting the quantity demanded, in equation (19.7), equal to the quantity supplied, in equation (19.6):

$$3,500 - 15P = -500 + 25P$$
$$40P = 4,000$$
$$P = 100.$$

The quantity demanded equals

$$Q_D = 3{,}500 - 15P = 3{,}500 - 15(100) = 2{,}000$$

And the quantity supplied equals the same amount:

$$Q_S = -500 + 25P = -500 + 25(100) = 2{,}000.$$

In other words, before the new regulation, the price of paper is $100 per ton and 2,000 thousands of tons are produced per week.

What is the effect of the new regulation on the price and output of paper? Suppose the regulation raises the marginal cost of producing paper by 25 percent. After the regulation, the marginal cost function of each paper producer is

$$MC = 1.25\ (20 + 40Q)$$
$$= 25 + 50Q$$

To maximize profit, each firm sets marginal cost equal to price, which means that

$$25 + 50Q = P$$
$$Q = -0.5 + 0.02P$$

Hence, the industry's postregulation supply curve is

$$Q'_S = 1{,}000(-0.5 + 0.02P)$$
$$= -500 + 20P \tag{19.8}$$

if all 1,000 paper producers stay in the industry. (Some may drop out if they cannot avoid losses. Recall Chapter 10.) To find the equilibrium price after the enactment of the new regulation, we set the quantity demanded in equation (19.7) equal to the quantity supplied in equation (19.8):

$$3{,}500 - 15P = -500 + 20P$$
$$35P = 4{,}000$$
$$P = 114.29$$

Hence, the postregulation quantity demanded equals

$$Q_D = 3{,}500 - 15P = 3{,}500 - 15(114.29) = 1{,}785.71$$

And, the quantity supplied equals the same amount:

$$Q'_S = -500 + 20P = -500 + 20(114.29) = 1{,}785.71$$

In other words, after the new regulation, the price of paper is $114.29 per ton and 1,785.71 thousands of tons of paper are produced per week.

Clearly, the new regulation results in an increase in price (from $100 to $114.29 per ton) and a reduction in output (from 2,000 to 1,785.71 thousands of tons per week). This typically is the effect of such regulations, but the

ANALYZING MANAGERIAL DECISIONS

Auctioning Off Spectrum Rights: Australia and the United States

In 1995, the Federal Communications Commission (FCC) completed the first auction for broadband personal communications services (PCS) licenses. In designing its auction, both the FCC and its economic advisers were aware auctions could backfire, as illustrated by a famous case in Australia. In April 1993, two licenses for satellite television service were auctioned off in Australia. When the sealed bids were received, the winners were Hi Vision Ltd. and Ucom Pty. Ltd.; their winning bids were about $140 million and $120 million, respectively. Because these bids were larger than expected and because these firms were not among the major players in the Australian television industry, the Australian government announced that the auction ushered in a "whole new era."

To the government's dismay, both Hi Vision and Ucom defaulted on their highest bids. Hence, the licenses had to be reawarded at the next-highest levels, which were also theirs. It soon became clear that each firm had submitted a large number of bids, each about $5 million higher than the next. After defaulting on a number of its bids, Ucom eventually paid about $80 million for one license and $50 million for the other. An Australian politician called it "one of the world's great media license fiascos," and Bob Collins, Australia's communications minister, almost was fired.

(a) What are the advantages of auctions over other schemes to choose who gets licenses? (b) What was the fundamental flaw in Australia's auction of licenses? (c) To help avoid such flaws, the FCC stipulated that firms had to make downpayments to the FCC and, if a high bidder were to withdraw its bid during the auction, it would be liable for the difference between its bid and the price ultimately obtained for the license. (For bids withdrawn after the auction, there would be a supplementary penalty of 3 percent.) Why would these stipulations help avoid such flaws?

SOLUTION (a) Auctions tend to reduce the costs and delays in choosing licenses. Hearings and lotteries, which are the principal alternative ways to allocate licenses, use up a great deal of resources, particularly the time of economic, engineering, and legal consultants. (b) The fundamental flaw in Australia's auction was the lack of a penalty for default, which implied that bids were really not meaningful. (c) These stipulations were aimed at preventing bidders from defaulting without penalty on their bids.*

*For further discussion, see John McMillan, "Selling Spectrum Rights," *Journal of Economic Perspectives*, Summer 1994.

extent of the price increase (and the output reduction) depends on the price elasticity of demand for the product. If the price elasticity is very low in absolute value, the price increase is greater (and the output reduction smaller) than if the price elasticity were very high in absolute value.

Public Goods

In addition to regulating the environment and the behavior of monopolists, the government performs a wide variety of economic functions, including the provision of goods and services. For example, the government is responsible for the provision of national defense, a critically important product in any society. Why does the government provide some goods and not others? One important reason is that some goods—so-called public goods—are unlikely to be produced in sufficient amounts by the private (nongovernmental) sector of the economy. Therefore, the government is given the task of providing these goods. Before concluding this chapter, we must describe briefly what is a public good and why the private sector is unlikely to provide a public good in sufficient amounts.

A major hallmark of a public good is that *it can be consumed by one person without diminishing the amount that other people consume of it.* Public goods tend to be relatively indivisible; they often come in such large units that they cannot be broken into pieces that can be bought or sold in ordinary markets. Also, *once such goods are produced, there is no way to bar citizens from consuming them.* Whether or not citizens contribute toward their cost, they benefit from them. Obviously, this means that it would be very difficult for any firm to market them effectively.

National defense is a public good. The benefits of expenditure on national defense apply to the entire nation. Extension of the benefits of national defense to an additional citizen does not mean that any other citizen gets less of these benefits. Also, there is no way of preventing citizens from benefiting from them, whether they contribute to the cost or not. Therefore, there is no way to use ordinary markets (such as exist for wheat, steel, or computers) to provide for national defense. Since it is a public good, national defense, if it is to reach an adequate level, must be provided by the government—similarly with flood control, environmental protection, and other such services.

However, it is important to recognize that, although these services are provided by the government, this does not mean that they must be produced entirely by the government. The U.S. Air Force does not produce the B-2 Stealth Bomber; Northrop Corporation (now part of Northrop Grumman) does. The U.S. Navy does not produce the F-14 fighter; Grumman (now also part of Northrop Grumman) does. Firms play a central role in developing and producing the weapons systems on which our military establishment relies, even though national defense is a public good.

CONCEPTS IN CONTEXT

Entrance Fees to National Parks

The United States has many national parks, such as Yellowstone, and there are frequent complaints that they are overcrowded. Some economists, such as Allen Sanderson of the University of Chicago, have suggested that the solution is to raise entrance fees. They point out that, when the National Park Service was set up in 1916, a family of five arriving by car could gain admission to Yellowstone for $7.50; in 1995, the price was only $10. If the 1916 price had risen in accord with the general rate of inflation, the 1995 fee would have been about $120.

According to Sanderson, "We are treating our national and historical treasures as free goods when they are not. We are ignoring the costs of maintaining these places and rationing by congestion—when it gets too crowded no more visitors are allowed—perhaps the most inefficient way to allocate scarce resources."*

*New York Times, September 30, 1995, 19.

Government agencies have a major influence over a wide variety of industries, not just defense contractors like Northrop Grumman. This chapter describes in detail many of the activities of government agencies that are of most importance to managers. Much more is said on this score in the next chapter, which deals with managerial economics in a global context.

In some cases, services exist that have some (but not all) of the characteristics of pure public goods. These are services like education. As a result, both the public and the private sectors provide such services, and consumers choose whether they want "free" public education or to pay market prices for private education.

Summary

1. Commissions regulating public utilities often set price at the level at which it equals average total cost, including a "fair" rate of return on the firm's investment. One difficulty with this arrangement is that, since the firm is guaranteed this rate of return (regardless of how well or poorly it performs), there is no incentive for the firm to increase its efficiency. Although regulatory lag results in some incentives of this sort, they often are relatively weak.

2. The Sherman Act outlaws any contract, combination, or conspiracy in restraint of trade and makes it illegal to monopolize or attempt to monopolize. The Clayton Act outlaws unjustified price discrimination and tying

contracts that reduce competition, among other things. The Robinson-Patman Act was aimed at preventing price discrimination in favor of chain stores that buy goods in large quantities. The Federal Trade Commission Act was designed to prevent undesirable and unfair competitive practices.

3. The real impact of the antitrust laws depends on the interpretation placed on these laws by the courts. In its early cases, the Supreme Court put forth and used the famous rule of reason—that only unreasonable combinations in restraint of trade, not all trusts, required conviction under the Sherman Act. The situation changed greatly in the 1940s, when the court decided that Alcoa, because it controlled practically all the nation's aluminum output, was in violation of the antitrust laws. In the early 1980s, two major antitrust cases, against American Telephone and Telegraph and the IBM Corporation, were decided.

4. The patent laws grant the inventor exclusive control over the use of an invention in exchange for his or her making the invention public knowledge. The patent system enables innovators to obtain a larger portion of the social benefits from their innovations than would be the case without it, but it frequently has only a limited effect on the rate at which imitators appear. Nonetheless, firms continue to make extensive use of the patent system.

5. An external economy occurs when an action taken by a firm or individual results in uncompensated benefits to others. An external diseconomy occurs when an action taken by a firm or individual results in uncompensated costs or harm to others. Firms and individuals that pollute our waterways and atmosphere are engaged in activities resulting in external diseconomies.

6. The socially optimal level of pollution (holding output constant) is at the point where the marginal cost of pollution equals the marginal cost of pollution control. In general, this is at a point where a nonzero amount of pollution occurs. To formulate incentives that lead to a more nearly optimal level of pollution, the government can establish effluent fees, issue transferable emissions permits, or enact direct regulations, among other things.

7. Regulations (and other measures) designed to reduce pollution tend to increase the costs of the regulated firms. The price of their products generally goes up, and industry output tends to go down. If the price elasticity of demand is relatively low in absolute value, more of the cost increase can be passed along to consumers in the form of a price increase than would be the case if the price elasticity of demand were relatively high in absolute value.

8. A public good can be consumed by one person without diminishing the amount of it that other people consume. Also, once a public good is produced, there is no way to bar citizens from consuming it. Public goods, such as national defense, are unlikely to be produced in sufficient

quantities by the private (nongovernmental) sector of the economy. Therefore, the government often is given the task of providing these goods.

Problems

1. In 1985, United Airlines purchased Pan Am's Pacific Division for $750 million. The Department of Justice opposed the purchase, but it was approved by the U.S. Department of Transportation. The percentage of total passengers carried across the Pacific by each airline in 1984 was as follows:

Firm	Percentage	Firm	Percentage
Northeast	27.5	United	7.3
JAL	21.9	China Airlines	6.8
Pan Am	18.5	Singapore Airlines	2.9
Korean Air	9.3	Other	5.8

   a. What was the concentration ratio before the purchase? Was it relatively high?
   b. What was the concentration ratio after the purchase?

2. The Chicago Board of Trade voted to create a private market for rights to emit sulfur dioxide. The Clean Air Act of 1990 established a limit, beginning in 1995, on total emissions of sulfur dioxide from 110 power plants. Firms finding it relatively expensive to cut down on their sulfur dioxide emissions are likely to buy pollution permits, because such permits cost less than cutting down on their emissions. Given that firms can exceed their legal limits and pay fines of $2,000 per ton, do you think that the price of a right to emit a ton of sulfur dioxide exceeds $2,000? Why or why not?

3. The Miller-Lyons Electric Company is engaged in a rate case with the local regulatory commission. The demand curve for the firm's product is

$$P = 1,000 - 2Q$$

where P is price per unit of output (in dollars) and Q is the output (in thousands of units per year). The total cost (excluding the opportunity cost of the capital invested in the firm by its owners) is

$$TC = 50 + 0.25Q$$

where TC is expressed in millions of dollars.

a. The Miller-Lyons Electric Company has requested an annual rate (that is, price) of $480. If the firm has assets of $100 million, what would be its rate of return on its assets if this request is granted?

b. How much greater would the firm's accounting profits be if it were deregulated?

4. The cost of pollution (in billions of dollars) originating in the paper industry is

$$C_P = 2P + P^2$$

where P is the quantity of pollutants emitted (in thousands of tons). The cost of pollution control (in billions of dollars) for this industry is

$$C_C = 5 - 3P$$

a. What is the optimal level of pollution?

b. At this level of pollution, what is the marginal cost of pollution?

c. At this level of pollution, what is the marginal cost of pollution control?

5. Seven firms produce kitchen tables. Suppose their sales in the year 2003 are as follows:

Firm	Sales (million of dollars)
A	100
B	50
C	40
D	30
E	20
F	5
G	5

a. What is the concentration ratio in this industry?

b. Would you regard this industry as oligopolistic? Why or why not?

c. Suppose that firm A merges with firm G. What now is the concentration ratio in this industry?

d. Suppose that, after they merge, firms A and G go out of business. What now is the concentration ratio in this industry?

6. The cost of pollution emanating from the chemical industry (in billions of dollars) is

$$C_P = 3P + 3P^2$$

where P is the quantity of pollutants emitted (in thousands of tons). The cost of pollution control (in billions of dollars) is

$$C_C = 7 - 5P$$

a. What is the optimal effluent fee?

b. If the cost of pollution control falls by $1 billion at each level of pollution, does this alter your answer to part a?

7. In the cardboard box industry, the minimum value of average cost is reached when a firm produces 1,000 units of output per month. At this output rate, average cost is $1 per unit of output. The demand curve for this product is as follows:

Price (dollars per unit of output)	Quantity (units demanded per month)
3.00	1,000
2.00	8,000
1.00	12,000
0.50	20,000

a. Is this industry a natural monopoly? Why or why not?

b. If the price is $2, how many firms, each of which is producing an output such that average cost is at a minimum, can the market support?

8. The Arena Company, which sells engines, has a uniform price of $500, which it charges all its customers. But, after its competitors begin to cut their prices in the California market to $400, Arena reduces its price to $400.

a. Does this tend to violate the Clayton Act?

b. If the Arena Company had cut its price to $300, might this tend to violate the Clayton Act?

c. Suppose the Arena Company decides to purchase enough of the stock of competing firms so that it can exercise control over them and see to it that the price-cutting in the California market stops. Is this legal? If not, what law does it violate?

9. Bethlehem and Youngstown, two major steel producers, accounted for about 21 percent of the national steel market in the late 1950s, when they proposed to merge.

a. Should the two steel companies have been allowed to merge? Why or why not?

b. According to the companies, Bethlehem sold most of its output in the East, whereas Youngstown sold most of its output in the Midwest. Was this fact of relevance? Why or why not?

c. In fact, the district court did not allow Bethlehem and Youngstown to merge. Yet in 1985 (as we saw in problem 1), the Department of Transportation allowed United Airlines (with about 7 percent of the service between Japan and the U.S. mainland) to acquire Pan Am's Pacific Division (with about 19 percent). How can you explain this?

10. One of the most celebrated antitrust cases in recent years involved East-man Kodak and Berkey Photo. Eastman Kodak has long been a dominant producer of cameras and film. Berkey Photo competed with Kodak as a photofinisher and, less successfully (until 1978), as a camera manufacturer. Berkey bought much of its film and photofinishing equipment and supplies from Kodak. In 1973, Berkey filed suit, saying that Kodak had violated the antitrust laws when, in 1972, it introduced its new 110 "Pocket Instamatic" camera. Because the camera was introduced with no advance notice to Kodak's competitors, Berkey could not introduce its own version of the new camera until late 1973 and did not reach a substantial sales volume until 1974. Berkey claimed that Kodak's failure to disclose the innovation to its competitors before introducing it violated Section 2 of the Sherman Act. Does withholding from others advance knowledge of a firm's new products ordinarily constitute valid and legal competitive conduct?

11. On August 28, 1991, the New York State Electric and Gas Corporation filed a request for a 10.7-percent increase in electric revenues. The reasons given to justify the increase were that the value of the firm's plant and equipment had increased by $140 million, operating costs had increased, and investors required a higher rate of return.

    a. Why should an increase in the value of the firm's plant and equipment result in an increase in the amount of revenue allowed by the Public Service Commission?

    b. Why should an increase in operating costs have the same effect?

    c. Why should the attitude of investors regarding what they require as a rate of return be relevant here?

12. During the 1990s, an enormous amount of attention was devoted to global warming. According to many scientific theories, increases in carbon dioxide and other so-called greenhouse gases may produce significant climatic changes over the next century. To cope with this potential problem, it has been suggested that firms reduce energy consumption and switch to non-fossil fuels. William Nordhaus, a leading expert on this topic, estimated that the worldwide costs (in 1989 U.S. dollars) of various percentage reductions in the quantity of greenhouse gases emitted into the atmosphere would be as in Figure 19.7.

    a. Does this graph show the cost of pollution or the cost of pollution control?

    b. Can this graph alone indicate the socially optimal amount of greenhouse gases that should be emitted into the atmosphere? Why or why not?

    c. If world output is about $20 trillion, by what percentage would that world output be reduced if the countries of the world agreed to cut greenhouse gas emission by 50 percent?

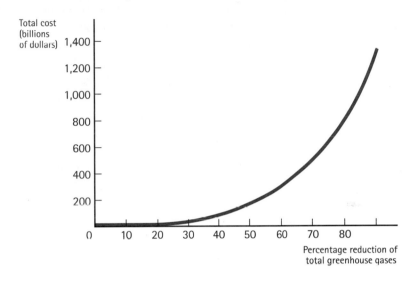

FIGURE
19.7

Cost of Greenhouse Gases in the Atmosphere

Source: R. Dornbusch and J. Poterba, eds., *Global Warming: Economic Policy Responses* (Cambridge, MA: MIT Press, 1991), p. 50.

d. The single most-common policy proposed to decrease greenhouse gas emission is a so-called carbon tax, a tax on fossil fuels in proportion to the amount of carbon they emit when burned. Why would such a tax have the desired effect?

13. On February 17, 1994, the Justice Department filed a criminal indictment against General Electric and deBeers, which are the dominant producers of industrial diamonds. According to the Justice Department, in November 1991, Peter Frenz of General Electric faxed price increases that his firm proposed to make to Philippe Liotier of Diamant Boart, a Belgian firm owned by Sibeka, which is 20 percent owned by deBeers. (Also, deBeers produces its industrial diamonds through a 50–50 joint venture with Sibeka.) In December 1991, Liotier provided Frenz with deBeers's proposed price increases. Subsequently, the two men met. According to Anne Bingaman, at that time chief of the Justice Department's antitrust division, "The division will not tolerate . . . sophisticated schemes that are used to fix prices and to disguise criminal activity."[14]

[14] *Wall Street Journal*, February 22, 1994.

a. About $600 million of industrial diamonds, used in cutting tools for construction and oil drilling, are sold per year; and General Electric and deBeers account for 80 percent of total sales. Is this the kind of market where collusion is relatively likely? Why or why not?

b. What law did the Justice Department charge the firms with violating?

c. This investigation by the federal government was stimulated by Edward Russell, a discharged General Electric executive, who alleged antitrust violations by General Electric and sued the company for improperly firing him. A day before the Justice Department's indictment, Russell settled his suit against General Electric. He received part of his legal costs and a package of benefits, and signed a statement that he did not have "any personal knowledge" of antitrust violations. What effect did this have on the strength or weakness of the government's case?

d. According to the *New York Times*, "The government's case depended on proving that Mr. Liotier was acting not as a General Electric customer, but for deBeers, which owned part of Diamant Boart's parent company."[15] Why did the case hinge on this issue?

e. Then General Electric chairman John F. Welch called the charges "outrageous." Was the Justice Department able to win the case?

[15]*New York Times*, December 6, 1994, D2.

Managerial Economics:
Taking a Global View

Managers are increasingly conducting business in global environments.

Many large firms are multinationals. Even small firms source their production overseas. Overseas firms are producing their products here. The supply chain for many goods is global. U.S. firms are acquiring firms abroad and non-U.S. firms are acquiring U.S. firms.

As an example, the U.S. auto market has changed dramatically in the last 30 years. The U.S. market was dominated by the big three domestic producers (General Motors, Ford, and Chrysler). But, in a short period of time, imports (primarily from Japan) had 25 percent of the market. Even when the U.S. firms caught up with the Japanese in quality and fuel efficiency, they could not reverse the market share numbers. As the exchange rate changed and protectionism in the United States increased, Japanese auto firms set up production facilities in the United States. In the last several years, mergers or alliances have occurred between Daimler Benz and Chrysler, Ford and Volvo, Renault and Nissan, and General Motors and Fiat.

Forty years ago, virtually all television sets and stereos consumed in the United States were manufactured in the United States. Today not a single TV is manufactured in the United States. The imbalance of maritime container traffic (net empty moving westbound from the West Coast of the United States) between the Far East and the United States is indicative of the trade activity and its direction. Most drug companies are multinationals, and oil companies are becoming multinational. Large commercial jet aircraft are produced by only two companies, Boeing (an American company) and Airbus (a joint French, English, German, and Spanish company). Smaller (regional) jet aircraft are dominated by two companies, Bombardier of Canada and Embraer of Brazil. Airlines from all over the world use their products. Governments may offer considerable aid to major industries. Boeing and Airbus spent many years accusing the other of receiving unfair advantages from their home governments. Brazil and Canada have had a long-running dispute on export credits involving Embraer and Bombardier before the World Trade Organization.

Governments also influence international trade flows through the use of tariffs, quotas, and embargoes. Managers playing the international market game must understand the relevant aspects of international economics. We take up the factors influencing whether a country will import or export a particular product, the determinants of exchange rates, and the nature and effects of tariffs, quotas, and strategic trade policy. We also discuss the factors that managers should consider in deciding whether to build a plant abroad, where to build it, how quickly, and in choosing whether—and, if so, how—to transfer technology abroad. Today, these topics are of central importance, when advances in transportation and communication have truly made this a shrinking world.

Foreign Trade

First, it is important to recognize that foreign trade is of great importance to the United States. As Table 20.1 shows, we exported a little over $1 trillion in goods and services in 2001. Goods accounted for about $729 billion of the exports, much of it in capital goods (except automotive) and industrial supplies and materials. We imported a little over $1.35 trillion in goods and services in 2001. About $1.14 trillion was imports of goods, much of it capital goods (except automotive), consumer goods (nonfood except automotive), industrial supplies and materials, and automotive vehicles, engines, and parts. As Table 20.2 shows, slightly less than half our export transactions went to Canada and Western Europe in 2001 and over half our imports were from Western Europe, Canada, and Japan. The biggest trade deficits were with other countries (where the deficit with China is large) but specific country deficits with Japan ($70.6 billion) and Canada ($55.4 billion) loom large. Also of interest is the $40.3 billion trade deficit with OPEC countries.

Why does trade occur among countries? As economists have pointed out for over a century, trade permits specialization, and specialization increases output. Because the United States can trade with other countries, it can specialize

TABLE
20.1

U.S. Goods and Services—Exports and Imports, 2001

Product	Exports amount (billions of dollars)	Imports amount (billions of dollars)	Trade surplus or (deficit) (billions of dollars)
Food, feeds, and beverages	49.4	46.6	2.8
Industrial supplies and materials	160.1	273.9	(113.8)
Capital goods except automotive	321.7	298.0	23.7
Automotive vehicles, parts, and engines	75.4	189.8	(114.4)
Consumer goods (nonfood except automotive)	88.3	284.3	(196.0)
Other	34.2	48.4	(14.2)
Total goods	729.1	1,141.0	(411.9)
Services	279.3	210.4	68.9
Total goods and services	1,008.4	1,351.4	(343.0)

Source: *Economic Report of the President,* 2003, Table B-106.

in the goods and services it produces well and cheaply. Then, it can trade them for goods and services that other countries are particularly good at producing. The result is that both we and our trading partners benefit.

International differences in resource endowments and the relative quantity of various types of human and nonhuman resources are important bases for specialization. Consider countries with lots of fertile soil, little capital, and much unskilled labor. They are likely to find it advantageous to produce agricultural goods, while countries with poor soil, much capital, and highly skilled labor probably do better to produce capital-intensive, high-technology goods. However, the bases for specialization do not remain fixed over time. Instead, as technology and the resource endowments of various nations change, the pattern of international specialization changes as well. For example, the United States specialized more in raw materials and foodstuffs a century ago than it does now.

TABLE
20.2

Geographical Distribution of U.S. Exports and Imports and Regional Trade Surplus and Deficits, 2001

Area	Percentage distribution		Trade surplus (deficit) (in billions of dollars)
	Exports	Imports	
Canada	22.72	19.09	(55.4)
Japan	7.78	11.04	(70.6)
Western Europe	23.85	21.03	(69.6)
Australia New Zealand and South Africa	1.47 0.70	0.57 0.58	4.1 (1.6)
OPEC	2.71	5.22	(40.3)
Eastern Europe	0.95	1.25	(7.5)
Other countries	39.83	41.23	(186.2)

Source: Economic Report of the President, 2003, Table B-105.

Comparative Advantage

Even if one country is able to produce everything more cheaply than another country, it still is likely that they both can benefit from specialization and trade. This proposition, known as the **law of comparative advantage**, must be understood. Suppose the United States is twice as efficient as China in producing computers and 50 percent more efficient than China in producing textiles. In particular, suppose that the United States can produce two computers or 6,000 pounds of textiles with one unit of resources, and China can produce one computer or 4,000 pounds of textiles with one unit of resources. In this case, the United States is a more efficient producer of both computers and textiles, but it has a comparative advantage in computers, not textiles. In other words, its efficiency advantage over China is greater in computers than in textiles, so its comparative advantage lies in computers. (Why is its efficiency advantage greater in computers than in textiles? Because it can produce twice as many computers, but only 50 percent more textiles, from a unit of resources than China.)

If countries specialize in producing goods and services in which they have a comparative advantage and trade with one another, each country can improve its standard of living. Figure 20.1 shows the **production possibilities curve** in the United States—the curve that shows the maximum number of computers that can be produced, given various outputs of textiles. The United States must give up one computer for every additional 3,000 pounds of textiles it produces;

FIGURE
20.1

Production and Trading Possibilities Curves, United States and China

Each country's trading possibilities curve lies above its production possibilities curve. This means that both countries can have more of both commodities by specializing and trading than by trying to be self-sufficient.

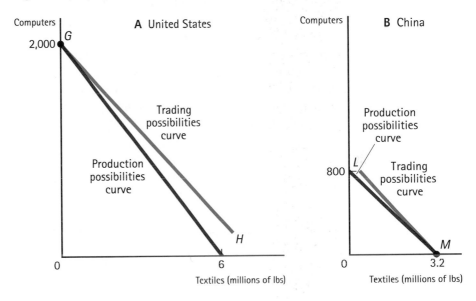

therefore, the slope of the U.S. production possibilities curve is $-1/3,000$. Also, Figure 20.1 shows China's production possibilities curve. Since China must give up one computer for every additional 4,000 pounds of textiles it produces, the slope of its production possibilities curve is $-1/4,000$.

Suppose that the United States has 1,000 units of resources and uses all of them to produce computers, while China has 800 units of resources and uses all of them to produce textiles.[1] In other words, the United States operates at point G on its production possibilities curve and China operates at point M on its production possibilities curve. Then, suppose that the United States trades its computers for China's textiles. The line GH in panel A of Figure 20.1 shows the various

[1]By *resources*, we mean here a combination of labor, capital, and other types of inputs, not just labor, so it is realistic to suppose that the United States has more resources than China. Note, too, that it generally is more realistic to assume that production possibilities curves are curvilinear, rather than linear (as in Figure 20.1). Usually, the slope of a production possibilities curve becomes steeper as one moves to the right along the horizontal axis. However, for present purposes, we assume that these curves are linear to keep the analysis as simple as possible.

amounts of computers and textiles the United States can end up with if it specializes in computers and trades them for Chinese textiles. The line *GH* is called the **trading possibilities curve** of the United States. The slope of *GH* is

$$-\frac{\text{Price of textiles (per pound)}}{\text{Price of a computer}}$$

which (in absolute value) equals the number of computers the United States must give up to get a pound of Chinese textiles. Similarly, the line *LM* in panel B of Figure 20.1 shows China's trading possibilities curve. That is, *LM* represents the various amounts of computers and textiles China can wind up with if it specializes in textiles and trades them for U.S. computers. The slope of the line is somewhere between −1/3,000 and −1/4,000, depending on the supply and demand curves for computers and textiles.

The big point to note about both panels of Figure 20.1 is that each country's trading possibilities curve (*GH* in panel A and *LM* in panel B) lies above its production possibilities curve. This means that both countries can have more of both commodities by specializing and trading than by trying to be self-sufficient, even though the United States is more efficient than China at producing both commodities. Moreover, firms in the United States can make money by producing computers and selling them in both countries, and firms in China can make money by producing textiles and selling them in both countries.

Changes in Comparative Advantage

Any good manager must recognize that, if a country has a comparative advantage in the production of a particular commodity, it cannot count on this situation to last indefinitely. To illustrate, consider the case of watches. In 1945, Switzerland produced about 90 percent of the world's watches and watch movements. The production of watches was labor intensive; about 60 percent of the production cost of a watch went for labor. The Swiss firms concentrated on making high-quality, expensive watches (so-called jewel-levered watches). Their watches were sold largely in jewelry stores (and some department stores), where profit margins were typically about 50 percent. During the 1950s and 1960s, Switzerland's share of world watch output declined, in part because Timex, a U.S. firm, successfully produced and marketed inexpensive watches that were popular and the Japanese became a bigger factor in the watch market. Nonetheless, the Swiss still produced about half the world's watches in 1970.

During the 1970s, the technology of watchmaking was revolutionized, resulting in the quartz watch. The new technology permitted the design of watches that were very accurate; also, it allowed miniaturization and the digital display of time. For analog quartz watches (those with the traditional face and hands), average variable production costs fell by about 83 percent between 1974 and 1979. By 1979, direct labor accounted for less than 20 percent of the production cost of an analog quartz watch. In the case of digital quartz watches, many semiconductor firms, often in the United States or Hong Kong, constructed fully automated production processes to make them.

By 1980, Switzerland no longer had a comparative advantage in watch manufacture. It produced only about 15 percent of the world's watches, less than Hong Kong or Japan. The leading producer was Hong Kong, where most watches were made by semiconductor firms, not the traditional watch manufacturers. What happened to the Swiss watch industry? It shrank. In 1980, it contained about half as many firms and employed about half as many employees as in 1970.

Clearly, the managers of any firm selling largely to foreign markets (or competing against foreign rivals in domestic markets) must constantly be on their guard against the loss of comparative advantage. In some cases, if such a loss occurs, the answer is to locate the firm's factories in some other part of the world, where costs are lower. For example, Timex produced overseas many of the watches it sold in the United States. In other cases, the firm may be best off to get out of the business and invest its resources elsewhere. Therefore, Jack Welch, chairman of General Electric, decided to sell its aerospace business to Martin Marietta Corporation.[2]

Using Demand and Supply Curves to Determine Which Country Will Export a Product

How can a manager tell whether his or her country has a comparative advantage in the production of a particular product? One important indicator is whether this country's firms can make money by producing and exporting the product. Consider the Wilton Company, the maker of a new product produced and sold only in Germany and the United States, the only two countries where this product has a significant market. In the United States, the demand curve for this product is such that[3]

$$Q_D^U = 100 - 2P_U \qquad (20.1)$$

---

[2]For further discussion, see D. Yoffie, *International Trade and Competition* (New York: McGraw-Hill, 1990).

[3]As was pointed out in Chapter 3, the demand curve for a product is an equation where price is on the left-hand side of the equation and quantity demanded is on the right-hand side. To derive equation (20.1) and equation (20.3), we move price to the right-hand side and quantity demanded to the left-hand side.

and the supply curve is such that[4]

$$Q_S^U = 5 + 2.6P_U \tag{20.2}$$

where P_U is the price of the product (in dollars) in the United States, Q_D^U is the quantity demanded (in millions of units) per month in the United States, and Q_S^U is the quantity supplied (in millions of units) per month in the United States. In Germany, the demand curve for this product is such that

$$Q_D^G = 120 - 4P_G \tag{20.3}$$

and the supply curve is such that

$$Q_S^G = 2 + 2P_G \tag{20.4}$$

where P_G is the price of the product (in euros) in Germany, Q_D^G is the quantity demanded (in millions of units) per month in Germany, and Q_S^G is the quantity supplied (in millions of units) per month in Germany.

Since the new product is being introduced for the first time in Germany and the United States, managers and analysts in both countries would like to predict whether, after markets in both countries settle down, this product will be exported and, if so, by which of these two countries. To answer this question, we must begin by noting that, if the cost of transporting this product from the United States to Germany (or back) is zero, the price of this product must be the same in both countries. Why? Because if it were different, a firm could make money by purchasing it in the country where its price is lower and selling it in the country where its price is higher. As this continues, the price would rise in the former country and fall in the latter country, until eventually the price in both countries would be equal.

But what do we mean by the prices in both countries being equal? Prices in the United States are quoted in dollars; prices in Germany are quoted in euros. What we mean is that, based on prevailing exchange rates, the prices in the two countries are the same. If the U.S. dollar exchanges (at banks and elsewhere) for 1.6 euros, a price of $10 in the United States is equivalent to a price of 16 euros in Germany. Consequently, if this is the exchange rate, what we mean when we say that the prices in the two countries are the same is that

$$P_G = 1.6P_U \tag{20.5}$$

---

[4]As pointed out in Chapter 10, the supply curve for a product is an equation where price is on the left-hand side of the equation, and quantity supplied is on the right-hand side. To derive equation (20.2), and equation (20.4), we move price to the right-hand side and quantity supplied to the left-hand side.

If there is no government intervention in the market for this product and the market is competitive, the price of this product will tend to be at the level where the total world demand for the product equals the total world supply. In other words, in equilibrium,

$$Q_D^U + Q_D^G = Q_S^U + Q_S^G \tag{20.6}$$

Using equations (20.1) to (20.4), we can express each of the values of Q in equation (20.6) as a function of P_U or P_G. Substituting each of these functions for each of the Q values in equation (20.6), we obtain

$$(100 - 2P_U) + (120 - 4P_G) = (5 + 2.6P_U) + (2 + 2P_G)$$

And substituting $1.6P_U$ for P_G we find that

$$(100 - 2P_U) + [120 - 4(1.6P_U)] = (5 + 2.6P_U) + [2 + 2(1.6P_U)]$$
$$220 - 8.4P_U = 7 + 5.8P_U$$
$$213 = 14.2P_U$$
$$P_U = \$15$$

Since $P_G = 1.6P_U$, $P_G = 1.6(15) = 24$ euros. In other words, the price of the product is $15 in the United States and 24 euros in Germany.

Given these prices, we can determine whether Germany or the United States will be an exporter of the product. Based on equation (20.1), the monthly demand in the United States will be $100 - 2P_U = 100 - 2(15) = 70$ millions of units. Based on equation (20.2), the amount supplied per month in the United States will be $5 + 2.6P_U = 5 + 2.6(15) = 44$ millions of units. Therefore, the United States will import $70 - 44 = 26$ millions of units per month. Based on equation (20.3), the monthly demand in Germany will be $120 - 4P_G = 120 - 4(24) = 24$ millions of units. Based on equation (20.4), the amount supplied per month in Germany will be $2 + 2P_G = 2 + 2(24) = 50$ million units per month. Therefore, Germany will export 26 million units per month.

In sum, the answer is that Germany will be the exporter of this new product and that its exports will be 26 million units per month.

Analyzing the Gains from Trade

We now view the gains from trade for both the United States and Germany in the preceding example. To do so, we use the concepts of consumer surplus (introduced in Chapter 4) and producer surplus (introduced in Chapter 10). Figure 20.2 shows the situation in the United States.

FIGURE
20.2

U.S. Demand and Supply and Gains from Trade[*]

The U.S. gain in consumer surplus is $B + C_1 + C_2$ and the U.S. loss in producer surplus is B, for a net societal gain of $C_1 + C_2$.

[*]P_{AT} = price after trade; P_{BT} = price before trade; Q_{SAT} = quantity supplied after trade; Q_{DAT} = quantity demanded after trade; Q_{BT} = quantity demanded and supplied before trade.

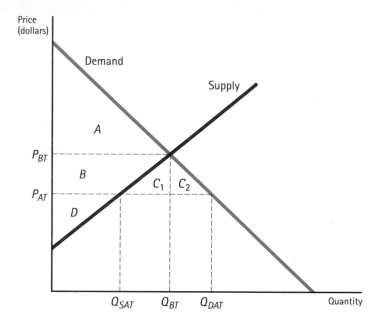

Before trade with Germany, the price of the product was approximately $20.65 and approximately 58.70 units were transacted. This left U.S. consumers with a consumer surplus of A and U.S. producers with a producer surplus of $B + D$. Because of the lower price ($15) after trade, consumers gain a consumer surplus (now $A + B + C_1 + C_2$). Thus, consumers gain $B + C_1 + C_2$. Prior to trade, U.S. producers received a producer surplus of $B + D$. Lowering the price reduces the producer surplus to D. Therefore, U.S. producers lose B in producer surplus because of the trade. The sum of the consumers gain and the producer surplus loss ($C_1 + C_2$) is the gains from trade. Its magnitude is $C_1 + C_2 = 0.5(\$20.65 - \$15)26 = \$73.45$. Society is better off because the societal welfare has increased from $A + B + D$ to $A + B + D + C_1 + C_2$, or by $C_1 + C_2$. While the producers have lost, in theory there are enough gains that they could be more than compensated for their loss.

For example, suppose that the government wrote the producers a check for $B + C_1$. Producers now have gained C_1 (i.e., $B + D - B + B + C_1 = B + D + C_1$

versus $B + D$ before the trade). Where did the government get the money to pay the producers? By taxing the recently better-off consumers. However, even after being taxed $B + C_1$, consumers are still better off because they have $A + B + C_1 + C_2 - (B + C_1) = A + C_2$, as compared to the A they had before the trade. Thus, trade makes a country better off and, depending on how the gains are distributed, can make both consumers and producers better off.

Figure 20.3 shows the situation in Germany. Before the trade, the good sold for 19.67 euros and 41.33 units of the good were transacted. German consumers enjoyed a consumer surplus of $W + X$, while German producers had a producer surplus of Z for a total German social welfare of $W + X + Z$.

After the trade, the price increased to 24 euros. This price increase hurts German consumers, and the consumer surplus falls to W (a loss of X). However, the price increase benefits German producers, and the producer surplus increases to $X + Y + Z$, a gain of $X + Y$. The producer gain more than offsets the consumer loss (by Y). The social welfare is now $W + X + Y + Z$ (up by Y). As measured previously, Y is $Y = 0.5(24 - 19.67)26 = 56.33$ euros or $56.33(\$1.6) = \$90.13$. Note that the gains in each country need not be equal, and in this case,

---

FIGURE
20.3

German Demand and Supply and Gains from Trade[*]

German loss in consumer surplus is X, and German gain in producer surplus is $X + Y$ for a net societal gain of Y.

[*]P_{AT} = price after trade; P_{BT} = price before trade; Q_{SAT} = quantity supplied after trade; Q_{DAT} = quantity demanded after trade; Q_{BT} = quantity demanded and supplied before trade.

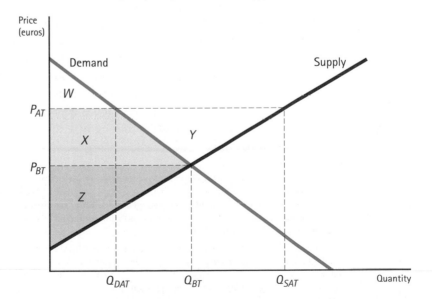

Germany has gained much more from the trade than the United States—but the point is that both have gained, giving each side incentive to join in the trade.

One thing, however, must be true in this two-good trading world: The U.S. imports (26) must equal the German exports (26). The 26 units imported is the U.S. physical trade deficit. The fiscal trade deficit is the 26 units multiplied by the "world" price of $15, or 26($15) = $390. Germany, on the other hand, is running a physical trade surplus of 26 and a fiscal trade surplus of 26(24) = 624 euros (or 624/1.6 = $390).

How does the United States obtain the euros to import goods from Germany? We can receive euros from Germans who use euros as payment when they import a good from the United States; from German tourists, who spend money in the United States; and from Germans who buy U.S. securities, services, and real estate. Alternatively, we have reserves of euros that were accrued in the past.

Exchange Rates

Practically any manager of a large firm (and many managers of small firms) must be concerned with exchange rates. For example, suppose that a U.S. firm wants to buy a machine tool from a German firm. To buy the machine tool, it must somehow get euros to pay the machine toolmaker, since this is the currency in which the toolmaker deals. Or, if the machine toolmaker agrees, the U.S. firm might pay in dollars; but the German firm would then have to exchange the dollars for euros, since its bills must be paid in euros. Whatever happens, either the U.S. firm or the German firm must somehow exchange dollars for euros, since international business transactions, unlike transactions within a country, involve two different currencies.

As pointed out in the previous section, the **exchange rate** is *the number of units of one currency that exchanges for a unit of another currency*. In May 2003, a U.S. dollar exchanged for about 1.17 euros; this was the exchange rate between these two currencies. Exchange rates can vary considerably over time; for example, when the euro first appeared in 1999, it traded close to 1 euro for $1.17 (or $1 bought 0.855 euros; see Figure 20.4). It then traded significantly below that rate. But in May 2003, the euro returned to a rate just about the same as its initial rate.[5]

---

[5]Prior to 1973, exchange rates generally were fixed by government agreements. The International Monetary Fund was established to maintain a stable system of fixed exchange rates and ensure that, when exchange rates had to be changed because of significant trade imbalances, disruption was minimized. This system, set up at the end of World War II, broke down and was replaced by flexible exchange rates in 1973.

However, governments still intervene to some extent in the currency markets. That is, they step in to buy and sell their currency. The United States has agreed that "when necessary and desirable," it would support the value of the dollar. Also, some European countries have attempted to maintain fixed exchange rates among their own currencies but to float jointly against other currencies.

FIGURE
20.4

Exchange Rate: German Marks and Euros Bought for a U.S. Dollar

The exchange rate between the dollar and the mark and euro has varied greatly in the last 30 years.

Source: Panel A: *Economic Report of the President,* 2000, Table B-108, p. 430. Panel B: *Economic Report of the President,* 2003, Table B-110.

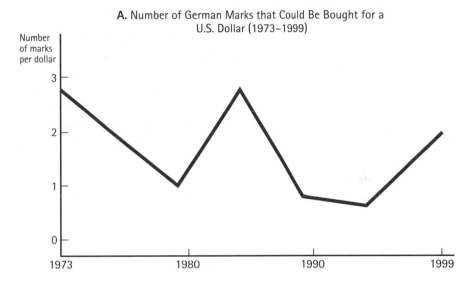

A. Number of German Marks that Could Be Bought for a U.S. Dollar (1973–1999)

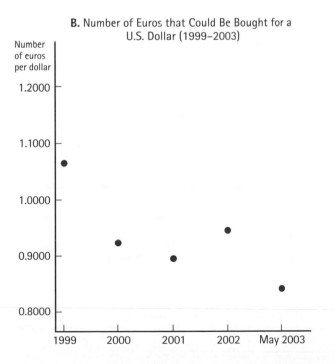

B. Number of Euros that Could Be Bought for a U.S. Dollar (1999–2003)

In the case of euros, what would be the exchange rate if the demand and supply curves were as represented in Figure 20.5? The demand curve shows the amount of euros that people with dollars demand at various prices of a euro. The supply curve shows the amount of euros that people with euros supply at various prices of a euro. Since the amount of euros supplied must equal the amount demanded in equilibrium, the equilibrium price of an euro is given by the intersection of the demand and supply curves. In Figure 20.5, this intersection is at $1.17.

Changes in exchange rates can have a big effect on practically any firm. For example, if the dollar goes up relative to other currencies, this means that U.S. goods and services go up in price relative to those of our foreign rivals. Consequently, it is harder for U.S. firms to sell abroad and easier for foreign producers to sell in the United States. In the early 1980s (peaking in 1985), the dollar went up relative to other major currencies (see Figure 20.6), and U.S. firms complained bitterly of the difficulties they were experiencing as a consequence of selling abroad and competing with imports. Recall the plight of Caterpillar Tractor, which had great difficulties in meeting the prices charged by its Japanese rival, Komatsu.

To understand why changes in exchange rates occur, we must look in more detail at the demand and supply curves in Figure 20.5. On the demand side

---

FIGURE
20.5

Demand and Supply Curves for Euros

The equilibrium price of a euro is $1.17.

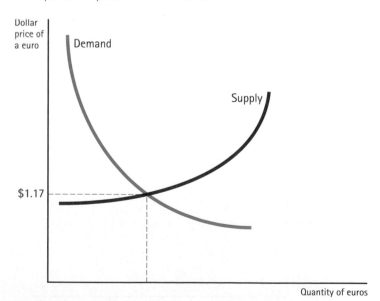

FIGURE
20.6

Value of a U.S. Dollar in Terms of the Major Foreign Currencies (Real Effective Exchange Rate), 1976–1998

The value of a dollar rose greatly (relative to other major currencies) in the early 1980s.
Source: Economic Report of the President, 2000, Chart 6–9, p. 234.

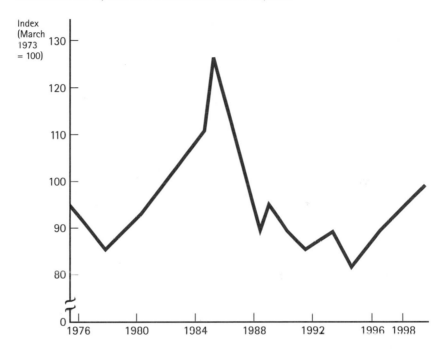

of the market are firms that want to import German goods into the United States, people who want to travel to Germany (where they need euros), firms that want to invest in facilities in Germany, and others with dollars who want German currency. The people on the supply side of the market are those who want to import U.S. goods into Germany, Germans who want to travel in the United States (where they need U.S. money), firms with euros that want to invest in facilities in the United States, and others with euros who want U.S. currency.

When U.S. firms and individuals demand more German goods and services, causing the demand curve in Figure 20.5 to shift upward and to the right, the price of the euro tends to increase. For example, if the demand curve for euros shifts as shown in Figure 20.7, the result is an increase in the equilibrium price of the euro from $1.17 to $1.25. On the other hand, when the Germans demand more U.S. goods and services, causing the supply curve

FIGURE
20.7

Effect of a Rightward Shift of the Demand Curve for Euros

Because of the rightward shift of the demand curve, the equilibrium price of a euro shifts from 117 to 125 cents.

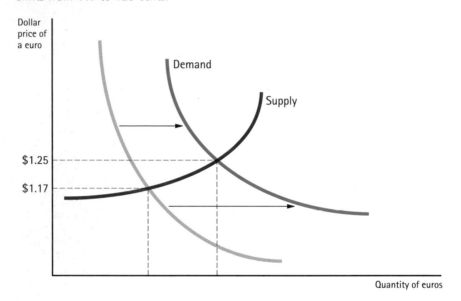

in Figure 20.5 to shift downward and to the right, the price of the euro tends to decrease.

Why does an increase in German demand for U.S. goods and services cause the supply curve in Figure 20.5 to shift downward and to the right? Because this supply curve shows the amount of euros to be supplied at each price of a euro. Since an increase in the German demand for U.S. goods and services is expected to result in a greater amount of euros being put forth at a given price of the euro, it would be expected to shift this supply curve downward and to the right.

Determinants of Exchange Rates

Having pointed out that exchange rates are determined by supply and demand, we must now cite some of the major factors that determine the position of these supply and demand curves. In the long run, according to the so-called purchasing power parity theory of exchange rate determination, the exchange rate between any two currencies may be expected to reflect differences in the price levels in the two countries. To see why, suppose that Germany and the United States are the only exporters or importers of automobiles and automobiles are the only product they export or import. If an automobile costs $10,000 in the United States and a comparable automobile costs 20,000 euros in Germany, what must be the exchange rate between the dollar and the euro? Clearly, an euro must be worth $0.50, because otherwise the two countries' automobiles would not be competitive in the world market. If a euro were set equal to $0.60, this would mean that an automobile in Germany would cost $12,000 (that is, 20,000 times $0.60), which is more than what it would cost in the United States. Hence, foreign buyers would obtain their automobiles in the United States.

On the basis of this theory, one would expect that, if the rate of inflation in Country A is higher than in Country B, Country A's currency is likely to fall in value relative to Country B's. Suppose that costs double in the United States but increase by only 50 percent in Germany. After this burst of inflation, an automobile costs $20,000 (that is, two times $10,000) in the United States and 30,000 euros (that is, 1.50 times 20,000 euros) in Germany. Based on the purchasing power parity theory, the new value of the euro must be $0.67, rather than the old value of $0.50. (Why $0.67? Because this is the exchange rate that makes the new cost of an automobile in the United States, $20,000, equivalent to the new cost of an automobile in Germany, 30,000 euros.) Because the rate of inflation is higher in the United States than in Germany, the dollar falls in value relative to the euro.

While relative price levels may play an important role in the long run, other factors tend to exert more influence on exchange rates in the short run. In particular, if one country's rate of economic growth is higher than the rest of the world's, its currency is likely to depreciate (that is, fall in value relative to other countries' currencies). If a country's economy is booming, this tends to increase its imports. If there is a boom in the United States, Americans tend to make more money and buy more of all goods, including foreign-made goods. If a country's imports tend to grow faster than its exports, its demand for foreign currency tends to grow more rapidly than the amount of foreign currency supplied to it. Consequently, its currency is likely to depreciate.

Furthermore, if the rate of interest in Germany is higher than in the United States, banks, multinational corporations, and other investors in the United States sell dollars and buy euros to invest in the high-yielding Germany securities. Also, German investors (and others) are less likely to find U.S. securities attractive. Therefore, the euro tends to appreciate (that is, rise in value) relative to the dollar, since the demand curve for euros shifts to the right and the supply curve for euros shifts to the left. In general, an increase in a country's interest rates leads to an appreciation of its currency, and a decrease in its interest rates leads to a depreciation of its currency. In the short run, interest rate differentials can have a major impact on exchange rates, since huge amounts of money are moved from country to country in response to differentials in interest rates.

Tariffs and Quotas

When an industry is threatened by foreign competition, it sometimes presses for a tariff, a tax that the government imposes on imports. The object of a tariff is to reduce imports in order to protect domestic industry and workers from foreign competition. Obviously, foreign firms faced with a tariff cut down on the amount they export to this country. Indeed, if the tariff is high enough (a so-called prohibitive tariff), foreign firms find it unprofitable to export to this country at all.

For example, during the early 1950s, watches imported from Switzerland rose from 38 to 58 percent of the U.S. market. In 1954, U.S. watch manufacturers petitioned the federal government to increase tariffs on Swiss watches. They argued that the Swiss had a cost advantage because of lower wage rates and watch manufacturing technology was important to national defense. The government agreed to increase tariffs by 50 percent on watches with one to 17 jewels.

In addition to tariffs, other barriers to free trade are quotas, which are limits that many countries impose on the quantities of certain commodities that can be imported annually. In many cases, a quota insulates local industry from foreign competition even more effectively than a tariff. Foreigners, if their costs are low enough, can surmount a tariff barrier; but if a quota exists, there is no way they can exceed the quota. The United States has imposed quotas on the imports of sugar and steel, among other commodities. In the case of sugar, imports in 1990 were limited to 1.6 million tons. In the case of steel, quotas were instituted in 1984, after U.S. steel firms experienced substantial losses in the early 1980s and turned to the government for help. By 1989, steel imports were limited to about 20 percent of the U.S. market. In early 1992, the George H. Bush administration, citing the improved position of U.S. steel firms, allowed the steel import quotas to expire. In March 2002, the administration of George W. Bush imposed significantly higher tariffs on steel.

While economists traditionally have argued for free trade, there are circumstances in which, from society's point of view, tariffs and quotas make sense. If a particular industry is essential for national defense, it may be reasonable to protect it in this way. Also, if an industry is young (a so-called infant industry), it may be sensible for the government to shelter it temporarily from the rigors of international competition, enabling it to develop to the point where it becomes strong and viable. However, even if there is a legitimate case on such grounds for protecting a domestic industry, government subsidies may be a more straightforward means to do so than tariffs or quotas.

The Effects of a Quota: The Case of the Wilton Company's Product

To illustrate the effects of a quota, we return to the Wilton Company, producer of the new product produced and sold only in Germany and the United States. According to the analysis presented earlier in this chapter, Germany would be expected to export 26 million units of this product to the United States per month. Suppose that the Wilton Company and other U.S. producers of the product succeed in getting the federal government to establish a quota of 3 million units per month on imports of this product from Germany. What would be the effect on the price of this product in the United States?

Since Q_D^U is the quantity demanded in the United States and Q_S^U is the quantity supplied in the United States, our imports of this product from Germany equal

$$Q_D^U - Q_S^U = (100 - 2P_U) - (5 + 2.6P_U) = 95 - 4.6P_U \qquad (20.7)$$

And, since the quota says that these imports must not exceed 3 million units, it follows that

$$95 - 4.6P_U = 3$$

which means that

$$P_U = 20$$

Therefore, the price of this product is $20 in the United States not $15, as it was before the quota. Clearly, this increase in price is a welcome development for the Wilton Company and other U.S. producers of the product but not for U.S. consumers.

The Presence of Protectionism

During most of the period since World War II, the United States has pushed for reductions in tariffs, quotas, and other barriers to global trade. In 1947, the United States and 22 other countries signed the General Agreement on Tariffs and Trade (GATT), which calls for all participating parties to meet periodically to negotiate bilaterally on tariff cuts. Any tariff cut negotiated in this way is extended to all participating countries. During the 1960s, the "Kennedy Round" negotiations took place among 40 countries in an effort to reduce taxes; and during the 1970s, representatives of over 100 countries met in Tokyo to further

CONCEPTS IN CONTEXT

Sweetening with Corn, Not Sugar

The Archer Daniels Midland Company, a huge manufacturer of agricultural products, made an estimated profit in 1994 of about $290 million from its corn sweeteners, which were used as a substitute for sugar. The world price for raw sugar had been about half of the domestic price in the United States, but because of sugar quotas, only a limited amount of sugar had been imported. Hence, corn sweetener, which cost about 12 cents a pound, found a ready market in making candy and soft drinks.

The U.S. Department of Commerce estimated that the quotas and other devices that kept relatively cheap imported sugar out of the United States cost about $3 billion a year. Consequently, critics said that Archer Daniels's profit was at a considerable cost to consumers. In rebuttal, it was claimed that makers of candy and soft drinks would not pass along the savings from cheaper sweeteners to consumers.

Source: "It's Dwayne's World," *New York Times*, January 16, 1996, D1.

reduce tariffs and promote free global trade. In 1994 after 7.5 years of discussion and debate, 125 nations signed the Uruguay Round. This agreement brought the greatest reform in free world trade since GATT. In addition to reducing tariffs and import duties, the agreement set up a dispute settlement system and a trade policy review mechanism. By 1999, tariffs on industrial products averaged less than 4 percent across industrial countries.

Despite this support for free trade, protectionism sentiment still exists in most countries, including the United States. For example, in the 1980s hundreds of petitions were filed by industry and labor, appealing to the federal government for protection from imports. Strong lobbying by the auto manufacturers and unions caused many on Capitol Hill to support mandatory restrictions on the number of autos imported into the United States. This led the Japanese auto manufacturers to voluntarily limit exports to the United States at 1.68 million units per year. As with most protectionist policies, consumers were burdened with the costs. Since the Japanese manufacturers restricted their supply, they could charge a higher price per auto. This, in turn, allowed U.S. manufacturers to increase their prices. Some economists estimated that each saved auto worker's job cost U.S. consumers about $160,000 per year.

One reason U.S. manufacturers felt so much pressure from their foreign rivals during this time was because of the strength of the U.S. dollar. As shown in Figure 20.6, the value of the dollar (relative to the other major currencies) increased by over 50 percent between 1980 and 1985. As well as making U.S.

goods more expensive to foreigners, which hurt our exports, this made foreign goods less expensive in the United States.

Although the dollar's strength has lessened in recent years, there is still sentiment for protectionism in certain industrial segments, despite economic evidence of a strong link between free trade and economic growth. Segments demanding this protection are generally concerned about their own performance, not the effect on the national economy or consumers. For example, in 1999, the steel industry strongly lobbied Congress to impose highly restrictive quotas on imported steel, even though U.S. steel mills shipped 102 million tons of steel in 1998 (the second highest total in over 20 years), these mills supplied over 66 percent of the steel used in the United States, and 11 of the 13 largest steel producers were profitable. Some economists estimate these protectionist efforts cost consumers about $60 billion per year in higher prices.

Strategic Trade Policy

Traditionally, economists have tended to argue that free trade is the best policy to promote the interests of society as a whole. They generally applauded the lowering of tariffs in the 1960s and early 1970s and looked with disfavor on the growth of protectionism during the 1980s. But some economists have begun to dispute these traditional beliefs. In their view, the U.S. government should control the access of foreign firms to our domestic markets, as well as promote the activities of our firms in foreign markets. For example, if particular high-technology industries result in large technological benefits to other domestic industries, the government may be justified in using subsidies or tariffs to protect and promote these industries. And if economies of scale mean that only two highly profitable producers can exist in the world market for a particular product, the government may be justified in using subsidies or tariffs to increase the chances that a U.S. firm is one of the lucky pair.

According to these economists, there are strategic industries that, from the point of view of a particular country, are worth protecting in this way. However, it is very difficult to identify which industries fall into this category and estimate how much the country would gain from such policies. Consequently, critics of such strategic trade policies worry that special-interest groups use such policies to advance their own interests, not those of the nation as a whole. Given the vagueness of the criteria for identifying which industries should be protected, many industries could use these ideas to justify protection for themselves and their allies, regardless of whether it is merited.[6]

[6]P. Krugman, *Journal of Economic Perspectives*, Fall 1987.

CONCEPTS IN CONTEXT

Why Bridgestone Paid $2.6 Billion for Firestone

The Bridgestone Tire Company is not only a large tire producer in Japan but also a large tire producer in the world. During the 1970s and 1980s, its sales grew rapidly in both Japan and the rest of the world. Because its tires are part of the original equipment on exported Japanese cars, many of its tires enter foreign markets with little or no effort on its part. But direct exports of its tires are also important, and Bridgestone's management wanted to expand its export sales.

In 1988, Bridgestone surprised many observers by buying Firestone Rubber, a major U.S. producer. Bridgestone paid Firestone $2.6 billion, for which it received five tire plants in North America (which provided at that time about 40 percent of the tires for North American cars built by Ford and 20 percent of those built by General Motors), and other plants in Europe and South America, as well as Firestone's nontire business.

To understand this key decision, you must look carefully at two topics emphasized in this chapter: the government imposition of tariffs and quotas and the movement of exchange rates. With regard to tariffs and quotas, Bridgestone's decision was influenced by actual and potential limitations by the U.S. government on U.S. imports of Japanese automobiles. These limitations led four major Japanese auto producers to start making cars in the United States, and all of them put U.S.-made tires on their U.S.-made cars. Clearly, the purchase of Firestone's plants enabled Bridgestone to elude many of the effects of these limitations.

Turning to the movement of exchange rates, Bridgestone's decision was also influenced by its need to keep its costs competitive with those in the United States. During the early 1980s, Bridgestone's costs were no higher than its U.S. competitors' (despite its much higher transportation costs) because of the low value of the yen relative to the U.S. dollar. But, in the late 1980s, the value of the yen increased, so that the price of tires in the United States, when expressed in yen, fell below Bridgestone's unit costs. By buying Firestone's plants, Bridgestone could prevent increases in the value of the yen from increasing the cost of its tires to its U.S. customers.

Further, its purchase of these plants reduced very significantly Bridgestone's transportation costs in serving the U.S. market. Because the cost of shipping a tire to the United States is relatively high ($3 to $12 per tire for Bridgestone), there are obvious problems in trying to sell tires in the United States except as part of original vehicle equipment. By buying Firestone's plants, Bridgestone cut its transportation costs greatly.

Returning to the central point here, you cannot understand why Bridgestone made this huge investment in Firestone unless you understand the nature and effects of import restrictions like tariffs and quotas and the implications for firms of changes in exchange rates.*

*For further discussion, see J. Daniels and L. Radebaugh, *International Business: Environments and Operations* (5th ed.; Reading, MA: Addison-Wesley, 1989). Information provided by Bridgestone/Firestone, Inc. is gratefully acknowledged.

FIGURE
20.8

Payoff Matrix: Airbus and Boeing

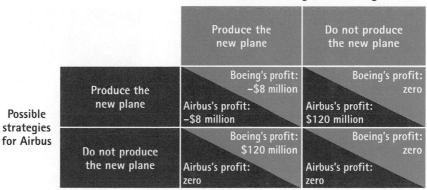

Possible strategies for Boeing

		Produce the new plane	Do not produce the new plane
Possible strategies for Airbus	Produce the new plane	Boeing's profit: −$8 million / Airbus's profit: −$8 million	Boeing's profit: zero / Airbus's profit: $120 million
	Do not produce the new plane	Boeing's profit: $120 million / Airbus's profit: zero	Boeing's profit: zero / Airbus's profit: zero

Airbus versus Boeing: Strategic Trade Policy in Action

To illustrate the workings of strategic trade policy, suppose that only two firms, Airbus and Boeing, are capable of producing a new 250-seat passenger aircraft. Each firm must decide whether or not to produce and market such a plane. Because Boeing has a headstart, it will be able to make this decision first. Figure 20.8 shows the payoff matrix for the two firms.[7] If either firm is the sole producer of the plane, it will make $120 million, but if both firms decide to produce and market such a plane, both will lose $8 million. Clearly Boeing, which has the first move in this game, will decide to produce the plane; and Airbus, once it realizes that Boeing is committed to this course of action, will decide not to produce it.

But Boeing is a U.S. firm, while Airbus is a joint venture of French, British, German, and Spanish aerospace firms (with their governments' blessings and participation). If these European governments decide to pay Airbus a subsidy of $10 million if it produces the plane, the game has quite a different outcome. Since the payoff matrix is now as shown in Figure 20.9, it is clear that Airbus will produce the plane, regardless of whether Boeing commits itself to produce it. And Boeing, recognizing that this will be Airbus's decision, will not find it profitable to produce it. Instead, Boeing will decide against production of the plane.

[7]The concept of a payoff matrix is discussed in detail in Chapter 14.

FIGURE
20.9

Payoff Matrix after Subsidy to Airbus

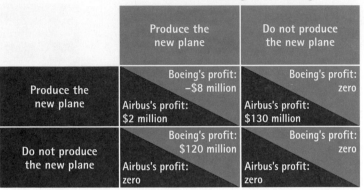

In effect, the European governments have taken the profit of $120 million away from Boeing and bestowed it on Airbus. Admittedly, they have to pay a subsidy of $10 million, but this is relatively small. Without question, this example seems to indicate that government intervention of this sort can pay off. But things are not so simple. For one thing, such government actions are likely to provoke retaliation. The U.S. government may retaliate by granting a $10 million subsidy to Boeing to produce the plane, with the result that both firms may produce it, although this is not economically desirable.

International Trade Disputes

Many U.S. industries are influenced in an important way by international trade disputes. For example, the semiconductor industry has been involved in a series of disputes with the Japanese. Among other things, the semiconductor firms charge that the Japanese dumped chips (that is, sold them at a lower price than in Japan, and perhaps below cost) in the United States and the Japanese have not allowed U.S. firms access to Japanese markets.

In 1974, Congress passed major legislation relating to international trade, often referred to as the 1974 Trade Act. Section 301 of this act gave the president of the United States the authority to take action to remove foreign trade barriers. In 1988, the Omnibus Trade and Competitiveness Act gave the U.S. trade representative the authority to determine whether a foreign trade practice was unfair. The trade representative, subject to presidential direction, could then choose what action to take.

These pieces of legislation have given the president considerable leeway in deciding what sorts of retaliatory action to take against other countries. The president can suspend or withdraw any trade concessions, impose tariffs or other restrictions on imports from the countries involved, and retaliate against goods or services other than those cited in the complaints. Section 301 can be invoked if U.S. firms file a complaint with the trade representative or if the trade representative, on his or her own, decides to do so.

In 1985, the semiconductor firms filed a petition with the federal government asking for the use of Section 301 against the Japanese. The trade representative expressed support for the semiconductor firms' position. The Japanese then agreed to increase their purchase of foreign-made chips and have their government monitor export prices on semiconductor products to prevent their going below fair market value in the United States and elsewhere. The United States, in turn, agreed to drop the Section 301 case. But problems continued. The semiconductor firms have complained repeatedly that the Japanese have violated this and other agreements.[8]

International trade disputes of this sort are very hard to resolve. Despite its obvious economic, political, and military strength, the United States cannot dictate to the rest of the world. Indeed, despite its superpower status, the United States sometimes has remarkably little influence over other countries' economic policies. Moreover, as in all disputes, there are two sides to the story, and it would be naive to believe that the United States has a monopoly on righteousness.

In late 1994, Congress approved an agreement to extend GATT. This agreement, which included over 100 countries, created a World Trade Organization, which was meant to enforce the accord. Reduction in tariffs (including agricultural tariffs) and quotas were called for under the agreement. Also, all countries agreed to protect intellectual property. However, there was no agreement on limiting government subsidies to civil aircraft producers, and shipping, steel, and telecommunications were largely exempted.

Making Direct Investments Abroad

To survive and prosper, many firms must produce and sell in a number of countries. One of the most important questions faced by a variety of industrial managers is whether—and if so, where—to establish sales outlets, manufacturing facilities, and R and D laboratories abroad. In other words, what sorts of direct investments should be made in other countries?

---

[8]See Yoffie, *International Trade and Competition*. Also, see D. Yoffie and B. Gomes-Casseres, *International Trade and Competition* (2d ed.; New York: McGraw-Hill, 1994).

ANALYZING MANAGERIAL DECISIONS

Is Airbus Playing by the Rules?

In March 1986, European and U.S. officials met in Geneva, Switzerland, to discuss allegations by both sides of unfair competitive practices, including an allegation by the United States about Airbus subsidies. There were rumors that the Reagan administration was considering a Section 301 case against Airbus; and the governments of France, Germany, and the United Kingdom (the biggest governments involved in the Airbus program) asked for the meeting.

The U.S. government charged that "direct program subsidies by [France, Germany, and the United Kingdom] . . . are leading to trade distortions in large transport aircraft. The United States believes that continued support of this type will result in increased trade tensions in the area of civil aircraft—a sector that has generally been one of cooperation in trade."* According to the president of Boeing's commercial aircraft unit, these governments had put about $10 billion into Airbus without regard to profit.

By 1990, the conflict had intensified, as Airbus's share of the world aircraft market rose to about 30 percent, as shown in the table. By 2001, there was virtual parity between the two companies, and in 2003, Airbus outsold Boeing.

| Company | Percent of passenger jet market (based on orders) | |
	1988	1990
Airbus	15	34
Boeing	59	45
McDonnell Douglas	22	15
Other	4	6
	100	100

(a) Why does the U.S. government say that it is unfair for the European governments to subsidize Airbus in this way? (b) The European governments retort that U.S. firms like Boeing also receive large government subsidies, since the work they do for the Department of Defense under government contracts yields great benefits to their civilian business. Is this true? (c) If the U.S. aircraft manufacturers feel that Airbus constitutes unfair competition, why has no Section 301 case been brought against Airbus?

SOLUTION (a) In the U.S. view, Airbus is selling its airplanes at well under their true cost, which the European governments refuse to divulge. (b) Yes. However, the United States points out that there was no direct U.S. government support for commercial aircraft programs, and it argues that there were "only negligible" indirect benefits to U.S. civil aircraft manufacturers from their defense work. (The latter argument is often challenged.) (c) Neither Boeing nor McDonnell Douglas filed a petition, because they feared that sanctions could disrupt the market. Many of the components of their aircraft are produced abroad, and many of their customers are in Europe. They feared that if the United States tried to get tough, the Europeans might retaliate.[†]

*U.S. press release, March 21, 1986, quoted by Yoffie, *International Trade and Competition*, p. 352.

[†]For further information, see J. Pierce and R. Robinson, *Cases in Strategic Management* (2d ed.; Homewood, IL: Irwin, 1991); Yoffie, *International Trade and Competition*; and *New York Times*, June 23, 1991.

Many firms are multinational; that is, they already have facilities in other countries (recall the case of Bridgestone, described earlier). In some industries, like aluminum and oil, firms establish overseas facilities to control foreign sources of raw materials. Frequently, firms invest overseas in an attempt to defend their competitive position. In many cases, firms set up foreign branches to exploit a technological lead. That is, after exporting a new product to a foreign market, a firm may decide to establish a plant overseas to supply that market. Once a foreign market is large enough to accommodate a plant of minimum efficient size, this decision does not conflict with economies of scale. Moreover, transport costs often can be reduced in this way; and in some cases, the only way a firm can introduce its innovation into a foreign market is by establishing a production facility there.

What factors are important in deciding where to locate a new plant? Firms seem to be particularly interested in the size of the local market, because a large local market both tends to reduce freight and delivery costs and means lower tariffs (since much of the plant's output is sold within the country where the plant is located). Another important factor is the country's investment and political climate—whether the country allows foreign ownership, its government is reasonably stable, and profits can be taken out of the country. Still another major factor is the availability of skilled labor and relevant technology or know-how in the country.

Establishing a Plant Abroad: Time-Cost Trade-Offs

If a firm decides to establish a plant overseas, there often is a time-cost trade-off that is somewhat similar to that which pertains to industrial innovation (recall Chapter 8). That is, if the firm decides to design and construct this plant in a relatively short period of time, the costs often are higher than if more time is taken to do the work. As additional engineers are brought on the project to speed the design work, diminishing returns can generally be expected. Attempts to reduce project time by speeding equipment procurement can also be expected to increase project costs. The available evidence indicates that the relationship between C, the present value of the costs of establishing the plant, and t, the number of months it takes to establish the plant, is generally like that shown in Figure 20.10.[9]

To determine how quickly to do the design and construction work, the firm must estimate, for each value of t, the present value of the gross profit if the

[9]E. Mansfield, A. Romeo, M. Schwartz, D. Teece, S. Wagner, and P. Brach, *Technology Transfer, Productivity, and Economic Policy* (New York: Norton, 1982).

FIGURE
20.10

Time–Cost Trade–off in Design and Construction of an Overseas Plant

The optimal duration of the project is *Y* months, since this is the value of *t* where the present value of net profit is highest.

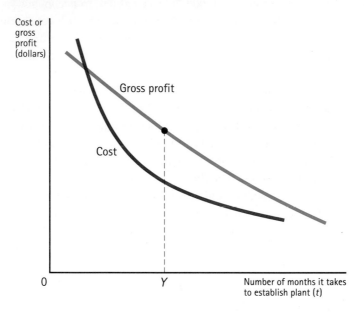

duration of the project is *t* months. If the results are as shown in Figure 20.10, the optimal duration of the project is *Y* months, since this is the value of *t* where the present value of the net profit is highest. To see that this is true, note that the present value of the *net profit* at each value of *t* is the vertical distance between the present value of the *gross profit* (given by the gross profit curve in Figure 20.10) and the present value of the costs (given by the cost curve in Figure 20.10). Clearly, this vertical distance is greatest when the duration of the project is *Y* months.

Channels of International Technology Transfer

In today's global economy, international technology transfer is of vital importance in many industries. Firms want to both make profitable use of their technology in other countries and obtain technology at minimum cost from foreign firms, universities, and other sources. Thus, international technology transfer is a two-way street. To understand the nature of international technology transfer, it is necessary to describe the principal ways in which technology can be transferred across national borders.

- *Export of goods.* The mere existence or availability of a good in a foreign country may result in the transfer of technology, since the good may provide information to the importers of the good. Therefore, the export of advanced computers to a particular country may result in technology transfer. In addition, the importing country may gain technology because the exporters of the good, to promote their sales, may help the importing country's personnel use the good efficiently—and this training is a form of technology transfer. Also, if the country that imports the good is able to reverse-engineer it (that is, take it apart to discover how it is constructed), there is the opportunity for further technology transfer.

- *Direct investment in wholly owned subsidiaries.* Another way of transferring technology is through direct investment in overseas subsidiaries. For example, firms like IBM and Hewlett-Packard have established global networks of facilities. They train foreign operatives and managers, communicate information and capabilities to foreign engineers and technicians, help the foreign users of their products to use them more effectively, and help foreign suppliers to upgrade their technology.

- *Licensing agreements.* Firms with significant new products or processes often engage in licensing agreements with foreigners covering patents, trademarks, franchises, technical assistance, and so on. Licensing agreements often call for the licensee to pay a certain percentage of its sales to the licensor, plus, in some cases, a flat fee for technical help. Some licensing agreements also require the licensee to buy certain inputs from the licensor.

- *Joint ventures.* Technology can also be transferred to other countries through the formation of a joint venture, an operation owned jointly by the firm with the technology and a firm or agency of the host country. The joint venture generally produces a good or service based on the technology in question. Joint venture agreements are often made by smaller firms that need capital to complement their technology.[10]

Choice among Transfer Channels

Which of these means of transferring their technology do firms generally prefer? According to the available evidence, direct investment in wholly owned subsidiaries is generally preferred, if firms can obtain the necessary resources and they believe

---

[10]Technology is transferred in other ways, too. For example, scientists and engineers exchange information at international meetings, and one country's scientists and engineers read the publications of other countries' scientists and engineers. Also, emigration can sometimes be an important channel of international technology transfer.

ANALYZING MANAGERIAL DECISIONS

Seagram Makes Vodka in Ukraine

In 1992, the Seagram Company, a leading liquor producer, established a plant to produce vodka in Ukraine. Attracted by low labor costs, a competent labor force, and a large market for vodka in Russia and Ukraine, Edgar Bronfman, CEO of Seagram, felt that this overseas investment was promising. Moreover, the Ukrainian government, in its original foreign investment law of 1992, offered a variety of tax breaks and stipulated that the conditions would not change for five years.

(a) After more than a year of negotiations, the Ukrainian government refused to give Seagram permission to produce for export markets. In its view, the export of spirits is a state monopoly. What effect did this have on the prospective profitability of Seagram's investment? (b) In December 1993, the Ukrainian government suddenly increased the excise tax on Seagram's vodka so that its price rose by about 150 percent. The aim was to increase government revenue, but the result has been an upsurge in the amount of liquor smuggled into the country. Why did smuggling increase? What was the effect of this tax increase on the quantity sold of Seagram's Ukrainian vodka? (c) In 1994, the price level rose by about 100 percent per month in Ukraine. What effect did this have on the efficiency of Seagram's operations

there? (d) Foreign business executives in Ukraine charge that widespread corruption exists. According to their statements, unless one contributes to the "minister's pension fund," government officials do not issue the permits needed to keep a business functioning. What difficulties does this produce for firms operating in Ukraine?

SOLUTION (a) The prospective profitability of Seagram's investment was reduced considerably because Seagram had intended to export from Ukraine into Russia, which is a very large market for vodka. (b) Smuggling increased because the price of vodka rose sharply and it became more profitable to smuggle it into Ukraine. Because it raised the price of Seagram's vodka, the tax increase reduced the quantity sold of Seagram's Ukrainian vodka. (c) Very rapid inflation makes it very difficult for firms to minimize costs and maximize profit because no one knows what the prices of various inputs and outputs will be even a month or two ahead. (d) According to Walter Kish, Seagram's manager in Ukraine (and, like Bronfman, of Ukrainian descent), "It is now impossible to do business in Ukraine legally and make a profit."*

*For further discussion, see *New York Times,* January 27, 1994.

that licensing gives away valuable know-how to foreign producers, who are likely to become competitors in the future. Of course, the longer the estimated life of the innovation, the less inclined a firm is to enter into a licensing agreement. Also, firms prefer direct investment over licensing when the technology is sophisticated and foreigners lack the know-how to assimilate it or a firm is concerned about protecting quality standards. For example, if a firm licenses technology to a less-than-capable foreign firm and the foreign firm produces defective merchandise, it may reflect adversely on the firm whose technology was used (or abused).

On the other hand, licensing is often preferred when the foreign market is too small to warrant direct investment, the firm with the technology lacks the resources required for direct investment, or advantages accrue through cross-licensing. Also, in some countries, direct investment has been discouraged by the government. (Particularly, the developing countries sometimes have shown considerable hostility toward multinational firms. Some governments feel that their sovereignty is threatened by the great power of the multinational firm over their national economy.) Joint ventures have advantages with regard to forging good relations with host countries, but they have disadvantages and problems in operation, personnel matters, and division of profits.

To the host country's government, the choice among these alternatives as a means of obtaining technology looks quite different than it does to the firm with the technology. To the host government, direct investment creates many problems, because the wholly owned subsidiary of a foreign firm is partly outside the government's control. The direct investor is only partly responsive to the host country's economic policies. The investor can draw on funds and resources outside the host country. Moreover, the investor has a global strategy, which may be at odds with the optimal operation of the subsidiary from the viewpoint of the host government. Joint ventures may overcome some of these disadvantages of direct investment, but they have the disadvantage that the host country must invest more capital. Licensing arrangements eliminate many of the problems of control, but they have the disadvantage that the firm with the technology has little commitment or incentive to help the licensee with managerial and technical problems.

The choice of the channel of technology transfer may in fact depend on the age of the technology being transferred. Consider the case of petrochemicals. When various important petrochemicals were relatively new, direct investment was the dominant form of technology transfer; but as they became mature, licensing became dominant. One reason for this sort of pattern lies in the changes over time in the relative bargaining positions of the innovating firm and the country wanting the technology. When the technology is quite new, it is closely held; and countries wanting the technology are under pressure to accept the firm's conditions, which often are a wholly owned subsidiary. But as time goes on, the technology becomes more widely known and the host country can take advantage of competition among technologically capable firms to obtain joint ventures or sometimes licenses. Eventually, the technology may become available in plants that can be acquired by the host country on a turnkey basis from independent engineering firms.

Strategic Alliances

In recent years, more and more firms have formed strategic alliances with firms in other countries (as well as firms in their own countries). In the auto

CONSULTANT'S CORNER

Reorganizing a Firm's Global R and D Network

Boehringer Ingelheim was the first German pharmaceutical firm to establish subsidiaries in the United States and Japan. The U.S. subsidiary (in Ridgefield, Connecticut) began to carry out research and development in about 1975; the Japanese subsidiary began to do so in the early 1980s. Decision making regarding R and D was completely decentralized. The head of research and development of each subsidiary could develop products for his or her own geographical markets. Therefore, the U.S. subsidiary could develop a new product for the U.S. market, and the Japanese subsidiary could develop a new product for the Japanese market. This seemed to be the best way for Boehringer Ingelheim to expand its market share in the U.S. and Japanese markets.

In the late 1980s, however, the firm's top managers became convinced that this was not the optimal way to manage its global network of R and D laboratories. Too much money was being spent on developing products that could not be transferred from one market to another. Given the very high costs of developing a new drug, there were obvious advantages in being able to spread these costs over a number of markets, not just one.

If you were a consultant to Boehringer Ingelheim, what changes would you recommend in the organization and administration of its global R and D activities?

Source: This case is based on material in P. Roussel, K. Saad, and T. Erickson, *Third Generation R and D* (Boston: Harvard Business School Press, 1991).

industry, major companies have cooperated in joint development and supply of complete vehicles, engines, and transmissions. For example, during the 1980s, Renault, a French firm, jointly produced transmissions with Volkswagen (Germany), gasoline engines with Volvo (Sweden) and Peugeot (France), and diesel engines with Fiat (Italy). Practically all the major firms in the auto industry are involved in this global cooperative network. Figure 20.11 shows the various links among the leading firms. As you can see, U.S. firms like General Motors have ties with a variety of Japanese and European auto producers.[11]

Many strategic alliances involve sharing technological information. In the semiconductor industry, U.S. firms often trade design information regarding their products for information concerning Japanese firms' production techniques. (There is evidence that Japanese firms tend to devote a larger proportion of their industrial R and D to processes than U.S. firms.) For example, in the alliance

[11]K. Clark and T. Fujimoto, *Product Development Performance* (Boston: Harvard Business School Press, 1991).

FIGURE 20.11

Global Network of Auto Producers

Practically all the major firms in the auto industry are involved in a global cooperative network.

Source: Clark and Fujimoto, *Product Development Performance*, p. 326.

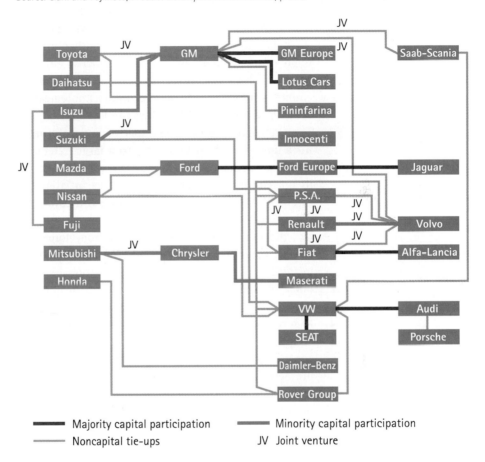

between VLSI Technology (United States) and Hitachi (Japan), VLSI Technology traded design technology for Hitachi's process technology in integrated circuits.[12]

Strategic alliances of this sort can be of considerable value, since they enable firms to gain access to technology complementary to their own and help them enter new markets or defend existing market positions. But, they also can be hazardous. If a firm provides valuable technology to others and gets little in

[12]D. Methé, *Technological Competition in Global Industries* (New York: Quorum Books, 1991).

return, such an alliance can be very costly. Unfortunately, some firms have had this happen. It is important that a firm's managers be clear as to exactly what benefits an alliance of this sort will bring—and how they can be reasonably sure that these benefits will be forthcoming.

Summary

1. If countries specialize in producing goods and services in which they have a comparative advantage and trade with one another, each country can improve its standard of living. Whether a particular country has a comparative advantage in the production of a given product depends on the country's resource endowments and technological expertise. Managers must constantly be on guard against the loss of comparative advantage.

2. The exchange rate is the number of units of one currency that exchanges for a unit of another currency. To a large extent, exchange rates currently are set by supply and demand. The value of a country's currency (relative to other currencies) tends to fall if its inflation rate or economic growth rate is high or if its interest rates are comparatively low.

3. A tariff is a tax imposed by the government on imports, the aim being to protect domestic industry and workers from foreign competition. Quotas are another major barrier to free trade. While tariffs and quotas can sometimes be justified (for example, on the basis of national security considerations), economists traditionally have felt that a tariff or quota tends to cost the general public more than the protected industry (and its workers and suppliers) gains.

4. In recent years, some economists have begun to argue that countries should adopt strategic trade policies. In their view, the U.S. government should control the access of foreign firms to our domestic markets, as well as promote the activities of our firms in foreign markets. If particular high-technology industries result in large technological benefits to other domestic industries, these economists believe that the government may be justified in using subsidies, tariffs, or quotas to protect and promote the industries.

5. The 1974 Trade Act and the 1988 Omnibus Trade and Competitiveness Act gave the president considerable leeway in deciding what retaliatory action to take against foreign trade practices that are regarded as unfair. The president can suspend or withdraw any trade concessions, impose tariffs or other restrictions on imports from the countries involved, and retaliate against goods and services other than those cited in the complaints.

6. Many firms must decide whether—and, if so, where—to establish facilities abroad. Whether a firm locates a plant in a particular country depends on the size of the market in that country, the country's investment climate, and the availability of skilled labor. If a firm decides to build a plant overseas, there often is a time-cost trade-off.

MANAGERIAL ECONOMICS IN CONTEXT

NAFTA: A Historic Agreement

For decades, there was talk about a free trade agreement for North America. All tariffs and quotas would be eliminated on trade among Canada, Mexico, and the United States. The result would be the world's largest free market, with about 400 million consumers and a total output of $6 trillion (about 25 percent larger than the original European Community). During the 1980s, this talk became much more serious. Indeed, in 1988, the Canada–U.S. Free Trade Agreement was signed by Prime Minister Brian Mulroney and President Ronald Reagan.*

According to some estimates, this agreement was supposed to create an additional 750,000 jobs in the United States and 150,000 in Canada. On both sides of the U.S.–Canadian border, there were misgivings about the agreement. On the Canadian side, people were concerned that they would lose their cultural identity and be overwhelmed by the economic and political juggernaut to their south. On the U.S. side, some people were worried that they would lose production and jobs to Canada. Nonetheless, on January 1, 1989, the historic agreement went into operation. All bilateral tariffs were to be removed in 10 equal, annual steps, which began on that date (except for those cases where the relevant industries agreed to a faster phaseout of the tariffs).

In late November 1990, Presidents George H. Bush and Carlos Salinas de Gortari met to launch trade talks between Mexico and the United States. Mexico wanted to weaken U.S. quotas on textiles and steel and open U.S. markets to its fruits and vegetables. The United States wanted Mexico to allow foreign investment in its oil industry. (Such investment was prohibited by the Mexican constitution.) As these talks continued, alarm bells went off among U.S. labor leaders, who feared the export of jobs to Mexico. Also, environmentalists warned that Mexico could degrade clean-air and toxic-waste standards across the continent. Industries that might be hurt by free trade with Mexico also were concerned. For example, Bill Becker, chairman of the Florida Citrus Commission, warned that the removal of the U.S. tariff on orange juice would "wipe out the Florida industry. We can't compete with our environmental constraints, labor constraints, and the other regulations."[†]

Actually, many of the barriers to trade between Mexico and the United States had already been torn down. Take the important case of automobiles. In 1991, Mexico produced over 1 million vehicles. With a North American Free Trade Agreement, many auto executives think that Mexican output could hit 3 million by the year 2000. But even if such an agreement had not been signed, many auto executives think that Mexican auto output could have hit 2 million. In fact, Mexican automobile output was over 1.8 million in 2001, up 50% since 1996.[***] However, by 2003, production fell to 1.54 million and the 2004 trend through August is lower still.

Many of these cars are made by Ford, Chrysler, and General Motors. For example, at Ramos Arizpe, General Motors makes the Buick Century and the Chevrolet Cavalier for export and local sale. At Hermosillo, Ford makes Tracers and Escorts for export to California and elsewhere. At Toluca, Chrysler's plant exports Shadows and Spirits. But Mexico is not the home of only U.S. auto producers; France's Renault, Japan's Nissan, and Germany's Volkswagen, among others, have plants there.

Why have auto producers moved into Mexico? One reason is low wages. An experienced welder at Chrysler's Toluca plant has made about $1.75 per hour, much less than the $16 an hour earned by experienced welders at Chrysler's Michigan plant. However, this is only part of the story. Surprising as it has been to many observers, the quality of the cars produced is high. Within two years after its startup in 1987, Ford's Hermosillo plant was winning quality awards. Ramos Arizpe, only five years old, is General Motors' top plant of its kind, outscoring other plants in Oklahoma City and Quebec.

According to auto executives, Mexico's young workers learn new industrial methods more quickly than their older counterparts in the United States. For example, the labor force at Ramos Arizpe quickly learned Japanese-style manufacturing techniques. Highly trained workers in small teams can substitute for one another and effectively monitor quality. In contrast, many U.S. plants still have rigid work rules. At Hermosillo, Ford provides trainees with a seven-week program where they study statistics and economics.

While U.S. auto companies are enthusiastic about their experiences in Mexico, the United Auto Workers (UAW) has been protesting loudly. Indeed, the UAW tried to torpedo the North American Free Trade Agreement. According to Owen Bieber, president of the UAW, the agreement means "you can kiss the jobs and livelihoods of thousands of Americans goodbye."[†]

On August 13, 1992, the United States, Canada, and Mexico announced a free trade agreement, which subsequently was ratified by lawmakers in the three countries. According to William Ethier of the University of Pennsylvania, the most important effect of this action was on Mexico. It is "a way for the current [Mexican] president to set in concrete the dramatic economic reforms that have been made in Mexico. [He] . . . wants to make sure that there is no backsliding in the future and an international agreement is one way of doing that."[§]

In late 1994, the value (in dollars) of the Mexican peso (Mexico's currency) dropped dramati-

cally, from about 29 cents to about 20 cents. To help restore investor confidence in Mexico, President Clinton expanded U.S. financial support for Mexico to $20 billion. This support included loan guarantees backed by claims on the proceeds from Mexican oil exports. Support of this sort was not dictated by the free trade agreement. In the words of President Clinton's Council of Economic Advisers, "The United States is providing support to Mexico because we have a stake in the stability of a country with whom we share a 2,000-mile border and important commercial ties. There is no commitment under NAFTA to do so."[∥]

Evidence in 2003 shows that neither significant job creation nor job loss can be attributed to NAFTA. Many U.S. operations on the Mexican side of the border have been shut down or significantly cut back.

(a) Does it appear that the United States has lost its comparative advantage in the production of automobiles? Is the evidence clear-cut?

(b) On February 12, 1992, the U.S. Customs Service ruled that Honda Motor Company had to pay tariffs of about $180 per car on the Civics it shipped from its plant in Alliston, Ontario, to the United States because, in its view, too little of these cars were produced in North America to allow them to enter the United States duty free. Some leading Canadians said Canada should abrogate its free trade agreements with the United States. Why were they so concerned?

(c) Have Ford, General Motors, and Chrysler transferred technology to Mexico? If so, through what channels have they done so? Why have they chosen these channels?

(d) Florida produces 95 percent of the winter tomato crop in the United States. According to Paul DiMare, whose family oversees a big Florida farm, field hands are paid $3 a day in Mexico whereas U.S. farm workers make $50 a day (plus Social Security and other benefits). As a result of NAFTA, Mexican producers ship tomatoes into the United

States for sale at \$3 to \$5 for a 25-pound box, compared with the \$8 to \$10 it costs DiMare to grow and ship the same amount.# Should this be allowed?

(e) A study published by the University of California at Los Angeles in late 1996 concluded that the near-collapse of the Mexican economy in 1995 had a much bigger effect on the number of trade-related jobs in the United States than NAFTA.** Did it increase or decrease the number of jobs among U.S. exporters?

(f) Environmentalists cite the sludge in the Rio Grande river and the smog over Mexico City. (The lower Rio Grande is the most polluted river in the United States.) How can one tell whether existing levels of pollution in these cases are excessive? If they are excessive, what can the government of Mexico and the United States do to reduce pollution?

*For background, see Daniels and Radebaugh, *International Business*.
†*Business Week*, May 27, 1991, p. 33.
†*Business Week*, March 16, 1992, p. 100.
§"An Economist's View of NAFTA," *Penn Arts and Sciences*, Winter 1994, p. 5.
‖*Economic Report of the President* (Washington, D.C.: Government Printing Office, 1995), p. 224.
#*Philadelphia Inquirer*, March 16, 1996, p. D1.
***New York Times*, December 19, 1996, p. D1.
***"Mexican Auto Industry Braces for Competition" at www.geocities.com/ericsquire/articles/ftaa/1t020526.htm

7. International technology transfer is of vital importance to many firms. Technology can be transferred across national borders in four principal ways: export of goods, direct investment in wholly owned foreign subsidiaries, licensing agreements, and joint ventures. Direct investment is often preferred by firms if they can obtain the necessary resources and believe that other methods of transfer give away valuable know-how to foreign producers, who are likely to become competitors in the future.

8. In recent years, more and more firms have been forming strategic alliances with firms in other countries (as well as firms in their own countries). Many strategic alliances involve sharing technological information. It is important that a firm's managers be clear as to exactly what benefits an alliance of this sort will bring and how they can be confident that these benefits are obtained.

Problems

1. Donald R. Keough, when president of the Coca-Cola Company, said, "Our single and relentless focus has been internationalizing this business."[13] In

[13]"For Coke, World Is Its Oyster," *New York Times*, November 21, 1991.

1991, Coke pushed the international contribution to its profits to 80 percent from 50 percent in 1985. By the year 2000, the United States may account for no more than 10 percent of the firm's profits.

a. At one time in the United States, per capita consumption of soft drinks made by Coca-Cola equalled 292 eight-ounce servings per year, whereas it equalled 48 in France and 112 in Japan. Does this help to account for the fact that Coke's unit sales grew at an annual rate of 8 to 10 percent overseas, as compared with 3.5 percent in the United States? If so, how?

b. Keough said, "When I think of Indonesia—a country on the Equator with 180 million people, a median age of 18, and a Muslim ban on alcohol, I feel I know what heaven looks like." Why was he so enthusiastic about Indonesia? (Note: Indonesia's per capita consumption of soft drinks made by Coca-Cola equalled four eight-ounce servings per year.)

c. In some countries, like Britain and Taiwan, Coke has used joint ventures with bottlers to enter foreign markets; in others, like France, it has established wholly owned bottling operations. What factors influence Coke's decision in this regard?

d. At one time, Coke's principal rival, Pepsi Cola, obtained less than 20 percent of its profits from outside the United States. At the same time, Coke had about 40 percent of the domestic soft drink market as compared with Pepsi's figure of about a third, it outsold Pepsi four to one outside the United States. According to some analysts, this helped to explain why Coke made three or four times as much profit per gallon sold in many overseas markets as in the United States. Why did they think that this is the explanation?

2. In 1991, local cement makers in Florida filed a complaint against Venezuelan firms, charging that they were dumping cement in Florida. According to U.S. law, dumping occurs when foreigners set their price below "fair market value," which is defined as either the price they establish at home or their cost of production. At that time, more than half of Florida's cement was supplied by local firms, such as a subsidiary of Texas-based Southdown, Inc. The rest came from overseas. The price of cement was roughly $60 in both Florida and Venezuela.[14]

a. Why was it profitable for Venezuelan firms to enter the Florida cement market? (Hint: Ocean transportation was and is cheap relative to railroads or trucks.)

b. If transportation and storage added about $10 to $15 per ton to the cost of sending Venezuelan cement to Florida, does it appear that the Venezuelan firms were selling cement at a lower price in Florida than in their home markets?

[14]"Cement Shoes for Venezuela," *New York Times*, September 25, 1991.

    c. According to Kenneth Clarkson of the University of Miami and Stephen Morrell of Barry University, both consultants for the Venezuelan firms, Florida consumers would pay over $600 million more for cement in the period 1991 to 1996 if foreign firms were no longer permitted to ship into the Florida market. If this were true, should foreign firms have been allowed to continue selling cement at $60 per ton in Florida?

3. Suppose that Japan and the United States are the only producers and consumers of a particular sort of flashbulb. The demand and supply curves for this flashbulb in the United States are as follows:

Price (dollars)	Quantity demanded (millions)	Quantity supplied (millions)
5	10	4
10	8	6
15	6	8
20	4	10

The demand and supply curves for this flashbulb in Japan are

Price (in dollar equivalent of Japanese yen)	Quantity demanded (millions)	Quantity supplied (millions)
5	5	2
10	4	6
15	3	10
20	2	14

    a. Suppose that there is free trade in these flashbulbs. What is the equilibrium price?

    b. Which country exports flashbulbs to the other country?

    c. How large are the exports?

    d. Suppose that the United States imposes a tariff of $10 per flashbulb. What happens to exports and imports?

4. According to a (hypothetical) government report, the United States can produce three computers or 3,000 cases of wine with one unit of resources, while Germany can produce one computer or 5,000 cases of wine with one unit of resources.

    a. If this report is accurate, will specialization increase the world output of computers and wine?

    b. If the maximum number of computers that can be produced per year in the United States is 1,000, draw the U.S. production possibilities curve on the following graph:

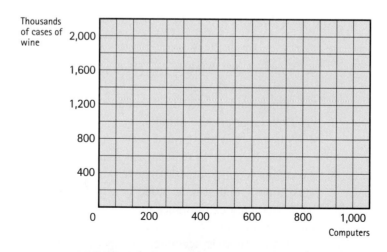

c. In this diagram, draw the trading possibilities curve if the United States produces only computers and trades them for German wine (at a price for each computer equivalent to 2,000 cases of German wine). Does this curve lie above the production possibilities curve?

d. If the maximum number of cases of wine that can be produced per year in Germany is 2 million, draw the German production possibilities curve in the following grid:

e. In this diagram, draw the trading possibilities curve if Germany produces only wine and trades it for U.S. computers (at a price for each computer equivalent to 2,000 cases of German wine). Does this curve lie above the production possibilities curve?

5. If labor is the only input, a study indicates that two countries, Honduras and Panama, can produce the following amounts of two commodities, bananas and coffee, with a day of labor.

	Bananas (lbs)	Coffee (lbs)
Honduras	20	6
Panama	10	8

   a. For both countries to gain from trade with one another, between what limits must the ratio of the prices lie?
   b. Suppose that there is free trade and the price of bananas increases relative to the price of coffee. Is this change in relative prices to the advantage of Honduras or Panama?

6. The supply curve for Japanese cameras to the U.S. market is shown next for two periods of time.
   a. One curve is before a depreciation of the dollar relative to the yen; one curve is after it. Which curve is which? Why?
   b. What is the effect of the depreciation on the dollar price of Japanese cameras?
   c. What is the effect on U.S. expenditures (in dollars) for Japanese cameras if the demand for them in the United States is price elastic?
   d. What is the effect on U.S. expenditures (in dollars) for Japanese cameras if the demand for them in the United States is price inelastic?

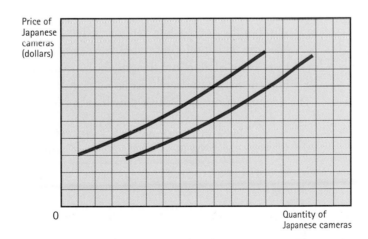

7. The demand curve in Italy for U.S. computers follows:
   a. If the euro depreciates relative to the U.S. dollar, does the quantity of computers sold in Italy at a dollar price of $8,000 rise or fall?
   b. Under these circumstances, does the demand curve rise or fall?

8. The demand and supply curves for the Swiss franc are as follows:

Price of franc (dollars)	Francs demanded (millions)	Francs supplied (millions)
0.80	600	800
0.70	640	740
0.60	680	680
0.50	720	620
0.40	760	560

a. What is the equilibrium rate of exchange for the dollar?
b. What is the equilibrium rate of exchange for the Swiss franc?
c. How many dollars are bought in the market?
d. How many Swiss francs are bought in the market?

9. The demand curve for British pounds is as follows:

Price of British pound (dollars)	Pounds demanded (millions)
2.00	400
2.10	380
2.20	360
2.30	340
2.40	320
2.50	300

a. Suppose the British government tries to maintain the exchange rate at $2.40 and the quantity of pounds supplied at this exchange rate is 360 million. Does the British government have to buy or sell pounds? If so, how many?

b. If the British government has to buy pounds with dollars, where does it get the dollars?

10. The Liverous Company is the maker of a new product made and bought only in Japan and the United States. In the United States, the demand curve for this product is such that

$$Q_D^U = 20 - 2P_U$$

and the supply curve is such that

$$Q_S^U = 5 + 3P_U$$

where P_U is the price of the product (in dollars) in the United States, Q_D^U is the quantity demanded (in thousands of units) per week in the United States, and Q_S^U is the quantity supplied (in thousands of units) per week in the United States. In Japan, the demand curve for this product is such that

$$Q_D^J = 45.5 - 3P_J$$

and the supply curve is such that

$$Q_S^J - -5 + 2P_J$$

where P_J is the price of the product (in yen) in Japan, Q_D^J is the quantity demanded (in thousands of units) per week in Japan, and Q_S^J is the quantity supplied (in thousands of units) per week in Japan. Assume that a U.S. dollar exchanges for 130 Japanese yen.

a. What is the price of this product in Japan? In the United States?

b. How much of this product does each country supply?

c. Is the United States an importer or an exporter of this product?

11. During the 1980s, Black and Decker (B&D), the manufacturer of power tools, encountered a number of problems. The recession of the early 1980s hurt B&D's sales, as did the subsequent strength of the U.S. dollar. Its rival, Japan's Mikita Electric Works, reduced its costs and was able to nearly equal B&D's 20 percent share of the world market. In part, B&D's problems were of its own making, according to some observers, for these reasons.

By 1982, B&D operated 25 manufacturing plants in 13 countries on six continents. It had three operating groups, as well as the headquarters in Maryland. Each group had its own staff. In addition, B&D companies, such as B&D of West Germany, operated autonomously in each of the more than 50 countries where B&D sells and services products. The company's philosophy had been to let each country adapt products and product lines to fit the unique characteristics of that market. The Italian firm produced power tools for Italians, the British subsidiary made power tools for the British, and so on.

As a result, countries did not communicate well with each other. Successful products in one country often took years to be introduced in others. To meet the tailor-made specifications of different markets, design centers were not being used efficiently. At one point, eight design centers around the world had produced 260 different motors, even though it was determined that the firm needed fewer than 10 different models.[15]

If you were asked by B&D's top managers to recommend changes to improve this situation, what advice would you give?

[15]J. Daniels and L. Radebaugh, *International Business*, (5th ed.; Reading, MA: Addison-Wesley, 1989), pp. 449–450.

Discounting and Present Values

When a manager chooses between two courses of action, *A* and *B*, he or she is choosing between the cash flows resulting if *A* is chosen and the cash flows if *B* is chosen. These cash flows generally occur over a number of periods. For example, if *A* is chosen, the firm may experience an outflow of $1 million this year and an inflow of $300,000 during each of the next five years. On the other hand, if *B* is chosen, the firm may experience an outflow of $1 million this year and an inflow of $250,000 for each of the next six years. How can a manager compare these two alternatives?

To answer this question, it is convenient to begin by pointing out one of the basic propositions in managerial economics: *A dollar received today is worth more than a dollar received a year from today.* Why? Because one can always invest money that is available now and obtain interest on it. If the interest rate is 6 percent, a dollar received now is equivalent to $1.06 received a year hence. Why? Because if you invest the dollar now, you'll get $1.06 in a year. Similarly, *a dollar received now is equivalent to $(1.06)^2$ dollars two years hence.* Why? Because if you invest the dollar now, you'll get 1.06 dollars in a year, and if you reinvest this amount for another year at 6 percent, you'll get $(1.06)^2$ dollars.

More generally, suppose that you can invest at a compound rate of i percent per year. What is the *present value*–that is, the value *today*–of a dollar received n years hence? Based on the foregoing argument, its present value is

$$\frac{1}{(1 + i)^n}. \tag{A.1}$$

Thus, if the interest rate is 0.10 and if $n = 4$ (which means that the dollar is received in four years), the present value of a dollar equals

$$\frac{1}{(1 + 0.10)^4} = \frac{1}{1.4641} = \$0.683.$$

In other words, the present value of the dollar is 68.3 cents.

To see that this answer is correct, let's see what would happen if you invested 68.3 cents today. As shown in Table A.1, this investment would be worth 75.1 cents after one year, 82.6 cents after two years, 90.9 cents after three years, and 1 dollar after four years. Thus, 68.3 cents is the present value of a dollar received four years hence, because if you invest 68.3 cents today, you will have exactly 1 dollar in four years.

Appendix Table 1 shows the value of $1/(1 + i)^n$, for various values of i and n. For example, according to this table, the present value of a dollar received ten years hence is 46.3 cents if the interest rate is 0.08. To see this, note that the figure in Appendix Table 1 corresponding to $n = 10$ and $i = 0.08$ is 0.46319.

Using this table, you can readily determine the present value of any amount received n years hence, not just 1 dollar. If you receive R_n dollars n years hence, the present value of this amount is

$$\frac{R_n}{(1 + i)^n}. \tag{A.2}$$

TABLE
A.1

Value of 68.3 Cents Invested at 10 Percent Interest

Number of years hence	Return received	Value of investment
1	68.301(0.10) = 6.830¢	68.301 + 6.830 = 75.13¢
2	75.131(0.10) = 7.513¢	75.131 + 7.513 = 82.64¢
3	82.643(0.10) = 8.264¢	82.645 + 8.265 = 90.91¢
4	90.907(0.10) = 9.091¢	90.909 + 9.091 = 100.00¢

Thus, to determine the present value of R_n, all that you have to do is multiply R_n by $1/(1 + i)^n$. Since Appendix Table 1 provides us with the value of $1/(1 + i)^n$, this is a simple calculation.

To illustrate, suppose you will receive $10,000 ten years hence and the interest rate is 0.12. According to equation (A.2), the present value of this amount equals $10,000[1/(1 + i)^n]$. Since Appendix Table 1 shows that $1/(1 + i)^n = 0.32197$ when $n = 10$ and $i = 0.12$, the present value of this amount is $10,000(0.32197) = $3,219.70.

Present Value of a Series of Payments

As pointed out at the beginning of this appendix, managers generally must consider situations in which cash flows occur at more than a single time. For example, investment in a new machine tool is likely to result in a cash outflow now and a series of cash inflows in the future. To determine the present value of such an investment, it is convenient to begin by considering the simple case in which you receive $1 per year for n years, the interest rate being i. More specifically, the n receipts of $1 occur one year from now, two years from now, . . . , and n years from now. The present value of this stream of $1 receipts is

$$\frac{1}{1 + i} + \frac{1}{(1 + i)^2} + \cdots + \frac{1}{(1 + i)^n} = \sum_{t=1}^{n} \frac{1}{(1 + i)^t}. \qquad (A.3)$$

For example, the present value of $1 to be received at the end of each of the next five years, if the interest rate is 0.10, is

$$\sum_{t=1}^{5} \frac{1}{(1 + 0.10)^t} = \frac{1}{(1 + 0.10)} + \frac{1}{(1 + 0.10)^2} + \frac{1}{(1 + 0.10)^3}$$

$$+ \frac{1}{(1 + 0.10)^4} + \frac{1}{(1 + 0.10)^5} = 0.90909 + 0.82645$$

$$+ 0.75131 + 0.68301 + 0.62092 = $3.79. \qquad (A.4)$$

To obtain each of the terms on the right in equation (A.4), we use Appendix Table 1. For example, the final term on the right is 0.62092, which is the present value of a dollar received five years hence (if the interest rate is 0.10), according to Appendix Table 1.

Table A.2 shows that $3.79 is indeed the present value of $1 to be received at the end of each of the next five years, if the interest rate is 0.10. As you can see, if you invest $3.79 at 10 percent interest, you will be able to withdraw $1 at the end of each year, with nothing left over or lacking. Since analysts

TABLE

A.2

Demonstration that $3.79 (Invested at 10 Percent Interest) Provides Exactly $1 at the End of Each of the Next Five Years

Number of years hence	Return received	Amount withdrawn	Net value of investment
1	$3.790(0.10) = $.3790	$1.00	$3.790 + 0.3790 − 1.00 = $3.169
2	3.169(0.10) = .3169	$1.00	3.169 + 0.3169 − 1.00 = 2.486
3	2.486(0.10) = .2486	$1.00	2.486 + 0.2486 − 1.00 = 1.735
4	1.735(0.10) = .1735	$1.00	1.735 + 0.1735 − 1.00 = .909
5	0.909(0.10) = .0909	$1.00	0.909 + 0.0909 − 1.00 = 0

frequently must calculate the present value of a dollar received at the end of each of the next n years, the expression in equation (A.3),

$$\sum_{t=1}^{n} 1/(1 + i)^t,$$

has been tabled; the results are shown in Appendix Table 2. For example, if you receive $1 at the end of each of the next ten years, and if the interest rate is 0.06, the present value is $7.36. To see this, note that the figure in Appendix Table 2 corresponding to $n = 10$ and $i = 0.06$ is 7.3601.

More generally, if you receive R dollars at the end of each of the next n years, and if the interest rate is i, the present value is

$$\sum_{t=1}^{n} \frac{R}{(1 + i)^t} = R \sum_{t=1}^{n} \frac{1}{(1 + i)^t}. \tag{A.5}$$

Thus, the present value of $5,000 to be received at the end of each of the next five years, if the interest rate is 0.08, is $5,000(3.9927) = $19,963.5, since Appendix Table 2 shows that the value of $\sum_{t=1}^{n} 1/(1 + i)^t = 3.9927$, when $n = 5$ and $i = 0.08$.

Finally, we must consider the case in which there is a series of unequal, not equal, payments. Suppose that a payment is received at the end of each of the next n years, that the amount received at the end of the tth year is R_t, and that the interest rate is i. The present value of this series of unequal payments is

$$\sum_{t=1}^{n} \frac{R_t}{(1 + i)^t}. \tag{A.6}$$

Present Value of Stream of Unequal Payments, Where $i = 0.10$ and $n = 3$

Number of years hence	(1) Amount received R_t	(2) $\dfrac{1}{(1 + 0.10)^t}$	(1) × (2) Present value of amount received
1	$3,000	0.90909	$2,727.27
2	2,000	0.82645	1,652.89
3	1,000	0.75131	751.31
			Total $5,131.48

Appendix Table 1 can be used to help carry out this computation. For example, suppose that $i = 0.10$, that $n = 3$, and that the amount received at the end of the first year is $3,000, the amount received at the end of the second year is $2,000, and the amount received at the end of the third year is $1,000. Table A.3 shows how to calculate the present value of this series of unequal payments, which in this case equals $5,131.48.

The Use of Periods Other Than a Year

Thus far, we have assumed that the interest or return from an invested amount is paid annually. In other words, we have assumed that a dollar invested at the beginning of a year earns interest of i percent at the end of that year. In many situations, this is not correct. Instead, interest, dividends, or other returns from an investment may be received semiannually, quarterly, monthly, or even daily. Because you earn a return in the next period on the return received in this period, the results differ from those given in previous sections of this appendix.

If interest is received *semiannually*, the present value of a dollar received n years hence is

$$\frac{1}{(1 + i/2)^{2n}}, \tag{A.7}$$

where i is the annual interest rate. To understand this expression, note that the interest rate for each semiannual period is $i/2$, and that there are $2n$ semiannual periods in n years. Bearing this in mind, this expression can be derived in the same way as expression (A.1).

If interest is received *quarterly*, the present value of a dollar received *n* years hence is

$$\frac{1}{(1 + i/4)^{4n}},$$ (A.8)

where *i* once again is the annual interest rate. To see why this is true, note that the interest rate for each quarterly period is $i/4$, and that there are $4n$ quarterly periods in *n* years. Bearing this in mind, this expression can be derived in the same way as expression (A.1).

More generally, suppose that interest is received *c* times per year. Under these circumstances, the present value of a dollar received *n* years hence is

$$\frac{1}{(1 + i/c)^{cn}}.$$ (A.9)

Appendix Table 1 can be used to determine present values under these circumstances. To evaluate expression (A.9), let the interest rate be i/c, and let the number of years be cn; using these values, Appendix Table 1 gives the correct answer. Thus, the present value of 1 dollar to be received 3 years hence, where the interest rate is 8 percent paid quarterly, can be obtained by finding in the table the present value of 1 dollar to be received 12 years hence where the interest rate is 2 percent. Specifically, the answer is 78.849 cents.

Determining the Internal Rate of Return

Previous sections of this appendix have been concerned entirely with determining the present value of a stream of cash flows. While this is of great importance in managerial economics, it also is important to calculate the internal rate of return—the interest rate that equates the present value of the cash inflows with the present value of the cash outflows. Put differently, the internal rate of return is the interest rate that makes the present value of a stream of cash flows equal zero. In other words, we want to find *i* where

$$R_0 + \frac{R_1}{1 + i} + \frac{R_2}{(1 + i)^2} + \cdots + \frac{R_n}{(1 + i)^n} = 0,$$

or

$$\sum_{t=0}^{n} \frac{R_t}{(1 + i)^t} = 0.$$ (A.10)

To solve equation (A.10) for i, it often is necessary to use trial and error (if you do not have access to a computer or calculator). The first step is to make a rough estimate of the value of i that will satisfy equation (A.10). The second step is to adjust this estimate. If the present value based on the original estimated rate of interest is *positive*, *increase* the value of i. If the present value based on the original estimated rate of return is *negative*, *reduce* the value of i. The third step is to continue to adjust this estimate until you find the value of i that will satisfy equation (A.10).

As an illustration, consider the following stream of cash flows: $R_0 = -\$5,980$, $R_1 = \$3,000$, $R_2 = \$2,000$, and $R_3 = \$2,000$. As a first step, we estimate (roughly) that the internal rate of return is in the neighborhood of 8 percent. As Table A.4 shows, the present value of this stream of cash flows, given that the interest rate is 8 percent, is $100.12, which is positive. Thus, a higher value of i must be tried. We choose 9 percent. As Table A.4 shows, the present value of this stream of cash flows, given that the interest rate is 9 percent, is virtually zero. Thus, the internal rate of return is 9 percent.

If the cash flows (in years other than year 0) are all equal, there is a simpler way to determine the internal rate of return. Under these circumstances, equation (A.10) can be written:

$$R_0 + \sum_{t=1}^{n} \frac{R}{(1 + i)^t} = 0,$$

where R is the cash flow in years 1 to n. Thus,

$$\sum_{t=1}^{n} \frac{1}{(1 + i)^t} = \frac{-R_0}{R}. \tag{A.11}$$

TABLE
A.4

Determination of the Internal Rate of Return

Year t	Cash flow R_t	$i = 8$ percent $\frac{1}{(1 + i)^t}$	Present value	$i = 9$ percent $\frac{1}{(1 + i)^t}$	Present value
0	$-\$5,980$	1.00000	$-\$5,980$	1.00000	$-\$5,980$
1	$\$3,000$	0.92593	$\$2,777.78$	0.91743	$\$2,752.29$
2	2,000	0.85734	1,714.68	0.84168	1,683.36
3	2,000	0.79383	1,587.66	0.77228	1,544.37
Total			100.12		0.02

Since we are given the value of $-R_0/R$, we can find the value of i in Appendix Table 2 where the entry in the nth row equals $-R_0/R$. This value of i is the internal rate of return.

To illustrate, suppose that a machine tool costs $10,000, and that it will result in a cash inflow of $2,500 for each of the next six years. Since $R_0 = -\$10,000$ and $R = \$2,500$, the value of $-R_0/R$ is 4. Looking in the row of Appendix Table 2 where $n = 6$, we look for the interest rate where the entry in the table is 4. Since the entry is 3.9976 when $i = 13$ percent, the internal rate of return is about 13 percent.

Finally, it is worth pointing out that if an investment yields an infinite series of equal cash flows, the present value of this series is

$$\sum_{t=1}^{\infty} \frac{R}{(1 + i)^t} = R \sum_{t=1}^{\infty} \frac{1}{(1 + i)^t} = \frac{R}{i}. \tag{A.12}$$

For example, if an investment yields a perpetual annual return of $4,000 per year, and if the interest rate is 8 percent, the present value of this perpetual stream of returns equals $4,000/0.08 = \$50,000$.

The Normal, t, and F Distributions

The formula for the probability distribution of a variable with a normal distribution is

$$f(x) = \frac{1}{(2\pi)^{0.5}\sigma} e^{-1/2[(x-\mu)/\sigma]^2}, \tag{B.1}$$

where μ is the variable's mean, σ is its standard deviation, e is approximately 2.718 and is the base of the natural logarithms, and π is approximately 3.1416. This is often called the **normal curve**.

Although normal curves vary in shape because of differences in mean and standard deviation, all normal curves have the following characteristics in common:

1. *All normal curves are symmetrical about the mean.* In other words, the height of the normal curve at a value that is a certain amount *below* the mean

Comparison between Any Normal Curve (When Distance from Mean Is Measured in Units of σ) and the Standard Normal Curve

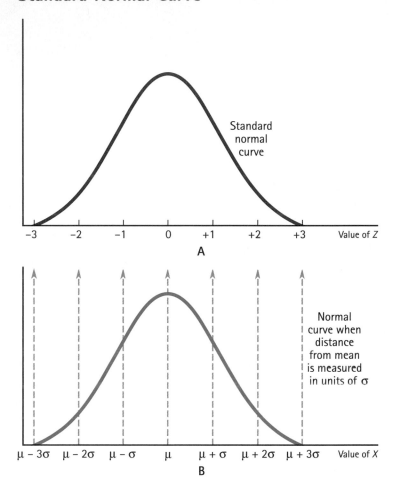

is equal to the height of the normal curve at a value that is the same amount *above* the mean. Besides being symmetrical, the normal curve is *bell shaped,* as in Figure B.1. (Note that a normal variable can assume values ranging from −∞ to +∞.)

2. Regardless of its mean or standard deviation, the probability that the value of a normal variable will lie within *one* standard deviation of its mean is 68.3 percent, the probability that it will lie within *two* standard deviations of its mean is 95.4 percent, and the probability that it will lie within *three*

standard deviations of its mean is 99.7 percent. Panel B of Figure B.1 shows the distance from the mean, μ, in units of the standard deviation, σ. Clearly, almost all the area under a normal curve lies within three standard deviations of the mean.

3. The location of a normal curve along the horizontal axis is determined entirely by its mean, μ. For example, if the mean of a normal curve equals four, it is centered at four; if its mean equals 400, it is centered at 400. The amount of spread in a normal curve is determined *entirely* by its standard deviation, σ. If σ increases, the curve's spread widens; if σ decreases, the curve's spread narrows.

If one expresses any normal variable as a deviation from its mean, and measures these deviations in units of its standard deviation, the resulting variable, called a **standard normal variable**, has the probability distribution shown in panel A of Figure B.1. This probability distribution is called the **standard normal curve**.

If any normal variable is expressed in standard units (that is, if it is expressed as a deviation from its mean, and measured in units of its standard deviation), its probability distribution is given by the standard normal curve. Thus, if a firm's sales are normally distributed and if we express them in standard units, their probability distribution is given by the standard normal curve. Put more formally, if X is a normally distributed variable, then

$$z = \frac{X - \mu}{\sigma} \tag{B.2}$$

has the standard normal distribution regardless of the values of μ and σ.

Appendix Table 3 shows the area under the standard normal curve from zero to the positive number (z) given in the left-hand column (and top) of the table. In other words, this table provides the probability that a standard normal variable lies between zero and z. Thus, the probability that a standard normal variable lies between zero and 1.10 equals 0.3643. Because of the symmetry of the normal curve, this is also the probability that it lies between zero and $-z$. Thus, the probability that a standard normal variable lies between zero and -1.10 equals 0.3643.

The t Distribution   The t distribution is really a family of distributions, each of which corresponds to a particular number of degrees of freedom. From a mathematical point of view, the number of degrees of freedom is simply a parameter in the formula for the t distribution. The shape of the t distribution is rather like that of the standard normal distribution. Figure B.2 compares the t distribution (with 2 degrees of freedom) with the standard normal distribution. As you can see, both are symmetrical, bell shaped, and have a mean of zero. The t distribution is somewhat flatter at the mean and somewhat higher in the

Comparison between Normal and *t* Distributions

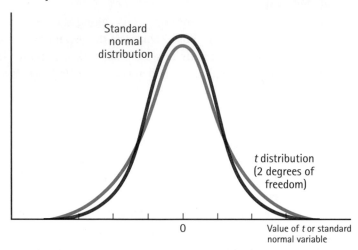

tails than the standard normal distribution. As the number of degrees of freedom becomes larger and larger, the *t* distribution tends to become exactly the same as the standard normal distribution. The *t* distribution is often called Student's *t* distribution because the statistician W. S. Gosset, who first derived this distribution, published his findings under the pseudonym Student.

To find the probability that the value of *t* exceeds a certain number, we can use Appendix Table 4. As you can see, each row of this table corresponds to a particular number of degrees of freedom. The numbers in each row are the numbers that are exceeded with the indicated probability by a *t* variable. For example, the first row indicates that if a *t* variable has 1 degree of freedom, there is a 0.40 probability that its value will exceed 0.325, a 0.25 probability that its value will exceed 1.000, a 0.05 probability that its value will exceed 6.314, a 0.01 probability that its value will exceed 31.821, and so on. Since the *t* distribution is symmetrical, it follows that if a *t* variable has 1 degree of freedom, there is a 0.40 probability that its value will lie below −0.325, a 0.25 probability that its value will lie below −1.000, and so on.

The *F* Distribution The *F* distribution, like the *t* distribution, is in reality a family of probability distributions, each corresponding to certain numbers of degrees of freedom. But unlike the *t* distribution, the *F* distribution has two numbers of degrees of freedom, not one. Figure B.3 shows the *F* distribution with 2 and 9 degrees of freedom. As you can see, the *F* distribution is skewed to the right. However, as both numbers of degrees of freedom become very large, the *F* distribution tends toward normality. Once again, it should be

The *F* Probability Distribution, with 2 and 9 Degrees of Freedom

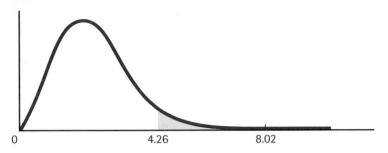

emphasized that any *F* random variable has *two* numbers of degrees of freedom. Be careful to keep these numbers of degrees of freedom in the *correct order,* because an *F* distribution with v_1 and v_2 degrees of freedom is not the same as an *F* distribution with v_2 and v_1 degrees of freedom.

Tables are available that show the values of *F* that are exceeded with certain probabilities, such as 0.05 and 0.01. Appendix Table 5 shows, for various numbers of degrees of freedom, the value of *F* that is exceeded with probability equal to 0.05. For example, if the numbers of degrees of freedom are 2 and 9, the value of *F* that is exceeded with probability equal to 0.05 is 4.26. Similarly, Appendix Table 6 shows, for various numbers of degrees of freedom, the value of *F* that is exceeded with probability equal to 0.01. For example, if the numbers of degrees of freedom are 2 and 9, the value of *F* exceeded with probability equal to 0.01 is 8.02. (In Appendix Tables 5 and 6, the first number of degrees of freedom is labeled "Degrees of freedom for numerator," and the second number is labeled "Degrees of freedom for denominator.")

ANSWERS

Brief Answers to Odd-Numbered End-of-Chapter Questions and Problems

Chapter 1

1. a. Yes. **b.** Yes. Yes.

3. They tend to exacerbate it, since the executive's pay is not so directly related to his or her effectiveness in raising the firm's profits.

5.

Number of years in the future	Profit (millions of dollars)	$\dfrac{1}{(1 + i)^t}$	Present value
1	8	0.90909	7.27272
2	10	0.82645	8.26450
3	12	0.75131	9.01572
4	14	0.68301	9.56214
5	15	0.62092	9.31380
6	16	0.56447	9.03152
7	17	0.51316	8.72372

Number of years in the future	Profit (millions of dollars)	$\dfrac{1}{(1 + i)^t}$	Present value
(cont'd)			
8	15	0.46651	6.99765
9	13	0.42410	5.51330
10	10	0.38554	3.85540
			Total 77.55056

Thus, the answer is $77.55056 million.

7. a. He will receive 80(50)($5) = $20,000, from which he must pay $3,000 for the umbrellas and 3($3,000) = $9,000 for rent. Thus, his accounting profit equals $20,000 − $3,000 − $9,000, or $8,000.

  b. Since he could earn $4,000 doing construction work, his economic profit is $8,000 − $4,000 = $4,000. (For simplicity, we ignore the fact that he could have earned interest on the money he invested in this business during the summer.)

9. No. No. The first group emphasized the demand side while the second group emphasized the supply side.

11. a. If the price were $65, the weekly operating profit would be $80,000, so it would take $8 million/$80,000 = 100 weeks for the operating profits to cover the $8 million investment. If the price were $75, the weekly operating profit would be $165,000, so it would take $8 million/$165,000 = 48.5 weeks for the operating profits to cover the $8 million investment. But note that it would take longer for the investors to get any return on their investment.

  b. Given that about two-thirds of Broadway shows have not broken even, investors in such shows obviously assume considerable risk.

  c. They do not take into account the likelihood that *Showboat* will play outside Broadway. Also, there may be profits from cast albums and other spin-offs from the show.

  d. Yes.

Chapter 2

1. a. Since the cost per patient-day $(Y) = C/X$, the desired relationship is

$$Y = \frac{4,700,000}{X} + 0.00013X.$$

  b. To find the value of X that minimizes the value of Y, we set the derivative of Y with respect to X equal to zero:

$$\frac{dY}{dX} = -\frac{4,700,000}{X^2} + 0.00013 = 0.$$

Thus, $X = \left(\dfrac{4,700,000}{0.00013}\right)^{0.5}$ or approximately 190,141.6476 patient-days.

c. Since $d^2Y/dX^2 = 2(4,700,000)/X^3$, d^2Y/dX^2 must be positive (since X is positive). Thus, Y must be a minimum, not a maximum, at the point where $dY/dX = 0$.

3. a. $5,000. - \$3,000.

   b. 7 units per day.

   c. No, because profit is higher at 9 units per day than at 7 units per day.

5. a. Since marginal cost equals $4 + 16Q$, it is 164 when $Q = 10$.

   b. $4 + 16(12) = 196$.

   c. $4 + 16(20) = 324$.

7. a. 6

   b. $24X$

   c. $48X^2$

   d. $8/X^3$

9. a. 2

   b. $12X^2$

   c. $0.8Z^{0.2} X^{-0.2} = 0.8\dfrac{Y}{X}$

   d. $-3Z/(4 + X)^2$

11. a. $\partial C/\partial X_1 = -3 + 4X_1 + X_2 = 0$

    $\partial C/\partial X_2 = -4 + 6X_2 + X_1 = 0$.

    Solving these two equations simultaneously,

    $X_1 = 14/23$ and $X_2 = 13/23$.

    b. The answer will not change.

13. a. The Lagrangian function is $L_{TC} = 7X_1^2 + 9X_2^2 - 1.5X_1X_2 + \lambda(10 - X_1 - X_2)$. Thus,

    $\partial L_{TC}/\partial X_1 = 14X_1 - 1.5X_2 - \lambda = 0$

    $\partial L_{TC}/\partial X_2 = 18X_2 - 1.5X_1 - \lambda = 0$

    $\partial L_{TC}/\partial \lambda = 10 - X_1 - X_2 = 0$

    From the first two of these equations, it follows that

    $X_1 = (195/155)X_2$,

    which, together with the third equation, implies that $X_1 = 195/35$ and $X_2 = 155/35$.

    b. Yes.

    c. If we substitute 195/35 for X_1, and 155/35 for X_2 in either of the first two equations, we find that $\lambda = 71.36$, which is the marginal cost of a rug at the cost-minimizing combination of types that total ten rugs per day.

Chapter 3

1. a. If $Q = 20$, $P = 2,000 - 50(20) = 1,000$. Thus, price would have to equal $1,000.

b. Since $500 = 2,000 - 50Q$, $Q = 1,500/50 = 30$. Thus, it will sell 30 per month.

c. Because $Q = (2,000 - P)/50 = 40 - 0.02P$, $dQ/dP = -0.02$. Thus,

$$\left(\frac{P}{Q}\right)\left(\frac{\partial Q}{\partial P}\right) = -0.02\frac{500}{30} = -0.33.$$

d. If $-0.02 \dfrac{P}{(2,000 - P)/50} = -1,$

$$-0.02\frac{50P}{2,000 - P} = -1,$$

$$P = 2,000 - P$$

$$= 2,000/2 = 1,000.$$

Thus, if price equals $1,000, the demand is of unitary elasticity.

3. a. $\dfrac{\partial Q}{\partial P}\left(\dfrac{P}{Q}\right) = \dfrac{-3(10)}{500 - 3(10) + 2(20) + 0.1(6,000)}$

$$= \frac{-30}{500 - 30 + 40 + 600} = \frac{-30}{1,110}.$$

b. $\dfrac{\partial Q}{\partial I}\left(\dfrac{I}{Q}\right) = \dfrac{0.1(6,000)}{1,110} = \dfrac{600}{1,110}.$

c. $\partial\dfrac{Q}{\partial P_r}\left(\dfrac{P_r}{Q}\right) = \dfrac{2(20)}{1,110} = \dfrac{40}{1,110}.$

d. Population is assumed to be essentially constant (or to have no significant effect on Q, other than via whatever effect it has on per capita disposable income).

5. Yes.

7. a. Because there are lots of very close substitutes for a particular brand, but not for cigarettes as a whole. It appears that the elasticity was less than -2.

b. No. More will be said about estimating demand functions in Chapter 5.

9. No. The fact that the elasticity of demand with respect to advertising is relatively low (0.003) does not necessarily mean that an additional dollar spent on advertising would not be profitable, or that the last dollar spent was not profitable.

11. a. -3.1.

b. Decreases.

c. 2.3.

d. 0.1.

e. The quantity demanded will increase by 10 percent. (Note that Q in this problem is defined as quantity demanded *per capita*.)

13. a. Price should be set equal to

$$MC\frac{1}{1 + 1/\eta} = 18\frac{1}{1 - 1/3} = \$27.$$

b. $18.

Chapter 4

1. a. His or her indifference curves are as follows:

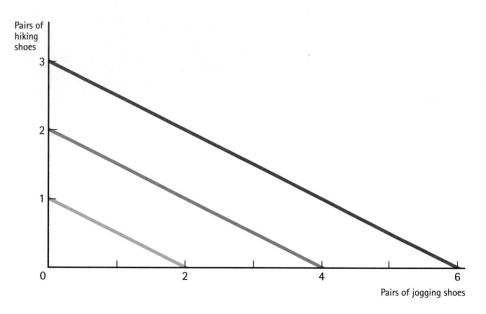

b. No. Indifference curves seldom are straight lines.

3.

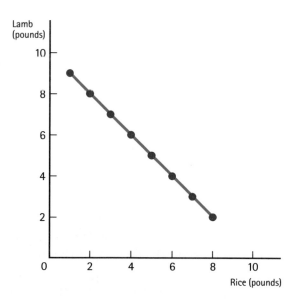

5. His budget line is as follows:

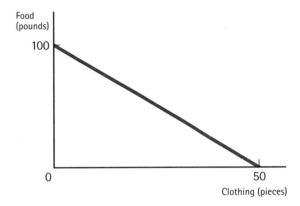

7. Maria will maximize utility at point *A*, where she purchases 15 units of both chips and salsa. Note that her indifference curves are 90-degree angles.

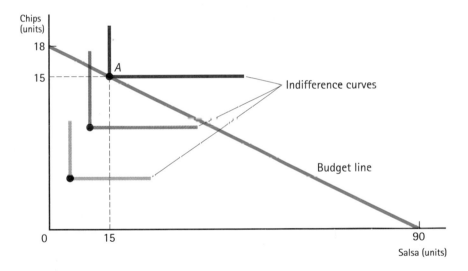

9. Since her marginal rate of substitution of opera tickets for movie tickets equals 5, and since the ratio of the price of an opera ticket to the price of a movie ticket is 10, it is impossible for her to set the marginal rate of substitution equal to the price ratio. She can increase satisfaction by substituting movie tickets for opera tickets because she is willing to give up only 5 movie tickets to get an extra opera ticket, but she has to give up 10 movie tickets to get an extra opera ticket. Thus, she will spend the entire $300 on movie tickets; she will buy 50 of them.

11. a. 150 miles   **b.** 300 miles   **c.** Yes. −0.5.   **d.** $3 billion.

Chapter 5

1. **a.** The evidence appears to be very strong that increases in the firm's advertising expenditure do have a positive effect on the quantity demanded of the firm's product.

   b. $Q = -104 + 3.2(5,000) + 1.5(20) + 1.6(1,000) - 2.1P$
   $= 17,526 - 2.1P.$

   Thus,

   $$P = \frac{17,526 - Q}{2.1} = 8,346 - 0.476Q.$$

   c. From the answer to part b,

   $Q = 17,526 - 2.1P.$

   Thus, if $P = 500$,

   $Q = 17,526 - 2.1(500) = 16,476.$

   d. Since R^2 equals 0.89, the regression equation seems to fit the data quite well. However, we have no way of knowing (from the information given here) whether the error terms are serially correlated or a nonlinear equation fits significantly better.

3. **a.** Let profit equal Y and sales equal X. Plotting Y against X, we get the following:

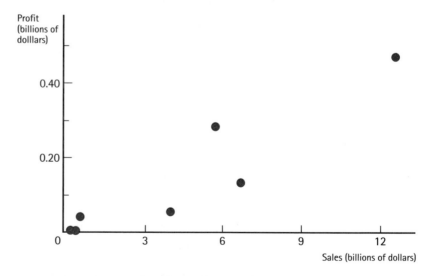

$\Sigma X = 30.0;\ \Sigma Y = 0.94;\ \Sigma X^2 = 248.72;\ \Sigma XY = 8.307;\ n = 7;$
$\Sigma Y^2 = 0.3030.$

$$b = \frac{7(8.307) - (30)(0.94)}{7(248.72) - 30^2} = \frac{58.149 - 28.200}{1,741.04 - 900} = \frac{29.949}{841.04} = 0.0356.$$

$a = 0.134 - (0.0356)(4.286) = 0.134 - .153 = -0.019.$

The regression line is $\hat{Y} = -0.019 + 0.0356X.$

b. $-0.019 + 0.0356(2) = -0.019 + 0.071 = 0.052$. Thus, the answer is about 0.05 billion dollars.

c. No. Prices and costs will be different in 2001 than in 1980.

5. a. 40.833.

 b. -1.025.

 c. 0.006667.

 d. 0.916.

 e. 1.361.

 f. Less than 0.001.

 g. Less than 0.001.

 h. 0.244.

 i. The average relationship is $C1 = 40.8 - 1.02\ C2 + 0.00667\ C3$. This relationship seems to fit the data quite well, R^2 being 0.916. There is a very small probability that the estimated effect of $C2$ (price) is due to chance, but a much higher probability (0.244) that the effect of $C3$ (disposable income) could be due to chance.

7. a. Let General Electric's profits be Y and gross domestic product be X. If we plot Y against X, we get the following graph:

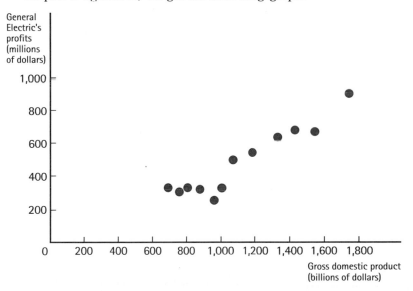

To calculate a and b, we can compute the following:

X	Y	X^2	Y^2	XY
688	355	473,344	126,025	244,240
753	339	567,009	114,921	255,267
796	361	633,616	130,321	287,356
868	357	753,424	127,449	309,876
936	278	876,096	77,284	260,208
982	363	964,324	131,769	356,466
1,063	510	1,129,969	260,100	542,130

	X	Y	X^2	Y^2	XY
(cont'd)					
	1,171	573	1,371,241	328,329	670,983
	1,306	661	1,705,636	436,921	863,266
	1,407	705	1,979,649	497,025	991,935
	1,529	688	2,337,841	473,344	1,051,952
	1,706	931	2,910,436	866,761	1,588,286
Sum	13,205	6,121	15,702,585	3,570,249	7,421,965
Mean	1,100.42	510.08			

The results are

$$b = \frac{12(7,421,965) - (13,205)(6,121)}{12(15,702,585) - 13,205^2}$$

$$= \frac{89,063,580 - 80,827,805}{188,431,020 - 174,372,025}$$

$$= \frac{8,235,775}{14,058,995} = 0.586$$

and

$$a = 510.08 - (0.586)(1,100.42) = 510.08 - 644.85 = -134.77.$$

Thus, the slope equals 0.586, and the intercept equals -134.77 millions of dollars.

b. On the average a \$1 increase in the GDP seems to be associated with a \$0.000586 increase in General Electric's profits (recalling that GDP is measured in billions of dollars, while General Electric's profits are measured in millions of dollars).

c. The forecast equals $-134.77 + 0.586(2,000) = -134.77 + 1,172 = 1,037.23$. That is, it equals 1,037.23 million dollars.

d. $r^2 - 0.90$.

e. No. No. A nonlinear relationship might be as good or better.

f. If nothing else is available, this model may be serviceable, but it is so crude that it is difficult to believe that the analyst could not improve upon it by taking other independent variables into account.

9. a. Taking antilogs,

$$Q = 102P^{-0.148}Z^{0.258}$$

$$\partial Q/\partial P = -0.148(102P^{-1.148}Z^{0.258}) = -0.148 \, Q/P.$$

Since the price elasticity of demand equals $(\partial Q/\partial P)(P/Q)$, it follows that the price elasticity of demand equals -0.148.

b. $\partial Q/\partial Z = 0.258(102P^{-0.148}Z^{-0.742}) = 0.258Q/Z.$

Since the cross elasticity of demand equals $(\partial Q/\partial Z)(Z/Q)$, it follows that the cross elasticity of demand equals 0.258.

c. The regression seems to provide a good fit. The fact that $\bar{R}^2$ equals 0.98 means that 98 percent of the variation in log Q can be explained by the regression (see the chapter appendix). See Figure 5.6.

11. a. No.

b. The market supply curve for wine.

Chapter 6

1. a. Yes. Room occupancy in August tends to be about 57 percent greater than in January.

   b. There are more tourists in the summer than in the winter. Because of the recession, there may have been fewer tourists, and hence the seasonal variation may have been less pronounced during the recession than before it.

   c. It might be of use in scheduling labor inputs and in ordering supplies. Certainly, the manager would want to take proper account of this seasonal variation in his or her hiring and purchasing decisions.

3. a. Because the seasonal index shows by what percent sales for a particular month tend to be above or below normal.

   b. Deseasonalized sales are as follows:

January	2.5/0.97 = $2.58 million
February	2.4/0.96 = $2.50 million
March	2.7/0.97 = $2.78 million
April	2.9/0.98 = $2.96 million
May	3.0/0.99 = $3.03 million
June	3.1/1.00 = $3.10 million
July	3.2/1.01 = $3.17 million
August	3.1/1.03 = $3.01 million
September	3.2/1.03 = $3.11 million
October	3.1/1.03 = $3.01 million
November	3.0/1.02 = $2.94 million
December	2.9/1.01 – $2.87 million

   c. Because they want to see how sales are changing, when the seasonal factor is deleted.

5. a. Yes. Yes.

   b. Yes. Yes.

7. a. $S_t = -5,744 + 2.9143t$.

   b. The forecast would have been $-5,744 + 2.9143(1991) = 58.4$ billion dollars, so the forecasting error would have been about 2 percent.

   c. The forecast would have been $-5,744 + 2.9143(1992) = 61.3$ billion dollars, so the forecasting error would have been about 17 percent.

9. a. Let $t' = 0$ when $t = 1963$. Let y be General Electric's sales.

t'	y	t'^2	y^2	$t'y$
−13	2.2	169	4.84	−28.6
−12	2.6	144	6.76	−31.2
−11	3.0	121	9.00	−33.0
−10	3.5	100	12.25	−35.0
−9	3.3	81	10.89	−29.7
−8	3.5	64	12.25	−28.0

	t'	y	t'^2	y^2	$t'y$
(cont'd)					
	−7	4.1	49	16.81	−28.7
	−6	4.3	36	18.49	−25.8
	−5	4.2	25	17.64	−21.0
	−4	4.5	16	20.25	−18.0
	−3	4.2	9	17.64	−12.6
	−2	4.5	4	20.25	−9.0
	−1	4.8	1	23.04	−4.8
	0	4.9	0	24.01	0.0
	1	4.9	1	24.01	4.9
	2	6.2	4	38.44	12.4
	3	7.2	9	51.84	21.6
	4	7.7	16	59.29	30.8
	5	8.4	25	70.56	42.0
	6	8.4	36	70.56	50.4
	7	8.8	49	77.44	61.6
	8	9.6	64	92.16	76.8
	9	10.5	81	110.25	94.5
	10	11.9	100	141.61	119.0
	11	13.9	121	193.21	152.9
	12	14.1	144	198.81	169.2
	13	15.7	169	246.49	204.1
Sum	0	180.9	1,638	1,588.79	734.8
Mean	0	6.7			

$$b = \frac{734.8 - (180.9)(0)}{1,638 - (0)(0)} = \frac{734.8}{1,638} = 0.449.$$

$$a = 6.7 - (0.449)(0) = 6.7.$$

Thus, the trend is $6.7 + 0.449t'$.

b. The graph is as follows:

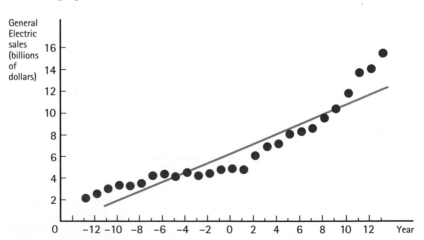

General Electric sales (billions of dollars)

    c. It appears from the graph that the trend may be curvilinear, and that an exponential or quadratic trend might do better.

    d. The forecast would be $6.7 + 0.449(31) = 20.619$ billion dollars, which was only about 30 percent higher than actual sales in 1976. In fact, GE's sales were about \$60 billion in 1994, which indicates how poor linear extrapolations of this sort can be, particularly when one is using them to forecast many years (18 years in this case) into the future.

Chapter Appendix

1. a. Let S_0 be the smoothed value for 1989, S_1 be the smoothed value for 1990, and so on.

$S_0 = 2$.
$S_1 = (1/4)(4) + (3/4)(2) = 2.50$.
$S_2 = (1/4)(8) + (3/4)(2.50) = 3.88$.
$S_3 = (1/4)(12) + (3/4)(3.88) = 5.91$.
$S_4 = (1/4)(20) + (3/4)(5.91) = 9.43$.
$S_5 = (1/4)(28) + (3/4)(9.43) = 14.07$.
$S_6 = (1/4)(38) + (3/4)(14.07) = 9.50 + 10.55 = 20.05$.
$S_7 = (1/4)(50) + (3/4)(20.05) = 12.50 + 15.04 = 27.54$.
$S_8 = (1/4)(70) + (3/4)(27.54) = 17.50 + 20.66 = 38.16$.
$S_9 = (1/4)(90) + (3/4)(38.16) = 22.50 + 28.62 = 51.12$.

b. $S_0 = 2$.
$S_1 = (1/2)(4) + (1/2)(2) = 3.00$.
$S_2 = (1/2)(8) + (1/2)(3.00) = 5.50$.
$S_3 = (1/2)(12) + (1/2)(5.50) = 8.75$.
$S_4 = (1/2)(20) + (1/2)(8.75) = 14.38$.
$S_5 = (1/2)(28) + (1/2)(14.38) = 21.19$.
$S_6 = (1/2)(38) + (1/2)(21.19) = 29.60$.
$S_7 = (1/2)(50) + (1/2)(29.60) = 39.80$.
$S_8 = (1/2)(70) + (1/2)(39.80) = 54.90$.
$S_9 = (1/2)(90) + (1/2)(54.90) = 72.45$.

c. $S_0 = 2$.
$S_1 = (3/4)(4) + (1/4)(2) = 3.50$.
$S_2 = (3/4)(8) + (1/4)(3.50) = 6.88$.
$S_3 = (3/4)(12) + (1/4)(6.88) = 10.72$.
$S_4 = (3/4)(20) + (1/4)(10.72) = 17.68$.
$S_5 = (3/4)(28) + (1/4)(17.68) = 25.42$.
$S_6 = (3/4)(38) + (1/4)(25.42) = 28.50 + 6.36 = 34.86$.
$S_7 = (3/4)(50) + (1/4)(34.86) = 37.50 + 8.72 = 46.22$.
$S_8 = (3/4)(70) + (1/4)(46.22) = 52.50 + 11.56 = 64.06$.
$S_9 = (3/4)(90) + (1/4)(64.06) = 67.50 + 16.02 = 83.52$.

Chapter 7

1. **a.** To see whether 400 hours of skilled labor and 100 hours of unskilled labor are the optimal input combination, recall from equation (7.11) that to minimize cost, the Elwyn Company should pick an input combination where

$$\frac{MP_S}{P_S} = \frac{MP_U}{P_U},$$

where MP_S is the marginal product of skilled labor, MP_U is the marginal product of unskilled labor, P_S is the price of skilled labor, and P_U is the price of unskilled labor. Since $P_S = 10$, $P_U = 5$, and

$$MP_S = \frac{\partial Q}{\partial S} = 300 - 0.4S$$

$$MP_U = \frac{\partial Q}{\partial U} = 200 - 0.6U,$$

it follows that the Elwyn Company should pick an input combination where

$$\frac{300 - 0.4S}{10} = \frac{200 - 0.6U}{5},$$

or

$1,500 - 2S = 2,000 - 6U$

$S = -250 + 3U.$

Thus, 400 hours of skilled labor and 100 hours of unskilled labor are not the optimal input combination, because, if $S = 400$ and $U = 100$, this equation does not hold.

b. If a total of $5,000 is spent on skilled and unskilled labor,

$10S + 5U = 5,000,$

since $P_S = 10$ and $P_U = 5$. From the answer to part a, we know that

$S = -250 + 3U.$

Solving these two equations simultaneously, $S = 392.9$ and $U = 214.3$. Thus, to maximize output, Elwyn should hire about 393 hours of skilled labor and about 214 hours of unskilled labor.

c. From equation 7.4, we know that $MP_U \bullet P$ must equal P_U, where P is the price of the product. (Under present circumstances, the marginal revenue product of unskilled labor equals $MP_U \bullet P$, and the marginal expenditure on unskilled labor equals P_U.) Thus, since $P = 10$, $P_U = 5$, and $MP_U = 200 - 0.6U$,

$10(200 - 0.6U) = 5$

$U = 332.5.$

To maximize profit, Elwyn should hire 332.5 hours of unskilled labor. (Note that we no longer assume that a total of $5,000 is spent on labor. Thus, the answer is different from that in part b.)

3. a. No.

  b. 50 pounds, since half of these amounts (that is, 50 pounds of hay and 125.1 pounds of grain) results in a 25-pound gain.

  c. $-(125.1 - 130.9)/(50 - 40) = 0.58$.

  d. No, because it is impossible to tell (from the information given in the question) how much hay and grain can be used to produce a 25-pound gain after the advance in technology.

5. a. No.

  b. General farms.

  c. No.

7. a. and b. The average and marginal products of grain when each amount is used are calculated as follows:

Amount of grain	Average product	Marginal product
1,200	5,917/1,200 = 4.93	
		$\dfrac{7,250 - 5,917}{1,800 - 1,200} = 2.22$
1,800	7,250/1,800 = 4.03	
		$\dfrac{8,379 - 7,250}{2,400 - 1,800} = 1.88$
2,400	8,379/2,400 = 3.49	
		$\dfrac{9,371 - 8,379}{3,000 - 2,400} = 1.65$
3,000	9,371/3,000 = 3.12	

  c. Yes. The marginal product of grain decreases as more of it is used.

9. a. To minimize cost, the firm should choose an input combination where $MP_L/P_L = MP_K/P_K$, where MP_L is the marginal product of labor, MP_K is the marginal product of capital, P_L is the price of labor, and P_K is the price of capital. Since

$$MP_L = \frac{\partial Q}{\partial L} = 5K \quad \text{and} \quad MP_K = \frac{\partial Q}{\partial K} = 5L,$$

  it follows that,

$$\frac{5K}{1} = \frac{5L}{2},$$

  or $K = L/2$. Since $Q = 20$, $K = 4/L$. Thus,

$$\frac{L}{2} = \frac{4}{L} \quad \text{or} \quad L^2 = 8,$$

  which means that the firm should use $2(2)^{0.5}$ units of labor and $(2)^{0.5}$ units of capital.

  b. If the price of labor is $2 per unit, the optimal value of K is 2, and the optimal value of L is 2. Thus, output per unit of labor is 20/2, or 10, whereas it formerly was $20/2 \times 2^{0.5}$ or $10/2^{0.5}$. Thus, output per unit of labor will rise.

  c. No, because a 1 percent increase in both K and L results in more than a 1 percent increase in Q.

11. a. Total annual cost equals $C = 40L/2 + (8,000)(1,000)/L$. Thus, $dC/dL = 20 - 8,000,000/L^2$, and the optimal lot size is

$$632.5 = \left(\frac{8,000 \times 1,000}{20}\right)^{0.5} = (400,000)^{0.5}$$

b. The optimal lot size is $2,000 = \left(\dfrac{8,000 \times 10,000}{20}\right)^{0.5} = (4,000,000)^{0.5}$

c. The optimal lot size is $6,324.6 = \left(\dfrac{8,000 \times 100,000}{20}\right)^{0.5} = (40,000)^{0.5}$

13. a. All other things equal, it often is less expensive to focus inputs in a particular area, rather than to spread them out.

b. The quicker cars are produced, the sooner the firm will sell them and receive the profit.

c. It costs money to maintain inventories, and reductions in inventories cut these costs.

Chapter 8

1. a. $\dfrac{200,000}{10(20,000) + 0.02(50,000) + 5(10,000)} = \dfrac{200,000}{251,000} = 0.797.$

b. $\dfrac{300,000}{10(30,000) + 0.02(100,000) + 5(14,000)} = \dfrac{300,000}{372,000} = 0.806.$

c. The base year is 2000.

3. a. $\log C = 5.1 - 0.25 \log 100$

$\qquad = 5.1 - 0.25(2)$

$\qquad = 4.6.$

Thus, $C = 39,811.$

b. $\log C = 5.1 - 0.25 \log 200$

$\qquad = 5.1 - 0.25\ (2.30)$

$\qquad = 4.525.$

Thus, $C = 33,497.$

c. $1 - 33,497/39,811 = 16$ percent.

5. $9.6 million. $7.68 million.

7. a. $0.5(\$1 \text{ million}) + 0.5(\$2 \text{ million}) = \$1.5$ million.

b. $0.75(\$1 \text{ million}) + 0.25(\$2 \text{ million}) + \$150,000 = \$1.4$ million. This assumes that whether each approach costs $1 million or $2 million is independent of what the other approach costs. Also, the total cost figure for each approach, if adopted, includes the $150,000. Thus only the $150,000 spent on the aborted approach is lost. The $150,000 spent on the approach that is adopted is part of the total cost figure given in the problem.

c. Comparing the answers to parts a and b, parallel approaches result in lower expected cost.

9. a. 0.6($5 million) + 0.4($3 million) = $4.2 million.
   b. 0.7($3 million) + 0.3($5 million) = $3.6 million.
   c. 0.18($5 million) + 0.82($3 million) + $500,000 = $3.86 million.

Chapter 9

1. a. It is the cheapest of these three ways of making steel. Using this method, cost per ton is $310.34, as compared with $368.86 and $401.73 with the other methods.
   b. If the price of scrap rises, the cost of producing steel based on the electric-furnace continuous-casting route will increase, because this route uses scrap. Thus, the cost advantage of this route will be reduced if the price of scrap goes up.
   c. It suggests that U.S. steel producers may have a hard time competing with steel producers in low-wage countries.
   d. If each figure is the minimum value of long-run average cost for a particular technique, it also equals the long-run marginal cost for the technique, since marginal cost equals average cost when the latter is a minimum.

3. a. If Q is the sales volume,
   $Q(\$200) - \$5,000 = \$10,000$,
   so Q must equal 75.
   b. Since $Q(\$250) - \$5,000 = \$10,000$, Q must equal 60.
   c. Since $Q(\$265) - \$5,000 = \$10,000$, Q must equal 56.6.

5. The table is as follows:

Total fixed cost	Total variable cost	Average fixed cost	Average variable cost
50	0	—	—
50	25	50	25
50	50	25	25
50	70	$16^2/_3$	$23^1/_3$
50	85	$12^1/_2$	$21^1/_4$
50	100	10	20
50	140	$8^1/_3$	$23^1/_3$
50	210	$7^1/_7$	30

7. a. Yes. Since $(\partial TC/\partial Q)(Q/TC) = \alpha_1$, this is true.
   b. Yes. If $\alpha_1 < 1$, a 1 percent increase in output results in a less than 1 percent increase in total cost, so average cost falls with increases in output; in other words, there are economies of scale. If $\alpha_1 > 1$, a 1 percent increase in output results in a more than 1 percent increase in total cost, so average cost increases with increases in output; in other words, there are diseconomies of scale.

    c. If we assume that a 1 percent increase in both P_L and P_K will result in a 1 percent increase in TC, $\alpha_2 + \alpha_3 = 1$. Thus,

$$\frac{TC}{P_K} = \alpha_0 Q^{\alpha_1} \left(\frac{P_L}{P_K} \right)^{\alpha_2},$$

and

$$\log \left(\frac{TC}{P_K} \right) = \log \alpha_0 + \alpha_1 \log Q + \alpha_2 \log \left(\frac{P_L}{P_K} \right).$$

If this is treated as a regression equation, one can estimate the αs, using the regression technique discussed in Chapter 5, subject to the caveats concerning various kinds of possible errors cited there.

3. a. Since marginal cost equals $dTVC/dQ$, it equals

$$MC = 50 - 20Q + 3Q^2.$$

It is a minimum when

$$\frac{dMC}{dQ} = -20 + 6Q = 0, \quad \text{or} \quad Q = 20/6.$$

    b. Average variable cost equals

$$AVC = \frac{TVC}{Q} = 50 - 10Q + Q^2.$$

It is a minimum when

$$\frac{dAVC}{dQ} = -10 + 2Q = 0, \quad \text{or} \quad Q = 5.$$

    c. If $Q = 5$, average variable cost equals $50 - 10(5) + 5^2 = 25$. Marginal cost equals $50 - 20(5) + 3(5^2) = 25$. Thus, marginal cost equals average variable cost at this output level.

11. a. Using equation (9.7), $S = (23,000 + 11,000 - 30,000)/30,000 = 0.13$.

    b. Production facilities used to make one product sometimes can be used to make another product, and by-products resulting from the production of one product may be useful in making other products.

Chapter 10

1. a. Since average cost (AC) must be a minimum, and since

$$AC = \frac{25,000}{Q} + 150 + 3Q,$$

$$\frac{dAC}{dQ} = \frac{-25,000}{Q^2} + 3 = 0.$$

Thus, $Q = \left(\frac{25,000}{3} \right)^{0.5} = 91.3$, and

$$AC = 25,000/91.3 + 150 + 3(91.3) = 697.7$$

so the price must be $697.7, since in long-run equilibrium, price equals the minimum value of average cost.

    b. 91.3 units.

3. a. Marginal cost equals

$$MC = \frac{dTC}{dQ} = 4 + 4Q.$$

Setting marginal cost equal to price, we have

$$4 + 4Q = 24$$
$$4Q = 20$$
$$Q = 5.$$

Thus, the optimal output rate is 5.

b. Profit equals total revenue minus total cost. Since total revenue equals $24Q$, profit equals

$$\pi = 24Q - 200 - 4Q - 2Q^2 = -200 + 20Q - 2Q^2.$$

Because $Q = 5$,

$$\pi = -200 + 20(5) - 2(5)^2 = -200 + 100 - 50 = -150.$$

Thus, the firm loses $150 (which is less than if it shuts down).

5. a. The White Company's marginal cost is $dTC/dQ = MC = 20 + 10Q$. Equating this to the market price $= P = 50$ and solving yields the optimal output Q, i.e., $P = 50 = 20 + 10Q = MC$ or $10Q = 30$ or $Q = 3$.

b. The White Company's total revenue (TR) is $TR = P*Q = 50*3 = 150$. The White Company's total cost (TC) is $TC + 1,000 + 20*3 + 5*3*3 = 1,000 + 60 + 45 - 1,105$. The White Company's economic profit is $TR - TC = 150 - 1,105 = -955$.

c. The White Company's average total cost (ATC) is $ATC = TC/Q = (1,000/Q) + 20 + 50 = (1,000/3) + 20 + 5*3 = 333.33 + 20 + 15 = 368.33$.

d. The industry is not in equilirium because the firms in the industry are losing money. In the long run, we would expect some firms to leave the industry such that in the long run, the typical firm would have long run average cost equal to long run marginal cost and no economic profits being made by any firm.

Chapter 11

1. a. Marginal revenue $= 100 - 2Q$; marginal cost $= 60 + 2Q$. Thus, if marginal revenue equals marginal cost, $100 - 2Q = 60 + 2Q$, so $Q = 10$.

b. Since $P = 100 - Q$, P must equal 90 if $Q = 10$. Thus, he should charge a price of $90.

3. a. Since $P = (8,300 - Q)/2.1 = 3,952 - 0.476Q$,

$$MR = 3,952 - 0.952Q.$$

b. $MC = 480 + 40Q$. If $MC = MR$,

$$480 + 40Q = 3,952 - 0.952Q$$
$$40.952Q = 3,472$$
$$Q = 84.8.$$

Thus, the firm would produce 84.8 lasers per month. If $Q = 84.8$, $P = 3,952 + 0.476(84.8) = 3,912$. Thus, the price should be $3,912.

c. The firm's monthly profit equals
$84.8(3,912) - [2,200 + 480(84.8) + 20(84.8)^2] = \$145,012.80$.

5. a. If the firm is producing 5 units in the first plant, the marginal cost in the first plant equals $20 + 2(5)$, or 30. Thus, if the firm is minimizing costs, marginal cost in the second plant must also equal 30; this means that
$10 + 5Q_2 = 30$
$Q_2 = 4$.

Thus, the second plant must be producing 4 units of output.

b. Since $MC_1 = MC_2 = MC$ and the firm's output, Q, equals $Q_1 + Q_2$,
$Q_1 = (MC_1/2) - 10$
$Q_2 = (MC_2/5) - 2$
$Q = Q_1 + Q_2 = 0.7MC - 12$
$MC = (1/0.7)(Q + 12)$.

c. No, because we do not have information concerning the fixed costs of each plant. But you can determine average variable cost.

7. a. It probably tended to increase because high profits induced entry. Also, the 1990–91 recession may have resulted in more demand for the services of pawnshops.

b. No. It is likely to be an oligopoly, since there generally is not a very large number of pawnshops in a small city.

c. Apparently not, but licensing requirements may exist.

9. a. The total revenue (TR) for diamonds is $TR_Z = P_Z{}^*Q_Z = (980 - 2Q_Z){}^*Q_Z = 980Q_Z - 2Q_Z{}^2$. The marginal revenue for diamonds is $dTR_Z/dQ_Z = MR_Z = 980 - 4Q_Z$. The marginal cost for diamonds is $MC_Z = dTC/dQ_Z = 50 + Q_Z$. To maximize profit, the monopolist sets $MR_Z = MC_Z$ or $MR_Z = 980 - 4Q_Z = 50 + Q_Z = MC_Z$ or $5Q_Z = 930$ or $Q_Z = 186$. Substituting $Q_Z = 186$ into the demand function yields $P_Z = 980 - 2{}^*186 = 980 - 372 = 608$. Consumer surplus (CS) is then $CS_Z = 0.5{}^*(980 - 608){}^*372 = 0.5{}^*372{}^*186 = 34,596$. Total revenue is $TR_Z = 608{}^*186 = 113,088$. Variable cost is $VC_Z = 50{}^*186 + 0.5{}^*1686{}^*186 = 9,300 + 17,298 = 26,598$. So variable cost profit = producer surplus = $PS_Z = TR_Z - VC_Z = 113,088 - 26,598 = 86,490$. Social welfare is $CS_Z + PS_Z = 34,596 + 86,490 = 121,086$.

b. If De Beers acts as a perfect competitor, they would set price = $P_Z = MC_Z$ or $P_Z = 980 - 2Q_Z = 50 + Q_Z = MC_Z$ or $3Q_Z = 930$ or $Q_Z = 310$. Substituting $Q_Z = 310$ into the demand fuction gives $P_Z = 980 - 2{}^*310 = 980 - 620 = 360$. Consumer surplus (CS) is then $CS_Z = 0.5{}^*(980 - 360){}^*310 = 0.5{}^*620{}^*310 = 96,100$. Total revenue is $TR_Z = 360{}^*310 = 111,600$. Variable cost is $VC_Z = 50{}^*310 + 0.5{}^*310{}^*310 = 15,500 + 48,050 = 63,550$. So variable cost profit = producer surplus = $PS_Z = TR_Z - VC_Z = 11,600 - 63,550 = 48,050$. Social welfare is $CS_Z + PS_Z = 96,100 + 48,050 = 144,150$.

    c. Social welfare increases by $144{,}150 - 121{,}086 = 23{,}064$.

11. a. To earn 20 percent on its total investment of $250,000, its profit must equal $50,000 per year. Thus, if it operates at 80 percent of capacity (and sells 10,000 units), it must set a price of $15 per unit. (Since average cost equals $10, profit per unit will be $5, so total profit per year will be $50,000.)

    b. From the information given, there is no assurance that it can sell 10,000 units per year if it charges a price of $15 per unit.

    c. Unless the markup bears the proper relationship to the price elasticity of demand, the firm probably is sacrificing profit.

13. a. Backus' total revenues equal

$$TR = P_X Q_X + P_Y Q_Y = (400 - Q_X)Q_X + (300 - 3Q_Y)Q_Y,$$

and since $Q_Y = 2Q_X$,

$$TR = (400 - Q_X)Q_X + (300 - 6Q_X)(2Q_X)$$
$$= 400Q_X - Q_X^2 + 600Q_X - 12Q_X^2 = 1{,}000Q_X - 13Q_X^2.$$

Thus, the firm's profit equals

$$\pi = 1{,}000Q_X - 13Q_X^2 - 500 - 3Q_X - 9Q_X^2$$
$$= -500 + 997Q_X - 22Q_X^2$$

Setting $d\pi/dQ_X = 997 - 44Q_X = 0$, we find that the profit-maximizing value of $Q_X = 997/44 = 22.66$. Thus, Backus should produce and sell 22.66 units of product X and 45.32 units of product Y per period of time.

    b. The price of product X must be $400 - 22.66 = \$377.34$, and the price of product Y must be $300 - 3(45.32) = \$164.05$.

    We have assumed that Backus sells all that it produces of both products. The marginal revenue of product X equals $400 - 2(22.66) = 354.68$, and the marginal revenue of product Y equals $300 - 6(45.32) = 28.09$. Since both are nonnegative, this assumption is true if Backus maximizes profit.

Chapter 12

1. a. The recommendation is not correct. Profit maximization requires the marginal revenue (MR) in each market be the same and equal to margial cost. Using the relationship that $MR = P(1 + [1/\eta])$, $MR_J = P_J(1 + [1/\eta_J])$, $P_J(1 + [1/-4]) = P_J(1 + [1/4]) = 0.75P_J$, $MR_{US} = P_{US}(1 + [1/\eta_{US}]) = P_{US}(1 + [1/-2]) = P_{US}(1 - [1/2]) = 0.5P_{US}$, and $MR_E = P_E(1 + [1/\eta_E]) = P_E(1 + [1/(-4/3)]) = P_E(1 - [3/4]) = 0.25P_E$, where J = Japan, US = United States, and E = Europe. Thus, profit maximization requires $MR_J = MR_{US} = MR_E$ or $0.75P_J = 0.5P_{US} = 0.25P_E$. $0.75P_J = 0.75*\$1{,}000 = \$750$, $0.5P_{US} = 0.5*\$2{,}000 = \$1{,}000$, and $0.25P_E = 0.25*\$3{,}000 = \$750$. Since $MR_J = MR_{US} = MR_E$ does not hold, this is not a profit maximizing pricing policy.

    b. Since the US price is too high (see a. above), we should not be suprised that the sales (Q) in the US are below expectations.

    c. The decision to lower the price in the US to \$1,500 results in $MR_J = MR_{US} = MR_E$ since $MR_{US} = 0.5P_{US} = 0.5*1,500 = 750$. We cannot tell if this is a wise decision because we don't know if the marginal cost of the Ridgeway Corporation is 750.

    d. We do not know if the Ridgeway Corporation is maximizing profit because we don't know their marginal cost. Profit maximization requires $MR_J = MR_{US} = MR_E = MC$.

3. a. $MR_1 = 160 - 16Q_1$

$MR_2 = 80 - 4Q_2$

$MC = 5 + (Q_1 + Q_2)$.

Therefore

$160 - 16Q_1 = 5 + Q_1 + Q_2$

  $80 - 4Q_2 = 5 + Q_1 + Q_2$.

Or

$155 - 17Q_1 = Q_2$

  $75 - 5Q_2 = Q_1$.

Thus,

$155 - 17(75 - 5Q_2) = Q_2$

$155 - 1,275 + 85Q_2 = Q_2$

$84Q_2 = 1,120$

  $Q_2 = 1,120/84 = 13\frac{1}{3}$

It should sell $13\frac{1}{3}$ units in the second market.

  b. $Q_1 = 75 - 5Q_2$

$= 75 - 5(1,120/84)$

$= 75 - 5,600/84$

$= 75 - 66\frac{2}{3}$

$= 8\frac{1}{3}$.

It should sell $8\frac{1}{3}$ units in the first market.

  c. $P_1 = 160 - 8(8\frac{1}{3}) = 93\frac{1}{3}$.

$P_2 = 80 - 2(13\frac{1}{3}) = 53\frac{1}{3}$.

5. a. The firm's profit equals $P_C Q_C + P_M Q_M - TC$, or

$\pi = (495 - 5Q_C)Q_C + (750 - 10Q_M)Q_M - 410 - 8(Q_C + Q_M)$.

Thus,

$$\frac{\partial \pi}{\partial Q_C} = 495 - 10Q_C - 8 = 0$$

$$\frac{\partial \pi}{\partial Q_M} = 750 - 20Q_M - 8 = 0.$$

Consequently, $Q_C = 48.7$ and $Q_M = 37.1$, so

$P_C = 495 - 5(48.7) = 251.5$.

  b. $P_M = 750 - 10(37.1) = 379$.

  c. Yes. Under these circumstances,

$$Q_C = \frac{495 - P}{5} \text{ and } Q_M = \frac{750 - P}{10},$$

so

$Q = Q_C + Q_M = 174 - 0.3P$

and

$P = (174 - Q)/0.3 = 580 - {}^{10}/_3 Q$.

Thus,

$\pi = (580 - {}^{10}/_3 Q)Q - 410 - 8Q$

$= -410 + 572Q - {}^{10}/_3 Q^2$.

If π is a maximum,

$\dfrac{\partial \pi}{dQ} = 572 - {}^{20}/_3 Q = 0$,

so $Q = 572(3/20) = 85.8$. Consequently,

$\pi = -410 + 572(85.8) - {}^{10}/_3(85.8^2) = 24{,}129$,

which compares with

$\pi = [495 - 5(48.7)]48.7 + [750 - 10(37.1)]37.1 - 410$

$\qquad - 8(48.7 + 37.1)$

$\qquad = 251.5(48.7) + 379(37.1) - 1{,}096.4$

$\qquad = 12{,}248.05 + 14{,}060.9 - 1{,}096.4 = 25{,}213$,

the value of profits when price discrimination is allowed.

So profits decrease by $1,084.

7. a. Yes. As stressed on page 507, to maximize the firm's overall profit, the transfer price should equal the price of the product in the external (competitive market).

b. When the production of phenol increased, the supply of acetone increased, since acetone was a by-product. Thus, since less isopropanol was demanded to make acetone, the demand curve for isopropanol shifted to the left (as shown below), and the price of isopropanol declined (from P_0 to P_1).

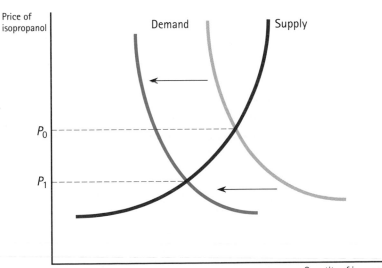

   c. Yes.

   d. Yes.

9. a. Since $P = (8,300 - Q)/2.1 = 3,952 - 0.476Q$,

     $MR = 3,952 - 0.952Q$.

   b. $MC = 480 + 40Q$. If $MC = MR$,

$$480 + 40Q = 3,952 - 0.952Q$$
$$40.952Q = 3,472$$
$$Q = 84.8.$$

Thus, the firm would produce 84.8 lasers per month. If $Q = 84.8$, $P = 3,952 + 0.476(84.8) = 3,912$. Thus, the price should be \$3,912.

   c. The firm's monthly profit equals

$$84.8(3,912) - [2,200 + 480(84.8) + 20(84.8)^2] = \$145,012.80.$$

11. a. If the firm is producing 5 units in the first plant, the marginal cost in the first plant equals $20 + 2(5)$, or 30. Thus, if the firm is minimizing costs, marginal cost in the second plant must also equal 30; this means that

$$10 + 5Q_2 = 30$$
$$Q_2 = 4.$$

Thus, the second plant must be producing 4 units of output.

   b. Since $MC_1 = MC_2 = MC$ and the firm's output, Q, equals $Q_1 + Q_2$,

$$Q_1 = (MC_1/2) - 10$$
$$Q_2 = (MC_2/5) - 2$$
$$Q = Q_1 + Q_2 = 0.7MC - 12$$
$$MC = (1/0.7)(Q + 12).$$

   c. No, because we do not have information concerning the fixed costs of each plant. But you can determine average variable cost.

13. a. It probably tended to increase because high profits induced entry. Also, the 1990–91 recession may have resulted in more demand for the services of pawnshops.

   b. No. It is likely to be an oligopoly, since there generally is not a very large number of pawnshops in a small city.

   c. Apparently not, but licensing requirements may exist.

15. Consider the price separately pricing system. The following table evaluates the profitability of each price separately price. Note that we only have to consider one demander in each class because if there were X demanders per class, profits would just be X times higher—but the largest profit for 1 would still be the largest profit if X demanders/class existed.

Price$_{CD1}$ $	Cost$_{CD1}$	Π/CD1	No. of CD1 demanded	Π from CD1
11	4	7	1	7
8	4	4	3	12 ← best
9	4	5	2	10

Chapter 13

1. a. They would want to set marginal revenue equal to the marginal cost of each firm, but this is impossible since Bergen's marginal cost is $410 and Gutenberg's marginal cost is $460. Because Bergen's marginal cost is always less than Gutenberg's, it will produce all the output. Equating its marginal cost to marginal revenue (MR),

$MR = 580 - 6Q = 410$,

so $Q = 170/6$. This is the output Bergen would produce.

b. Nothing.

c. Not unless Gutenberg receives an attractive share of the profit from Bergen's output even though it produces nothing.

3. a. $9,000. **b.** 6.

5. a. To find the profit-maximizing price, the IATA should construct the marginal cost curve for the cartel as a whole. Then, as shown in Figure 11.2, it should determine the amount of traffic (which is the output of this industry) where marginal revenue equals marginal cost. The price that will elicit this amount of traffic is the profit-maximizing price.

b. If IATA wants to maximize profit, it will allocate this traffic among the airlines in such a way that the marginal cost of all airlines is equal. (However, for reasons discussed on page 432, it may not want to maximize profit.)

c. No. This would not maximize profit.

7. a. Letting Alliance's profit be π_1,

$\pi_1 = Q_1[200,000 - 6(Q_1 + Q_2)] - 8,000\,Q_1$.

Letting Bangor's profit be π_2,

$\pi_2 = Q_2[200,000 - 6(Q_1 + Q_2)] - 12,000\,Q_2$.

If Alliance maximizes its profit, assuming that Bangor will hold its output constant,

$$\frac{\partial \pi_1}{\partial Q_1} = 192,000 - 6Q_2 - 12Q_1 = 0.$$

If Bangor maximizes its profit, assuming that Alliance will hold its output constant,

$$\frac{\partial \pi_2}{\partial Q_2} = 188,000 - 6Q_1 - 12Q_2 = 0.$$

Solving these equations simultaneously, $Q_1 = 196,000/18, = 10,888.89$, and

$Q_2 = (188,000 - 196,000/3)/12 = 122,667/12 = 10,222.22$,

so

$P - 200,000 - 6(10,888.89 + 10,222.22) = 73,333.33$ dollars.

b. Alliance's output is 10,888.89, and Bangor's output is 10,222.22.

    c. Alliance's profit is 10,888.89(73,333.33 − 8,000), or approximately $711.41 million.

    Bangor's profit is

    10,222(73,333.33 − 12,000), or approximately $626.96 million.

9. a. Obviously, Procter and Gamble must be concerned with its own costs. If it adopts a tactic that is far more costly to itself than to a potential entrant, it may cost more than it is worth. If the costs of the strategy outweigh the benefits, Proctor and Gamble, on net, will lose.

    b. The point of these tactics is to raise the cost to a potential entrant, thus discouraging entry.

    c. Whether Procter and Gamble should have cut its price depends on whether the discount brands (and Kimberly-Clark, which had become a major rival) would cut their prices in response, and by how much. In fact, Procter and Gamble did reduce its price substantially (by 16 percent in the case of Luvs). According to the chairperson of Procter and Gamble, "We believe our profits are going to grow because we're going to get volume back."

    d. Yes. Procter and Gamble wanted to reduce what it regarded as improper imitation of its technology. On the other hand, firms that are sued often regard such suits as attempts to intimidate them.

11. a. The size of a firm is often measured by its total revenue. Perhaps a firm might feel that a higher total revenue would make the firm more visible to investors and customers. Also, its managers may be more interested in the growth of the firm than in profits. (However, they are likely to feel that profits should not fall below some minimum level.)

    b. To maximize its total revenue, it should set

$$\frac{d(PQ)}{dQ} = \frac{d(28Q - 0.14Q^2)}{dQ} = 28 - 0.28Q = 0.$$

    Thus, Q should equal 100, and P should equal $14.

    c. If it maximizes profit, it sets

$$MR = 28 - 0.28Q = 14 = MC$$

    so $Q = 50$. Consequently, the firm produces 50,000 units more than it would if it maximized profit.

Chapter 14

1. a. Yes. Fortnum should focus on magazines, and Maison should focus on newspapers.

    b. Fortnum's profit is $9 million, and Maison's profit is $8 million.

    c. No.

3.

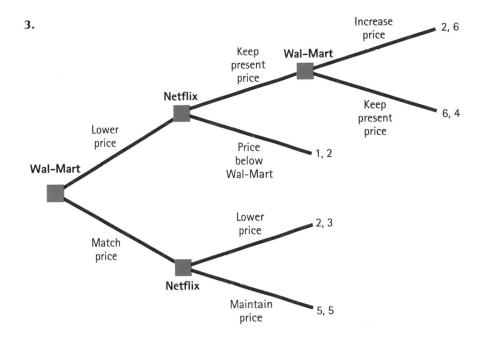

Using backward induction, the equilibrium is for Wal-Mart to lower price, Netflix to keep its present price, and Wal-Mart to respond by keeping its present price. The final payoff to Wal-Mart is 6, and Netflix receives 4.

5. a. Each firm will choose to cheat on the agreement. They will each earn $28 million.

b. No, as long as the horizon is finite, behavior will not change.

c. Yes, this is an example of prisoner's dilemma.

7. If Rose cannot ascertain the strategy of its rival then it cannot implement a tit-for-tat strategy because it will not know which strategy to play. A tit-for-tat strategy requires a player to mimic the strategy played by a rival in the previous period. For example, if Rose's rival played cheat in period n, then Rose would choose cheat in period $n + 1$.

Chapter 15

1. a. The expected present value is $10.7 million, the standard deviation is $5.06 million, and the coefficient of variation is 47 percent.

b. The expected present value is $11.0 million, the standard deviation is $1.95 million, and the coefficient of variation is 18 percent.

c. Investment X.

d. Investment Y, since she is a risk averter (as indicated by the fact that

U increases at a decreasing rate as P rises). Investment Y has both a higher expected present value and a lower standard deviation than investment X and because $E(U_X) = 62.099 < 63.752 = E(U_Y)$, i.e., X's expected utility is less than Y's.

3. **a.** No.

   b. It is very conservative, as discussed on pages 558 to 559.

   c. No, because no probability distribution of the outcome can be given.

5. **a.** 3. **b.** −0.6. **c.** −1.2.

7. **a.**

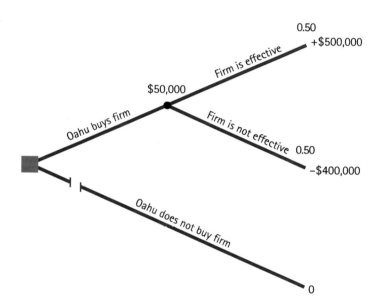

   b. There is only one: whether to buy the firm.

   c. There is only one: whether the firm becomes an effective producer of washing machine parts or not.

   d. Yes, it should buy the firm.

   e. (1) Yes.

   (2) Three mutually exclusive outcomes are: (a) The firm becomes an effective producer of washing machine parts. (b) The firm does not become an effective producer of washing parts and is sold to the Saudis. (c) The firm does not become an effective producer of washing machine parts and cannot be sold to the Saudis.

   (3) The probability of the first outcome (in part 2) is 0.5, the probability of the second outcome is 0.5(0.2), or 0.1, and the probability of the third outcome is (0.5)(0.8), or 0.4.

   (4) The extra profit to Oahu from the first outcome is $500,000; the extra profit from the second outcome is $100,000; the extra profit from the third outcome is −$400,000.

f. Oahu should buy the firm. The expected extra profit if it does so is 0.5($500,000) + 0.1($100,000) + 0.4(−$400,000) = $100,000.

g. (1) If the extra profit if the firm is made into an effective producer of washing machine parts is $400,000 or less, the decision will be reversed. Put differently, if the *error* was an *overstatement* of this extra profit by $100,000 or more, the decision will be reversed.

(2) If the extra profit if the firm is made into an effective producer of washing machine parts is $300,000 or less, the decision will be reversed. Put differently, if the *error* was an *overstatement* of this extra profit by $200,000 or more, the decision will be reversed.

9. a.

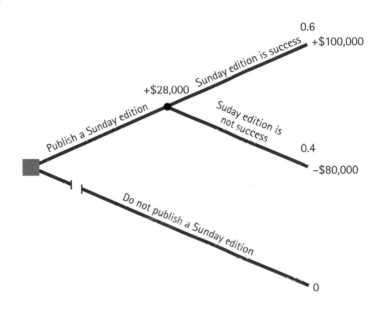

If the publisher is risk neutral, she wants to maximize expected profit. Thus, she should publish the Sunday edition.

b. Whether to publish the Sunday edition is a decision fork. Whether it is a success, if published, is a chance fork.

Chapter 16

1. Expected Value or EV($45) = 1,750($4.05)(.35) + 1,975($4.05)(.20) + 2,220($4.05)(.30) + 2,445($4.05)(.15).

EV($45) = $2,480.63 + $1,599.75 + $2,697.30 + $1,485.34 or $8,263.02.

EV($50) = 1,200($4.50)(.35) + 1,415($4.50)(.20) + 2,001($4.50)(.30) + 2,305($4.50)(.15).

EV($50) = $1,890 + $1,273.50 + $2,701.35 + $1,555.88 or $7,420.73

EV(auction) = $2,480.63 + 1,599.75 + 2,701.35 + 1,555.88 = $8,337.61.

The value of information would be worth,

EV($45) = 1,750($4.05)(.35) + 1,975($4.05)(.20) + 2,220($4.05)(.30) + 2,445($4.05)(.15).

EV($45) = **$2,480.63 + $1,599.75** + $2,697.30 + $1,485.34 or $8,263.02.

EV($50) = 1,200($4.50)(.35) + 1,415($4.50)(.20) + 2,001($4.50)(.30) + 2,305($4.50)(.15).

EV($50) = $1,890 + $1,273.50 + **$2,701.35** + **$1,555.88** or $7,420.73

EV(auction) = $2,480.63 + 1,599.75 + 2,701.35 + 1,555.88 = $8,337.61.

So, the value of information = $8,337.61 − $8,263.02 or $74.59.

3. **a.** The mean value is 67.91.

   b. (80 − 67.91)/(63.64 = .04573; z score of .04573 = .4820. Hence the probability of a reservation price being less than 80 is approximately 19 percent.

5. If they choose to price their PSLs at $6,000, their expected revenue is: $58,802,000 + $58,800,000 + **$60,000** = $177,602,000. If they choose to price their PSLs at $7,000, their expected revenue is: **$60,214,000** + 58,803,500 + 56,000,000 = 175,017,500. If they choose to prices their PSLs at $8,000, their expected revenue is: $56,030,000 + **$61,610,500** + $50,000,000 = $167,640,500. So, if they set the price and don't use an auction, they should charge $6,000/PSL. If the Eagles use a modified Dutch auction, then their expected revenue is: $60,214,000 + $61,610,500 + $60,000 = $181,824,500. So relative to setting a price of $6,000/PSL, the auction would increase expected revenue by $4,222,500. But since auction costs are $5,100,000, the Eagles are better off pricing the PSLs at $6,000.

Chapter 17

1. **a.** Flat salary:

   If effort is low, utility = 758.29. If effort is high, utility = 658.29. The manager chooses low effort since it gives higher expected utility. Your expected profit will be 0.3($5 million) + 0.4($10 million) + 0.3($15 million) − $0.575 million = $9.425 million.

   b. Six percent of profit:

   Expected utility of manager with

   Low effort is $0.3\sqrt{0.06(\$5 \text{ million})} + 0.4\sqrt{0.06(\$10 \text{ million})} + 0.3\sqrt{0.06(15 \text{ million})} = 758.76.$

   High effort is $-100 + 0.3\sqrt{0.06(\$7 \text{ million})} + 0.4\sqrt{0.06(\$12 \text{ million})} + 0.3\sqrt{0.06(\$17 \text{ million})} = 736.82.$

   The manager chooses low effort since it gives higher expected utility. Given the manager's choice of low effort, your expected profit will be the expected profit of $10 million minus 6 percent which is {0.3($5 million) + 0.4($10 million) + 0.3($15 million)}

$(1 - 0.06) = \$9.4m$.

c. Five hundred thousand dollars plus half of profits in excess of $15 million:

Expected utility of manager with

Low effort is $\sqrt{(\$0.5 \text{ million})} = 707.11$.

High effort is $-100 + 0.7\sqrt{(\$0.5 \text{ million})} +$

$\qquad 0.3\sqrt{^1/_2(\$17 \text{ million} - \$15 \text{ million}) + \$0.5 \text{ million}} = 762.40$.

The manager chooses high effort since it gives higher expected utility. Your expected profit will be the expected profit of $12 million minus expected compensation which is $\{\$0.5m + 0.3(0.5(\$2m))\} = \$800,000$.

$\{0.3(\$7m) + 0.4(\$12m) + 0.3(\$17m)\} - \$0.8m = \$11.2m$.

You will choose the third plan (c) since it gives highest profit after deducting the manager's compensation.

3. If the manager does not work hard, she will receive,

$[100]^{0.5} = 10$.

If the manager works hard, she will receive

$[100 + x(15,000 - 13,000)]^{0.5} - 1$.

To calculate the minimum level of x necessary to ensure that expected compensation will be higher with hard work, set the expected utility with hard work equal to that without hard work:

$[100 + x(15,000 - 13,000)]^{0.5} - 1 = 10$

$[100 + x(15,000 - 13,000)]^{0.5} \quad = 11 \qquad$ (square both sides to get)

$[100 + x(15,000 - 13,000)] \quad = 11^2 - 121$

$x = \dfrac{121 - 100}{15,000 - 13,000} = 0.0105$

Thus, if the manager gets a little over 0.105 times equity in excess of 13,000 she will work hard.

5. Total value of firm:

$$V = 500 + 300 - 700\,\frac{0.2}{1 + s} - s = 800 - \frac{140}{1 + s} - s.$$

To calculate the value of s that maximizes total value, set the derivative of value with respect to s equal to zero:

$$\frac{dV}{ds} = \frac{140}{(1 + s)^2} - 1 = 0.$$

So, $S = 10.83$.

Therefore, the value of firm is

$$800 - \frac{140}{11.83} - 10.83 = 777.3.$$

Division 1 is riskless and has a stand-alone value of 500. Since all the risk comes from division 2, we must consider the chosen level of safety of this unit as a stand-alone entity. In calculating this value recollect that its value is 300 if no liability arises. However, if a loss of 700 occurs, it simply cannot pay more than the original 300 stand-alone value (because of limited liability). So, the stand-alone value of division 2 is:

$$300 - 300 \frac{0.2}{1 + s} - s = 300 - \frac{60}{1 + s} - s$$

Set the derivative equal to zero to maximize the division 2 stand-alone value:

$$\frac{dV}{ds} = \frac{60}{(1 + s)^2} - 1 = 0. \text{ So, } s = 6.746.$$

So, the stand-alone value of division 2 is:

$$300 - \frac{60}{7.746} - 6.746 = 285.5.$$

Total value with split up

500 + 285.5 = 785.5.

So the gain from split up is 785.55 − 777.34 = 8.21.

7. There is an asset-substitution problem. To show this, we should value the firm as a whole, and each of the stakeholders' claims, first assuming A is chosen then assuming B is chosen. We can then see which project selection leads to the higher value of equity. This is the one share-holders would naturally favor.

Value of the firm if project A is chosen:

First, note that the value of the firm will be either 720 (300 from existing operations and 420 from the new project) or 1020 (600 from existing operations and 420 from the new project) depending on the success of existing operations. This value must be divided up by first paying off old debt, next new debt, and finally equity.

Value of the firm   0.5(720 + 1020) = 870
Old debt   0.5(250 + 250) = 250
New debt   0.5(400 + 400) = 400
Equity   0.5(70) + 370) = 220

Value of the firm if project B is chosen

The value of the firm will be either 300, 600, 1000, or 1300. These figures come from the different combinations of the two possible values for the existing operations (300 and 600) and the two values for the new project (0 and 700).

Value of the firm   0.25(300 + 600 + 1000 + 1300) = 800
Old debt   0.25(250 + 250 + 250 + 250) = 250
New debt   0.25(50 + 350 + 400 + 400) = 300
Equity   0.25(0 + 0 + 350 + 650) = 250

Shareholders would like to choose B after they had creditors' money. But since investors would pay only 300 for new debt, this cannot be funded. So neither project can be undertaken if debt financing is used. The analysis can be repeated using equity financing for the new project. The values of the firm will be the same as above, but these will be allocated first to the existing debt (for which 250 is owing) and any residual will accrue to equity.

Value of the firm if project A is chosen

Value of the firm	$0.5(720 + 1020) = 870$
Old debt	$0.5(250 + 250) = 250$
Equity	$0.5(470 + 770) = 620$

Value of the firm if project B is chosen

Value of the firm	$0.25(300 + 600 + 1000 + 1300) = 800$
Old debt	$0.25(250 + 250 + 250 + 250) = 250$
Equity	$0.25(50 + 350 + 750 + 1050) = 550$

Now, shareholders will naturally choose the higher Net Present Value project A since it has the higher equity value. The asset-substitution problem is solved.

Chapter 18

1. First, note that buyers will not be willing to pay $10,000 for any used car since there is a chance that it is lemon. So the obvious price to contemplate is a price reflecting the average quality; i.e., there is a 75% chance the car will be "good" and worth $10,000 and a 25% chance the car will be "bad" and worth $5,000.

    Average value $(0.75)(\$10,000) + (0.25)(\$5,000) = \$8,750$

    But, sellers of high quality cars, knowing there vehicles are really worth $10,000, will not be willing to sell at this price. So, only sellers of low quality vehicles will offer their cars for sale. But buyers can anticipate that only low quality cars will be offered, therefore they will only be willing to pay $5,000 for any second hand Corolla on the second hand market. Thus, only low quality cars are sold and the price is $5,000.

3. Form the following table if all are considering buying insurance:

Group	Initial Car Value	Ending Car Value If Accident	Probability of Accident	Expected Claim
A	10,000	5,000	0.2	1,000
B	10,000	5,000	0.3	1,500
C	10,000	5,000	0.4	2,000

    Thus, if all purchased insurance, the expected claims would be 1,000 + 1,500 + 2,000 = 4,500 and hence the premium would have to be 4,500/3 = 1,500. But this requires that ALL types buy the policy. Let's see if they will. Would A buy insurance if the premium was 1,500? If A self insures (does not buy insurance), his/her expected utility would be:

    $EU_a = 0.8(10,000)0.5 + 0.2(5,000)0.5 = 0.8(100) + 0.2(70.711) = 80 + 14.142 = 94.142$

If A buys a full coverage policy for 1,500, A's expected utility will be
EUa = (10,000 − 1,500)0.5 = (8,500)0.5 = 92.195
Thus, A will self insure since 94.142 > 92.195
Thus, the premium can not be 1,500 since A is not buying insurance.
So, if the type A's drop out of the insurance pool, we are left with the B's and C's. If only B and C are interested in buying, the expected claims are 1,500 + 2,000 = 3,500 and the premium must be 3,500/2 = 1,750.
But would B buy insurance at the premium of 1,750? If B self insures, their expected utility would be:
EUb = 0.7(10,000)0.5 + 0.3(5,000)0.5 = 0.7(100) + 0.3(70.711) = 70 + 21.213 = 91.213
If B buys a full coverage policy for 1,750, B's expected utility will be
EUb = (10,000 − 1,750)0.5 = (8,250)0.5 = 90.830
Thus, B will self insure since 91.213 > 90.830.
Thus, the premium cannot be 1,750 since B is not buying insurance.
If only C is interested in buying insurance, then the premium must be 2,000
If C self insures, their expected utility would be:
EUc = 0.6(10,000)0.5 + 0.4(5,000)0.5 = 0.6(100) + 0.4(70.711)
    = 60 + 28.284 = 88.284
If C buys a full coverage policy for 2,000, C's expected utility will be:
EUc = (10,000 − 2,000)0.5 = (8,000)0.5 = 89.443
Since 89.443 > 88.284, C will buy the insurance for a premium of 2,000.
However, No-State can sell the policy for a higher price. Type C's certainty equivalent will be (88.284)2 = 7,794.11. Thus, Type C's would be willing to pay up to 10,000 − 7,794.11 = 2,205.89 for such a policy. Since the question required that the premium must be sufficient to cover expected claims and the expected claims for type C's are
0.4(5,000) = 2,000, a premium of 2,205.90 would certainly fill the bill.

5. The following table charts the maximum price people are willing to pay.
Formula =
1.1(x)($50,000) for less risk averse
1.3(x)($50,000) for more risk averse

	Poor health Life expectancy = 9 years	Good health Life expectancy = 11 years
Less risk averse Pay up to 1.1 times expected value	495	605
More risk averse Pay up to 1.3 times expected value	585	715

At a price of $550,000, the product will be purchased by all those in good health and the more risk averse in poor health.

The expected profit can now be calculated

More risk averse in poor health   (50 times $550,000) − (50 times 9 times $50,000) = $5,000,000

Less risk averse in good health   (50 times $550,000) − (50 times 11 times $50,000) = $0

More risk averse in poor health   (50 times $550,000) − (50 times 11 times $50,000) = $0

TOTAL PROFIT = $5,000,000

Chapter 19

1. a. It equaled $27.5 + 21.9 + 18.5 + 9.3 = 77.2$ percent. Yes.

b. It was $27.5 + 21.9 + (18.5 + 7.3) + 9.3 = 84.5$ percent if we simply combine United's and Pan Am's shares to approximate United's post-purchase share.

3. a. If $P = 480$, $Q = 260$, according to the demand curve. Thus, the firm's total revenue equals 260(480) thousand dollars, or $124,800,000. The firm's total cost equals $50 + 0.25(260) = 115$ million dollars. Thus, the firm's accounting profit is $9,800,000; this means that its rate of return is 9.8 percent.

b. If it were deregulated, it would maximize
$$\pi = (1/1,000)[Q(1,000 - 2Q)] - 50 - 0.25Q$$
$$= -50 + 0.75Q - 0.002Q^2.$$
Setting $d\pi/dQ = 0.75 - 0.004Q = 0$, $Q = 187.5$. Thus, under deregulation, $\pi = -50 + 0.75(187.5) - 0.002(187.5^2) = \$20.3125$ million.
So, the difference is $\$20.3125 - \$9.8 = \$10.5125$ million.

5. a. $220/250 = 88$ percent.

b. Yes, because it is dominated by a few firms.

c. $225/250 = 90$ percent.

d. $140/145 = 97$ percent.

7. a. No. If price is $1, 12 firms of optimal size can exist in the market.

b. Eight.

9. a. The district court ruled against the merger.

b. The court held that transportation costs were small enough so that competition on a national basis was practical.

c. Obviously, the views of courts and government agencies change over time. The prevailing climate of opinion was quite different in the 1980s than in the 1950s.

11. a. Because the commission tries to provide the firm with a "fair" rate of return on its investment.

     b. Because this increase reduced the firm's profit.

     c. See pages 645 to 646.

13. a. Yes. If there are only a very few sellers, collusion is much more likely than if there are many sellers.

     b. Sherman Act.

     c. It weakened the case.

     d. There is nothing wrong with G.E. discussing price increases with a customer.

     e. No. On December 5, 1994, District Court Judge George Smith ruled that there was not enough evidence to warrant sending the case to a jury.

Chapter 20

1. a. Yes. Since consumption levels are much less in other countries, there appears to be far more room for growth than in the United States.

     b. Because the conditions in Indonesia seem to be very favorable to the consumption of soft drinks, and at present, Coca-Cola is selling relatively little there, it appears that great sales growth there is quite possible.

     c. Trade barriers and regulatory considerations are important. So are costs and local custom.

     d. Because Coke does not have to compete so aggressively against Pepsi, it can spend much less on marketing than domestically and thus increase its profits abroad.

3. a. $10.

     b. Japan.

     c. 2 million flashbulbs.

     d. They will cease.

5. a. The price of a pound of bananas must be between $^3/_{10}$ and $^8/_{10}$ of the price of a pound of coffee.

     b. Honduras.

7. a. It will fall.

     b. It will fall.

9. a. Buy; 40 million pounds.

     b. From its reserves.

11. Basically, much more effort should be devoted to coordinating the work and planning of B&D's farflung (and largely uncoordinated) subsidiaries.

Brief Answers to "Consultant's Corner"

Planning to Meet Peak Engineering Requirements (Chapter 2)

The firm wanted an estimate of when the number of engineers required to carry out this project would reach a maximum. Since $a = 18$ and $b = 1$,

$$Y = 18t - t^2$$

and

$$\frac{dY}{dt} = 18 - 2t.$$

Setting dY/dt equal to zero,

$$18 - 2t = 0$$
$$t = 9.$$

Thus, Y reaches a maximum when $t = 9$. (Because $d^2Y/dt^2 = -2$, we can be sure that this is a maximum, not a minimum.)

The firm also wanted an estimate of the maximum number of engineers that would be required to carry out this project. To obtain such an estimate, we find the value of Y when $t = 9$.

$$Y = 18(9) - (9)^2 = 81.$$

Thus, when engineering requirements for this project reach their peak, 81 engineers will be needed.

To sum up, the engineering requirements for this project will reach their peak nine months after the project begins, when 81 engineers will be needed.

Estimating the Demand for Rail Passenger Business by Amtrak (Chapter 3)

(a) Disposable personal income: the quantity demanded for service is influenced by how well the economy is doing. As the economy does better, there is more business and leisure travel. As the note already implies, the sign of the coefficient is positive.

Amtrak fare: the quantity demanded for a service is influenced by its price. We would expect that fare would have a negative sign.

Amtrak fare/airline fare: air travel is a major competitor for Amtrak (even in the short-haul northeast corridor market between New York and Boston and between New York and Washington, DC). We expect that this variable will have a negative sign, indicating that if Amtrak's fare relative to its air competitor becomes higher, more travelers will opt for air travel.

Gasoline prices: another major competitor for Amtrak is the automobile, and the major "fare" of driving is the price of fuel. As the price of fuel increases, we expect more people to use the train, and hence, this variable would have a positive sign.

Dummies: while we don't have all the dummies used, we would expect increased traffic over the holidays and during bad weather. In addition, leisure travel increases in the summer season (because children are out of school and because many vacations are scheduled then).

(b) Since revenues are price times quantity, with the quantity estimate provided by the regression, multiplying the quantity estimate by the average rail fare (price) will give the estimate of systemwide revenues. **(c)** Income elasticity is $\eta_I = \Delta Q/\Delta I$ so if ΔI is 1% and if ΔQ is 1.8 percent, the implied income elasticity is 1.8. If disposable personal income per capita increases from \$24,000 to \$25,000, this is a 4.17% increase. Thus, an estimate of %ΔQ is $(\eta_I)(\%\Delta I) = 1.8*4.17\% = 7.5\%$. Elasticities account for only small percentage changes in the denominator. The 4.17% change in per capita disposable personal income isn't very small, so we wouldn't expect our estimate to be 100% accurate. In addition, since regression analysis uses past data, the model is only good if the future is going to be like the past. Major structural changes in how a market behaves may render this condition inappropriate. **(d)** As disposable personal income has risen, it's had a positive impact on air and auto travel also. Air fares for leisure travel have increased below the increase in the Consumer Price Index (so the real price of leisure air travel has decreased). Automobile acquisitions have increased such that there are now more registered passenger vehicles and light trucks (SUVs, pickups, vans), than there are licensed drivers in the United States. On a real price basis (except for a spike in late 1999 through early 2000 and in spring of 2001), gasoline prices have been as inexpensive as they ever have been. Cheap gas and air prices and auto availability all point to an explosion in travel by these modes.

The Trade-off between Risk and Return (Chapter 4)

These indifference curves slope *upward* to the right because this investor prefers less risk to more risk when the expected return is held constant. If there is an increase in risk, she must receive a higher expected return if she is to maintain the same level of satisfaction. She must choose some point on line *RT*. The point on this line which is on the highest indifference curve (and which therefore maximizes her satisfaction) is point *S*, where the expected return is 7.5 percent, which indicates that she invests half in U.S. government securities and half in common stocks. (Recall that the expected return from U.S. government securities is 5 percent and the expected return from common stocks is 10 percent.)

Marketing Plans at the Stafford Company (Chapter 5)

If the total market is 10,000 units, the relationship between price and quantity demanded is as follows:

Price	Quantity demanded
$ 800	10,000 (0.110) = 1,100
900	10,000 (0.102) = 1,020
1,000	10,000 (0.092) = 920
1,100	10,000 (0.084) = 840
1,200	10,000 (0.075) = 750
1,300	10,000 (0.066) = 660
1,400	10,000 (0.056) = 560

To obtain a simple equation expressing quantity demanded as a function of price, regression analysis can be used, the independent variable being price and the dependent variable being quantity demanded. The resulting regression equation is

$$Y = 1822 - 0.8964X,$$

where Y is the quantity demanded and X is price (in dollars). The equation seems to be reliable in the sense that it fits the above data very well, as indicated by the fact that $r^2 = 0.999$. However, the above data may or may not be very reliable, depending on how thoroughly the market research department did its job. It is risky to extrapolate a regression equation beyond the range to which the data apply. Thus, the firm cannot safely assume that this equation can predict quantity demanded if price is $1,500 or $1,600.

Without data on the costs of producing and marketing the electrical drive, one cannot say what the price should be.

Deciding Whether to Finance the Purchase of an Oil Field (Chapter 6)

In deciding whether to approve this loan application, the bank's forecasts of the price of oil are very important. Yet the simple extrapolation technique that is used is very crude. It is clear from the figures that this forecast was the result of a simple trend extrapolation that assumed a steady increase, beginning at $25 in 1986 and reaching $49 in 1998. Econometric models based on a more sophisticated analysis of the demand and supply of oil might be more effective. In fact, the bank's forecasts were very poor. For example, the price was about $13, not $25, in 1986, and about $20, not $31, in 1989.

Choosing the Size of an Oil Tanker (Chapter 7)

The company should build an oil tanker of 200,000 tonnes, not 20,000 tonnes. Because of the large economies of scale in tanker construction and operation, costs decrease as the size of the tanker increases. For example, a 280,000-tonne tanker costs roughly $75 million to construct. A 28,000-tonne tanker costs over $15 million to construct. Operating expenses show similar savings. For example, to operate a 280,000-tonne tanker does not require a crew size 10 times that of a 28,000-tonne tanker.

Mr. Martin Gets Chewed Out by the Boss (Chapter 9)

All the president's points are relevant. The fact that the product mix changes with increases in output may be quite important. It may be misleading to lump all three products together as the accountant did. Also, contrary to the assumption that the total cost curve is linear, the marginal cost of the first type of desk would increase with increases in output. Further, the price used for the second type of desk is not the relevant one.

Forecasting the Price of Salmon (Chapter 10)

If the quantity supplied three years ahead is in accord with the firm's estimate, regardless of whatever price changes occur, the quantity demanded must increase by about 15 percent to close the gap between the quantity supplied and the quantity demanded. Since the price elasticity of demand is about -1.5, a 10 percent decrease in price would increase the quantity demanded by about 15 percent. Thus, a very rough estimate would be that the price would fall by about 10 percent.

Using a Price Announcement to Preempt a Market (Chapter 12)

It seems doubtful that such a price announcement would have the desired effect. Since this firm will not be the lowest-cost producer of the next generation of products, it will not be able to announce a price that is low enough to make it unprofitable for all its rivals to enter the market. Unless it announces a price that is so low that it, as well as its rivals, would lose money, it is unlikely to induce its rivals to drop their plans to develop their own new products of the relevant kind. Moreover, even if it did announce a price at which it would lose money, it seems likely that its rivals would not take it too seriously, because announcements of this sort are not regarded as binding. Thus, such an announcement might well be regarded as a bluff. To be effective, an announcement must be credible. The firm's rivals would have to be convinced that the firm really would sell the product at a price that would impose unacceptable losses on them.

Settling Some Strife over a Pricing Formula
(Chapter 13)

From our discussion of transfer pricing, we know that if there is a competitive market for ethane, the transfer price should equal the price in this market. However, it must be recognized that there can be heated disputes between divisions over transfer pricing. In this case, the petrochemical division may resist the increase in the transfer price of ethane because it will make the petrochemical division look less profitable—and make the division's managers appear less successful.

Choosing Areas for Research Regarding Pollution
Costs (Chapter 14)

The expected value of perfect information seems to be greatest for a remote plant with low-sulfur coal available and least for an urban plant with low-sulfur coal available. However, this tells us nothing about the costs involved in obtaining perfect information. Unless you have some idea of these costs, it is very difficult to say much about the relative desirability of various areas of research.

A Dispute over a Requested Gas Rate Increase
(Chapter 19)

To reduce the adverse effects of regulatory lag, you might suggest that the firm file for an interim rate increase (besides the permanent rate increase). The firm might promise to refund any difference between the interim rate and the permanent rate if the former turned out to be higher than the latter. (In fact, this is what the company proposed.) To see which of the two estimates of the cost of equity capital is closer to the truth, you might study the historical rate of growth of the firm's dividends, the object being to estimate g. Also, you might try to forecast the growth of the firm's dividends, based on various estimates published by brokerage firms as well as on statistical analysis.

Reorganizing a Firm's Global R and D Network
(Chapter 20)

There are advantages in coordinating decisions regarding which products to develop with an eye toward the total world market, not just regional markets. In fact, Boehringer Ingelheim has altered its organization in this way. Decisions regarding which products to develop are now made centrally, but all the subsidiaries have a voice in these decisions, which are made by an International Steering Committee, composed of executives from all the major subsidiaries as well as from Germany.

Brief Answers to "Managerial Economics in Context"

Part 2 How to Forecast the Sales of Paper, According to McKinsey

    a. Yes. One can calculate a regression where the quantity demanded of plain-paper copy paper is the dependent variable, while cents per copy and gross domestic product are the independent variables. However, in a time-series analysis of this sort, one must be careful to recognize that serial correlation may be present.

    b. The multiple coefficient of determination.

    c. On the basis of the graph on page 235, one cannot calculate the elasticity of demand for plain-paper copy paper with respect to cost per copy, because there are no numbers along the horizontal axis. But if these numbers were supplied, such a calculation could be made. This elasticity might be of use because it would indicate how sensitive the quantity demanded is to changes in cost per copy.

    d. Not necessarily. The annual rate of growth of the quantity demanded may have varied from one year to another. If an exponential curve fits well, the annual rate of growth is relatively constant from year to year.

    e. No. The procedures described on pages 209 to 213 might be used to calculate such a seasonal index. To make monthly or quarterly forecasts, a seasonal index would be useful.

    f. If the multiple regression described in the answer to question a were calculated, one would need forecasts of gross domestic product and of cents per copy to forecast quantity demanded. Econometric models might be used to forecast gross domestic product.

Part 4 A Rocky Road for Caterpillar Tractor

    a. Oligopoly.

    b. Caterpillar clearly has not maintained a constant percentage markup of price over average cost. During the 1980s, its profit margins often were less than in earlier years. As shown on page 439, its profits were negative in the early 1980s and early 1990s.

    c. No. It charged a price that was higher than that of its rivals in 1981.

    d. Faced with large losses, Caterpillar cut back on many expense items that would probably have not been cut so much otherwise. As was pointed out on page 439, the firm engaged in a major cost-reduction program in 1983 and 1984.

    e. It is worthwhile to spend money on them up to the point where the extra expenditure equals the extra savings. There are some technical improvements of this sort that require little expenditure relative to the savings they produce. Others require greater expenditure and yield smaller savings. Eventually one reaches a point where it is worthwhile to spend no more on such improvements, since the extra savings are less than the extra expenditures.

    f. No. It is wise only if the longer-term improved results are worth more than the short-term profits that are sacrificed. If a firm sacrifices $2 million in profits this year to obtain $1 million in profits five years from now, this is not a wise policy. Caterpillar estimated that the longer-term improved results were well worth the sacrifice.

    g. Cost reduction would allow the firm more latitude in keeping its prices down. However, bad labor relations can raise costs if productivity suffers.

Part 6 NAFTA: A Historic Agreement

    a. On the basis of the fact that U.S. auto plants have found it difficult to compete with the Japanese and others, some observers have argued that the United States has lost its comparative advantage, but it is a complex question, and more time is required to settle it.

b. Canadians felt that this ruling put their exporters at a disadvantage and that it would discourage investment in their country.

c. Yes. Direct investment in subsidiaries located in Mexico has been very important, for reasons cited in Chapter 20.

d. Florida tomato growers obviously are hurt by such imports, but U.S. consumers benefit.

e. It decreased the number of jobs.

f. In theory, one should carry out the sort of analysis shown in Figure 19.5, but in practice, it is very difficult to do this with any precision. They can use transferable emissions permits, effluent fees, and/or direct regulation.

TABLES

Appendix Tables

APPENDIX TABLE 1

Value of $\dfrac{1}{(1 + i)^n}$

Value of i

n	1%	2%	3%	4%	5%	6%	7%	8%	9%	10%
1	.99010	.98039	.97007	.96154	.95233	.94340	.93458	.92593	.91743	.90909
2	.98030	.96117	.94260	.92456	.90703	.89000	.87344	.85734	.84168	.82645
3	.97059	.94232	.91514	.88900	.86384	.83962	.81639	.79383	.77228	.75131
4	.96098	.92385	.88849	.85480	.82270	.79209	.76290	.73503	.70883	.68301
5	.95147	.90573	.86261	.82193	.78353	.74726	.71299	.68058	.64993	.62092
6	.94204	.88797	.83748	.79031	.74622	.70496	.66634	.63017	.59627	.56447
7	.93272	.87056	.81309	.75992	.71063	.66506	.62275	.58349	.54705	.51316
8	.92348	.85349	.78941	.73069	.67684	.62741	.58201	.54027	.50189	.46651
9	.91434	.83675	.76642	.70259	.64461	.59190	.54393	.50025	.46043	.42410
10	.90529	.82035	.74409	.67556	.61391	.55839	.50835	.46319	.42241	.38554
11	.89632	.80426	.72242	.64958	.58468	.52679	.47509	.42888	.38753	.35049
12	.88745	.78849	.70138	.62460	.55684	.49697	.44401	.39711	.35553	.31683
13	.87866	.77303	.68095	.60057	.53032	.46884	.41496	.36770	.32618	.28966
14	.86996	.75787	.66112	.57747	.50507	.44230	.38782	.34046	.29925	.26333
15	.86135	.74301	.64186	.55526	.48102	.41726	.36245	.31524	.27454	.23939
16	.85282	.72845	.62317	.53391	.45811	.39365	.33873	.29189	.25187	.21763
17	.84436	.71416	.60502	.51337	.43630	.37136	.31657	.27027	.23107	.19784
18	.83602	.70016	.58739	.49363	.41552	.35034	.29586	.25025	.21199	.17986
19	.82774	.68643	.57029	.47464	.39573	.33051	.27651	.23171	.19449	.16354
20	.81954	.67297	.55367	.45639	.37689	.31180	.25842	.21455	.17843	.14864
21	.81143	.65978	.53755	.44883	.35894	.29415	.24151	.19866	.16370	.13513
22	.80340	.64684	.52189	.42195	.34185	.27750	.22571	.18394	.15018	.12285
23	.79544	.63414	.50669	.40573	.32557	.26180	.21095	.17031	.13778	.11168
24	.78757	.62172	.49193	.39012	.31007	.24698	.19715	.15770	.12640	.10153
25	.77977	.60953	.47760	.37512	.29530	.23300	.18425	.14602	.11597	.09230

APPENDIX
TABLE
1

Value of $\dfrac{1}{(1+i)^n}$ (Continued)

Value of i

n	11%	12%	13%	14%	15%	16%	17%	18%	19%	20%	24%
1	.90090	.89286	.88496	.87719	.86957	.86207	.85470	.84746	.84043	.83333	.8065
2	.81162	.79719	.78315	.76947	.75614	.74316	.73051	.71818	.70616	.69444	.6504
3	.73119	.71178	.69305	.67497	.65752	.64066	.62437	.60863	.59342	.57870	.5245
4	.65873	.63552	.61332	.59208	.57175	.55229	.53365	.51579	.49867	.48225	.4230
5	.59345	.56743	.54276	.51937	.49718	.47611	.45611	.43711	.41905	.40188	.3411
6	.53464	.50663	.48032	.45559	.43233	.41044	.38984	.37043	.35214	.33490	.2751
7	.48166	.45235	.42506	.39964	.37594	.35383	.33320	.31392	.29592	.27908	.2218
8	.43393	.40388	.37616	.35056	.32690	.30503	.28478	.26604	.24867	.23257	.1789
9	.39092	.36061	.33288	.30751	.28426	.26295	.24340	.22546	.20897	.19381	.1443
10	.35218	.32197	.29459	.26974	.24718	.22668	.20804	.19106	.17560	.16151	.1164
11	.31728	.28748	.26070	.23662	.21494	.19542	.17781	.16192	.14756	.13459	.0938
12	.28584	.25667	.23071	.20756	.18691	.16846	.15197	.13722	.12400	.11216	.0757
13	.25751	.22917	.20416	.18207	.16253	.14523	.12989	.11629	.10420	.09346	.0610
14	.23199	.20462	.18068	.15971	.14133	.12520	.11102	.09855	.08757	.07789	.0492
15	.20900	.18270	.15989	.14010	.12289	.10793	.09489	.08352	.07359	.06491	.0397
16	.18829	.16312	.14150	.12289	.10686	.09304	.08110	.07073	.06184	.05409	.0320
17	.16963	.14564	.12522	.10780	.09293	.08021	.06932	.05998	.05196	.04507	.0258
18	.15282	.13004	.11081	.09456	.08080	.06914	.05925	.05083	.04367	.03756	.0208
19	.13768	.11611	.09806	.08295	.07026	.05961	.05064	.04308	.03669	.03130	.0168
20	.12403	.10367	.08678	.07276	.06110	.05139	.04328	.03651	.03084	.02608	.0135
21	.11174	.09256	.07680	.06383	.05313	.04430	.03699	.03094	.02591	.02174	.0109
22	.10067	.08264	.06796	.05599	.04620	.03819	.03162	.02622	.02178	.01811	.0088
23	.09069	.07379	.06014	.04911	.04017	.03292	.02702	.02222	.01830	.01509	.0071
24	.08170	.06588	.05322	.04308	.03493	.02838	.02310	.01883	.01538	.01258	.0057
25	.07361	.05882	.04710	.03779	.03038	.02447	.01974	.01596	.01292	.01048	.0046

APPENDIX
TABLE
2

Value of $\sum_{t=1}^{n} \dfrac{1}{(1 + i)^t}$

					Value of i					
n	1%	2%	3%	4%	5%	6%	7%	8%	9%	10%
1	.9901	.9804	.9709	.9615	.9524	.9434	.9346	.9259	.9174	.9091
2	1.9704	1.9416	1.9135	1.8861	1.8594	1.8334	1.8080	1.7833	1.7591	1.7355
3	2.9410	2.8839	2.8286	2.7751	2.7233	2.6730	2.6243	2.5771	2.5313	2.4868
4	3.9020	3.8077	3.7171	3.6299	3.5459	3.4651	3.3872	3.3121	3.2397	3.1699
5	4.8535	4.7134	4.5797	4.4518	4.3295	4.2123	4.1002	3.9927	3.8896	3.7908
6	5.7955	5.6014	5.4172	5.2421	5.0757	4.9173	4.7665	4.6229	4.4859	4.3553
7	6.7282	6.4720	6.2302	6.0020	5.7863	5.5824	5.3893	5.2064	5.0329	4.8684
8	7.6517	7.3254	7.0196	6.7327	6.4632	6.2093	5.9713	5.7466	5.5348	5.3349
9	8.5661	8.1622	7.7861	7.4353	7.1078	6.8017	6.5152	6.2469	5.9852	5.7590
10	9.4714	8.9825	8.7302	8.1109	7.7217	7.3601	7.0236	6.7101	6.4176	6.1446
11	10.3677	9.7868	9.2526	8.7604	8.3064	7.8868	7.4987	7.1389	6.8052	6.4951
12	11.2552	10.5753	9.9589	9.3850	8.8632	8.3838	7.9427	7.5361	7.1601	6.8137
13	12.1338	11.3483	10.6349	9.9856	9.3935	8.8527	8.3576	7.9038	7.4869	7.1034
14	13.0088	12.1062	11.2960	10.5631	9.8986	9.2950	8.7454	8.2442	7.7860	7.3667
15	13.8651	12.8492	11.9379	11.1183	10.3796	9.7122	9.1079	8.5595	8.0607	7.6061
16	14.7180	13.5777	12.5610	11.6522	10.8377	10.1059	9.4466	8.8514	8.3126	7.8237
17	15.5624	14.2918	13.1660	12.1656	11.2740	10.4772	9.7632	9.1216	8.5435	8.0215
18	16.3984	14.9920	13.7534	12.6592	11.6895	10.8276	10.0591	9.3719	8.7556	8.2014
19	17.2201	15.2684	14.3237	13.1339	12.0853	11.1581	10.3356	9.6036	8.9501	8.3649
20	18.0457	16.3514	14.8774	13.5903	12.4622	11.4699	10.5940	9.8181	9.1285	8.5136
21	18.8571	17.0111	15.4149	14.0291	12.8211	11.7640	10.8355	10.0168	9.2922	8.6487
22	19.6605	17.6581	15.9368	14.4511	13.1630	12.0416	11.0612	10.2007	9.4424	8.7715
23	20.4559	18.2921	16.4435	14.8568	13.4885	12.3033	11.2722	10.3710	9.5802	8.8832
24	21.2435	18.9139	16.9355	15.2469	13.7986	12.5503	11.4693	10.5287	9.7066	8.9847
25	22.0233	19.5234	17.4181	15.6220	14.9039	12.7833	11.6536	10.6748	9.8226	9.0770

APPENDIX
TABLE
2

Value of $\sum_{t=1}^{n} \dfrac{1}{(1+i)^t}$ (Continued)

Value of i

n	11%	12%	13%	14%	15%	16%	17%	18%	19%	20%	24%
1	.9009	.8929	.8850	.8772	.8696	.8621	.8547	.8475	.8403	.8333	.8065
2	1.7125	1.6901	1.6681	1.6467	1.6257	1.6052	1.5852	1.5656	1.5465	1.5278	1.4568
3	2.4437	2.4018	2.3612	2.3126	2.2832	2.2459	2.2096	2.1743	2.1399	2.1065	1.9813
4	3.1024	3.0373	2.9745	2.9137	2.8550	2.7982	2.7432	2.6901	2.6386	2.5887	2.4043
5	3.6959	3.6048	3.5172	3.4331	3.3522	3.2743	3.1993	3.1272	3.0576	2.9906	2.7454
6	4.2305	4.1114	3.9976	3.8887	3.7845	3.6847	3.5892	3.4976	3.4098	3.3255	3.0205
7	4.7122	4.5638	4.4226	4.2883	4.1604	4.0386	3.9224	3.8115	3.7057	3.6046	3.2423
8	5.1461	4.9676	4.7988	4.6389	4.4873	4.3436	4.2072	4.0776	3.9544	3.8372	3.4212
9	5.5370	5.3282	5.1317	4.9464	4.7716	4.6065	4.4506	4.3030	4.1633	4.0310	3.5655
10	5.8892	5.6502	5.4262	5.2161	5.0188	4.8332	4.6586	4.4941	4.3389	4.1925	3.6819
11	6.2065	5.9377	5.6869	5.4527	5.2337	5.0286	4.8364	4.6560	4.4865	4.3271	3.7757
12	6.4924	6.1944	5.9176	5.6603	5.4206	5.1971	4.9884	4.7932	4.6105	4.4392	3.8514
13	6.7499	6.4235	6.1218	5.8424	5.5831	5.3423	5.1183	4.9095	4.7147	4.5327	3.9124
14	6.9819	6.6282	6.3025	6.0021	5.7245	5.4675	5.2293	5.0081	4.8023	4.6106	3.9616
15	7.1909	6.8109	6.4624	6.1422	5.8474	5.5755	5.3242	5.0916	4.8759	4.6755	4.0013
16	7.3792	6.9740	6.6039	6.2651	5.9542	5.6685	5.4053	5.1624	4.9377	4.7296	4.0333
17	7.5488	7.1196	6.7291	6.3729	6.0472	5.7487	5.4746	5.2223	4.9897	4.7746	4.0591
18	7.7016	7.2497	6.8399	6.4674	6.1280	5.8178	5.5339	5.2732	5.0333	4.8122	4.0799
19	7.8393	7.3650	6.9380	6.5504	6.1982	5.8775	5.5845	5.3176	5.0700	4.8435	4.0967
20	7.9633	7.4694	7.0248	6.6231	6.2593	5.9288	5.6278	5.3527	5.1009	4.8696	4.1103
21	8.0751	7.5620	7.1016	6.6870	6.3125	5.9731	5.6648	5.3837	5.1268	4.8913	4.1212
22	8.1757	7.6446	7.1695	6.7429	6.3587	6.0113	5.6964	5.4099	5.1486	4.9094	4.1300
23	8.2664	7.7184	7.2297	6.7921	6.3988	6.0442	5.7234	5.4321	5.1668	4.9245	4.1371
24	8.3481	7.7843	7.2829	6.8351	6.4338	6.0726	5.7465	5.4509	5.1822	4.9371	4.1428
25	8.4217	7.8431	7.3300	6.8729	6.4641	6.0971	5.7662	5.4669	5.1951	4.9476	4.1474

APPENDIX
TABLE
3

Areas under the Standard Normal Curve

This table shows the area between zero (the mean of a standard normal variable) and z. For example, if $z = 1.50$, this is the shaded area shown below, which equals .4332.

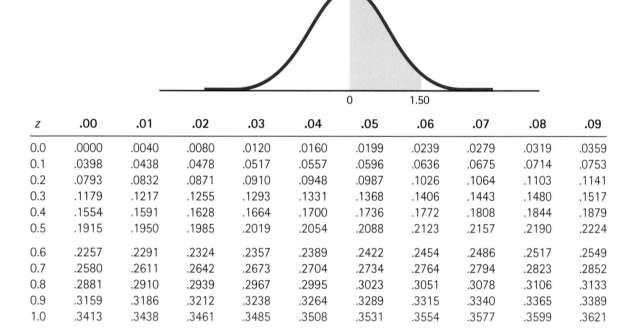

z	.00	.01	.02	.03	.04	.05	.06	.07	.08	.09
0.0	.0000	.0040	.0080	.0120	.0160	.0199	.0239	.0279	.0319	.0359
0.1	.0398	.0438	.0478	.0517	.0557	.0596	.0636	.0675	.0714	.0753
0.2	.0793	.0832	.0871	.0910	.0948	.0987	.1026	.1064	.1103	.1141
0.3	.1179	.1217	.1255	.1293	.1331	.1368	.1406	.1443	.1480	.1517
0.4	.1554	.1591	.1628	.1664	.1700	.1736	.1772	.1808	.1844	.1879
0.5	.1915	.1950	.1985	.2019	.2054	.2088	.2123	.2157	.2190	.2224
0.6	.2257	.2291	.2324	.2357	.2389	.2422	.2454	.2486	.2517	.2549
0.7	.2580	.2611	.2642	.2673	.2704	.2734	.2764	.2794	.2823	.2852
0.8	.2881	.2910	.2939	.2967	.2995	.3023	.3051	.3078	.3106	.3133
0.9	.3159	.3186	.3212	.3238	.3264	.3289	.3315	.3340	.3365	.3389
1.0	.3413	.3438	.3461	.3485	.3508	.3531	.3554	.3577	.3599	.3621

Areas under the Standard Normal Curve (Continued)

z	.00	.01	.02	.03	.04	.05	.06	.07	.08	.09
1.1	.3643	.3665	.3686	.3708	.3729	.3749	.3770	.3790	.3810	.3830
1.2	.3849	.3869	.3888	.3907	.3925	.3944	.3962	.3980	.3997	.4015
1.3	.4032	.4049	.4066	.4082	.4099	.4115	.4131	.4147	.4162	.4177
1.4	.4192	.4207	.4222	.4236	.4251	.4265	.4279	.4292	.4306	.4319
1.5	.4332	.4345	.4357	.4370	.4382	.4394	.4406	.4418	.4429	.4441
1.6	.4452	.4463	.4474	.4484	.4495	.4505	.4515	.4525	.4535	.4545
1.7	.4554	.4564	.4573	.4582	.4591	.4599	.4608	.4616	.4625	.4633
1.8	.4641	.4649	.4656	.4664	.4671	.4678	.4686	.4693	.4699	.4706
1.9	.4713	.4719	.4726	.4732	.4738	.4744	.4750	.4756	.4761	.4767
2.0	.4772	.4778	.4783	.4788	.4793	.4798	.4803	.4808	.4812	.4817
2.1	.4821	.4826	.4830	.4834	.4838	.4842	.4846	.4850	.4854	.4857
2.2	.4861	.4864	.4868	.4871	.4875	.4878	.4881	.4884	.4887	.4890
2.3	.4893	.4896	.4898	.4901	.4904	.4906	.4909	.4911	.4913	.4916
2.4	.4918	.4920	.4922	.4925	.4927	.4929	.4931	.4932	.4934	.4936
2.5	.4938	.4940	.4941	.4943	.4945	.4946	.4948	.4949	.4951	.4952
2.6	.4953	.4955	.4956	.4957	.4959	.4960	.4961	.4962	.4963	.4964
2.7	.4965	.4966	.4967	.4968	.4969	.4970	.4971	.4972	.4973	.4974
2.8	.4974	.4975	.4976	.4977	.4977	.4978	.4979	.4979	.4980	.4981
2.9	.4981	.4982	.4982	.4983	.4984	.4984	.4985	.4985	.4986	.4986
3.0	.4987	.4987	.4987	.4988	.4988	.4989	.4989	.4989	.4990	.4990

Source: This table is adapted from National Bureau of Standards, *Tables of Normal Probability Functions,* Applied Mathematics Series 23, U.S. Department of Commerce, 1953.

APPENDIX TABLE 4

Values of *t* That Will Be Exceeded with Specified Probabilities

This table shows the value of *t* where the area under the *t* distribution exceeding this value of *t* equals the specified amount. For example, the probability that a *t* variable with 14 degrees of freedom will exceed 1.345 equals .10.

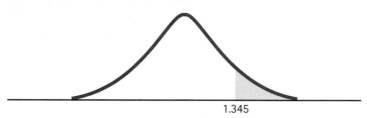

1.345

Degrees of freedom	Probability						
	.40	.25	.10	.05	.025	.01	.005
1	0.325	1.000	3.078	6.314	12.706	31.821	63.657
2	.289	0.816	1.886	2.920	4.303	6.965	9.925
3	.277	.765	1.638	2.353	3.182	4.541	5.841
4	.271	.741	1.533	2.132	2.776	3.747	4.604
5	0.267	0.727	1.476	2.015	2.571	3.365	4.032
6	.265	.718	1.440	1.943	2.447	3.143	3.707
7	.263	.711	1.415	1.895	2.365	2.998	3.499
8	.262	.706	1.397	1.860	2.306	2.896	3.355
9	.261	.703	1.383	1.833	2.262	2.821	3.250
10	0.260	0.700	1.372	1.812	2.228	2.764	3.169
11	.260	.697	1.363	1.796	2.201	2.718	3.106
12	.259	.695	1.356	1.782	2.179	2.681	3.055
13	.259	.694	1.350	1.771	2.160	2.650	3.012
14	.258	.692	1.345	1.761	2.145	2.624	2.977
15	0.258	0.691	1.341	1.753	2.131	2.602	2.947
16	.258	.690	1.337	1.746	2.120	2.583	2.921
17	.257	.689	1.333	1.740	2.110	2.567	2.898
18	.257	.688	1.330	1.734	2.101	2.552	2.878
19	.257	.688	1.328	1.729	2.093	2.539	2.861
20	0.257	0.687	1.325	1.725	2.086	2.528	2.845
21	.257	.686	1.323	1.721	2.080	2.518	2.831
22	.256	.686	1.321	1.717	2.074	2.508	2.819
23	.256	.685	1.319	1.714	2.069	2.500	2.807
24	.256	.685	1.318	1.711	2.064	2.492	2.797

APPENDIX
TABLE
4

Values of *t* That Will Be Exceeded with Specified Probabilities (Continued)

This table shows the value of *t* where the area under the *t* distribution exceeding this value of *t* equals the specified amount. For example, the probability that a *t* variable with 14 degrees of freedom will exceed 1.345 equals .10.

Degrees of freedom	Probability						
	.40	.25	.10	.05	.025	.01	.005
25	0.256	0.684	1.316	1.708	2.060	2.485	2.787
26	.256	.684	1.315	1.706	2.056	2.479	2.779
27	.256	.684	1.314	1.703	2.052	2.473	2.771
28	.256	.683	1.313	1.701	2.048	2.467	2.763
29	.256	.683	1.311	1.699	2.045	2.462	2.756
30	0.256	0.683	1.310	1.697	2.042	2.457	2.750
40	.255	.681	1.303	1.684	2.021	2.423	2.704
60	.254	.679	1.296	1.671	2.000	2.390	2.660
120	.254	.677	1.289	1.658	1.980	2.358	2.617
∞	.253	.674	1.282	1.645	1.960	2.326	2.576

Source: Biometrika Tables for Statisticians (Cambridge, U.K.: Cambridge University, 1954).

Value of an *F* Variable That Is Exceeded with Probability Equal to .05

	Degrees of freedom for numerator								
	1	2	3	4	5	6	7	8	9
1	161.4	199.5	215.7	224.6	230.2	234.0	236.8	238.9	240.5
2	18.51	19.00	19.16	19.25	19.30	19.33	19.35	19.37	19.38
3	10.13	9.55	9.28	9.12	9.01	8.94	8.89	8.85	8.81
4	7.71	6.94	6.59	6.39	6.26	6.16	6.09	6.04	6.00
5	6.61	5.79	5.41	5.19	5.05	4.95	4.88	4.82	4.77
6	5.99	5.14	4.76	4.53	4.39	4.28	4.21	4.15	4.10
7	5.59	4.74	4.35	4.12	3.97	3.87	3.79	3.73	3.68
8	5.32	4.46	4.07	3.84	3.69	3.58	3.50	3.44	3.39
9	5.12	4.26	3.86	3.63	3.48	3.37	3.29	3.23	3.18
10	4.96	4.10	3.71	3.48	3.33	3.22	3.14	3.07	3.02
11	4.84	3.98	3.59	3.36	3.20	3.09	3.01	2.95	2.90
12	4.75	3.89	3.49	3.26	3.11	3.00	2.91	2.85	2.80
13	4.67	3.81	3.41	3.18	3.03	2.92	2.83	2.77	2.71
14	4.60	3.74	3.34	3.11	2.96	2.85	2.76	2.70	2.65
15	4.54	3.68	3.29	3.06	2.90	2.79	2.71	2.64	2.59
16	4.49	3.63	3.24	3.01	2.85	2.74	2.66	2.59	2.54
17	4.45	3 59	3.20	2.96	2.81	2.70	2.61	2.55	2.49
18	4.41	3.55	3.16	2.93	2.77	2.66	2.58	2.51	2.46
19	4.38	3.52	3.13	2.90	2.74	2.63	2.54	2.48	2.42
20	4.35	3.49	3.10	2.87	2.71	2.60	2.51	2.45	2.39
21	4.32	3.47	3.07	2.84	2.68	2.57	2.49	2.42	2.37
22	4.30	3.44	3.05	2.82	2.66	2.55	2.46	2.40	2.34
23	4.28	3.42	3.03	2.80	2.64	2.53	2.44	2.37	2.32
24	4.26	3.40	3.01	2.78	2.62	2.51	2.42	2.36	2.30
25	4.24	3.39	2.99	2.76	2.60	2.49	2.40	2.34	2.28
26	4.23	3.37	2.98	2.74	2.59	2.47	2.39	2.32	2.27
27	4.21	3.35	2.96	2.73	2.57	2.46	2.37	2.31	2.25
28	4.20	3.34	2.95	2.71	2.56	2.45	2.36	2.29	2.24
29	4.18	3.33	2.93	2.70	2.55	2.43	2.35	2.28	2.22
30	4.17	3.32	2.92	2.69	2.53	2.42	2.33	2.27	2.21
40	4.08	3.23	2.84	2.61	2.45	2.34	2.25	2.18	2.12
60	4.00	3.15	2.76	2.53	2.37	2.25	2.17	2.10	2.04
120	3.92	3.07	2.68	2.45	2.29	2.17	2.09	2.02	1.96
∞	3.84	3.00	2.60	2.37	2.21	2.10	2.01	1.94	1.88

Degrees of freedom for denominator

Value of an *F* Variable That Is Exceeded with Probability Equal to .05 (Continued)

Degrees of freedom for numerator

		10	12	15	20	24	30	40	60	120	∞
	1	241.9	243.9	245.9	248.0	249.1	250.1	251.1	252.2	253.3	254.3
	2	19.40	19.41	19.43	19.45	19.45	19.46	19.47	19.48	19.49	19.50
	3	8.79	8.74	8.70	8.66	8.64	8.62	8.59	8.57	8.55	8.53
	4	5.96	5.91	5.86	5.80	5.77	5.75	5.72	5.69	5.66	5.63
	5	4.74	4.68	4.62	4.56	4.53	4.50	4.46	4.43	4.40	4.36
	6	4.06	4.00	3.94	3.87	3.84	3.81	3.77	3.74	3.70	3.67
	7	3.64	3.57	3.51	3.44	3.41	3.38	3.34	3.30	3.27	3.23
	8	3.35	3.28	3.22	3.15	3.12	3.08	3.04	3.01	2.97	2.93
	9	3.14	3.07	3.01	2.94	2.90	2.86	2.83	2.79	2.75	2.71
Degrees of freedom for denominator	10	2.98	2.91	2.85	2.77	2.74	2.70	2.66	2.62	2.58	2.54
	11	2.85	2.79	2.72	2.65	2.61	2.57	2.53	2.49	2.45	2.40
	12	2.75	2.69	2.62	2.54	2.51	2.47	2.43	2.38	2.34	2.30
	13	2.67	2.60	2.53	2.46	2.42	2.38	2.34	2.30	2.25	2.21
	14	2.60	2.53	2.46	2.39	2.35	2.31	2.27	2.22	2.18	2.13
	15	2.54	2.48	2.40	2.33	2.29	2.25	2.20	2.16	2.11	2.07
	16	2.49	2.42	2.35	2.28	2.24	2.19	2.15	2.11	2.06	2.01
	17	2.45	2.38	2.31	2.23	2.19	2.15	2.10	2.06	2.01	1.96
	18	2.41	2.34	2.27	2.19	2.15	2.11	2.06	2.02	1.97	1.92
	19	2.38	2.31	2.23	2.16	2.11	2.07	2.03	1.98	1.93	1.88
	20	2.35	2.28	2.20	2.12	2.08	2.04	1.99	1.95	1.90	1.84
	21	2.32	2.25	2.18	2.10	2.05	2.01	1.96	1.92	1.87	1.81
	22	2.30	2.23	2.15	2.07	2.03	1.98	1.94	1.89	1.84	1.78
	23	2.27	2.20	2.13	2.05	2.01	1.96	1.91	1.86	1.81	1.76
	24	2.25	2.18	2.11	2.03	1.98	1.94	1.89	1.84	1.79	1.73
	25	2.24	2.16	2.09	2.01	1.96	1.92	1.87	1.82	1.77	1.71
	26	2.22	2.15	2.07	1.99	1.95	1.90	1.85	1.80	1.75	1.69
	27	2.20	2.13	2.06	1.97	1.93	1.88	1.84	1.79	1.73	1.67
	28	2.19	2.12	2.04	1.96	1.91	1.87	1.82	1.77	1.71	1.65
	29	2.18	2.10	2.03	1.94	1.90	1.85	1.81	1.75	1.70	1.64
	30	2.16	2.09	2.01	1.93	1.89	1.84	1.79	1.74	1.68	1.62
	40	2.08	2.00	1.92	1.84	1.79	1.74	1.69	1.64	1.58	1.51
	60	1.99	1.92	1.84	1.75	1.70	1.65	1.59	1.53	1.47	1.39
	120	1.91	1.83	1.75	1.66	1.61	1.55	1.50	1.43	1.35	1.25
	∞	1.83	1.75	1.67	1.57	1.52	1.46	1.39	1.32	1.22	1.00

Source: Biometrika Tables for Statisticians.

APPENDIX TABLE 6

Value of an *F* Variable That Is Exceeded with Probability Equal to .01

Degrees of freedom for numerator

	1	2	3	4	5	6	7	8	9
1	4052	4999.5	5403	5625	5764	5859	5928	5982	6022
2	98.50	99.00	99.17	99.25	99.30	99.33	99.36	99.37	99.39
3	34.12	30.82	29.46	28.71	28.24	27.91	27.67	27.49	27.35
4	21.20	18.00	16.69	15.98	15.52	15.21	14.98	14.80	14.66
5	16.26	13.27	12.06	11.39	10.97	10.67	10.46	10.29	10.16
6	13.75	10.92	9.78	9.15	8.75	8.47	8.26	8.10	7.98
7	12.25	9.55	8.45	7.85	7.46	7.19	6.99	6.84	6.72
8	11.26	8.65	7.59	7.01	6.63	6.37	6.18	6.03	5.91
9	10.56	8.02	6.99	6.42	6.06	5.80	5.61	5.47	5.35
10	10.04	7.56	6.55	5.99	5.64	5.39	5.20	5.06	4.94
11	9.65	7.21	6.22	5.67	5.32	5.07	4.89	4.74	4.63
12	9.33	6.93	5.95	5.41	5.06	4.82	4.64	4.50	4.39
13	9.07	6.70	5.74	5.21	4.86	4.62	4.44	4.30	4.19
14	8.86	6.51	5.56	5.04	4.69	4.46	4.28	4.14	4.03
15	8.68	6.36	5.42	4.89	4.56	4.32	4.14	4.00	3.89
16	8.53	6.23	5.29	4.77	4.44	4.20	4.03	3.89	3.78
17	8.40	6.11	5.18	4.67	4.34	4.10	3.93	3.79	3.68
18	8.29	6.01	5.09	4.58	4.25	4.01	3.84	3.71	3.60
19	8.18	5.93	5.01	4.50	4.17	3.94	3.77	3.63	3.52
20	8.10	5.85	4.94	4.43	4.10	3.87	3.70	3.56	3.46
21	8.02	5.78	4.87	4.37	4.04	3.81	3.64	3.51	3.40
22	7.95	5.72	4.82	4.31	3.99	3.76	3.59	3.45	3.35
23	7.88	5.66	4.76	4.26	3.94	3.71	3.54	3.41	3.30
24	7.82	5.61	4.72	4.22	3.90	3.67	3.50	3.36	3.26
25	7.77	5.57	4.68	4.18	3.85	3.63	3.46	3.32	3.22
26	7.72	5.53	4.64	4.14	3.82	3.59	3.42	3.29	3.18
27	7.68	5.49	4.60	4.11	3.78	3.56	3.39	3.26	3.15
28	7.64	5.45	4.57	4.07	3.75	3.53	3.36	3.23	3.12
29	7.60	5.42	4.54	4.04	3.73	3.50	3.33	3.20	3.09
30	7.56	5.39	4.51	4.02	3.70	3.47	3.30	3.17	3.07
40	7.31	5.18	4.31	3.83	3.51	3.29	3.12	2.99	2.89
60	7.08	4.98	4.13	3.65	3.34	3.12	2.95	2.82	2.72
120	6.85	4.79	3.95	3.48	3.17	2.96	2.79	2.66	2.56
∞	6.63	4.61	3.78	3.32	3.02	2.80	2.64	2.51	2.41

Degrees of freedom for denominator

Value of an *F* Variable That is Exceeded with Probability Equal to .01 (Continued)

Degrees of freedom for numerator

	10	12	15	20	24	30	40	60	120	∞
1	6056	6106	6157	6209	6235	6261	6287	6313	6339	6366
2	99.40	99.42	99.43	99.45	99.46	99.47	99.47	99.48	99.49	99.50
3	27.23	27.05	26.87	26.69	26.60	26.50	26.41	26.32	26.22	26.13
4	14.55	14.37	14.20	14.02	13.93	13.84	13.75	13.65	13.56	13.46
5	10.05	9.89	9.72	9.55	9.47	9.38	9.29	9.20	9.11	9.02
6	7.87	7.72	7.56	7.40	7.31	7.23	7.14	7.06	6.97	6.88
7	6.62	6.47	6.31	6.16	6.07	5.99	5.91	5.82	5.74	5.65
8	5.81	5.67	5.52	5.36	5.28	5.20	5.12	5.03	4.95	4.86
9	5.26	5.11	4.96	4.81	4.73	4.65	4.57	4.48	4.40	4.31
10	4.85	4.71	4.56	4.41	4.33	4.25	4.17	4.08	4.00	3.91
11	4.54	4.40	4.25	4.10	4.02	3.94	3.86	3.78	3.69	3.60
12	4.30	4.16	4.01	3.86	3.78	3.70	3.62	3.54	3.45	3.36
13	4.10	3.96	3.82	3.66	3.59	3.51	3.43	3.34	3.25	3.17
14	3.94	3.80	3.66	3.51	3.43	3.35	3.27	3.18	3.09	3.00
15	3.80	3.67	3.52	3.37	3.29	3.21	3.13	3.05	2.96	2.87
16	3.69	3.55	3.41	3.26	3.18	3.10	3.02	2.93	2.84	2.75
17	3.59	3.46	3.31	3.16	3.08	3.00	2.92	2.83	2.75	2.65
18	3.51	3.37	3.23	3.08	3.00	2.92	2.84	2.75	2.66	2.57
19	3.43	3.30	3.15	3.00	2.92	2.84	2.76	2.67	2.58	2.49
20	3.37	3.23	3.09	2.94	2.86	2.78	2.69	2.61	2.52	2.42
21	3.31	3.17	3.03	2.88	2.80	2.72	2.64	2.55	2.46	2.36
22	3.26	3.12	2.98	2.83	2.75	2.67	2.58	2.50	2.40	2.31
23	3.21	3.07	2.93	2.78	2.70	2.62	2.54	2.45	2.35	2.26
24	3.17	3.03	2.89	2.74	2.66	2.58	2.49	2.40	2.31	2.21
25	3.13	2.99	2.85	2.70	2.62	2.54	2.45	2.36	2.27	2.17
26	3.09	2.96	2.81	2.66	2.58	2.50	2.42	2.33	2.23	2.13
27	3.06	2.93	2.78	2.63	2.55	2.47	2.38	2.29	2.20	2.10
28	3.03	2.90	2.75	2.60	2.52	2.44	2.35	2.26	2.17	2.06
29	3.00	2.87	2.73	2.57	2.49	2.41	2.33	2.23	2.14	2.03
30	2.98	2.84	2.70	2.55	2.47	2.39	2.30	2.21	2.11	2.01
40	2.80	2.66	2.52	2.37	2.29	2.20	2.11	2.02	1.92	1.80
60	2.63	2.50	2.35	2.20	2.12	2.03	1.94	1.84	1.73	1.60
120	2.47	2.34	2.19	2.03	1.95	1.86	1.76	1.66	1.53	1.38
∞	2.32	2.18	2.04	1.88	1.79	1.70	1.59	1.47	1.32	1.00

Degrees of freedom for denominator (row labels)

Source: Biometrika Tables for Statisticians.

APPENDIX TABLE 7

Values of d_L and d_U for the Durbin–Watson Test

A. Significance level = .05

n	k = 1 d_L	k = 1 d_U	k = 2 d_L	k = 2 d_U	k = 3 d_L	k = 3 d_U	k = 4 d_L	k = 4 d_U	k = 5 d_L	k = 5 d_U
15	1.08	1.36	0.95	1.54	0.82	1.75	0.69	1.97	0.56	2.21
16	1.10	1.37	0.98	1.54	0.86	1.73	0.74	1.93	0.62	2.15
17	1.13	1.38	1.02	1.54	0.90	1.71	0.78	1.90	0.67	2.10
18	1.16	1.39	1.05	1.53	0.93	1.69	0.82	1.87	0.71	2.06
19	1.18	1.40	1.08	1.53	0.97	1.68	0.86	1.85	0.75	2.02
20	1.20	1.41	1.10	1.54	1.00	1.68	0.90	1.83	0.79	1.99
21	1.22	1.42	1.13	1.54	1.03	1.67	0.93	1.81	0.83	1.96
22	1.24	1.43	1.15	1.54	1.05	1.66	0.96	1.80	0.86	1.94
23	1.26	1.44	1.17	1.54	1.08	1.66	0.99	1.79	0.90	1.92
24	1.27	1.45	1.19	1.55	1.10	1.66	1.01	1.78	0.93	1.90
25	1.29	1.45	1.21	1.55	1.12	1.66	1.04	1.77	0.95	1.89
26	1.30	1.46	1.22	1.55	1.14	1.65	1.06	1.76	0.98	1.88
27	1.32	1.47	1.24	1.56	1.16	1.65	1.08	1.76	1.01	1.86
28	1.33	1.48	1.26	1.56	1.18	1.65	1.10	1.75	1.03	1.85
29	1.34	1.48	1.27	1.56	1.20	1.65	1.12	1.74	1.05	1.84
30	1.35	1.49	1.28	1.57	1.21	1.65	1.14	1.74	1.07	1.83
31	1.36	1.50	1.30	1.57	1.23	1.65	1.16	1.74	1.09	1.83
32	1.37	1.50	1.31	1.57	1.24	1.65	1.18	1.73	1.11	1.82
33	1.38	1.51	1.32	1.58	1.26	1.65	1.19	1.73	1.13	1.81
34	1.39	1.51	1.33	1.58	1.27	1.65	1.21	1.73	1.15	1.81
35	1.40	1.52	1.34	1.58	1.28	1.65	1.22	1.73	1.16	1.80
36	1.41	1.52	1.35	1.59	1.29	1.65	1.24	1.73	1.18	1.80
37	1.42	1.53	1.36	1.59	1.31	1.66	1.25	1.72	1.19	1.80
38	1.43	1.54	1.37	1.59	1.32	1.66	1.26	1.72	1.21	1.79
39	1.43	1.54	1.38	1.60	1.33	1.66	1.27	1.72	1.22	1.79
40	1.44	1.54	1.39	1.60	1.34	1.66	1.29	1.72	1.23	1.79
45	1.48	1.57	1.43	1.62	1.38	1.67	1.34	1.72	1.29	1.78
50	1.50	1.59	1.46	1.63	1.42	1.67	1.38	1.72	1.34	1.77
55	1.53	1.60	1.49	1.64	1.45	1.68	1.41	1.72	1.38	1 77
60	1.55	1.62	1.51	1.65	1.48	1.69	1.44	1.73	1.41	1.77
65	1.57	1.63	1.54	1.66	1.50	1.70	1.47	1.73	1.44	1.77
70	1.58	1.64	1.55	1.67	1.52	1.70	1.49	1.74	1.46	1.77
75	1.60	1.65	1.57	1.68	1.54	1.71	1.51	1.74	1.49	1.77
80	1.61	1.66	1.59	1.69	1.56	1.72	1.53	1.74	1.51	1.77
85	1.62	1.67	1.60	1.70	1.57	1.72	1.55	1.75	1.52	1.77
90	1.63	1.68	1.61	1.70	1.59	1.73	1.57	1.75	1.54	1.78
95	1.64	1.69	1.62	1.71	1.60	1.73	1.58	1.75	1.56	1.78
100	1.65	1.69	1.63	1.72	1.61	1.74	1.59	1.76	1.57	1.78

Values of d_L and d_U for the Durbin-Watson Test (Continued)

B. Significance level = .025

n	k = 1 d_L	k = 1 d_U	k = 2 d_L	k = 2 d_U	k = 3 d_L	k = 3 d_U	k = 4 d_L	k = 4 d_U	k = 5 d_L	k = 5 d_U
15	0.95	1.23	0.83	1.40	0.71	1.61	0.59	1.84	0.48	2.09
16	0.98	1.24	0.86	1.40	0.75	1.59	0.64	1.80	0.53	2.03
17	1.01	1.25	0.90	1.40	0.79	1.58	0.68	1.77	0.57	1.98
18	1.03	1.26	0.93	1.40	0.82	1.56	0.72	1.74	0.62	1.93
19	1.06	1.28	0.96	1.41	0.86	1.55	0.76	1.72	0.66	1.90
20	1.08	1.28	0.99	1.41	0.89	1.55	0.79	1.70	0.70	1.87
21	1.10	1.30	1.01	1.41	0.92	1.54	0.83	1.69	0.73	1.84
22	1.12	1.31	1.04	1.42	0.95	1.54	0.86	1.68	0.77	1.82
23	1.14	1.32	1.06	1.42	0.97	1.54	0.89	1.67	0.80	1.80
24	1.16	1.33	1.08	1.43	1.00	1.54	0.91	1.66	0.83	1.79
25	1.18	1.34	1.10	1.43	1.02	1.54	0.94	1.65	0.86	1.77
26	1.19	1.35	1.12	1.44	1.04	1.54	0.96	1.65	0.88	1.76
27	1.21	1.36	1.13	1.44	1.06	1.54	0.99	1.64	0.91	1.75
28	1.22	1.37	1.15	1.45	1.08	1.54	1.01	1.64	0.93	1.74
29	1.24	1.38	1.17	1.45	1.10	1.54	1.03	1.63	0.96	1.73
30	1.25	1.38	1.18	1.46	1.12	1.54	1.05	1.63	0.98	1.73
31	1.26	1.39	1.20	1.47	1.13	1.55	1.07	1.63	1.00	1.72
32	1.27	1.40	1.21	1.47	1.15	1.55	1.08	1.63	1.02	1.71
33	1.28	1.41	1.22	1.48	1.16	1.55	1.10	1.63	1.04	1.71
34	1.29	1.41	1.24	1.48	1.17	1.55	1.12	1.63	1.06	1.70
35	1.30	1.42	1.25	1.48	1.19	1.55	1.13	1.63	1.07	1.70
36	1.31	1.43	1.26	1.49	1.20	1.56	1.15	1.63	1.09	1.70
37	1.32	1.43	1.27	1.49	1.21	1.56	1.16	1.62	1.10	1.70
38	1.33	1.44	1.28	1.50	1.23	1.56	1.17	1.62	1.12	1.70
39	1.34	1.44	1.29	1.50	1.24	1.56	1.19	1.63	1.13	1.69
40	1.35	1.45	1.30	1.51	1.25	1.57	1.20	1.63	1.15	1.69
45	1.39	1.48	1.34	1.53	1.30	1.58	1.25	1.63	1.21	1.69
50	1.42	1.50	1.38	1.54	1.34	1.59	1.30	1.64	1.26	1.69
55	1.45	1.52	1.41	1.56	1.37	1.60	1.33	1.64	1.30	1.69
60	1.47	1.54	1.44	1.57	1.40	1.61	1.37	1.65	1.33	1.69
65	1.49	1.55	1.46	1.59	1.43	1.62	1.40	1.66	1.36	1.69
70	1.51	1.57	1.48	1.60	1.45	1.63	1.42	1.66	1.39	1.70
75	1.53	1.58	1.50	1.61	1.47	1.64	1.45	1.67	1.42	1.70
80	1.54	1.59	1.52	1.62	1.49	1.65	1.47	1.67	1.44	1.70
85	1.56	1.60	1.53	1.63	1.51	1.65	1.49	1.68	1.46	1.71
90	1.57	1.61	1.55	1.64	1.53	1.66	1.50	1.69	1.48	1.71
95	1.58	1.62	1.56	1.65	1.54	1.67	1.52	1.69	1.50	1.71
100	1.59	1.63	1.57	1.65	1.55	1.67	1.53	1.70	1.51	1.72

Values of d_L and d_U for the Durbin–Watson Test (Continued)

C. Significance level = 0.01

n	k = 1		k = 2		k = 3		k = 4		k = 5	
	d_L	d_U	d_L	d_U	d_L	d_U	d_L	d_U	d_L	d_U
15	0.81	1.07	0.70	1.25	0.59	1.46	0.49	1.70	0.39	1.96
16	0.84	1.09	0.74	1.25	0.63	1.44	0.53	1.66	0.44	1.90
17	0.87	1.10	0.77	1.25	0.67	1.43	0.57	1.63	0.48	1.85
18	0.90	1.12	0.80	1.26	0.71	1.42	0.61	1.60	0.52	1.80
19	0.93	1.13	0.83	1.26	0.74	1.41	0.65	1.58	0.56	1.77
20	0.95	1.15	0.86	1.27	077	1.41	0.68	1.57	0.60	1.74
21	0.97	1.16	0.89	1.27	0.80	1.41	0.72	1.55	0.63	1.71
22	1.00	1.17	0.91	1.28	0.83	1.40	0.75	1.54	0.66	1.69
23	1.02	1.19	0.94	1.29	0.86	1.40	0.77	1.53	0.70	1.67
24	1.04	1.20	0.96	1.30	0.88	1.41	0.80	1.53	0.72	1.66
25	1.05	1.21	0.98	1.30	0.90	1.41	0.83	1.52	0.75	1.65
26	1.07	1.22	1.00	1.31	0.93	1.41	0.85	1.52	0.78	1.64
27	1.09	1.23	1.02	1.32	0.95	1.41	0.88	1.51	0.81	1.63
28	1.10	1.24	1.04	1.32	0.97	1.41	0.90	1.51	0.83	1.62
29	1.12	1.25	1.05	1.33	0.99	1.42	0.92	1.51	0.85	1.61
30	1.13	1.26	1.07	1.34	1.01	1.42	0.94	1.51	0.88	1.61
31	1.15	1.27	1.08	1.34	1.02	1.42	0.96	1.51	0.90	1.60
32	1.16	1.28	1.10	1.35	1.04	1.43	0.98	1.51	0.92	1.60
33	1.17	1.29	1.11	1.36	1.05	1.43	1.00	1.51	0.94	1.59
34	1.18	1.30	1.13	1.36	1.07	1.43	1.01	1.51	0.95	1.59
35	1.19	1.31	1.14	1.37	1.08	1.44	1.03	1.51	0.97	1.59
36	1.21	1.32	1.15	1.38	1.10	1.44	1.04	1.51	0.99	1.59
37	1.22	1.32	1.16	1.38	1.11	1.45	1.06	1.51	1.00	1.59
38	1.23	1.33	1.18	1.39	1.12	1.45	1.07	1.52	1.02	1.58
39	1.24	1.34	1.19	1.39	1.14	1.45	1.09	1.52	1.03	1.58
40	1.25	1.34	1.20	1.40	1.15	1.46	1.10	1.52	1.05	1.58
45	1.29	1.38	1.24	1.42	1.20	1.48	1.16	1.53	1.11	1.58
50	1.32	1.40	1.28	1.45	1.24	1.49	1.20	1.54	1.16	1.59
55	1.36	1.43	1.32	1.47	1.28	1.51	1.25	1.55	1.21	1.59
60	1.38	1.45	1.35	1.48	1.32	1.52	1.28	1.56	1.25	1.60
65	1.41	1.47	1.38	1.50	1.35	1.53	1.31	1.57	1.28	1.61
70	1.43	1.49	1.40	1.52	1.37	1.55	1.34	1.58	1.31	1.61
75	1.45	1.50	1.42	1.53	1.39	1.56	1.37	1.59	1.34	1.62
80	1.47	1.52	1.44	1.54	1.42	1.57	1.39	1.60	1.36	1.62
85	1.48	1.53	1.46	1.55	1.43	1.58	1.41	1.60	1.39	1.63
90	1.50	1.54	1.47	1.56	1.45	1.59	1.43	1.61	1.41	1.64
95	1.51	1.55	1.49	1.57	1.47	1.60	1.45	1.62	1.42	1.64
100	1.52	1.56	1.50	1.58	1.48	1.60	1.46	1.63	1.44	1.65

Source: J. Durbin and G. S. Watson, "Testing for Serial Correlation in Least Squares Regression," *Biometrika 38* (June 1951).

PHOTO CREDITS

INDEX